Blackstone's Statutes on

Medical Law

Blackstone's Statutes on
Medical Law

8th edition

Edited by

Anne E. Morris
Honorary Senior Research Fellow in Law at the University of Liverpool

Michael A. Jones
Emeritus Professor of Law at the University of Liverpool

OXFORD
UNIVERSITY PRESS

OXFORD
UNIVERSITY PRESS

Great Clarendon Street, Oxford, OX2 6DP,
United Kingdom

Oxford University Press is a department of the University of Oxford.
It furthers the University's objective of excellence in research, scholarship,
and education by publishing worldwide. Oxford is a registered trade mark of
Oxford University Press in the UK and in certain other countries

First published by Blackstone Press 1992
Fifth edition 2007
Sixth edition 2009
Seventh edition 2011
Eighth edition 2015

Impression: 1

Published in the United States of America by Oxford University Press
198 Madison Avenue, New York, NY 10016, United States of America

British Library Cataloguing in Publication Data

Data available

ISBN 978–0–19–967862–4

Printed in Italy by
L.E.G.O. S.p.A.

Preface

This collection of statutory and non-statutory materials is intended for students of Medical Law in all its different guises. It is clear from the comments of reviewers that there are many variants of the subject taught at undergraduate, post-graduate and professional levels. We have focused on including material likely to be relevant in the majority of those courses, although space constraints mean no collection can be entirely comprehensive. The new edition has taken account of feedback from users and we have excised some of the more regulatory material (for example, the NHS (General Medical Services) Contracts Regulations) in favour of including more international materials. We have updated the section on General Medical Council Guidance and, as ever, we are grateful to the GMC for permission to reproduce this.

We are conscious that a primary purpose of the Blackstone's Statute series is that it may be used in examinations. We remain of the view, therefore, that we should not include material which explains or describes the legislation. This is why we continue to omit, for example, the Mental Capacity Act Code of Practice.

It is frequently the case that new legislation takes effect by amending earlier statutes, rather than by repealing them. In line with our previous practice, we have incorporated changes into the existing Act, including those not yet in force. This means that the changes may not be apparent, but we believe the result is more readily comprehensible and coherent. It also means that the amending legislation may not appear in full. This is the case, for example, with the Health and Social Care Act 2012 which amends the National Health Service Act 2006. Legislation that has received the Royal Assent appears as though in force. We have assumed, not too optimistically we hope, that the Order in Council establishing the Medical Practitioners Tribunal Service (MPTS) as a statutory committee of the GMC and the consequent amendments to the Medical Act 1983 will come into force in due course and have amended the 1983 Act accordingly (see the General Medical Council (Fitness to Practise and Over-arching Objective) and the Professional Standards Authority for Health and Social Care (References to Court) Order 2015).

As legislation—both primary and secondary—becomes more complex and lengthy the decision as to what to include or omit becomes more difficult. We hope that this selection is representative of what students will find useful.

We reiterate, once again, our apologies for being unable, for reasons of space, to include a fully comprehensive section on Scottish and Welsh materials.

We would like to record our thanks to the staff at Oxford University Press for the remarkable efficiency and patience that they always display.

The law is stated as at April 2015.

Anne Morris
Michael Jones

New to this edition

The eighth edition of *Blackstone's Statutes on Medical Law* has been fully updated to incorporate relevant statutory and non-statutory materials through to April 2015 and the international section has been expanded, including:

- Health and Social Care Act 2012
- Care Act 2014
- Social Action, Responsibility and Heroism Act 2015
- National Health Service (Clinical Negligence Scheme) Regulations 2015
- GMC Guidance on Personal beliefs and medical practice (2013)
- GMC Guidance on Maintaining a professional boundary between you and your patient (2013)
- GMC Guidance on Financial and commercial arrangements and conflicts of interest (2013)
- GMC Guidance on Good practice in prescribing and managing medicines and devices (2013)
- Human Fertilisation and Embryology Code of Practice (updated 2015)
- Mental Health Act 1983 Code of Practice 2015
- International Covenant on Economic, Social and Cultural Rights 1966
- Universal Declaration on the Human Genome and Human Rights 1997
- Optional Protocol to the Convention against Torture and other Cruel, Inhuman or Degrading Treatment or Punishment 2002
- United Nations Declaration on Human Cloning 2005
- Convention on the Rights of Persons with Disabilities 2006

Contents

Alphabetical contents

Chronological contents

Statutes

Offences Against the Person Act 1861

(1861, c. 100)

Attempts to procure abortion

58 Administering drugs or using instruments to procure abortion

Every woman, being with child, who, with intent to procure her own miscarriage, shall unlawfully administer to herself any poison or other noxious thing, or shall unlawfully use any instrument or other means whatsoever with the like intent, and whosoever, with intent to procure the miscarriage of any woman, whether she be or be not with child, shall unlawfully administer to her or cause to be taken by her any poison or other noxious thing, or shall unlawfully use any instrument or other means whatsoever with the like intent, shall be guilty of felony, and being convicted thereof shall be liable to be kept in penal servitude for life.

59 Procuring drugs, &c. to cause abortion

Whosoever shall unlawfully supply or procure any poison or other noxious thing, or any instrument or thing whatsoever, knowing that the same is intended to be unlawfully used or employed with intent to procure the miscarriage of any woman, whether she be or be not with child, shall be guilty of a misdemeanor, and being convicted thereof shall be liable to be kept in penal servitude.

Infant Life (Preservation) Act 1929

(1929, c. 34)

1 Punishment for child destruction

(1) Subject as hereinafter in this subsection provided, any person who, with intent to destroy the life of a child capable of being born alive, by any wilful act causes a child to die before it has an existence independent of its mother, shall be guilty of felony, to wit, of child destruction, and shall be liable on conviction thereof on indictment to penal servitude for life:

Provided that no person shall be found guilty of an offence under this section unless it is proved that the act which caused the death of the child was not done in good faith for the purpose only of preserving the life of the mother.

(2) For the purposes of this Act, evidence that a woman had at any material time been pregnant for a period of twenty-eight weeks or more shall be prima facie proof that she was at that time pregnant of a child capable of being born alive.

2 Prosecution of offences

...

(2) Where upon the trial of any person for the murder or manslaughter of any child, or for infanticide, or for an offence under section fifty-eight of the Offences against the Person Act 1861 (which

relates to administering drugs or using instruments to procure abortion), the jury are of opinion that the person charged is not guilty of murder, manslaughter or infanticide, or of an offence under the said section fifty-eight, as the case may be, but that he is shown by the evidence to be guilty of the felony of child destruction, the jury may find him guilty of that felony, and thereupon the person convicted shall be liable to be punished as if he had been convicted upon an indictment for child destruction.

(3) Where upon the trial of any person for the felony of child destruction the jury are of opinion that the person charged is not guilty of that felony, but that he is shown by the evidence to be guilty of an offence under the said section fifty-eight of the Offences against the Person Act 1861, the jury may find him guilty of that offence, and thereupon the person convicted shall be liable to be punished as if he had been convicted upon an indictment under that section.

Children and Young Persons Act 1933

(1933, c. 12)

1   Cruelty to persons under sixteen

(1) If any person who has attained the age of sixteen years and has responsibility for any child or young person under that age, wilfully assaults, ill-treats, neglects, abandons, or exposes him, or causes or procures him to be assaulted, ill-treated, neglected, abandoned, or exposed, in a manner likely to cause him unnecessary suffering or injury to health (including injury to or loss of sight, or hearing, or limb, or organ of the body, and any mental derangement), that person shall be guilty of a misdemeanor, and shall be liable –

    (a) on conviction on indictment, to a fine or alternatively, or in addition thereto, to imprisonment for any term not exceeding ten years;

    (b) on summary conviction, to a fine not exceeding the prescribed sum, or alternatively, or in addition thereto, to imprisonment for any term not exceeding six months.

(2) For the purposes of this section –

    (a) a parent or other person legally liable to maintain a child or young person, or the legal guardian of a child or young person, shall be deemed to have neglected him in a manner likely to cause injury to his health if he has failed to provide adequate food, clothing, medical aid or lodging for him, or if, having been unable otherwise to provide such food, clothing, medical aid or lodging, he has failed to take steps to procure it to be provided under the enactments applicable in that behalf;

(3) A person may be convicted of an offence under this section –

    (a) notwithstanding that actual suffering or injury to health, or the likelihood of actual suffering or injury to health, was obviated by the action of another person;

    (b) notwithstanding the death of the child or young person in question.

Suicide Act 1961

(1961, c. 60)

1   Suicide to cease to be a crime

The rule of law whereby it is a crime for a person to commit suicide is hereby abrogated.

2   Criminal liability for complicity in another's suicide

(1) A person ('D') commits an offence if –

    (a) D does an act capable of encouraging or assisting the suicide or attempted suicide of another person, and

    (b) D's act was intended to encourage or assist suicide or an attempt at suicide.

(1A) The person referred to in subsection (1)(a) need not be a specific person (or class of persons) known to, or identified by, D.

(1B) D may commit an offence under this section whether or not a suicide, or an attempt at suicide, occurs.

(1C) An offence under this section is triable on indictment and a person convicted of such an offence is liable to imprisonment for a term not exceeding 14 years.

(2) If on the trial of an indictment for murder or manslaughter of a person it is proved that the deceased person committed suicide, and the accused committed an offence under subsection (1) in relation to that suicide, the jury may find the accused guilty of the offence under subsection (1).

(4) No proceedings shall be instituted for an offence under this section except by or with the consent of the Director of Public Prosecutions.

Abortion Act 1967

(1967, c. 87)

1 Medical termination of pregnancy

(1) Subject to the provisions of this section, a person shall not be guilty of an offence under the law relating to abortion when a pregnancy is terminated by a registered medical practitioner if two registered medical practitioners are of the opinion, formed in good faith –

    (a) that the pregnancy has not exceeded its twenty-fourth week and that the continuance of the pregnancy would involve risk, greater than if the pregnancy were terminated, of injury to the physical or mental health of the pregnant woman or any existing children of her family; or

    (b) that the termination is necessary to prevent grave permanent injury to the physical or mental health of the pregnant woman; or

    (c) that the continuance of the pregnancy would involve risk to the life of the pregnant woman, greater than if the pregnancy were terminated; or

    (d) that there is a substantial risk that if the child were born it would suffer from such physical or mental abnormalities as to be seriously handicapped.

(2) In determining whether the continuance of a pregnancy would involve such risk of injury to health as is mentioned in paragraph (a) or (b) of subsection (1) of this section, account may be taken of the pregnant woman's actual or reasonably foreseeable environment.

(3) Except as provided by subsection (4) of this section, any treatment for the termination of pregnancy must be carried out in a hospital vested in the Secretary of State for the purposes of his functions under the National Health Service Act 2006 or the National Health Service (Scotland) Act 1978 or in a hospital vested in a National Health Service trust or an NHS foundation trust or in a place approved for the purposes of this section by the Secretary of State.

(3A) The power under subsection (3) of this section to approve a place includes power, in relation to treatment consisting primarily in the use of such medicines as may be specified in the approval and carried out in such manner as may be so specified, to approve a class of places.

(4) Subsection (3) of this section, and so much of subsection (1) as relates to the opinion of two registered medical practitioners, shall not apply to the termination of a pregnancy by a registered medical practitioner in a case where he is of the opinion, formed in good faith, that the termination is immediately necessary to save the life or to prevent grave permanent injury to the physical or mental health of the pregnant woman.

2 Notification

(1) The Secretary of State in respect of England and Wales, and the Secretary of State in respect of Scotland, shall by statutory instrument make regulations to provide –

(a) for requiring any such opinion as is referred to in section 1 of this Act to be certified by the practitioners or practitioners concerned in such form and at such time as may be prescribed by the regulations, and for requiring the preservation and disposal of certificates made for the purposes of the regulations;

(b) for requiring any registered medical practitioner who terminates a pregnancy to give notice of the termination and such other information relating to the termination as may be so prescribed;

(c) for prohibiting the disclosure, except to such persons or for such purposes as may be so prescribed, of notices given or information furnished pursuant to the regulations.

(2) The information furnished in pursuance of regulations made by virtue of paragraph (b) of subsection (1) of this section shall be notified solely to the Chief Medical Officer of the Department of Health, or of the Welsh Office, or of the Scottish Administration.

(3) Any person who wilfully contravenes or wilfully fails to comply with the requirements of regulations under subsection (1) of this section shall be liable on summary conviction to a fine not exceeding level 5 on the standard scale.

4   Conscientious objection to participation in treatment

(1) Subject to subsection (2) of this section, no person shall be under any duty, whether by contract or by any statutory or other legal requirement, to participate in any treatment authorised by this Act to which he has a conscientious objection:
Provided that in any legal proceedings the burden of proof of conscientious objection shall rest on the person claiming to rely on it.

(2) Nothing in subsection (1) of this section shall affect any duty to participate in treatment which is necessary to save the life or to prevent grave permanent injury to the physical or mental health of a pregnant woman.

5   Supplementary provisions

(1) No offence under the Infant Life (Preservation) Act 1929 shall be committed by a registered medical practitioner who terminates a pregnancy in accordance with the provisions of this Act.

(2) For the purposes of the law relating to abortion, anything done with intent to procure a woman's miscarriage (or, in the case of a woman carrying more than one foetus, her miscarriage of any foetus) is unlawfully done unless authorised by section 1 of this Act and, in the case of a woman carrying more than one foetus, anything done with intent to procure her miscarriage of any foetus is authorised by that section if –

(a) the ground for termination of the pregnancy specified in subsection (1)(d) of that section applies in relation to any foetus and the thing is done for the purpose of procuring the miscarriage of that foetus, or

(b) any of the other grounds for termination of the pregnancy specified in that section applies.

6   Interpretation

In this Act, the following expressions have meanings hereby assigned to them: –
'the law relating to abortion' means sections 58 and 59 of the Offences against the Person Act 1861, and any rule of law relating to the procurement of abortion.

Family Law Reform Act 1969

(1969, c. 46)

1   Reduction of age of majority from 21 to 18

(1) As from the date on which this section comes into force a person shall attain full age on attaining the age of eighteen instead of on attaining the age of twenty-one; and a person shall

attain full age on that date if he has then already attained the age of eighteen but not the age of twenty-one.

8   Consent by persons over 16 to surgical, medical and dental treatment

(1) The consent of a minor who has attained the age of sixteen years to any surgical, medical or dental treatment which, in the absence of consent, would constitute a trespass to his person, shall be as effective as it would be if he were of full age; and where a minor has by virtue of this section given an effective consent to any treatment it shall not be necessary to obtain any consent for it from his parent or guardian.

(3) In this section 'surgical, medical or dental treatment' includes any procedure undertaken for the purposes of diagnosis, and this section applies to any procedure (including, in particular, the administration of an anaesthetic) which is ancillary to any treatment as it applies to that treatment.

(4) Nothing in this section shall be construed as making ineffective any consent which would have been effective if this section had not been enacted.

Congenital Disabilities (Civil Liability) Act 1976

(1976, c. 28)

1   Civil liability to child born disabled

(1) If a child is born disabled as the result of such an occurrence before its birth as is mentioned in subsection (2) below, and a person (other than the child's own mother) is under this section answerable to the child in respect of the occurrence, the child's disabilities are to be regarded as damage resulting from the wrongful act of that person and actionable accordingly at the suit of the child.

(2) An occurrence to which this section applies is one which –
  (a) affected either parent of the child in his or her ability to have a normal, healthy child; or
  (b) affected the mother during her pregnancy, or affected her or the child in the course of its birth, so that the child is born with disabilities which would not otherwise have been present.

(3) Subject to the following subsections, a person (here referred to as 'the defendant') is answerable to the child if he was liable in tort to the parent or would, if sued in due time have been so; and it is no answer that there could not have been such liability because the parent suffered no actionable injury, if there was a breach of legal duty which, accompanied by injury, would have given rise to the liability.

(4) In the case of an occurrence preceding the time of conception, the defendant is not answerable to the child if at that time either or both of the parents knew the risk of their child being born disabled (that is to say, the particular risk created by the occurrence); but should it be the child's father who is the defendant, this subsection does not apply if he knew of the risk and the mother did not.

(4A) In the case of a child who has a parent by virtue of section 42 or 43 of the Human Fertilisation and Embryology Act 2008, the reference in subsection (4) to the child's father includes a reference to the woman who is a parent by virtue of that section.

(5) The defendant is not answerable to the child, for anything he did or omitted to do when responsible in a professional capacity for treating or advising the parent, if he took reasonable care having due regard to then received professional opinion applicable to the particular class of case; but this does not mean that he is answerable only because he departed from received opinion.

(6) Liability to the child under this section may be treated as having been excluded or limited by contract made with the parent affected, to the same extent and subject to the same restrictions as liability in the parent's own case; and a contract term which could have been set up by the

defendant in an action by the parent, so as to exclude or limit his liability to him or her, operates in the defend-ant's favour to the same, but no greater, extent in an action under this section by the child.

(7) If in the child's action under this section it is shown that the parent affected shared the responsibility for the child being born disabled, the damages are to be reduced to such extent as the court thinks just and equitable having regard to the extent of the parent's responsibility.

1A   Extension of section 1 to cover infertility treatments

(1) In any case where –

    (a) a child carried by a woman as the result of the placing in her of an embryo or of sperm and eggs or her artificial insemination is born disabled,

    (b) the disability results from an act or omission in the course of the selection, or the keeping or use outside the body, of the embryo carried by her or of the gametes used to bring about the creation of the embryo, and

    (c) a person is under this section answerable to the child in respect of the act or omission, the child's disabilities are to be regarded as damage resulting from the wrongful act of that person and actionable accordingly at the suit of the child.

(2) Subject to subsection (3) below and the applied provisions of section 1 of this Act, a person (here referred to as 'the defendant') is answerable to the child if he was liable in tort to one or both of the parents (here referred to as 'the parent or parents concerned') or would, if sued in due time, have been so; and it is no answer that there could not have been such liability because the parent or parents concerned suffered no actionable injury, if there was a breach of legal duty which, accompanied by injury, would have given rise to the liability.

(3) The defendant is not under this section answerable to the child if at the time the embryo, or the sperm and eggs, are placed in the woman or the time of her insemination (as the case may be) either or both of the parents knew the risk of their child being born disabled (that is to say, the particular risk created by the act or omission).

(4) Subsections (5) to (7) of section 1 of this Act apply for the purposes of this section as they apply for the purposes of that but as if references to the parent or the parent affected were references to the parent or parents concerned.

2   Liability of woman driving when pregnant

A woman driving a motor vehicle when she knows (or ought reasonably to know) herself to be pregnant is to be regarded as being under the same duty to take care for the safety of her unborn child as the law imposes on her with respect to the safety of other people; and if in consequence of her breach of that duty her child is born with disabilities which would not otherwise have been present, those disabilities are to be regarded as damage resulting from her wrongful act and actionable accordingly at the suit of the child.

4   Interpretation and other supplementary provisions

(1) References in this Act to a child being born disabled or with disabilities are to its being born with any deformity, disease or abnormality, including predisposition (whether or not susceptible of immediate prognosis) to physical or mental defect in the future.

(2) In this Act –

    (a) 'born' means born alive (the moment of a child's birth being when it first has a life separate from its mother), and 'birth' has a corresponding meaning; and

    (b) 'motor vehicle' means a mechanically propelled vehicle intended or adapted for use on roads,

and reference to embryos shall be construed in accordance with section 1(1) of the Human Fertilisation and Embryology Act 1990 and any regulations under section 1(6) of that Act.

(3) Liability to a child under section 1, 1A or 2 of this Act is to be regarded –

    (a) as respects all its incidents and any matters arising or to arise out of it; and

    (b) subject to any contrary context or intention, for the purpose of construing references in enactments and documents to personal or bodily injuries and cognate matters,

as liability for personal injuries sustained by the child immediately after its birth.

(4) No damages shall be recoverable under any of those sections in respect of any loss of expectation of life, nor shall any such loss be taken into account in the compensation payable in respect of a child under the Nuclear Installations Act 1965 as extended by section 3, unless (in either case) the child lives for at least 48 hours.

(4A) In any case where a child carried by a woman as the result of the placing in her of an embryo or of sperm and eggs or her artificial insemination is born disabled, any reference in section 1 of this Act to a parent includes a reference to a person who would be a parent but for sections 27 to 29 of the Human Fertilisation and Embryology Act 1990 or sections 33 to 47 of the Human Fertilisation and Embryology Act 2008.

(5) This Act applies in respect of births after (but not before) its passing, and in respect of any such birth it replaces any law in force before its passing, whereby a person could be liable to a child in respect of disabilities with which it might be born; but in section 1(3) of this Act the expression 'liable in tort' does not include any reference to liability by virtue of this Act, or to liability by virtue of any such law.

Unfair Contract Terms Act 1977

(1977, c. 50)

1 Scope of Part I

(1) For the purposes of this Part of this Act, 'negligence' means the breach –

    (a) of any obligation, arising from the express or implied terms of a contract, to take reasonable care or exercise reasonable skill in the performance of the contract;

    (b) of any common law duty to take reasonable care or exercise reasonable skill (but not any stricter duty);

(3) In the case of both contract and tort, sections 2 to 7 apply (except where the contrary is stated in section 6(4)) only to business liability, that is liability for breach of obligations or duties arising –

    (a) from things done or to be done by a person in the course of a business (whether his own business or another's) …

(4) In relation to any breach of duty or obligation, it is immaterial for any purpose of this Part of this Act whether the breach was inadvertent or intentional, or whether liability for it arises directly or vicariously.

2 Negligence liability

(1) A person cannot by reference to any contract term or to a notice given to persons generally or to particular persons exclude or restrict his liability for death or personal injury resulting from negligence.

(2) In the case of other loss or damage, a person cannot so exclude or restrict his liability for negligence except in so far as the term or notice satisfies the requirement of reasonableness.

(3) Where a contract term or notice purports to exclude or restrict liability for negligence a per-son's agreement to or awareness of it is not of itself to be taken as indicating his voluntary acceptance of any risk.

Vaccine Damage Payments Act 1979

(1979, c. 17)

1   Payments to persons severely disabled by vaccination

(1) If, on consideration of a claim, the Secretary of State is satisfied –

    (a) that a person is, or was immediately before his death, severely disabled as a result of vaccination against any of the diseases to which this Act applies; and

    (b) that the conditions of entitlement which are applicable in accordance with section 2 below are fulfilled,

he shall in accordance with this Act make a payment of the relevant statutory sum to or for the benefit of that person or to his personal representatives.

(1A) In subsection (1) above 'statutory sum' means £120,000 or such other sum as is specified by the Secretary of State for the purposes of this Act by order made by statutory instrument with the consent of the Treasury; and the relevant statutory sum for the purposes of that subsection is the statutory sum at the time when a claim for payment is first made.

(2) The diseases to which this Act applies are –

    (a) diphtheria,

    (b) tetanus,

    (c) whooping cough,

    (d) poliomyelitis,

    (e) measles,

    (f) mumps,

    (g) rubella,

    (h) tuberculosis,

    (i) smallpox, and

    (j) any other disease which is specified by the Secretary of State for the purpose of this Act by order made by statutory instrument.

(3) Subject to section 2(3) below, this Act has effect with respect to a person who is severely disabled as a result of a vaccination given to his mother before he was born as if the vaccination had been given directly to him and, in such circumstances as may be prescribed by regulations under this Act, this Act has effect with respect to a person who is severely disabled as a result of contracting a disease through contact with a third person who was vaccinated against it as if the vaccination had been given to him and the disablement resulted from it.

(4) For the purposes of this Act, a person is severely disabled if he suffers disablement to the extent of 60 per cent. or more, assessed as for the purposes of section 103 of the Social Security Contributions and Benefits Act 1992...

2   Conditions of entitlement

(3) In a case where this Act has effect by virtue of section 1(3) above, the reference in sub-section (1)(b) above to the person to whom a vaccination was given is a reference to the person to whom it was actually given and not to the disabled person.

6   Payments to or for the benefit of disabled persons

(4) The making of a claim for, or the receipt of, a payment under section 1(1) above does not prejudice the right of any person to institute or carry on proceedings in respect of disablement suffered as a result of vaccination against any disease to which this Act applies; but in any civil proceedings brought in respect of disablement resulting from vaccination against such a disease, the court shall treat a payment made to or in respect of the disabled person concerned under section 1(1) above as paid on account of any damages which the court awards in respect of such disablement.

Senior Courts Act 1981

(1981, c. 54)

33   Powers of High Court exercisable before commencement of action

(2) On the application, in accordance with rules of court, of a person who appears to the High Court to be likely to be a party to subsequent proceedings in that court the High Court shall, in such circumstances as may be specified in the rules, have power to order a person who appears to the court to be likely to be a care to the proceedings and to be likely to have or to have had in his possession, custody or power any documents which are relevant to an issue arising or likely to arise out of that claim –

    (a) to disclose whether those documents are in his possession, custody or power; and

    (b) to produce such of those documents as are in his possession, custody or power to the applicant or, on such conditions as may be specified in the order –

        (i)   to the applicant's legal advisers; or

        (ii) to the applicant's legal advisers and any medical or other professional adviser of the applicant; or

        (iii) if the applicant has no legal adviser, to any medical or other professional adviser of the applicant.

34   Power of High Court to order disclosure of documents, inspection of property etc. in proceedings for personal injuries or death

(2) On the application, in accordance with rules of court, of a party to any proceedings, the High Court shall, in such circumstances as may be specified in the rules, have power to order a person who is not a party to the proceedings and who appears to the court to be likely to have in his possession, custody or power any documents which are relevant to an issue arising out of the said claim –

    (a) to disclose whether those documents are in his possession, custody or power; and

    (b) to produce such of those documents as are in his possession, custody or power to the applicant or, on such conditions as may be specified in the order –

        (i)   to the applicant's legal advisers; or

        (ii) to the applicant's legal advisers and any medical or other professional adviser of the applicant; or

        (iii) if the applicant has no legal adviser, to any medical or other professional adviser of the applicant;

(4) The preceding provisions of this section are without prejudice to the exercise by the High Court of any power to make orders which is exercisable apart from those provisions.

Supply of Goods and Services Act 1982

(1982, c. 29)

12   The contracts concerned

(1) In this Act a 'relevant contract for the supply of a service' means, subject to subsection (2) below, a contract under which a person ('the supplier') agrees to carry out a service.

13   Implied term about care and skill

In a relevant contract for the supply of a service where the supplier is acting in the course of a business, there is an implied term that the supplier will carry out the service with reasonable care and skill.

Mental Health Act 1983

(1983, c. 20)

PART I APPLICATION OF ACT

1   Application of Act: 'mental disorder'

(1) The provisions of this Act shall have effect with respect to the reception, care and treatment of mentally disordered patients, the management of their property and other related matters.

(2) In this Act –

'mental disorder' means any disorder or disability of the mind; and 'mentally disordered' shall be construed accordingly;

and other expressions shall have the meanings assigned to them in section 145 below.

(2A) But a person with learning disability shall not be considered by reason of that disability to be –

    (a) suffering from mental disorder for the purposes of the provisions mentioned in subsection (2B) below; or

    (b) requiring treatment in hospital for mental disorder for the purposes of sections 17E and 50 to 53 below, unless that disability is associated with abnormally aggressive or seriously irresponsible conduct on his part.

(2B) The provisions are –

    (a) sections 3, 7, 17A, 20 and 20A below;

    (b) sections 35 to 38, 45A, 47, 48 and 51 below; and

    (c) section 72(1)(b) and (c) and (4) below.

(3) Dependence on alcohol or drugs is not considered to be a disorder or disability of the mind for the purposes of subsection (2) above.

(4) In subsection (2A) above, 'learning disability' means a state of arrested or incomplete development of the mind which includes significant impairment of intelligence and social functioning.

PART II COMPULSORY ADMISSION TO HOSPITAL AND GUARDIANSHIP

Procedure for hospital admission

2   Admission for assessment

(1) A patient may be admitted to a hospital and detained there for the period allowed by subsection (4) below in pursuance of an application (in this Act referred to as 'an application for admission for assessment') made in accordance with subsections (2) and (3) below.

(2) An application for admission for assessment may be made in respect of a patient on the grounds that –

    (a) he is suffering from mental disorder of a nature or degree which warrants the detention of the patient in a hospital for assessment (or for assessment followed by medical treatment) for at least a limited period; and

    (b) he ought to be so detained in the interests of his own health or safety or with a view to the protection of other persons.

(3) An application for admission for assessment shall be founded on the written recommendations in the prescribed form of two registered medical practitioners, including in each case a statement that in the opinion of the practitioner the conditions set out in subsection (2) above are complied with.

(4) Subject to the provisions of section 29(4) below, a patient admitted to hospital in pursuance of an application for admission for assessment may be detained for a period not exceeding 28 days beginning with the day on which he is admitted, but shall not be detained after the expiration of

that period unless before it has expired he has become liable to be detained by virtue of a subsequent application, order or direction under the following provisions of this Act.

3   Admission for treatment

(1) A patient may be admitted to a hospital and detained there for the period allowed by the following provisions of this Act in pursuance of an application (in this Act referred to as 'an application for admission for treatment') made in accordance with this section.

(2) An application for admission for treatment may be made in respect of a patient on the grounds that –

(a) he is suffering from mental disorder of a nature or degree which makes it appropriate for him to receive medical treatment in a hospital; and

(c) it is necessary for the health or safety of the patient or for the protection of other persons that he should receive such treatment and it cannot be provided unless he is detained under this section; and

(d) appropriate medical treatment is available for him.

(3) An application for admission for treatment shall be founded on the written recommendations in the prescribed form of two registered medical practitioners, including in each case a statement that in the opinion of the practitioner the conditions set out in subsection (2) above are complied with; and each such recommendation shall include –

(a) such particulars as may be prescribed of the grounds for that opinion so far as it relates to the conditions set out in paragraphs (a) and (d) of that subsection; and

(b) a statement of the reasons for that opinion so far as it relates to the conditions set out in paragraph (c) of that subsection, specifying whether other methods of dealing with the patient are available and, if so, why they are not appropriate.

(4) In this Act, references to appropriate medical treatment, in relation to a person suffering from mental disorder, are references to medical treatment which is appropriate in his case, taking into account the nature and degree of the mental disorder and all other circumstances of his case.

4   Admission for assessment in cases of emergency

(1) In any case of urgent necessity, an application for admission for assessment may be made in respect of a patient in accordance with the following provisions of this section, and any application so made is in this Act referred to as 'an emergency application'.

(2) An emergency application may be made either by an approved mental health professional or by the nearest relative of the patient; and every such application shall include a statement that it is of urgent necessity for the patient to be admitted and detained under section 2 above, and that compliance with the provisions of this Part of this Act relating to applications under that section would involve undesirable delay.

(3) An emergency application shall be sufficient in the first instance if founded on one of the medical recommendations required by section 2 above, given, if practicable, by a practitioner who has previous acquaintance with the patient and otherwise complying with the requirements of section 12 below so far as applicable to a single recommendation, and verifying the statement referred to in subsection (2) above.

(4) An emergency application shall cease to have effect on the expiration of a period of 72 hours from the time when the patient is admitted to the hospital unless –

(a) the second medical recommendation required by section 2 above is given and received by the managers within that period; and

(b) that recommendation and the recommendation referred to in subsection (3) above together comply with all the requirements of section 12 below (other than the requirement as to the time of signature of the second recommendation).

(5) In relation to an emergency application, section 11 below shall have effect as if in subsection (5) of that section for the words 'the period of 14 days ending with the date of the application' there were substituted the words 'the previous 24 hours'.

5 Application in respect of patient already in hospital

(1) An application for the admission of a patient to a hospital may be made under this Part of this Act notwithstanding that the patient is already an in-patient in that hospital or, in the case of an application for admission for treatment that the patient is for the time being liable to be detained in the hospital in pursuance of an application for admission for assessment; and where an application is so made the patient shall be treated for the purposes of this Part of this Act as if he had been admitted to the hospital at the time when that application was received by the managers.

(2) If, in the case of a patient who is an in-patient in a hospital, it appears to the registered medical practitioner or approved clinician in charge of the treatment of the patient that an application ought to be made under this Part of this Act for the admission of the patient to hospital, he may furnish to the managers a report in writing to that effect; and in any such case the patient may be detained in the hospital for a period of 72 hours from the time when the report is so furnished.

(3) The registered medical practitioner or approved clinician in charge of the treatment of a patient in a hospital may nominate one (but not more than one) other registered medical practitioner on the staff of that hospital to act for him under subsection (2) above in his absence.

(3A) For the purposes of subsection (3) above –
  (a) the registered medical practitioner may nominate another registered medical practitioner, or an approved clinician, on the staff of the hospital; and
  (b) the approved clinician may nominate another approved clinician, or a registered medical practitioner, on the staff of the hospital.

(4) If, in the case of a patient who is receiving treatment for mental disorder as an in-patient in a hospital, it appears to a nurse of the prescribed class –
  (a) that the patient is suffering from mental disorder to such a degree that it is necessary for his health or safety or for the protection of others for him to be immediately restrained from leaving the hospital; and
  (b) that it is not practicable to secure the immediate attendance of a practitioner or clinician for the purpose of furnishing a report under subsection (2) above, the nurse may record that fact in writing; and in that event the patient may be detained in the hospital for a period of six hours from the time when that fact is so recorded or until the earlier arrival at the place where the patient is detained of a practitioner or clinician having power to furnish a report under that subsection.

(5) A record made under subsection (4) above shall be delivered by the nurse (or by a person authorised by the nurse in that behalf) to the managers of the hospital as soon as possible after it is made; and where a record is made under that subsection the period mentioned in subsection (2) above shall begin at the time when it is made.

(6) The reference in subsection (1) above to an in-patient does not include an in-patient who is liable to be detained in pursuance of an application under this Part of this Act or a community patient and the references in subsections (2) and (4) above do not include an in-patient who is liable to be detained in a hospital under this Part of this Act or a community patient.

(7) In subsection (4) above 'prescribed' means prescribed by an order made by the Secretary of State.

6 Effect of application for admission

(1) An application for the admission of a patient to a hospital under this Part of this Act, duly completed in accordance with the provisions of this Part of this Act, shall be sufficient authority for the applicant, or any person authorised by the applicant, to take the patient and convey him to the hospital at any time within the following period, that is to say –

(a) in the case of an application other than an emergency application, the period of 14 days beginning with the date on which the patient was last examined by a registered medical practitioner before giving a medical recommendation for the purposes of the application;

(b) in the case of an emergency application, the period of 24 hours beginning at the time when the patient was examined by the practitioner giving the medical recommendation which is referred to in section 4(3) above, or at the time when the application is made, whichever is the earlier.

(2) Where a patient is admitted within the said period to the hospital specified in such an application as is mentioned in subsection (1) above, or, being within that hospital, is treated by virtue of section 5 above as if he had been so admitted, the application shall be sufficient authority for the managers to detain the patient in the hospital in accordance with the provisions of this Act.

(3) Any application for the admission of a patient under this Part of this Act which appears to be duly made and to be founded on the necessary medical recommendations may be acted upon without further proof of the signature or qualification of the person by whom the application or any such medical recommendation is made or given or of any matter of fact or opinion stated in it.

(4) Where a patient is admitted to a hospital in pursuance of an application for admission for treatment, any previous application under this Part of this Act by virtue of which he was liable to be detained in a hospital or subject to guardianship shall cease to have effect.

Guardianship

7 Application for guardianship

(1) A patient who has attained the age of 16 years may be received into guardianship, for the period allowed by the following provisions of this Act, in pursuance of an application (in this Act referred to as 'a guardianship application') made in accordance with this section.

(2) A guardianship application may be made in respect of a patient on the grounds that –

(a) he is suffering from mental disorder of a nature or degree which warrants his reception into guardianship under this section; and

(b) it is necessary in the interests of the welfare of the patient or for the protection of other persons that the patient should be so received.

(3) A guardianship application shall be founded on the written recommendations in the prescribed form of two registered medical practitioners, including in each case a statement that in the opinion of the practitioner the conditions set out in subsection (2) above are complied with; and each such recommendation shall include –

(a) such particulars as may be prescribed of the grounds for that opinion so far as it relates to the conditions set out in paragraph (a) of that subsection; and

(b) a statement of the reasons for that opinion so far as it relates to the conditions set out in paragraph (b) of that subsection.

(4) A guardianship application shall state the age of the patient or, if his exact age is not known to the applicant, shall state (if it be the fact) that the patient is believed to have attained the age of 16 years.

(5) The person named as guardian in a guardianship application may be either a local social services authority or any other person (including the applicant himself); but a guardianship application in which a person other than a local social services authority is named as guardian shall be of no effect unless it is accepted on behalf of that person by the local social services authority for the area in which he resides, and shall be accompanied by a statement in writing by that person that he is willing to act as guardian.

8 Effect of guardianship application, etc.

(1) Where a guardianship application, duly made under the provisions of this Part of this Act and forwarded to the local social services authority within the period allowed by subsection (2) below is accepted by that authority, the application shall, subject to regulations made by the

Secretary of State, confer on the authority or person named in the application as guardian, to the exclusion of any other person –

    (a) the power to require the patient to reside at a place specified by the authority or person named as guardian;

    (b) the power to require the patient to attend at places and times so specified for the purpose of medical treatment, occupation, education or training;

    (c) the power to require access to the patient to be given, at any place where the patient is residing, to any registered medical practitioner, approved mental health professional or other person so specified.

(2) The period within which a guardianship application is required for the purposes of this section to be forwarded to the local social services authority is the period of 14 days beginning with the date on which the patient was last examined by a registered medical practitioner before giving a medical recommendation for the purposes of the application.

(3) A guardianship application which appears to be duly made and to be founded on the necessary medical recommendations may be acted upon without further proof of the signature or qualification of the person by whom the application or any such medical recommendation is made or given, or of any matter of fact or opinion stated in the application.

(4) If within the period of 14 days beginning with the day on which a guardianship application has been accepted by the local social services authority the application, or any medical recommendation given for the purposes of the application, is found to be in any respect incorrect or defective, the application or recommendation may, within that period and with the consent of that authority, be amended by the person by whom it was signed; and upon such amendment being made the application or recommendation shall have effect and shall be deemed to have had effect as if it had been originally made as so amended.

(5) Where a patient is received into guardianship in pursuance of a guardianship application, any previous application under this Part of this Act by virtue of which he was subject to guardianship or liable to be detained in a hospital shall cease to have effect.

10   Transfer of guardianship in case of death, incapacity, etc., of guardian

(1) If any person (other than a local social services authority) who is the guardian of a patient received into guardianship under this Part of this Act –

    (a) dies; or

    (b) gives notice in writing to the local social services authority that he desires to relinquish the functions of guardian,

the guardianship of the patient shall thereupon vest in the local social services authority, but without prejudice to any power to transfer the patient into the guardianship of another person in pursuance of regulations under section 19 below.

(2) If any such person, not having given notice under subsection (1)(b) above, is incapacitated by illness or any other cause from performing the functions of guardian of the patient, those functions may, during his incapacity, be performed on his behalf by the local social services authority or by any other person approved for the purposes by that authority.

(3) If it appears to the county court, upon application made by an approved mental health professional acting on behalf of the local social services authority that any person other than a local social services authority having the guardianship of a patient received into guardianship under this Part of this Act has performed his functions negligently or in a manner contrary to the interests of the welfare of the patient, the court may order that the guardianship of the patient be transferred to the local social services authority or to any other person approved for the purpose by that authority.

(4) Where the guardianship of a patient is transferred to a local social services authority or other person by or under this section, subsection (2)(c) of section 19 below shall apply as if the patient had been transferred into the guardianship of that authority or person in pursuance of regulations under that section.

(5) In this section 'the local social services authority', in relation to a person (other than a local social services authority) who is the guardian of a patient, means the local social services authority for the area in which that person resides (or resided immediately before his death).

General provisions as to applications and recommendations

11   General provisions as to applications

(1) Subject to the provisions of this section, an application for admission for assessment, an application for admission for treatment and a guardianship application may be made either by the nearest relative of the patient or by an approved mental health professional; and every such application shall specify the qualification of the applicant to make the application.

(1A) No application mentioned in subsection (1) above shall be made by an approved mental health professional if the circumstances are such that there would be a potential conflict of interest for the purposes of regulations under section 12A below.

(2) Every application for admission shall be addressed to the managers of the hospital to which admission is sought and every guardianship application shall be forwarded to the local social services authority named in the application as guardian, or, as the case may be, to the local social services authority for the area in which the person so named resides.

(3) Before or within a reasonable time after an application for the admission of a patient for assessment is made by an approved mental health professional, that professional shall take such steps as are practicable to inform the person (if any) appearing to be the nearest relative of the patient that the application is to be or has been made and of the power of the nearest relative under section 23(2) (a) below.

(4) An approved mental health professional may not make an application for admission for treatment or a guardianship application in respect of a patient in either of the following cases –

(a) the nearest relative of the patient has notified that professional, or the local social services authority on whose behalf the professional is acting, that he objects to the application being made; or

(b) that professional has not consulted the person (if any) appearing to be the nearest relative of the patient, but the requirement to consult that person does not apply if it appears to the professional that in the circumstances such consultation is not reasonably practicable or would involve unreasonable delay.

(5) None of the applications mentioned in subsection (1) above shall be made by any person in respect of a patient unless that person has personally seen the patient within the period of 14 days ending with the date of the application.

(7) Each of the applications mentioned in subsection (1) above shall be sufficient if the recommendations on which it is founded are given either as separate recommendations, each signed by a registered medical practitioner, or as a joint recommendation signed by two such practitioners.

12   General provisions as to medical recommendations

(1) The recommendations required for the purposes of an application for the admission of a patient under this Part of this Act or a guardianship application (in this Act referred to as 'medical recommendations') shall be signed on or before the date of the application, and shall be given by practitioners who have personally examined the patient either together or separately, but where they have examined the patient separately not more than five days must have elapsed between the days on which the separate examination took place.

(2) Of the medical recommendations given for the purposes of any such application, one shall be given by a practitioner approved for the purposes of this section by the Secretary of State as having special experience in the diagnosis or treatment of mental disorder; and unless that practitioner has previous acquaintance with the patient, the other such recommendation shall, if practicable, be given by a registered medical practitioner who has such previous acquaintance.

(2A) A registered medical practitioner who is an approved clinician shall be treated as also approved for the purposes of this section under subsection (2) above as having special experience as mentioned there.

(3) No medical recommendation shall be given for the purposes of an application mentioned in subsection (1) above if the circumstances are such that there would be a potential conflict of interest for the purposes of regulations under section 12A below.

12A Conflicts of interest

(1) The appropriate national authority may make regulations as to the circumstances in which there would be a potential conflict of interest such that –

    (a) an approved mental health professional shall not make an application mentioned in section 11(1) above;

    (b) a registered medical practitioner shall not give a recommendation for the purposes of an application mentioned in section 12(1) above.

13 Duty of approved mental health professionals to make applications for admission or guardianship

(1) If a local social services authority have reason to think that an application for admission to hospital or a guardianship application may need to be made in respect of a patient within their area, they shall make arrangements for an approved mental health professional to consider the patient's case on their behalf.

(1A) If that professional is –

    (a) satisfied that such an application ought to be made in respect of the patient; and

    (b) of the opinion, having regard to any wishes expressed by relatives of the patient or any other relevant circumstances, that it is necessary or proper for the application to be made by him,

he shall make the application.

(1B) Subsection (1C) below applies where –

    (a) a local social services authority makes arrangements under subsection (1) above in respect of a patient;

    (b) an application for admission for assessment is made under subsection (1A) above in respect of the patient;

    (c) while the patient is liable to be detained in pursuance of that application, the authority have reason to think that an application for admission for treatment may need to be made in respect of the patient; and

    (d) the patient is not within the area of the authority.

(1C) Where this subsection applies, subsection (1) above shall be construed as requiring the authority to make arrangements under that subsection in place of the authority mentioned there.

(2) Before making an application for the admission of a patient to hospital an approved mental health professional shall interview the patient in a suitable manner and satisfy himself that detention in a hospital is in all the circumstances of the case the most appropriate way of providing the care and medical treatment of which the patient stands in need.

(3) An application under subsection (1A) above may be made outside the area of the local social services authority on whose behalf the approved mental health professional is considering the patient's case.

(4) It shall be the duty of a local social services authority, if so required by the nearest relative of a patient residing in their area, to make arrangements under subsection (1) above for an approved mental health professional to consider the patient's case with a view to making an application for his admission to hospital; and if in any such case that professional decides not to make an application he shall inform the nearest relative of his reasons in writing.

(5) Nothing in this section shall be construed as authorising or requiring an application to be made by an approved mental health professional in contravention of the provisions of section 11(4)

above or of regulations under section 12A above, or as restricting the power of a local social services authority to make arrangements with an approved mental health professional to consider a patient's case or of an approved mental health professional to make any application under this Act.

14 Social reports

Where a patient is admitted to a hospital in pursuance of an application (other than an emergency application) made under this Part of this Act by his nearest relative, the managers of the hospital shall as soon as practicable give notice of that fact to the local social services authority for the area in which the patient resided immediately before his admission; and that authority shall as soon as practicable arrange for an approved mental health professional to interview the patient and provide the managers with a report of his social circumstances.

15 Rectification of applications and recommendations

(1) If within the period of 14 days beginning with the day on which a patient has been admitted to a hospital in pursuance of an application for admission for assessment or for treatment the application, or any medical recommendation given for the purpose of the application, is found to be in any respect incorrect or defective, the application or recommendation may, within that period and with the consent of the managers of the hospital, be amended by the person by whom it was signed; and upon such amendment being made the application or recommendation shall have effect and shall be deemed to have had effect as if it had been originally made as so amended.

(2) Without prejudice to subsection (1) above, if within the period mentioned in that subsection it appears to the managers of the hospital that one of the two medical recommendations on which an application for the admission of a patient is founded is insufficient to warrant the detention of the patient in pursuance of the application, they may, within that period, give notice in writing to that effect to the applicant; and where any such notice is given in respect of a medical recommendation, that recommendation shall be disregarded, but the application shall be, and shall be deemed always to have been, sufficient if –

(a) a fresh medical recommendation complying with the relevant provisions of this Part of this Act (other than the provisions relating to the time of signature and the interval between examinations) is furnished to the managers within that period; and

(b) that recommendation, and the other recommendation on which the application is founded, together comply with those provisions.

(3) Where the medical recommendations upon which an application for admission is founded are, taken together, insufficient to warrant the detention of the patient in pursuance of the application, a notice under subsection (2) above may be given in respect of either of those recommendations.

(4) Nothing in this section shall be construed as authorising the giving of notice in respect of an application made as an emergency application, or the detention of a patient admitted in pursuance of such an application, after the period of 72 hours referred to in section 4(4) above, unless the conditions set out in paragraphs (a) and (b) of that section are complied with or would be complied with apart from any error or defect to which this section applies.

Position of patients subject to detention or guardianship

17 Leave of absence from hospital

(1) The responsible clinician may grant to any patient who is for the time being liable to be detained in a hospital under this Part of this Act leave to be absent from the hospital subject to such conditions (if any) as that clinician considers necessary in the interests of the patient or for the protection of other persons.

(2) Leave of absence may be granted to a patient under this section either indefinitely or on specified occasions or for any specified period; and where leave is so granted for a specified period, that period may be extended by further leave granted in the absence of the patient.

(2A) But longer-term leave may not be granted to a patient unless the responsible clinician first considers whether the patient should be dealt with under section 17A instead.

(2B) For these purposes, longer-term leave is granted to a patient if –

(a) leave of absence is granted to him under this section either indefinitely or for a specified period of more than seven consecutive days; or

(b) a specified period is extended under this section such that the total period for which leave of absence will have been granted to him under this section exceeds seven consecutive days.

(3) Where it appears to the responsible clinician that it is necessary so to do in the interests of the patient or for the protection of other persons, he may, upon granting leave of absence under this section, direct that the patient remain in custody during his absence; and where leave of absence is so granted the patient may be kept in the custody of any officer on the staff of the hospital, or of any other person authorised in writing by the managers of the hospital or, if the patient is required in accordance with conditions imposed on the grant of leave of absence to reside in another hospital, of any officer on the staff of that other hospital.

(4) In any case where a patient is absent from a hospital in pursuance of leave of absence granted under this section, and it appears to the responsible clinician that it is necessary so to do in the interests of the patient's health or safety or for the protection of other persons, that clinician may, subject to subsection (5) below, by notice in writing given to the patient or to the person for the time being in charge of the patient, revoke the leave of absence and recall the patient to the hospital.

(5) A patient to whom leave of absence is granted under this section shall not be recalled under subsection (4) above after he has ceased to be liable to be detained under this Part of this Act.

17A   Community treatment orders

(1) The responsible clinician may by order in writing discharge a detained patient from hospital subject to his being liable to recall in accordance with section 17E below.

(2) A detained patient is a patient who is liable to be detained in a hospital in pursuance of an application for admission for treatment.

(3) An order under subsection (1) above is referred to in this Act as a 'community treatment order'.

(4) The responsible clinician may not make a community treatment order unless –

(a) in his opinion, the relevant criteria are met; and

(b) an approved mental health professional states in writing –

(i)   that he agrees with that opinion; and

(ii)   that it is appropriate to make the order.

(5) The relevant criteria are –

(a) the patient is suffering from mental disorder of a nature or degree which makes it appropriate for him to receive medical treatment;

(b) it is necessary for his health or safety or for the protection of other persons that he should receive such treatment;

(c) subject to his being liable to be recalled as mentioned in paragraph (d) below, such treatment can be provided without his continuing to be detained in a hospital;

(d) it is necessary that the responsible clinician should be able to exercise the power under section 17E(1) below to recall the patient to hospital; and

(e) appropriate medical treatment is available for him.

(6) In determining whether the criterion in subsection (5)(d) above is met, the responsible clinician shall, in particular, consider, having regard to the patient's history of mental disorder and any other relevant factors, what risk there would be of a deterioration of the patient's condition if he were not detained in a hospital (as a result, for example, of his refusing or neglecting to receive the medical treatment he requires for his mental disorder).

(7) In this Act –

'community patient' means a patient in respect of whom a community treatment order is in force; 'the community treatment order', in relation to such a patient, means the community treatment order in force in respect of him; and

'the responsible hospital', in relation to such a patient, means the hospital in which he was liable to be detained immediately before the community treatment order was made, subject to section 19A below.

17B   Conditions

(1) A community treatment order shall specify conditions to which the patient is to be subject while the order remains in force.

(2) But, subject to subsection (3) below, the order may specify conditions only if the responsible clinician, with the agreement of the approved mental health professional mentioned in section 17A(4)(b) above, thinks them necessary or appropriate for one or more of the following purposes –

    (a) ensuring that the patient receives medical treatment;

    (b) preventing risk of harm to the patient's health or safety;

    (c) protecting other persons.

(3) The order shall specify –

    (a) a condition that the patient make himself available for examination under section 20A below; and

    (b) a condition that, if it is proposed to give a certificate under Part 4A of this Act that falls within section 64C(4) below in his case, he make himself available for examination so as to enable the certificate to be given.

(4) The responsible clinician may from time to time by order in writing vary the conditions specified in a community treatment order.

(5) He may also suspend any conditions specified in a community treatment order.

(6) If a community patient fails to comply with a condition specified in the community treatment order by virtue of subsection (2) above, that fact may be taken into account for the purposes of exercising the power of recall under section 17E(1) below.

(7) But nothing in this section restricts the exercise of that power to cases where there is such a failure.

17C   Duration of community treatment order

A community treatment order shall remain in force until –

    (a) the period mentioned in section 20A(1) below (as extended under any provision of this Act) expires, but this is subject to sections 21 and 22 below;

    (b) the patient is discharged in pursuance of an order under section 23 below or a direction under section 72 below;

    (c) the application for admission for treatment in respect of the patient otherwise ceases to have effect; or

    (d) the order is revoked under section 17F below, whichever occurs first.

17D   Effect of community treatment order

(1) The application for admission for treatment in respect of a patient shall not cease to have effect by virtue of his becoming a community patient.

(2) But while he remains a community patient –

    (a) the authority of the managers to detain him under section 6(2) above in pursuance of that application shall be suspended; and

    (b) reference (however expressed) in this or any other Act, or in any subordinate legislation (within the meaning of the Interpretation Act 1978), to patients liable to be detained, or detained, under this Act shall not include him.

(3) And section 20 below shall not apply to him while he remains a community patient.

(4) Accordingly, authority for his detention shall not expire during any period in which that authority is suspended by virtue of subsection (2)(a) above.

17E   Power to recall to hospital

(1) The responsible clinician may recall a community patient to hospital if in his opinion –

(a) the patient requires medical treatment in hospital for his mental disorder; and

(b) there would be a risk of harm to the health or safety of the patient or to other persons if the patient were not recalled to hospital for that purpose.

(2) The responsible clinician may also recall a community patient to hospital if the patient fails to comply with a condition specified under section 17B(3) above.

(3) The hospital to which a patient is recalled need not be the responsible hospital.

(4) Nothing in this section prevents a patient from being recalled to a hospital even though he is already in the hospital at the time when the power of recall is exercised; references to recalling him shall be construed accordingly.

(5) The power of recall under subsections (1) and (2) above shall be exercisable by notice in writing to the patient.

(6) A notice under this section recalling a patient to hospital shall be sufficient authority for the managers of that hospital to detain the patient there in accordance with the provisions of this Act.

17F   Powers in respect of recalled patients

(1) This section applies to a community patient who is detained in a hospital by virtue of a notice recalling him there under section 17E above.

(2) The patient may be transferred to another hospital in such circumstances and subject to such conditions as may be prescribed in regulations made by the Secretary of State (if the hospital in which the patient is detained is in England) or the Welsh Ministers (if that hospital is in Wales).

(3) If he is so transferred to another hospital, he shall be treated for the purposes of this section (and section 17E above) as if the notice under that section were a notice recalling him to that other hospital and as if he had been detained there from the time when his detention in hospital by virtue of the notice first began.

(4) The responsible clinician may by order in writing revoke the community treatment order if –

(a) in his opinion, the conditions mentioned in section 3(2) above are satisfied in respect of the patient; and

(b) an approved mental health professional states in writing –

(i)   that he agrees with that opinion; and

(ii)   that it is appropriate to revoke the order.

(5) The responsible clinician may at any time release the patient under this section, but not after the community treatment order has been revoked.

(6) If the patient has not been released, nor the community treatment order revoked, by the end of the period of 72 hours, he shall then be released.

(7) But a patient who is released under this section remains subject to the community treatment order.

(8) In this section –

(a) 'the period of 72 hours' means the period of 72 hours beginning with the time when the patient's detention in hospital by virtue of the notice under section 17E above begins; and

(b) references to being released shall be construed as references to being released from that detention (and accordingly from being recalled to hospital).

17G   Effect of revoking community treatment order

(1) This section applies if a community treatment order is revoked under section 17F above in respect of a patient.

(2) Section 6(2) above shall have effect as if the patient had never been discharged from hospital by virtue of the community treatment order.

(3) The provisions of this or any other Act relating to patients liable to be detained (or detained) in pursuance of an application for admission for treatment shall apply to the patient as they did before the community treatment order was made, unless otherwise provided.

(4) If, when the order is revoked, the patient is being detained in a hospital other than the responsible hospital, the provisions of this Part of this Act shall have effect as if –

    (a) the application for admission for treatment in respect of him were an application for admission to that other hospital; and

    (b) he had been admitted to that other hospital at the time when he was originally admitted in pursuance of the application.

(5) But, in any case, section 20 below shall have effect as if the patient had been admitted to hospital in pursuance of the application for admission for treatment on the day on which the order is revoked.

18   Return and readmission of patients absent without leave

(1) Where a patient who is for the time being liable to be detained under this Part of this Act in a hospital –

    (a) absents himself from the hospital without leave granted under section 17 above; or

    (b) fails to return to the hospital on any occasion on which, or at the expiration of any period for which, leave of absence was granted to him under that section, or upon being recalled under that section; or

    (c) absents himself without permission from any place where he is required to reside in accordance with conditions imposed on the grant of leave of absence under that section, he may, subject to the provisions of this section, be taken into custody and returned to the hospital or place by any approved mental health professional, by any officer on the staff of the hospital, by any constable, or by any person authorised in writing by the managers of the hospital.

(2) Where the place referred to in paragraph (c) of subsection (1) above is a hospital other than the one in which the patient is for the time being liable to be detained, the references in that subsection to an officer on the staff of the hospital and the managers of the hospital shall respectively include references to an officer on the staff of the first-mentioned hospital and the managers of that hospital.

(2A) Where a community patient is at any time absent from a hospital to which he is recalled under section 17E above, he may, subject to the provisions of this section, be taken into custody and returned to the hospital by any approved mental health professional, by any officer on the staff of the hospital, by any constable, or by any person authorised in writing by the responsible clinician or the managers of the hospital.

(3) Where a patient who is for the time being subject to guardianship under this Part of this Act absents himself without the leave of the guardian from the place at which he is required by the guardian to reside, he may, subject to the provisions of this section, be taken into custody and returned to that place by any officer on the staff of a local social services authority, by any constable, or by any person authorised in writing by the guardian or a local social services authority.

(4) A patient shall not be taken into custody under this section after the later of –

    (a) the end of the period of six months beginning with the first day of his absence without leave; and

    (b) the end of the period for which (apart from section 21 below) he is liable to be detained or subject to guardianship or, in the case of a community patient, the community treatment order is in force.

(4A) In determining for the purposes of subsection (4)(b) above or any other provision of this Act whether a person who is or has been absent without leave is at any time liable to be detained or subject to guardianship, a report furnished under section 20 or 21B below before the first day of his absence without leave shall not be taken to have renewed the authority for his detention or guardianship unless the period of renewal began before that day.

(4B) Similarly, in determining for those purposes whether a community treatment order is at any time in force in respect of a person who is or has been absent without leave, a report furnished under section 20A or 21B below before the first day of his absence without leave shall not be taken to have extended the community treatment period unless the extension began before that day.

(5) A patient shall not be taken into custody under this section if the period for which he is liable to be detained is that specified in section 2(4), 4(4) or 5(2) or (4) above and that period has expired.

(6) In this Act 'absent without leave' means absent from any hospital or other place and liable to be taken into custody and returned under this section, and related expressions shall be construed accordingly.

Duration of authority and discharge

20   Duration of authority

(1) Subject to the following provisions of this Part of this Act, a patient admitted to hospital in pursuance of an application for admission for treatment, and a patient placed under guardianship in pursuance of a guardianship application, may be detained in a hospital or kept under guardianship for a period not exceeding six months beginning with the day on which he was so admitted, or the day on which the guardianship application was accepted, as the case may be, but shall not be so detained or kept for any longer period unless the authority for his detention or guardianship is renewed under this section.

(2) Authority for the detention or guardianship of a patient may, unless the patient has previously been discharged under section 23 below, be renewed –

(a) from the expiration of the period referred to in subsection (1) above, for a further period of six months;

(b) from the expiration of any period of renewal under paragraph (a) above, for a further period of one year,

and so on for periods of one year at a time.

(3) Within the period of two months ending on the day on which a patient who is liable to be detained in pursuance of an application for admission for treatment would cease under this section to be so liable in default of the renewal of the authority for his detention, it shall be the duty of the responsible clinician –

(a) to examine the patient; and

(b) if it appears to him that the conditions set out in subsection (4) below are satisfied, to furnish to the managers of the hospital where the patient is detained a report to that effect in the prescribed form; and where such a report is furnished in respect of a patient the managers shall, unless they discharge the patient under section 23 below, cause him to be informed.

(4) The conditions referred to in subsection (3) above are that –

(a) the patient is suffering from mental disorder of a nature or degree which makes it appropriate for him to receive medical treatment in a hospital; and

(c) it is necessary for the health or safety of the patient or for the protection of other persons that he should receive such treatment and that it cannot be provided unless he continues to be detained; and

(d) appropriate medical treatment is available for him.

(5) Before furnishing a report under subsection (3) above the responsible clinician shall consult one or more other persons who have been professionally concerned with the patient's medical treatment.

(5A) But the responsible clinician may not furnish a report under subsection (3) above unless a person –

(a) who has been professionally concerned with the patient's medical treatment; but

(b) who belongs to a profession other than that to which the responsible clinician belongs, states in writing that he agrees that the conditions set out in subsection (4) above are satisfied.

(6) Within the period of two months ending with the day on which a patient who is subject to guardianship under this Part of this Act would cease under this section to be so liable in default of the renewal of the authority for his guardianship, it shall be the duty of the appropriate practitioner –

(a) to examine the patient; and

(b) if it appears to him that the conditions set out in subsection (7) below are satisfied, to furnish to the guardian and, where the guardian is a person other than a local social services authority, to the responsible local social services authority a report to that effect in the prescribed form;

and where such a report is furnished in respect of a patient, the local social services authority shall, unless they discharge the patient under section 23 below, cause him to be informed.

(7) The conditions referred to in subsection (6) above are that –

(a) the patient is suffering from mental disorder of a nature or degree which warrants his reception into guardianship; and

(b) it is necessary in the interests of the welfare of the patient or for the protection of other persons that the patient should remain under guardianship.

(8) Where a report is duly furnished under subsection (3) or (6) above, the authority for the detention or guardianship of the patient shall be thereby renewed for the period prescribed in that case by subsection (2) above.

20A Community treatment period

(1) Subject to the provisions of this Part of this Act, a community treatment order shall cease to be in force on expiry of the period of six months beginning with the day on which it was made.

(2) That period is referred to in this Act as 'the community treatment period'.

(3) The community treatment period may, unless the order has previously ceased to be in force, be extended –

(a) from its expiration for a period of six months;

(b) from the expiration of any period of extension under paragraph (a) above for a further period of one year, and so on for periods of one year at a time.

(4) Within the period of two months ending on the day on which the order would cease to be in force in default of an extension under this section, it shall be the duty of the responsible clinician –

(a) to examine the patient; and

(b) if it appears to him that the conditions set out in subsection (6) below are satisfied and if a statement under subsection (8) below is made, to furnish to the managers of the responsible hospital a report to that effect in the prescribed form.

(5) Where such a report is furnished in respect of the patient, the managers shall, unless they discharge him under section 23 below, cause him to be informed.

(6) The conditions referred to in subsection (4) above are that –

(a) the patient is suffering from mental disorder of a nature or degree which makes it appropriate for him to receive medical treatment;

(b) it is necessary for his health or safety or for the protection of other persons that he should receive such treatment;

(c) subject to his continuing to be liable to be recalled as mentioned in paragraph (d) below, such treatment can be provided without his being detained in a hospital;

(d) it is necessary that the responsible clinician should continue to be able to exercise the power under section 17E(1) above to recall the patient to hospital; and

(e) appropriate medical treatment is available for him.

(7) In determining whether the criterion in subsection (6)(d) above is met, the responsible clinician shall, in particular, consider, having regard to the patient's history of mental disorder and any other relevant factors, what risk there would be of a deterioration of the patient's condition if he were to continue not to be detained in a hospital (as a result, for example, of his refusing or neglecting to receive the medical treatment he requires for his mental disorder).

(8) The statement referred to in subsection (4) above is a statement in writing by an approved mental health professional –

(a) that it appears to him that the conditions set out in subsection (6) above are satisfied; and

(b) that it is appropriate to extend the community treatment period.

(9) Before furnishing a report under subsection (4) above the responsible clinician shall consult one or more other persons who have been professionally concerned with the patient's medical treatment.

(10) Where a report is duly furnished under subsection (4) above, the community treatment period shall be thereby extended for the period prescribed in that case by subsection (3) above.

20B   Effect of expiry of community treatment order

(1) A community patient shall be deemed to be discharged absolutely from liability to recall under this Part of this Act, and the application for admission for treatment cease to have effect, on expiry of the community treatment order, if the order has not previously ceased to be in force.

(2) For the purposes of subsection (1) above, a community treatment order expires on expiry of the community treatment period as extended under this Part of this Act, but this is subject to sections 21 and 22 below.

21   Special provisions as to patients absent without leave

(1) Where a patient is absent without leave –

(a) on the day on which (apart from this section) he would cease to be liable to be detained or subject to guardianship under this Part of this Act or, in the case of a community patient, the community treatment order would cease to be in force; or

(b) within the period of one week ending with that day,

he shall not cease to be so liable or subject, or the order shall not cease to be in force, until the relevant time.

(2) For the purposes of subsection (1) above the relevant time –

(a) where the patient is taken into custody under section 18 above, is the end of the period of one week beginning with the day on which he is returned to the hospital or place where he ought to be;

(b) where the patient returns himself to the hospital or place where he ought to be within the period during which he can be taken into custody under section 18 above, is the end of the period of one week beginning with the day on which he so returns himself; and

(c) otherwise, is the end of the period during which he can be taken into custody under section 18 above.

(3) Where a patient is absent without leave on the day on which (apart from this section) the managers would be required under section 68 below to refer the patient's case to the appropriate tribunal, that requirement shall not apply unless and until –

(a) the patient is taken into custody under section 18 above and returned to the hospital where he ought to be; or

(b) the patient returns himself to the hospital where he ought to be within the period during which he can be taken into custody under section 18 above.

(4) Where a community patient is absent without leave on the day on which (apart from this section) the 72-hour period mentioned in section 17F above would expire, that period shall not expire until the end of the period of 72 hours beginning with the time when –

(a) the patient is taken into custody under section 18 above and returned to the hospital where he ought to be; or

(b) the patient returns himself to the hospital where he ought to be within the period during which he can be taken into custody under section 18 above.

(5) Any reference in this section, or in sections 21A to 22 below, to the time when a community treatment order would cease, or would have ceased, to be in force shall be construed as a reference to the time when it would cease, or would have ceased, to be in force by reason only of the passage of time.

21A Patients who are taken into custody or return within 28 days

(1) This section applies where a patient who is absent without leave is taken into custody under section 18 above, or returns himself to the hospital or place where he ought to be, not later than the end of the period of 28 days beginning with the, first day of his absence without leave.

(2) Where the period for which the patient is liable to be detained or subject to guardianship is extended by section 21 above, any examination and report to be made and furnished in respect of the patient under section 20(3) or (6) above may be made and furnished within the period as so extended.

(3) Where the authority for the detention or guardianship of the patient is renewed by virtue of subsection (2) above after the day on which (apart from section 21 above) that authority would have expired, the renewal shall take effect as from that day.

(4) In the case of a community patient, where the period for which the community treatment order is in force is extended by section 21 above, any examination and report to be made and furnished in respect of the patient under section 20A(4) above may be made and furnished within the period as so extended.

(5) Where the community treatment period is extended by virtue of subsection (4) above after the day on which (apart from section 21 above) the order would have ceased to be in force, the extension shall take effect as from that day.

21B Patients who are taken into custody or return after more than 28 days

(1) This section applies where a patient who is absent without leave is taken into custody under section 18 above, or returns himself to the hospital or place where he ought to be, later than the end of the period of 28 days beginning with the first day of his absence without leave.

(2) It shall be the duty of the appropriate practitioner, within the period of one week beginning with the day on which the patient is returned or returns himself to the hospital or place where he ought to be (his 'return day') –

(a) to examine the patient; and

(b) if it appears to him that the relevant conditions are satisfied, to furnish to the appropriate body a report to that effect in the prescribed form;

and where such a report is furnished in respect of the patient the appropriate body shall cause him to be informed.

(3) Where the patient is liable to be detained or is a community patient (as opposed to subject to guardianship), the appropriate practitioner shall, before furnishing a report under subsection (2) above, consult –

(a) one or more other persons who have been professionally concerned with the patient's medical treatment; and

(b) an approved mental health professional.

(4) Where –

(a) the patient would (apart from any renewal of the authority for his detention or guardianship on or after his return day) be liable to be detained or subject to guardianship after the end of the period of one week beginning with that day; or

(b) in the case of a community patient, the community treatment order would (apart from any extension of the community treatment period on or after that day) be in force after the end of that period, he shall cease to be so liable or subject, or the community treatment period shall be deemed to expire, at the end of that period unless a report is duly furnished in respect of him under subsection (2) above.

(4A) If, in the case of a community patient, the community treatment order is revoked under section 17F above during the period of one week beginning with his return day –

(a) subsections (2) and (4) above shall not apply; and

(b) any report already furnished in respect of him under subsection (2) above shall be of no effect.

(5) Where the patient would (apart from section 21 above) have ceased to be liable to be detained or subject to guardianship on or before the day on which a report is duly furnished in respect of him under subsection (2) above, the report shall renew the authority for his detention or guardianship for the period prescribed in that case by section 20(2) above.

(6) Where the authority for the detention or guardianship of the patient is renewed by virtue of subsection (5) above –

(a) the renewal shall take effect as from the day on which (apart from section 21 above and that subsection) the authority would have expired; and

(b) if (apart from this paragraph) the renewed authority would expire on or before the day on which the report is furnished, the report shall further renew the authority, as from the day on which it would expire, for the period prescribed in that case by section 20(2) above.

(6A) In the case of a community patient, where the community treatment order would (apart from section 21 above) have ceased to be in force on or before the day on which a report is duly furnished in respect of him under subsection (2) above, the report shall extend the community treatment period for the period prescribed in that case by section 20A(3) above.

(6B) Where the community treatment period is extended by virtue of subsection (6A) above –

(a) the extension shall take effect as from the day on which (apart from section 21 above and that subsection) the order would have ceased to be in force; and

(b) if (apart from this paragraph) the period as so extended would expire on or before the day on which the report is furnished, the report shall further extend that period, as from the day on which it would expire, for the period prescribed in that case by section 20A(3) above.

(7) Where the authority for the detention or guardianship of the patient would expire within the period of two months beginning with the day on which a report is duly furnished in respect of him under subsection (2) above, the report shall, if it so provides, have effect also as a report duly furnished under section 20(3) or (6) above; and the reference in this subsection to authority includes any authority renewed under subsection (5) above by the report.

(7A) In the case of a community patient, where the community treatment order would (taking account of any extension under subsection (6A) above) cease to be in force within the period of two months beginning with the day on which a report is duly furnished in respect of him under subsection (2) above, the report shall, if it so provides, have effect also as a report duly furnished under section 20A(4) above.

(10) In this section –

'the appropriate body' means –

(a) in relation to a patient who is liable to be detained in a hospital, the managers of the hospital;

(b) in relation to a patient who is subject to guardianship, the responsible local social services authority;

(c) in relation to a community patient, the managers of the responsible hospital; and

the relevant conditions' means –

(a) in relation to a patient who is liable to be detained in a hospital, the conditions set out in subsection (4) of section 20 above; and

(b) in relation to a patient who is subject to guardianship, the conditions set out in subsection (7) of that section.

(c) in relation to a community patient, the conditions set out in section 20A(6) above.

22   Special provisions as to patients sentenced to imprisonment, etc.

(1) If –

(a) a qualifying patient is detained in custody in pursuance of any sentence or order passed or made by a court in the United Kingdom (including an order committing or remanding him in custody); and

(b) he is so detained for a period exceeding, or for successive periods exceeding in the aggregate, six months,

the relevant application shall cease to have effect on expiry of that period.

(2) A patient is a qualifying patient for the purposes of this section if –

(a) he is liable to be detained by virtue of an application for admission for treatment;

(b) he is subject to guardianship by virtue of a guardianship application; or

(c) he is a community patient.

(3) 'The relevant application', in relation to a qualifying patient, means –

(a) in the case of a patient who is subject to guardianship, the guardianship application in respect of him;

(b) in any other case, the application for admission for treatment in respect of him.

(4) The remaining subsections of this section shall apply if a qualifying patient is detained in custody as mentioned in subsection (1)(a) above but for a period not exceeding, or for successive periods not exceeding in the aggregate, six months.

(5) If apart from this subsection –

(a) the patient would have ceased to be liable to be detained or subject to guardianship by virtue of the relevant application on or before the day on which he is discharged from custody; or

(b) in the case of a community patient, the community treatment order would have ceased to be in force on or before that day,

he shall not cease and shall be deemed not to have ceased to be so liable or subject, or the order shall not cease and shall be deemed not to have ceased to be in force, until the end of that day.

(6) In any case (except as provided in subsection (8) below), sections 18, 21 and 21A above shall apply in relation to the patient as if he had absented himself without leave on that day.

(7) In its application by virtue of subsection (6) above section 18 above shall have effect as if –

(a) in subsection (4) for the words from 'later of' to the end there were substituted 'end of the period of 28 days beginning with the first day of his absence without leave'; and

(b) subsections (4A) and (4B) were omitted.

(8) In relation to a community patient who was not recalled to hospital under section 17E above at the time when his detention in custody began –

(a) section 18 above shall not apply; but

(b) sections 21 and 21A above shall apply as if he had absented himself without leave on the day on which he is discharged from custody and had returned himself as provided in those sections on the last day of the period of 28 days beginning with that day.

23   Discharge of patients

(1) Subject to the provisions of this section and section 25 below, a patient who is for the time being liable to be detained or subject to guardianship under this Part of this Act shall cease to be so liable or subject if an order in writing discharging him absolutely from detention or guardianship is made in accordance with this section.

(1A) Subject to the provisions of this section and section 25 below, a community patient shall cease to be liable to recall under this Part of this Act, and the application for admission for treatment cease to have effect, if an order in writing discharging him from such liability is made in accordance with this section.

(1B) An order under subsection (1) or (1A) above shall be referred to in this Act as 'an order for discharge'.

(2) An order for discharge may be made in respect of a patient –

    (a) where the patient is liable to be detained in a hospital in pursuance of an application for admission for assessment or for treatment by the responsible clinician, by the managers or by the nearest relative of the patient;

    (b) where the patient is subject to guardianship, by the responsible clinician, by the responsible local social services authority or by the nearest relative of the patient;

    (c) where the patient is a community patient, by the responsible clinician, by the managers of the responsible hospital or by the nearest relative of the patient.

(6) The powers conferred by this section on any NHS foundation trust may be exercised by any three or more persons authorised by the board of the trust in that behalf, each of whom is neither an executive director of the board nor an employee of the trust.

24   Visiting and examination of patients

(1) For the purpose of advising as to the exercise by the nearest relative of a patient who is liable to be detained or subject to guardianship under this Part of this Act, or who is a community patient, of any power to order his discharge, any registered medical practitioner or approved clinician authorised by or on behalf of the nearest relative of the patient may, at any reasonable time, visit the patient and examine him in private.

(2) Any registered medical practitioner or approved clinician authorised for the purposes of subsection (1) above to visit and examine a patient may require the production of and inspect any records relating to the detention or treatment of the patient in any hospital or to any after-care services provided for the patient under section 117 below.

25   Restrictions on discharge by nearest relative

(1) An order for the discharge of a patient who is liable to be detained in a hospital shall not be made under section 23 above by his nearest relative except after giving not less than 72 hours' notice in writing to the managers of the hospital; and if, within 72 hours after such notice has been given, the responsible clinician furnishes to the managers a report certifying that in the opinion of that clinician the patient, if discharged, would be likely to act in a manner dangerous to other persons or to himself –

    (a) any order for the discharge of the patient made by that relative in pursuance of the notice shall be of no effect; and

    (b) no further order for the discharge of the patient shall be made by that relative during the period of six months beginning with the date of the report.

(1A) Subsection (1) above shall apply to an order for the discharge of a community patient as it applies to an order for the discharge of a patient who is liable to be detained in a hospital, but with the reference to the managers of the hospital being read as a reference to the managers of the responsible hospital.

(2) In any case where a report under subsection (1) above is furnished in respect of a patient who is liable to be detained in pursuance of an application for admission for treatment, or in

respect of a community patient, the managers shall cause the nearest relative of the patient to be informed.

Functions of relatives of patients

26 Definition of 'relative' and 'nearest relative'

(1) In this Part of this Act 'relative' means any of the following persons: –

(a) husband or wife or civil partner;

(b) son or daughter;

(c) father or mother;

(d) brother or sister;

(e) grandparent;

(f) grandchild;

(g) uncle or aunt;

(h) nephew or niece.

(2) In deducing relationships for the purposes of this section, any relationship of the half-blood shall be treated as a relationship of the whole blood, and an illegitimate person shall be treated as the legitimate child of

(a) his mother, and

(b) if his father has parental responsibility for him within the meaning of section 3 of Children Act 1989, his father

(3) In this Part of this Act, subject to the provisions of this section and to the following provisions of this Part of this Act, the 'nearest relative' means the person first described in subsection (1) above who is for the time being surviving, relatives of the whole blood being preferred to relatives of the same description of the half-blood and the elder or eldest of two or more relatives described in any paragraph of that subsection being preferred to the other or others of those relatives, regardless of sex.

(4) Subject to the provisions of this section and to the following provisions of this Part of this Act, where the patient ordinarily resides with or is cared for by one or more of his relatives (or, if he is for the time being an in-patient in a hospital, he last ordinarily resided with or was cared for by one or more of his relatives) his nearest relative shall be determined –

(a) by giving preference to that relative or those relatives over the other or others; and

(b) as between two or more such relatives, in accordance with subsection (3) above.

(5) Where the person who, under subsection (3) or (4) above, would be the nearest relative of a patient –

(a) in the case of a patient ordinarily resident in the United Kingdom, the Channel Islands or the Isle of Man, is not so resident; or

(b) is the husband or wife or civil partner of the patient, but is permanently separated from the patient, either by agreement or under an order of a court, or has deserted or has been deserted by the patient for a period which has not come to an end; or

(c) is a person other than the husband, wife, civil partner, father or mother of the patient, and is for the time being under 18 years of age;

the nearest relative of the patient shall be ascertained as if that person were dead.

(6) In this section 'husband', 'wife' and 'civil partner' include a person who is living with the patient as the patient's husband or wife or as if they were civil partners, as the case may be (or, if the patient is for the time being an in-patient in a hospital, was so living until the patient was admitted), and has been or had been so living for a period of not less than six months; but a person shall not be treated by virtue of this subsection as the nearest relative of a married patient or a patient in a civil partnership unless the husband, wife or civil partner of the patient is disregarded by virtue of paragraph (b) of subsection (5) above.

(7) A person, other than a relative, with whom the patient ordinarily resides (or, if the patient is for the time being an in-patient in a hospital, last ordinarily resided before he was admitted), and

with whom he has or had been ordinarily residing for a period of not less than five years, shall be treated for the purposes of this Part of this Act as if he were a relative but –

    (a) shall be treated for the purposes of subsection (3) above as if mentioned last in subsection (1) above; and

    (b) shall not be treated by virtue of this subsection as the nearest relative of a married patient or a patient in a civil partnership unless the husband, wife or civil partner of the patient is disregarded by virtue of paragraph (b) of subsection (5) above.

27 Children and young persons in care

Where –

    (a) a patient who is a child or young person is in the care of a local authority by virtue of a care order within the meaning of the Children Act 1989; or

    (b) the rights and powers of a parent of a patient who is a child or young person are vested in a local authority by virtue of section 16 of the Social Work (Scotland) Act 1968, the authority shall be deemed to be the nearest relative of the patient in preference to any person except the patient's husband, wife or civil partner (if any).

28 Nearest relative of minor under guardianship etc.

(1) Where –

    (a) a guardian has been appointed for a person who has not attained the age of eighteen years; or

    (b) a person is named in a child arrangement (as defined by section 8 of the Children Act 1989) as a person with whom a person who has not attained the age of eighteen years is to live,

the guardian (or guardians, where there is more than one) or the person so named (or the persons so named, where there is more than one) shall, to the exclusion of any other person, be deemed to be his nearest relative.

(2) Subsection (5) of section 26 above shall apply in relation to a person who is, or who is one of the persons, deemed to be the nearest relative of a patient by virtue of this section as it applies in relation to a person who would be the nearest relative under subsection (3) of that section.

(3) In this section 'guardian' includes a special guardian (within the meaning of the Children Act 1989), but does not include a guardian under this Part of this Act.

29 Appointment by court of acting nearest relative

(1) The county court may, upon application made in accordance with the provisions of this section in respect of a patient, by order direct that the functions of the nearest relative of the patient under this Part of this Act and sections 66 and 69 below shall, during the continuance in force of the order, be exercisable by the person specified in the order.

(1A) If the court decides to make an order on an application under subsection (1) above, the following rules have effect for the purposes of specifying a person in the order –

    (a) if a person is nominated in the application to act as the patient's nearest relative and that person is, in the opinion of the court, a suitable person to act as such and is willing to do so, the court shall specify that person (or, if there are two or more such persons, such one of them as the court thinks fit);

    (b) otherwise, the court shall specify such person as is, in its opinion, a suitable person to act as the patient's nearest relative and is willing to do so.

(2) An order under this section may be made on the application of –

    (za) the patient;

    (a) any relative of the patient;

(b) any other person with whom the patient is residing (or, if the patient is then an in-patient in a hospital, was last residing before he was admitted); or

(c) an approved mental health professional.

(3) An application for an order under this section may be made upon any of the following grounds, that is to say –

(a) that the patient has no nearest relative within the meaning of this Act, or that it is not reasonably practicable to ascertain whether he has such a relative, or who that relative is;

(b) that the nearest relative of the patient is incapable of acting as such by reason of mental disorder or other illness;

(c) that the nearest relative of the patient unreasonably objects to the making of an application for admission for treatment or a guardianship application in respect of the patient;

(d) that the nearest relative of the patient has exercised without due regard to the welfare of the patient or the interests of the public his power to discharge the patient under this Part of this Act, or is likely to do so; or

(e) that the nearest relative of the patient is otherwise not a suitable person to act as such.

(4) If, immediately before the expiration of the period for which a patient is liable to be detained by virtue of an application for admission for assessment, an application under this section, which is an application made on the ground specified in subsection (3)(c) or (d) above, is pending in respect of the patient, that period shall be extended –

(a) in any case, until the application under this section has been finally disposed of; and

(b) if an order is made in pursuance of the application under this section, for a further period of seven days;

and for the purposes of this subsection an application under this section shall be deemed to have been finally disposed of at the expiration of the time allowed for appealing from the decision of the court or, if notice of appeal has been given within that time, when the appeal has been heard or withdrawn, and 'pending' shall be construed accordingly.

(5) An order made on the ground specified in subsection (3)(a), (b) or (e) above may specify a period for which it is to continue in force unless previously discharged under section 30 below.

(6) While an order made under this section is in force, the provisions of this Part of this Act (other than this section and section 30 below) and sections 66, 69, 132(4) and 133 below shall apply in relation to the patient as if for any reference to the nearest relative of the patient there were substituted a reference to the person having the functions of that relative and (without prejudice to section 30 below) shall so apply notwithstanding that the person who was the patient's nearest relative when the order was made is no longer his nearest relative; but this subsection shall not apply to section 66 below in the case mentioned in paragraph (h) of subsection (1) of that section.

30 Discharge and variation of orders under s. 29

(1) An order made under section 29 above in respect of a patient may be discharged by the county court upon application made –

(a) in any case, by the patient or the person having the functions of the nearest relative of the patient by virtue of the order;

(b) where the order was made on the ground specified in paragraph (a), (b) or (e) of section 29(3) above, or where the person who was the nearest relative of the patient when the order was made has ceased to be his nearest relative, on the application of the nearest relative of the patient.

(1A) But, in the case of an order made on the ground specified in paragraph (e) of section 29(3) above, an application may not be made under subsection (1)(b) above by the person who was the nearest relative of the patient when the order was made except with leave of the county court.

(2) An order made under section 29 above in respect of a patient may be varied by the county court, on the application of the person having the functions of the nearest relative by virtue of the order or on the application of the patient or of an approved mental health professional, by substituting another person for the person having those functions.

(2A) If the court decides to vary an order on an application under subsection (2) above, the following rules have effect for the purposes of substituting another person –

(a) if a person is nominated in the application to act as the patient's nearest relative and that person is, in the opinion of the court, a suitable person to act as such and is willing to do so, the court shall specify that person (or, if there are two or more such persons, such one of them as the court thinks fit);

(b) otherwise, the court shall specify such person as is, in its opinion, a suitable person to act as the patient's nearest relative and is willing to do so.

(3) If the person having the functions of the nearest relative of a patient by virtue of an order under section 29 above dies –

(a) subsections (1) and (2) above shall apply as if for any reference to that person there were substituted a reference to any relative of the patient, and

(b) until the order is discharged or varied under those provisions the functions of the nearest relative under this Part of this Act and sections 66 and 69 below shall not be exercisable by any person.

(4) An order made on the ground specified in paragraph (c) or (d) of section 29(3) above shall, unless previously discharged under subsection (1) above, cease to have effect as follows –

(a) if –

(i) on the date of the order the patient was liable to be detained or subject to guardianship by virtue of a relevant application, order or direction; or

(ii) he becomes so liable or subject within the period of three months beginning with that date; or

(iii) he was a community patient on the date of the order,

it shall cease to have effect when he is discharged under section 23 above or 72 below or the relevant application, order or direction otherwise ceases to have effect (except as a result of his being transferred in pursuance of regulations under section 19 above);

(b) otherwise, it shall cease to have effect at the end of the period of three months beginning with the date of the order.

(4A) In subsection (4) above, reference to a relevant application, order or direction is to any of the following –

(a) an application for admission for treatment;

(b) a guardianship application;

(c) an order or direction under Part 3 of this Act (other than under section 35, 36 or 38).

(4B) An order made on the ground specified in paragraph (a), (b) or (e) of section 29(3) above shall –

(a) if a period was specified under section 29(5) above, cease to have effect on expiry of that period, unless previously discharged under subsection (1) above;

(b) if no such period was specified, remain in force until it is discharged under subsection (1) above.

Supplemental

33   Special provisions as to wards of court

(1) An application for the admission to hospital of a minor who is a ward of court may be made under this Part of this Act with the leave of the court; and section 11(4) above shall not apply in relation to an application so made.

(2) Where a minor who is a ward of court is liable to be detained in a hospital by virtue of an application for admission under this Part of this Act, or is a community patient any power

exercisable under this Part of this Act or under section 66 below in relation to the patient by his nearest relative shall be exercisable by or with the leave of the court.

(3) Nothing in this Part of this Act shall be construed as authorising the making of a guardianship application in respect of a minor who is a ward of court, or the transfer into guardianship of any such minor.

(4) Where a community treatment order has been made in respect of a minor who is a ward of court, the provisions of this Part of this Act relating to community treatment orders and community patients have effect in relation to the minor subject to any order which the court makes in the exercise of its wardship jurisdiction; but this does not apply as regards any period when the minor is recalled to hospital under section 17E above.

34 Interpretation of Part II

(1) In this Part of this Act –

'the appropriate practitioner' means –

  (a) in the case of a patient who is subject to the guardianship of a person other than a local social services authority, the nominated medical attendant of the patient; and

  (b) in any other case, the responsible clinician;

'the responsible clinician' means –

  (a) in relation to a patient liable to be detained by virtue of an application for admission for assessment or an application for admission for treatment, or a community patient, the approved clinician with overall responsibility for the patient's case;

  (b) in relation to a patient subject to guardianship, the approved clinician authorised by the responsible local social services authority to act (either generally or in any particular case or for any particular purpose) as the responsible clinician…

PART III PATIENTS CONCERNED IN CRIMINAL PROCEEDINGS OR UNDER SENTENCE

Remands to hospital

35 Remand to hospital for report on accused's mental condition

(1) Subject to the provisions of this section, the Crown Court or a magistrates court may remand an accused person to a hospital specified by the court for a report on his mental condition.

(2) For the purposes of this section an accused person is –

  (a) in relation to the Crown Court, any person who is awaiting trial before the court for an offence punishable with imprisonment or who has been arraigned before the court for such an offence and has not yet been sentenced or otherwise dealt with for the offence on which he has been arraigned;

  (b) in relation to a magistrates' court, any person who has been convicted by the court of an offence punishable on summary conviction with imprisonment and any person charged with such an offence if the court is satisfied that he did the act or made the omission charged or he has consented to the exercise by the court of the powers conferred by this section.

(3) Subject to subsection (4) below, the powers conferred by this section may be exercised if –

  (a) the court is satisfied, on the written or oral evidence of a registered medical practitioner, that there is reason to suspect that the accused person is suffering from mental disorder; and

  (b) the court is of the opinion that it would be impracticable for a report on his mental condition to be made if he were remanded on bail; but those powers shall not be exercised by the Crown Court in respect of a person who has been convicted before the court if the sentence for the offence of which he has been convicted is fixed by law.

(4) The court shall not remand an accused person to a hospital under this section unless satisfied, on the written or oral evidence of the approved clinician who would be responsible for making the report or of some other person representing the managers of the hospital, that arrangements have been made for his admission to that hospital and for his admission to it within the period of seven days beginning with the date of the remand; and if the court is so satisfied it may, pending his admission, give directions for his conveyance to and detention in a place of safety.

(5) Where a court has remanded an accused person under this section it may further remand him if it appears to the court, on the written or oral evidence of the approved clinician responsible for making the report, that a further remand is necessary for completing the assessment of the accused person's mental condition.

(6) The power of further remanding an accused person under this section may be exercised by the court without his being brought before the court if he is represented by counsel or a solicitor and his counsel or solicitor is given an opportunity of being heard.

(7) An accused person shall not be remanded or further remanded under this section for more than 28 days at a time or for more than 12 weeks in all; and the court may at any time terminate the remand if it appears to the court that it is appropriate to do so.

(8) An accused person remanded to hospital under this section shall be entitled to obtain at his own expense an independent report on his mental condition from a registered medical practitioner or approved clinician chosen by him and to apply to the court on the basis of it for his remand to be terminated under subsection (7) above.

(9) Where an accused person is remanded under this section –

(a) a constable or any other person directed to do so by the court shall convey the accused person to the hospital specified by the court within the period mentioned in subsection (4) above; and

(b) the managers of the hospital shall admit him within that period and thereafter detain him in accordance with the provisions of this section.

(10) If an accused person absconds from a hospital to which he has been remanded under this section, or while being conveyed to or from that hospital, he may be arrested without warrant by any constable and shall, after being arrested, be brought as soon as practicable before the court that remanded him; and the court may thereupon terminate the remand and deal with him in any way in which it could have dealt with him if he had not been remanded under this section.

36 Remand of accused person to hospital for treatment

(1) Subject to the provisions of this section, the Crown Court may, instead of remanding an accused person in custody, remand him to a hospital specified by the court if satisfied, on the written or oral evidence of two registered medical practitioners, that

(a) he is suffering from mental disorder of a nature or degree which makes it appropriate for him to be detained in a hospital for medical treatment; and

(b) appropriate medical treatment is available for him.

(2) For the purposes of this section an accused person is any person who is in custody awaiting trial before the Crown Court for an offence punishable with imprisonment (other than an offence the sentence for which is fixed by law) or who at any time before sentence is in custody in the course of a trial before that court for such an offence.

(3) The court shall not remand an accused person under this section to a hospital unless it is satisfied, on the written or oral evidence of the approved clinician who would have overall responsibility for his case or of some other person representing the managers of the hospital, that arrangements have been made for his admission to that hospital and for his admission to it within the

period of seven days beginning with the date of the remand; and if the court is so satisfied it may, pending his admission, give directions for his conveyance to and detention in a place of safety.

(4) Where a court has remanded an accused person under this section it may further remand him if it appears to the court, on the written or oral evidence of the responsible clinician, that a further remand is warranted.

(5) The power of further remanding an accused person under this section may be exercised by the court without his being brought before the court if he is represented by counsel or a solicitor and his counsel or solicitor is given an opportunity of being heard.

(6) An accused person shall not be remanded or further remanded under this section for more than 28 days at a time or for more than 12 weeks in all; and the court may at any time terminate the remand if it appears to the court that it is appropriate to do so.

(7) An accused person remanded to hospital under this section shall be entitled to obtain at his own expense an independent report on his mental condition from a registered medical practitioner or approved clinician chosen by him and to apply to the court on the basis of it for his remand to be terminated under subsection (6) above.

(8) Subsections (9) and (10) of section 35 above shall have effect in relation to a remand under this section as they have effect in relation to a remand under that section.

Hospital and guardianship orders

37 Powers of courts to order hospital admission or guardianship

(1) Where a person is convicted before the Crown Court of an offence punishable with imprisonment other than an offence the sentence for which is fixed by law, or is convicted by a magistrates' court of an offence punishable on summary conviction with imprisonment, and the conditions mentioned in subsection (2) below are satisfied, the court may by order authorise his admission to and detention in such hospital as may be specified in the order or, as the case may be, place him under the guardianship of a local social services authority or of such other person approved by a local social services authority as may be so specified.

(2) The conditions referred to in subsection (1) above are that –

    (a) the court is satisfied, on the written or oral evidence of two registered medical practitioners, that the offender is suffering from mental disorder and that either –

        (i) the mental disorder from which the offender is suffering is of a nature or degree which makes it appropriate for him to be detained in a hospital for medical treatment and appropriate medical treatment is available for him; or

        (ii) in the case of an offender who has attained the age of 16 years, the mental disorder is of a nature or degree which warrants his reception into guardianship under this Act; and

    (b) the court is of the opinion, having regard to all the circumstances including that nature of the offence and the character and antecedents of the offender, and to the other available methods of dealing with him, that the most suitable method of disposing of the case is by means of an order under this section.

(3) Where a person is charged before a magistrates' court with any act or omission as an offence and the court would have power, on convicting him of that offence, to make an order under subsection (1) above in his case, then, if the court is satisfied that the accused did the act or made the omission charged, the court may, if it thinks fit, make such an order without convicting him.

(4) An order for the admission of an offender to a hospital (in this Act referred to as 'a hospital order') shall not be made under this section unless the court is satisfied on the written or oral evidence of the approved clinician who would have overall responsibility for his case or of some other person representing the managers of the hospital that arrangements have been made for his admission to that hospital, and for his admission to it within the period of 28 days beginning with the date of the making of such an order; and the court may, pending his admission within that period, give such directions as it thinks fit for his conveyance to and detention in a place of safety.

(5) If within the said period of 28 days it appears to the Secretary of State that by reason of an emergency or other special circumstances it is not practicable for the patient to be received into the hospital specified in the order, he may give directions for the admission of the patient to such other hospital as appears to be appropriate instead of the hospital so specified; and where such directions are given –

(a) the Secretary of State shall cause the person having the custody of the patient to be informed, and

(b) the hospital order shall have effect as if the hospital specified in the directions were substituted for the hospital specified in the order.

(6) An order placing an offender under the guardianship of a local social services authority or of any other person (in this Act referred to as 'a guardianship order') shall not be made under this section unless the court is satisfied that that authority or person is willing to receive the offender into guardianship.

(8) Where an order is made under this section, the court shall not

(a) pass sentence of imprisonment or impose a fine or make a community order (within the meaning of Part 12 of the Criminal Justice Act 2003) in respect of the offence;

(b) if the order under this section is a hospital order, make a referral order (within the meaning of the Powers of Criminal Courts (Sentencing) Act 2000 in respect of the offence; or

(c) make in respect of the offender a supervision order (within the meaning of that Act) or an order under section 150 of that Act (binding over of parent or guardian),

but the court may make any other order which it has power to make apart from this section; and for the purposes of this subsection 'sentence of imprisonment' includes any sentence or order for detention.

38   Interim hospital orders

(1) Where a person is convicted before the Crown Court of an offence punishable with imprisonment (other than an offence the sentence for which is fixed by law) or is convicted by a magistrates' court of an offence punishable on summary conviction with imprisonment and the court before or by which he is convicted is satisfied, on the written or oral evidence of two registered medical practitioners –

(a) that the offender is suffering from mental disorder; and

(b) that there is reason to suppose that the mental disorder from which the offender is suffering is such that it may be appropriate for a hospital order to made in his case, the court may, before making a hospital order or dealing with him in some other way, make an order (in this Act referred to as 'an interim hospital order') authorising his admission to such hospital as may be specified in the order and his detention there in accordance with this section.

(2) In the case of an offender who is subject to an interim hospital order the court may make a hospital order without his being brought before the court if he is represented by counsel or a solicitor and his counsel or solicitor is given an opportunity of being heard.

(3) At least one of the registered medical practitioners whose evidence is taken into account under subsection (1) above shall be employed at the hospital which is to be specified in the order.

(4) An interim hospital order shall not be made for the admission of an offender to a hospital unless the court is satisfied, on the written or oral evidence of the approved clinician who would have overall responsibility for his case or of some other person representing the managers of the hospital, that arrangements have been made for his admission to that hospital and for his admission to it within the period of 28 days beginning with the date of the order; and if the court is so satisfied the court may, pending his admission, give directions for his conveyance to and detention in a place of safety.

(5) An interim hospital order –

(a) shall be in force for such period, not exceeding 12 weeks, as the court may specify when making the order; but

(b) may be renewed for further periods of not more than 28 days at a time if it appears to the court, on the written or oral evidence of the responsible clinician, that the continuation of the order is warranted;

but no such order shall continue in force for more than six months in all and the court shall terminate the order if it makes a hospital order in respect of the offender or decides after considering the written or oral evidence of the responsible clinician to deal with the offender in some other way.

(6) The power of renewing an interim hospital order may be exercised without the offender being brought before the court if he is represented by counsel or a solicitor and his counsel or solicitor is given an opportunity of being heard.

(7) If an offender absconds from a hospital in which he is detained in pursuance of an interim hospital order, or while being conveyed to or from such a hospital, he may be arrested without warrant by a constable and shall, after being arrested, be brought as soon as practicable before the court that made the order; and the court may thereupon terminate the order and deal with him in any way in which it could have dealt with him if no such order had been made.

40   Effect of hospital orders, guardianship orders and interim hospital orders

(1) A hospital order shall be sufficient authority –

(a) for a constable, an approved mental health professional or any other person directed to do so by the court to convey the patient to the hospital specified in the order within a period of 28 days; and

(b) for the managers of the hospital to admit him at any time within that period and thereafter detain him in accordance with the provisions of this Act.

(2) A guardianship order shall confer on the authority or person named in the order as guardian the same powers as a guardianship application made and accepted under Part II of this Act.

(3) Where an interim hospital order is made in respect of an offender –

(a) a constable or any other person directed to do so by the court shall convey the offender to the hospital specified in the order within the period mentioned in section 38(4) above; and

(b) the managers of the hospital shall admit him within that period and thereafter detain him in accordance with the provisions of section 38 above.

(4) A patient who is admitted to a hospital in pursuance of a hospital order, or placed under guardianship by a guardianship order, shall, subject to the provisions of this subsection, be treated for the purposes of the provisions of this Act mentioned in Part I of Schedule 1 to this Act as if he had been so admitted or placed on the date of the order in pursuance of an application for admission for treatment or a guardianship application, as the case may be, duly made under Part II of this Act, but subject to any modifications of those provisions specified in that Part of that Schedule.

(5) Where a patient is admitted to a hospital in pursuance of a hospital order, or placed under guardianship by a guardianship order, any previous application, hospital order or guardianship order by virtue of which he was liable to be detained in a hospital or subject to guardianship shall cease to have effect; but if the first-mentioned order, or the conviction on which it was made, is quashed on appeal, this subjection shall not apply and section 22 above shall have effect as if during any period for which the patient was liable to be detained or subject to guardianship under the order, he had been detained in custody as mentioned in that section.

(6) Where –

(a) a patient admitted to a hospital in pursuance of a hospital order is absent without leave;

(b) a warrant to arrest him has been issued under section 72 of the Criminal Justice Act 1967; and

    (c) he is held pursuant to the warrant in any country or territory other than the United
        Kingdom, any of the Channel Islands and the Isle of Man,

he shall be treated as having been taken into custody under section 18 above on first being so held.

Restriction orders

41   Power of higher courts to restrict discharge from hospital

(1) Where a hospital order is made in respect of an offender by the Crown Court, and it appears to the court, having regard to the nature of the offence, the antecedents of the offender and the risk of his committing further offences if set at large, that it is necessary for the protection of the public from serious harm so to do, the court may, subject to the provisions of this section, further order that the offender shall be subject to the special restrictions set out in this section; and an order under this section shall be known as 'a restriction order'.

(2) A restriction order shall not be made in the case of any person unless at least one of the registered medical practitioners whose evidence is taken into account by the court under section 37 (2)(a) above has given evidence orally before the court.

(3) The special restrictions applicable to a patient in respect of whom a restriction order is in force are as follows –

    (a) none of the provisions of Part II of this Act relating to the duration, renewal and expiration of authority for the detention of patients shall apply, and the patient shall continue to be liable to be detained by virtue of the relevant hospital order until he is duly discharged under the said Part II or absolutely discharged under section 42, 73, 74 or 75 below;

    (aa) none of the provisions of Part II of this Act relating to community treatment orders and community patients shall apply;

    (b) no application shall be made to the appropriate tribunal in respect of a patient under section 66 or 69(1) below;

    (c) the following powers shall be exercisable only with the consent of the Secretary of State, namely –

        (i) power to grant leave of absence to the patient under section 17 above;

        (ii) power to transfer the patient in pursuance of regulations under section 19 above or in pursuance of subsection (3) of that section; and

        (iii) power to order the discharge of the patient under section 23 above;

        and if leave of absence is granted under the said section 17 power to recall the patient under that section shall vest in the Secretary of State as well as the responsible clinician; and

    (d) the power of the Secretary of State to recall the patient under the said section 17 and power to take the patient into custody and return him under section 18 above may be exercised at any time;

and in relation to any such patient section 40(4) above shall have effect as if it referred to Part II of Schedule 1 to this Act instead of Part I of that Schedule.

(4) A hospital order shall not cease to have effect under section 40(5) above if a restriction order in respect of the patient is in force at the material time.

(5) Where a restriction order in respect of a patient ceases to have effect while the relevant hospital order continues in force, the provisions of section 40 above and Part I of Schedule 1 to this Act shall apply to the patient as if he had been admitted to the hospital in pursuance of a hospital order (without a restriction order) made on the date on which the restriction order ceased to have effect.

(6) While a person is subject to a restriction order the responsible clinician shall at such intervals (not exceeding one year) as the Secretary of State may direct examine and report to the Secretary of State on that person; and every report shall contain such particulars as the Secretary of State may require.

42   Powers of Secretary of State in respect of patients subject to restriction orders

(1) If the Secretary of State is satisfied that in the case of any patient a restriction order is no longer required for the protection of the public from serious harm, he may direct that the patient shall cease to be subject to the special restrictions set out in section 41(3) above; and where the Secretary of State so directs, the restriction order shall cease to have effect, and section 41(5) above shall apply accordingly.

(2) At any time while a restriction order is in force in respect of a patient, the Secretary of State may, if he thinks fit, by warrant discharge the patient from hospital, either absolutely or subject to conditions; and where a person is absolutely discharged under this subsection, he shall thereupon cease to be liable to be detained by virtue of the relevant hospital order, and the restriction order shall cease to have effect accordingly.

(3) The Secretary of State may at any time during the continuance in force of a restriction order in respect of a patient who has been conditionally discharged under subsection (2) above by warrant recall the patient to such hospital as may be specified in the warrant.

(4) Where a patient is recalled as mentioned in subsection (3) above –

  (a) if the hospital specified in the warrant is not the hospital from which the patient was conditionally discharged, the hospital order and the restriction order shall have effect as if the hospital specified in the warrant were substituted for the hospital specified in the hospital order;

  (b) in any case, the patient shall be treated for the purposes of section 18 above as if he had absented himself without leave from the hospital specified in the warrant.

(5) If a restriction order in respect of a patient ceases to have effect after the patient has been conditionally discharged under this section, the patient shall, unless previously recalled under subsection (3) above, be deemed to be absolutely discharged on the date when the order ceases to have effect, and shall cease to be liable to be detained by virtue of the relevant hospital order accordingly.

(6) The Secretary of State may, if satisfied that the attendance at any place in Great Britain of a patient who is subject to a restriction order is desirable in the interests of justice or for the purposes of any public inquiry, direct him to be taken to that place; and where a patient is directed under this subsection to be taken to any place he shall, unless the Secretary of State otherwise directs, be kept in custody while being so taken, while at that place and while being taken back to the hospital in which he is liable to be detained.

43   Power of magistrates' courts to commit for restriction order

(1) If in the case of a person of or over the age of 14 years who is convicted by a magistrates' court of an offence punishable on summary conviction with imprisonment –

  (a) the conditions which under section 37(1) above are required to be satisfied for the making of a hospital order are satisfied in respect of the offender; but

  (b) it appears to the court, having regard to the nature of the offence, the antecedents of the offender and the risk of his committing further offences if set at large, that if a hospital order is made a restriction order should also be made,

the court may, instead of making a hospital order or dealing with him in any other manner, commit him in custody to the Crown Court to be dealt with in respect of the offence.

(2) Where an offender is committed to the Crown Court under this section, the Crown Court shall inquire into the circumstances of the case and may –

  (a) if that court would have power so to do under the foregoing provisions of this Part of this Act upon the conviction of the offender before that court of such an offence as is described in section 37(1) above, make a hospital order in his case, with or without a restriction order;

  (b) if the court does not make such an order, deal with the offender in any other manner in which the magistrates' court might have dealt with him.

(3) The Crown Court shall have the same power to make orders under sections 35, 36 and 38 above in the case of a person committed to the court under this section as the Crown Court has under those sections in the case of an accused person within the meaning of section 35 or 36 above or of a person convicted before that court as mentioned in section 38 above.

(4) The power of a magistrates' court under section 3 of the Powers of Criminal Courts (Sentencing) Act 2000 (which enables such a court to commit an offender to the Crown Court where the court is of the opinion that greater punishment should be inflicted for the offence than the court has power to inflict) shall also be exercisable by a magistrates' court where it is of the opinion that greater punishment should be inflicted as aforesaid on the offender unless a hospital order is made in his case with a restriction order.

(5) The power of the Crown Court to make a hospital order, with or without a restriction order, in the case of a person convicted before that court of an offence may, in the same circumstances and subject to the same conditions, be exercised by such a court in the case of a person committed to the court under section 5 of the Vagrancy Act 1824 (which provides for the committal to the Crown Court of persons who are incorrigible rogues within the meaning of that section).

44   Committal to hospital under s. 43

(1) Where an offender is committed under section 43(1) above and the magistrates' court by which he is committed is satisfied on written or oral evidence that arrangements have been made for the admission of the offender to a hospital in the event of an order being made under this section, the court may, instead of committing him in custody, by order direct him to be admitted to that hospital, specifying it, and to be detained there until the case is disposed of by the Crown Court, and may give such directions as it thinks fit for his production from the hospital to attend the Crown Court by which his case is to be dealt with.

(2) The evidence required by subsection (1) above shall be given by the approved clinician who would have overall responsibility for the offender's case or by some other person representing the managers of the hospital in question.

(3) The power to give directions under section 37(4) above, section 37(5) above and section 40(1) above shall apply in relation to an order under this section as they apply in relation to a hospital order, but as if references to the period of 28 days mentioned in section 40(1) above were omitted; and subject as aforesaid an order under this section shall, until the offender's case is disposed of by the Crown Court, have the same effect as a hospital order together with a restriction order.

45   Appeals from magistrates' courts

(1) Where on the trial of an information charging a person with an offence a magistrates' court makes a hospital order or guardianship order in respect of him without convicting him, he shall have the same right of appeal against the order as if it had been made on his conviction; and on any such appeal the Crown Court shall have the same powers as if the appeal had been against both conviction and sentence.

(2) An appeal by a child or young person with respect to whom any such order has been made, whether the appeal is against the order or against the finding upon which the order was made, may be brought by him or by his parent or guardian on his behalf.

Transfer to hospital of prisoners, etc.

47   Removal to hospital of persons serving sentences of imprisonment, etc.

(1) If in the case of a person serving a sentence of imprisonment the Secretary of State is satisfied, by reports from at least two registered medical practitioners –

(a) that the said person is suffering from mental disorder; and

(b) that the mental disorder from which that person is suffering is of a nature or degree which makes it appropriate for him to be detained in a hospital for medical treatment; and

(c) that appropriate medical treatment is available for him;

the Secretary of State may, if he is of the opinion having regard to the public interest and all the circumstances that it is expedient so to do, by warrant direct that that person be removed to and detained in such hospital (not being a mental nursing home) as may be specified in the direction; and a direction under this section shall be known as 'a transfer direction'.

(2) A transfer direction shall cease to have effect at the expiration of the period of 14 days beginning with the date on which it is given unless within that period the person with respect to whom it was given has been received into the hospital specified in the direction.

(3) A transfer direction with respect to any person shall have the same effect as a hospital order made in his case.

(5) References in this Part of this Act to a person serving a sentence of imprisonment include references –
  (a) to a person detained in pursuance of any sentence or order for detention made by a court in criminal proceedings (other than an order made in consequence of a finding of insanity or unfitness to stand trial);
  (b) to a person committed to custody under section 115(3) of the Magistrates' Courts Act 1980 (which relates to persons who fail to comply with an order to enter into recognisances to keep the peace or be of good behaviour); and
  (c) to a person committed by a court to a prison or other institution to which the Prison Act 1952 applies in default of payment of any sum adjudged to be paid on his conviction.

48   Removal to hospital of other prisoners

(1) If in the case of a person to whom this section applies the Secretary of State is satisfied by the same reports as are required for the purposes of section 47 above that –
  (a) that person is suffering from mental disorder of a nature or degree which makes it appropriate for him to be detained in a hospital for medical treatment;
  (b) he is in urgent need of such treatment; and
  (c) appropriate medical treatment is available for him;
the Secretary of State shall have the same power of giving a transfer direction in respect of him under that section as if he were serving a sentence of imprisonment.

(2) This section applies to the following persons, that is to say –
  (a) persons detained in a prison or remand centre, not being persons serving a sentence of imprisonment or persons falling within the following paragraphs of this subsection;
  (b) persons remanded in custody by a magistrates' court;
  (c) civil prisoners, that is to say, persons committed by a court to prison for a limited term, who are not persons falling to be dealt with under section 47 above;
  (d) persons detained under the Immigration Act 1971 or under section 62 of the Nationality, Immigration and Asylum Act 2002 (detention by the Secretary of State).

(3) Subsections (2) and (3) of section 47 above shall apply for the purposes of this section and of any transfer direction given by virtue of this section as they apply for the purposes of that section and of any transfer direction under that section.

49   Restriction on discharge of prisoners removed to hospital

(1) Where a transfer direction is given in respect of any person, the Secretary of State, if he thinks fit, may by warrant further direct that that person shall be subject to the special restrictions set out in section 41 above; and where the Secretary of State gives a transfer direction in respect of any such person as is described in paragraph (a) or (b) of section 48(2) above, he shall also give a direction under this section applying those restrictions to him.

(2) A direction under this section shall have the same effect as a restriction order made under section 41 above and shall be known as 'a restriction direction'.

(3) While a person is subject to a restriction direction the responsible clinician shall at such intervals (not exceeding one year) as the Secretary of State may direct examine and report to the

Secretary of State on that person; and every report shall contain such particulars as the Secretary of State may require.

50   Further provisions as to prisoners under sentence

(1) Where a transfer direction and a restriction direction have been given in respect of a person serving a sentence of imprisonment and before his release date the Secretary of State is notified by the responsible clinician, any other approved clinician or the appropriate tribunal that that person no longer requires treatment in hospital for mental disorder or that no effective treatment for his disorder can be given in the hospital to which he has been removed, the Secretary of State may –

(a) by warrant direct that he be remitted to any prison or other institution in which he might have been detained if he had not been removed to hospital, there to be dealt with as if he had not been so removed; or

(b) exercise any power of releasing him on licence or discharging him under supervision which would have been exercisable if he had been remitted to such a prison or institution as aforesaid,

and on his arrival in the prison or other institution or, as the case may be, his release or discharge as aforesaid, the transfer direction and the restriction direction shall cease to have effect.

(2) A restriction direction in the case of a person serving a sentence of imprisonment shall cease to have effect on his release date.

(3) In this section, references to a person's release date are to the day (if any) on which he would be entitled to be released (whether unconditionally or on licence) from any prison or other institution in which he might have been detained if the transfer direction had not been given; and in determining that day there shall be disregarded –

(a) any powers that would be exercisable by the Parole Board if he were detained in such a prison or other institution; and

(b) any practice of the Secretary of State in relation to the early release under discretionary powers of persons detained in such a prison or other institution.

(4) For the purposes of section 49(2) of the Prison Act 1952 (which provides for discounting from the sentences of certain prisoners periods while they are unlawfully at large) a patient who, having been transferred in pursuance of a transfer direction from any such institution as is referred to in that section, is at large in circumstances in which he is liable to be taken into custody under any provision of this Act, shall be treated as unlawfully at large and absent from that institution.

51   Further provisions as to detained persons

(1) This section has effect where a transfer direction has been given in respect of any such person as is described in paragraph (a) of section 48(2) above and that person is in this section referred to as 'the detainee'.

(2) The transfer direction shall cease to have effect when the detainee's case is disposed of by the court having jurisdiction to try or otherwise deal with him, but without prejudice to any power of that court to make a hospital order or other order under this Part of this Act in his case.

(3) If the Secretary of State is notified by the responsible clinician, any other approved clinician or the appropriate tribunal at any time before the detainee's case is disposed of by that court –

(a) that the detainee no longer requires treatment in hospital for mental disorder; or

(b) that no effective treatment for his disorder can be given at the hospital to which he has been removed,

the Secretary of State may by warrant direct that he be remitted to any place where he might have been detained if he had not been removed to hospital, there to be dealt with as if he had not been so removed, and on his arrival at the place to which he is so remitted the transfer direction shall cease to have effect.

(4) If (no direction having been given under subsection (3) above) the court having jurisdiction to try or otherwise deal with the detainee is satisfied on the written or oral evidence of the responsible clinician –

    (a) that the detainee no longer requires treatment in hospital for mental disorder; or

    (b) that no effective treatment for his disorder can be given at the hospital to which he has been removed,

the court may order him to be remitted to any such place as is mentioned in subsection (3) above or, subject to section 25 of the Criminal Justice and Public Order Act 1994, released on bail and on his arrival at that place or, as the case may be, his release on bail the transfer direction shall cease to have effect.

(5) If (no direction or order having been given or made under subsection (3) or (4) above) it appears to the court having jurisdiction to try or otherwise deal with the detainee –

    (a) that it is impracticable or inappropriate to bring the detainee before the court; and

    (b) that the conditions set out in subsection (6) below are satisfied,

the court may make a hospital order (with or without a restriction order) in his case in his absence and, in the case of a person awaiting trial, without convicting him.

(6) A hospital order may be made in respect of a person under subsection (5) above if the court –

    (a) is satisfied, on the written or oral evidence of at least two registered medical practitioners, that

        (i)   the detainee is suffering from mental disorder of a nature or degree which makes it appropriate for the patient to be detained in a hospital for medical treatment; and

        (ii) appropriate medical treatment is available for him; and

    (b) is of the opinion, after considering any depositions or other documents required to be sent to the proper officer of the court, that it is proper to make such an order.

(7) Where a person committed to the Crown Court to be dealt with under section 43 above is admitted to a hospital in pursuance of an order under section 44 above, subsections (5) and (6) above shall apply as if he were a person subject to a transfer direction.

52   Further provisions as to persons remanded by magistrates' courts

(1) This section has effect where a transfer direction has been given in respect of any such person as is described in paragraph (b) of section 48(2) above; and that person is in this section referred to as 'the accused'.

(2) Subject to subsection (5) below, the transfer direction shall cease to have effect on the expiration of the period of remand unless the accused is sent in custody to the Crown Court for trial or to be otherwise dealt with.

(3) Subject to subsection (4) below, the power of further remanding the accused under section 128 of the Magistrates' Courts Act 1980 may be exercised by the court without his being brought before the court; and if the court further remands the accused in custody (whether or not he is brought before the court) the period of remand shall, for the purposes of this section, be deemed not to have expired.

(4) The court shall not under subsection (3) above further remand the accused in his absence unless he has appeared before the court within the previous six months.

(5) If the magistrates' court is satisfied, on the written or oral evidence of the responsible clinician –

    (a) that the accused no longer requires treatment in hospital for mental disorder; or

    (b) that no effective treatment for his disorder can be given in the hospital to which he has been removed,

the court may direct that the transfer direction shall cease to have effect notwithstanding that the period of remand has not expired or that the accused is sent to the Crown Court as mentioned in subsection (2) above.

(6) If the accused is sent to the Crown Court as mentioned in subsection (2) above and the transfer direction has not ceased to have effect under subsection (5) above, section 51 above shall apply as if the transfer direction given in his case were a direction given in respect of a person falling within that section.

(7) The magistrates' court may, in the absence of the accused, send him to the Crown Court for trial under section 51 or 51A of the Crime and Disorder Act 1998 if –

    (a) the court is satisfied, on the written or oral evidence of the responsible clinician, that the accused is unfit to take part in the proceedings; and

    (b) the accused is represented by counsel or a solicitor.

53   Further provisions as to civil prisoners and persons detained under the Immigration Act 1971

(1) Subject to subsection (2) below, a transfer direction given in respect of any such person as is described in paragraph (c) or (d) of section 48(2) above shall cease to have effect on the expiration of the period during which he would, but for his removal to hospital, be liable to be detained in the place from which he was removed.

(2) Where a transfer direction and a restriction direction have been given in respect of any such person as is mentioned in subsection (1) above, then, if the Secretary of State is notified by the responsible clinician, any approved clinician or the appropriate tribunal at any time before the expiration of the period there mentioned –

    (a) that that person no longer requires treatment in hospital for mental disorder; or

    (b) that no effective treatment for his disorder can be given in the hospital to which he has been removed,

the Secretary of State may be warrant direct that he be remitted to any place where he might have been detained if he had not been removed to hospital, and on his arrival at the place to which he is so remitted the transfer direction and the restriction direction shall cease to have effect.

Supplemental

54   Requirements as to medical evidence

(1) The registered medical practitioner whose evidence is taken into account under section 35(3) (a) above and at least one of the registered medical practitioners whose evidence is taken into account under sections 36(1), 37(2)(a), 38(1), 45A(2) and 51(6)(a) above and whose reports are taken into account under sections 47(1) and 48(1) above shall be a practitioner approved for the purposes of section 12 above by the Secretary of State or by another person by virtue of section 12ZA or 12ZB above, as having special experience in the diagnosis or treatment of mental disorder.

(2) For the purposes of any provision of this Part of this Act under which a court may act on the written evidence of any person, a report in writing purporting to be signed by that person may, subject to the provisions of this section, be received in evidence without proof of the following –

    (a) the signature of the person; or

    (b) his having the requisite qualifications or approval or authority or being of the requisite description to give the report.

(2A) But the court may require the signatory of any such report to be called to give oral evidence.

(3) Where, in pursuance of a direction of the court, any such report is tendered in evidence otherwise than by or on behalf of the person who is the subject of the report, then –

    (a) if that person is represented by counsel or a solicitor, a copy of the report shall be given to his counsel or solicitor;

    (b) if that person is not so represented, the substance of the report shall be disclosed to him or, where he is a child or young person, to his parent or guardian if present in court; and

    (c) except where the report relates only to arrangements for his admission to a hospital, that person may require the signatory of the report to be called to give oral evidence, and evidence to rebut the evidence contained in the report may be called by or on behalf of that person.

55 Interpretation of Part III

(1) In this Part of this Act –

'child' and 'young person' have the same meaning as in the Children and Young Persons Act 1933; 'civil prisoner' has the meaning given to it by section 48(2)(c) above;

'guardian', in relation to a child or young person, has the same meaning as in the Children and Young Persons Act 1933;

'place of safety', in relation to a person who is not a child or young person, means any police station, prison or remand centre, or any hospital the managers of which are willing temporarily to receive him, and in relation to a child or young person has the same meaning as in the Children and Young Persons Act 1933;

'responsible clinician', in relation to a person liable to be detained in a hospital within the meaning of Part 2 of this Act, means the approved clinician with overall responsibility for the patient's case.

PART IV CONSENT TO TREATMENT

56 Patients to whom Part IV applies

(1) Section 57 and, so far as relevant to that section, sections 59 to 62 below apply to any patient.

(2) Subject to that and to subsection (5) below, this Part of this Act applies to a patient only if he falls within subsection (3) or (4) below.

(3) A patient falls within this subsection if he is liable to be detained under this Act but not if –

    (a) he is so liable by virtue of an emergency application and the second medical recommendation referred to in section 4(4)(a) above has not been given and received;

    (b) he is so liable by virtue of section 5(2) or (4) or 35 above or section 135 or 136 below or by virtue of a direction for his detention in a place of safety under section 37(4) or 45A(5) above; or

    (c) he has been conditionally discharged under section 42(2) above or section 73 or 74 below and he is not recalled to hospital.

(4) A patient falls within this subsection if –

    (a) he is a community patient; and

    (b) he is recalled to hospital under section 17E above.

(5) Section 58A and, so far as relevant to that section, sections 59 to 62 below also apply to any patient who –

    (a) does not fall within subsection (3) above;

    (b) is not a community patient; and

    (c) has not attained the age of 18 years.

57 Treatment requiring consent and a second opinion

(1) This section applies to the following forms of medical treatment for mental disorder –

    (a) any surgical operation for destroying brain tissue or for destroying the functioning of brain tissue; and

    (b) such other forms of treatment as may be specified for the purposes of this section by regulations made by the Secretary of State.

(2) Subject to section 62 below, a patient shall not be given any form of treatment to which this section applies unless he has consented to it and –

    (a) a registered medical practitioner appointed for the purposes of this Part of this Act by the regulatory authority (not being the responsible clinician (if there is one) or the person in charge of the treatment in question) and two other persons appointed for the purposes of this paragraph by the regulatory authority (not being registered medical practitioners) have certified in writing that the patient is capable of understanding the nature, purpose and likely effects of the treatment in question and has consented to it; and

(b) the registered medical practitioner referred to in paragraph (a) above has certified in writing that it is appropriate for the treatment to be given.

(3) Before giving a certificate under subsection (2)(b) above the registered medical practitioner concerned shall consult two other persons who have been professionally concerned with the patient's medical treatment, but of those persons –

(a) one shall be a nurse and the other shall be neither a nurse nor a registered medical practitioner; and

(b) neither shall be the responsible clinician (if there is one) or the person in charge of the treatment in question.

(4) Before making any regulations for the purpose of this section the Secretary of State shall consult such bodies as appear to him to be concerned.

58   Treatment requiring consent or a second opinion

(1) This section applies to the following forms of medical treatment for mental disorder –

(a) such forms of treatment as may be specified for the purposes of this section by regulations made by the Secretary of State;

(b) the administration of medicine to a patient by any means (not being a form of treatment specified under paragraph (a) above or section 57 above or section 58A(1)(b) below) at any time during a period for which he is liable to be detained as a patient to whom this Part of this Act applies if three months or more have elapsed since the first occasion in that period when medicine was administered to him by any means for his mental disorder.

(2) The Secretary of State may by order vary the length of the period mentioned in subsection (1)(b) above.

(3) Subject to section 62 below, a patient shall not be given any form of treatment to which this section applies unless –

(a) he has consented to that treatment and either the approved clinician in charge of it or a registered medical practitioner appointed for the purposes of this Part of this Act by the regulatory authority has certified in writing that the patient is capable of understanding its nature, purpose and likely effects and has consented to it; or

(b) a registered medical practitioner appointed as aforesaid (not being the responsible clinician or the approved clinician in charge of the treatment in question) has certified in writing that the patient is not capable of understanding the nature, purpose and likely effects of that treatment or being so capable has not consented to it but that it is appropriate for the treatment to be given.

(4) Before giving a certificate under subsection (3)(b) above the registered medical practitioner concerned shall consult two other persons who have been professionally concerned with the patient's medical treatment, but of those persons –

(a) one shall be a nurse and the other shall be neither a nurse nor a registered medical practitioner; and

(b) neither shall be the responsible clinician (if there is one) or the person in charge of the treatment in question.

(5) Before making any regulations for the purposes of this section the Secretary of State shall consult such bodies as appear to him to be concerned.

58A   Electro-convulsive therapy, etc.

(1) This section applies to the following forms of medical treatment for mental disorder –

(a) electro-convulsive therapy; and

    (b) such other forms of treatment as may be specified for the purposes of this section by regulations made by the appropriate national authority.

(2) Subject to section 62 below, a patient shall not be given any form of treatment to which this section applies unless he falls within subsection (3), (4) or (5) below.

(3) A patient falls within this subsection if –

    (a) he has attained the age of 18 years;

    (b) he has consented to the treatment in question; and

    (c) either the approved clinician in charge of it or a registered medical practitioner appointed as mentioned in section 58(3) above has certified in writing that the patient is capable of understanding the nature, purpose and likely effects of the treatment and has consented to it.

(4) A patient falls within this subsection if –

    (a) he has not attained the age of 18 years; but

    (b) he has consented to the treatment in question; and

    (c) a registered medical practitioner appointed as aforesaid (not being the approved clinician in charge of the treatment) has certified in writing –

        (i)   that the patient is capable of understanding the nature, purpose and likely effects of the treatment and has consented to it; and

        (ii) that it is appropriate for the treatment to be given.

(5) A patient falls within this subsection if a registered medical practitioner appointed as aforesaid (not being the responsible clinician, if there is one, or the approved clinician in charge of the treatment in question) has certified in writing –

    (a) that the patient is not capable of understanding the nature, purpose and likely effects of the treatment; but

    (b) that it is appropriate for the treatment to be given; and

    (c) that giving him the treatment would not conflict with –

        (i)   an advance decision which the registered medical practitioner concerned is satisfied is valid and applicable; or

        (ii) a decision made by a donee or deputy or by the Court of Protection.

(6) Before giving a certificate under subsection (5) above the registered medical practitioner concerned shall consult two other persons who have been professionally concerned with the patient's medical treatment but, of those persons –

    (a) one shall be a nurse and the other shall be neither a nurse nor a registered medical practitioner; and

    (b) neither shall be the responsible clinician (if there is one) or the approved clinician in charge of the treatment in question.

(7) This section shall not by itself confer sufficient authority for a patient who falls within section 56(5) above to be given a form of treatment to which this section applies if he is not capable of understanding the nature, purpose and likely effects of the treatment (and cannot therefore consent to it).

(8) Before making any regulations for the purposes of this section, the appropriate national authority shall consult such bodies as appear to it to be concerned.

(9) In this section –

    (a) a reference to an advance decision is to an advance decision (within the meaning of the Mental Capacity Act 2005) made by the patient;

    (b) 'valid and applicable', in relation to such a decision, means valid and applicable to the treatment in question in accordance with section 25 of that Act;

    (c) a reference to a donee is to a donee of a lasting power of attorney (within the meaning of section 9 of that Act) created by the patient, where the donee is acting within the scope of his authority and in accordance with that Act; and

    (d) a reference to a deputy is to a deputy appointed for the patient by the Court of Protection under section 16 of that Act, where the deputy is acting within the scope of his authority and in accordance with that Act.

  (10) In this section, 'the appropriate national authority' means –

    (a) in a case where the treatment in question would, if given, be given in England, the Secretary of State;

    (b) in a case where the treatment in question would, if given, be given in Wales, the Welsh Ministers.

59   Plans of treatment

Any consent or certificate under section 57, 58 or 58A above may relate to a plan of treatment under which the patient is to be given (whether within a specified period or otherwise) one or more of the forms of treatment to which that section applies.

60   Withdrawal of consent

    (1) Where the consent of a patient to any treatment has been given for the purposes of section 57, 58 or 58A above, the patient may, subject to section 62 below, at any time before the completion of the treatment withdraw his consent, and those sections shall then apply as if the remainder of the treatment were a separate form of treatment.

    (1A) Subsection (1B) below applies where –

    (a) the consent of a patient to any treatment has been given for the purposes of section 57, 58 or 58A above; but

    (b) before the completion of the treatment, the patient ceases to be capable of understanding its nature, purpose and likely effects.

    (1B) The patient shall, subject to section 62 below, be treated as having withdrawn his consent, and those sections shall then apply as if the remainder of the treatment were a separate form of treatment.

    (1C) Subsection (1D) below applies where –

    (a) a certificate has been given under section 58 or 58A above that a patient is not capable of understanding the nature, purpose and likely effects of the treatment to which the certificate applies; but

    (b) before the completion of the treatment, the patient becomes capable of understanding its nature, purpose and likely effects.

    (1D) The certificate shall, subject to section 62 below, cease to apply to the treatment and those sections shall then apply as if the remainder of the treatment were a separate form of treatment.

    (2) Without prejudice to the application of subsections (1) to (1D) above to any treatment given under the plan of treatment to which a patient has consented, a patient who has consented to such a plan may, subject to section 62 below, at any time withdraw his consent to further treatment, or to further treatment of any description, under the plan.

61   Review of treatment

    (1) Where a patient is given treatment in accordance with section 57(2), 58(3)(b) or 58A(4) or (5) above or by virtue of section 62A below in accordance with a Part 4A certificate (within the meaning of that section) that falls within section 64C(4) below, a report on the treatment and the patient's condition shall be given by the approved clinician in charge of the treatment to the regulatory authority –

    (a) on the next occasion on which the responsible clinician furnishes a report in respect of the patient under section 20(3), 20A(4) or 21B(2) above in respect of the patient; and

    (b) at any other time if so required by the regulatory authority.

    (2) In relation to a patient who is subject to a restriction order, limitation direction or restriction direction subsection (1) above shall have effect as if paragraph (a) required the report to be made –

    (a) in the case of treatment in the period of six months beginning with the date of the order or direction, at the end of that period;

(b) in the case of treatment at any subsequent time, on the next occasion on which the responsible clinician makes a report in respect of the patient under section 41(6) or 49(3) above.

(3) The regulatory authority may at any time give notice directing that, subject to section 62 below, a certificate given in respect of a patient under section 57(2), 58(3)(b) or 58A(4) or (5) above shall not apply to treatment given to him (whether in England or Wales) after a date specified in the notice and sections 57, 58 and 58A above shall then apply to any such treatment as if that certificate had not been given.

(3A) The notice under subsection (3) above shall be given to the approved clinician in charge of the treatment.

62   Urgent treatment

(1) Sections 57 and 58 above shall not apply to any treatment –

(a) which is immediately necessary to save the patient's life; or

(b) which (not being irreversible) is immediately necessary to prevent a serious deterioration of his condition; or

(c) which (not being irreversible or hazardous) is immediately necessary to alleviate serious suffering by the patient; or

(d) which (not being irreversible or hazardous) is immediately necessary and represents the minimum interference necessary to prevent the patient from behaving violently or being a danger to himself or to others.

(1A) Section 58A above, in so far as it relates to electro-convulsive therapy by virtue of subsection (1)(a) of that section, shall not apply to any treatment which falls within paragraph (a) or (b) of subsection (1) above.

(1B) Section 58A above, in so far as it relates to a form of treatment specified by virtue of subsection (1)(b) of that section, shall not apply to any treatment which falls within such of paragraphs (a) to (d) of subsection (1) above as may be specified in regulations under that section.

(1C) For the purposes of subsection (1B) above, the regulations –

(a) may make different provision for different cases (and may, in particular, make different provision for different forms of treatment);

(b) may make provision which applies subject to specified exceptions; and

(c) may include transitional, consequential, incidental or supplemental provision.

(2) Sections 60 and 61(3) above shall not preclude the continuation of any treatment or of treatment under any plan pending compliance with section 57, 58 or 58A above if the approved clinician in charge of the treatment considers that the discontinuance of the treatment or of treatment under the plan would cause serious suffering to the patient.

(3) For the purposes of this section treatment is irreversible if it has unfavourable irreversible physical or psychological consequences and hazardous if it entails significant physical hazard.

62A   Treatment on recall of community patient or revocation of order

(1) This section applies where –

(a) a community patient is recalled to hospital under section 17E above; or

(b) a patient is liable to be detained under this Act following the revocation of a community treatment order under section 17F above in respect of him.

(2) For the purposes of section 58(1)(b) above, the patient is to be treated as if he had remained liable to be detained since the making of the community treatment order.

(3) But section 58 above does not apply to treatment given to the patient if –

(a) the certificate requirement is met for the purposes of section 64C or 64E below; or

(b) as a result of section 64B(4) or 64E(4) below, the certificate requirement would not apply (were the patient a community patient not recalled to hospital under section 17E above).

(4) Section 58A above does not apply to treatment given to the patient if there is authority to give the treatment, and the certificate requirement is met, for the purposes of section 64C or 64E below.

(5) In a case where this section applies and the Part 4A certificate falls within section 64C(4) below, the certificate requirement is met only in so far as –

(a) the Part 4A certificate expressly provides that it is appropriate for one or more specified forms of treatment to be given to the patient in that case (subject to such conditions as may be specified); or

(b) a notice having been given under subsection (5) of section 64H below, treatment is authorised by virtue of subsection (8) of that section.

(6) Subsection (5)(a) above shall not preclude the continuation of any treatment, or of treatment under any plan, pending compliance with section 58 or 58A above or 64B or 64E below if the approved clinician in charge of the treatment considers that the discontinuance of the treatment, or of the treatment under the plan, would cause serious suffering to the patient.

(6A) In a case where this section applies and the certificate requirement is no longer met for the purposes of section 64C(4A) below, the continuation of any treatment, or of treatment under any plan, pending compliance with section 58 or 58A above or 64B or 64E below shall not be precluded if the approved clinician in charge of the treatment considers that the discontinuance of the treatment, or of treatment under the plan, would cause serious suffering to the patient.

(7) In a case where subsection (1)(b) above applies, subsection (3) above only applies pending compliance with section 58 above.

(8) In subsection (5) above –

'Part 4A certificate' has the meaning given in section 64H below; and

'specified', in relation to a Part 4A certificate, means specified in the certificate.

63   Treatment not requiring consent

The consent of a patient shall not be required for any medical treatment given to him for the mental disorder from which he is suffering, not being a form of treatment to which section 57, 58 or 58A above applies, if the treatment is given by or under the direction of the approved clinician in charge of the treatment.

64   Supplementary provisions for Part IV

(1) In this Part of this Act 'the responsible clinician' means the approved clinician with overall responsibility for the case of the patient in question and 'hospital' includes a registered establishment.

(1A) References in this Part of this Act to the approved clinician in charge of a patient's treatment shall, where the treatment in question is a form of treatment to which section 57 above applies, be construed as references to the person in charge of the treatment.

(1B) References in this Part of this Act to the approved clinician in charge of a patient's treatment shall, where the treatment in question is a form of treatment to which section 58A above applies and the patient falls within section 56(5) above, be construed as references to the person in charge of the treatment.

(1C) Regulations made by virtue of section 32(2)(d) above apply for the purposes of this Part as they apply for the purposes of Part 2 of this Act.

(2) Any certificate for the purposes of this Part of this Act shall be in such form as may be prescribed by regulations made by the Secretary of State.

(3) For the purposes of this Part of this Act, it is appropriate for treatment to be given to a patient if the treatment is appropriate in his case, taking into account the nature and degree of the mental disorder from which he is suffering and all other circumstances of his case.

PART IVA TREATMENT OF COMMUNITY PATIENTS NOT RECALLED TO HOSPITAL

64A   Meaning of 'relevant treatment'

In this Part of this Act 'relevant treatment', in relation to a patient, means medical treatment which –

    (a) is for the mental disorder from which the patient is suffering; and

    (b) is not a form of treatment to which section 57 above applies.

64B   Adult community patients

    (1) This section applies to the giving of relevant treatment to a community patient who –

        (a) is not recalled to hospital under section 17E above; and

        (b) has attained the age of 16 years.

    (2) The treatment may not be given to the patient unless –

        (a) there is authority to give it to him; and

        (b) if it is section 58 type treatment or section 58A type treatment, the certificate requirement is met.

    (3) But the certificate requirement does not apply if –

        (a) giving the treatment to the patient is authorised in accordance with section 64G below; or

        (b) the treatment is immediately necessary and –

            (i) the patient has capacity to consent to it and does consent to it; or

            (ii) a donee or deputy or the Court of Protection consents to the treatment on the patient's behalf.

    (4) Nor does the certificate requirement apply in so far as the administration of medicine to the patient at any time during the period of one month beginning with the day on which the community treatment order is made is section 58 type treatment.

    (5) The reference in subsection (4) above to the administration of medicine does not include any form of treatment specified under section 58(1)(a) above.

64C   Section 64B: supplemental

    (1) This section has effect for the purposes of section 64B above.

    (2) There is authority to give treatment to a patient if –

        (a) he has capacity to consent to it and does consent to it;

        (b) a donee or deputy or the Court of Protection consents to it on his behalf; or

        (c) giving it to him is authorised in accordance with section 64D or 64G below.

    (3) Relevant treatment is section 58 type treatment or section 58A type treatment if, at the time when it is given to the patient, section 58 or 58A above (respectively) would have applied to it, had the patient remained liable to be detained at that time (rather than being a community patient).

    (4) The certificate requirement is met in respect of treatment to be given to a patient if –

        (a) a registered medical practitioner appointed for the purposes of Part 4 of this Act (not being the responsible clinician or the person in charge of the treatment) has certified in writing that it is appropriate for the treatment to be given or for the treatment to be given subject to such conditions as may be specified in the certificate; and

        (b) if conditions are so specified, the conditions are satisfied.

    (4A) Where there is authority to give treatment by virtue of subsection (2)(a), the certificate requirement is also met in respect of the treatment if the approved clinician in charge of the treatment has certified in writing that the patient has capacity to consent to the treatment and has consented to it.

    (4B) But, if the patient has not attained the age of 18, subsection (4A) does not apply to section 58A type treatment.

(5) In a case where the treatment is section 58 type treatment, treatment is immediately necessary if –

    (a) it is immediately necessary to save the patient's life; or

    (b) it is immediately necessary to prevent a serious deterioration of the patient's condition and is not irreversible; or

    (c) it is immediately necessary to alleviate serious suffering by the patient and is not irreversible or hazardous; or

    (d) it is immediately necessary, represents the minimum interference necessary to prevent the patient from behaving violently or being a danger to himself or others and is not irreversible or hazardous.

(6) In a case where the treatment is section 58A type treatment by virtue of subsection (1)(a) of that section, treatment is immediately necessary if it falls within paragraph (a) or (b) of subsection (5) above.

(7) In a case where the treatment is section 58A type treatment by virtue of subsection (1)(b) of that section, treatment is immediately necessary if it falls within such of paragraphs (a) to (d) of subsection (5) above as may be specified in regulations under that section.

(9) Subsection (3) of section 62 above applies for the purposes of this section as it applies for the purposes of that section.

64D   Adult community patients lacking capacity

(1) A person is authorised to give relevant treatment to a patient as mentioned in section 64C(2) (c) above if the conditions in subsections (2) to (6) below are met.

(2) The first condition is that, before giving the treatment, the person takes reasonable steps to establish whether the patient lacks capacity to consent to the treatment.

(3) The second condition is that, when giving the treatment, he reasonably believes that the patient lacks capacity to consent to it.

(4) The third condition is that –

    (a) he has no reason to believe that the patient objects to being given the treatment; or

    (b) he does have reason to believe that the patient so objects, but it is not necessary to use force against the patient in order to give the treatment.

(5) The fourth condition is that –

    (a) he is the person in charge of the treatment and an approved clinician; or

    (b) the treatment is given under the direction of that clinician.

(6) The fifth condition is that giving the treatment does not conflict with –

    (a) an advance decision which he is satisfied is valid and applicable; or

    (b) a decision made by a donee or deputy or the Court of Protection.

(7) In this section –

    (a) reference to an advance decision is to an advance decision (within the meaning of the Mental Capacity Act 2005) made by the patient; and

    (b) 'valid and applicable', in relation to such a decision, means valid and applicable to the treatment in question in accordance with section 25 of that Act.

64E   Child community patients

(1) This section applies to the giving of relevant treatment to a community patient who –

    (a) is not recalled to hospital under section 17E above; and

    (b) has not attained the age of 16 years.

(2) The treatment may not be given to the patient unless –

    (a) there is authority to give it to him; and

    (b) if it is section 58 type treatment or section 58A type treatment, the certificate requirement is met.

(3) But the certificate requirement does not apply if –

    (a) giving the treatment to the patient is authorised in accordance with section 64G below; or

    (b) in a case where the patient is competent to consent to the treatment and does consent to it, the treatment is immediately necessary.

(4) Nor does the certificate requirement apply in so far as the administration of medicine to the patient at any time during the period of one month beginning with the day on which the community treatment order is made is section 58 type treatment.

(5) The reference in subsection (4) above to the administration of medicine does not include any form of treatment specified under section 58(1)(a) above.

(6) For the purposes of subsection (2)(a) above, there is authority to give treatment to a patient if –

    (a) he is competent to consent to it and he does consent to it; or

    (b) giving it to him is authorised in accordance with section 64F or 64G below.

(7) Subsections (3) to (4A) and (5) to (9) of section 64C above have effect for the purposes of this section as they have effect for the purposes of section 64B above; and for the purpose of this subsection, subsection (4A) of section 64C above has effect as if –

    (a) the references to treatment were references only to section 58 type treatment,

    (b) the reference to subsection (2)(a) of section 64C were a reference to subsection (6)(a) of this section, and

    (c) the reference to capacity to consent were a reference to competence to consent.

(8) Regulations made by virtue of section 32(2)(d) above apply for the purposes of this section as they apply for the purposes of Part 2 of this Act.

64F   Child community patients lacking competence

(1) A person is authorised to give relevant treatment to a patient as mentioned in section 64E(6)(b) above if the conditions in subsections (2) to (5) below are met.

(2) The first condition is that, before giving the treatment, the person takes reasonable steps to establish whether the patient is competent to consent to the treatment.

(3) The second condition is that, when giving the treatment, he reasonably believes that the patient is not competent to consent to it.

(4) The third condition is that –

    (a) he has no reason to believe that the patient objects to being given the treatment; or

    (b) he does have reason to believe that the patient so objects, but it is not necessary to use force against the patient in order to give the treatment.

(5) The fourth condition is that –

    (a) he is the person in charge of the treatment and an approved clinician; or

    (b) the treatment is given under the direction of that clinician.

64FA   Withdrawal of consent

(1) Where the consent of a patient to any treatment has been given as mentioned in section 64C(2)(a) above for the purposes of section 64B or 64E above, the patient may at any time before the completion of the treatment withdraw his consent, and those sections shall then apply as if the remainder of the treatment were a separate form of treatment.

(2) Subsection (3) below applies where –

    (a) the consent of a patient to any treatment has been given as mentioned in section 64C(2)(a) above for the purposes of section 64B or 64E above; but

    (b) before the completion of the treatment, the patient loses capacity or (as the case may be) competence to consent to the treatment.

(3) The patient shall be treated as having withdrawn his consent and section 64B or (as the case may be) section 64E above shall then apply as if the remainder of the treatment were a separate form of treatment.

(4) Without prejudice to the application of subsections (1) to (3) above to any treatment given under the plan of treatment to which a patient has consented, a patient who has consented to such a plan may at any time withdraw his consent to further treatment, or to further treatment of any description, under the plan.

(5) This section shall not preclude the continuation of any treatment, or of treatment under any plan, pending compliance with section 58, 58A, 64B or 64E above if the approved clinician in charge of the treatment considers that the discontinuance of the treatment, or of treatment under the plan, would cause serious suffering to the patient.

64G Emergency treatment for patients lacking capacity or competence

(1) A person is also authorised to give relevant treatment to a patient as mentioned in section 64C(2)(c) or 64E(6)(b) above if the conditions in subsections (2) to (4) below are met.

(2) The first condition is that, when giving the treatment, the person reasonably believes that the patient lacks capacity to consent to it or, as the case may be, is not competent to consent to it.

(3) The second condition is that the treatment is immediately necessary.

(4) The third condition is that if it is necessary to use force against the patient in order to give the treatment –

    (a) the treatment needs to be given in order to prevent harm to the patient; and

    (b) the use of such force is a proportionate response to the likelihood of the patient's suffering harm, and to the seriousness of that harm.

(5) Subject to subsections (6) to (8) below, treatment is immediately necessary if –

    (a) it is immediately necessary to save the patient's life; or

    (b) it is immediately necessary to prevent a serious deterioration of the patient's condition and is not irreversible; or

    (c) it is immediately necessary to alleviate serious suffering by the patient and is not irreversible or hazardous; or

    (d) it is immediately necessary, represents the minimum interference necessary to prevent the patient from behaving violently or being a danger to himself or others and is not irreversible or hazardous.

(6) Where the treatment is section 58A type treatment by virtue of subsection (1)(a) of that section, treatment is immediately necessary if it falls within paragraph (a) or (b) of subsection (5) above.

(7) Where the treatment is section 58A type treatment by virtue of subsection (1)(b) of that section, treatment is immediately necessary if it falls within such of paragraphs (a) to (d) of subsection (5) above as may be specified in regulations under section 58A above.

(9) Subsection (3) of section 62 above applies for the purposes of this section as it applies for the purposes of that section.

64H Certificates: supplementary provisions

(1) A certificate under section 64B(2)(b) or 64E(2)(b) above (a 'Part 4A certificate') may relate to a plan of treatment under which the patient is to be given (whether within a specified period or otherwise) one or more forms of section 58 type treatment or section 58A type treatment.

(2) A Part 4A certificate shall be in such form as may be prescribed by regulations made by the appropriate national authority; and the regulations may make different provision for the different descriptions of Part 4A certificate.

(3) Before giving a Part 4A certificate that falls within section 64C(4) above, the registered medical practitioner concerned shall consult two other persons who have been professionally concerned with the patient's medical treatment but, of those persons –

    (a) at least one shall be a person who is not a registered medical practitioner; and

(b) neither shall be the patient's responsible clinician or the person in charge of the treatment in question.

(4) Where a patient is given treatment in accordance with a Part 4A certificate that falls within section 64C(4) above, a report on the treatment and the patient's condition shall be given by the person in charge of the treatment to the appropriate national authority if required by that authority.

(5) The appropriate national authority may at any time give notice directing that a Part 4A certificate that falls within section 64C(4) above shall not apply to treatment given to a patient after a date specified in the notice, and the relevant section shall then apply to any such treatment as if that certificate had not been given.

(6) The relevant section is –

    (a) if the patient is not recalled to hospital in accordance with section 17E above, section 64B or 64E above;

    (b) if the patient is so recalled or is liable to be detained under this Act following revocation of the community treatment order under section 17F above –

        (i) section 58 above, in the case of section 58 type treatment;

        (ii) section 58A above, in the case of section 58A type treatment; (subject to section 62A(2) above).

(7) The notice under subsection (5) above shall be given to the person in charge of the treatment in question.

(8) Subsection (5) above shall not preclude the continuation of any treatment or of treatment under any plan pending compliance with the relevant section if the person in charge of the treatment considers that the discontinuance of the treatment or of treatment under the plan would cause serious suffering to the patient.

64I   Liability for negligence

Nothing in section 64D, 64F or 64G above excludes a person's civil liability for loss or damage, or his criminal liability, resulting from his negligence in doing anything authorised to be done by that section.

64J   Factors to be considered in determining whether patient objects to treatment

(1) In assessing for the purposes of this Part whether he has reason to believe that a patient objects to treatment, a person shall consider all the circumstances so far as they are reasonably ascertainable, including the patient's behaviour, wishes, feelings, views, beliefs and values.

(2) But circumstances from the past shall be considered only so far as it is still appropriate to consider them.

64K   Interpretation of Part IVA

(1) This Part of this Act is to be construed as follows.

(2) References to a patient who lacks capacity are to a patient who lacks capacity within the meaning of the Mental Capacity Act 2005.

(3) References to a patient who has capacity are to be read accordingly.

(4) References to a donee are to a donee of a lasting power of attorney (within the meaning of section 9 of the Mental Capacity Act 2005) created by the patient, where the donee is acting within the scope of his authority and in accordance with that Act.

(5) References to a deputy are to a deputy appointed for the patient by the Court of Protection under section 16 of the Mental Capacity Act 2005, where the deputy is acting within the scope of his authority and in accordance with that Act.

(6) Reference to the responsible clinician shall be construed as a reference to the responsible clinician within the meaning of Part 2 of this Act.

(7) References to a hospital include a registered establishment.

(8) Section 64(3) above applies for the purposes of this Part of this Act as it applies for the purposes of Part 4 of this Act.

PART V MENTAL HEALTH REVIEW TRIBUNALS

Applications and references concerning Part II patients

66 Applications to tribunals

(1) Where –

   (a) a patient is admitted to a hospital in pursuance of an application for admission for assessment; or

   (b) a patient is admitted to a hospital in pursuance of an application for admission for treatment; or

   (c) a patient is received into guardianship in pursuance of a guardianship application; or

   (ca) a community treatment order is made in respect of a patient; or

   (cb) a community treatment order is revoked under section 17F above in respect of a patient; or

   (e) a patient is transferred from guardianship to a hospital in pursuance of regulations made under section 19 above; or

   (f) a report is furnished under section 20 above in respect of a patient and the patient is not discharged under section 23 above; or

   (fza) a report is furnished under section 20A above in respect of a patient and the patient is not discharged under section 23 above; or

   (fa) a report is furnished under subsection (2) of section 21B above in respect of a patient and subsection (5) of the section applies (or subsections (5) and (6)(b) of that section apply) in the case of the report; or

   (faa) a report is furnished under subsection (2) of section 21B above in respect of a community patient and subsection (6A) of that section applies (or subsections (6A) and (6B) (b) of that section apply) in the case of the report; or

   (g) a report is furnished under section 25 above in respect of a patient who is detained in pursuance of an application for admission for treatment or a community patient; or

   (h) an order is made under section 29 above on the ground specified in paragraph (c) or (d) of subsection (3) of that section in respect of a patient who is or subsequently becomes liable to be detained or subject to guardianship under Part II of this Act or who is a community patient,

an application may be made to the appropriate tribunal within the relevant period –

   (i)   by the patient (except in the cases mentioned in paragraphs (g) and (h) above);

   (ii) in the cases mentioned in paragraphs (g) and (h) above, by his nearest relative.

(2) In subsection (1) above 'the relevant period' means –

   (a) in the cases mentioned in paragraph (a) of that subsection, 14 days beginning with the day on which the patient is admitted as so mentioned;

   (b) in the case mentioned in paragraph (b) of that subsection, six months beginning with the day on which the patient is admitted as so mentioned;

   (c) in the case mentioned in paragraphs (c) of that subsection, six months beginning with the day on which the application is accepted;

   (ca) in the case mentioned in paragraph (ca) of that subsection, six months beginning with the day on which the community treatment order is made;

   (cb) in the case mentioned in paragraph (cb) of that subsection, six months beginning with the day on which the community treatment order is revoked;

   (d) in the case mentioned in paragraph (g) of that subsection, 28 days beginning with the day on which the applicant is informed that the report has been furnished;

   (e) in the case mentioned in paragraph (e) of that subsection, six months beginning with the day on which the patient is transferred;

(f)   in the case mentioned in paragraph (f) or (fa) of that subsection, the period or periods for which authority for the patient's detention or guardianship is renewed by virtue of the report;

(fza)   in the cases mentioned in paragraphs (fza) and (faa) of that subsection, the period or periods for which the community treatment period is extended by virtue of the report;

(g)   in the case mentioned in paragraph (h) of that subsection, 12 months beginning with the date of the order, and in any subsequent period of 12 months during which the order continues in force.

(2A)   Nothing in subsection (1)(b) above entitles a community patient to make an application by virtue of that provision even if he is admitted to a hospital on being recalled there under section 17E above.

(4)   In this Act 'the appropriate tribunal' means the First-tier Tribunal or the Mental Health Review Tribunal for Wales.

(3)   Section 32 above shall apply for the purposes of this section as it applies for the purposes of Part II of this Act.

67   References to tribunals by Secretary of State concerning Part II patients

(1)   The Secretary of State may, if he thinks fit, at any time refer to the appropriate tribunal the case of any patient who is liable to be detained or subject to guardianship under Part II of this Act or of any community patient.

(2)   For the purpose of furnishing information for the purposes of a reference under subsection (1) above any registered medical practitioner or approved clinician authorised by or on behalf of the patient may, at any reasonable time, visit the patient and examine him in private and require the production of and inspect any records relating to the detention or treatment of the patient in any hospital or to any aftercare services provided for the patient under section 117 below.

(3)   Section 32 above shall apply for the purposes of this section as it applies for the purposes of Part II of this Act.

68   Duty of managers of hospitals to refer cases to tribunal

(1)   This section applies in respect of the following patients –

(a)   a patient who is admitted to a hospital in pursuance of an application for admission for assessment;

(b)   a patient who is admitted to a hospital in pursuance of an application for admission for treatment;

(c)   a community patient;

(d)   a patient whose community treatment order is revoked under section 17F above;

(e)   a patient who is transferred from guardianship to a hospital in pursuance of regulations made under section 19 above.

(2)   On expiry of the period of six months beginning with the applicable day, the managers of the hospital shall refer the patient's case to the appropriate tribunal.

(3)   But they shall not do so if during that period –

(a)   any right has been exercised by or in respect of the patient by virtue of any of paragraphs (b), (ca), (cb), (e), (g) and (h) of section 66(1) above;

(b)   a reference has been made in respect of the patient under section 67(1) above, not being a reference made while the patient is or was liable to be detained in pursuance of an application for admission for assessment; or

(c)   a reference has been made in respect of the patient under subsection (7) below.

(4) A person who applies to a tribunal but subsequently withdraws his application shall be treated for these purposes as not having exercised his right to apply, and if he withdraws his application on a date after expiry of the period mentioned in subsection (2) above, the managers shall refer the patient's case as soon as possible after that date.

(5) In subsection (2) above, 'the applicable day' means –

    (a) in the case of a patient who is admitted to a hospital in pursuance of an application for admission for assessment, the day on which the patient was so admitted;

    (b) in the case of a patient who is admitted to a hospital in pursuance of an application for admission for treatment –

        (i)   the day on which the patient was so admitted; or

        (ii) if, when he was so admitted, he was already liable to be detained in pursuance of an application for admission for assessment, the day on which he was originally admitted in pursuance of the application for admission for assessment;

    (c) in the case of a community patient or a patient whose community treatment order is revoked under section 17F above, the day mentioned in sub-paragraph (i) or (ii), as the case may be, of paragraph (b) above;

    (d) in the case of a patient who is transferred from guardianship to a hospital, the day on which he was so transferred.

(6) The managers of the hospital shall also refer the patient's case to the appropriate tribunal if a period of more than three years (or, if the patient has not attained the age of 18 years, one year) has elapsed since his case was last considered by such a tribunal, whether on his own application or otherwise.

(7) If, in the case of a community patient, the community treatment order is revoked under section 17F above, the managers of the hospital shall also refer the patient's case to the appropriate tribunal as soon as possible after the order is revoked.

(8) For the purposes of furnishing information for the purposes of a reference under this section, a registered medical practitioner or approved clinician authorised by or on behalf of the patient may at any reasonable time –

    (a) visit and examine the patient in private; and

    (b) require the production of and inspect any records relating to the detention or treatment of the patient in any hospital or any after-care services provided for him under section 117 below.

(9) Reference in this section to the managers of the hospital –

    (a) in relation to a community patient, is to the managers of the responsible hospital;

    (b) in relation to any other patient, is to the managers of the hospital in which he is liable to be detained.

68A   Power to reduce periods under section 68

(1) The appropriate national authority may from time to time by order amend subsection (2) or (6) of section 68 above so as to substitute for a period mentioned there such shorter period as is specified in the order.

Applications and references concerning Part III patients

69   Applications to tribunals concerning patients subject to hospital and guardianship orders

(1) Without prejudice to any provision of section 66(1) above as applied by section 40(4) above, an application to the appropriate tribunal may also be made –

    (a) in respect of a patient liable to be detained in pursuance of a hospital order or a community patient who was so liable before he became a community patient, by the nearest relative of the patient in any period in which an application may be made by the patient under any such provision as so applied;

(b) in respect of a patient placed under guardianship by a guardianship order –

    (i)   by the patient, within the period of six months beginning with the date of the order;

    (ii) by the nearest relative of the patient, within the period of 12 months beginning with the date of the order and in any subsequent period of 12 months.

(2) Where a person detained in a hospital –

    (a) is treated as subject to a hospital order, hospital direction or transfer direction by virtue of section 41(5) above or section 80B(2), 82(2) or 85(2) below; or

    (b) is subject to a direction having the same effect as a hospital order by virtue of section 47(3) or 48(3) above,

then, without prejudice to any provision of Part II of this Act as applied by section 40 above, that person may make an application to the appropriate tribunal in the period of six months beginning with the date of the order or direction mentioned in paragraph (a) above or, as the case may be, the date of the direction mentioned in paragraph (b) above.

(3) The provisions of section 66 above as applied by section 40(4) above are subject to subsection (4) below.

(4) If the initial detention period has not elapsed when the relevant application period begins, the right of a hospital order patient to make an application by virtue of paragraph (ca) or (cb) of section 66(1) above shall be exercisable only during whatever remains of the relevant application period after the initial detention period has elapsed.

(5) In subsection (4) above –

    (a) 'hospital order patient' means a patient who is subject to a hospital order, excluding a patient of a kind mentioned in paragraph (a) or (b) of subsection (2) above;

    (b) 'the initial detention period', in relation to a hospital order patient, means the period of six months beginning with the date of the hospital order; and

    (c) 'the relevant application period' means the relevant period mentioned in paragraph (ca) or (cb), as the case may be, of section 66(2) above.

70 Applications to tribunals concerning restricted patients

A patient who is a restricted patient within the meaning of section 79 below and is detained in a hospital may apply to the appropriate tribunal –

    (a) in the period between the expiration of six months and the expiration of 12 months beginning with the date of the relevant hospital order, hospital direction or transfer direction; and

    (b) in any subsequent period of 12 months.

71 References by Secretary of State concerning restricted patients

(1) The Secretary of State may at any time refer the case of a restricted patient to the appropriate tribunal.

(2) The Secretary of State shall refer to the appropriate tribunal the case of any restricted patient detained in a hospital whose case has not been considered by such a tribunal, whether on his own application or otherwise, within the last three years.

(3) The Secretary of State may by order vary the length of the period mentioned in subsection (2) above.

Discharge of patients

72 Powers of tribunals

(1) Where application is made to the appropriate tribunal by or in respect of a patient who is liable to be detained under this Act or is a community patient, the tribunal may in any case direct that the patient be discharged, and –

    (a) the tribunal shall direct the discharge of a patient liable to be detained under section 2 above if it is not satisfied –

(i)   that he is then suffering from mental disorder or from mental disorder of a nature or degree which warrants his detention in a hospital for assessment (or for assessment followed by medical treatment) for at least a limited period; or

(ii) that his detention as aforesaid is justified in the interests of his own health or safety or with a view to the protection of other persons;

(b) the tribunal shall direct the discharge of a patient liable to be detained otherwise than under section 2 above if it is not satisfied –

(i)   that he is then suffering from mental disorder or from mental disorder of a nature or degree which makes it appropriate for him to be liable to be detained in a hospital for medical treatment; or

(ii) that it is necessary for the health of safety of the patient or for the protection of other persons that he should receive such treatment; or

(iia) that appropriate medical treatment is available for him; or

(iii) in the case of an application by virtue of paragraph (g) of section 66(1) above, that the patient, if released, would be likely to act in a manner dangerous to other persons or to himself.

(c) the tribunal shall direct the discharge of a community patient if it is not satisfied –

(i)   that he is then suffering from mental disorder or mental disorder of a nature or degree which makes it appropriate for him to receive medical treatment; or

(ii) that it is necessary for his health or safety or for the protection of other persons that he should receive such treatment; or

(iii) that it is necessary that the responsible clinician should be able to exercise the power under section 17E(1) above to recall the patient to hospital; or

(iv) that appropriate medical treatment is available for him; or

(v)   in the case of an application by virtue of paragraph (g) of section 66(1) above, that the patient, if discharged, would be likely to act in a manner dangerous to other persons or to himself.

(1A) In determining whether the criterion in subsection (1)(c)(iii) above is met, the tribunal shall, in particular, consider, having regard to the patient's history of mental disorder and any other relevant factors, what risk there would be of a deterioration of the patient's condition if he were to continue not to be detained in a hospital (as a result, for example, of his refusing or neglecting to receive the medical treatment he requires for his mental disorder).

(3) A tribunal may under subsection (1) above direct the discharge of a patient on a future date specified in the direction; and where a tribunal does not direct the discharge of a patient under that subsection the tribunal may –

(a) with a view to facilitating his discharge on a future date, recommend that he be granted leave of absence or transferred to another hospital or into guardianship; and

(b) further consider his case in the event of any such recommendation not being complied with.

(3A) Subsection (1) above does not require a tribunal to direct the discharge of a patient just because it thinks it might be appropriate for the patient to be discharged (subject to the possibility of recall) under a community treatment order; and a tribunal –

(a) may recommend that the responsible clinician consider whether to make a community treatment order; and

(b) may (but need not) further consider the patient's case if the responsible clinician does not make an order.

(4) Where application is made to the appropriate tribunal by or in respect of a patient who is subject to guardianship under this Act, the tribunal may in any case direct that the patient be discharged, and shall so direct if it is satisfied –

(a) that he is not then suffering from mental disorder; or

(b) that it is not necessary in the interests of the welfare of the patient, or for the protection of other persons, that the patient should remain under such guardianship.

(6) Subsections (1) to (4) above apply in relation to references to the appropriate tribunal as they apply in relation to applications made to such a tribunal by or in respect of a patient.

(7) Subsection (1) above shall not apply in the case of a restricted patient except as provided in section 73 and 74 below.

73   Power to discharge restricted patients

(1) Where an application to the appropriate tribunal is made by a restricted patient who is subject to a restriction order, or where the case of such a patient is referred to the appropriate tribunal, the tribunal shall direct the absolute discharge of the patient if –

(a) the tribunal is not satisfied as to the matters mentioned in paragraph (b)(i), (ii) or (iia) of section 72(1) above; and

(b) the tribunal is satisfied that it is not appropriate for the patient to remain liable to be recalled to hospital for further treatment.

(2) Where in the case of any such patient as is mentioned in subsection (1) above –

(a) paragraph (a) of that subsection applies; but

(b) paragraph (b) of that subsection does not apply, the tribunal shall direct the conditional discharge of the patient.

(3) Where a patient is absolutely discharged under this section he shall thereupon cease to be liable to be detained by virtue of the relevant hospital order, and the restriction order shall cease to have effect accordingly.

(4) Where a patient is conditionally discharged under this section –

(a) he may be recalled by the Secretary of State under subsection (3) of section 42 above as if he had been conditionally discharged under subsection (2) of that section; and

(b) the patient shall comply with such conditions (if any) as may be imposed at the time of discharge by the tribunal or at any subsequent time by the Secretary of State.

(5) The Secretary of State may from time to time vary any condition imposed (whether by the tribunal or by him) under subsection (4) above.

(6) Where a restriction order in respect of a patient ceases to have effect after he has been conditionally discharged under his section the patient shall, unless previously recalled, be deemed to be absolutely discharged on the date when the order ceases to have effect and shall cease to be liable to be detained by virtue of the relevant hospital order.

(7) A tribunal may defer a direction for the conditional discharge of a patient until such arrangements as appear to the tribunal to be necessary for that purpose have been made to its satisfaction; and where by virtue of any such deferment no direction has been given on an application or reference before the time when the patient's case comes before the tribunal on a subsequent application or reference, the previous application or reference shall be treated as one on which no direction under this section can be given.

(8) This section is without prejudice to section 42 above.

74   Restricted patients subject to restriction directions

(1) Where an application to the appropriate tribunal is made by a restricted patient who is subject to a restriction direction, or where the case of such a patient is referred to the appropriate tribunal, the tribunal –

(a) shall notify the Secretary of State whether, in its opinion, the patient would, if subject to a limitation direction or a restriction order, be entitled to be absolutely or conditionally discharged under section 73 above; and

(b) if the tribunal notifies him that the patient would be entitled to be conditionally discharged, may recommend that in the event of his not being discharged under his section he should continue to be detained in hospital.

(2) If in the case of a patient not falling within subsection (4) below –

(a) the tribunal notifies the Secretary of State that the patient would be entitled to be absolutely or conditionally discharged; and

(b) within the period of 90 days beginning with the date of that notification the Secretary of State gives notice to the tribunal that the patient may be so discharged,

the tribunal shall direct the absolute or, as the case may be, the conditional discharge of the patient.

(3) Where a patient continues to be liable to be detained in a hospital at the end of the period referred to in subsection (2)(b) above because the Secretary of State has not given the notice there mentioned, the managers of the hospital shall, unless the tribunal has made a recommendation under subsection (1)(b) above, transfer the patient to a prison or other institution in which he might have been detained if he had not been removed to hospital, there to be dealt with as if he had not been so removed.

(4) If, in the case of a patient who is subject to a transfer direction under section 48 above, the tribunal notify the Secretary of State that the patient would be entitled to be absolutely or conditionally discharged, the Secretary of State shall, unless the tribunal have made a recommendation under subsection (1)(b) above, by warrant direct that the patient be remitted to a prison or other institution in which he might have been detained if he had not been removed to hospital, there to be dealt with as if he had not been so removed.

(5) Where a patient is transferred or remitted under subsection (3) or (4) above the relevant hospital direction and the limitation direction or, as the case may be, the relevant transfer direction and the restriction direction shall cease to have effect on his arrival in the prison or other institution.

(5A) Where the tribunal has made a recommendation under subsection (1)(b) above in the case of a patient who is subject to a restriction direction or a limitation direction –

(a) the fact that the restriction direction or limitation direction remains in force does not prevent the making of any application or reference to the Parole Board by or in respect of him or the exercise by him of any power to require the Secretary of State to refer his case to the Parole Board; and

(b) if the Parole Board make a direction or recommendation by virtue of which the patient would become entitled to be released (whether unconditionally or on licence) from any prison or other institution in which he might have been detained if he had not been removed to hospital, the restriction direction or limitation direction shall cease to have effect at the time when he would become entitled to be so released.

(6) Subsections (3) to (8) of section 73 above shall have effect in relation to this section as they have effect in relation to that section, taking references to the relevant hospital order and the restriction order as references to the transfer direction and the restriction direction.

(7) This section is without prejudice to sections 50 to 53 above in their application to patients who are not discharged under this section.

75 Applications and references concerning conditionally discharged restricted patients

(1) Where a restricted patient has been conditionally discharged under section 42(2), 73 or 74 above and is subsequently recalled to hospital –

(a) the Secretary of State shall, within one month of the day on which the patient returns or is returned to hospital, refer his case to the appropriate tribunal; and

(b) section 70 above shall apply to the patient as if the relevant hospital order, hospital direction or transfer direction had been made on that day.

(2) Where a restricted patient has been conditionally discharged as aforesaid but has not been recalled to hospital he may apply to the appropriate tribunal –

(a) in the period between the expiration of 12 months and the expiration of two years beginning with the date on which he was conditionally discharged; and

(b) in any subsequent period of two years.

(3) Sections 73 and 74 above shall not apply to an application under subsection (2) above but on any such application the tribunal may –

    (a) vary any condition to which the patient is subject in connection with his discharge or impose any condition which might have been imposed in connection therewith; or

    (b) direct that the restriction order, limitation direction or restriction direction to which he is subject shall cease to have effect;

and if the tribunal give a direction under paragraph (b) above the patient shall cease to be liable to be detained by virtue of the relevant hospital order, hospital direction or transfer direction.

General

76 Visiting and examination of patients

(1) For the purpose of advising whether an application to the appropriate tribunal should be made by or in respect of a patient who is liable to be detained or subject to guardianship under Part II of this Act or a community patient or of furnishing information as to the condition of a patient for the purposes of such an application, any registered medical practitioner or approved clinician authorised by or on behalf of the patient or other person who is entitled to make or has made the application –

    (a) may at any reasonable time visit the patient and examine him in private, and

    (b) may require the production of and inspect any records relating to the detention or treatment of the patient in any hospital or to any after-care services provided for the patient under section 117 below.

(2) Section 32 above shall apply for the purposes of this section as it applies for the purposes of Part II of this Act.

77 General provisions concerning tribunal applications

(1) No application shall be made to the appropriate tribunal by or in respect of a patient except in such cases and at such times as are expressly provided by this Act.

(3) Subject to subsection (4) below an application to a tribunal authorised to be made by or in respect of a patient under this Act shall be made by notice in writing addressed –

    (a) in the case of a patient who is liable to be detained in a hospital, to the First-tier Tribunal where that hospital is in England and to the Mental Health Review Tribunal for Wales where that hospital is in Wales;

    (b) in the case of a community patient, to the First-tier Tribunal where the responsible hospital is in England and to the Mental Health Review Tribunal for Wales where that hospital is in Wales;

    (c) in the case of a patient subject to guardianship, to the First-tier Tribunal where the patient resides in England and to the Mental Health Review Tribunal for Wales where the patient resides in Wales.

79 Interpretation of Part V

(1) In this Part of this Act 'restricted patient' means a patient who is subject to a restriction order, limitation direction or restriction direction and this Part of this Act shall, subject to the provisions of this section, have effect in relation to any person who –

    (a) is treated by virtue of any enactment as subject to a hospital order and a restriction order; or

    (c) is treated as subject to a hospital order and a restriction order or to a hospital direction order and a limitation direction or to transfer direction and a restriction direction by virtue of any provision of Part 6 of this Act (except sections 80D(3), 82A(2) or 85A(2) below, as it has effect in relation to a restricted patient.

PART VIII MISCELLANEOUS FUNCTIONS OF LOCAL AUTHORITIES AND THE SECRETARY OF STATE

Approved mental health professionals

114 Approval by local social services authority

(1) A local social services authority may approve a person to act as an approved mental health professional for the purposes of this Act.

(2) But a local social services authority may not approve a registered medical practitioner to act as an approved mental health professional.

(3) Before approving a person under subsection (1) above, a local social services authority shall be satisfied that he has appropriate competence in dealing with persons who are suffering from mental disorder.

115 Powers of entry and inspection

(1) An approved mental health professional may at all reasonable times enter and inspect any premises (other than a hospital) in which a mentally disordered patient is living, if he has reasonable cause to believe that the patient is not under proper care.

(2) The power under subsection (1) above shall be exercisable only after the professional has produced, if asked to do so, some duly authenticated document showing that he is an approved mental health professional.

Visiting patients

116 Welfare of certain hospital patients

(1) Where a patient to whom this section applies is admitted to a hospital, independent hospital or care home in England and Wales (whether for treatment for mental disorder or for any other reason) then, without prejudice to their duties in relation to the patient apart from the provisions of this section, the authority shall arrange for visits to be made to him on behalf of the authority, and shall take such other steps in relation to the patient while in the hospital, independent hospital or care home as would be expected to be taken by his parents.

(2) This section applies to –
- (a) a child or young person –
    - (i)   who is in the care of a local authority by virtue of a care order within the meaning of the Children Act 1989, or
    - (ii) in respect of whom the rights and powers of a parent are vested in a local authority by virtue of section 16 of the Social Work (Scotland) Act 1968;
- (b) a person who is subject to the guardianship of a local social services authority under the provisions of this Act; or
- (c) a person the functions of whose nearest relative under this Act are for the time being transferred to a local social services authority.

After-care

117 After-care

(1) This section applies to persons who are detained under section 3 above, or admitted to a hospital in pursuance of a hospital order made under section 37 above, or transferred to a hospital in pursuance of a hospital direction made under section 45A above or a transfer direction made under section 47 or 48 above, and then cease to be detained and (whether or not immediately after so ceasing) leave hospital.

(2) It shall be the duty of the clinical commissioning group or Local Health Board and of the local social services authority to provide or arrange for provision of, in co-operation with relevant voluntary agencies, after-care services for any person to whom this section applies until such time

as the clinical commissioning group or Local Health Board and the local social services authority are satisfied that the person concerned is no longer in need of such services; but they shall not be so satisfied in the case of a community patient while he remains such a patient.

(2B) Section 32 above shall apply for the purposes of this section as it applies for the purposes of Part II of this Act.

(3) In this section 'the clinical commissioning group or Local Health Board' means the clinical commissioning group or Local Health Board, and 'the local social services authority' means the local social services authority

(a) if, immediately before being detained, the person concerned was ordinarily resident in England, for the area in England in which he was ordinarily resident;

(b) if, immediately before being detained, the person concerned was ordinarily resident in Wales, for the area in Wales in which he was ordinarily resident; or

(c) in any other case, for the area in which the person concerned is resident or to which he is sent on discharge by the hospital in which he was detained.

Functions of the Secretary of State

118 Code of practice

(1) The Secretary of State shall prepare, and from time to time revise, a code of practice –

(a) for the guidance of registered medical practitioners, approved clinicians, managers and staff of hospitals, independent hospitals and care homes and approved mental health professionals in relation to the admission of patients to hospitals and registered establishments under this Act and to guardianship and community patients under this Act; and

(b) for the guidance of registered medical practitioners and members of other professions in relation to the medical treatment of patients suffering from mental disorder.

(2) The code shall, in particular, specify forms of medical treatment in addition to any specified by regulations made for the purposes of section 57 above which in the opinion of the Secretary of State give rise to special concern and which should accordingly not be given by a registered medical practitioner unless the patient has consented to the treatment (or to a plan of treatment including that treatment) and a certificate in writing as to the matters mentioned in subsection (2)(a) and(b) of that section has been given by another registered medical practitioner, being a practitioner appointed for the purposes of this section by the regulatory authority.

(2A) The code shall include a statement of the principles which the Secretary of State thinks should inform decisions under this Act.

(2B) In preparing the statement of principles the Secretary of State shall, in particular, ensure that each of the following matters is addressed –

(a) respect for patients' past and present wishes and feelings,

(b) respect for diversity generally including, in particular, diversity of religion, culture and sexual orientation (within the meaning of section 35 of the Equality Act 2006),

(c) minimising restrictions on liberty,

(d) involvement of patients in planning, developing and delivering care and treatment appropriate to them,

(e) avoidance of unlawful discrimination,

(f) effectiveness of treatment,

(g) views of carers and other interested parties,

(h) patient well-being and safety, and

(i) public safety.

(2C) The Secretary of State shall also have regard to the desirability of ensuring –

(a) the efficient use of resources, and

(b) the equitable distribution of services.

(2D) In performing functions under this Act persons mentioned in subsection (1)(a) or (b) shall have regard to the code.

(3) Before preparing the code or making any alteration in it the Secretary of State shall consult such bodies as appear to him to be concerned.

119   Practitioners approved for Part IV and s. 118

(2) A registered medical practitioner or other person appointed for the purposes of the provisions mentioned in subsection (1) above may, for the purpose of exercising his functions under those provisions or under Part 4A of this Act, at any reasonable time –

    (a) visit and interview and, in the case of a registered medical practitioner, examine in private any patient detained in a hospital or registered establishment or any community patient in a hospital or establishment of any description or (if access is granted) other place; and

    (b) require the production of and inspect any records relating to the treatment of the patient there.

(3) In this section, 'establishment of any description' shall be construed in accordance with section 4(8) of the Care Standards Act 2000.

120   General protection of relevant patients

(1) The regulatory authority must keep under review and, where appropriate, investigate the exercise of the powers and the discharge of the duties conferred or imposed by this Act so far as relating to the detention of patients or their reception into guardianship or to relevant patients.

(2) Relevant patients are –

    (a) patients liable to be detained under this Act,

    (b) community patients, and

    (c) patients subject to guardianship.

(3) The regulatory authority must make arrangements for persons authorised by it to visit and interview relevant patients in private –

    (a) in the case of relevant patients detained under this Act, in the place where they are detained, and

    (b) in the case of other relevant patients, in hospitals and regulated establishments and, if access is granted, other places.

(4) The regulatory authority must also make arrangements for persons authorised by it to investigate any complaint as to the exercise of the powers or the discharge of the duties conferred or imposed by this Act in respect of a patient who is or has been detained under this Act or who is or has been a relevant patient.

(7) For the purposes of a review or investigation under subsection (1) or the exercise of functions under arrangements made under this section, a person authorised by the regulatory authority may at any reasonable time –

    (a) visit and interview in private any patient in a hospital or regulated establishment,

    (b) if the authorised person is a registered medical practitioner or approved clinician, examine the patient in private there, and

    (c) require the production of and inspect any records relating to the detention or treatment of any person who is or has been detained under this Act or who is or has been a community patient or a patient subject to guardianship.

PART IX OFFENCES

127   Ill-treatment of patients

(1) It shall be an offence for any person who is an officer on the staff of or otherwise employed in, or who is one of the managers of, a hospital, independent hospital or care home –

    (a) to ill-treat or wilfully to neglect a patient for the time being receiving treatment for mental disorder as an in-patient in that hospital or home; or

(b) to ill-treat or wilfully to neglect, on the premises of which the hospital or home forms part, a patient for the time being receiving such treatment there as an outpatient.

(2) It shall be an offence for any individual to ill-treat or wilfully to neglect a mentally disordered patient who is for the time being subject to his guardianship under this Act or otherwise in his custody or care (whether by virtue of any legal or moral obligation or otherwise).

(3) Any person guilty of an offence under this section shall be liable –

(a) on summary conviction, to imprisonment for a term not exceeding six months or to a fine not exceeding the statutory maximum, or to both;

(b) on conviction on indictment, to imprisonment for a term not exceeding five years or to a fine of any amount, or to both.

(4) No proceedings shall be instituted for an offence under this section except by or with the consent of the Director of Public Prosecutions.

PART X MISCELLANEOUS AND SUPPLEMENTARY

Miscellaneous provisions

130A Independent mental health advocates: England

(1) A local social services authority whose area is in England shall make such arrangements as it considers reasonable to enable persons ('independent mental health advocates') to be available to help qualifying patients.

(4) In making arrangements under this section, a local social services authority shall have regard to the principle that any help available to a patient under the arrangements should, so far as practicable, be provided by a person who is independent of any person who is professionally concerned with the patient's medical treatment.

(5) For the purposes of subsection (4) above, a person is not to be regarded as professionally concerned with a patient's medical treatment merely because he is representing him in accordance with arrangements –

(a) under section 35 of the Mental Capacity Act 2005; or

(b) of a description specified in regulations under this section.

130B Arrangements under section 130A

(1) The help available to a qualifying patient under arrangements under section 130A above shall include help in obtaining information about and understanding –

(a) the provisions of this Act by virtue of which he is a qualifying patient;

(b) any conditions or restrictions to which he is subject by virtue of this Act;

(c) what (if any) medical treatment is given to him or is proposed or discussed in his case;

(d) why it is given, proposed or discussed;

(e) the authority under which it is, or would be, given; and

(f) the requirements of this Act which apply, or would apply, in connection with the giving of the treatment to him.

(2) The help available under the arrangements to a qualifying patient shall also include –

(a) help in obtaining information about and understanding any rights which may be exercised under this Act by or in relation to him; and

(b) help (by way of representation or otherwise) in exercising those rights.

(3) For the purpose of providing help to a patient in accordance with the arrangements, an independent mental health advocate may –

(a) visit and interview the patient in private;

(b) visit and interview any person who is professionally concerned with his medical treatment;

(c) require the production of and inspect any records relating to his detention or treatment in any hospital or registered establishment or to any after-care services provided for him under section 117 above;

(d) require the production of and inspect any records of, or held by, a local social services authority which relate to him.

(4) But an independent mental health advocate is not entitled to the production of, or to inspect, records in reliance on subsection (3)(c) or (d) above unless –

(a) in a case where the patient has capacity or is competent to consent, he does consent; or

(b) in any other case, the production or inspection would not conflict with a decision made by a donee or deputy or the Court of Protection and the person holding the records, having regard to such matters as may be prescribed in regulations under section 130A above, considers that –

(i)   the records may be relevant to the help to be provided by the advocate; and

(ii)   the production or inspection is appropriate.

(5) For the purpose of providing help to a patient in accordance with the arrangements, an independent mental health advocate shall comply with any reasonable request made to him by any of the following for him to visit and interview the patient –

(a) the person (if any) appearing to the advocate to be the patient's nearest relative;

(b) the responsible clinician for the purposes of this Act;

(c) an approved mental health professional.

(6) But nothing in this Act prevents the patient from declining to be provided with help under the arrangements.

(7) In subsection (4) above –

(a) the reference to a patient who has capacity is to be read in accordance with the Mental Capacity Act 2005;

(b) the reference to a donee is to a donee of a lasting power of attorney (within the meaning of section 9 of that Act) created by the patient, where the donee is acting within the scope of his authority and in accordance with that Act;

(c) the reference to a deputy is to a deputy appointed for the patient by the Court of Protection under section 16 of that Act, where the deputy is acting within the scope of his authority and in accordance with that Act.

130C   Section 130A: supplemental

(1) This section applies for the purposes of section 130A above.

(2) A patient is a qualifying patient if he is –

(a) liable to be detained under this Act (otherwise than by virtue of section 4 or 5(2) or (4) above or section 135 or 136 below) and the hospital or registered establishment in which he is liable to be detained is situated in England;

(b) subject to guardianship under this Act and the area of the responsible local social services authority within the meaning of section 34(3) above is situated in England;

(c) a community patient and the responsible hospital is situated in England.

(3) A patient is also a qualifying patient if the patient is to be regarded as being in England for the purposes of this subsection and –

(a) not being a qualifying patient falling within subsection (2) above, he discusses with a registered medical practitioner or approved clinician the possibility of being given a form of treatment to which section 57 above applies; or

(b) not having attained the age of 18 years and not being a qualifying patient falling within subsection (2) above, he discusses with a registered medical practitioner or approved clinician the possibility of being given a form of treatment to which section 58A above applies.

(4) Where a patient who is a qualifying patient falling within subsection (3) above is informed that the treatment concerned is proposed in his case, he remains a qualifying patient falling within that subsection until –

(a) the proposal is withdrawn; or

(b) the treatment is completed or discontinued.

(4A) A local social services authority is responsible for a qualifying patient if –
    (a) in the case of a qualifying patient falling within subsection (2)(a) above, the hospital or registered establishment in which he is liable to be detained is situated in that authority's area;
    (b) in the case of a qualifying patient falling within subsection (2)(b) above, that authority is the responsible local social services authority within the meaning of section 34(3) above;
    (c) in the case of a qualifying patient falling within subsection (2)(c), the responsible hospital is situated in that authority's area;
    (d) in the case of a qualifying patient falling within subsection (3) –
        (i)   in a case where the patient has capacity or is competent to do so, he nominates that authority as responsible for him for the purposes of section 130A above, or
        (ii) in any other case, a donee or deputy or the Court of Protection, or a person engaged in caring for the patient or interested in his welfare, nominates that authority on his behalf as responsible for him for the purposes of that section.
(4B) In subsection (4A)(d) above –
    (a) the reference to a patient who has capacity is to be read in accordance with the Mental Capacity Act 2005;
    (b) the reference to a donee is to a donee of a lasting power of attorney (within the meaning of section 9 of that Act) created by the patient, where the donee is acting within the scope of his authority and in accordance with that Act;
    (c) the reference to a deputy is to a deputy appointed for the patient by the Court of Protection under section 16 of that Act, where the deputy is acting within the scope of his authority and in accordance with that Act.

130D Duty to give information about independent mental health advocates

(1) The responsible person in relation to a qualifying patient (within the meaning given by section 130C above) shall take such steps as are practicable to ensure that the patient understands –
    (a) that help is available to him from an independent mental health advocate; and
    (b) how he can obtain that help.
(2) In subsection (1) above, 'the responsible person' means –
    (a) in relation to a qualifying patient falling within section 130C(2)(a) above (other than one also falling within paragraph (b) below), the managers of the hospital or registered establishment in which he is liable to be detained;
    (b) in relation to a qualifying patient falling within section 130C(2)(a) above and conditionally discharged by virtue of section 42(2), 73 or 74 above, the responsible clinician;
    (c) in relation to a qualifying patient falling within section 130C(2)(b) above, the responsible local social services authority within the meaning of section 34(3) above;
    (d) in relation to a qualifying patient falling within section 130C(2)(c) above, the managers of the responsible hospital;
    (e) in relation to a qualifying patient falling within section 130C(3) above, the registered medical practitioner or approved clinician with whom the patient first discusses the possibility of being given the treatment concerned.
(3) The steps to be taken under subsection (1) above shall be taken –
    (a) where the responsible person falls within subsection (2)(a) above, as soon as practicable after the patient becomes liable to be detained;
    (b) where the responsible person falls within subsection (2)(b) above, as soon as practicable after the conditional discharge;
    (c) where the responsible person falls within subsection (2)(c) above, as soon as practicable after the patient becomes subject to guardianship;
    (d) where the responsible person falls within subsection (2)(d) above, as soon as practicable after the patient becomes a community patient;

(e) where the responsible person falls within subsection (2)(e) above, while the discussion with the patient is taking place or as soon as practicable thereafter.

(4) The steps to be taken under subsection (1) above shall include giving the requisite information both orally and in writing.

(5) The responsible person in relation to a qualifying patient falling within section 130C(2) above (other than a patient liable to be detained by virtue of Part 3 of this Act) shall, except where the patient otherwise requests, take such steps as are practicable to furnish the person (if any) appearing to the responsible person to be the patient's nearest relative with a copy of any information given to the patient in writing under subsection (1) above.

(6) The steps to be taken under subsection (5) above shall be taken when the information concerned is given to the patient or within a reasonable time thereafter.

131   Informal admission of patients

(1) Nothing in this Act shall be construed as preventing a patient who requires treatment for mental disorder from being admitted to any hospital or mental nursing home in pursuance of arrangements made in that behalf and without any application, order or direction rendering him liable to be detained under this Act, or from remaining in any hospital or mental nursing home in pursuance of such arrangements after he has ceased to be so liable to be detained.

(2) Subsections (3) and (4) below apply in the case of a patient aged 16 or 17 years who has capacity to consent to the making of such arrangements as are mentioned in subsection (1) above.

(3) If the patient consents to the making of the arrangements, they may be made, carried out and determined on the basis of that consent even though there are one or more persons who have parental responsibility for him.

(4) If the patient does not consent to the making of the arrangements, they may not be made, carried out or determined on the basis of the consent of a person who has parental responsibility for him.

(5) In this section –
(a) the reference to a patient who has capacity is to be read in accordance with the Mental Capacity Act 2005; and
(b) 'parental responsibility' has the same meaning as in the Children Act 1989.

131A   Accommodation, etc. for children

(1) This section applies in respect of any patient who has not attained the age of 18 years and who –
(a) is liable to be detained in a hospital under this Act; or
(b) is admitted to, or remains in, a hospital in pursuance of such arrangements as are mentioned in section 131(1) above.

(2) The managers of the hospital shall ensure that the patient's environment in the hospital is suitable having regard to his age (subject to his needs).

(3) For the purpose of deciding how to fulfil the duty under subsection (2) above, the managers shall consult a person who appears to them to have knowledge or experience of cases involving patients who have not attained the age of 18 years which makes him suitable to be consulted.

(4) In this section, 'hospital' includes a registered establishment.

132   Duty of managers of hospitals to give information to detained patients

(1) The managers of a hospital or registered establishment in which a patient is detained under this Act shall take such steps as are practicable to ensure that the patient understands –
(a) under which of the provisions of this Act he is for the time being detained and the effect of that provision; and

(b) what rights of applying to a tribunal are available to him in respect of his detention under that provision; and those steps shall be taken as soon as practicable after the commencement of the patient's detention under the provision in question.

(2) The managers of a hospital or registered establishment in which a patient is detained as aforesaid shall also take such steps as are practicable to ensure that the patient understands the effect, so far as relevant in his case, of sections 23, 25, 56 to 64, 66(1)(g), 118 and 120 above and section 134 below; and those steps shall be taken as soon as practicable after the commencement of the patient's detention in the hospital or registered establishment.

(3) The steps to be taken under subsections (1) and (2) above shall include giving the requisite information both orally and in writing.

(4) The managers of a hospital or registered establishment in which a patient is detained as aforesaid shall, except where the patient otherwise requests, take such steps as are practicable to furnish the person (if any) appearing to them to be his nearest relative with a copy of any information given to him in writing under subsections (1) and (2) above; and those steps shall be taken when the information is given to the patient or within a reasonable time thereafter.

133   Duty of managers of hospitals to inform nearest relatives of discharge

(1) Where a patient liable to be detained under this Act in a hospital or mental nursing home is to be discharged otherwise than by virtue of an order for discharge made by his nearest relative, the managers of the hospital or mental nursing home shall, subject to subsection (2) below, take such steps as are practicable to inform the person (if any) appearing to them to be the nearest relative of the patient; and that information shall, if practicable, be given at least seven days before the date of discharge.

(1A) The reference in subsection (1) above to a patient who is to be discharged includes a patient who is to be discharged from hospital under section 17A above.

(1B) Subsection (1) above shall also apply in a case where a community patient is discharged under section 23 or 72 above (otherwise than by virtue of an order for discharge made by his nearest relative), but with the reference in that subsection to the managers of the hospital or registered establishment being read as a reference to the managers of the responsible hospital.

(2) Subsection (1) above shall not apply if the patient or his nearest relative has requested that information about the patient's discharge should not be given under this section.

134   Correspondence of patients

(1) A postal packet addressed to any person by a patient detained in a hospital under this Act and delivered by the patient for dispatch may be withheld from the postal operator concerned –

(a) if that person has requested that communications addressed to him by the patient should be withheld; or

(b) subject to subsection (3) below, if the hospital is one at which high security psychiatric services are provided and the managers of the hospital consider that the postal packet is likely –

(i) to cause distress to the person to whom it is addressed or to any other person (not being a person on the staff of the hospital); or

(ii) to cause danger to any person;

and any request for the purposes of paragraph (a) above shall be made by a notice in writing given to the managers of the hospital, or the approved clinician with overall responsibility for the patient's case.

(2) Subject to subsection (3) below, a postal packet addressed to a patient detained under this Act in a hospital at which high security psychiatric services are provided may be withheld from the patient if, in the opinion of the managers of the hospital, it is necessary to do so in the interests of the safety of the patient or for the protection of other persons.

(4) The managers of a hospital may inspect and open any postal packet for the purposes of determining –

    (a) whether it is one to which subsection (1) or (2) applies, and

    (b) in the case of a postal packet to which subsection (1) or (2) above applies, whether or not if should be withheld under that subsection;

and the power to withhold a postal packet under either of those subsections includes power to withhold anything contained in it.

(5) Where a postal packet or anything contained in it is withheld under subsection (1) or (2) above the managers of the hospital shall record that fact in writing.

(6) Where a postal packet or anything contained in it is withheld under subsection (1)(b) or (2) above the managers of the hospital shall within seven days give notice of that fact to the patient and, in the case of a packet withheld under subsection (2) above, to the person (if known) by whom the postal packet was sent; and any such notice shall be given in writing and shall contain a statement of the effect of section 134A(1) to (4).

Section 134A omitted

135   Warrant to search for and remove patients

(1) If it appears to a justice of the peace, on information on oath laid by an approved mental health professional, that there is reasonable cause to suspect that a person believed to be suffering from mental disorder –

    (a) has been, or is being, ill-treated, neglected or kept otherwise than under proper control, in any place within the jurisdiction of the justice, or

    (b) being unable to care for himself, is living alone in any such place, the justice may issue a warrant authorising any constable to enter, if need be by force, any premises specified in the warrant in which that person is believed to be, and, if thought fit, to remove him to a place of safety with a view to the making of an application in respect of him under Part II of this Act, or of other arrangements for his treatment or care.

(2) If it appears to a justice of the peace, on information on oath laid by any constable or other person who is authorised by or under this Act ... to take a patient to any place, or to take into custody or retake a patient who is liable under this Act ... to be so taken or retaken –

    (a) that there is reasonable cause to believe that the patient is to be found on premises within the jurisdiction of the justice; and

    (b) that admission to the premises has been refused or that a refusal of such admission is apprehended,

the justice may issue a warrant authorising any constable to enter the premises, if need be by force, and remove the patient.

(3) A patient who is removed to a place of safety in the execution of a warrant issued under this section may be detained there for a period not exceeding 72 hours.

(3A) A constable, an approved mental health professional or a person authorised by either of them for the purposes of this subsection may, before the end of the period of 72 hours mentioned in subsection (3) above, take a person detained in a place of safety under that subsection to one or more other places of safety.

(3B) A person taken to a place of safety under subsection (3A) above may be detained there for a period ending no later than the end of the period of 72 hours mentioned in subsection (3) above.

(4) In the execution of a warrant issued under subsection (1) above, a constable shall be accompanied by an approved mental health professional and by a registered medical practitioner, and in the execution of a warrant issued under subsection (2) above a constable may be accompanied –

    (a) by a registered medical practitioner;

    (b) by any person authorised by or under this Act ... to take or retake the patient.

(5) It shall not be necessary in any information or warrant under subsection (1) above to name the patient concerned.

(6) In this section 'place of safety' means residential accommodation provided by a local social services authority under Part III of the National Assistance Act 1948, a hospital as defined by this Act, a police station, an independent hospital or care home for mentally disordered persons or any other suitable place the occupier of which is willing temporarily to receive the patient.

136 Mentally disordered persons found in public places

(1) If a constable finds in a place to which the public have access a person who appears to him to be suffering from mental disorder and to be in immediate need of care or control, the constable may, if he thinks it necessary to do so in the interests of that person or for the protection of other persons, remove that person to a place of safety within the meaning of section 135 above.

(2) A person removed to a place of safety under this section may be detained there for a period not exceeding 72 hours for the purpose of enabling him to be examined by a registered medical practitioner and to be interviewed by an approved mental health professional and of making any necessary arrangements for his treatment or care.

(3) A constable, an approved mental health professional or a person authorised by either of them for the purposes of this subsection may, before the end of the period of 72 hours mentioned in subsection (2) above, take a person detained in a place of safety under that subsection to one or more other places of safety.

(4) A person taken to a place of safety under subsection (3) above may be detained there for a purpose mentioned in subsection (2) above for a period ending no later than the end of the period of 72 hours mentioned in that subsection.

139 Protection for acts done in pursuance of this Act

(1) No person shall be liable, whether on the ground of want of jurisdiction or on any other ground, to any civil or criminal proceedings to which he would have been liable apart from this section in respect of any act purporting to be done in pursuance of this Act or any regulations or rules made under this Act, unless the act was done in bad faith or without reasonable care.

(2) No civil proceedings shall be brought against any person in any court in respect of any such act without the leave of the High Court; and no criminal proceedings shall be brought against any person in any court in respect of any such act except by or with the consent of the Director of Public Prosecutions.

(3) This section does not apply to proceedings for an offence under this Act, being proceedings which, under any other provision of this Act, can be instituted only by or with the consent of the Director of Public Prosecutions.

(4) This section does not apply to proceedings against the Secretary of State or against the National Health Service Commissioning Board, a clinical commissioning group, Local Health Board or Special Health Authority or against a National Health Service trust established under the National Health Service Act 2006 or the National Health Service (Wales) Act 2006 or NHS foundation trust or against the Department of Justice in Northern Ireland or against a person who has functions under this Act by virtue of section 12ZA in so far as the proceedings relate to the exercise of those functions.

140 Notification of hospitals having arrangements for special cases

It shall be the duty of every clinical commissioning group and of every Local Health Board to give notice to every local social services authority for an area wholly or partly comprised within the area of the clinical commissioning group or Local Health Board, as the case may be, of the Authority specifying the hospital or hospitals administered by or otherwise available to the clinical commissioning group or Local Health Board in which arrangements are from time to time in force –

  (a) for the reception of patients in cases of special urgency;

(b) for the provision of accommodation or facilities designed so as to be specially suitable for patients who have not attained the age of 18 years.

Supplemental

145 Interpretation

(1) In this Act, unless the context otherwise requires –

'absent without leave' has the meaning given to it by section 18 above and related expressions (including expressions relating to a patient's liability to be returned to a hospital or other place) shall be construed accordingly;

'application for admission for assessment' has the meaning given in section 2 above;

'application for admission for treatment' has the meaning given in section 3 above;

'the appropriate tribunal' has the meaning given to it by section 66(4) above;

'approved clinician' means a person approved by the Secretary of State or another person by virtue of section 12ZA or 12ZB above (in relation to England) or by the Welsh Ministers (in relation to Wales) to act as an approved clinician for the purposes of this Act;

'approved mental health professional' has the meaning given in section 114 above;

'care home' has the same meaning as in the Care Standards Act 2000;

'community patient' has the meaning given in section 17A above;

'community treatment order' and 'the community treatment order' have the meanings given in section 17A above;

'the community treatment period' has the meaning given in section 20A above;

'high security psychiatric services' has the same meaning as in section 4 of the National Health Service Act 2006 or section 4 of the National Health Service (Wales) Act 2006;

'hospital' means –

(a) any health service hospital within the meaning of the National Health Service Act 2006 or the National Health Service (Wales) Act 2006; and

(b) any accommodation provided by a local authority and used as a hospital by or on behalf of the Secretary of State under that Act;

and 'hospital within the meaning of Part II of this Act' has the meaning given in section 34 above;

'hospital order' and 'guardianship order' have the meanings respectively given in section 37 above;

'medical treatment' includes nursing, psychological intervention and specialist mental health habilitation, rehabilitation and care (but see also subsection (4) below);

'mental disorder' has the meaning given in section 1 above (subject to section 86(4));

'nearest relative', in relation to a patient, has the meaning given in Part II of this Act;

'patient' means a person suffering or appearing to be suffering from mental disorder;

'registered establishment' has the meaning given in section 34 above;

'the regulatory authority' means –

(a) in relation to England, the Care Quality Commission;

(b) in relation to Wales, the Welsh Ministers;

'the responsible hospital' has the meaning given in section 17A above;

'restriction order' has the meaning given to it by section 41 above;

(1AA) Where high security psychiatric services and other services are provided at a hospital, the part of the hospital at which high security psychiatric services are provided and the other part shall be treated as separate hospitals for the purposes of this Act.

(1AB) References in this Act to appropriate medical treatment shall be construed in accordance with section 3(4) above.

(4) Any reference in this Act to medical treatment, in relation to mental disorder, shall be construed as a reference to medical treatment the purpose of which is to alleviate, or prevent a worsening of, the disorder or one or more of its symptoms or manifestations.

Medical Act 1983

(1983, c. 54)

PART I PRELIMINARY

The General Medical Council

1 The General Medical Council

(1) There shall continue to be a body corporate known as the General Medical Council (in this Act referred to as 'the General Council') having the functions assigned to them by this Act.

(1A) The over-arching objective of the General Council in exercising their functions is the protection of the public.

(1B) The pursuit by the General Council of their over-arching objective involves the pursuit of the following objectives –

(a) to protect, promote and maintain the health, safety and well-being of the public,

(b) to promote and maintain public confidence in the medical profession, and

(c) to promote and maintain proper professional standards and conduct for members of that profession.

(2) The General Council shall be constituted as provided by order of the Privy Council under this section subject to the provisions of Part I of Schedule 1 to this Act.

(3) The General Council shall have the following committees –

(c) one or more Registration Panels,

(d) one or more Registration Appeals Panels,

(e) the Investigation Committee,

(g) the Medical Practitioners Tribunal Service ('the MPTS'),

(h) one or more Medical Practitioners Tribunals,

(i) one or more Interim Orders Tribunals,

constituted in accordance with Part III of Schedule 1 to this Act and having the functions assigned to them by or under this Act.

(3A) The committees of the General Council specified in subsection (3) above are referred to in this Act as 'the statutory committees'.

2 Registration of medical practitioners

(1) There shall continue to be kept by the registrar of the General Council (in this Act referred to as 'the Registrar') a register of medical practitioners registered under this Act containing the names of those registered and the qualifications they are entitled to have registered under this Act.

(2) The register referred to is 'the register of medical practitioners' consisting of the following lists, namely –

(a) the principal list,

(aa) if anyone is registered under section 18A, the emergency powers doctors list,

(c) the visiting overseas doctors list, and

(d) the list of visiting medical practitioners from relevant European States.

(3) Medical practitioners shall be registered as fully registered medical practitioners or provisionally as provided in Parts II and III of this Act and in the appropriate list of the register of medical practitioners as provided in Part IV of this Act.

(4) Section 35C(2)(da) (the necessary knowledge of English) shall not apply in determining whether a person's fitness to practise is impaired for the purposes of registration under this Act.

PART V FITNESS TO PRACTISE AND MEDICAL ETHICS

35   General Council's power to advise on conduct, performance or ethics

The powers of the General Council shall include the power to provide, in such manner as the Council think fit, advice for members of the medical profession on –

    (a) standards of professional conduct;

    (b) standards of professional performance; or

    (c) medical ethics.

35A   General Council's power to require disclosure of information

    (1) For the purpose of assisting the General Council or any of their committees or the Registrar in carrying out functions in respect of a practitioner's fitness to practise, or for the purpose of assisting the Registrar in carrying out functions in respect of identifying any person registered by virtue of section 18A(1)(b) a person authorised by the Council may require –

    (a) a practitioner (except the practitioner in respect of whom the information or document is sought); or

    (b) any other person,

who in his opinion is able to supply information or produce any document which appears relevant to the discharge of any such function, to supply such information or produce such a document.

    (1A) The Registrar may by notice in writing require a practitioner, within such period as is specified in the notice, to supply such information or produce such documents as the Registrar considers necessary –

    (a) for the purpose of assisting the General Council or any of their committees or the Registrar in carrying out functions in respect of the practitioner's fitness to practise;

    (b) for the purpose of assisting the Registrar in carrying out functions in respect of identifying whether the practitioner is a person registered by virtue of section 18A(1)(b).

    (2) As soon as is reasonably practicable after the relevant date, the General Council shall require, from a practitioner in respect of whom a decision mentioned in subsection (3) has been made, details of any person –

    (a) by whom the practitioner is employed to provide services in, or in relation to, any area of medicine; or

    (b) with whom he has an arrangement to do so.

    (3) For the purposes of this section and section 35B below the relevant date is the date specified by the General Council by rules under paragraph 1 of Schedule 4 of this Act.

    (4) Nothing in this section shall require or permit any disclosure of information which is prohibited by or under any other enactment.

    (5) But where information is held in a form in which the prohibition operates because the information is capable of identifying an individual, the person referred to in subsection (1) or (1A) may, in exercising his functions under that subsection, require that the information be put into a form which is not capable of identifying that individual.

    (5A) In determining for the purposes of subsection (4) above whether a disclosure is not prohibited, by reason of being a disclosure of personal data which is exempt from non-disclosure provisions of the Data Protection Act 1998 by virtue of section 35(1) of that Act, it shall be assumed that the disclosure is required by this section.

    (6) Subsections (1) and (1A) above do not apply in relation to the supplying of information or the production of any document which a person could not be compelled to supply or produce in civil proceedings before the court (within the meaning of section 40(5) below).

    (6A) If a person fails to supply any information or produce any document within 14 days of his being required to do so under subsection (1) above, the General Council may seek an order of the relevant court requiring the information to be supplied or the document to be produced.

(6B) For the purposes of subsection (6A), 'the relevant court' means the county court or, in Scotland, the sheriff in whose sheriffdom is situated the address –

(a) which is shown in the register as the address of the person concerned; or

(b) which would have been so shown if the person concerned were registered.

(6C) If a person fails to comply with a requirement imposed under subsection (1A), the Registrar may refer that matter to the MPTS for them to arrange for it to be considered by a Medical Practitioners Tribunal.

(6D) Where a matter is referred to the MPTS under subsection (6C), the MPTS must arrange for it to be considered by a Medical Practitioners Tribunal.

(6E) Sub-paragraphs (3D) to (5A) of paragraph 5A of Schedule 4 apply to a matter being considered by a Medical Practitioners Tribunal under subsection (6D) as if it were a matter being considered by the Tribunal under sub-paragraph (3B) of that paragraph; and a reference in this Act to any of sub-paragraphs (3D) to (5A) of that paragraph is to be read as including a reference to that sub-paragraph as so applied.

(8) For the purposes of this section and section 35B, a 'practitioner' means a fully registered person or a provisionally registered person.

35B Notification and disclosure by the General Council

(1) As soon as is reasonably practicable after the relevant date, the General Council shall notify the following of an investigation by the General Council of a practitioner's fitness to practise –

(a) the Secretary of State, the Scottish Ministers, the Department of Health, Social Services and Public Safety in Northern Ireland and the National Assembly for Wales; and

(b) any person in the United Kingdom of whom the General Council are aware –

(i) by whom the practitioner concerned is employed to provide services in, or in relation to, any area of medicine, or

(ii) with whom he has an arrangement to do so.

(2) The General Council may, if they consider it to be in the public interest to do so, publish, or disclose to any person, information –

(a) which relates to a particular practitioner's fitness to practise, whether the matter to which the information relates arose before or after his registration, or arose in the United Kingdom or elsewhere; or

(b) of a particular description related to fitness to practise in relation to every practitioner, or to every practitioner of a particular description.

(3) For the purposes of subsection (2)(b) above, the General Council need not consider whether it is in the public interest to publish or disclose the information in question in relation to each individual practitioner to whom it relates.

(4) Subject to subsection (5), the General Council shall publish in such manner as they see fit –

(a) decisions of a Medical Practitioners Tribunal that relate to a finding that a person's fitness to practise is impaired (including decisions in respect of a direction relating to such a finding that follow a review of an earlier direction relating to such a finding);

(b) decisions of a Medical Practitioners Tribunal to make an order under section 38(1) or (2) below;

(c) decisions of a Medical Practitioners Tribunal to refuse an application for restoration to the register or to give a direction under section 41(9) below;

(d) decisions of an Interim Orders Tribunal or a Medical Practitioners Tribunal to make an order under section 41A below (including decisions in respect of orders varying earlier orders under that section);

(e) warnings of a Medical Practitioners Tribunal regarding a person's future conduct or performance;

(f) warnings of the Investigation Committee regarding a person's future conduct or performance; and

    (g) undertakings that have been agreed in accordance with rules made under paragraph 1(2A) of Schedule 4.

    (5) The General Council may withhold from publication under subsection (4) above information concerning the physical or mental health of a person which the General Council consider to be confidential.

35C   Functions of the Investigation Committee

    (1) This section applies where an allegation is made to the General Council against –

      (a) a fully registered person; or

      (b) a person who is provisionally registered, that his fitness to practise is impaired.

    (2) A person's fitness to practise shall be regarded as 'impaired' for the purposes of this Act by reason only of –

      (a) misconduct;

      (b) deficient professional performance;

      (c) a conviction or caution in the British Islands for a criminal offence, or a conviction elsewhere for an offence which, if committed in England and Wales, would constitute a criminal offence;

      (d) adverse physical or mental health; or

      (da) not having the necessary knowledge of English (but see section 2(4));

      (e) a determination by a body in the United Kingdom responsible under any enactment for the regulation of a health or social care profession to the effect that his fitness to practise as a member of that profession is impaired, or a determination by a regulatory body elsewhere to the same effect;

      (f) the Independent Barring Board including the person in a barred list (within the meaning of the Safeguarding Vulnerable Groups Act 2006 or the Safeguarding Vulnerable Groups (Northern Ireland) Order 2007); or

      (g) the Scottish Ministers including the person in the children's list or the adults' list (within the meaning of the Protection of Vulnerable Groups (Scotland) Act 2007).

    (3) This section is not prevented from applying because –

      (a) the allegation is based on a matter that is alleged to have occurred –

        (i)   outside the United Kingdom, or

        (ii) at a time when the person was not registered; or

      (b) in relation to a person who is a participant in a revalidation pilot scheme, the allegation is based on information obtained in the course of or otherwise in connection with the per-son's revalidation under that scheme.

    (4) The Investigation Committee shall investigate the allegation and decide whether it should be considered by a Medical Practitioners Tribunal.

    (5) If the Investigation Committee decide that the allegation ought to be considered by a Medical Practitioners Tribunal –

      (a) they shall give a direction to that effect to the Registrar;

      (b) the Registrar shall refer the allegation to the MPTS for them to arrange for the allegation to be considered by a Medical Practitioners Tribunal; and

      (c) the Registrar shall serve a notification of the Committee's decision on the person who is the subject of the allegation and the person making the allegation (if any).

    (6) If the Investigation Committee decide that the allegation ought not to be considered by a Medical Practitioners Tribunal, they may give a warning to the person who is the subject of the allegation regarding his future conduct or performance.

    (6A) In deciding whether to give a warning under subsection (6), the Investigation Committee must have regard to the over-arching objective.

    (7) If the Investigation Committee decide that the allegation ought not to be considered by a Medical Practitioners Tribunal, but that no warning should be given under subsection (6) above –

      (a) they shall give a direction to that effect to the Registrar; and

(b) the Registrar shall serve a notification of the Committee's decision on the person who is the subject of the allegation and the person making the allegation (if any).

(8) If the Investigation Committee are of the opinion that an Interim Orders Tribunal or a Medical Practitioners Tribunal should consider making an order for interim suspension or interim conditional registration under section 41A below in relation to the person who is the subject of the allegation –

(a) they shall give a direction to that effect to the Registrar;

(b) the Registrar shall refer the matter to the MPTS for them to arrange for an Interim Orders Tribunal or a Medical Practitioners Tribunal to decide whether to make such an order; and

(c) the Registrar shall serve notification of the decision on the person who is the subject of the allegation and the person making the allegation (if any).

35D   Functions of a Medical Practitioners Tribunal

(1) Where an allegation against a person is referred under section 35C(5)(b) above to the MPTS –

(a) the MPTS must arrange for the allegation to be considered by a Medical Practitioners Tribunal, and

(b) subsections (2) and (3) below shall apply.

(2) Where the Medical Practitioners Tribunal finds that the person's fitness to practise is impaired they may, if they think fit –

(a) except in a health case or language case, direct that the person's name shall be erased from the register;

(b) direct that his registration in the register shall be suspended (that is to say, shall not have effect) during such period not exceeding twelve months as may be specified in the direction; or

(c) direct that his registration shall be conditional on his compliance, during such period not exceeding three years as may be specified in the direction, with such requirements so specified as the Tribunal thinks fit to impose for the protection of members of the public or in his interests.

(3) Where the Tribunal find that the person's fitness to practise is not impaired they may nevertheless give him a warning regarding his future conduct or performance.

(4) Where a Medical Practitioners Tribunal has given a direction that a person's registration be suspended –

(a) under subsection (2) above;

(b) under subsection (10) or (12) below; or

(c) under rules made by virtue of paragraph 5A(3E) of Schedule 4 to this Act,

subsections (4A) and (4B) below apply.

(4A) The Tribunal may direct that the direction is to be reviewed by another Medical Practitioners Tribunal prior to the expiry of the period of suspension; and, where the Tribunal do so direct, the MPTS must arrange for the direction to be reviewed by another Medical Practitioners Tribunal prior to that expiry.

(4B) The Registrar may, at any time prior to the expiry of the period of suspension, refer the matter to the MPTS for them to arrange for the direction to be reviewed by a Medical Practitioners Tribunal prior to that expiry; and, where a matter is referred to the MPTS under this subsection, the MPTS must arrange for the direction to be reviewed by a Medical Practitioners Tribunal.

(5) On a review arranged under subsection (4A) or (4B), a Medical Practitioners Tribunal may, if they think fit –

(a) direct that the current period of suspension shall be extended for such further period from the time when it would otherwise expire as may be specified in the direction;

(b) except in a health case or language case, direct that the person's name shall be erased from the register;

(c) direct that the person's registration shall, as from the expiry of the current period of suspension or from such date before that expiry as may be specified in the direction, be conditional on his compliance, during such period not exceeding three years as may be specified in the direction, with such requirements so specified as the Tribunal think fit to impose for the protection of members of the public or in his interests, but, subject to subsection (6) below, the Tribunal shall not extend any period of suspension under this section for more than twelve months at a time; or

(d) revoke the direction for the remainder of the current period of suspension.

(6) In a health case or language case, a Medical Practitioners Tribunal may give a direction in relation to a person whose registration has been suspended under this section extending his period of suspension indefinitely where –

(a) the period of suspension will, on the date on which the direction takes effect, have lasted for at least two years; and

(b) the direction is made not more than two months before the date on which the period of suspension would otherwise expire.

(7) Where a Medical Practitioners Tribunal have given a direction under subsection (6) above for a person's period of suspension to be extended indefinitely, the Registrar shall refer the matter to the MPTS for them to arrange for a Medical Practitioners Tribunal to review the direction if –

(a) the person makes a request to the Registrar for there to be such a review;

(b) at least two years have elapsed since the date on which the direction took effect; and

(c) if the direction has previously been reviewed under this subsection, at least two years have elapsed since the date of the previous review.

(8) Where a matter is referred to the MPTS under subsection (7), the MPTS must arrange for the direction to be reviewed by a Medical Practitioners Tribunal; and on such a review, the Tribunal may –

(a) confirm the direction;

(b) direct that the suspension be terminated; or

(c) direct that the person's registration be conditional on his compliance, during such period not exceeding three years as may be specified in the direction, with such requirements so specified as the Tribunal think fit to impose for the protection of members of the public or in his interests.

(9) Where –

(a) a direction that a person's registration be subject to conditions has been given under –

(i)   subsection (2), (5) or (8) above,

(ii) subsection (12) below,

(iii) rules made by virtue of paragraph 5A(3E) of Schedule 4 to this Act, or

(iv) section 41A below; and

(b) the Registrar is of the opinion that that person has failed to comply with any requirement imposed on the person as such a condition,

subsection (9A) below applies.

(9A) The Registrar may refer the matter to the MPTS for them to arrange for the direction to be reviewed by a Medical Practitioners Tribunal; and, where a matter is referred to the MPTS under this subsection, the MPTS must arrange for the direction to be reviewed by a Medical Practitioners Tribunal.

(10) Where, on a review arranged under subsection (9A), the Tribunal judge the person concerned to have failed to comply with a requirement imposed as a condition such as is mentioned in subsection (9)(a), the Tribunal may, if they think fit –

(a) except in a health case or language case, direct that the person's name shall be erased from the register; or

(b) direct that the person's registration in the register shall be suspended during such period not exceeding twelve months as may be specified in the direction.

(11) Where, in a case which does not come within subsection (9) above, a direction that a person's registration be subject to conditions has been given under subsection (2), (5) or (8) above or paragraph 5A(3D) or 5C(4) of Schedule 4 to this Act, subsections (11A) and (11B) below apply.

(11A) The Tribunal may direct that the direction is to be reviewed by another Medical Practitioners Tribunal prior to the expiry of the period for which the conditions apply; and, where the Tribunal do so direct, the MPTS must arrange for the direction to be reviewed by another Medical Practitioners Tribunal prior to that expiry.

(11B) The Registrar may, at any time prior to the expiry of the period for which the conditions apply, refer the matter to the MPTS for them to arrange for the direction to be reviewed by a Medical Practitioners Tribunal; and, where a matter is referred to the MPTS under this subsection, the MPTS must arrange for the direction to be reviewed by a Medical Practitioners Tribunal.

(12) On a review arranged under subsection (11A) or (11B), a Medical Practitioners Tribunal may, if they think fit –

    (a) except in a health case or language case, direct that the person's name shall be erased from the register;

    (b) direct that the person's registration in the Register shall be suspended during such period not exceeding twelve months as may be specified in the direction;

    (c) direct that the current period of conditional registration shall be extended for such further period from the time when it would otherwise expire as may be specified in the direction; or

    (d) revoke the direction, or revoke or vary any of the conditions imposed by the direction, for the remainder of the current period of conditional registration,

but the Tribunal shall not extend any period of conditional registration under this section for more than three years at a time.

(13) Where a Medical Practitioners Tribunal have yet to hold a hearing to consider a case in which they would have the power to give or make a direction, revocation or variation under subsection (5), (6), (8), (10) or (12) above, but the person concerned and the General Council have agreed in writing to the terms of such a direction, revocation or variation –

    (a) the Tribunal, on considering the matter on the papers, or the chair of the Tribunal, on doing so instead of the Tribunal, may give a direction or make a revocation or variation on the agreed terms; or

    (b) if the Tribunal or chair (as the case may be) acting under paragraph (a) determines that the Tribunal should hold a hearing to consider the matter, the MPTS must arrange for a hearing of the Tribunal for that purpose.

(14) A direction, revocation or variation given or made under subsection (13)(a) by a Tribunal or the chair of a Tribunal is to be treated for the purposes of this Act as if it had been given or made by the Tribunal under subsection (5), (6), (8), (10) or (12) above (as the case may be).

35E   Provisions supplementary to section 35D

(3) While a person's registration in the register is suspended by virtue of a direction under section 35D –

    (a) he shall be treated as not being registered in the register notwithstanding that his name still appears in it, but

    (b) sections 31A, 35C, 35CC and 35D above, this section and section 39 below shall continue to apply to him.

(3A) In exercising a function under section 35D, a Medical Practitioners Tribunal must have regard to the over-arching objective.

(4) In section 35D above, 'health case' means any case in which a Medical Practitioners Tribunal have determined that –

    (a) a person's fitness to practise is impaired by reason of a matter falling within paragraph (d) of subsection (2) of section 35C above, but

(b) the person's fitness to practise is not impaired by any matter falling within any other paragraph of that subsection other than paragraph (da).

(5) In section 35D, 'language case' means any case in which a Medical Practitioners Tribunal has determined that –

(a) a person's fitness to practise is impaired by reason of a matter falling within paragraph (da) of subsection (2) of section 35C, but

(b) that person's fitness to practise is not impaired by any matter falling within any other paragraph of that subsection other than paragraph (d).

38 Power to order immediate suspension etc. after a finding of impairment of fitness to practise

(1) On giving a direction for erasure or a direction for suspension under section 35D(2), (10) or (12) above, or under paragraph 5A(3) of Schedule 4 to this Act, in respect of any person the Medical Practitioners Tribunal , if satisfied that to do so is necessary for the protection of members of the public or is otherwise in the public interest, or is in the best interests of that person, may order that his registration in the register shall be suspended forthwith in accordance with this section.

(2) On giving a direction for conditional registration under section 35D(2) above, or under paragraph 5A(3) of Schedule 4 to this Act, in respect of any person the Medical Practitioners Tribunal , if satisfied that to do so is necessary for the protection of members of the public or is otherwise in the public interest, or is in the best interests of that person, may order that his registration be made conditional forthwith in accordance with this section.

(3) Where, on the giving of a direction, an order under subsection (1) or (2) above is made in respect of a person, his registration in the register shall, subject to subsection (4) below, be suspended (that is to say, shall not have effect) or made conditional, as the case may be, from the time when the order is made until the time when –

(a) the direction takes effect in accordance with –

(i) paragraph 10 or 10A of Schedule 4 to this Act; or

(b) an appeal against it under section 40 below or paragraph 5A(5) of Schedule 4 of this Act is (otherwise than by the dismissal of the appeal) determined.

(4) Where a Medical Practitioners Tribunal makes an order under subsection (1) or (2) above, the Registrar shall forthwith serve a notification of the order on the person to whom it applies.

(5) If, when an order under subsection (1) or (2) above is made, the person to whom it applies is neither present nor represented at the proceedings, subsection (3) above shall have effect as if, for the reference to the time when the order is made, there were substituted a reference to the time of service of a notification of the order as determined for the purposes of paragraph 8 of Schedule 4 to this Act.

(6) Except as provided in subsection (7) below, while a person's registration in the register is suspended by virtue of subsection (1) above, he shall be treated as not being registered in the register notwithstanding that his name still appears in it.

(7) Notwithstanding subsection (6) above, sections 35C to 35E above shall continue to apply to a person whose registration in the register is suspended.

(8) The relevant court may terminate any suspension of a person's registration in the register imposed under subsection (1) above or any conditional registration imposed under subsection (2) above, and the decision of the court on any application under this subsection shall be final.

(9) In this section 'the relevant court' has the same meaning as in section 40(5) below.

39 Fraud or error in relation to registration

(1) If the Registrar is satisfied that any entry in the register has been fraudulently procured or incorrectly made, he may erase the entry from the register.

(2) Where the Registrar decides to erase a person's name under this section, the Registrar shall forthwith serve on that person notification of the decision and of his right to appeal against the decision under Schedule 3A to this Act.

40   Appeals by persons subject to decisions by Tribunals

(1) The following decisions are appealable decisions for the purposes of this section, that is to say –

    (a) a decision of a Medical Practitioners Tribunal under section 35D above giving a direction for erasure, for suspension or for conditional registration or varying the conditions imposed by a direction for conditional registration;

    (b) a decision of a Medical Practitioners Tribunal under section 41(9) below giving a direction that the right to make further application under that section shall be suspended indefinitely; or

(1A) A decision under regulations made –

    (a) under section 31 above by virtue of subsection (8) of that section; or

    (b) under section 31A(1)(c) above,

not to restore a person's name to the register for a reason that relates to his fitness to practise is also an appealable decision for the purposes of this section.

(3) In subsection (1) above –

    (a) references to a direction for suspension include a reference to a direction extending a period of suspension; and

    (b) references to a direction for conditional registration include a reference to a direction extending a period of conditional registration.

(4) A person in respect of whom an appealable decision falling within subsection (1) has been taken may, before the end of the period of 28 days beginning with the date on which notification of the decision was served under section 35E(1) above, or section 41(10) below, appeal against the decision to the relevant court.

(4A) A person in respect of whom an appealable decision falling within subsection (1A) has been taken may, before the end of the period of 28 days beginning with the date on which notification of the decision was served, appeal against the decision to the relevant court.

(5) In subsections (4) and (4A) above, 'the relevant court' –

    (a) in the case of a person whose address in the register is (or if he were registered would be) in Scotland, means the Court of Session;

    (b) in the case of a person whose address in the register is (or if he were registered would be) in Northern Ireland, means the High Court of Justice in Northern Ireland; and

    (c) in the case of any other person, means the High Court of Justice in England and Wales.

(7) On an appeal under this section from a Medical Practitioners Tribunal, the court may –

    (a) dismiss the appeal;

    (b) allow the appeal and quash the direction or variation appealed against;

    (c) substitute for the direction or variation appealed against any other direction or variation which could have been given or made by a Medical Practitioners Tribunal; or

    (d) remit the case to the MPTS for them to arrange for a Medical Practitioners Tribunal to dispose of the case in accordance with the directions of the court,

and may make such order as to costs (or, in Scotland, expenses) as it thinks fit.

(7A) Where a case is referred under subsection (7)(d) to the MPTS, the MPTS must arrange for the case to be disposed of by a Medical Practitioners Tribunal in accordance with the directions of the court.

(8) On an appeal under this section from the General Council, the court (or the sheriff) may –

    (a) dismiss the appeal;

    (b) allow the appeal and quash the direction appealed against; or

    (c) remit the case to the General Council to dispose of the case in accordance with the directions of the court (or the sheriff),

and may make such order as to costs (or, in Scotland, expenses) as it (or he) thinks fit.

(9) On an appeal under this section from a Medical Practitioners Tribunal, the General Council may appear as respondent; and for the purpose of enabling directions to be given as to the costs

of any such appeal the Council shall be deemed to be a party thereto, whether they appear on the hearing of the appeal or not.

40A   Appeals by General Council

(1) This section applies to any of the following decisions by a Medical Practitioners Tribunal –

(a) a decision under section 35D giving –

(i)   a direction for suspension, including a direction extending a period of suspension;

(ii)   a direction for conditional registration, including a direction extending a period of conditional registration;

(iii) a direction varying any of the conditions imposed by a direction for conditional registration;

(b) a decision under paragraph 5A(3D) or 5C(4) of Schedule 4 giving –

(i)   a direction for suspension;

(ii)   a direction for conditional registration;

(c) a decision under section 35D –

(i)   giving a direction that a suspension be terminated;

(ii)   revoking a direction for conditional registration or a condition imposed by such a direction;

(d) a decision not to give a direction under section 35D;

(e) a decision under section 41 giving a direction that a person's name be restored to the register;

(f) a decision not to give a direction under paragraph 5A(3D) or 5C(4) of Schedule 4.

(2) A decision to which this section applies is referred to below as a 'relevant decision'.

(3) The General Council may appeal against a relevant decision to the relevant court if they consider that the decision is not sufficient (whether as to a finding or a penalty or both) for the protection of the public.

(4) Consideration of whether a decision is sufficient for the protection of the public involves consideration of whether it is sufficient –

(a) to protect the health, safety and well-being of the public;

(b) to maintain public confidence in the medical profession; and

(c) to maintain proper professional standards and conduct for members of that profession.

(5) The General Council may not bring an appeal under this section after the end of the period of 28 days beginning with the day on which notification of the relevant decision was served on the person to whom the decision relates.

(6) On an appeal under this section, the court may –

(a) dismiss the appeal;

(b) allow the appeal and quash the relevant decision;

(c) substitute for the relevant decision any other decision which could have been made by the Tribunal; or

(d) remit the case to the MPTS for them to arrange for a Medical Practitioners Tribunal to dispose of the case in accordance with the directions of the court,

and may make such order as to costs (or, in Scotland, expenses) as it thinks fit.

(7) In this section and section 40B, 'relevant court' has the meaning given by section 40(5).

41   Restoration of names to the register

(1) Subject to subsections (2) and (6) below, where the name of a person has been erased from the register under section 35D above, or section 44B(4)(b) below, a Medical Practitioners Tribunal, if they think fit, direct that his name be restored to the register.

(2) No application for the restoration of a name to the register under this section shall be made –

(a) before the expiration of five years from the date of erasure; or

(b) in any period of twelve months in which an application for the restoration of his name has already been made by or on behalf of the person whose name has been erased.

(3) An application under this section shall be made to the Registrar who shall refer the application to the MPTS for them to arrange for the application to be determined by a Medical Practitioners Tribunal.

(4) In the case of a person who was provisionally registered under section 15, 15A, 21 or 21C above before his name was erased, a direction under subsection (1) above shall be a direction that his name be restored by way of provisional registration under section 15, 15A, 21 or 21C above, as the case requires.

(5) The requirements of Part II or Part III of this Act as to the experience required for registration as a fully registered medical practitioner shall not apply to registration in pursuance of a direction under subsection (1) above.

(6) Before determining whether to give a direction under subsection (1) above, a Medical Practitioners Tribunal shall require an applicant for restoration to provide such evidence as the Tribunal directs as to his fitness to practise; and the Tribunal shall not give such a direction if that evidence does not satisfy it.

(7) A Medical Practitioners Tribunal shall not give a direction under subsection (1) above unless at the same time they direct that the practitioner's licence to practise be restored.

(9) Where, during the same period of erasure, a second or subsequent application for the restoration of a name to the register, made by or on behalf of the person whose name has been erased, is unsuccessful, a Medical Practitioners Tribunal may direct that his right to make any further such applications shall be suspended indefinitely.

(10) Where a Medical Practitioners Tribunal give a direction under subsection (9) above, the MPTS shall without delay serve on the person in respect of whom it has been made a notification of the direction and of his right to appeal against it in accordance with section 40 above.

(11) Any person in respect of whom a direction has been given under subsection (9) above may, after the expiration of three years from the date on which the direction was given, apply to the Registrar for that direction to be referred to the MPTS for them to arrange for the direction to be reviewed by a Medical Practitioners Tribunal and, thereafter, may make further applications for review; but no such application may be made before the expiration of three years from the date of the most recent review decision.

(12) In exercising a function under this section, a Medical Practitioners Tribunal must have regard to the over-arching objective.

41A   Interim orders

(A1) Where a matter is referred under section 35C(8) to the MPTS, the MPTS must arrange for an Interim Orders Tribunal or a Medical Practitioners Tribunal to decide whether to make an order as mentioned in that provision.

(1) Where an Interim Orders Tribunal or a Medical Practitioners Tribunal in arrangements made under subsection (A1), or a Medical Practitioners Tribunal on their consideration of the matter are satisfied that it is necessary for the protection of members of the public or is otherwise in the public interest, or is in the interests of a fully registered person, for the registration of that person to be suspended or to be made subject to conditions, the Tribunal may make an order –

(a) that his registration in the register shall be suspended (that is to say, shall not have effect) during such period not exceeding eighteen months as may be specified in the order (an 'interim suspension order'); or

(b) that his registration shall be conditional on his compliance, during such period not exceeding eighteen months as may be specified in the order, with such requirements so specified as the Tribunal thinks fit to impose (an 'order for interim conditional registration').

(2) Subject to subsection (9) below, where an Interim Orders Tribunal or a Medical Practitioners Tribunal have made an order under subsection (1) above, the Interim Orders Tribunal or the Medical Practitioners Tribunal –

    (a) shall review it within the period of six months beginning on the date on which the order was made, and shall thereafter, for so long as the order continues in force, further review it –

        (i) before the end of the period of six months beginning on the date of the decision of the immediately preceding review; or

        (ii) if after the end of the period of three months beginning on the date of the decision of the immediately preceding review the person concerned requests an earlier review, as soon as practicable after that request; and

    (b) may review it where new evidence relevant to the order has become available after the making of the order.

(3) Where an interim suspension order or an order for interim conditional registration has been made in relation to any person under any provision of this section (including this subsection), an Interim Orders Tribunal or a Medical Practitioners Tribunal may, subject to subsection (4) below –

    (a) revoke the order or revoke any condition imposed by the order;

    (b) vary any condition imposed by the order;

    (c) if satisfied that to do so is necessary for the protection of members of the public or is otherwise in the public interest, or is in the interests of the person concerned, replace an order for interim conditional registration with an interim suspension order having effect for the remainder of the term of the former; or

    (d) if satisfied that to do so is necessary for the protection of members of the public, or is otherwise in the public interest, or is in the interests of the person concerned, replace an interim suspension order with an order for interim conditional registration having effect for the remainder of the term of the former.

(3A) Where an Interim Orders Tribunal or a Medical Practitioners Tribunal have yet to hold a hearing to consider a case in which they would have the power to make an order under subsection (3) above, but the person concerned and the General Council have already agreed in writing to the terms of such an order –

    (a) the Tribunal, on considering the matter on the papers, or the chair of the Tribunal, on doing so instead of the Tribunal, may make an order on the agreed terms; or

    (b) if the Tribunal or chair (as the case may be) acting under paragraph (a) determines that the Tribunal should hold a hearing to consider the matter, the MPTS must arrange for a hearing of the Tribunal for that purpose.

(3B) An order made under subsection (3A)(a) by a Tribunal or the chair of a Tribunal is to be treated for the purposes of this Act as if it had been made by the Tribunal under subsection (3).

(4) No order under subsection (1) or (3)(b) to (d) above shall be made by a Tribunal in respect of any person unless he has been afforded an opportunity of appearing before the Tribunal and being heard on the question of whether such an order should be made in his case.

(5) If an order is made under any provision of this section, the MPTS shall without delay serve a notification of the order on the person to whose registration it relates.

(6) The General Council may apply to the relevant court for an order made by an Interim Orders Tribunal or a Medical Practitioners Tribunal under subsection (1) or (3) above to be extended, and may apply again for further extensions.

(7) On such an application the relevant court may extend (or further extend) for up to 12 months the period for which the order has effect.

(8) Any reference in this section to an interim suspension order, or to an order for interim conditional registration, includes a reference to such an order as so extended.

(9) For the purposes of subsection (2) above the first review after the relevant court's extension of an order made by an Interim Orders Tribunal or a Medical Practitioners Tribunal or after a

replacement order made by an Interim Orders Tribunal or a Medical Practitioners Tribunal under subsection (3)(c) or (d) above shall take place –

    (a) if the order (or the order which has been replaced) had not been reviewed at all under subsection (2), within the period of six months beginning on the date on which the relevant court ordered the extension or on which a replacement order under subsection (3) (c) or (d) was made; and

    (b) if it had been reviewed under the provision, within the period of three months beginning on that date.

  (10) Where an order has effect under any provision of this section, the relevant court may –

    (a) in the case of an interim suspension order, terminate the suspension;

    (b) in the case of an order for interim conditional registration, revoke or vary any condition imposed by the order;

    (c) in either case, substitute for the period specified in the order (or in the order extending it) some other period which could have been specified in the order when it was made (or in the order extending it),

and the decision of the relevant court under any application under this subsection shall be final.

  (11) Except as provided in subsection (12) below, while a person's registration in the register is suspended by virtue of an interim suspension order under this section he shall be treated as not being registered in the register notwithstanding that his name still appears in the register.

  (12) Notwithstanding subsection (11) above, sections 31A, 35C to 35E and 39 above shall continue to apply to a person whose registration in the register is suspended.

  (13) This section applies to a provisionally registered person whether or not the circumstances are such that he falls within the meaning in this Act of the expression 'fully registered person'.

  (14) In this section 'the relevant court' has the same meaning as in section 40(5) above.

44 Effect of disqualification in another relevant European State on registration in the United Kingdom

  (1) A person who is subject to a disqualifying decision in a relevant European State in which he is or has been established in medical practice shall not be entitled to be registered by virtue of section 3(1)(b) above for so long as the decision remains in force in relation to him.

  (2) A disqualifying decision in respect of a person is a decision, made by responsible authorities of the relevant European State in which he was established in medical practice or in which he acquired a medical qualification, and –

    (a) expressed to be made on the grounds that he has committed a criminal offence or on grounds related to his professional conduct, professional performance or physical or mental health; and

    (b) having in that State the effect either that he is no longer registered or otherwise officially recognised as a medical practitioner, or that he is prohibited from practising medicine there.

  (3) If a person has been registered by virtue of section 3(1)(b) above and it is subsequently shown to the satisfaction of the Registrar that he was subject to a disqualifying decision in force at the time of registration, and that the decision remains in force, the Registrar shall remove the person's name from the register.

  (4) A decision under –

    (a) subsection (1) above not to register a person; or

    (b) subsection (3) above to remove a person's name from the register, is an appealable registration decision for the purposes of Schedule 3A to this Act.

  (5) If a person has been registered as a fully registered medical practitioner by virtue of section 3(1)(b) above at a time when a disqualifying decision was in force in respect of him, and he has been so registered for a period of not less than one month throughout which the decision had effect –

    (a) a Medical Practitioners Tribunal may, if the matter is referred to it by the Registrar, direct that the person's registration be suspended for such period, not exceeding the length of the first-mentioned period, as the Tribunal thinks fit, and the period of suspension shall begin on a date to be specified in the Tribunal's direction; and

(b) sections 35E(1) and (3) and 40 and paragraphs 8, 9, 10 and 12 of Schedule 4 to this Act shall have effect, with any necessary modifications, in relation to suspension under this subsection.

(5A) In deciding whether to give a direction under subsection (5)(a), a Medical Practitioners Tribunal must have regard to the over-arching objective.

(6) Where on or after the date on which a person was registered by virtue of section 3(1)(b), 14A or 19A above a disqualifying decision relating to him comes into force, this Part of this Act shall apply, with any necessary modifications, as if it had been found that he had been convicted of the criminal offence referred to in the disqualifying decision, or that his professional performance or physical or mental health had been such as is imputed to him by that decision, as the case may be.

44B   Provision of information in respect of fitness to practise matters

(1) If a person has been registered by virtue of any provision of this Act, other than Schedule 2A, and it is subsequently shown to the satisfaction of the Registrar that –

(a) his fitness to practise was impaired at the time of his registration as a result of serious, specific circumstances or because of a problem with his physical or mental health; and

(b) he had not informed the Registrar of that matter or problem before his registration, the Registrar may erase that person's name from the register.

(2) The General Council may by regulations make provision for the information to be provided to the Registrar –

(a) by or in respect of a person seeking registration by virtue of any provision of this Act, other than Schedule 2A, for the purpose of determining whether his fitness to practise is impaired;

(b) by or in respect of a person who is fully registered otherwise than by virtue of Schedule 2A, or provisionally registered, for the purpose of determining whether his fitness to practise was impaired at the time of his registration as a result of serious, specific circumstances or a problem with his physical or mental health.

(3) In subsections (1) and (2) above, 'serious, specific circumstances' has the same meaning as in article 56(2) of the Directive (exchange between authorities of information about disciplinary action etc).

(4) The Registrar may –

(a) refuse to register (even if he is directed by the General Council to do so) any person who fails to comply with, or in respect of whom there is a failure to comply with, regulations made under subsection (2)(a) above;

(b) erase from the register the name of any person who fails to comply with, or in respect of whom there is a failure to comply with, regulations made under subsection (2)(b) above.

44BA   Fitness to practise of exempt persons: sufficient evidence

(1) Subsections (2) to (5) apply in relation to an exempt person ('E') who applies for registration under section 3(1)(b), 14A or 19A of this Act.

(2) For the purpose of determining whether E's fitness to practise is impaired, the Registrar shall accept as sufficient evidence of E's good health a certificate which –

(a) attests to E's good physical and mental health; and

(b) is required of a person who wishes to practise medicine in E's attesting state.

(3) If no such certificate is required of persons who wish to practise medicine in E's attesting State, for the purpose of determining whether E's fitness to practise is impaired, the Registrar shall accept as sufficient evidence of E's good health a certificate which –

(a) attests to E's good physical and mental health; and

(b) is issued by a competent authority in E's attesting State.

(4) For the purpose of determining whether E's fitness to practise is impaired, the Registrar shall accept as sufficient evidence of E's good character a certificate which –

    (a) attests to E's good character or good repute; and

    (b) is issued by a competent authority in E's attesting State.

(5) If no such certificate is issued by a competent authority in E's attesting State, for the purpose of determining whether E's fitness to practise is impaired, the Registrar shall accept as sufficient evidence of E's good character a certificate –

    (a) attesting to the authenticity of a declaration on oath made by E –

        (i) before a competent judicial or administrative authority, notary or qualified profes-sional body of E's attesting State, and

        (ii) attesting to E's good character; and

    (b) issued by the authority, notary or body referred to in paragraph (a)(i).

In this subsection, 'declaration on oath' includes a solemn declaration.

(6) In subsections (2) to (5) the 'attesting State', in relation to E, is –

    (a) the relevant European State in which E obtained his medical qualification; or

    (b) (if different) the relevant European State from which E comes to the United Kingdom.

(7) The Registrar shall not accept any certificate referred to in subsection (2), (3), (4) or (5) if it is presented more than three months after the date on which it was issued.

44C Indemnity arrangements

(1) A person who holds a licence to practise as a medical practitioner, and practises as such, must have in force in relation to him an indemnity arrangement which provides appropriate cover for practising as such.

(2) For the purposes of this section, an 'indemnity arrangement' may comprise –

    (a) a policy of insurance;

    (b) an arrangement for the purposes of indemnifying a person;

    (c) a combination of the two.

(3) For the purposes of this section, 'appropriate cover', in relation to practice as a medical practitioner, means cover against liabilities that may be incurred in practising as such which is ap-propriate, having regard to the nature and extent of the risks of practising as such.

(4) The General Council may make regulations in connection with the information to be pro-vided to the Registrar –

    (a) by or in respect of a person seeking a licence to practise for the purpose of determining whether, if he is granted such a licence, there will be in force in relation to him by the time he begins to practise an indemnity arrangement which provides appropriate cover; and

    (b) by or in respect of a person who holds a licence to practise for the purpose of deter-mining whether there is in force in relation to him an indemnity arrangement which provides appropriate cover.

(5) Regulations made under subsection (4)(b) may require the information mentioned there to be provided –

    (a) at the request of the Registrar; or

    (b) on such dates or at such intervals as the Registrar may determine, either generally or in relation to individual practitioners or practitioners of a particular description.

(6) The General Council may also make regulations requiring a person who holds a licence to practise to inform the Registrar if there ceases to be in force in relation to him an indemnity arrangement which provides appropriate cover.

(7) The General Council may also make regulations requiring a person who holds a licence to practise to inform the Registrar if there is in force in relation to him appropriate cover provided under an indemnity arrangement by an employer.

(8) A licensing authority may refuse to grant a licence to practise to any person who fails to comply, or in respect of whom there is a failure to comply, with regulations made under sub-section (4)(a).

(9) Where a person who holds a licence to practise is in breach of subsection (1) or there is a failure to comply with regulations made under subsection (4)(b) in relation to him –

    (a) a licensing authority may withdraw that person's licence to practise; or

    (b) the breach or failure may be treated as misconduct for the purposes of section 35C(2)
       (a) , and the Registrar may accordingly refer the matter to the Investigation Committee
       under section 35C(4).

(11) This section does not apply to a person who holds a licence to practise as a result of registration under Schedule 2A (visiting medical practitioners from relevant European States).

44D   Approved practice settings

(1) Unless the Registrar otherwise directs in relation to a particular person, a person who is registered under section 3(1)(a) or 21B above after the coming into force of this section shall, before his first revalidation in accordance with Part 3A above after he is registered, practise medicine in the United Kingdom only in a practice setting –

    (a) where he is subject to a governance system that includes, but is not limited to, provision
       for appropriate supervision and appraisal arrangements or assessments; and

    (b) which is, or which is of a type which is, for the time being recognised by the General
       Council, either generally or in relation to him or to practitioners of his class, as being
       acceptable for a practitioner who is newly fully registered.

(2) Unless the Registrar otherwise directs in relation to a particular person, a person whose name is restored to the register after the coming into force of this section shall, before his first revalidation in accordance with Part 3A above after his name is restored to the register, practise medicine in the United Kingdom only in a practice setting –

    (a) where he is subject to a governance system that includes, but is not limited to, provision
       for appropriate supervision and appraisal arrangements or assessments; and

    (b) which is, or which is of a type which is, for the time being recognised by the General
       Council, either generally or in relation to him or to practitioners of his class, as being
       acceptable for a practitioner who is newly restored to the register.

(3) The General Council may limit their recognition of –

    (a) a particular practice setting so that it is recognised in relation only to one or more par-
       ticular practitioners or particular classes of practitioner;

    (b) a particular type of practice setting so that it is recognised in relation only to one or
       more particular classes of practitioner.

(4) The General Council may exclude a particular practice setting from their recognition of a particular type of practice setting –

    (a) in relation to all practitioners; or

    (b) in relation to one or more particular classes of practitioner.

(5) The General Council may at any time vary or withdraw their recognition from a particular practice setting or a particular type of practice setting.

(6) An example of a valid reason for withdrawing recognition from a particular practice setting, or excluding a particular practice setting from recognition of a particular type of practice setting, is that the relevant governance system operated there is not quality assured by a body that is acceptable to the General Council as a provider of quality assurance.

(7) If –

    (a) a person starts practising medicine in a practice setting that is, or is of a type that is,
       recognised under whichever is appropriate of subsection (1)(b) or (2)(b) above, either
       generally or in relation to practitioners of his class; and

    (b) while he is practising medicine there, it ceases to be so recognised,

it is to be treated as continuing to be recognised in relation to the particular practitioner while he continues to practise medicine there.

(8) The General Council may by regulations make provision for the information to be provided to the Registrar by or in respect of a fully registered person for the purposes of determining whether or not he is in breach of subsection (1) or (2) above.

(9) If a fully registered person –

    (a) is in breach of subsection (1) or (2) above; or

    (b) fails to comply with regulations made under subsection (8) above, or there is a failure to comply with those regulations in respect of him,

the breach or failure may be treated as misconduct for the purposes of section 35C(2)(a) above, and the Registrar may refer the matter to the Investigation Committee for investigation by them under section 35C(4) above.

(11) The General Council may publish guidance for practitioners who –

    (a) are newly fully registered or whose names are newly restored to the register; but

    (b) are not subject to the requirements imposed by subsection (1) and (2),

on what are suitable practice settings for them before their first revalidation in accordance with Part 3A above after being registered or before their names are restored to the register.

PART VA RESPONSIBLE OFFICERS

45A Requirement to nominate or appoint responsible officer

(1) The appropriate authority may by regulations make provision for or in connection with requiring designated bodies to nominate or appoint persons who are to have such responsibilities as may be conferred on them by virtue of section 45B.

(2) A person who is so nominated or appointed by a designated body is to be known as its responsible officer (but this is subject to any provision made by virtue of subsection (5)(e)).

(3) In this Part 'designated body' means –

    (a) a body falling within any description of bodies prescribed for the purposes of this section, or

    (b) any other body prescribed for those purposes.

(4) The descriptions of bodies, or particular bodies, that may be so prescribed are descriptions of bodies, or particular bodies, appearing to the appropriate authority –

    (a) to provide, or arrange for the provision of, health care, or

    (b) to employ or contract with medical practitioners.

(5) Regulations under this section may make provision –

    (a) for conditions that must be satisfied in relation to a person if that person is to be nominated or appointed as, or remain as, a responsible officer of a designated body,

    (b) authorising or requiring a designated body to nominate or appoint more than one responsible officer,

    (c) for a single person to be nominated or appointed as the responsible officer for each of two or more designated bodies where those bodies are satisfied as to the prescribed matters,

    (d) requiring a designated body that has a responsible officer to provide to the officer, or, if that designated body does not employ the officer, to the employer of the officer, funds and other resources necessary for enabling the officer to discharge the officer's prescribed responsibilities as a responsible officer for the designated body,

    (e) for the persons nominated or appointed as mentioned in subsection (1) to be known by such name as is prescribed, and

    (f) for making such amendments of any enactment as appear to the appropriate authority to be required in connection with any provision made by virtue of paragraph (e).

(6) The conditions imposed under subsection (5)(a) may in particular include a requirement for the designated body to consult the General Council before nominating or appointing any person as a responsible officer for the body.

(7) Regulations under this section may in prescribed cases provide that a responsible officer for a designated body is to be nominated by the appropriate authority instead of the designated body.

(8) In this section –

'health care' means services provided to individuals for or in connection with the prevention, diagnosis or treatment of illness;

'illness' has the same meaning as in section 25(1) of the Health Act 2006.

PART VI PRIVILEGES OF REGISTERED PRACTITIONERS

46   Recovery of fees

(1) Except as provided in subsection (2A) below, no person shall be entitled to recover any charge in any court of law for any medical advice or attendance, or for the performance of any operation, unless he proves that he is fully registered and holds a licence to practise.

(2A) Subsection (1) above shall not apply to fees in respect of medical services lawfully provided –

(a) under arrangements to provide services as part of the health service, the Northern Ireland health service or the Scottish health service (those terms having the same meaning here as in section 29G(3) above);

(b) by any person who is not a medical practitioner but who is entitled to provide those medical services by virtue of an enforceable EU right;

(c) by a person who is a member of a profession regulated by a body, apart from the General Council, mentioned in section 25(3) of the National Health Service Reform and Health Care Professions Act 2002.

(3) Where a practitioner is a fellow of a college of physicians, fellows of which are prohibited by byelaw from recovering by law their expenses, charges or fees, then, notwithstanding that he is fully registered and holds a licence to practise, the prohibitory byelaw, so long as it is in force, may be pleaded in bar of any legal proceedings instituted by him for the recovery of expenses, charges or fees.

47   Appointments not to be held except by fully registered practitioners who hold licences to practise

(1) Subject to subsection (2) below, only a person who is fully registered and who holds a licence to practise may hold any appointment as physician, surgeon or other medical officer –

(a) in the naval, military or air service,

(b) in any hospital or other place for the reception of persons suffering from mental disorder, or in any other hospital, infirmary or dispensary not supported wholly by voluntary contributions,

(c) in any prison, or

(d) in any other public establishment, body or institution, or to any friendly or other society for providing mutual relief in sickness, infirmity or old age.

(2) Nothing in this section shall prevent any person who is not a Commonwealth citizen from being and acting as the resident physician or medical officer of any hospital established exclusively for the relief of foreigners in sickness, so long as he –

(a) has obtained from a foreign university a degree or diploma of doctor in medicine and has passed the regular examinations entitling him to practise medicine in his own country, and

(b) is engaged in no medical practise except as such a resident physician or medical officer.

(3) None of the suspension events mentioned in subsection (4) below shall terminate any appointment such as is mentioned in subsection (1) above but the person suspended shall not perform the duties of such an appointment during the suspension.

(4) The suspension events are –

(a) the suspension of registration of a person by a Medical Practitioners Tribunal –

(i) following a finding of impairment of fitness to practise by reason of deficient professional performance or adverse physical or mental health under section 35D above, or

(ii) under paragraph 5A(3) of Schedule 4 to this Act;

(b) an order for immediate suspension by a Medical Practitioners Tribunal under section 38(1) above; or

(c) an interim suspension order by an Interim Orders Tribunal or a Medical Practitioners Tribunal under section 41A above (or such an order as extended under that section).

48   Certificates invalid if not signed by fully registered practitioners who hold licences to practise

A certificate required by any enactment, whether passed before or after the commencement of this Act, from any physician, surgeon, licentiate in medicine and surgery or other medical practitioner shall not be valid unless the person signing it is fully registered and holds a licence to practise.

49   Penalty for pretending to be registered

(1)   Any person who wilfully and falsely pretends to be or takes or uses the name or title of physician, doctor of medicine, licentiate in medicine and surgery, bachelor of medicine, surgeon, general practitioner or apothecary, or any name, title, addition or description implying that he is registered under any provision of this Act, or that he is recognised by law as a physician or surgeon or licentiate in medicine and surgery or a practitioner in medicine or an apothecary, shall be liable on summary conviction to a fine not exceeding level 5 on the standard scale.

49A   Penalty for pretending to hold a licence to practise

(1)   If a person who does not hold a licence to practise –

(a) holds himself out as having such a licence; or

(b) engages in conduct calculated to suggest that he has such a licence, he shall be liable on summary conviction to a fine not exceeding level 5 on the standard scale.

Surrogacy Arrangements Act 1985

(1985, c. 49)

1   Meaning of 'surrogate mother', 'surrogacy arrangement' and other terms

(1)   The following provisions shall have effect for the interpretation of this Act.

(2)   'Surrogate mother' means a woman who carries a child in pursuance of an arrangement –

(a) made before she began to carry the child, and

(b) made with a view to any child carried in pursuance of it being handed over to, and parental responsibility being met (so far as practicable) by, another person or other persons.

(3)   An arrangement is a surrogacy arrangement if, were a woman to whom the arrangement relates to carry a child in pursuance of it, she would be a surrogate mother.

(4)   In determining whether an arrangement is made with such a view as is mentioned in subsection (2) above regard may be had to the circumstances as a whole (and, in particular, where there is a promise or understanding that any payment will or may be made to the woman or for her benefit in respect of the carrying of any child in pursuance of the arrangement, to that promise or understanding).

(5)   An arrangement may be regarded as made with such a view though subject to conditions relating to the handing over of any child.

(6)   A woman who carries a child is to be treated for the purposes of subsection (2)(a) above as beginning to carry it at the time of the insemination or of the placing in her of an embryo, of an egg in the process of fertilisation or of sperm and eggs, as the case may be, that results in her carrying the child.

(7)   'Body of persons' means a body of persons corporate or unincorporate.

(7A) 'Non-profit making body' means a body of persons whose activities are not carried on for profit.

(8) 'Payment' means payment in money or money's worth.

(9) This Act applies to arrangements whether or not they are lawful.

1A Surrogacy arrangements unenforceable

No surrogacy arrangement is enforceable by or against any of the persons making it.

2 Negotiating surrogacy arrangements on a commercial basis, etc.

(1) No person shall on a commercial basis do any of the following acts in the United Kingdom, that is –

    (a) initiate any negotiations with a view to the making of a surrogacy arrangement, (aa) take part in any negotiations with a view to the making of a surrogacy arrangement,

    (b) offer or agree to negotiate the making of a surrogacy arrangement, or

    (c) compile any information with a view to its use in making, or negotiating the making of, surrogacy arrangements;

and no person shall in the United Kingdom knowingly cause another to do any of those acts on a commercial basis.

(2) A person who contravenes subsection (1) above is guilty of an offence; but it is not a contravention of that subsection –

    (a) for a woman, with a view to becoming a surrogate mother herself, to do any act mentioned in that subsection or to cause such an act to be done, or

    (b) for any person, with a view to a surrogate mother carrying a child for him, to do such an act or to cause such an act to be done.

(2A) A non-profit making body does not contravene subsection (1) merely because –

    (a) the body does an act falling within subsection (1)(a) or (c) in respect of which any reasonable payment is at any time received by it or another, or

    (b) it does an act falling within subsection (1)(a) or (c) with a view to any reasonable payment being received by it or another in respect of facilitating the making of any surrogacy arrangement.

(2B) A person who knowingly causes a non-profit making body to do an act falling within subsection (1)(a) or (c) does not contravene subsection (1) merely because –

    (a) any reasonable payment is at any time received by the body or another in respect of the body doing the act, or

    (b) the body does the act with a view to any reasonable payment being received by it or another person in respect of the body facilitating the making of any surrogacy arrangement.

(2C) Any reference in subsection (2A) or (2B) to a reasonable payment in respect of the doing of an act by a non-profit making body is a reference to a payment not exceeding the body's costs reasonably attributable to the doing of the act.

(3) For the purposes of this section, a person does an act on a commercial basis (subject to subsection (4) below) if –

    (a) any payment is at any time received by himself or another in respect of it, or

    (b) he does it with a view to any payment being received by himself or another in respect of making, or negotiating or facilitating the making of, any surrogacy arrangement. In this subsection 'payment' does not include payment to or for the benefit of a surrogate mother or prospective surrogate mother.

(4) In proceedings against a person for an offence under subsection (1) above, he is not to be treated as doing an act on a commercial basis by reason of any payment received by another in respect of the act if it is proved that –

    (a) in a case where the payment was received before he did the act, he did not do the act knowing or having reasonable cause to suspect that any payment had been received in respect of the act; and

    (b) in any other case, he did not do the act with a view to any payment being received in respect of it.

  (5) Where –

    (a) a person acting on behalf of a body of persons takes any part in negotiating or facilitating the making of a surrogacy arrangement in the United Kingdom, and

    (b) negotiating or facilitating the making of surrogacy arrangements is an activity of the body, then, if the body at any time receives any payment made by or on behalf of –

      (i)　a woman who carries a child in pursuance of the arrangement,

      (ii)　the person or persons for whom she carries it, or

      (iii)　any person connected with the woman or with that person or those persons, the body is guilty of an offence.

For the purposes of this subsection, a payment received by a person connected with a body is to be treated as received by the body.

  (5A)　A non-profit making body is not guilty of an offence under subsection (5), in respect of the receipt of any payment described in that subsection, merely because a person acting on behalf of the body takes part in facilitating the making of a surrogacy arrangement.

  (6)　In proceedings against a body for an offence under subsection (5) above, it is a defence to prove that the payment concerned was not made in respect of the arrangement mentioned in paragraph (a) of that subsection.

  (7)　A person who in the United Kingdom takes part in the management or control –

    (a) of any body of persons, or

    (b) of any of the activities of any body of persons,

is guilty of an offence if the activity described in subsection (8) below is an activity of the body concerned.

  (8)　The activity referred to in subsection (7) above is negotiating or facilitating the making of surrogacy arrangements in the United Kingdom, being –

    (a) arrangements the making of which is negotiated or facilitated on a commercial basis, or

    (b) arrangements in the case of which payments are received (or treated for the purposes of subsection (5) above as received) by the body concerned in contravention of subsection (5) above.

  (8A)　A person is not guilty of an offence under subsection (7) if –

    (a) the body of persons referred to in that subsection is a non-profit making body, and

    (b) the only activity of that body which falls within subsection (8) is facilitating the making of surrogacy arrangements in the United Kingdom.

  (8B)　In subsection (8A)(b) 'facilitating the making of surrogacy arrangements' is to be construed in accordance with subsection (8).

  (9)　In proceedings against a person for an offence under subsection (7) above, it is a defence to prove that he neither knew nor had reasonable cause to suspect that the activity described in subsection (8) above was an activity of the body concerned; and for the purposes of such proceedings any arrangement falling within subsection (8)(b) above shall be disregarded if it is proved that the payment concerned was not made in respect of the arrangement.

3　Advertisements about surrogacy

  (1)　This section applies to any advertisement containing an indication (however expressed) –

    (a) that any person is or may be willing to enter into a surrogacy arrangement or to negotiate or facilitate the making of a surrogacy arrangement, or

    (b) that any person is looking for a woman willing to become a surrogate mother or for persons wanting a woman to carry a child as a surrogate mother.

  (1A)　This section does not apply to any advertisement placed by, or on behalf of, a non-profit making body if the advertisement relates only to the doing by the body of acts that would not contravene section 2(1) even if done on a commercial basis (within the meaning of section 2).

(2) Where a newspaper or periodical containing an advertisement to which this section applies is published in the United Kingdom, any proprietor, editor or publisher of the newspaper or periodical is guilty of an offence.

(3) Where an advertisement to which this section applies is conveyed by means of a telecommunication system so as to be seen or heard (or both) in the United Kingdom, any person who in the United Kingdom causes it to be so conveyed knowing it to contain such an indication as is mentioned in subsection (1) above is guilty of an offence.

(4) A person who publishes or causes to be published in the United Kingdom an advertisement to which this section applies (not being an advertisement contained in a newspaper or periodical or conveyed by means of a telecommunication system) is guilty of an offence.

(5) A person who distributes or causes to be distributed in the United Kingdom an advertisement to which this section applies (not being an advertisement contained in a newspaper or periodical published outside the United Kingdom or an advertisement conveyed by means of a telecommunication system) knowing it to contain such an indication as is mentioned in subsection (1) above is guilty of an offence.

4 Offences

(1) A person guilty of an offence under this Act shall be liable on summary conviction –

    (a) in the case of an offence under section 2 to a fine not exceeding level 5 on the standard scale or to imprisonment for a term not exceeding 3 months or both,

    (b) in the case of an offence under section 3 to a fine not exceeding level 5 on the standard scale.

In this subsection 'the standard scale' has the meaning given by section 75 of the Criminal Justice Act 1982.

(2) No proceedings for an offence under this Act shall be instituted –

    (a) in England and Wales, except by or with the consent of the Director of Public Prosecutions; and

    (b) in Northern Ireland, except by or with the consent of the Director of Public Prosecutions for Northern Ireland.

Family Law Reform Act 1987

(1987, c. 42)

27 Artificial insemination

(1) Where after the coming into force of this section a child is born in England and Wales as the result of the artificial insemination of a woman who –

    (a) was at the time of the insemination a party to a marriage (being a marriage which had not at that time been dissolved or annulled); and

    (b) was artificially inseminated with the semen of some person other than the other party to that marriage,

then, unless it is proved to the satisfaction of any court by which the matter has to be determined that the other party to that marriage did not consent to the insemination, the child shall be treated in law as the child of the parties to that marriage and shall not be treated as the child of any person other than the parties to that marriage.

(2) Any reference in this section to a marriage includes a reference to a void marriage if at the time of the insemination resulting in the birth of the child both or either of the parties reasonably believed that the marriage was valid; and for the purposes of this section it shall be

presumed, unless the contrary is shown, that one of the parties so believed at that time that the marriage was valid.*

Consumer Protection Act 1987

(1987, c. 43)

PART I PRODUCT LIABILITY

1 Purpose and construction of Part I

(1) This Part shall have effect for the purpose of making such provision as is necessary in order to comply with the product liability Directive and shall be construed accordingly.

(2) In this Part, except in so far as the context otherwise requires –

'dependant' and 'relative' have the same meaning as they have in, respectively, the Fatal Accidents Act 1976 and the Damages (Scotland) Act 2011;

'producer', in relation to a product, means –

(a) the person who manufactured it;

(b) in the case of a substance which has not been manufactured but has been won or abstracted, the person who won or abstracted it;

(c) in the case of a product which has not been manufactured, won or abstracted but essential characteristics of which are attributable to an industrial or other process having been carried out (for example, in relation to agricultural produce), the person who carried out that process;

'product' means any goods or electricity and (subject to subsection (3) below) includes a product which is comprised in another product, whether by virtue of being a component part or raw material or otherwise; and

'the product liability Directive' means the Directive of the Council of the European Communities, dated 25th July 1985 (No. 85/374/EEC) on the approximation of the laws, regulations and administrative provisions of the member States concerning liability for defective products.

(3) For the purposes of this Part a person who supplies any product in which products are comprised, whether by virtue of being component parts or raw materials or otherwise, shall not be treated by reason only of his supply of that product as supplying any of the products so comprised.

2 Liability for defective products

(1) Subject to the following provisions of this Part, where any damage is caused wholly or partly by a defect in a product, every person to whom subsection (2) below applies shall be liable for the damage.

(2) This subsection applies to –

(a) the producer of the product;

(b) any person who, by putting his name on the product or using a trade mark or other distinguishing mark in relation to the product, has held himself out to be the producer of the product;

(c) any person who has imported the product into a member State from a place outside the member States in order, in the course of any business of his, to supply it to another.

(3) Subject as aforesaid, where any damage is caused wholly or partly by a defect in a product, any person who supplied the product (whether to the person who suffered the damage, to the

---

* **Editors' note:** See also the Human Fertilisation and Embryology Acts 1990 and 2008.

producer of any product in which the product in question is comprised or to any other person) shall be liable for the damage if –

    (a) the person who suffered the damage requests the supplier to identify one or more of the persons (whether still in existence or not) to whom subsection (2) above applies in relation to the product;

    (b) that request is made within a reasonable period after the damage occurs and at a time when it is not reasonably practicable for the person making the request to identify all those persons; and

    (c) the supplier fails, within a reasonable period after receiving the request, either to comply with the request or to identify the person who supplied the product to him.

(5) Where two or more persons are liable by virtue of this Part for the same damage, their liability shall be joint and several.

(6) This section shall be without prejudice to any liability arising otherwise than by virtue of this Part.

3 Meaning of 'defect'

(1) Subject to the following provisions of this section, there is a defect in a product for the purposes of this Part if the safety of the product is not such as persons generally are entitled to expect; and for those purposes 'safety', in relation to a product, shall include safety with respect to products comprised in that product and safety in the context of risks of damage to property, as well as in the context of risks of death or personal injury.

(2) In determining for the purposes of subsection (1) above what persons generally are entitled to expect in relation to a product all the circumstances shall be taken into account, including –

    (a) the manner in which, and purposes for which, the product has been marketed, its get-up, the use of any mark in relation to the product and any instructions for, or warnings with respect to, doing or refraining from doing anything with or in relation to the product;

    (b) what might reasonably be expected to be done with or in relation to the product; and

    (c) the time when the product was supplied by its producer to another; and nothing in this section shall require a defect to be inferred from the fact alone that the safety of a product which is supplied after that time is greater than the safety of the product in question.

4 Defences

(1) In any civil proceedings by virtue of this Part against any person ('the person proceeded against') in respect of a defect in a product it shall be a defence for him to show –

    (a) that the defect is attributable to compliance with any requirement imposed by or under any enactment or with any EU obligation; or

    (b) that the person proceeded against did not at any time supply the product to another; or

    (c) that the following conditions are satisfied, that is to say –

        (i) that the only supply of the product to another by the person proceeded against was otherwise than in the course of a business of that person's; and

        (ii) that section 2(2) above does not apply to that person or applies to him by virtue only of things done otherwise than with a view to profit; or

    (d) that the defect did not exist in the product at the relevant time; or

    (e) that the state of scientific and technical knowledge at the relevant time was not such that a producer of products of the same description as the product in question might be expected to have discovered the defect if it had existed in his products while they were under his control; or

    (f) that the defect –

        (i) constituted a defect in a product ('the subsequent product') in which the product in question had been comprised; and

        (ii) was wholly attributable to the design of the subsequent product or to compliance by the producer of the product in question with instructions given by the producer of the subsequent product.

(2) In this section 'the relevant time', in relation to electricity, means the time at which it was generated, being a time before it was transmitted or distributed, and in relation to any other product, means –

    (a) if the person proceeded against is a person to whom subsection (2) of section 2 above applies in relation to the product, the time when he supplied the product to another;

    (b) if that subsection does not apply to that person in relation to the product, the time when the product was last supplied by a person to whom that subsection does apply in relation to the product.

5 Damage giving rise to liability

(1) Subject to the following provisions of this section, in this Part 'damage' means death or personal injury or any loss of or damage to any property (including land).

(2) A person shall not be liable under section 2 above in respect of any defect in a product for the loss of or any damage to the product itself or for the loss of or any damage to the whole or any part of any product which has been supplied with the product in question comprised in it.

(3) A person shall not be liable under section 2 above for any loss of or damage to any property which, at the time it is lost or damaged, is not –

    (a) of a description of property ordinarily intended for private use, occupation or consumption; and

    (b) intended by the person suffering the loss or damage mainly for his own private use, occupation or consumption.

(4) No damages shall be awarded to any person by virtue of this Part in respect of any loss of or damage to any property if the amount which would fall to be so awarded to that person, apart from this subsection and any liability for interest, does not exceed £275.

(5) In determining for the purposes of this Part who has suffered any loss of or damage to property and when any such loss or damage occurred, the loss or damage shall be regarded as having occurred at the earliest time at which a person with an interest in the property had knowledge of the material facts about the loss or damage.

(6) For the purposes of subsection (5) above the material facts about any loss of or damage to any property are such facts about the loss or damage as would lead a reasonable person with an interest in the property to consider the loss or damage sufficiently serious to justify his instituting proceedings for damages against a defendant who did not dispute liability and was able to satisfy a judgment.

(7) For the purposes of subsection (5) above a person's knowledge includes knowledge which he might reasonably have been expected to acquire –

    (a) from facts observable or ascertainable by him; or

    (b) from facts ascertainable by him with the help of appropriate expert advice which it is reasonable for him to seek;

but a person shall not be taken by virtue of this subsection to have knowledge of a fact ascertainable by him only with the help of expert advice unless he has failed to take all reasonable steps to obtain (and, where appropriate, to act on) that advice.

(8) Subsections (5) to (7) above shall not extend to Scotland.

6 Application of certain enactments etc.

(1) Any damage for which a person is liable under section 2 above shall be deemed to have been caused –

    (a) for the purposes of the Fatal Accidents Act 1976, by that person's wrongful act, neglect or default;

(2) Where –

    (a) a person's death is caused wholly or partly by a defect in a product, or a person dies after suffering damage which has been so caused;

    (b) a request such as mentioned in paragraph (a) of subsection (3) of section 2 above is made to a supplier of the product by that person's personal representatives or, in the case of a person whose death is caused wholly or partly by the defect, by any dependant or relative of that person; and

(c) the conditions specified in paragraphs (b) and (c) of that subsection are satisfied in relation to that request,

this Part shall have effect for the purposes of the Law Reform (Miscellaneous Provisions) Act 1934, the Fatal Accidents Act 1976 and the Damages (Scotland) Act 2011 as if liability of the supplier to that person under that subsection did not depend on that person having requested the supplier to identify certain persons or on the said conditions having been satisfied in relation to a request made by that person.

(3) Section 1 of the Congenital Disabilities (Civil Liability) Act 1976 shall have effect for the purposes of this Part as if –

(a) a person were answerable to a child in respect of an occurrence caused wholly or partly by a defect in a product if he is or has been liable under section 2 above in respect of any effect of the occurrence on a parent of the child, or would be so liable if the occurrence caused a parent of the child to suffer damage;

(b) the provisions of this Part relating to liability under section 2 above applied in relation to liability by virtue of paragraph (a) above under the said section 1; and

(c) subsection (6) of the said section 1 (exclusion of liability) were omitted.

(4) Where any damage is caused partly by a defect in a product and partly by the fault of the person suffering the damage, the Law Reform (Contributory Negligence) Act 1945 and section 5 of the Fatal Accidents Act 1976 (contributory negligence) shall have effect as if the defect were the fault of every person liable by virtue of this Part for the damage caused by the defect.

(5) In subsection (4) above 'fault' has the same meaning as in the said Act of 1945.

(7) It is hereby declared that liability by virtue of this Part is to be treated as liability in tort for the purposes of any enactment conferring jurisdiction on any court with respect to any matter.

7   Prohibition on exclusions from liability

The liability of a person by virtue of this Part to a person who has suffered damage caused wholly or partly by a defect in a product, or to a dependant or relative of such a person, shall not be limited or excluded by any contract term, by any notice or by any other provision.

Access to Medical Reports Act 1988

(1988, c. 28)

1   Right of access

It shall be the right of an individual to have access, in accordance with the provisions of this Act, to any medical report relating to the individual which is to be, or has been, supplied by a medical practitioner for employment purposes or insurance purposes.

2   Interpretation

(1) In this Act –

'the applicant' means the person referred to in section 3(1) below;

'care' includes examination, investigation or diagnosis for the purposes of, or in connection with, any form of medical treatment;

'employment purposes', in the case of any individual, means the purposes in relation to the individual of any person by whom he is or has been, or is seeking to be, employed (whether under a contract of service or otherwise);

'health professional' has the same meaning as in the Data Protection Act 1998.

'insurance purposes', in a case of any individual who has entered into, or is seeking to enter into, a contract of insurance with an insurer, means the purposes of that insurer in relation to that individual;

'insurer' means –

    (a) a person who has permission under Part 4A of the Financial Services and Markets Act 2000 to effect or carry out contracts of insurance;

    (b) an EEA firm of the kind mentioned in paragraph 5(d) of Schedule 3 to that Act, which has permission under paragraph 15 of that Schedule (as a result of qualifying for authorisation under paragraph 12 of that Schedule) to effect or carry out relevant contracts of insurance;

'medical practitioner' means a person registered under the Medical Act 1983;

'medical report', in the case of an individual, means a report relating to the physical or mental health of the individual prepared by a medical practitioner who is or has been responsible for the clinical care of the individual.

(1A) The definitions of 'insurance purposes' and 'insurer' in subsection (1) must be read with –

    (a) section 22 of the Financial Services and Markets Act 2002;

    (b) any relevant order under that section; and

    (c) Schedule 2 to that Act.

(2) Any reference in this Act to the supply of a medical report for employment or insurance purposes shall be construed –

    (a) as a reference to the supply of such a report for employment or insurance purposes which are purposes of the person who is seeking to be supplied with it; or

    (b) (in the case of a report that has already been supplied) as a reference to the supply of such a report for employment or insurance purposes which, at the time of its being supplied, were purposes of the person to whom it was supplied.

3   Consent to applications for medical reports for employment or insurance purposes

(1) A person shall not apply to a medical practitioner for a medical report relating to any individual to be supplied to him for employment or insurance purposes unless –

    (a) that person ('the applicant') has notified the individual that he proposes to make the application; and

    (b) the individual has notified the applicant that he consents to the making of the application.

(2) Any notification given under subsection (1)(a) above must inform the individual of his right to withhold his consent to the making of the application, and of the following rights under this Act, namely –

    (a) the rights arising under sections 4(1) to (3) and 6(2) below with respect to access to the report before or after it is supplied,

    (b) the right to withhold consent under subsection (1) of section 5 below, and

    (c) the right to request the amendment of the report under subsection (2) of that section, as well as of the effect of section 7 below.

4   Access to reports before they are supplied

(1) An individual who gives his consent under section 3 above to the making of an application shall be entitled, when giving his consent, to state that he wishes to have access to the report to be supplied in response to the application before it is so supplied; and, if he does so, the applicant shall –

    (a) notify the medical practitioner of that fact at the time when the application is made, and

    (b) at the same time notify the individual of the making of the application; and each such notification shall contain a statement of the effect of subsection (2) below.

(2) Where a medical practitioner is notified by the applicant under subsection (1) above that the individual in question wishes to have access to the report before it is supplied, the practitioner shall not supply the report unless –

    (a) he has given the individual access to it and any requirements of section 5 below have been complied with, or

(b) the period of 21 days beginning with the date of the making of the application has elapsed without his having received any communication from the individual concerning arrangements for the individual to have access to it.

(3) Where a medical practitioner –

    (a) receives an application for a medical report to be supplied for employment or insurance purposes without being notified by the applicant as mentioned in subsection (1) above, but

    (b) before supplying the report receives a notification from the individual that he wishes to have access to the report before it is supplied, the practitioner shall not supply the report unless –

        (i) he has given the individual access to it and any requirements of section 5 below have been complied with, or

        (ii) the period of 21 days beginning with the date of that notification has elapsed without his having received (either with that notification or otherwise) any communication from the individual concerning arrangements for the individual to have access to it.

(4) References in this section and section 5 below to giving an individual access to a medical report are references to –

    (a) making the report or a copy of it available for his inspection; or

    (b) supplying him with a copy of it;

and where a copy is supplied at the request, or otherwise with the consent, of the individual the practitioner may charge a reasonable fee to cover the costs of supplying it.

5   Consent to supplying of report and correction of errors

(1) Where an individual has been given access to a report under section 4 above the report shall not be supplied in response to the application in question unless the individual has notified the medical practitioner that he consents to its being so supplied.

(2) The individual shall be entitled, before giving his consent under subsection (1) above, to request the medical practitioner to amend any part of the report which the individual considers to be incorrect or misleading; and, if the individual does so, the practitioner –

    (a) if he is to any extent prepared to accede to the individual's request, shall amend the report accordingly;

    (b) if he is to any extent not prepared to accede to it but the individual requests him to attach to the report a statement of the individual's views in respect of any part of the report which he is declining to amend, shall attach such a statement to the report.

(3) Any request made by an individual under subsection (2) above shall be made in writing.

6   Retention of reports

(1) A copy of any medical report which a medical practitioner has supplied for employment or insurance purposes shall be retained by him for at least six months from the date on which it was supplied.

(2) A medical practitioner shall, if so requested by an individual, give the individual access to any medical report relating to him which the practitioner has supplied for employment or insurance purposes in the previous six months.

(3) The reference in subsection (2) above to giving an individual access to a medical report is a reference to –

    (a) making a copy of the report available for his inspection; or

    (b) supplying him with a copy of it;

and where a copy is supplied at the request, or otherwise with the consent, of the individual the practitioner may charge a reasonable fee to cover the costs of supplying it.

7   Exemptions

(1) A medical practitioner shall not be obliged to give an individual access, in accordance with the provisions of section 4(4) or 6(3) above, to any part of a medical report whose disclosure would in

the opinion of the practitioner be likely to cause serious harm to the physical or mental health of the individual or others or would indicate the intentions of the practitioner in respect of the individual.

(2) A medical practitioner shall not be obliged to give an individual access, in accordance with those provisions, to any part of a medical report whose disclosure would be likely to reveal information about another person, or to reveal the identity of another person who has supplied information to the practitioner about the individual, unless –

(a) that person has consented; or

(b) that person is a health professional who has been involved in the care of the individual and the information relates to or has been provided by the professional in that capacity.

(3) Where it appears to a medical practitioner that subsection (1) or (2) above is applicable to any part (but not the whole) of a medical report –

(a) he shall notify the individual of that fact; and

(b) references in the preceding sections of this Act to the individual being given access to the report shall be construed as references to his being given access to the remainder of it; and other references to the report in sections 4(4), 5(2) and 6(3) above shall similarly be construed as references to the remainder of the report.

(4) Where it appears to a medical practitioner that subsection (1) or (2) above is applicable to the whole of a medical report –

(a) he shall notify the individual of that fact; but

(b) he shall not supply the report unless he is notified by the individual that the individual consents to its being supplied;

and accordingly, if he is so notified by the individual, the restrictions imposed by section 4(2) and (3) above on the supply of the report shall not have effect in relation to it.

8 Application to the court

(1) If a court is satisfied on the application of an individual that any person, in connection with a medical report relating to that individual, has failed or is likely to fail to comply with any requirement of this Act, the court may order that person to comply with that requirement.

(2) The jurisdiction conferred by this section shall be exercisable by the county court or, in Scotland, by the sheriff.

9 Notifications under this Act

Any notification required or authorised to be given under this Act –

(a) shall be given in writing; and

(b) may be given by post.

Children Act 1989

(1989, c. 41)

PART I INTRODUCTORY

1 Welfare of the child

(1) When a court determines any question with respect to –

(a) the upbringing of a child; or

(b) the administration of a child's property or the application of any income arising from it, the child's welfare shall be the court's paramount consideration.

(1A) Where a child –

(a) has a parent by virtue of section 42 of the Human Fertilisation and Embryology Act 2008; or

(b) has a parent by virtue of section 43 of that Act and is a person to whom section 1(3) of the Family Law Reform Act 1987 applies,

the child's mother and the other parent shall each have parental responsibility for the child.

(2) In any proceedings in which any question with respect to the upbringing of a child arises, the court shall have regard to the general principle that any delay in determining the question is likely to prejudice the welfare of the child.

(2A) A court, in the circumstances mentioned in subsection (4)(a) or (7), is as respects each parent within subsection (6)(a) to presume, unless the contrary is shown, that involvement of that parent in the life of the child concerned will further the child's welfare.

(2B) In subsection (2A) 'involvement' means involvement of some kind, either direct or indirect, but not any particular division of a child's time.

(3) In the circumstances mentioned in subsection (4), a court shall have regard in particular to –

    (a) the ascertainable wishes and feelings of the child concerned (considered in the light of his age and understanding);

    (b) his physical, emotional and educational needs;

    (c) the likely effect on him of any change in his circumstances;

    (d) his age, sex, background and any characteristics of his which the court considers relevant;

    (e) any harm which he has suffered or is at risk of suffering;

    (f) how capable each of his parents, and any other person in relation to whom the court considers the question to be relevant, is of meeting his needs;

    (g) the range of powers available to the court under this Act in the proceedings in question.

(4) The circumstances are that –

    (a) the court is considering whether to make, vary or discharge a section 8 order, and the making, variation or discharge of the order is opposed by any party to the proceedings; or

    (b) the court is considering whether to make, vary or discharge a special guardianship order or an order under Part IV.

(5) Where a court is considering whether or not to make one or more orders under this Act with respect to a child, it shall not make the order or any of the orders unless it considers that doing so would be better for the child than making no order at all.

2   Parental responsibility for children

(1) Where a child's father and mother were married to each other at the time of his birth, they shall each have parental responsibility for the child.

(1A) Where a child –

    (a) has a parent by virtue of section 42 of the Human Fertilisation and Embryology Act 2008; or

    (b) has a parent by virtue of section 43 of that Act and is a person to whom section 1(3) of the Family Law Reform Act 1987 applies,

the child's mother and the other parent shall each have parental responsibility for the child.

(2) Where a child's father and mother were not married to each other at the time of his birth –

    (a) the mother shall have parental responsibility for the child;

    (b) the father shall have parental responsibility for the child if he has acquired it (and has not ceased to have it) in accordance with the provisions of this Act.

(2A) Where a child has a parent by virtue of section 43 of the Human Fertilisation and Embryology Act 2008 and is not a person to whom section 1(3) of the Family Law Reform Act 1987 applies –

    (a) the mother shall have parental responsibility for the child;

    (b) the other parent shall have parental responsibility for the child if she has acquired it (and has not ceased to have it) in accordance with the provisions of this Act.

(3) References in this Act to a child whose father and mother were, or (as the case may be) were not, married to each other at the time of his birth must be read with section 1 of the Family Law Reform Act 1987 (which extends their meaning).

(4) The rule of law that a father is the natural guardian of his legitimate child is abolished.

(5) More than one person may have parental responsibility for the same child at the same time.

(6) A person who has parental responsibility for a child at any time shall not cease to have that responsibility solely because some other person subsequently acquires parental responsibility for the child.

(7) Where more than one person has parental responsibility for a child, each of them may act alone and without the other (or others) in meeting that responsibility; but nothing in this Part shall be taken to affect the operation of any enactment which requires the consent of more than one person in a matter affecting the child.

(8) The fact that a person has parental responsibility for a child shall not entitle him to act in any way which would be incompatible with any order made with respect to the child under this Act.

(9) A person who has parental responsibility for a child may not surrender or transfer any part of that responsibility to another but may arrange for some or all of it to be met by one or more persons acting on his behalf.

(10) The person with whom any such arrangement is made may himself be a person who already has parental responsibility for the child concerned.

(11) The making of any such arrangement shall not affect any liability of the person making it which may arise from any failure to meet any part of his parental responsibility for the child concerned.

3   Meaning of 'parental responsibility'

(1) In this Act 'parental responsibility' means all the rights, duties, powers, responsibilities and authority which by law a parent of a child has in relation to the child and his property.

(2) It also includes the rights, powers and duties which a guardian of the child's estate (appointed, before the commencement of section 5, to act generally) would have had in relation to the child and his property.

(3) The rights referred to in subsection (2) include, in particular, the right of the guardian to receive or recover in his own name, for the benefit of the child, property of whatever description and wherever situated which the child is entitled to receive or recover.

(4) The fact that a person has, or does not have, parental responsibility for a child shall not affect –
  (a) any obligation which he may have in relation to the child (such as a statutory duty to maintain the child); or
  (b) any rights which, in the event of the child's death, he (or any other person) may have in relation to the child's property.

(5) A person who –
  (a) does not have parental responsibility for a particular child; but
  (b) has care of the child,
may (subject to the provisions of this Act) do what is reasonable in all the circumstances of the case for the purpose of safeguarding or promoting the child's welfare.

4   Acquisition of parental responsibility by father

(1) Where a child's father and mother were not married to each other at the time of his birth the father shall acquire parental responsibility if –
  (a) he becomes registered as the child's father under any of the enactments specified in subsection (1A);
  (b) he and the child's mother make an agreement (a 'parental responsibility agreement') providing for him to have parental responsibility for the child; or

(c) the court, on his application, orders that he shall have parental responsibility for the child.

(1A) The enactments referred to in subsection (1)(a) are –

(a) paragraphs (a), (b) and (c) of section 10(1) and of section 10A(1) of the Births and Deaths Registration Act 1953;

(2A) A person who has acquired parental responsibility under subsection (1) shall cease to have that responsibility only if the court so orders.

(3) The court may make an order under subsection (2A) on the application –

(a) of any person who has parental responsibility for the child; or

(b) with the leave of the court, of the child himself,

subject, in the case of parental responsibility acquired under subsection (1)(c), to section 12(4).

(4) The court may only grant leave under subsection (3)(b) if it is satisfied that the child has sufficient understanding to make the proposed application.

4ZA   Acquisition of parental responsibility by second female parent

(1) Where a child has a parent by virtue of section 43 of the Human Fertilisation and Embryology Act 2008 and is not a person to whom section 1(3) of the Family Law Reform Act 1987 applies, that parent shall acquire parental responsibility for the child if –

(a) she becomes registered as a parent of the child under any of the enactments specified in subsection (2);

(b) she and the child's mother make an agreement providing for her to have parental responsibility for the child; or

(c) the court, on her application, orders that she shall have parental responsibility for the child.

(2) The enactments referred to in subsection (1)(a) are –

(a) paragraphs (a), (b) and (c) of section 10(1B) and of section 10A(1B) of the Births and Deaths Registration Act 1953;

(4) An agreement under subsection (1)(b) is also a 'parental responsibility agreement', and section 4(2) applies in relation to such an agreement as it applies in relation to parental responsibility agreements under section 4.

(5) A person who has acquired parental responsibility under subsection (1) shall cease to have that responsibility only if the court so orders.

(6) The court may make an order under subsection (5) on the application –

(a) of any person who has parental responsibility for the child; or

(b) with the leave of the court, of the child himself, subject, in the case of parental responsibility acquired under subsection (1)(c), to section 12(4).

(7) The court may only grant leave under subsection (6)(b) if it is satisfied that the child has sufficient understanding to make the proposed application.

PART II ORDERS WITH RESPECT TO CHILDREN IN FAMILY PROCEEDINGS

General

8   Child arrangements orders and other orders with respect to children

(1) In this Act –

'child arrangements order' means an order regulating arrangements relating to any of the following –

(a) with whom a child is to live, spend time or otherwise have contact, and

(b) when a child is to live, spend time or otherwise have contact with any person;

'a prohibited steps order' means an order that no step which could be taken by a parent in meeting his parental responsibility for a child, and which is of a kind specified in the order, shall be taken by any person without the consent of the court;

'a specific issue order' means an order giving directions for the purpose of determining a specific question which has arisen, or which may arise, in connection with any aspect of parental responsibility for a child.

(2) In this Act 'a section 8 order' means any of the orders mentioned in subsection (1) and any order varying or discharging such an order.

9   Restrictions on making section 8 orders

(1) No court shall make any section 8 order, other than a child arrangements order to which subsection (6B) applies with respect to a child who is in the care of a local authority.

(2) No application may be made by a local authority for a child arrangements order and no court shall make such an order in favour of a local authority.

(5) No court shall exercise its powers to make a specific issue order or prohibited steps order –

    (a) with a view to achieving a result which could be achieved by making a child arrangements order or an order under section 51A of the Adoption and Children Act 2002 (post-adoption contact); or

    (b) in any way which is denied to the High Court (by section 100(2)) in the exercise of its inherent jurisdiction with respect to children.

(6) No court shall make a section 8 order which is to have effect for a period which will end after the child has reached the age of sixteen unless it is satisfied that the circumstances of the case are exceptional.

(7) No court shall make any section 8 order, other than one varying or discharging such an order, with respect to a child who has reached the age of sixteen unless it is satisfied that the circumstances of the case are exceptional.

10   Power of court to make section 8 orders

(1) In any family proceedings in which a question arises with respect to the welfare of any child, the court may make a section 8 order with respect to the child if –

    (a) an application for the order has been made by a person who –

        (i)   is entitled to apply for a section 8 order with respect to the child; or

        (ii) has obtained the leave of the court to make the application; or

    (b) the court considers that the order should be made even though no such application has been made.

(2) The court may also make a section 8 order with respect to any child on the application of a person who –

    (a) is entitled to apply for a section 8 order with respect to the child; or

    (b) has obtained the leave of the court to make the application.

(3) This section is subject to the restrictions imposed by section 9.

(4) The following persons are entitled to apply to the court for any section 8 order with respect to a child –

    (a) any parent or guardian, or special guardian of the child;

    (aa) any person who by virtue of section 4A has parental responsibility for the child;

    (b) any person who is named, in a child arrangements order that is in force with respect to the child, as a person with whom the child is to live.

(8) Where the person applying for leave to make an application for a section 8 order is the child concerned, the court may only grant leave if it is satisfied that he has sufficient understanding to make the proposed application for the section 8 order.

(9) Where the person applying for leave to make an application for a section 8 order is not the child concerned, the court shall, in deciding whether or not to grant leave, have particular regard to –

    (a) the nature of the proposed application for the section 8 order;

    (b) the applicant's connection with the child;

    (c) any risk there might be of that proposed application disrupting the child's life to such an extent that he would be harmed by it; and

    (d) where the child is being looked after by a local authority – (i) the authority's plans for the child's future; and

    (e) the wishes and feelings of the child's parents.

PART IV CARE AND SUPERVISION

General

31   Care and supervision orders

    (1) On the application of any local authority or authorised person, the court may make an order –

        (a) placing the child with respect to whom the application is made in the care of a designated local authority.

    (2) A court may only make a care order or supervision order if it is satisfied –

        (a) that the child concerned is suffering, or is likely to suffer, significant harm; and

        (b) that the harm, or likelihood of harm, is attributable to –

            (i)   the care given to the child, or likely to be given to him if the order were not made, not being what it would be reasonable to expect a parent to give to him; or

            (ii) the child's being beyond parental control.

    (3) No care order or supervision order may be made with respect to a child who has reached the age of seventeen (or sixteen, in the case of a child who is married).

    (5) The court may –

        (a) on an application for a care order, make a supervision order;

        (b) on an application for a supervision order, make a care order.

    (9) In this section –

'harm' means ill-treatment or the impairment of health or development including, for example, impairment suffered from seeing or hearing the ill-treatment of another;

'development' means physical, intellectual, emotional, social or behavioural development;

'health' means physical or mental health; and

'ill-treatment' includes sexual abuse and forms of ill-treatment which are not physical.

    (10) Where the question of whether harm suffered by a child is significant turns on the child's health or development, his health or development shall be compared with that which could reasonably be expected of a similar child.

Care orders

33   Effect of care order

    (1) Where a care order is made with respect to a child it shall be the duty of the local authority designated by the order to receive the child into their care and to keep him in their care while the order remains in force.

    (3) While a care order is in force with respect to a child, the local authority designated by the order shall –

        (a) have parental responsibility for the child; and

        (b) have the power (subject to the following provisions of this section) to determine the extent to which

            (i)   a parent, guardian or special guardian of the child; or

            (ii) a person who by virtue of section 4A has parental responsibility for the child, may meet his parental responsibility for him.

    (4) The authority may not exercise the power in subsection (3)(b) unless they are satisfied that it is necessary to do so in order to safeguard or promote the child's welfare.

    (5) Nothing in subsection (3)(b) shall prevent a person mentioned in that provision who has care of the child from doing what is reasonable in all the circumstances of the case for the purpose of safeguarding or promoting his welfare.

PART V PROTECTION OF CHILDREN

43 Child assessment orders

(1) On the application of a local authority or authorised person for an order to be made under this section with respect to a child, the court may make the order if, but only if, it is satisfied that –

    (a) the applicant has reasonable cause to suspect that the child is suffering, or is likely to suffer, significant harm;

    (b) an assessment of the state of the child's health or development, or of the way in which he has been treated, is required to enable the applicant to determine whether or not the child is suffering, or is likely to suffer, significant harm; and

    (c) it is unlikely that such an assessment will be made, or be satisfactory, in the absence of an order under this section.

(2) In this Act 'a child assessment order' means an order under this section.

(3) A court may treat an application under this section as an application for an emergency protection order.

(4) No court shall make a child assessment order if it is satisfied –

    (a) that there are grounds for making an emergency protection order with respect to the child; and

    (b) that it ought to make such an order rather than a child assessment order.

(5) A child assessment order shall –

    (a) specify the date by which the assessment is to begin; and

    (b) have effect for such period, not exceeding 7 days beginning with that date, as may be specified in the order.

(6) Where a child assessment order is in force with respect to a child it shall be the duty of any person who is in a position to produce the child –

    (a) to produce him to such person as may be named in the order; and

    (b) to comply with such directions relating to the assessment of the child as the court thinks fit to specify in the order.

(7) A child assessment order authorises any person carrying out the assessment, or any part of the assessment, to do so in accordance with the terms of the order.

(8) Regardless of subsection (7), if the child is of sufficient understanding to make an informed decision he may refuse to submit to a medical or psychiatric examination or other assessment.

(9) The child may only be kept away from home –

    (a) in accordance with directions specified in the order;

    (b) if it is necessary for the purposes of the assessment; and

    (c) for such period or periods as may be specified in the order.

(10) Where the child is to be kept away from home, the order shall contain such directions as the court thinks fit with regard to the contact that he must be allowed to have with other persons while away from home.

(11) Any person making an application for a child assessment order shall take such steps as are reasonably practicable to ensure that notice of the application is given to –

    (a) the child's parents;

    (b) any person who is not a parent of his but who has parental responsibility for him;

    (c) any other person caring for the child;

    (d) any person named in a child arrangements order as a person with whom the child is to spend time or otherwise have contact;

    (e) any person who is allowed to have contact with the child by virtue of an order under section 34; and

    (f) the child,

before the hearing of the application.

(12) Rules of court may make provision as to the circumstances in which –

    (a) any of the persons mentioned in subsection (11); or

(b) such other person as may be specified in the rules, may apply to the court for a child assessment order to be varied or discharged.

100   Restrictions on use of wardship jurisdiction

(2) No court shall exercise the High Court's inherent jurisdiction with respect to children –

(a) so as to require a child to be placed in the care, or put under the supervision, of a local authority;

(b) so as to require a child to be accommodated by or on behalf of a local authority;

(c) so as to make a child who is the subject of a care order a ward of court; or

(d) for the purpose of conferring on any local authority power to determine any question which has arisen, or which may arise, in connection with any aspect of parental responsibility for a child.

(3) No application for any exercise of the court's inherent jurisdiction with respect to children may be made by a local authority unless the authority have obtained the leave of the court.

(4) The court may only grant leave if it is satisfied that –

(a) the result which the authority wish to achieve could not be achieved through the making of any order of a kind to which subsection (5) applies; and

(b) there is reasonable cause to believe that if the court's inherent jurisdiction is not exercised with respect to the child he is likely to suffer significant harm.

(5) This subsection applies to any order –

(a) made otherwise than in the exercise of the court's inherent jurisdiction; and

(b) which the local authority is entitled to apply for (assuming, in the case of any application which may only be made with leave, that leave is granted).

SCHEDULE 3   SUPERVISION ORDERS

Meaning of 'responsible person'

1. In this Schedule, 'the responsible person', in relation to a supervised child, means –

(a) any person who has parental responsibility for the child; and

(b) any other person with whom the child is living.

Psychiatric and medical examinations

4.—(1) A supervision order may require the supervised child –

(a) to submit to a medical or psychiatric examination; or

(b) to submit to any such examination from time to time as directed by the supervisor.

(2) Any such examination shall be required to be conducted –

(a) by, or under the direction of, such registered medical practitioner as may be specified in the order;

(b) at a place specified in the order and at which the supervised child is to attend as a non-resident patient; or

(c) at –

(i)   a health service hospital; or

(ii) in the case of a psychiatric examination, a hospital, independent hospital or care home, at which the child is, or is to attend as, a resident patient.

(3) A requirement of a kind mentioned in sub-paragraph (2)(c) shall not be included unless the court is satisfied, on the evidence of a registered medical practitioner, that –

(a) the child may be suffering from a physical or mental condition that requires, and may be susceptible to, treatment; and

(b) a period as a resident patient is necessary if the examination is to be carried out properly.

(4) No court shall include a requirement under this paragraph in a supervision order unless it is satisfied that –

(a) where the child has sufficient understanding to make an informed decision, he consents to its inclusion; and

(b) satisfactory arrangements have been, or can be, made for the examination.

Psychiatric and medical treatment

5.—(1) Where a court which proposes to make or vary a supervision order is satisfied, on the evidence of a registered medical practitioner approved for the purposes of section 12 of the Mental Health Act 1983, that the mental condition of the supervised child –

    (a) is such as requires, and may be susceptible to, treatment; but

    (b) is not such as to warrant his detention in pursuance of a hospital order under Part III of that Act,

the court may include in the order a requirement that the supervised child shall, for a period specified in the order, submit to such treatment as is so specified.

    (2) The treatment specified in accordance with sub-paragraph (1) must be –

    (a) by, or under the direction of, such registered medical practitioner as may be specified in the order;

    (b) as a non-resident patient at such a place as may be so specified; or

    (c) as a resident patient in a hospital, independent hospital or care home.

    (3) Where a court which proposes to make or vary a supervision order is satisfied, on the evidence of a registered medical practitioner, that the physical condition of the supervised child is such as requires, and may be susceptible to, treatment, the court may include in the order a requirement that the supervised child shall, for a period specified in the order, submit to such treatment as is so specified.

    (4) The treatment specified in accordance with sub-paragraph (3) must be –

    (a) by, or under the direction of, such registered medical practitioner as may be specified in the order;

    (b) as a non-resident patient at such place as may be so specified; or

    (c) as a resident patient in a health service hospital.

    (5) No court shall include a requirement under this paragraph in a supervision order unless it is satisfied –

    (a) where the child has sufficient understanding to make an informed decision, that he consents to its inclusion; and

    (b) that satisfactory arrangements have been, or can be, made for the treatment.

    (6) If a medical practitioner by whom or under whose direction a supervised person is being treated in pursuance of a requirement included in a supervision order by virtue of this paragraph is unwilling to continue to treat or direct the treatment of the supervised child or is of the opinion that –

    (a) the treatment should be continued beyond the period specified in the order;

    (b) the supervised child needs different treatment;

    (c) he is not susceptible to treatment; or

    (d) he does not require further treatment,

the practitioner shall make a report in writing to that effect to the supervisor.

Access to Health Records Act 1990

(1990, c. 23)

Preliminary

1 'Health record' and related expressions

    (1) In this Act 'health record' means a record which –

    (a) consists of information relating to the physical or mental health of an individual who can be identified from that information, or from that and other information in the possession of the holder of the record; and

    (b) has been made by or on behalf of a health professional in connection with the care of that individual.

(2) In this Act 'holder', in relation to a health record, means –

    (a) in the case of a record made by a health professional performing primary medical services under a general medical services contract made with the National Health Service Commissioning Board or a Local Health Board, the person or body who entered into the contract with the Board (or, in a case where more than one person so entered into the contract, any such person);

    (aa) in the case of a record made by a health professional performing such services in accordance with arrangements under section 92 or 107 of the National Health Service Act 2006, or section 50 or 64 of the National Health Service (Wales) Act 2006, with the National Health Service Commissioning Board or a Local Health Board, the person or body which made the arrangements with the Board (or, in a case where more than one person so made the arrangements, any such person);

    (b) in the case of a record made by a health professional for purposes connected with the provision of health services by a health service body (and not falling within paragraph (aa) above), the health service body by which or on whose behalf the record is held;

    (c) in any other case, the health professional by whom or on whose behalf the record is held;

(3) In this Act 'patient', in relation to a health record, means the individual in connection with whose care the record has been made.

2   Health professionals

In this Act 'health professional' has the same meaning as in the Data Protection Act 1998.

Main provisions

3   Right of access to health records

(1) An application for access to a health record, or to any part of a health record, may be made to the holder of the record by any of the following, namely –

    (f) where the patient has died, the patient's personal representative and any person who may have a claim arising out of the patient's death;

    (g) where the patient has died, a medical examiner exercising functions by virtue of section 20 of the Coroners and Justice Act 2009 in relation to the death.

(2) Subject to section 4 below, where an application is made under subsection (1) above the holder shall, within the requisite period, give access to the record, or the part of a record, to which the application relates –

    (a) in the case of a record, by allowing the applicant to inspect the record or, where section 5 below applies, an extract setting out so much of the record as is not excluded by that section;

    (b) in the case of a part of a record, by allowing the applicant to inspect an extract setting out that part or, where that section applies, so much of that part as is not so excluded; or

    (c) in either case, if the applicant so requires, by supplying him with a copy of the record or extract.

(3) Where any information contained in a record or extract which is so allowed to be inspected, or a copy of which is so supplied, is expressed in terms which are not intelligible without explanation, an explanation of those terms shall be provided with the record or extract, or supplied with the copy.

4   Cases where right of access may be wholly excluded

(3) Where an application is made under subsection (1)(f) of section 3 above, access shall not be given under subsection (2) of that section if the record includes a note, made at the patient's request, that he did not wish access to be given on such an application.

5 Cases where right of access may be partially excluded

(1) Access shall not be given under section 3(2) above to any part of a health record –

(a) which, in the opinion of the holder of the record, would disclose –

    (i) information likely to cause serious harm to the physical or mental health of any individual; or

    (ii) information relating to or provided by an individual, other than the patient, who could be identified from that information; or

(b) which was made before the commencement of this Act.

(2) Subsection (1)(a)(ii) above shall not apply –

(a) where the individual concerned has consented to the application; or

(b) where that individual is a health professional who has been involved in the care of the patient;

and subsection (1)(b) above shall not apply where and to the extent that, in the opinion of the holder of the record, the giving of access is necessary in order to make intelligible any part of the record to which access is required to be given under section 3(2) above.

(3) Access shall not be given under section 3(2) to any part of a health record which, in the opinion of the holder of the record, would disclose –

(a) information provided by the patient in the expectation that it would not be disclosed to the applicant; or

(b) information obtained as a result of any examination or investigation to which the patient consented in the expectation that the information would not be so disclosed.

(4) Where an application is made under subsection (1)(f) of section 3 above, access shall not be given under subsection (2) of that section to any part of the record which, in the opinion of the holder of the record, would disclose information which is not relevant to any claim which may arise out of the patient's death.

6 Correction of inaccurate health records

(1) Where a person considers that any information contained in a health record, or any part of a health record, to which he has been given access under section 3(2) above is inaccurate, he may apply to the holder of the record for the necessary correction to be made.

(2) On an application under subsection (1) above, the holder of the record shall –

(a) if he is satisfied that the information is inaccurate, make the necessary correction;

(b) if he is not so satisfied, make in the part of the record in which the information is contained a note of the matters in respect of which the information is considered by the applicant to be inaccurate; and

(c) in either case, without requiring any fee, supply the applicant with a copy of the correction or note.

(3) In this section 'inaccurate' means incorrect, misleading or incomplete.

7 Duty of health service bodies etc. to take advice

(1) A health service body shall take advice from the appropriate health professional before they decide whether they are satisfied as to any matter for the purposes of this Act, or form an opinion as to any matter for those purposes.

(2) In this section 'the appropriate health professional', in relation to a health service body means –

(a) where, for purposes connected with the provision of health services by the body, one or more medical or dental practitioners are currently responsible for the clinical care of the patient, that practitioner or, as the case may be, such one of those practitioners as is the most suitable to advise the body on the matter in question;

(b) where paragraph (a) above does not apply but one or more medical or dental practitioners are available who, for purposes connected with the provision of such services by the body, have been responsible for the clinical care of the patient, that practitioner or, as the case may be, such one of those practitioners as was most recently so responsible; and

(c) where neither paragraph (a) nor paragraph (b) above applies, a health professional who has the necessary experience and qualifications to advise the body on the matter in question.

Supplemental

8   Applications to the court

(1)   Subject to subsection (2) below, where the court is satisfied, on an application made by the person concerned within such period as may be prescribed by rules of court, that the holder of a health record has failed to comply with any requirement of this Act, the court may order the holder to comply with that requirement.

(2)   The court shall not entertain an application under subsection (1) above unless it is satisfied that the applicant has taken all such steps to secure compliance with the requirement as may be prescribed by regulations made by the Secretary of State.

(3)   For the purposes of subsection (2) above, the Secretary of State may by regulations require the holders of health records to make such arrangements for dealing with complaints that they have failed to comply with any requirements of this Act as may be prescribed by the regulations.

(4)   For the purpose of determining any question whether an applicant is entitled to be given access under section 3(2) above to any health record, or any part of a health record, the court –

(a) may require the record or part to be made available for its own inspection; but

(b) shall not, pending determination of that question in the applicant's favour, require the record or part to be disclosed to him or his representatives whether by discovery (or, in Scotland, recovery) or otherwise.

(5)   The jurisdiction conferred by this section shall be exercisable by the High Court or a county court or, in Scotland, by the Court of Session or the sheriff.

9   Avoidance of certain contractual terms

Any term or condition of a contract shall be void in so far as it purports to require an individual to supply any other person with a copy of a health record, or of an extract from a health record, to which he has been given access under section 3(2) above.

11   Interpretation

In this Act –

'application' means an application in writing and 'apply' shall be construed accordingly;

'care' includes examination, investigation, diagnosis and treatment;

'health service body' means –

(a) a Local Health Board, Health Authority or Special Health Authority;

(b) a Health Board;

(d) a National Health Service trust first established under section 5 of the National Health Service and Community Care Act 1990, section 25 of the National Health Service Act 2006 or section 18 of the National Health Service (Wales) Act 2006 or section 12A of the National Health Service (Scotland) Act 1978;

(e) an NHS foundation trust;

(f) the Health and Social Care Information Centre;

'information', in relation to a health record, includes any expression of opinion about the patient;

'make', in relation to such a record, includes compile.

Human Fertilisation and Embryology Act 1990

(1990, c. 37)

Principal terms used

1   Meaning of 'embryo', 'gamete' and associated expressions
    (1) In this Act (except in section 4A or in the term 'human admixed embryo') –
        (a) embryo means a live human embryo and does not include a human admixed embryo (as defined by section 4A(6)), and
        (b) references to an embryo include an egg that is in the process of fertilisation or is undergoing any other process capable of resulting in an embryo.
    (2) This Act, so far as it governs bringing about the creation of an embryo, applies only to bringing about the creation of an embryo outside the human body; and in this Act –
        (a) references to embryos the creation of which was brought about *in vitro* (in their application to those where fertilisation or any other process by which an embryo is created is complete) are to those where fertilisation or any other process by which the embryo was created began outside the human body whether or not it was completed there, and
        (b) references to embryos taken from a woman do not include embryos whose creation was brought about *in vitro*.
    (3) This Act, so far as it governs the keeping or use of an embryo, applies only to keeping or using an embryo outside the human body.
    (4) In this Act (except in section 4A) –
        (a) references to eggs are to live human eggs, including cells of the female germ line at any stage of maturity, but (except in subsection (1)(b)) not including eggs that are in the process of fertilisation or are undergoing any other process capable of resulting in an embryo,
        (b) references to sperm are to live human sperm, including cells of the male germ line at any stage of maturity, and
        (c) references to gametes are to be read accordingly.
    (5) For the purposes of this Act, sperm is to be treated as partner-donated sperm if the donor of the sperm and the recipient of the sperm declare that they have an intimate physical relationship.
    (6) If it appears to the Secretary of State necessary or desirable to do so in the light of developments in science or medicine, regulations may provide that in this Act (except in section 4A) 'embryo', 'eggs', 'sperm' or 'gametes' includes things specified in the regulations which would not otherwise fall within the definition.
    (7) Regulations made by virtue of subsection (6) may not provide for anything containing any nuclear or mitochondrial DNA that is not human to be treated as an embryo or as eggs, sperm or gametes.

1A   Reference to Directives
In this Act –
  'the first Directive' means Directive 2004/23/EC of the European Parliament and of the Council of 31 March 2004 on setting standards of quality and safety for the donation, procurement, testing, processing, preservation, storage and distribution of human tissues and cells,
  'the second Directive' means Commission Directive 2006/17/EC of 8 February 2006 implementing Directive 2004/23/EC of the European Parliament and of the Council as regards certain technical requirements for the donation, procurement and testing of human tissues and cells, as amended by Commission Directive 2012/39/EU and

'the third Directive' means Commission Directive 2006/86/EC of 24 October 2006 implementing Directive 2004/23/EC of the European Parliament and of the Council as regards traceability requirements, notification of serious adverse reactions and events and certain technical requirements for the coding, processing, preservation, storage and distribution of human tissues and cells.

2   Other terms

(1) In this Act –

'the Authority' means the Human Fertilisation and Embryology Authority established under section 5 of this Act,

'basic partner treatment services' means treatment services that are provided for a woman and a man together without using –

    (a) the gametes of any other person, or

    (b) embryos created outside the woman's body,

'competent authority', in relation to an EEA state other than the United Kingdom or in relation to Gibraltar, means an authority designated in accordance with the law of that state or territory as responsible for implementing the requirements of the first, second and third Directives,

'directions' means directions under section 23 of this Act,

'distribution', in relation to gametes or embryos intended for human application, means transportation or delivery, and related terms are to be interpreted accordingly,

'human application' means use in a human recipient,

'licence' means a licence under Schedule 2 to this Act and, in relation to a licence, 'the person responsible' has the meaning given by section 17 of this Act,

'non-medical fertility services' means any services that are provided, in the course of a business, for the purpose of assisting women to carry children, but are not medical, surgical or obstetric services,

'nuclear DNA', in relation to an embryo, includes DNA in the pronucleus of the embryo,

'processing', in relation to gametes or embryos intended for human application, means any operation involved in their preparation, manipulation or packaging, and related terms are to be interpreted accordingly,

'procurement', in relation to gametes or embryos intended for human application, means any process by which they are made available, and related terms are to be interpreted accordingly,

'serious adverse event' means –

    (a) any untoward occurrence which may be associated with the procurement, testing, processing, storage or distribution of gametes or embryos intended for human application and which, in relation to a donor of gametes or a person who receives treatment services or non-medical fertility services –

        (i) might lead to the transmission of a communicable disease, to death, or life-threatening, disabling or incapacitating conditions, or

        (ii) might result in, or prolong, hospitalisation or illness, or

    (b) any type of gametes or embryo misidentification or mix-up,

'serious adverse reaction' means an unintended response, including a communicable disease, in a donor of gametes intended for human application or a person who receives treatment services or non-medical fertility services, which may be associated with the procurement or human application of gametes or embryos and which is fatal, life-threatening, disabling, incapacitating or which results in, or prolongs, hospitalisation or illness,

'store', in relation to gametes, embryos or human admixed embryos, means preserve, whether by cryopreservation or in any other way, and 'storage' and 'stored' are to be interpreted accordingly,

'traceability' means the ability –

    (a) to identify and locate gametes and embryos during any step from procurement to use for human application or disposal,

(b) to identify the donor and recipient of particular gametes or embryos,

(c) to identify any person who has carried out any activity in relation to particular gametes or embryos, and

(d) to identify and locate all relevant data relating to products and materials coming into contact with particular gametes or embryos and which can affect their quality or safety, and 'treatment services' means medical, surgical or obstetric services provided to the public or a section of the public for the purpose of assisting women to carry children.

(2) References in this Act to keeping, in relation to embryos, gametes or human admixed embryos, include keeping while preserved in storage.

(2A) For the purposes of this Act, a person who, from any premises, controls the provision of services for transporting gametes or embryos is to be taken to distribute gametes or embryos on those premises.

(2B) In this Act, any reference to a requirement of a provision of the first, second or third Directive is a reference to a requirement which that provision requires to be imposed.

(3) For the purposes of this Act, a woman is not to be treated as carrying a child until the embryo has become implanted.

2A   Third party agreements

(1) For the purposes of this Act, a 'third party agreement' is an agreement in writing between a person who holds a licence and another person which is made in accordance with any licence conditions imposed by the Authority for the purpose of securing compliance with the requirements of Article 24 of the first Directive (relations between tissue establishments and third parties) and under which the other person –

(a) procures, tests or processes gametes or embryos (or both), on behalf of the holder of the licence, or

(b) supplies to the holder of the licence any goods or services (including distribution services) which may affect the quality or safety of gametes or embryos.

(2) In this Act –

'relevant third party premises', in relation to a licence, means any premises (other than premises to which the licence relates) –

(a) on which a third party procures, tests, processes or distributes gametes or embryos on behalf of any person in connection with activities carried out by that person under a licence, or

(b) from which a third party provides any goods or services which may affect the quality or safety of gametes or embryos to any person in connection with activities carried out by that person under a licence;

'third party' means a person with whom a person who holds a licence has a third party agreement.

(3) References in this Act to the persons to whom a third party agreement applies are to –

(a) the third party,

(b) any person designated in the third party agreement as a person to whom the agreement applies, and

(c) any person acting under the direction of a third party or of any person so designated.

Activities governed by the Act

3   Prohibitions in connection with embryos

(1) No person shall bring about the creation of an embryo except in pursuance of a licence.

(1A) No person shall keep or use an embryo except –

(a) in pursuance of a licence, or

(b) in the case of –

(i)   the keeping, without storage, of an embryo intended for human application, or

(ii) the processing, without storage, of such an embryo, in pursuance of a third party agreement.

(1B) No person shall procure or distribute an embryo intended for human application except in pursuance of a licence or a third party agreement.

(2) No person shall place in a woman –
(a) an embryo other than a permitted embryo (as defined by section 3ZA), or
(b) any gametes other than permitted eggs or permitted sperm (as so defined).

(3) A licence cannot authorise –
(a) keeping or using an embryo after the appearance of the primitive streak,
(b) placing an embryo in any animal, or
(c) keeping or using an embryo in any circumstances in which regulations prohibit its keeping or use, or

(4) For the purposes of subsection (3)(a) above, the primitive streak is to be taken to have appeared in an embryo not later than the end of the period of 14 days beginning with the day on which the process of creating the embryo began, not counting any time during which the embryo is stored.

3ZA Permitted eggs, permitted sperm and permitted embryos

(1) This section has effect for the interpretation of section 3(2).

(2) A permitted egg is one –
(a) which has been produced by or extracted from the ovaries of a woman, and
(b) whose nuclear or mitochondrial DNA has not been altered.

(3) Permitted sperm are sperm –
(a) which have been produced by or extracted from the testes of a man, and
(b) whose nuclear or mitochondrial DNA has not been altered.

(4) An embryo is a permitted embryo if –
(a) it has been created by the fertilisation of a permitted egg by permitted sperm,
(b) no nuclear or mitochondrial DNA of any cell of the embryo has been altered, and
(c) no cell has been added to it other than by division of the embryo's own cells.

(5) Regulations may provide that –
(a) an egg can be a permitted egg, or
(b) an embryo can be a permitted embryo,
even though the egg or embryo has had applied to it in prescribed circumstances a prescribed process designed to prevent the transmission of serious mitochondrial disease.

(6) In this section –
(a) 'woman' and 'man' include respectively a girl and a boy (from birth), and
(b) 'prescribed' means prescribed by regulations.

3A Prohibition in connection with germ cells

(1) No person shall, for the purpose of providing fertility services for any woman, use female germ cells taken or derived from an embryo or a foetus or use embryos created by using such cells.

(2) In this section –
'female germ cells' means cells of the female germ line and includes such cells at any stage of maturity and accordingly includes eggs; and
'fertility services' means medical, surgical or obstetric services provided for the purpose of assisting women to carry children.

4 Prohibitions in connection with gametes

(1) No person shall –
(a) store any gametes, or
(b) in the course of providing treatment services for any woman, use –
(i) any sperm, other than partner-donated sperm which has been neither processed nor stored,

(ii) the woman's eggs after processing or storage, or

(iii) the eggs of any other woman,

except in pursuance of a licence.

(1A) No person shall procure, test, process or distribute any gametes intended for human application except in pursuance of a licence or a third party agreement.

(2) A licence cannot authorise storing or using gametes in any circumstances in which regulations prohibit their storage or use.

(3) No person shall place sperm and eggs in a woman in any circumstances specified in regulations except in pursuance of a licence.

(4) Regulations made by virtue of subsection (3) above may provide that, in relation to licences only to place sperm and eggs in a woman in such circumstances, sections 12 to 22 of this Act shall have effect with such modifications as may be specified in the regulations.

(5) Activities regulated by this section or section 3 or 4A of this Act are referred to in this Act as 'activities governed by this Act'.

4A Prohibitions in connection with genetic material not of human origin

(1) No person shall place in a woman –

(a) a human admixed embryo,

(b) any other embryo that is not a human embryo, or

(c) any gametes other than human gametes.

(2) No person shall –

(a) mix human gametes with animal gametes,

(b) bring about the creation of a human admixed embryo, or

(c) keep or use a human admixed embryo, except in pursuance of a licence.

(3) A licence cannot authorise keeping or using a human admixed embryo after the earliest of the following –

(a) the appearance of the primitive streak, or

(b) the end of the period of 14 days beginning with the day on which the process of creating the human admixed embryo began, but not counting any time during which the human admixed embryo is stored.

(4) A licence cannot authorise placing a human admixed embryo in an animal.

(5) A licence cannot authorise keeping or using a human admixed embryo in any circumstances in which regulations prohibit its keeping or use.

(6) For the purposes of this Act a human admixed embryo is –

(a) an embryo created by replacing the nucleus of an animal egg or of an animal cell, or two animal pronuclei, with –

(i) two human pronuclei,

(ii) one nucleus of a human gamete or of any other human cell, or

(iii) one human gamete or other human cell,

(b) any other embryo created by using –

(i) human gametes and animal gametes, or

(ii) one human pronucleus and one animal pronucleus,

(c) a human embryo that has been altered by the introduction of any sequence of nuclear or mitochondrial DNA of an animal into one or more cells of the embryo,

(d) a human embryo that has been altered by the introduction of one or more animal cells, or

(e) any embryo not falling within paragraphs (a) to (d) which contains both nuclear or mito-chondrial DNA of a human and nuclear or mitochondrial DNA of an animal ('animal DNA') but in which the animal DNA is not predominant.

(7) In subsection (6) –

(a) references to animal cells are to cells of an animal or of an animal embryo, and

(b) references to human cells are to cells of a human or of a human embryo.

(8) For the purposes of this section an 'animal' is an animal other than man.

(9) In this section 'embryo' means a live embryo, including an egg that is in the process of fertilisation or is undergoing any other process capable of resulting in an embryo.

(10) In this section –

   (a) references to eggs are to live eggs, including cells of the female germ line at any stage of maturity, but (except in subsection (9)) not including eggs that are in the process of fertilisation or are undergoing any other process capable of resulting in an embryo, and

   (b) references to gametes are to eggs (as so defined) or to live sperm, including cells of the male germ line at any stage of maturity.

(11) If it appears to the Secretary of State necessary or desirable to do so in the light of developments in science or medicine, regulations may –

   (a) amend (but not repeal) paragraphs (a) to (e) of subsection (6);

   (b) provide that in this section 'embryo', 'eggs' or 'gametes' includes things specified in the regulations which would not otherwise fall within the definition.

(12) Regulations made by virtue of subsection (11)(a) may make any amendment of subsection (7) that appears to the Secretary of State to be appropriate in consequence of any amendment of subsection (6).

The Human Fertilisation and Embryology Authority, its functions and procedure

5   The Human Fertilisation and Embryology Authority

(1) There shall be a body corporate called the Human Fertilisation and Embryology Authority.

(2) The Authority shall consist of –

   (a) a chairman and deputy chairman, and

   (b) such number of other members as the Secretary of State appoints.

(3) Schedule 1 to this Act (which deals with the membership of the Authority, etc.) shall have effect.

8   General functions of the authority

(1) The Authority shall –

   (a) keep under review information about embryos and any subsequent development of embryos and about the provision of treatment services and activities governed by this Act, and advise the Secretary of State, if he asks it to do so, about those matters,

   (b) publicise the services provided to the public by the Authority or provided in pursuance of licences,

   (c) provide, to such extent as it considers appropriate, advice and information for persons to whom licences apply or who are receiving treatment services or providing gametes or embryos for use for the purposes of activities governed by this Act, or may wish to do so, and

   (ca) maintain a statement of the general principles which it considers should be followed –

      (i)   in the carrying-on of activities governed by this Act, and

      (ii) in the carrying-out of its functions in relation to such activities, (cb) promote, in relation to activities governed by this Act, compliance with –

      (i)   requirements imposed by or under this Act, and

      (ii) the code of practice under section 25 of this Act, and

   (d) perform such other functions as may be specified in regulations.

(2) The Authority may, if it thinks fit, charge a fee for any advice provided under subsection (1)(c).

Scope of licences

11   Licences for treatment, storage and research

(1) The Authority may grant the following and no other licences –

   (a) licences under paragraph 1 of Schedule 2 to this Act authorising activities in the course of providing treatment services, (aa) licences under paragraph 1A of that Schedule authorising activities in the course of providing non-medical fertility services,

(b) licences under that Schedule authorising the storage of gametes, embryos or human admixed embryos, and

(c) licences under paragraph 3 of that Schedule authorising activities for the purpose of a project of research.

(2) Paragraph 4 of that Schedule has effect in the case of all licences.

Licence conditions

12   General conditions

(1) The following shall be conditions of every licence granted under this Act –

(a) except to the extent that the activities authorised by the licence fall within paragraph (aa), that those activities shall be carried on only on the premises to which the licence relates and under the supervision of the person responsible,

(aa) that any activities to which section 3(1A)(b) or (1B) or 4(1A) applies shall be carried on only on the premises to which the licence relates or on relevant third party premises,

(b) that any member or employee of the Authority, on production, if so required, of a document identifying the person as such, shall at all reasonable times be permitted to enter those premises and inspect them (which includes inspecting any equipment or records and observing any activity),

(c) except in relation to the use of gametes in the course of providing basic partner treatment services that the provisions of Schedule 3 to this Act shall be complied with,

(d) that proper records shall be maintained in such form as the Authority may specify in directions,

(e) that no money or other benefit shall be given or received in respect of any supply of gametes, embryos or human admixed embryos unless authorised by directions,

(f) that, where gametes, embryos or human admixed embryos are supplied to a person to whom another licence applies, that person shall also be provided with such information as the Authority may specify in directions, and

(g) that the Authority shall be provided, in such form and at such intervals as it may specify in directions, with such copies of or extracts from the records, or such other information, as the directions may specify.

(2) Subsection (3) applies to –

(a) every licence under paragraph 1 or 1A of Schedule 2,

(b) every licence under paragraph 2 of that Schedule, so far as authorising the storage of gametes or embryos intended for human application, and

(c) every licence under paragraph 3 of that Schedule, so far as authorising activities in connection with the derivation from embryos of stem cells that are intended for human application.

(3) It shall be a condition of every licence to which this subsection applies that –

(a) such information as is necessary to facilitate the traceability of gametes and embryos, and

(b) any information relating to the quality or safety of gametes or embryos, shall be recorded and provided to the Authority upon request.

13   Conditions of licences for treatment

(1) The following shall be conditions of every licence under paragraph 1 of Schedule 2 to this Act.

(2) Such information shall be recorded as the Authority may specify in directions about the following –

(a) the persons for whom services are provided in pursuance of the licence,

(b) the services provided for them,

(c) the persons whose gametes are kept or used for the purposes of services provided in pursuance of the licence or whose gametes have been used in bringing about the creation of embryos so kept or used,

(d) any child appearing to the person responsible to have been born as a result of treatment in pursuance of the licence,

(e) any mixing of egg and sperm and any taking of an embryo from a woman or other acquisition of an embryo, and

(f) such other matters as the Authority may specify in directions.

(3) The records maintained in pursuance of the licence shall include any information recorded in pursuance of subsection (2) above and any consent of a person whose consent is required under Schedule 3 to this Act.

(4) No information shall be removed from any records maintained in pursuance of the licence before the expiry of such period as may be specified in directions for records of the class in question.

(5) A woman shall not be provided with treatment services unless account has been taken of the welfare of any child who may be born as a result of the treatment (including the need of that child for supportive parenting), and of any other child who may be affected by the birth.

(6) A woman shall not be provided with treatment services of a kind specified in Part 1 of Schedule 3ZA unless she and any man or woman who is to be treated together with her have been given a suitable opportunity to receive proper counselling about the implications of her being provided with treatment services of that kind, and have been provided with such relevant information as is proper.

(6A) A woman shall not be provided with treatment services after the happening of any event falling within any paragraph of Part 2 of Schedule 3ZA unless (before or after the event) she and the intended second parent have been given a suitable opportunity to receive proper counselling about the implications of the woman being provided with treatment services after the happening of that event, and have been provided with such relevant information as is proper.

(6B) The reference in subsection (6A) to the intended second parent is a reference to –

(a) any man as respects whom the agreed fatherhood conditions in section 37 of the Human Fertilisation and Embryology Act 2008 ('the 2008 Act') are for the time being satisfied in relation to treatment provided to the woman mentioned in subsection (6A), and

(b) any woman as respects whom the agreed female parenthood conditions in section 44 of the 2008 Act are for the time being satisfied in relation to treatment provided to the woman mentioned in subsection (6A).

(6C) In the case of treatment services falling within paragraph 1 of Schedule 3ZA (use of gametes of a person not receiving those services) or paragraph 3 of that Schedule (use of embryo taken from a woman not receiving those services), the information provided by virtue of subsection (6) or (6A) must include such information as is proper about –

(a) the importance of informing any resulting child at an early age that the child results from the gametes of a person who is not a parent of the child, and

(b) suitable methods of informing such a child of that fact.

(6D) Where the person responsible receives from a person ('X') notice under section 37(1)(c) or 44(1)(c) of the 2008 Act of X's withdrawal of consent to X being treated as the parent of any child resulting from the provision of treatment services to a woman ('W'), the person responsible –

(a) must notify W in writing of the receipt of the notice from X, and

(b) no person to whom the licence applies may place an embryo or sperm and eggs in W, or artificially inseminate W, until W has been so notified.

(6E) Where the person responsible receives from a woman ('W') who has previously given notice under section 37(1)(b) or 44(1)(b) of the 2008 Act that she consents to another person

('X') being treated as a parent of any child resulting from the provision of treatment services to W –

    (a) notice under section 37(1)(c) or 44(1)(c) of the 2008 Act of the withdrawal of W's consent, or

    (b) a notice under section 37(1)(b) or 44(1)(b) of the 2008 Act in respect of a person other than X,

the person responsible must take reasonable steps to notify X in writing of the receipt of the notice mentioned in paragraph (a) or (b).

(7) Suitable procedures shall be maintained –

    (a) for determining the persons providing gametes or from whom embryos are taken for use in pursuance of the licence, and

    (b) for the purpose of securing that consideration is given to the use of practices not requiring the authority of a licence as well as those requiring such authority.

(8) Subsections (9) and (10) apply in determining any of the following –

    (a) the persons who are to provide gametes for use in pursuance of the licence in a case where consent is required under paragraph 5 of Schedule 3 for the use in question;

    (b) the woman from whom an embryo is to be taken for use in pursuance of the licence, in a case where her consent is required under paragraph 7 of Schedule 3 for the use of the embryo;

    (c) which of two or more embryos to place in a woman.

(9) Persons or embryos that are known to have a gene, chromosome or mitochondrion abnormality involving a significant risk that a person with the abnormality will have or develop –

    (a) a serious physical or mental disability,

    (b) a serious illness, or

    (c) any other serious medical condition,

must not be preferred to those that are not known to have such an abnormality.

(10) Embryos that are known to be of a particular sex and to carry a particular risk, compared with embryos of that sex in general, that any resulting child will have or develop –

    (a) a gender-related serious physical or mental disability,

    (b) a gender-related serious illness, or

    (c) any other gender-related serious medical condition, must not be preferred to those that are not known to carry such a risk.

(11) For the purposes of subsection (10), a physical or mental disability, illness or other medical condition is gender-related if –

    (a) it affects only one sex, or

    (b) it affects one sex significantly more than the other.

(12) No embryo appropriated for the purpose mentioned in paragraph 1(1)(ca) of Schedule 2 (training in embryological techniques) shall be kept or used for the provision of treatment services.

(13) The person responsible shall comply with any requirement imposed on that person by section 31ZD.

13A   Conditions of licences for non-medical fertility services

(1) The following shall be conditions of every licence under paragraph 1A of Schedule 2.

(2) The requirements of section 13(2) to (4) and (7) shall be complied with.

(3) A woman shall not be provided with any non-medical fertility services involving the use of sperm other than partner-donated sperm unless the woman being provided with the services has been given a suitable opportunity to receive proper counselling about the implications of taking the proposed steps, and has been provided with such relevant information as is proper.

14   Conditions of storage licences

(1) The following shall be conditions of every licence authorising the storage of gametes, embryos or human admixed embryos –

    (a) that gametes of a person shall be placed in storage only if –

        (i) received from that person,

      (ii) acquired in circumstances in which by virtue of paragraph 9 or 10 of Schedule 3 that person's consent to the storage is not required, or

      (iii) acquired from a person to whom a licence or third party agreement applies,

  (aa) that an embryo taken from a woman shall be placed in storage only if –

      (i) received from that woman, or

      (ii) acquired from a person to whom a licence or third party agreement applies,

  (ab) that an embryo the creation of which has been brought about *in vitro* otherwise than in pursuance of that licence shall be placed in storage only if acquired from a person to whom a licence or third party agreement applies,

  (ac) that a human admixed embryo the creation of which has been brought about *in vitro* otherwise than in pursuance of that licence shall be placed in storage only if acquired from a person to whom a licence under paragraph 2 or 3 of Schedule 2 applies,

  (b) that gametes or embryos which are or have been stored shall not be supplied to a person otherwise than in the course of providing treatment services unless that person is a person to whom a licence applies,

  (ba) that human admixed embryos shall not be supplied to a person unless that person is a person to whom a licence applies,

  (c) that no gametes, embryos or human admixed embryos shall be kept in storage for longer than the statutory storage period and, if stored at the end of the period, shall be allowed to perish, and

  (d) that such information as the Authority may specify in directions as to the persons whose consent is required under Schedule 3 to this Act, the terms of their consent and the circumstances of the storage and as to such other matters as the Authority may specify in directions shall be included in the records maintained in pursuance of the licence.

(2) No information shall be removed from any record maintained in pursuance of such a licence before the expiry of such period as may be specified in directions for records of the class in question.

(3) The statutory storage period in respect of gametes is such period not exceeding ten years as the licence may specify.

(4) The statutory storage period in respect of embryos is such period not exceeding ten years as the licence may specify.

(4A) The statutory storage period in respect of human admixed embryos is such period not exceeding ten years as the licence may specify.

(5) Regulations may provide that subsection (3), (4) or (4A) above shall have effect as if for ten years there were substituted –

  (a) such shorter period, or

  (b) in such circumstances as may be specified in the regulations, such longer period, as may be specified in the regulations.

Grant, revocation and suspension of licences

17 The person responsible

(1) It shall be the duty of the individual under whose supervision the activities authorised by a licence are carried on (referred to in this Act as the 'person responsible') to secure –

  (a) that the other persons to whom the licence applies are of such character, and are so qualified by training and experience, as to be suitable persons to participate in the activities authorised by the licence,

  (b) that proper equipment is used,

  (c) that proper arrangements are made for the keeping of gametes, embryos and human admixed embryos and for the disposal of gametes, embryos or human admixed embryos that have been allowed to perish,

(d) that suitable practices are used in the course of the activities, and

(e) that the conditions of the licence are complied with,

(f) that conditions of third party agreements relating to the procurement, testing, processing or distribution of gametes or embryos are complied with, and

(g) that the Authority is notified and provided with a report analysing the cause and the ensuing outcome of any serious adverse event or serious adverse reaction.

25 Code of practice

(1) The Authority shall maintain a code of practice giving guidance about the proper conduct of activities carried on in pursuance of a licence under this Act and the proper discharge of the functions of the person responsible and other persons to whom the licence applies.

(2) The guidance given by the code shall include guidance for those providing treatment services about the account to be taken of the welfare of children who may be born as a result of treatment services (including a child's need for supportive parenting), and of other children who may be affected by such births.

(2A) The code shall also give guidance about –

(a) the giving of a suitable opportunity to receive proper counselling, and

(b) the provision of such relevant information as is proper,

in accordance with any condition that is by virtue of section 13(6) or (6A) a condition of a licence under paragraph 1 of Schedule 2.

(3) The code may also give guidance about the use of any technique involving the placing of sperm and eggs in a woman.

(4) The Authority may from time to time revise the whole or any part of the code.

*Status**

27 Meaning of 'mother'

(1) The woman who is carrying or has carried a child as a result of the placing in her of an embryo or of sperm and eggs, and no other woman, is to be treated as the mother of the child.

(6) Subsection (1) above does not apply to any child to the extent that the child is treated by virtue of adoption as not being the woman's child.

(7) Subsection (1) above applies whether the woman was in the United Kingdom or elsewhere at the time of the placing in her of the embryo or the sperm and eggs.

28 Meaning of 'father'

(1) Subject to subsections (5A) to (5I) below, this section applies in the case of a child who is being or has been carried by a woman as the result of the placing in her of an embryo or of sperm and eggs or her artificial insemination.

(2) If –

(a) at the time of the placing in her of the embryo or the sperm and eggs or of her insemination, the woman was a party to a marriage, and

(b) the creation of the embryo carried by her was not brought about with the sperm of the other party to the marriage,

then, subject to subsection (5) below, the other party to the marriage shall be treated as the father of the child unless it is shown that he did not consent to the placing in her of the embryo or the sperm and eggs or to her insemination (as the case may be).

(3) If no man is treated, by virtue of subsection (2) above, as the father of the child but –

(a) the embryo or the sperm and eggs were placed in the woman, or she was artificially inseminated, in the course of treatment services provided for her and a man together by a person to whom a licence applies, and

---

* **Editors' note:** For children born as a result of treatment provided after 6 April 2009, see Human Fertilisation and Embryology Act 2008, below.

(b) the creation of the embryo carried by her was not brought about with the sperm of
that man,

then, subject to subsection (5) below, that man shall be treated as the father of the child.

(4) Where a person is treated as the father of the child by virtue of subsection (2) or (3) above,
no other person is to be treated as the father of the child.

(5A) If –

(a) a child has been carried by a woman as the result of the placing in her of an embryo or
of sperm and eggs or her artificial insemination,

(b) the creation of the embryo carried by her was brought about by using the sperm of
a man after his death, or the creation of the embryo was brought about using the
sperm of a man before his death but the embryo was placed in the woman after his
death,

(c) the woman was a party to a marriage with the man immediately before his death,

(d) the man consented in writing (and did not withdraw the consent) –

(i)   to the use of his sperm after his death which brought about the creation of the
embryo carried by the woman or (as the case may be) to the placing in the woman
after his death of the embryo which was brought about using his sperm before his
death, and

(ii) to being treated for the purpose mentioned in subsection (5I) below as the father
of any resulting child,

(e) the woman has elected in writing not later than the end of the period of 42 days from
the day on which the child was born for the man to be treated for the purpose mentioned in subsection (5I) below as the father of the child, and

(f) no-one else is to be treated as the father of the child by virtue of subsection (2) or
(3) above or by virtue of adoption or the child being treated as mentioned in paragraph
(a) or (b) of subsection (5) above,

then the man shall be treated for the purpose mentioned in subsection (5I) below as the father of
the child.

(5B) If –

(a) a child has been carried by a woman as the result of the placing in her of an embryo or
of sperm and eggs or her artificial insemination,

(b) the creation of the embryo carried by her was brought about by using the sperm of
a man after his death, or the creation of the embryo was brought about using the
sperm of a man before his death but the embryo was placed in the woman after his
death,

(c) the woman was not a party to a marriage with the man immediately before his death
but treatment services were being provided for the woman and the man together before
his death either by a person to whom a licence applies or outside the United Kingdom,

(d) the man consented in writing (and did not withdraw the consent) –

(i)   to the use of his sperm after his death which brought about the creation of the
embryo carried by the woman or (as the case may be) to the placing in the woman
after his death of the embryo which was brought about using his sperm before his
death, and

(ii) to being treated for the purpose mentioned in subsection (5I) below as the father
of any resulting child,

(e) the woman has elected in writing not later than the end of the period of 42 days from
the day on which the child was born for the man to be treated for the purpose mentioned in subsection (5I) below as the father of the child, and

(f) no-one else is to be treated as the father of the child by virtue of subsection (2) or
(3) above or by virtue of adoption or the child being treated as mentioned in paragraph
(a) or (b) of subsection (5) above,

then the man shall be treated for the purpose mentioned in subsection (5I) below as the father of
the child.

(5C) If –
  (a) a child has been carried by a woman as the result of the placing in her of an embryo,
  (b) the embryo was created at a time when the woman was a party to a marriage,
  (c) the creation of the embryo was not brought about with the sperm of the other party to the marriage,
  (d) the other party to the marriage died before the placing of the embryo in the woman,
  (e) the other party to the marriage consented in writing (and did not withdraw the consent) –
      (i)   to the placing of the embryo in the woman after his death, and
      (ii) to being treated for the purpose mentioned in subsection (5I) below as the father of any resulting child,
  (f) the woman has elected in writing not later than the end of the period of 42 days from the day on which the child was born for the other party to the marriage to be treated for the purpose mentioned in subsection (5I) below as the father of the child, and
  (g) no-one else is to be treated as the father of the child by virtue of subsection (2) or (3) above or by virtue of adoption or the child being treated as mentioned in paragraph (a) or (b) of subsection (5) above,
then the other party to the marriage shall be treated for the purpose mentioned in subsection (5I) below as the father of the child.

(5D) If –
  (a) a child has been carried by a woman as the result of the placing in her of an embryo,
  (b) the embryo was not created at a time when the woman was a party to a marriage but was created in the course of treatment services provided for the woman and a man together either by a person to whom a licence applies or outside the United Kingdom,
  (c) the creation of the embryo was not brought about with the sperm of that man,
  (d) the man died before the placing of the embryo in the woman,
  (e) the man consented in writing (and did not withdraw the consent) –
      (i)   to the placing of the embryo in the woman after his death, and
      (ii) to being treated for the purpose mentioned in subsection (5I) below as the father of any resulting child,
  (f) the woman has elected in writing not later than the end of the period of 42 days from the day on which the child was born for the man to be treated for the purpose mentioned in subsection (5I) below as the father of the child, and
  (g) no-one else is to be treated as the father of the child by virtue of subsection (2) or (3) above or by virtue of adoption or the child being treated as mentioned in paragraph (a) or (b) of subsection (5) above,
then the man shall be treated for the purpose mentioned in subsection (5I) below as the father of the child.

29   Effect of sections 27 and 28

(1) Where by virtue of section 27 or 28 of this Act a person is to be treated as the mother or father of a child, that person is to be treated in law as the mother or, as the case may be, father of the child for all purposes.

(2) Where by virtue of section 27 or 28 of this Act a person is not be treated as the mother or father of a child, that person is to be treated in law as not being the mother or, as the case may be, father of the child for any purpose.

Information

31   Register of information

(1) The Authority shall keep a register which is to contain any information which falls within subsection (2) and which –
  (a) immediately before the coming into force of section 24 of the Human Fertilisation and Embryology Act 2008, was contained in the register kept under this section by the Authority, or
  (b) is obtained by the Authority.

(2) Subject to subsection (3), information falls within this subsection if it relates to –

    (a) the provision for any identifiable individual of treatment services other than basic partner treatment services,

    (b) the procurement or distribution of any sperm, other than sperm which is partner-donated sperm and has not been stored, in the course of providing non-medical fertility services for any identifiable individual,

    (c) the keeping of the gametes of any identifiable individual or of an embryo taken from any identifiable woman,

    (d) the use of the gametes of any identifiable individual other than their use for the purpose of basic partner treatment services, or

    (e) the use of an embryo taken from any identifiable woman, or if it shows that any identifiable individual is a relevant individual.

(3) Information does not fall within subsection (2) if it is provided to the Authority for the purposes of any voluntary contact register as defined by section 31ZF(1).

(4) In this section 'relevant individual' means an individual who was or may have been born in consequence of –

    (a) treatment services, other than basic partner treatment services, or

    (b) the procurement or distribution of any sperm (other than partner-donated sperm which has not been stored) in the course of providing non-medical fertility services.

31ZA   Request for information as to genetic parentage etc.

(1) A person who has attained the age of 16 ('the applicant') may by notice to the Authority require the Authority to comply with a request under subsection (2).

(2) The applicant may request the Authority to give the applicant notice stating whether or not the information contained in the register shows that a person ('the donor') other than a parent of the applicant would or might, but for the relevant statutory provisions, be the parent of the applicant, and if it does show that –

    (a) giving the applicant so much of that information as relates to the donor as the Authority is required by regulations to give (but no other information), or

    (b) stating whether or not that information shows that there are other persons of whom the donor is not the parent but would or might, but for the relevant statutory provisions, be the parent and if so –

        (i)   the number of those other persons,

        (ii) the sex of each of them, and

        (iii) the year of birth of each of them.

(3) The Authority shall comply with a request under subsection (2) if –

    (a) the information contained in the register shows that the applicant is a relevant individual, and

    (b) the applicant has been given a suitable opportunity to receive proper counselling about the implications of compliance with the request.

(4) Where a request is made under subsection (2)(a) and the applicant has not attained the age of 18 when the applicant gives notice to the Authority under subsection (1), regulations cannot require the Authority to give the applicant any information which identifies the donor.

(5) Regulations cannot require the Authority to give any information as to the identity of a person whose gametes have been used or from whom an embryo has been taken if a person to whom a licence applied was provided with the information at a time when the Authority could not have been required to give information of the kind in question.

(6) The Authority need not comply with a request made under subsection (2)(b) by any applicant if it considers that special circumstances exist which increase the likelihood that compliance with the request would enable the applicant –

    (a) to identify the donor, in a case where the Authority is not required by regulations under subsection (2)(a) to give the applicant information which identifies the donor, or

    (b) to identify any person about whom information is given under subsection (2)(b).

(7) In this section –

'relevant individual' has the same meaning as in section 31;

'the relevant statutory provisions' means sections 27 to 29 of this Act and sections 33 to 47 of the Human Fertilisation and Embryology Act 2008.

31ZC Power of Authority to inform donor of request for information

(1) Where –

    (a) the Authority has received from a person ('the applicant') a notice containing a request under subsection (2)(a) of section 31ZA, and

    (b) compliance by the Authority with its duty under that section has involved or will involve giving the applicant information relating to a person other than the parent of the applicant who would or might, but for the relevant statutory provisions, be a parent of the applicant ('the donor'),

the Authority may notify the donor that a request under section 31ZA(2)(a) has been made, but may not disclose the identity of the applicant or any information relating to the applicant.

(2) In this section 'the relevant statutory provisions' has the same meaning as in section 31ZA.

31ZD Provision to donor of information about resulting children

(1) This section applies where a person ('the donor') has consented under Schedule 3 (whether before or after the coming into force of this section) to –

    (a) the use of the donor's gametes, or an embryo the creation of which was brought about using the donor's gametes, for the purposes of treatment services provided under a licence, or

    (b) the use of the donor's gametes for the purposes of non-medical fertility services provided under a licence.

(2) In subsection (1) –

    (a) 'treatment services' do not include treatment services provided to the donor, or to the donor and another person together, and

    (b) 'non-medical fertility services' do not include any services involving partner-donated sperm.

(3) The donor may by notice request the appropriate person to give the donor notice stating –

    (a) the number of persons of whom the donor is not a parent but would or might, but for the relevant statutory provisions, be a parent by virtue of the use of the gametes or embryos to which the consent relates,

    (b) the sex of each of those persons, and

    (c) the year of birth of each of those persons.

(4) Subject to subsections (5) to (7), the appropriate person shall notify the donor whether the appropriate person holds the information mentioned in subsection (3) and, if the appropriate person does so, shall comply with the request.

(5) The appropriate person need not comply with a request under subsection (3) if the appropriate person considers that special circumstances exist which increase the likelihood that compliance with the request would enable the donor to identify any of the persons falling within paragraphs (a) to (c) of subsection (3).

(6) In the case of a donor who consented as described in subsection (1)(a), the Authority need not comply with a request made to it under subsection (3) where the person who held the licence referred to in subsection (1)(a) continues to hold a licence under paragraph 1 of Schedule 2, unless the donor has previously made a request under subsection (3) to the person responsible and the person responsible –

    (a) has notified the donor that the information concerned is not held, or

    (b) has failed to comply with the request within a reasonable period.

(7) In the case of a donor who consented as described in subsection (1)(b), the Authority need not comply with a request made to it under subsection (3) where the person who held the licence referred to in subsection (1)(b) continues to hold a licence under paragraph 1A of Schedule 2,

unless the donor has previously made a request under subsection (3) to the person responsible and the person responsible –

    (a) has notified the donor that the information concerned is not held, or

    (b) has failed to comply with the request within a reasonable period.

(8) In this section 'the appropriate person' means –

    (a) in the case of a donor who consented as described in paragraph (a) of subsection (1) –

        (i) where the person who held the licence referred to in that paragraph continues to hold a licence under paragraph 1 of Schedule 2, the person responsible, or

        (ii) the Authority, and

    (b) in the case of a donor who consented as described in paragraph (b) of subsection (1) –

        (i) where the person who held the licence referred to in that paragraph continues to hold a licence under paragraph 1A of Schedule 2, the person responsible, or

        (ii) the Authority.

(9) In this section 'the relevant statutory provisions' has the same meaning as in section 31ZA.

31ZE Provision of information about donor-conceived genetic siblings

(1) For the purposes of this section two relevant individuals are donor-conceived genetic siblings of each other if a person ('the donor') who is not the parent of either of them would or might, but for the relevant statutory provisions, be the parent of both of them.

(2) Where –

    (a) the information on the register shows that a relevant individual ('A') is the donor-conceived genetic sibling of another relevant individual ('B'),

    (b) A has provided information to the Authority ('the agreed information') which consists of or includes information which enables A to be identified with the request that it should be disclosed to –

        (i) any donor-conceived genetic sibling of A, or

        (ii) such siblings of A of a specified description which includes B, and

    (c) the conditions in subsection (3) are satisfied,

then, subject to subsection (4), the Authority shall disclose the agreed information to B.

(3) The conditions referred to in subsection (2)(c) are –

    (a) that each of A and B has attained the age of 18,

    (b) that B has requested the disclosure to B of information about any donor-conceived genetic sibling of B, and

    (c) that each of A and B has been given a suitable opportunity to receive proper counselling about the implications of disclosure under subsection (2).

(4) The Authority need not disclose any information under subsection (2) if it considers that the disclosure of information will lead to A or B identifying the donor unless –

    (a) the donor has consented to the donor's identity being disclosed to A or B, or

    (b) were A or B to make a request under section 31ZA(2)(a), the Authority would be required by regulations under that provision to give A or B information which would identify the donor.

(5) In this section –

'relevant individual' has the same meaning as in section 31;

'the relevant statutory provisions' has the same meaning as in section 31ZA.

31ZF Power of Authority to keep voluntary contact register

(1) In this section and section 31ZG, a 'voluntary contact register' means a register of persons who have expressed their wish to receive information about any person to whom they are genetically related as a consequence of the provision to any person of treatment services in the United Kingdom before 1 August 1991.

(2) The Authority may –

    (a) set up a voluntary contact register in such manner as it thinks fit,

    (b) keep a voluntary contact register in such manner as it thinks fit,

(c) determine criteria for eligibility for inclusion on the register and the particulars that may be included,

(d) charge a fee to persons who wish their particulars to be entered on the register,

(e) arrange for samples of the DNA of such persons to be analysed at their request,

(f) make such arrangements as it thinks fit for the disclosure of information on the register between persons who appear to the Authority to be genetically related, and

(g) impose such conditions as it thinks fit to prevent a person ('A') from disclosing information to a person to whom A is genetically related ('B') where that information would identify any person who is genetically related to both A and B.

32 Information to be provided to Registrar General

(1) This section applies where a claim is made before the Registrar General that a person is or is not the parent of a child and it is necessary or desirable for the purpose of any function of the Registrar General to determine whether the claim is or may be well-founded.

(2) The Authority shall comply with any request made by the Registrar General by notice to the Authority to disclose whether any information on the register kept in pursuance of section 31 of this Act tends to show that the person may be a parent of the child by virtue of any of the relevant statutory provisions and, if it does, disclose that information.

33A Disclosure of information

(1) No person shall disclose any information falling within section 31(2) which the person obtained (whether before or after the coming into force of section 24 of the Human Fertilisation and Embryology Act 2008) in the person's capacity as –

(a) a member or employee of the Authority,

(b) any person exercising functions of the Authority by virtue of section 8B or 8C of this Act (including a person exercising such functions by virtue of either of those sections as a member of staff or as an employee),

(c) any person engaged by the Authority to provide services to the Authority,

(d) any person employed by, or engaged to provide services to, a person mentioned in paragraph (c),

(e) a person to whom a licence applies,

(f) a person to whom a third party agreement applies, or

(g) a person to whom directions have been given.

(2) Subsection (1) does not apply where –

(h) the disclosure is of information other than identifying donor information and is made with the consent required by section 33B,

(i) the disclosure –

(i) is made by a person who is satisfied that it is necessary to make the disclosure to avert an imminent danger to the health of an individual ('P'),

(ii) is of information falling within section 31(2)(a) which could be disclosed by virtue of paragraph (h) with P's consent or could be disclosed to P by virtue of subsection (5), and

(iii) is made in circumstances where it is not reasonably practicable to obtain P's consent,

(j) the disclosure is of information which has been lawfully made available to the public before the disclosure is made,

(k) the disclosure is made in accordance with sections 31ZA to 31ZE,

(t) the disclosure is made necessarily for –

(i) the purpose of the investigation of any offence (or suspected offence), or

(ii) any purpose preliminary to proceedings, or for the purposes of, or in connection with, any proceedings.

(3) Subsection (1) does not apply to the disclosure of information in so far as –

(a) the information identifies a person who, but for sections 27 to 29 of this Act or sections 33 to 47 of the Human Fertilisation and Embryology Act 2008, would or might be a parent of a person who instituted proceedings under section 1A of the Congenital Disabilities (Civil Liability) Act 1976, and

(b) the disclosure is made for the purpose of defending such proceedings, or instituting connected proceedings for compensation against that parent.

33D Disclosure for the purposes of medical or other research

(1) Regulations may –

(a) make such provision for and in connection with requiring or regulating the processing of protected information for the purposes of medical research as the Secretary of State considers is necessary or expedient in the public interest or in the interests of improving patient care, and

(b) make such provision for and in connection with requiring or regulating the processing of protected information for the purposes of any other research as the Secretary of State considers is necessary or expedient in the public interest.

34 Disclosure in interests of justice

(1) Where in any proceedings before a court the question whether a person is or is not the parent of a child by virtue of sections 27 to 29 of this Act or sections 33 to 47 of the Human Fertilisation and Embryology Act 2008 falls to be determined, the court may on the application of any party to the proceedings make an order requiring the Authority –

(a) to disclose whether or not any information relevant to that question is contained in the register kept in pursuance of section 31 of this Act, and

(b) if it is, to disclose so much of it as is specified in the order,

but such an order may not require the Authority to disclose any information falling within section 31(2)(c) to (e) of this Act.

(2) The court must not make an order under subsection (1) above unless it is satisfied that the interests of justice require it to do so, taking into account –

(a) any representations made by any individual who may be affected by the disclosure, and

(b) the welfare of the child, if under 18 years old, and of any other person under that age who may be affected by the disclosure.

35 Disclosure in interests of justice: congenital disabilities, etc.

(1) Where for the purpose of instituting proceedings under section 1 of the Congenital Disabilities (Civil Liability) Act 1976 (civil liability to child born disabled) it is necessary to identify a person who would or might be the parent of a child but for the relevant statutory provisions, the court may, on the application of the child, make an order requiring the Authority to disclose any information contained in the register kept in pursuance of section 31 of this Act identifying that person.

Mitochondrial donation

35A Mitochondrial donation

(1) Regulations may provide for any of the relevant provisions to have effect subject to specified modifications in relation to cases where –

(a) an egg which is a permitted egg for the purposes of section 3(2) by virtue of regulations made under section 3ZA(5), or

(b) an embryo which is a permitted embryo for those purposes by virtue of such regulations, has been created from material provided by two women.

Conscientious objection

38 Conscientious objection

(1) No person who has a conscientious objection to participating in any activity governed by this Act shall be under any duty, however arising, to do so.

(2) In any legal proceedings the burden of proof of conscientious objection shall rest on the person claiming to rely on it.

(3) In any proceedings before a court in Scotland, a statement on oath by any person to the effect that he has a conscientious objection to participating in a particular activity governed by this Act shall be sufficient evidence of that fact for the purpose of discharging the burden of proof imposed by subsection (2) above.

Offences

41 Offences

(1) A person who –
- (a) contravenes section 3(2), 3A or 4A(1) or (2) of this Act, or
- (b) does anything which, by virtue of section 3(3) of this Act, cannot be authorised by a licence,

is guilty of an offence and liable on conviction on indictment to imprisonment for a term not exceeding ten years or a fine or both.

(2) A person who –
- (a)   contravenes section 3(1) or (1A) of this Act, otherwise than by doing something which, by virtue of section 3(3) of this Act, cannot be authorised by a licence,
- (aa) contravenes section 3(1B) of this Act,
- (b)   keeps any gametes in contravention of section 4(1)(a) of this Act, (ba) uses any gametes in contravention of section 4(1)(b),
- (bb) contravenes section 4(1A) of this Act,
- (c)   contravenes section 4(3) of this Act, or
- (d)   fails to comply with any directions given by virtue of section 24(5D) of this Act, is guilty of an offence.

(3) If a person –
- (a) provides any information for the purposes of the grant of a licence, being information which is false or misleading in a material particular, and
- (b) either he knows the information to be false or misleading in a material particular or he provides the information recklessly,

he is guilty of an offence.

(4) A person guilty of an offence under subsection (2) or (3) above is liable –
- (a) on conviction on indictment, to imprisonment for a term not exceeding two years or a fine or both, and
- (b) on summary conviction, to imprisonment for a term not exceeding six months or a fine not exceeding the statutory maximum or both.

(5) A person who discloses any information in contravention of section 33A of this Act is guilty of an offence and liable –
- (a) on conviction on indictment, to imprisonment for a term not exceeding two years or a fine or both, and
- (b) on summary conviction, to imprisonment for a term not exceeding six months or a fine not exceeding the statutory maximum or both.

42 Consent to prosecution

No proceedings for an offence under this Act shall be instituted –
- (a) in England and Wales, except by or with the consent of the Director of Public Prosecutions, and
- (b) in Northern Ireland, except by or with the consent of the Director of Public Prosecutions for Northern Ireland.

Miscellaneous and general

47   Index

The expressions listed in the left-hand column below are respectively defined or (as the case may be) are to be interpreted in accordance with the provisions of this Act listed in the right-hand column in relation to those expressions.

Expression	Relevant provision
Activities governed by this Act	Section 4(5)
Authority	Section 2(1)
Basic partner treatment services	Section 2(1)
Carry, in relation to a child	Section 2(3)
Embryo	Section 1
Gametes, eggs or sperm	Section 1
Human application	Section 2(1)
Keeping, in relation to embryos or gametes	Section 2(2)
Licence	Section 2(1)
Person responsible	Section 17(1)
Statutory storage period	Section 14(3) to (5)
Store, and similar expressions, in relation to embryos or gametes	Section 2(1)
Treatment services	Section 2(1)

49   Short title, commencement, etc.

(3) Section 27 to 29 of this Act shall have effect only in relation to children carried by women as a result of the placing in them of embryos or of sperm and eggs, or of their artificial insemination (as the case may be), after the commencement of those sections.

(4) Section 27 of the Family Law Reform Act 1987 (artificial insemination) does not have effect in relation to children carried by women as the result of their artificial insemination after the commencement of sections 27 to 29 of this Act.

SCHEDULES

SCHEDULE 2 ACTIVITIES FOR WHICH LICENCES MAY BE GRANTED

Licences for treatment

1.—(1) A licence under this paragraph may authorise any of the following in the course of providing treatment services –

    (a) bringing about the creation of embryos *in vitro,*

    (b) procuring, keeping, testing, processing or distributing embryos,

    (c) procuring, testing, processing, distributing or using gametes,

    (ca) using embryos for the purpose of training persons in embryo biopsy, embryo storage or other embryological techniques,

    (d) other practices designed to secure that embryos are in a suitable condition to be placed in a woman,

   (e) placing any permitted embryo in a woman,
   (f) mixing sperm with the egg of a hamster, or other animal specified in directions, for
       the purpose of testing the fertility or normality of the sperm, but only where anything
       which forms is destroyed when the test is complete and, in any event, not later than the
       two cell stage, and
   (g) such other practices, apart from practices falling within section 4A(2), as may be speci-
       fied in, or determined in accordance with, regulations.
   (2) Subject to the provisions of this Act, a licence under this paragraph may be granted subject
to such conditions as may be specified in the licence and may authorise the performance of any of
the activities referred to in sub-paragraph (1) above in such manner as may be so specified.
   (3) A licence under this paragraph cannot authorise any activity unless it appears to the
Authority to be necessary or desirable for the purpose of providing treatment services.
   (4) A licence under this paragraph cannot authorise altering the nuclear or mitochondrial
DNA of a cell while it forms part of an embryo, except for the purpose of creating something that
will by virtue of regulations under section 3ZA(5) be a permitted embryo.
   (4A) A licence under this paragraph cannot authorise the use of embryos for the purpose mentioned in sub-paragraph (1)(ca) unless the Authority is satisfied that the proposed use of embryos
is necessary for that purpose.
   (5) A licence under this paragraph shall be granted for such period not exceeding five years as
may be specified in the licence.
   (6) In this paragraph, references to a permitted embryo are to be read in accordance with
section 3ZA.

Embryo testing

   1ZA.—(1) A licence under paragraph 1 cannot authorise the testing of an embryo, except for
one or more of the following purposes –
   (a) establishing whether the embryo has a gene, chromosome or mitochondrion abnor-
       mality that may affect its capacity to result in a live birth,
   (b) in a case where there is a particular risk that the embryo may have any gene, chromo-
       some or mitochondrion abnormality, establishing whether it has that abnormality or
       any other gene, chromosome or mitochondrion abnormality,
   (c) in a case where there is a particular risk that any resulting child will have or develop –
       (i)   a gender-related serious physical or mental disability,
       (ii) a gender-related serious illness, or
       (iii) any other gender-related serious medical condition, establishing the sex of the
             embryo,
   (d) in a case where a person ('the sibling') who is the child of the persons whose gametes
       are used to bring about the creation of the embryo (or of either of those persons) suffers
       from a serious medical condition which could be treated by umbilical cord blood stem
       cells, bone marrow or other tissue of any resulting child, establishing whether the tis-
       sue of any resulting child would be compatible with that of the sibling, and
   (e) in a case where uncertainty has arisen as to whether the embryo is one of those whose
       creation was brought about by using the gametes of particular persons, establishing
       whether it is.
   (2) A licence under paragraph 1 cannot authorise the testing of embryos for the purpose mentioned in sub-paragraph (1)(b) unless the Authority is satisfied –
   (a) in relation to the abnormality of which there is a particular risk, and
   (b) in relation to any other abnormality for which testing is to be authorised under
       sub-paragraph (1)(b),
that there is a significant risk that a person with the abnormality will have or develop a serious
physical or mental disability, a serious illness or any other serious medical condition. (3) For the

purposes of sub-paragraph (1)(c), a physical or mental disability, illness or other medical condition is gender-related if the Authority is satisfied that –

    (a) it affects only one sex, or

    (b) it affects one sex significantly more than the other.

    (4) In sub-paragraph (1)(d) the reference to 'other tissue' of the resulting child does not include a reference to any whole organ of the child.

Sex selection

    1ZB.—(1) A licence under paragraph 1 cannot authorise any practice designed to secure that any resulting child will be of one sex rather than the other.

    (2) Sub-paragraph (1) does not prevent the authorisation of any testing of embryos that is capable of being authorised under paragraph 1ZA.

    (3) Sub-paragraph (1) does not prevent the authorisation of any other practices designed to secure that any resulting child will be of one sex rather than the other in a case where there is a particular risk that a woman will give birth to a child who will have or develop –

    (a) a gender-related serious physical or mental disability,

    (b) a gender-related serious illness, or

    (c) any other gender-related serious medical condition.

    (4) For the purposes of sub-paragraph (3), a physical or mental disability, illness or other medical condition is gender-related if the Authority is satisfied that –

    (a) it affects only one sex, or

    (b) it affects one sex significantly more than the other.

Licences for non-medical fertility services

    1A.—(1) A licence under this paragraph may authorise any of the following in the course of providing non-medical fertility services –

    (a) procuring sperm, and

    (b) distributing sperm.

    (1A) A licence under this paragraph cannot authorise the procurement or distribution of sperm to which there has been applied any process designed to secure that any resulting child will be of one sex rather than the other.

    (2) Subject to the provisions of this Act, a licence under this paragraph may be granted subject to such conditions as may be specified in the licence and may authorise the performance of any of the activities referred to in sub-paragraph (1) above in such manner as may be so specified.

    (3) A licence under this paragraph shall be granted for such period not exceeding five years as may be specified in the licence.

Licences for storage

    2.—(1) A licence under this paragraph or paragraph 1 or 3 of this Schedule may authorise the storage of gametes or embryos or both.

    (1A) A licence under this paragraph or paragraph 3 may authorise the storage of human admixed embryos (whether or not the licence also authorises the storage of gametes or embryos or both).

    (3) A licence under this paragraph shall be granted for such period not exceeding five years as may be specified in the licence.

Licences for research

    3.—(1) A licence under this paragraph may authorise any of the following –

    (a) bringing about the creation of embryos *in vitro,* and

    (b) keeping or using embryos,

for the purposes of a project of research specified in the licence.

(2) A licence under this paragraph may authorise mixing sperm with the egg of a hamster, or other animal specified in directions, for the purpose of developing more effective techniques for determining the fertility or normality of sperm, but only where anything which forms is destroyed when the research is complete and, in any event, no later than the two cell stage.

(3) A licence under this paragraph may authorise any of the following –

    (a) bringing about the creation of human admixed embryos *in vitro*, and

    (b) keeping or using human admixed embryos, for the purposes of a project of research specified in the licence.

(4) A licence under sub-paragraph (3) may not authorise the activity which may be authorised by a licence under sub-paragraph (2).

(5) No licence under this paragraph is to be granted unless the Authority is satisfied that any proposed use of embryos or human admixed embryos is necessary for the purposes of the research.

(8) A licence under this paragraph may be granted for such period not exceeding three years as may be specified in the licence.

(9) This paragraph has effect subject to paragraph 3A.

Purposes for which activities may be licensed under paragraph 3

3A.—(1) A licence under paragraph 3 cannot authorise any activity unless the activity appears to the Authority –

    (a) to be necessary or desirable for any of the purposes specified in sub-paragraph (2) ('the principal purposes'),

    (b) to be necessary or desirable for the purpose of providing knowledge that, in the view of the Authority, may be capable of being applied for the purposes specified in sub-paragraph (2)(a) or (b), or

    (c) to be necessary or desirable for such other purposes as may be specified in regulations.

(2) The principal purposes are –

    (a) increasing knowledge about serious disease or other serious medical conditions,

    (b) developing treatments for serious disease or other serious medical conditions,

    (c) increasing knowledge about the causes of any congenital disease or congenital medical condition that does not fall within paragraph (a),

    (d) promoting advances in the treatment of infertility,

    (e) increasing knowledge about the causes of miscarriage,

    (f) developing more effective techniques of contraception,

    (g) developing methods for detecting the presence of gene, chromosome or mitochondrion abnormalities in embryos before implantation, or

    (h) increasing knowledge about the development of embryos.

SCHEDULE 3 CONSENTS TO USE OR STORAGE OF GAMETES, EMBRYOS OR HUMAN ADMIXED EMBRYOS ETC.

Consent

1.—(1) A consent under this Schedule, and any notice under paragraph 4 varying or withdrawing a consent under this Schedule, must be in writing and, subject to sub-paragraph (2), must be signed by the person giving it.

(2) A consent under this Schedule by a person who is unable to sign because of illness, injury or physical disability (a 'person unable to sign'), and any notice under paragraph 4 by a person unable to sign varying or withdrawing a consent under this Schedule, is to be taken to comply with the requirement of sub-paragraph (1) as to signature if it is signed at the direction of the person unable

to sign, in the presence of the person unable to sign and in the presence of at least one witness who attests the signature.

(3) In this Schedule 'effective consent' means a consent under this Schedule which has not been withdrawn.

2.—(1) A consent to the use of any embryo must specify one or more of the following purposes –

    (a) use in providing treatment services to the person giving consent, or that person and another specified person together,

    (b) use in providing treatment services to persons not including the person giving consent,

      (ba) use for the purpose of training persons in embryo biopsy, embryo storage or other embryological techniques, or

    (c) use for the purposes of any project of research, and may specify conditions subject to which the embryo may be so used.

(1A) A consent to the use of any human admixed embryo must specify use for the purposes of any project of research and may specify conditions subject to which the human admixed embryo may be so used.

(2) A consent to the storage of any gametes, any embryo or any human admixed embryo must –

    (a) specify the maximum period of storage (if less than the statutory storage period),

    (b) except in a case falling within paragraph (c), state what is to be done with the gametes, embryo or human admixed embryo if the person who gave the consent dies or is unable, because the person lacks capacity to do so, to vary the terms of the consent or to withdraw it, and

    (c) where the consent is given by virtue of paragraph 8(2A) or 13(2), state what is to be done with the embryo or human admixed embryo if the person to whom the consent relates dies,

and may (in any case) specify conditions subject to which the gametes, embryo or human admixed embryo may remain in storage.

(2A) A consent to the use of a person's human cells to bring about the creation *in vitro* of an embryo or human admixed embryo is to be taken unless otherwise stated to include consent to the use of the cells after the person's death.

(4) A consent under this Schedule may apply –

    (a) to the use or storage of a particular embryo or human admixed embryo, or

    (b) in the case of a person providing gametes or human cells, to the use or storage of –

        (i) any embryo or human admixed embryo whose creation may be brought about using those gametes or those cells, and

        (ii) any embryo or human admixed embryo whose creation may be brought about using such an embryo or human admixed embryo.

(5) In the case of a consent falling within sub-paragraph (4)(b), the terms of the consent may be varied, or the consent may be withdrawn, in accordance with this Schedule either generally or in relation to –

    (a) a particular embryo or particular embryos, or

    (b) a particular human admixed embryo or particular human admixed embryos.

Procedure for giving consent

3.—(1) Before a person gives consent under this Schedule –

    (a) he must be given a suitable opportunity to receive proper counselling about the implications of taking the proposed steps, and

    (b) he must be provided with such relevant information as is proper.

(2) Before a person gives consent under this Schedule he must be informed of the effect of paragraph 4 and, if relevant, paragraph 4A below.

Variation and withdrawal of consent

4.—(1) The terms of any consent under this Schedule may from time to time be varied, and the consent may be withdrawn, by notice given by the person who gave the consent to the person keeping the gametes, human cells, embryo or human admixed embryo to which the consent is relevant.

(2) Subject to sub-paragraph (3), the terms of any consent to the use of any embryo cannot be varied, and such consent cannot be withdrawn, once the embryo has been used –

(a)   in providing treatment services,

(aa) in training persons in embryo biopsy, embryo storage or other embryological techniques, or

(b)   for the purposes of any project of research.

(3) Where the terms of any consent to the use of an embryo ('embryo A') include consent to the use of an embryo or human admixed embryo whose creation may be brought about *in vitro* using embryo A, that consent to the use of that subsequent embryo or human admixed embryo cannot be varied or withdrawn once embryo A has been used for one or more of the purposes mentioned in subparagraph (2)(a) or (b).

(4) Subject to sub-paragraph (5), the terms of any consent to the use of any human admixed embryo cannot be varied, and such consent cannot be withdrawn, once the human admixed embryo has been used for the purposes of any project of research.

(5) Where the terms of any consent to the use of a human admixed embryo ('human admixed embryo A') include consent to the use of a human admixed embryo or embryo whose creation may be brought about *in vitro* using human admixed embryo A, that consent to the use of that subsequent human admixed embryo or embryo cannot be varied or withdrawn once human admixed embryo A has been used for the purposes of any project of research.

4A.—(1) This paragraph applies where –

(a) a permitted embryo, the creation of which was brought about *in vitro*, is in storage,

(b) it was created for use in providing treatment services,

(c) before it is used in providing treatment services, one of the persons whose gametes were used to bring about its creation ('P') gives the person keeping the embryo notice withdrawing P's consent to the storage of the embryo, and

(d) the embryo was not to be used in providing treatment services to P alone.

(2) The person keeping the embryo must as soon as possible take all reasonable steps to notify each interested person in relation to the embryo of P's withdrawal of consent.

(3) For the purposes of sub-paragraph (2), a person is an interested person in relation to an embryo if the embryo was to be used in providing treatment services to that person.

(4) Storage of the embryo remains lawful until –

(a) the end of the period of 12 months beginning with the day on which the notice mentioned in sub-paragraph (1) was received from P, or

(b) if, before the end of that period, the person keeping the embryo receives a notice from each person notified of P's withdrawal under sub-paragraph (2) stating that the person consents to the destruction of the embryo, the time at which the last of those notices is received.

(5) The reference in sub-paragraph (1)(a) to a permitted embryo is to be read in accordance with section 3ZA.

Use of gametes for treatment of others

5.—(1) A person's gametes must not be used for the purposes of treatment services or non-medical fertility services unless there is an effective consent by that person to their being so used and they are used in accordance with the terms of the consent.

(2) A person's gametes must not be received for use for those purposes unless there is an effective consent by that person to their being so used.

(3) This paragraph does not apply to the use of a person's gametes for the purpose of that person, or that person and another together, receiving treatment services.

In vitro fertilisation and subsequent use of embryo

6.—(1) A person's gametes or human cells must not be used to bring about the creation of any embryo *in vitro* unless there is an effective consent by that person to any embryo, the creation of which may be brought about with the use of those gametes or human cells, being used for one or more of the purposes mentioned in paragraph 2(1)(a), (b) and (c) above.

(2) An embryo the creation of which was brought about *in vitro* must not be received by any person unless there is an effective consent by each relevant person in relation to the embryo to the use for one or more of the purposes mentioned in paragraph 2(1)(a), (b), (ba) and (c) above of the embryo.

(3) An embryo the creation of which was brought about *in vitro* must not be used for any purpose unless there is an effective consent by each relevant person in relation to the embryo to the use for that purpose of the embryo and the embryo is used in accordance with those consents.

(3A) If the Authority is satisfied that the parental consent conditions in paragraph 15 are met in relation to the proposed use under a licence of the human cells of a person who has not attained the age of 18 years ('C'), the Authority may in the licence authorise the application of sub-paragraph (3B) in relation to C.

(3B) Where the licence authorises the application of this sub-paragraph, the effective consent of a person having parental responsibility for C –

(a) to the use of C's human cells to bring about the creation of an embryo *in vitro* for use for the purposes of a project of research, or

(b) to the use for those purposes of an embryo in relation to which C is a relevant person by reason only of the use of C's human cells,

is to be treated for the purposes of sub-paragraphs (1) to (3) as the effective consent of C.

(3C) If C attains the age of 18 years or the condition in paragraph 15(3) ceases to be met in relation to C, paragraph 4 has effect in relation to C as if any effective consent previously given under subparagraphs (1) to (3) by a person having parental responsibility for C had been given by C but, subject to that, sub-paragraph (3B) ceases to apply in relation to C.

(3D) Sub-paragraphs (1) to (3) have effect subject to paragraphs 16 and 20.

(3E) For the purposes of sub-paragraphs (2), (3) and (3B), each of the following is a relevant person in relation to an embryo the creation of which was brought about *in vitro* ('embryo A') –

(a) each person whose gametes or human cells were used to bring about the creation of embryo A,

(b) each person whose gametes or human cells were used to bring about the creation of any other embryo, the creation of which was brought about *in vitro*, which was used to bring about the creation of embryo A, and

(c) each person whose gametes or human cells were used to bring about the creation of any human admixed embryo, the creation of which was brought about *in vitro*, which was used to bring about the creation of embryo A.

(4) Any consent required by this paragraph is in addition to any consent that may be required by paragraph 5 above.

Embryos obtained by lavage, etc.

7.—(1) An embryo taken from a woman must not be used for any purpose unless there is an effective consent by her to the use of the embryo for that purpose and it is used in accordance with the consent.

(2) An embryo taken from a woman must not be received by any person for use for any purpose unless there is an effective consent by her to the use of the embryo for that purpose.

(3) Sub-paragraphs (1) and (2) do not apply to the use, for the purpose of providing a woman with treatment services, of an embryo taken from her.

(4) An embryo taken from a woman must not be used to bring about the creation of any embryo *in vitro* or any human admixed embryo *in vitro*.

Storage of gametes and embryos

8.—(1) A person's gametes must not be kept in storage unless there is an effective consent by that person to their storage and they are stored in accordance with the consent.

(2) An embryo the creation of which was brought about *in vitro* must not be kept in storage unless there is an effective consent, by each relevant person in relation to the embryo, to the storage of the embryo and the embryo is stored in accordance with those consents.

(2A) Where a licence authorises the application of paragraph 6(3B) in relation to a person who has not attained the age of 18 years ('C'), the effective consent of a person having parental responsibility for C to the storage of an embryo in relation to which C is a relevant person by reason only of the use of C's human cells is to be treated for the purposes of sub-paragraph (2) as the effective consent of C.

(2B) If C attains the age of 18 years or the condition in paragraph 15(3) ceases to be met in relation to C, paragraph 4 has effect in relation to C as if any effective consent previously given under sub-paragraph (2) by a person having parental responsibility for C had been given by C but, subject to that, sub-paragraph (2A) ceases to apply in relation to C.

(2C) For the purposes of sub-paragraphs (2) and (2A), each of the following is a relevant person in relation to an embryo the creation of which was brought about *in vitro* ('embryo A') –

   (a) each person whose gametes or human cells were used to bring about the creation of embryo A,
   (b) each person whose gametes or human cells were used to bring about the creation of any other embryo, the creation of which was brought about *in vitro*, which was used to bring about the creation of embryo A, and
   (c) each person whose gametes or human cells were used to bring about the creation of any human admixed embryo, the creation of which was brought about *in vitro*, which was used to bring about the creation of embryo A.

(3) An embryo taken from a woman must not be kept in storage unless there is an effective consent by her to its storage and it is stored in accordance with the consent.

(4) Sub-paragraph (1) has effect subject to paragraphs 9 and 10; and sub-paragraph (2) has effect subject to paragraphs 4A(4), 16 and 20.

Cases where consent is not required for storage

9.—(1) The gametes of a person ('C') may be kept in storage without C's consent if the following conditions are met.

(2) Condition A is that the gametes are lawfully taken from or provided by C before C attains the age of 18 years.

(3) Condition B is that, before the gametes are first stored, a registered medical practitioner certifies in writing that C is expected to undergo medical treatment and that in the opinion of the registered medical practitioner –

   (a) the treatment is likely to cause a significant impairment of C's fertility, and
   (b) the storage of the gametes is in C's best interests.

(4) Condition C is that, at the time when the gametes are first stored, either –

   (a) C has not attained the age of 16 years and is not competent to deal with the issue of consent to the storage of the gametes, or
   (b) C has attained that age but, although not lacking capacity to consent to the storage of the gametes, is not competent to deal with the issue of consent to their storage.

(5) Condition D is that C has not, since becoming competent to deal with the issue of consent to the storage of the gametes –

   (a) given consent under this Schedule to the storage of the gametes, or

(b) given written notice to the person keeping the gametes that C does not wish them to continue to be stored.

10.—(1) The gametes of a person ('P') may be kept in storage without P's consent if the following conditions are met.

(2) Condition A is that the gametes are lawfully taken from or provided by P after P has attained the age of 16 years.

(3) Condition B is that, before the gametes are first stored, a registered medical practitioner certifies in writing that P is expected to undergo medical treatment and that in the opinion of the registered medical practitioner –

(a) the treatment is likely to cause a significant impairment of P's fertility,

(b) P lacks capacity to consent to the storage of the gametes,

(c) P is likely at some time to have that capacity, and

(d) the storage of the gametes is in P's best interests.

(4) Condition C is that, at the time when the gametes are first stored, P lacks capacity to consent to their storage.

(5) Condition D is that P has not subsequently, at a time when P has capacity to give a consent under this Schedule –

(a) given consent to the storage of the gametes, or

(b) given written notice to the person keeping the gametes that P does not wish them to continue to be stored.

11.—A person's gametes must not be kept in storage by virtue of paragraph 9 or 10 after the person's death.

Creation, use and storage of human admixed embryos

12.—(1) A person's gametes or human cells must not be used to bring about the creation of any human admixed embryo *in vitro* unless there is an effective consent by that person to any human admixed embryo, the creation of which may be brought about with the use of those gametes or human cells, being used for the purposes of any project of research.

(2) A human admixed embryo the creation of which was brought about *in vitro* must not be received by any person unless there is an effective consent by each relevant person in relation to the human admixed embryo to the use of the human admixed embryo for the purposes of any project of research.

(3) A human admixed embryo the creation of which was brought about *in vitro* must not be used for the purposes of a project of research unless –

(a) there is an effective consent by each relevant person in relation to the human admixed embryo to the use of the human admixed embryo for that purpose, and

(b) the human admixed embryo is used in accordance with those consents.

(4) If the Authority is satisfied that the parental consent conditions in paragraph 15 are met in relation to the proposed use under a licence of the human cells of a person who has not attained the age of 18 years ('C'), the Authority may in the licence authorise the application of sub-paragraph (5) in relation to C.

(5) Where the licence authorises the application of this sub-paragraph, the effective consent of a person having parental responsibility for C –

(a) to the use of C's human cells to bring about the creation of a human admixed embryo *in vitro* for use for the purposes of a project of research, or

(b) to the use for those purposes of a human admixed embryo in relation to which C is a relevant person by reason only of the use of C's human cells,

is to be treated for the purposes of sub-paragraphs (1) to (3) as the effective consent of C.

(6) If C attains the age of 18 years or the condition in paragraph 15(3) ceases to be met in relation to C, paragraph 4 has effect in relation to C as if any effective consent previously given under subparagraphs (1) to (3) by a person having parental responsibility for C had been given by C but, subject to that, sub-paragraph (5) ceases to apply in relation to C.

(7) Sub-paragraphs (1) to (3) have effect subject to paragraphs 16 and 20.

13.—(1) A human admixed embryo the creation of which was brought about *in vitro* must not be kept in storage unless –

    (a) there is an effective consent by each relevant person in relation to the human admixed embryo to the storage of the human admixed embryo, and

    (b) the human admixed embryo is stored in accordance with those consents.

(2) Where a licence authorises the application of paragraph 12(5) in relation to a person who has not attained the age of 18 years ('C'), the effective consent of a person having parental responsibility for C to the storage of a human admixed embryo in relation to which C is a relevant person by reason only of the use of C's human cells is to be treated for the purposes of sub-paragraph (1) as the effective consent of C.

(3) If C attains the age of 18 years or the condition in paragraph 15(3) ceases to be met in relation to C, paragraph 4 has effect in relation to C as if any effective consent previously given under sub-paragraph (1) by a person having parental responsibility for C had been given by C but, subject to that, sub-paragraph (2) ceases to apply in relation to C.

(4) Sub-paragraph (1) has effect subject to paragraphs 16 and 20.

14.—For the purposes of paragraphs 12 and 13, each of the following is a relevant person in relation to a human admixed embryo the creation of which was brought about *in vitro* ('human admixed embryo A') –

    (a) each person whose gametes or human cells were used to bring about the creation of human admixed embryo A,

    (b) each person whose gametes or human cells were used to bring about the creation of any embryo, the creation of which was brought about *in vitro*, which was used to bring about the creation of human admixed embryo A, and

    (c) each person whose gametes or human cells were used to bring about the creation of any other human admixed embryo, the creation of which was brought about *in vitro*, which was used to bring about the creation of human admixed embryo A.

Parental consent conditions

15.—(1) In relation to a person who has not attained the age of 18 years ('C'), the parental consent conditions referred to in paragraphs 6(3A) and 12(4) are as follows.

(2) Condition A is that C suffers from, or is likely to develop, a serious disease, a serious physical or mental disability or any other serious medical condition.

(3) Condition B is that either –

    (a) C is not competent to deal with the issue of consent to the use of C's human cells to bring about the creation *in vitro* of an embryo or human admixed embryo for use for the purposes of a project of research, or

    (b) C has attained the age of 16 years but lacks capacity to consent to such use of C's human cells.

(4) Condition C is that any embryo or human admixed embryo to be created *in vitro* is to be used for the purposes of a project of research which is intended to increase knowledge about –

    (a) the disease, disability or medical condition mentioned in sub-paragraph (2) or any similar disease, disability or medical condition, or

    (b) the treatment of, or care of persons affected by, that disease, disability or medical condition or any similar disease, disability or medical condition.

(5) Condition D is that there are reasonable grounds for believing that research of comparable effectiveness cannot be carried out if the only human cells that can be used to bring about the creation *in vitro* of embryos or human admixed embryos for use for the purposes of the project are the human cells of persons who –

    (a) have attained the age of 18 years and have capacity to consent to the use of their human cells to bring about the creation *in vitro* of an embryo or human admixed embryo for use for the purposes of the project, or

(b) have not attained that age but are competent to deal with the issue of consent to such use of their human cells.

Adults lacking capacity: exemption relating to use of human cells etc.

16.—(1) If, in relation to the proposed use under a licence of the human cells of a person who has attained the age of 18 years ('P'), the Authority is satisfied –

(a) that the conditions in paragraph 17 are met,

(b) that paragraphs (1) to (4) of paragraph 18 have been complied with, and

(c) that the condition in paragraph 18(5) is met,

the Authority may in the licence authorise the application of this paragraph in relation to P.

(2) Where a licence authorises the application of this paragraph, this Schedule does not require the consent of P –

(a) to the use (whether during P's life or after P's death) of P's human cells to bring about the creation *in vitro* of an embryo or human admixed embryo for use for the purposes of a project of research,

(b) to the storage or the use for those purposes (whether during P's life or after P's death) of an embryo or human admixed embryo in relation to which P is a relevant person by reason only of the use of P's human cells.

(3) This paragraph has effect subject to paragraph 19.

Consent to use of human cells etc. not required: adult lacking capacity

17.—(1) The conditions referred to in paragraph 16(1)(a) are as follows.

(2) Condition A is that P suffers from, or is likely to develop, a serious disease, a serious physical or mental disability or any other serious medical condition.

(3) Condition B is that P lacks capacity to consent to the use of P's human cells to bring about the creation *in vitro* of an embryo or human admixed embryo for use for the purposes of a project of research.

(4) Condition C is that the person responsible under the licence has no reason to believe that P had refused such consent at a time when P had that capacity.

(5) Condition D is that it appears unlikely that P will at some time have that capacity.

(6) Condition E is that any embryo or human admixed embryo to be created *in vitro* is to be used for the purposes of a project of research which is intended to increase knowledge about –

(a) the disease, disability or medical condition mentioned in sub-paragraph (2) or any similar disease, disability or medical condition, or

(b) the treatment of, or care of persons affected by, that disease, disability or medical condition or any similar disease, disability or medical condition.

(7) Condition F is that there are reasonable grounds for believing that research of comparable effectiveness cannot be carried out if the only human cells that can be used to bring about the creation *in vitro* of embryos or human admixed embryos for use for the purposes of the project are the human cells of persons who –

(a) have attained the age of 18 years and have capacity to consent to the use of their human cells to bring about the creation *in vitro* of an embryo or human admixed embryo for use for the purposes of the project, or

(b) have not attained that age but are competent to deal with the issue of consent to such use of their human cells.

(8) In this paragraph and paragraph 18 references to the person responsible under the licence are to be read, in a case where an application for a licence is being made, as references to the person who is to be the person responsible.

Consulting carers etc. in case of adult lacking capacity

18.—(1) This paragraph applies in relation to a person who has attained the age of 18 years ('P') where the person responsible under the licence ('R') wishes to use P's human cells to bring about the creation *in vitro* of an embryo or human admixed embryo for use for the purposes of a project of research, in a case where P lacks capacity to consent to their use.

(2) R must take reasonable steps to identify a person who –

    (a) otherwise than in a professional capacity or for remuneration, is engaged in caring for P or is interested in P's welfare, and

    (b) is prepared to be consulted by R under this paragraph of this Schedule.

(3) If R is unable to identify such a person R must nominate a person who –

    (a) is prepared to be consulted by R under this paragraph of this Schedule, but

    (b) has no connection with the project.

(4) R must provide the person identified under sub-paragraph (2) or nominated under sub-paragraph (3) ('F') with information about the proposed use of human cells to bring about the creation *in vitro* of embryos or human admixed embryos for use for the purposes of the project and ask F what, in F's opinion, P's wishes and feelings about the use of P's human cells for that purpose would be likely to be if P had capacity in relation to the matter.

(5) The condition referred to in paragraph 16(1)(c) is that, on being consulted, F has not advised R that in F's opinion P's wishes and feelings would be likely to lead P to decline to consent to the use of P's human cells for that purpose.

Effect of acquiring capacity

19.—(1) Paragraph 16 does not apply to the use of P's human cells to bring about the creation *in vitro* of an embryo or human admixed embryo if, at a time before the human cells are used for that purpose, P –

    (a) has capacity to consent to their use, and

    (b) gives written notice to the person keeping the human cells that P does not wish them to be used for that purpose.

(2) Paragraph 16 does not apply to the storage or use of an embryo or human admixed embryo whose creation *in vitro* was brought about with the use of P's human cells if, at a time before the embryo or human admixed embryo is used for the purposes of the project of research, P –

    (a) has capacity to consent to the storage or use, and

    (b) gives written notice to the person keeping the human cells that P does not wish them to be used for that purpose.

Use of cells or cell lines in existence before relevant commencement date

20.—(1) Where a licence authorises the application of this paragraph in relation to qualifying cells, this Schedule does not require the consent of a person ('P') –

    (a) to the use of qualifying cells of P to bring about the creation *in vitro* of an embryo or human admixed embryo for use for the purposes of a project of research, or

    (b) to the storage or the use for those purposes of an embryo or human admixed embryo in relation to which P is a relevant person by reason only of the use of qualifying cells of P.

(2) 'Qualifying cells' are human cells which –

    (a) were lawfully stored for research purposes immediately before the commencement date, or

    (b) are derived from human cells which were lawfully stored for those purposes at that time.

(3) The 'commencement date' is the date on which paragraph 9(2)(a) of Schedule 3 to the Human Fertilisation and Embryology Act 2008 (requirement for consent to use of human cells to create an embryo) comes into force.

Conditions for grant of exemption in paragraph 20

21.—(1) A licence may not authorise the application of paragraph 20 unless the Authority is satisfied –

    (a) that there are reasonable grounds for believing that scientific research will be adversely affected to a significant extent if the only human cells that can be used to bring about the creation *in vitro* of embryos or human admixed embryos for use for the purposes of the project of research are –

    (i)   human cells in respect of which there is an effective consent to their use to bring about the creation *in vitro* of embryos or human admixed embryos for use for those purposes, or

    (ii) human cells which by virtue of paragraph 16 can be used without such consent, and

  (b) that any of the following conditions is met in relation to each of the persons whose human cells are qualifying cells which are to be used for the purposes of the project of research.

(2) Condition A is that –

  (a) it is not reasonably possible for the person responsible under the licence ('R') to identify the person falling within sub-paragraph (1)(b) ('P'), and

  (b) where any information that relates to P (without identifying P or enabling P to be identified) is available to R, that information does not suggest that P would have objected to the use of P's human cells to bring about the creation *in vitro* of an embryo or human admixed embryo for use for the purposes of the project.

(3) Condition B is that –

  (a) the person falling within sub-paragraph (1)(b) ('P') is dead or the person responsible under the licence ('R') believes on reasonable grounds that P is dead,

  (b) the information relating to P that is available to R does not suggest that P would have objected to the use of P's human cells to bring about the creation *in vitro* of an embryo or human admixed embryo for use for the purposes of the project, and

  (c) a person who stood in a qualifying relationship to P immediately before P died (or is believed to have died) has given consent in writing to the use of P's human cells to bring about the creation *in vitro* of an embryo or human admixed embryo for use for the purposes of the project.

(4) Condition C is that –

  (a) the person responsible under the licence ('R') has taken all reasonable steps to contact –

    (i)   the person falling within sub-paragraph (1)(b) ('P'), or

    (ii) in a case where P is dead or R believes on reasonable grounds that P is dead, persons who could give consent for the purposes of sub-paragraph (3)(c), but has been unable to do so, and

  (b) the information relating to P that is available to R does not suggest that P would have objected to the use of P's human cells to bring about the creation *in vitro* of an embryo or human admixed embryo for use for the purposes of the project.

(5) The HTA consent provisions apply in relation to consent for the purposes of sub-paragraph (3)(c) as they apply in relation to consent for the purposes of section 3(6)(c) of the Human Tissue Act 2004; and for the purposes of this sub-paragraph the HTA consent provisions are to be treated as if they extended to Scotland.

(6) In sub-paragraph (5) 'the HTA consent provisions' means subsections (4), (5), (6), (7) and (8)(a) and (b) of section 27 of the Human Tissue Act 2004.

(7) In this paragraph references to the person responsible under the licence are to be read, in a case where an application for a licence is being made, as references to the person who is to be the person responsible.

(8) Paragraphs 1 to 4 of this Schedule do not apply in relation to a consent given for the purposes of sub-paragraph (3)(c).

Interpretation

22.—(1) In this Schedule references to human cells are to human cells which are not –

  (a) cells of the female or male germ line, or

  (b) cells of an embryo.

(2) References in this Schedule to an embryo or a human admixed embryo which was used to bring about the creation of an embryo ('embryo A') or a human admixed embryo ('human admixed embryo A') include an embryo or, as the case may be, a human admixed embryo which was used to bring about the creation of –

    (a) an embryo or human admixed embryo which was used to bring about the creation of embryo A or human admixed embryo A, and

    (b) the predecessor of that embryo or human admixed embryo mentioned in paragraph (a), and

    (c) the predecessor of that predecessor, and so on.

(3) References in this Schedule to an embryo or a human admixed embryo whose creation may be brought about using an embryo or a human admixed embryo are to be read in accordance with sub-paragraph (2).

(4) References in this Schedule (however expressed) to the use of human cells to bring about the creation of an embryo or a human admixed embryo include the use of human cells to alter the embryo or, as the case may be, the human admixed embryo.

(5) References in this Schedule to parental responsibility are –

    (a) in relation to England and Wales, to be read in accordance with the Children Act 1989,

(6) References in this Schedule to capacity are, in relation to England and Wales, to be read in accordance with the Mental Capacity Act 2005.

SCHEDULE 3ZA CIRCUMSTANCES IN WHICH OFFER OF COUNSELLING REQUIRED AS CONDITION OF LICENCE FOR TREATMENT

PART 1 KINDS OF TREATMENT IN RELATION TO WHICH COUNSELLING MUST BE OFFERED

1. The treatment services involve the use of the gametes of any person and that person's consent is required under paragraph 5 of Schedule 3 for the use in question.

2. The treatment services involve the use of any embryo the creation of which was brought about *in vitro*.

3. The treatment services involve the use of an embryo taken from a woman and the consent of the woman from whom the embryo was taken was required under paragraph 7 of Schedule 3 for the use in question.

PART 2 EVENTS IN CONNECTION WITH WHICH COUNSELLING MUST BE OFFERED

4. A man gives the person responsible a notice under paragraph (a) of subsection (1) of section 37 of the Human Fertilisation and Embryology Act 2008 (agreed fatherhood conditions) in a case where the woman for whom the treatment services are provided has previously given a notice under paragraph (b) of that subsection referring to the man.

5. The woman for whom the treatment services are provided gives the person responsible a notice under paragraph (b) of that subsection in a case where the man to whom the notice relates has previously given a notice under paragraph (a) of that subsection.

6. A woman gives the person responsible notice under paragraph (a) of subsection (1) of section 44 of that Act (agreed female parenthood conditions) in a case where the woman for whom the treatment services are provided has previously given a notice under paragraph (b) of that subsection referring to her.

7. The woman for whom the treatment services are provided gives the person responsible a notice under paragraph (b) of that subsection in a case where the other woman to whom the notice relates has previously given a notice under paragraph (a) of that subsection.

Health Service Commissioners Act 1993

(1993, c. 46)

Health Service Commissioner

1   The Commissioner

(1) For the purpose of conducting investigations in accordance with this Act, there shall continue to be –

(a) a Health Service Commissioner for England.

Health service bodies subject to investigation

2   The bodies subject to investigation

(1) The bodies subject to investigation by the Commissioner are –

(c) Special Health Authorities to which this section applies not exercising functions only or mainly in Wales,

(d) National Health Service trusts managing a hospital, or other establishment or facility, in England,

(db)   NHS foundation trusts,

(dc)   the National Health Service Commissioning Board,

(dd)   clinical commissioning groups.

Persons subject to investigation

2A   Health service providers subject to investigation

(1) Persons are subject to investigation by the Commissioner if they are or were at the time of the action complained of –

(a) persons (whether individuals or bodies) providing services under a contract entered into by them with the National Health Service Commissioning Board under section 84, 100 or 117 of the National Health Service Act 2006;

(b) persons (whether individuals or bodies) undertaking to provide in England pharmaceutical services under that Act; or

(c) individuals performing in England primary medical services or primary dental services in accordance with arrangements made under section 92 or 107 of that Act (except as employees of, or otherwise on behalf of, a health service body or an independent provider).

(4) In this Act –

(a) references to a family health service provider are to any person mentioned in subsection (1);

(b) references to family health services are to any of the services so mentioned.

2B   Independent providers subject to investigation

(1) Persons are subject to investigation by the Commissioner if –

(a) they are or were at the time of the action complained of persons (whether individuals or bodies) providing services in England under arrangements with health service bodies or family health service providers, and

(b) they are not or were not at the time of the action complained of themselves health service bodies or family health service providers.

(4) The services provided under arrangements mentioned in subsection (1)(a) may be services of any kind.

(5) In this Act references to an independent provider are to any person providing services as mentioned in subsection (1).

Matters subject to investigation

3 General remit of Commissioner

(1) On a complaint duly made to the Commissioner by or on behalf of a person that he has sustained injustice or hardship in consequence of –

    (a) a failure in a service provided by a health service body,

    (b) a failure of such a body to provide a service which it was a function of the body to provide, or

    (c) maladministration connected with any other action taken by or on behalf of such a body,

the Commissioner may, subject to the provisions of this Act, investigate the alleged failure or other action.

(1A) Where a family health service provider has undertaken to provide any family health services and a complaint is duly made to the Commissioner by or on behalf of a person that he has sustained injustice or hardship in consequence of –

    (a) action taken by the family health service provider in connection with the services,

    (b) action taken in connection with the services by a person employed by the family health service provider in respect of the services,

    (c) action taken in connection with the services by a person acting on behalf of the family health service provider in respect of the services, or

    (d) action taken in connection with the services by a person to whom the family health service provider has delegated any functions in respect of the services,

the Commissioner may, subject to the provisions of this Act, investigate the alleged action.

(1C) Where an independent provider has made an arrangement with a health service body or a family health service provider to provide a service (of whatever kind) and a complaint is duly made to the Commissioner by or on behalf of a person that he has sustained injustice or hardship in consequence of –

    (a) a failure in the service provided by the independent provider,

    (b) a failure of the independent provider to provide the service, or

    (c) maladministration connected with any other action taken in relation to the service,

the Commissioner may, subject to the provisions of this Act, investigate the alleged failure or other action.

(1D) Any failure or maladministration mentioned in subsection (1C) may arise from action of –

    (a) the independent provider,

    (b) a person employed by the provider,

    (c) a person acting on behalf of the provider, or

    (d) a person to whom the provider has delegated any functions.

(1E) Where a complaint is duly made to the Commissioner by or on behalf of a person that the person has sustained injustice or hardship in consequence of maladministration by any person or body in the exercise of any function under section 113 of the Health and Social Care (Community Health and Standards) Act 2003 (complaints about health care), the Commissioner may, subject to the provisions of this Act, investigate the alleged maladministration.

(2) In determining whether to initiate, continue or discontinue an investigation under this Act, the Commissioner shall act in accordance with his own discretion.

(3) Any question whether a complaint is duly made to the Commissioner shall be determined by him.

(4) Nothing in this Act authorises or requires the Commissioner to question the merits of a decision taken without maladministration by a health service body in the exercise of a discretion vested in that body.

(5) Nothing in this Act authorises or requires the Commissioner to question the merits of a decision taken without maladministration by –

    (a) a family health service provider,

    (b) a person employed by a family health service provider,

    (c) a person acting on behalf of a family health service provider, or

    (d) a person to whom a family health service provider has delegated any functions.

(6) Nothing in this Act authorises or requires the Commissioner to question the merits of a decision taken without maladministration by –

    (a) an independent provider,

    (b) a person employed by an independent provider,

    (c) a person acting on behalf of an independent provider, or

    (d) a person to whom an independent provider has delegated any functions.

(7) Subsections (4) to (6) do not apply to the merits of a decision to the extent that it was taken in consequence of the exercise of clinical judgment.

Matters excluded from investigation

4 Availability of other remedy

(1) The Commissioner shall not conduct an investigation in respect of action in relation to which the person aggrieved has or had –

    (a) a right of appeal, reference or review to or before a tribunal constituted by or under any enactment or by virtue of Her Majesty's prerogative, or

    (b) a remedy by way of proceedings in any court of law,

unless the Commissioner is satisfied that in the particular circumstances it is not reasonable to expect that person to resort or have resorted to it.

(2) The Commissioner shall not conduct an investigation in respect of action which has been, or is, the subject of an inquiry under section 84 of the National Health Service Act 1977.

(4) Subsection (5) applies where –

    (a) action by reference to which a complaint is made under section 3(1), (1A), (1C) or (1F)(a) or (b) is action by reference to which a complaint can be made under section 113(1) or (2) of the Health and Social Care (Community Health and Standards) Act 2003 under section 14 of the NHS Redress Act 2006 or under a procedure operated by a health service body, a family health service provider or an independent provider, and

    (b) subsection (1), (2) or (3) does not apply as regards the action.

(5) In such a case the Commissioner shall not conduct an investigation in respect of the action unless he is satisfied that –

    (a) the other procedure has been invoked and exhausted, or

    (b) in the particular circumstances it is not reasonable to expect that procedure to be invoked or (as the case may be) exhausted.

6 General health services and service committees

(3) The Commissioner shall not conduct an investigation in respect of action taken by a Primary Care Trust or Health Authority in the exercise of its functions under the National Health Service (Service Committees and Tribunal) Regulations 1992, or any instrument amending or replacing those regulations.

(5) The Commissioner shall not conduct an investigation in respect of action taken by a Primary Care Trust or Health Authority in the exercise of its functions under regulations made under section 126 or 129 of the National Health Service Act 2006 by virtue of section 17 of the Health and Medicines Act 1988 (investigations of matters relating to services).

7 Personnel, contracts etc.

(1) The Commissioner shall not conduct an investigation in respect of action taken in respect of appointments or removals, pay, discipline, superannuation or other personnel matters in

relation to service under the National Health Service Act 2006 or the National Health Service (Wales) Act 2006.

(2) The Commissioner shall not conduct an investigation in respect of action taken in matters relating to contractual or other commercial transactions, except for –

(a) matters relating to NHS contracts (as defined by section 9 of the National Health Service Act 2006),

(b) matters arising from arrangements between a health service body and an independent provider for the provision of services by the provider,

(c) matters arising from arrangements between a family health service provider and an independent provider for the provision of services by the independent provider and,

(d) matters arising from settlement agreements entered into under a scheme established under section 1 of the NHS Redress Act 2006.

(3A) The Commissioner shall not conduct an investigation in pursuance of a complaint if –

(a) the complaint is in respect of action taken in any matter relating to arrangements made by a health service body and a family health service provider for the provision of family health services,

(b) the action is taken by or on behalf of the body or by the provider, and

(c) the complaint is made by the provider or the body.

(3B) Nothing in the preceding provisions of this section prevents the Commissioner conducting an investigation in respect of action taken by a health service body in operating a procedure established to examine complaint.

Complaints

8   Individuals or bodies entitled to complain

(1) A complaint under this Act may be made by an individual or a body of persons, whether incorporated or not, other than a public authority.

9   Requirements to be complied with

(1) The following requirements apply in relation to a complaint, made to the Commissioner.

(2) A complaint must be made in writing.

(3) The complaint shall not be entertained unless it is made –

(a) by the person aggrieved, or

(b) where the person by whom a complaint might have been made has died or is for any reason unable to act for himself, by –

(i)   his personal representative,

(ii) a member of his family, or

(iii) some body or individual suitable to represent him.

(4) The Commissioner shall not entertain the complaint if it is made more than a year after the day on which the person aggrieved first had notice of the matters alleged in the complaint, unless he considers it reasonable to do so.

(4A) In the case of a complaint against a person who is no longer of a description set out in section 2A(1) or (2), but was of such a description at the time of the action complained of, the Commissioner shall not entertain the complaint if it is made more than three years after the last day on which the person was a family health service provider.

(4B) In the case of a complaint against a person falling within section 2B(1) or (2) in relation to whom there are no longer any such arrangements as are mentioned there, the Commissioner shall not entertain the complaint if it is made more than three years after the last day on which the person was an independent provider.

10   Referral of complaint by health service body

(1) A health service body may itself refer to the Commissioner a complaint made to that body that a person has, in consequence of a failure or maladministration for which the body is responsible, sustained such injustice or hardship as is mentioned in section 3(1).

(2) A complaint may not be so referred unless it was made –
    (a) in writing,
    (b) by the person aggrieved or by a person authorised by section 9(3)(b) to complain to the Commissioner on his behalf, and
    (c) not more than a year after the person aggrieved first had notice of the matters alleged in the complaint, or such later date as the Commissioner considers appropriate in any particular case.

(3) A health service body may not refer a complaint under this section after the period of one year beginning with the day on which the body received the complaint.

(4) Any question whether a complaint has been duly referred to the Commissioner under this section shall be determined by him.

(5) A complaint referred to the Commissioner under this section shall be deemed to be duly made to him.

Investigations

11 Procedure in respect of investigations

(1) Where the Commissioner proposes to conduct an investigation pursuant to a complaint under section 3(1), he shall afford –
    (a) to the health service body concerned, and
    (b) to any other person who is alleged in the complaint to have taken or authorised the action complained of,
an opportunity to comment on any allegations contained in the complaint.

(1A) Where the Commissioner proposes to conduct an investigation pursuant to a complaint under section 3(1A), he shall afford –
    (a) to the family health service provider, and
    (b) to any person by reference to whose action the complaint is made (if different from the family health service provider),
an opportunity to comment on any allegations contained in the complaint.

(1B) Where the Commissioner proposes to conduct an investigation pursuant to a complaint under section 3(1C) he shall afford –
    (a) to the independent provider concerned, and
    (b) to any other person who is alleged in the complaint to have taken or authorised the action complained of,
an opportunity to comment on any allegations contained in the complaint.

(1C) Where the Commissioner proposes to conduct an investigation pursuant to a complaint under section 3(1E) or (1F), he shall afford to the person or body whose maladministration is complained of an opportunity to comment on any allegations contained in the complaint.

(2) An investigation shall be conducted in private.

(3) In other respects, the procedure for conducting an investigation shall be such as the Commissioner considers appropriate in the circumstances of the case, and in particular –
    (a) he may obtain information from such persons and in such manner, and make such inquiries, as he thinks fit, and
    (b) he may determine whether any person may be represented, by counsel or solicitor or otherwise, in the investigation.

(5) The conduct of an investigation pursuant to a complaint under section 3(1) shall not affect any action taken by the health service body concerned, or any power or duty of that body to take further action with respect to any matters subject to the investigation.

(5A) The conduct of an investigation pursuant to a complaint under section 3(1A) or (1C) shall not affect any action taken by the family health service provider or independent provider concerned, or any power or duty of that provider to take further action with respect to any matters subject to the investigation.

12   Evidence

(1) For the purposes of an investigation pursuant to a complaint under section 3(1) the Commissioner may require any officer or member of the health service body concerned or any other person who in his opinion is able to supply information or produce documents relevant to the investigation to supply any such information or Produce any such document.

(1A) For the purposes of an investigation pursuant to a complaint under section 3(1A) or (1C), (1E) or (1F) the Commissioner may require any person who in his opinion is able to supply information or produce documents relevant to the investigation to supply any such information or produce any such document.

(2) For the purposes of an investigation the Commissioner shall have the same powers as the Court in respect of –
- (a) the attendance and examination of witnesses (including the administration of oaths and affirmations and the examination of witnesses abroad), and
- (b) the production of documents.

(3) No obligation to maintain secrecy or other restriction on the disclosure of information obtained by or supplied to persons in Her Majesty's service, whether imposed by any enactment or by any rule of law, shall apply to the disclosure of information for the purposes of an investigation.

(4) The Crown shall not be entitled in relation to an investigation to any such privilege in respect of the production of documents or the giving of evidence as is allowed by law in legal proceedings.

(6) Subject to subsections (3) and (4), no person shall be compelled for the purposes of an investigation to give any evidence or produce any document which he could not be compelled to give or produce in civil proceedings before the Court.

13   Obstruction and contempt

(1) The Commissioner may certify an offence to the Court where –
- (a) a person without lawful excuse obstructs him or any of his officers in the performance of his functions, or
- (b) a person is guilty of any act or omission in relation to an investigation which, if that investigation were a proceeding in the Court, would constitute contempt of court.

(2) Where an offence is so certified the Court may inquire into the matter and after hearing –
- (a) any witnesses who may be produced against or on behalf of the person charged with the offence, and
- (b) any statement that may be offered in defence,

the Court may deal with the person charged with the offence in any manner in which it could deal with him if he had committed the like offence in relation to the Court.

(3) Nothing in this section shall be construed as applying to the taking of any such action as is mentioned in section 11(5).

Reports

14   Reports by the Commissioner

(1) In any case where the Commissioner conducts an investigation pursuant to a complaint under section 3(1) he shall send a report of the results of the investigation –
- (a) to the person who made the complaint,
- (b) to any member of the House of Commons who to the Commissioner's knowledge assisted in the making of the complaint (or if he is no longer a member to such other member as the Commissioner thinks appropriate),
- (c) to the health service body who at the time the report is made provides the service, or has the function, in relation to which the complaint was made,
- (d) to any person who is alleged in the complaint to have taken or authorised the action complained of, and
- (e) to the Secretary of State,

(2) In any case pursuant to a complaint under section 3(1) where the Commissioner decides not to conduct an investigation pursuant to a complaint under section 3(1) he shall send a statement of his reasons –

    (a) to the person who made the complaint,

    (b) to any such member of the House of Commons as is mentioned in subsection (1)(b), and

(2A) In any case where the Commissioner conducts an investigation pursuant to a complaint under section 3(1A) he shall send a report of the results of the investigation –

    (a) to the person who made the complaint,

    (b) to any member of the House of Commons who to the Commissioner's knowledge assisted in the making of the complaint (or if he is no longer a member to such other member as the Commissioner thinks appropriate),

    (c) to any person by reference to whose action the complaint is made,

    (d) to the family health service provider (if he does not fall within paragraph (c)),

    (e) to any health service body with whom the family health service provider is subject to an undertaking to provide family health services, and

    (f) to the Secretary of State.

(2B) In any case where the Commissioner decides not to conduct an investigation pursuant to a complaint under section 3(1A) he shall send a statement of his reasons –

    (a) to the person who made the complaint, and

    (b) to any such member of the House of Commons as is mentioned in subsection (2A)(b).

(2C) In any case where the Commissioner conducts an investigation pursuant to a complaint under section 3(1C) he shall send a report of the results of the investigation –

    (a) to the person who made the complaint,

    (b) to any member of the House of Commons who to the Commissioner's knowledge assisted in the making of the complaint (or if he is no longer a member to such other member as the Commissioner thinks appropriate),

    (c) to any person who is alleged in the complaint to have taken or authorised the action complained of,

    (d) to the independent provider,

    (e) to the health service body or family health service provider with whom the independent provider made the arrangement to provide the service concerned, and

    (f) to the Secretary of State.

(2D) In any case where the Commissioner decides not to conduct an investigation pursuant to a complaint under section 3(1C) he shall send a statement of his reasons –

    (a) to the person who made the complaint, and

    (b) to any such member of the House of Commons as is mentioned in subsection (2C)(b).

(2E) In any case where the Commissioner conducts an investigation pursuant to a complaint under section 3(1E) he shall send a report of the results of the investigation –

    (a) to the person who made the complaint;

    (b) to any member of the House of Commons who to the Commissioner's knowledge assisted in the making of the complaint (or if he is no longer a member to such other member as the Commissioner thinks appropriate);

    (c) to the person or body whose maladministration is complained of;

    (d) to any person or body whose action was complained of in the complaint made to the person or body whose maladministration is complained of;

    (e) to the Secretary of State.

(2F) In any case where Commissioner decides not to conduct an investigation pursuant to a complaint under section 3(1E) he shall send a statement of his reasons –

    (a) to the person who made the complaint; or

    (b) to any such member of the House of Commons as is mentioned in subsection (2E)(b).

(2G) In any case where the Commissioner conducts an investigation pursuant to a complaint under section 3(1F) he shall send a report of the results of the investigation –

(a) to the person who made the complaint,

(b) to any member of the House of Commons who to the Commissioner's knowledge assisted in the making of the complaint (or if he is no longer a member to such other member as the Commissioner thinks appropriate),

(c) to the person or body whose maladministration is complained of,

(d) in the case of a complaint under section 3(1F)(c), to any person or body whose action was complained of in the complaint made to the person or body whose maladministration is complained of, and

(e) to the Secretary of State.

(2H) In any case where the Commissioner decides not to conduct an investigation pursuant to a complaint under section 3(1F) he shall send a statement of his reasons –

(a) to the person who made the complaint, and

(b) to any such member of the House of Commons as is mentioned in subsection (2G)(b).

(2HA) Where the Commissioner has not concluded an investigation before the end of the 12 month period beginning with the date the complaint was received, the Commissioner must send a statement explaining the reason for the delay to the person who made the complaint.

(3) If after conducting an investigation it appears to the Commissioner that –

(a) the person aggrieved has sustained such injustice or hardship as is mentioned in section 3(1), (1A) or (1C) and

(b) the injustice or hardship has not been and will not be remedied, he may if he thinks fit lay before each House of Parliament a special report on the case.

(4) The Commissioner –

(a) shall annually lay before each House of Parliament a general report on the performance of his functions under this Act, and

(b) may from time to time lay before each House of Parliament such other reports with respect to those functions as he thinks fit.

(4A) The general report laid under subsection (4)(a) must include information about –

(a) how long investigations that were concluded in the year to which the report relates took to be concluded,

(b) how many of those investigations took more than 12 months to be concluded, and

(c) the action being taken with a view to all investigations being concluded within 12 months.

(5) For the purposes of the law of defamation, the publication of any matter by the Commissioner in sending or making a report or statement in pursuance of this section shall be absolutely privileged.

Information and consultation

15   Confidentiality of information

(1) Information obtained by the Commissioner or his officers in the course of or for the purposes of an investigation shall not be disclosed except –

(a) for the purposes of the investigation and any report to be made in respect of it,

(b) for the purposes of any proceedings for –

(i) an offence under the Official Secrets Acts 1911 to 1989 alleged to have been committed in respect of information obtained by virtue of this Act by the Commissioner or any of his officers, or

(ii) an offence of perjury alleged to have been committed in the course of the investigation,

(c) for the purposes of an inquiry with a view to the taking of such proceedings as are mentioned in paragraph (b),

(d) for the purposes of any proceedings under section 13 (offences of obstruction and contempt), or

(e) where the information is to the effect that any person is likely to constitute a threat to the health or safety of patients as permitted by subsection (1B).

(1B) In a case within subsection (1)(e) the Commissioner may disclose the information to any persons to whom he thinks it should be disclosed in the interests of the health and safety of patients.

(1C) If the Commissioner discloses information as permitted by subsection (1B) he shall –

(a) where he knows the identity of the person mentioned in subsection (1)(e), inform that person that he has disclosed the information and of the identity of any person to whom he has disclosed it, and

(b) inform the person from whom the information was obtained that he has disclosed it.

(2) Neither the Commissioner nor his officers nor his advisers shall be called on to give evidence in any proceedings, other than proceedings mentioned in subsection (1), of matters coming to his or their knowledge in the course of an investigation under this Act.

(3) The reference in subsection (2) to a Commissioner's advisers is a reference to persons from whom the Commissioner obtains advice under paragraph 13 of Schedule 1.

(4) Information obtained from the Information Commissioner by virtue of section 76 of the Freedom of Information Act 2000 shall be treated for the purposes of subsection (1) as obtained for the purposes of an investigation and, in relation to such information, the reference in paragraph (a) of that subsection to the investigation shall have effect as a reference to any investigation.

16 Information prejudicial to the safety of the State

(1) A Minister of the Crown may give notice in writing to the Commissioner with respect to any document or information specified in the notice that in the Minister's opinion the disclosure of the document or information would be prejudicial to the safety of the State or otherwise contrary to the public interest.

(5) Where such a notice is given to a Commissioner, nothing in this Act shall be construed as authorising or requiring him or any of his officers to communicate to any person or for any purpose any document or information specified in the notice.

(6) References above to a document or information include references to a class of document or a class of information.

Data Protection Act 1998

(1998, c. 29)

PART I PRELIMINARY

1 Basic interpretative provisions

(1) In this Act, unless the context otherwise requires – 'data' means information which –

(a) is being processed by means of equipment operating automatically in response to instructions given for that purpose,

(b) is recorded with the intention that it should be processed by means of such equipment,

(c) is recorded as part of a relevant filing system or with the intention that it should form part of a relevant filing system,

(d) does not fall within paragraph (a), (b) or (c) but forms part of an accessible record as defined by section 68, or

(e) is recorded information held by a public authority and does not fall within any of the paragraphs (a) to (d);

'data controller' means, subject to subsection (4), a person who (either alone or jointly or in common with other persons) determines the purposes for which and the manner in which any personal data are, or are to be, processed;

'data processor', in relation to personal data, means any person (other than an employee of the data controller) who processes the data on behalf of the data controller;

'data subject' means an individual who is the subject of personal data;

'personal data' means data which relate to a living individual who can be identified –

(a) from those data, or

(b) from those data and other information which is in the possession of, or is likely to come into the possession of, the data controller,

and includes any expression of opinion about the individual and any indication of the intentions of the data controller or any other person in respect of the individual;

'processing', in relation to information or data, means obtaining, recording or holding the information or data or carrying out any operation or set of operations on the information or data, including –

(a) organisation, adaptation or alteration of the information or data,

(b) retrieval, consultation or use of the information or data,

(c) disclosure of the information or data by transmission, dissemination or otherwise making available, or

(d) alignment, combination, blocking, erasure or destruction of the information or data;

'public authority' has the same meaning as in the Freedom of Information Act 2000;

'relevant filing system' means any set of information relating to individuals to the extent that, although the information is not processed by means of equipment operating automatically in response to instructions given for that purpose, the set is structured, either by reference to individuals or by reference to criteria relating to individuals, in such a way that specific information relating to a particular individual is readily accessible.

(2) In this Act, unless the context otherwise requires –

(a) 'obtaining' or 'recording', in relation to personal data, includes obtaining or recording the information to be contained in the data, and

(b) 'using' or 'disclosing', in relation to personal data, includes using or disclosing the information contained in the data.

(3) In determining for the purposes of this Act whether any information is recorded with the intention –

(a) that it should be processed by means of equipment operating automatically in response to instructions given for that purpose, or

(b) that it should form part of a relevant filing system, it is immaterial that it is intended to be so processed or to form part of such a system only after being transferred to a country or territory outside the European Economic Area.

(4) Where personal data are processed only for purposes for which they are required by or under any enactment to be processed, the person on whom the obligation to process the data is imposed by or under that enactment is for the purposes of this Act the data controller.

2 Sensitive personal data

In this Act 'sensitive personal data' means personal data consisting of information as to –

(a) the racial or ethnic origin of data subject,

(b) his political opinions,

(c) his religious beliefs or other beliefs of a similar nature,

(d) whether he is a member of a trade union (within the meaning of the Trade Union and Labour Relations (Consolidation) Act 1992),

(e) his physical or mental health or condition,

(f) his sexual life,

(g) the commission or alleged commission by him of any offence, or

(h) any proceedings for any offence committed or alleged to have been committed by him, the disposal of such proceedings or the sentence of any court in such proceedings.

3   The special purposes

In this Act 'the special purposes' means any one or more of the following –

    (a) the purposes of journalism,

    (b) artistic purposes, and

    (c) literary purposes.

4   The data protection principles

(1) References in this Act to the data protection principles are to the principles set out in Part I of Schedule 1.

(2) Those principles are to be interpreted in accordance with Part II of Schedule 1.

(3) Schedule 2 (which applies to all personal data) and Schedule 3 (which applies only to sensitive personal data) set out conditions applying for the purposes of the first principle; and Schedule 4 sets out cases in which the eighth principle does not apply.

(4) Subject to section 27(1), it shall be the duty of a data controller to comply with the data protection principles in relation to all personal data with respect to which he is the data controller.

5   Application of Act

(1) Except as otherwise provided by or under section 54, this Act applies to a data controller in respect of any data only if –

    (a) the data controller is established in the United Kingdom and the data are processed in the context of that establishment, or

    (b) the data controller is established neither in the United Kingdom nor in any other EEA State but uses equipment in the United Kingdom for processing the data otherwise than for the purposes of transit through the United Kingdom.

(1A) Subsection (1) is subject to regulation 50 of the Criminal Justice and Data Protection (Protocol No. 36) Regulations 2014.

(2) A data controller falling within subsection (1)(b) must nominate for the purposes of this Act a representative established in the United Kingdom.

(3) For the purposes of subsections (1) and (2), each of the following is to be treated as established in the United Kingdom –

    (a) an individual who is ordinarily resident in the United Kingdom,

    (b) a body incorporated under the law of, or of any part of, the United Kingdom,

    (c) a partnership or other unincorporated association formed under the law of any part of the United Kingdom, and

    (d) any person who does not fall within paragraph (a), (b) or (c) but maintains in the United Kingdom –

        (i)   an office, branch or agency through which he carries on any activity, or

        (ii) a regular practice;

and the reference to establishment in any other EEA State has a corresponding meaning.

6   The Commissioner and the Tribunal

(1) For the purposes of this Act and of the Freedom of Information Act 2000 there shall be an officer known as the Information Commissioner (in this Act referred to as the Commissioner).

PART II RIGHTS OF DATA SUBJECTS AND OTHERS

7   Right of access to personal data

(1) Subject to the following provisions of this section and to sections 8 and 9 and 9A, an individual is entitled –

    (a) to be informed by any data controller whether personal data of which that individual is the data subject are being processed by or on behalf of that data controller,

    (b) if that is the case, to be given by the data controller a description of –
        (i)   the personal data of which that individual is the data subject,
        (ii) the purposes for which they are being or are to be processed, and
        (iii) the recipients or classes of recipients to whom they are or may be disclosed,
    (c) to have communicated to him in an intelligible form –
        (i)   the information constituting any personal data of which that individual is the data subject, and
        (ii) any information available to the data controller as to the source of those data, and
    (d) where the processing by automatic means of personal data of which that individual is the data subject for the purpose of evaluating matters relating to him such as, for example, his performance at work, his creditworthiness, his reliability or his conduct, has constituted or is likely to constitute the sole basis for any decision significantly affecting him, to be informed by the data controller of the logic involved in that decision-taking.

(2) A data controller is not obliged to supply any information under subsection (1) unless he has received –
    (a) a request in writing, and
    (b) except in prescribed cases, such fee (not exceeding the prescribed maximum) as he may require.

(3) Where a data controller –
    (a) reasonably requires further information in order to satisfy himself as to the identity of the person making a request under this section and to locate the information which that person seeks, and
    (b) has informed him of that requirement, the data controller is not obliged to comply with the request unless he is supplied with that further information.

(4) Where a data controller cannot comply with the request without disclosing information relating to another individual who can be identified from that information, he is not obliged to comply with the request unless –
    (a) the other individual has consented to the disclosure of the information to the person making the request, or
    (b) it is reasonable in all the circumstances to comply with the request without the consent of the other individual.

(5) In subsection (4) the reference to information relating to another individual includes a reference to information identifying that individual as the source of the information sought by the request; and that subsection is not to be construed as excusing a data controller from communicating so much of the information sought by the request as can be communicated without disclosing the identity of the other individual concerned, whether by the omission of names or other identifying particulars or otherwise.

(6) In determining for the purposes of subsection (4)(b) whether it is reasonable in all the circumstances to comply with the request without the consent of the other individual concerned, regard shall be had, in particular, to –
    (a) any duty of confidentiality owed to the other individual,
    (b) any steps taken by the data controller with a view to seeking the consent of the other individual,
    (c) whether the other individual is capable of giving consent, and
    (d) any express refusal of consent by the other individual.

(7) An individual making a request under this section may, in such cases as may be prescribed, specify that his request is limited to personal data of any prescribed description.

(8) Subject to subsection (4), a data controller shall comply with a request under this section promptly and in any event before the end of the prescribed period beginning with the relevant day.

(9) If a court is satisfied on the application of any person who has made a request under the foregoing provisions of this section that the data controller in question has failed to comply with the request in contravention of those provisions, the court may order him to comply with the request.

(10) In this section –

'prescribed' means prescribed by the Secretary of State by regulations;

'the prescribed maximum' means such amount as may be prescribed;

'prescribed period' means forty days or such other period as may be prescribed;

'the relevant day', in relation to a request under this section, means the day on which the data controller receives the request or, if later, the first day on which the data controller has both the required

fee and the information referred to in subsection (3).

(11) Different amounts or periods may be prescribed under this section in relation to different cases.

8   Provisions supplementary to section 7

(1) The Secretary of State may by regulations provide that, in such cases as may be prescribed, a request for information under any provision of subsection (1) of section 7 is to be treated as extending also to information under other provisions of that subsection.

(2) The obligation imposed by section 7(1)(c)(i) must be complied with by supplying the data subject with a copy of the information in permanent form unless –

(a) the supply of such a copy is not possible or would involve disproportionate effort, or

(b) the data subject agrees otherwise;

and where any of the information referred to in section 7(1)(c)(i) is expressed in terms which are not intelligible without explanation the copy must be accompanied by an explanation of those terms.

(3) Where a data controller has previously complied with a request made under section 7 by an individual, the data controller is not obliged to comply with a subsequent identical or similar request under that section by that individual unless a reasonable interval has elapsed between compliance with the previous request and the making of the current request.

(4) In determining for the purposes of subsection (3) whether requests under section 7 are made at reasonable intervals, regard shall be had to the nature of the data, the purpose for which the data are processed and the frequency with which data are altered.

(5) Section 7(1)(d) is not to be regarded as requiring the provision of information as to the logic involved in any decision-taking if, and to the extent that, the information constitutes a trade secret.

(6) The information to be supplied pursuant to a request under section 7 must be supplied by reference to the data in question at the time when the request is received, except that it may take account of any amendment or deletion made between that time and the time when the information is supplied, being an amendment or deletion that would have been made regardless of the receipt of the request.

(7) For the purposes of section 7(4) and (5) another individual can be identified from the information being disclosed if he can be identified from that information, or from that and any other information which, in the reasonable belief of the data controller, is likely to be in, or to come into, the possession of the data subject making the request.

10   Right to prevent processing likely to cause damage or distress

(1) to subsection (2), an individual is entitled at any time by notice in writing to a data controller to require the data controller at the end of such period as is reasonable in the circumstances to cease, or not to begin, processing, or processing for a specified purpose or in a specified manner, any personal data in respect of which he is the data subject, on the ground that, for specified reasons –

(a) the processing of those data or their processing for that purpose or in that manner is causing or is likely to cause substantial damage or substantial distress to him or to another, and

(b) that damage or distress is or would be unwarranted.

(2) Subsection (1) does not apply –

    (a) in a case where any of the conditions in paragraphs 1 to 4 of Schedule 2 is met, or

    (b) in such other cases as may be prescribed by the Secretary of State by order.

(3) The data controller must within twenty-one days of receiving a notice under subsection (1) ('the data subject notice') give the individual who gave it a written notice –

    (a) stating that he has complied or intends to comply with the data subject notice, or

    (b) stating his reasons for regarding the data subject notice as to any extent unjustified and the extent (if any) to which he has complied or intends to comply with it.

(4) If a court is satisfied, on the application of any person who has given a notice under subsection (1) which appears to the court to be justified (or to be justified to any extent), that the data controller in question has failed to comply with the notice, the court may order him to take such steps for complying with the notice (or for complying with it to that extent) as the court thinks fit.

(5) The failure by a data subject to exercise the right conferred by subsection (1) or section 11 (1) does not affect any other right conferred on him by this Part.

13 Compensation for failure to comply with certain requirements

(1) An individual who suffers damage by reason of any contravention by a data controller of any of the requirements of this Act is entitled to compensation from the data controller for that damage.

(2) An individual who suffers distress by reason of any contravention by a data controller of any of the requirements of this Act is entitled to compensation from the data controller for that distress if–

    (a) the individual also suffers damage by reason of the contravention, or

    (b) the contravention relates to the processing of personal data for the special purposes.

(3) In proceedings brought against a person by virtue of this section it is a defence to prove that he had taken such care as in all the circumstances was reasonably required to comply with the requirement concerned.

14 Rectification, blocking, erasure and destruction

(1) If a court is satisfied on the application of a data subject that personal data of which the applicant is the subject are inaccurate, the court may order the data controller to rectify, block, erase or destroy those data and any other personal data in respect of which he is the data controller and which contain an expression of opinion which appears to the court to be based on the inaccurate data.

PART III NOTIFICATION BY DATA CONTROLLERS

16 Preliminary

(1) In this Part 'the registrable particulars', in relation to a data controller, means –

    (a) his name and address,

    (b) if he has nominated a representative for the purposes of this Act, the name and address of the representative,

    (c) a description of the personal data being or to be processed by or on behalf of the data controller and of the category or categories of data subject to which they relate,

    (d) a description of the purpose or purposes for which the data are being or are to be processed,

    (e) a description of any recipient or recipients to whom the data controller intends or may wish to disclose the data,

    (f) the names, or a description of, any countries or territories outside the European Economic Area to which the data controller directly or indirectly transfers, or intends or may wish directly or indirectly to transfer, the data,

    (ff) where the data controller is a public authority, a statement of that fact,

    (g) in any case where –
        (i)   personal data are being, or are intended to be, processed in circumstances in
              which the prohibition in subsection (1) of section 17 is excluded by subsection
              (2) or (3) of that section, and
        (ii) the notification does not extend to those data, a statement of that fact.

17   Prohibition on processing without registration

(1) Subject to the following provisions of this section, personal data must not be processed
unless an entry in respect of the data controller is included in the register maintained by the
Commissioner under section 19 (or is treated by notification regulations made by virtue of section
19(3) as being so included).

(2) Except where the processing is assessable processing for the purposes of section 22, subsection (1) does not apply in relation to personal data consisting of information which falls neither
within paragraph (a) of the definition of 'data' in section 1(1) nor within paragraph (b) of that
definition.

(3) If it appears to the Secretary of State that processing of a particular description is unlikely
to prejudice the rights and freedoms of data subjects, notification regulations may provide that,
in such cases as may be prescribed, subsection (1) is not to apply in relation to processing of that
description.

(4) Subsection (1) does not apply in relation to any processing whose sole purpose is the maintenance of a public register.

18   Notification by data controllers

(1) Any data controller who wishes to be included in the register maintained under section 19
shall give a notification to the Commissioner under this section.

19   Register of notifications

(1) The Commissioner shall –
    (a) maintain a register of persons who have given notification under section 18, and
    (b) make an entry in the register in pursuance of each notification received by him under
        that section from a person in respect of whom no entry as data controller was for the
        time being included in the register.

20   Duty to notify changes

(1) For the purpose specified in subsection (2), notification regulations shall include provision
imposing on every person in respect of whom an entry as a data controller is for the time being
included in the register maintained under section 19 a duty to notify to the Commissioner, in such
circumstances and at such time or times and in such form as may be prescribed, such matters relating to the registrable particulars and measures taken as mentioned in section 18(2)(b) as may
be prescribed.

(2) The purpose referred to in subsection (1) is that of ensuring, so far as practicable, that at
any time –
    (a) the entries in the register maintained under section 19 contain current names and
        addresses and describe the current practice or intentions of the data controller with
        respect to the processing of personal data, and
    (b) the Commissioner is provided with a general description of measures currently being
        taken as mentioned in section 18(2)(b).

(4) On receiving any notification under notification regulations made by virtue of subsection (1),
the Commissioner shall make such amendments of the relevant entry in the register maintained under
section 19 as are necessary to take account of the notification.

21   Offences

(1) If section 17(1) is contravened, the data controller is guilty of an offence.

(2) Any person who fails to comply with the duty imposed by notification regulations made by virtue of section 20(1) is guilty of an offence.

(3) It shall be a defence for a person charged with an offence under subsection (2) to show that he exercised all due diligence to comply with the duty.

22   Preliminary assessment by the Commissioner

(1) In this section 'assessable processing' means processing which is of a description specified in an order made by the Secretary of State as appearing to him to be particularly likely –

    (a) to cause substantial damage or substantial distress to data subjects, or

    (b) otherwise significantly to prejudice the rights and freedoms of data subjects.

(2) On receiving notification from any data controller under section 18 or under notification regulations made by virtue of section 20 the Commissioner shall consider –

    (a) whether any of the processing to which the notification relates is assessable processing, and

    (b) if so, whether the assessable processing is likely to comply with the provisions of this Act.

(3) Subject to subsection (4), the Commissioner shall, within the period of twenty-eight days beginning with the day on which he receives a notification which relates to assessable processing, give a notice to the data controller stating the extent to which the Commissioner is of the opinion that the processing is likely or unlikely to comply with the provisions of this Act.

(4) Before the end of the period referred to in subsection (3) the Commissioner may, by reason of special circumstances, extend that period on one occasion only by notice to the data controller by such further period not exceeding fourteen days as the Commissioner may specify in the notice.

(5) No assessable processing in respect of which a notification has been given to the Commissioner as mentioned in subsection (2) shall be carried on unless either –

    (a) the period of twenty-eight days beginning with the day on which the notification is received by the Commissioner (or, in a case falling within subsection (4), that period as extended under that subsection) has elapsed, or

    (b) before the end of that period (or that period as so extended) the data controller has received a notice from the Commissioner under subsection (3) in respect of the processing.

(6) Where subsection (5) is contravened, the data controller is guilty of an offence.

(7) The Secretary of State may by order amend subsections (3), (4) and (5) by substituting for the number of days for the time being specified there a different number specified in the order.

23   Power to make provision for appointment of data protection supervisors

(1) The Secretary of State may by order –

    (a) make provision under which a data controller may appoint a person to act as a data protection supervisor responsible in particular for monitoring in an independent manner the data controller's compliance with the provisions of this Act, and

    (b) provide that, in relation to any data controller who has appointed a data protection supervisor in accordance with the provisions of the order and who complies with such conditions as may be specified in the order, the provisions of this Part are to have effect subject to such exemptions or other modifications as may be specified in the order.

(2) An order under this section may –

    (a) impose duties on data protection supervisors in relation to the Commissioner, and

    (b) confer functions on the Commissioner in relation to data protection supervisors.

24   Duty of certain data controllers to make certain information available

(1) Subject to subsection (3), where personal data are processed in a case where –

    (a) by virtue of subsection (2) or (3) of section 17, subsection (1) of that section does not apply to the processing, and

    (b) the data controller has not notified the relevant particulars in respect of that processing under section 18, the data controller must, within twenty-one days of receiving a written request from any person, make the relevant particulars available to that person in writing free of charge.

(2) In this section 'the relevant particulars' means the particulars referred to in paragraphs (a) to (f) of section 16(1).

(3) This section has effect subject to any exemption conferred for the purposes of this section by notification regulations.

(4) Any data controller who fails to comply with the duty imposed by subsection (1) is guilty of an offence.

(5) It shall be a defence for a person charged with an offence under subsection (4) to show that he exercised all due diligence to comply with the duty.

30   Health education and social work

(1) The Secretary of State may by order exempt from the subject information provisions, or modify those provisions in relation to, personal data consisting of information as to the physical or mental health or condition of the data subject.

31   Regulatory activity

(1) Personal data processed for the purposes of discharging functions to which this subsection applies are exempt from the subject information provisions in any case to the extent to which the application of those provisions to the data would be likely to prejudice the proper discharge of those functions.

(2) Subsection (1) applies to any relevant function which is designed –

    (a) for protecting members of the public against –

        (iii) dishonesty, malpractice or other seriously improper conduct by, or the unfitness or incompetence of, persons authorised to carry on any profession or other activity,

    (b) for protecting charities against misconduct or mismanagement (whether by trustees or other persons) in their administration,

    (c) for protecting the property of charities from loss or misapplication,

    (d) for the recovery of the property of charities,

    (e) for securing the health, safety and welfare of persons at work, or

    (f) for protecting persons other than persons at work against risk to health or safety arising out of or in connection with the actions of persons at work.

(3) In subsection (2) 'relevant function' means –

    (a) any function conferred on any person by or under any enactment,

    (b) any function of the Crown, a Minister of the Crown or a government department, or

    (c) any other function which is of a public nature and is exercised in the public interest.

(4) Personal data processed for the purpose of discharging any function which –

    (a) is conferred by or under any enactment on –

        (iii) the Health Service Commissioner for England, and

    (b) is designed for protecting members of the public against –

        (i) maladministration by public bodies,

        (ii) failures in services provided by public bodies, or

        (iii) a failure of a public body to provide a service which it was a function of the body to provide,

are exempt from the subject information provisions in any case to the extent to which the application of those provisions to the data would be likely to prejudice the proper discharge of that function.

(6) Personal data processed for the purpose of the function of considering a complaint under section 113(1) or (2) or 114(1) or (3) of the Health and Social Care (Community Health and Standards) Act 2003, or section 24D, 26, 26ZA or 26ZB of the Children Act 1989, are exempt from

the subject information provisions in any case to the extent to which the application of those provisions to the data would be likely to prejudice the proper discharge of that function.

32 Journalism, literature and art

(1) Personal data which are processed only for the special purposes are exempt from any provision to which this subsection relates if –

    (a) the processing is undertaken with a view to the publication by any person of any journalistic, literary or artistic material,

    (b) the data controller reasonably believes that, having regard in particular to the special importance of the public interest in freedom of expression, publication would be in the public interest, and

    (c) the data controller reasonably believes that, in all the circumstances, compliance with that provision is incompatible with the special purposes.

(2) Subsection (1) relates to the provisions of –

    (a) the data protection principles except the seventh data protection principle,

    (b) section 7,

    (c) section 10,

    (d) section 12, and

    (e) section 14(1) to (3).

(6) For the purposes of this Act 'publish', in relation to journalistic, literary or artistic material, means make available to the public or any section of the public.

33 Research, history and statistics

(1) In this section –

'research purposes' includes statistical or historical purposes;

'the relevant conditions', in relation to any processing of personal data, means the conditions –

    (a) that the data are not processed to support measures or decisions with respect to particular individuals, and

    (b) that the data are not processed in such a way that substantial damage or substantial distress is, or is likely to be, caused to any data subject.

(2) For the purposes of the second data protection principle, the further processing of personal data only for research purposes in compliance with the relevant conditions is not to be regarded as incompatible with the purposes for which they were obtained.

(3) Personal data which are processed only for research purposes in compliance with the relevant conditions may, notwithstanding the fifth data protection principle, be kept indefinitely.

(4) Personal data which are processed only for research purposes are exempt from section 7 if –

    (a) they are processed in compliance with the relevant conditions, and

    (b) the results of the research or any resulting statistics are not made available in a form which identifies data subjects or any of them.

(5) For the purposes of subsections (2) to (4) personal data are not to be treated as processed otherwise than for research purposes merely because the data are disclosed –

    (a) to any person, for research purposes only,

    (b) to the data subject or a person acting on his behalf,

    (c) at the request, or with the consent, of the data subject or a person acting on his behalf, or

    (d) in circumstances in which the person making the disclosure has reasonable grounds for believing that the disclosure falls within paragraph (a), (b) or (c).

33A Manual data held by public authorities

(1) Personal data falling within paragraph (e) of the definition of 'data' in section 1(1) are exempt from –

    (a) the first, second, third, fifth, seventh and eighth data protection principles,

    (b) the sixth data protection principle except so far as it relates to the rights conferred on data subjects by sections 7 and 14,

(c) sections 10 to 12,

(d) section 13, except so far as it relates to damage caused by a contravention of section 7 or of the fourth data protection principle and to any distress which is also suffered by reason of that contravention,

(e) Part III, and

(f) section 55.

(2) Personal data which fall within paragraph (e) of the definition of 'data' in section 1(1) and relate to appointments or removals, pay, discipline, superannuation or other personnel matters, in relation to –

(a) service in any of the armed forces of the Crown,

(b) service in any office or employment under the Crown or under any public authority, or

(c) service in any office or employment, or under any contract for services, in respect of which power to take action, or to determine or approve the action taken, in such matters is vested in Her Majesty, any Minister of the Crown, the National Assembly for Wales, any Northern Ireland Minister (within the meaning of the Freedom of Information Act 2000) or any public authority, are also exempt from the remaining data protection principles and the remaining provisions of Part II.

35   Disclosures required by law or made in connection with legal proceedings etc.

(1) Personal data are exempt from the non-disclosure provisions where the disclosure is required by or under any enactment, by any rule of law or by the order of a court.

(2) Personal data are exempt from the non-disclosure provisions where the disclosure is necessary

(a) for the purpose of, or in connection with, any legal proceedings (including prospective legal proceedings), or

(b) for the purpose of obtaining legal advice,

or is otherwise necessary for the purposes of establishing, exercising or defending legal rights.

PART V   ENFORCEMENT

40   Enforcement notices

(1) If the Commissioner is satisfied that a data controller has contravened or is contravening any of the data protection principles, the Commissioner may serve him with a notice (in this Act referred to as 'an enforcement notice') requiring him, for complying with the principle or principles in question, to do either or both of the following –

(a) to take within such time as may be specified in the notice, or to refrain from taking after such time as may be so specified, such steps as are so specified, or

(b) to refrain from processing any personal data, or any personal data of a description specified in the notice, or to refrain from processing them for a purpose so specified or in a manner so specified, after such time as may be so specified.

(2) In deciding whether to serve an enforcement notice, the Commissioner shall consider whether the contravention has caused or is likely to cause any person damage or distress.

PART VI   MISCELLANEOUS

Unlawful obtaining etc. of personal data

55   Unlawful obtaining etc. of personal data

(1) A person must not knowingly or recklessly, without the consent of the data controller –

(a) obtain or disclose personal data or the information contained in personal data, or

(b) procure the disclosure to another person of the information contained in personal data.

(2) Subsection (1) does not apply to a person who shows –

(a) that the obtaining, disclosing or procuring –

    (i) was necessary for the purpose of preventing or detecting crime, or

    (ii) was required or authorised by or under any enactment, by any rule of law or by the order of a court,

(b) that he acted in the reasonable belief that he had in law the right to obtain or disclose the data or information or, as the case may be, to procure the disclosure of the information to the other person,

(c) that he acted in the reasonable belief that he would have had the consent of the data controller if the data controller had known of the obtaining, disclosing or procuring and the circumstances of it, or

(ca) that he acted –

    (i) for the special purposes,

    (ii) with a view to the publication by any person of any journalistic, literary or artistic material, and

    (iii) in the reasonable belief that in the particular circumstances the obtaining, disclosing or procuring was justified as being in the public interest, or

(d) that in the particular circumstances the obtaining, disclosing or procuring was justified as being in the public interest.

(3) A person who contravenes subsection (1) is guilty of an offence.

(4) A person who sells personal data is guilty of an offence if he has obtained the data in contravention of subsection (1).

(5) A person who offers to sell personal data is guilty of an offence if –

(a) he has obtained the data in contravention of subsection (1), or

(b) he subsequently obtains the data in contravention of that subsection.

(6) For the purposes of subsection (5), an advertisement indicating that personal data are or may be for sale is an offer to sell the data.

(7) Section 1(2) does not apply for the purposes of this section; and for the purposes of subsections (4) to (6), 'personal data' includes information extracted from personal data.

(8) References in this section to personal data do not include references to personal data which by virtue of section 28 or 33A are exempt from this section.

55A Power of Commissioner to impose monetary penalty

(1) The Commissioner may serve a data controller with a monetary penalty notice if the Commissioner is satisfied that –

(a) there has been a serious contravention of section 4(4) by the data controller,

(b) the contravention was of a kind likely to cause substantial damage or substantial distress, and

(c) subsection (2) or (3) applies.

(2) This subsection applies if the contravention was deliberate.

(3) This subsection applies if the data controller –

(a) knew or ought to have known –

    (i) that there was a risk that the contravention would occur, and

    (ii) that such a contravention would be of a kind likely to cause substantial damage or substantial distress, but

(b) failed to take reasonable steps to prevent the contravention.

(4) A monetary penalty notice is a notice requiring the data controller to pay to the Commissioner a monetary penalty of an amount determined by the Commissioner and specified in the notice.

(5) The amount determined by the Commissioner must not exceed the prescribed amount.

(8) Any sum received by the Commissioner by virtue of this section must be paid into the Consolidated Fund.

57   Avoidance of certain contractual terms relating to health record

(1) Any term or condition of a contract is void in so far as it purports to require an individual –

    (a) to supply any other person with a record to which this section applies, or with a copy of such a record or a part of such a record, or

    (b) to produce to any other person such a record, copy or part.

(2) This section applies to any record which –

    (a) has been or is to be obtained by a data subject in the exercise of the right conferred by section 7, and

    (b) consists of the information contained in any health record as defined by section 68(2).

68   Meaning of 'accessible record'

(1) In this Act 'accessible record' means –

    (a) a health record as defined by subsection (2),

    (b) an educational record as defined by Schedule 11, or

    (c) an accessible public record' as defined by Schedule 12.

(2) In subsection (1)(a) 'health record' means any record which –

    (a) consists of information relating to the physical or mental health or condition of an individual, and

    (b) has been made by or on behalf of a health professional in connection with the care of that individual.

69   Meaning of 'health professional'

(1) In this Act 'health professional' means any of the following –

    (a) a registered medical practitioner,

    (b) a registered dentist as defined by section 53(1) of the Dentists Act 1984,

    (c) a registered dispensing optician or a registered optometrist within the meaning of the Opticians Act 1989,

    (d) a registered pharmacist or registered pharmacy technician within the meaning of the Pharmacists and Pharmacy Technicians Order 2007,

    (e) a registered nurse or midwife,

    (f) a registered osteopath as defined by section 41 of the Osteopaths Act 1993,

    (g) a registered chiropractor as defined by section 43 of the Chiropractors Act 1994,

    (h) any person who is registered as a member of a profession to which the Health Professions Order 2001 for the time being extends,

    (i) a child psychotherapist, and

    (k) a scientist employed by a health service body as head of a department.

(2) In subsection (1)(a) 'registered medical practitioner' includes any person who is provisionally registered under section 15 or 21 of the Medical Act 1983 and is engaged in such employment as is mentioned in subsection (3) of that section.

70   Supplementary definitions

(1) In this Act, unless the context otherwise requires –

'business' includes any trade or profession;

'the Commissioner' means the Information Commissioner;

'the Data Protection Directive' means Directive 95/46/EC on the protection of individuals with regard to the processing of personal data and on the free movement of such data;

'EEA State' means a State which is a contracting party to the Agreement on the European Economic

Area signed at Oporto on 2nd May 1992 as adjusted by the Protocol signed at Brussels on 17th March 1993:

'public register' means any register which pursuant to a requirement imposed –

(a) by or under any enactment, or

(b) in pursuance of any international agreement,

is open to public inspection or open to inspection by any person having a legitimate interest;

'recipient', in relation to any personal data, means any person to whom the data are disclosed, including any person (such as an employee or agent of the data controller, a data processor or an employee or agent of a data processor) to whom they are disclosed in the course of processing the data for the data controller, but does not include any person to whom disclosure is or may be made as a result of, or with a view to, a particular inquiry by or on behalf of that person made in the exercise of any power conferred by law;

'third party', in relation to personal data, means any person other than –

(a) the data subject,

(b) the data controller, or

(c) any data processor or other person authorised to process data for the data controller or processor;

'the Tribunal' in relation to any appeal under this Act, means –

(a) the Upper Tribunal, in any case where it is determined by or under Tribunal Procedure Rules that the Upper Tribunal is to hear the appeal; or

(b) the First-tier Tribunal, in any other case.

(2) For the purposes of this Act data are inaccurate if they are incorrect or misleading as to any matter of fact.

SCHEDULES

SCHEDULE 1   THE DATA PROTECTION PRINCIPLES

PART I THE PRINCIPLES

1. Personal data shall be processed fairly and lawfully and, in particular, shall not be processed unless –

(a) at least one of the conditions in Schedule 2 is met, and

(b) in the case of sensitive personal data, at least one of the conditions in Schedule 3 is also met.

2. Personal data shall be obtained only for one or more specified and lawful purposes, and shall not be further processed in any manner incompatible with that purpose or those purposes.

3. Personal data shall be adequate, relevant and not excessive in relation to the purpose or purposes for which they are processed.

4. Personal data shall be accurate and, where necessary, kept up to date.

5. Personal data processed for any purpose or purposes shall not be kept for longer than is necessary for that purpose or those purposes.

6. Personal data shall be processed in accordance with the rights of data subjects under this Act.

7. Appropriate technical and organisational measures shall be taken against unauthorised or unlawful processing of personal data and against accidental loss or destruction of, or damage to, personal data.

8. Personal data shall not be transferred to a country or territory outside the European Economic Area unless that country or territory ensures an adequate level of protection for the rights and freedoms of data subjects in relation to the processing of personal data.

PART II INTERPRETATION OF THE PRINCIPLES IN PART I

The first principle

1.—(1) In determining for the purposes of the first principle whether personal data are processed fairly, regard is to be had to the method by which they are obtained, including in particular whether any person from whom they are obtained is deceived or misled as to the purpose or purposes for which they are to be processed.

(2) Subject to paragraph 2, for the purposes of the first principle data are to be treated as obtained fairly if they consist of information obtained from a person who –

(a) is authorised by or under any enactment to supply it, or

(b) is required to supply it by or under any enactment or by any convention or other instrument imposing an international obligation on the United Kingdom.

2.—(1) Subject to paragraph 3, for the purposes of the first principle personal data are not to be treated as processed fairly unless –

(a) in the case of data obtained from the data subject, the data controller ensures so far as practicable that the data subject has, is provided with, or has made readily available to him, the information specified in sub-paragraph (3), and

(b) in any other case, the data controller ensures so far as practicable that, before the relevant time or as soon as practicable after that time, the data subject has, is provided with, or has made readily available to him, the information specified in sub-paragraph (3).

(2) In sub-paragraph (1)(b) 'the relevant time' means –

(a) the time when the data controller first processes the data, or

(b) in a case where at that time disclosure to a third party within a reasonable period is envisaged –

(i) if the data are in fact disclosed to such a person within that period, the time when the data are first disclosed,

(ii) if within that period the data controller becomes, or ought to become, aware that the data are unlikely to be disclosed to such a person within that period, the time when the data controller does become, or ought to become, so aware, or

(iii) in any other case, the end of that period.

(3) The information referred to in sub-paragraph (1) is as follows, namely –

(a) the identity of the data controller,

(b) if he has nominated a representative for the purposes of this Act, the identity of that representative,

(c) the purpose or purposes for which the data are intended to be processed, and

(d) any further information which is necessary, having regard to the specific circumstances in which the data are or are to be processed, to enable processing in respect of the data subject to be fair.

3.—(1) Paragraph 2(1)(b) does not apply where either of the primary conditions in sub-paragraph (2), together with such further conditions as may be prescribed by the Secretary of State by order, are met.

(2) The primary conditions referred to in sub-paragraph (1) are –

(a) that the provision of that information would involve a disproportionate effort, or

(b) that the recording of the information to be contained in the data by, or the disclosure of the data by, the data controller is necessary for compliance with any legal obligation to which the data controller is subject, other than an obligation imposed by contract.

4.—(1) Personal data which contain a general identifier falling within a description prescribed by the Secretary of State by order are not to be treated as processed fairly and lawfully unless they are processed in compliance with any conditions so prescribed in relation to general identifiers of that description.

(2) In sub-paragraph (1) 'a general identifier' means any identifier (such as, for example, a number or code used for identification purposes) which –

    (a) relates to an individual, and

    (b) forms part of a set of similar identifiers which is of general application.

The second principle

5. The purpose or purposes for which personal data are obtained may in particular be specified –

    (a) in a notice given for the purposes of paragraph 2 by the data controller to the data subject, or

    (b) in a notification given to the Commissioner under Part III of this Act.

6. In determining whether any disclosure of personal data is compatible with the purpose or purposes for which the data were obtained, regard is to be had to the purpose or purposes for which the personal data are intended to be processed by any person to whom they are disclosed.

The fourth principle

7. The fourth principle is not to be regarded as being contravened by reason of any inaccuracy in personal data which accurately record information obtained by the data controller from the data subject or a third party in a case where –

    (a) having regard to the purpose or purposes for which the data were obtained and further processed, the data controller has taken reasonable steps to ensure the accuracy of the data, and

    (b) if the data subject has notified the data controller of the data subject's view that the data are inaccurate, the data indicate that fact.

The sixth principle

8. A person is to be regarded as contravening the sixth principle if, but only if –

    (a) he contravenes section 7 by failing to supply information in accordance with that section,

    (b) he contravenes section 10 by failing to comply with a notice given under subsection (1) of that section to the extent that the notice is justified or by failing to give a notice under subsection (3) of that section,

    (c) he contravenes section 11 by failing to comply with a notice given under subsection (1) of that section, or

    (d) he contravenes section 12 by failing to comply with a notice given under subsection (1) or (2)(b) of that section or by failing to give a notification under subsection (2)(a) of that section or a notice under subsection (3) of that section.

The seventh principle

9. Having regard to the state of technological development and the cost of implementing any measures, the measures must ensure a level of security appropriate to –

    (a) the harm that might result from such unauthorised or unlawful processing or accidental loss, destruction or damage as are mentioned in the seventh principle, and

    (b) the nature of the data to be protected.

10. The data controller must take reasonable steps to ensure the reliability of any employees of his who have access to the personal data.

11. Where processing of personal data is carried out by a data processor on behalf of a data controller, the data controller must in order to comply with the seventh principle –

    (a) choose a data processor providing sufficient guarantees in respect of the technical and organisational security measures governing the processing to be carried out, and

    (b) take reasonable steps to ensure compliance with those measures.

12. Where processing of personal data is carried out by a data processor on behalf of a data controller, the data controller is not to be regarded as complying with the seventh principle unless –

    (a) the processing is carried out under a contract –

        (i) which is made or evidenced in writing, and

        (ii) under which the data processor is to act only on instructions from the data controller, and

    (b) the contract requires the data processor to comply with obligations equivalent to those imposed on a data controller by the seventh principle.

The eighth principle

13. An adequate level of protection is one which is adequate in all the circumstances of the case, having regard in particular to –

    (a) the nature of the personal data,

    (b) the country or territory of origin of the information contained in the data,

    (c) the country or territory of final destination of that information,

    (d) the purposes for which and period during which the data are intended to be processed,

    (e) the law in force in the country or territory in question,

    (f) the international obligations of that country or territory,

    (g) any relevant codes of conduct or other rules which are enforceable in that country or territory (whether generally or by arrangement in particular cases), and

    (h) any security measures taken in respect of the data in that country or territory.

14. The eighth principle does not apply to a transfer falling within any paragraph of Schedule 4, except in such circumstances and to such extent as the Secretary of State may by order provide.

15.—(1) Where –

    (a) in any proceedings under this Act any question arises as to whether the requirement of the eighth principle as to an adequate level of protection is met in relation to the transfer of any personal data to a country or territory outside the European Economic Area, and

    (b) a Community finding has been made in relation to transfers of the kind in question, that question is to be determined in accordance with that finding.

(2) In sub-paragraph (1) 'Community finding' means a finding of the European Commission, under the procedure provided for in Article 31(2) of the Data Protection Directive, that a country or territory outside the European Economic Area does, or does not, ensure an adequate level of protection within the meaning of Article 25(2) of the Directive.

SCHEDULE 2 CONDITIONS RELEVANT FOR PURPOSES OF THE FIRST PRINCIPLE: PROCESSING OF ANY PERSONAL DATA

1. The data subject has given his consent to the processing.

2. The processing is necessary –

    (a) for the performance of a contract to which the data subject is a party, or

    (b) for the taking of steps at the request of the data subject with a view to entering into a contract.

3. The processing is necessary for compliance with any legal obligation to which the data controller is subject, other than an obligation imposed by contract.

4. The processing is necessary in order to protect the vital interests of the data subject.

5. The processing is necessary –

    (a)   for the administration of justice,

    (aa) for the exercise of any functions of either House of Parliament,

    (b)   for the exercise of any functions conferred on any person by or under any enactment,

(c) for the exercise of any functions of the Crown, a Minister of the Crown or a government department, or

(d) for the exercise of any other functions of a public nature exercised in the public interest by any person.

6.—(1) The processing is necessary for the purposes of legitimate interests pursued by the data controller or by the third party or parties to whom the data are disclosed, except where the processing is unwarranted in any particular case by reason of prejudice to the rights and freedoms or legitimate interests of the data subject.

(2) The Secretary of State may by order specify particular circumstances in which this condition is, or is not, to be taken to be satisfied.

SCHEDULE 3 CONDITIONS RELEVANT FOR PURPOSES OF THE FIRST PRINCIPLE: PROCESSING OF SENSITIVE PERSONAL DATA

1. The data subject has given his explicit consent to the processing of the personal data.

2.—(1) The processing is necessary for the purposes of exercising or performing any right or obligation which is conferred or imposed by law on the data controller in connection with employment.

(2) The Secretary of State may by order –

(a) exclude the application of sub-paragraph (1) in such cases as may be specified, or

(b) provide that, in such cases as maybe specified, the condition in sub-paragraph (1) is not to be regarded as satisfied unless such further conditions as may be specified in the order are also satisfied.

3. The processing is necessary –

(a) in order to protect the vital interests of the data subject or another person, in a case where –

(i) consent cannot be given by or on behalf of the data subject, or

(ii) the data controller cannot reasonably be expected to obtain the consent of the data subject, or

(b) in order to protect the vital interests of another person, in a case where consent by or on behalf of the data subject has been unreasonably withheld.

4. The processing –

(a) is carried out in the course of its legitimate activities by any body or association which –

(i) is not established or conducted for profit, and

(ii) exists for political, philosophical, religious or trade-union purposes,

(b) is carried out with appropriate safeguards for the rights and freedoms of data subjects,

(c) relates only to individuals who either are members of the body or association or have regular contact with it in connection with its purposes, and

(d) does not involve disclosure of the personal data to a third party without the consent of the data subject.

5. The information contained in the personal data has been made public as a result of steps deliberately taken by the data subject.

6. The processing –

(a) is necessary for the purpose of, or in connection with, any legal proceedings (including prospective legal proceedings),

(b) is necessary for the purpose of obtaining legal advice, or

(c) is otherwise necessary for the purposes of establishing, exercising or defending legal rights.

7.—(1) The processing is necessary –

(a) for the administration of justice,

(aa) for the exercise of any functions of either House of Parliament,
(b)   for the exercise of any functions conferred on any person by or under an enactment, or
(c)   for the exercise of any functions of the Crown, a Minister of the Crown or a government department.

(2) The Secretary of State may by order –
(a) exclude the application of sub-paragraph (1) in such cases as may be specified, or
(b) provide that, in such cases as may be specified, the condition in sub-paragraph (1) is not to be regarded as satisfied unless such further conditions as may be specified in the order are also satisfied.

8.—(1) The processing is necessary for medical purposes and is undertaken by –
(a) a health professional, or
(b) a person who in the circumstances owes a duty of confidentiality which is equivalent to that which would arise if that person were a health professional.

(2) In this paragraph 'medical purposes' includes the purposes of preventative medicine, medical diagnosis, medical research, the provision of care and treatment and the management of healthcare services.

9.—(1) The processing –
(a) is of sensitive personal data consisting of information as to racial or ethnic origin,
(b) is necessary for the purpose of identifying or keeping under review the existence or absence of equality of opportunity or treatment between persons of different racial or ethnic origins, with a view to enabling such equality to be promoted or maintained, and
(c) is carried out with appropriate safeguards for the rights and freedoms of data subjects.
(2) The Secretary of State may by order specify circumstances in which processing falling within sub-paragraph (1)(a) and (b) is, or is not, to be taken for the purposes of sub-paragraph (1)(c) to be carried out with appropriate safeguards for the rights and freedoms of data subjects.

10. The personal data are processed in circumstances specified in an order made by the Secretary of State for the purposes of this paragraph.

SCHEDULE 4 CASES WHERE THE EIGHTH PRINCIPLE DOES NOT APPLY

1. The data subject has given his consent to the transfer.
2. The transfer is necessary –
(a) for the performance of a contract between the data subject and the data controller, or
(b) for the taking of steps at the request of the data subject with a view to his entering into a contract with the data controller.
3. The transfer is necessary –
(a) for the conclusion of a contract between the data controller and a person other than the data subject which –
(i)   is entered into at the request of the data subject, or
(ii) is in the interests of the data subject, or
(b) for the performance of such a contract.
4.—(1) The transfer is necessary for reasons of substantial public interest. (2) The Secretary of State may by order specify –
(a) circumstances in which a transfer is to be taken for the purposes of sub-paragraph (1) to be necessary for reasons of substantial public interest, and
(b) circumstances in which a transfer which is not required by or under an enactment is not to be taken for the purpose of sub-paragraph (1) to be necessary for reasons of substantial public interest.

5. The transfer –
   (a) is necessary for the purpose of, or in connection with, any legal proceedings (including prospective legal proceedings),
   (b) is necessary for the purpose of obtaining legal advice, or
   (c) is otherwise necessary for the purposes of establishing, exercising or defending legal rights.
6. The transfer is necessary in order to protect the vital interests of the data subject.
7. The transfer is of part of the personal data on a public register and any conditions subject to which the register is open to inspection are complied with by any person to whom the data are or may be disclosed after the transfer.
8. The transfer is made on terms which are of a kind approved by the Commissioner as ensuring adequate safeguards for the rights and freedoms of data subjects.
9. The transfer has been authorised by the Commissioner as being made in such a manner as to ensure adequate safeguards for the rights and freedoms of data subjects.

SCHEDULE 7 MISCELLANEOUS EXEMPTIONS

Confidential references given by the data controller

1. Personal data are exempt from section 7 if they consist of a reference given or to be given in confidence by the data controller for the purposes of –
   (a) the education, training or employment, or prospective education, training or employment, of the data subject,
   (b) the appointment, or prospective appointment, of the data subject to any office, or
   (c) the provision, or prospective provision, by the data subject of any service.

Human Rights Act 1998

(1998, c. 42)

Introduction

1.—(1) In this Act 'the Convention rights' means the rights and fundamental freedoms set out in –
   (a) Articles 2 to 12 and 14 of the Convention,
   (b) Articles 1 to 3 of the First Protocol, and
   (c) Article 1 of the Thirteenth Protocol,
as read with Articles 16 to 18 of the Convention.
   (2) Those Articles are to have effect for the purposes of this Act subject to any designated derogation or reservation (as to which see sections 14 and 15).
   (3) The Articles are set out in Schedule 1.
2.—(1) A court or tribunal determining a question which has arisen in connection with a Convention right must take into account any –
   (a) judgment, decision, declaration or advisory opinion of the European Court of Human Rights,
   (b) opinion of the Commission given in a report adopted under Article 31 of the Convention, or
   (c) decision of the Commission in connection with Article 26 or 27(2) of the Convention, or
   (d) decision of the Committee of Ministers taken under Article 46 of the Convention, whenever made or given, so far as, in the opinion of the court or tribunal, it is relevant to the proceedings in which that question has arisen.

Legislation

3.—(1) So far as it is possible to do so, primary legislation and subordinate legislation must be read and given effect in a way which is compatible with the Convention rights.

Public authorities

6.—(1) It is unlawful for a public authority to act in a way which is incompatible with a Convention right.

(2) Subsection (1) does not apply to an act if –

    (a) as the result of one or more provisions of primary legislation, the authority could not have acted differently; or

    (b) in the case of one or more provisions of, or made under, primary legislation which cannot be read or given effect in a way which is compatible with the Convention rights, the authority was acting so as to give effect to or enforce those provisions.

(3) In this section 'public authority' includes –

    (a) a court or tribunal, and

    (b) any person certain of whose functions are functions of a public nature, but does not include either House of Parliament or a person exercising functions in connection with proceedings in Parliament.

7.—(1) A person who claims that a public authority has acted (or proposes to act) in a way which is made unlawful by section 6(1) may –

    (a) bring proceedings against the authority under this Act in the appropriate court or tribunal, or

    (b) rely on the Convention right or rights concerned in any legal proceedings, but only if he is (or would be) a victim of the unlawful act.

(2) In subsection (1)(a) 'appropriate court or tribunal' means such court or tribunal as may be determined in accordance with rules; and proceedings against an authority include a counterclaim or similar proceeding.

(3) If the proceedings are brought on an application for judicial review, the applicant is to be taken to have a sufficient interest in relation to the unlawful act only if he is, or would be, a victim of that act.

(7) For the purposes of this section, a person is a victim of an unlawful act only if he would be a victim for the purposes of Article 34 of the Convention if proceedings were brought in the European Court of Human Rights in respect of that act.

(8) Nothing in this Act creates a criminal offence.

8.—(1) In relation to any act (or proposed act) of a public authority which the court finds is (or would be) unlawful, it may grant such relief or remedy, or make such order, within its powers as it considers just and appropriate.

(2) But damages may be awarded only by a court which has power to award damages, or to order the payment of compensation, in civil proceedings.

(3) No award of damages is to be made unless, taking account of all the circumstances of the case, including –

    (a) any other relief or remedy granted, or order made, in relation to the act in question (by that or any other court), and

    (b) the consequences of any decision (of that or any other court) in respect of that act, the court is satisfied that the award is necessary to afford just satisfaction to the person in whose favour it is made.

(4) In determining –

    (a) whether to award damages, or

    (b) the amount of an award,

the court must take into account the principles applied by the European Court of Human Rights in relation to the award of compensation under Article 41 of the Convention.

SCHEDULE

SCHEDULE 1   THE ARTICLES

PART I THE CONVENTION

Rights and freedoms

Article 2   Right to life

1. Everyone's right to life shall be protected by law. No one shall be deprived of his life intentionally save in the execution of a sentence of a court following his conviction of a crime for which this penalty is provided by law.

2. Deprivation of life shall not be regarded as inflicted in contravention of this Article when it results from the use of force which is no more than absolutely necessary:

    (a) in defence of any person from unlawful violence;

    (b) in order to effect a lawful arrest or to prevent the escape of a person lawfully detained;

    (c) in action lawfully taken for the purpose of quelling a riot or insurrection.

Article 3   Prohibition of torture

No one shall be subjected to torture or to inhuman or degrading treatment or punishment.

Article 5   Right to liberty and security

1. Everyone has the right to liberty and security of person. No one shall be deprived of his liberty save in the following cases and in accordance with a procedure prescribed by law:

    (e) the lawful detention of persons for the prevention of the spreading of infectious diseases, of persons of unsound mind, alcoholics or drug addicts or vagrants;

2. Everyone who is arrested shall be informed promptly, in a language which he understands, of the reasons for his arrest and of any charge against him.

4. Everyone who is deprived of his liberty by arrest or detention shall be entitled to take proceedings by which the lawfulness of his detention shall be decided speedily by a court and his release ordered if the detention is not lawful.

5. Everyone who has been the victim of arrest or detention in contravention of the provisions of this Article shall have an enforceable right to compensation.

Article 6   Right to a fair trial

1. In the determination of his civil rights and obligations or of any criminal charge against him, everyone is entitled to a fair and public hearing within a reasonable time by an independent and impartial tribunal established by law. Judgment shall be pronounced publicly but the press and public may be excluded from all or part of the trial in the interest of morals, public order or national security in a democratic society, where the interests of juveniles or the protection of the private life of the parties so require, or to the extent strictly necessary in the opinion of the court in special circumstances where publicity would prejudice the interests of justice.

Article 8   Right to respect for private and family life

1. Everyone has the right to respect for his private and family life, his home and his correspondence.

2. There shall be no interference by a public authority with the exercise of this right except such as is in accordance with the law and is necessary in a democratic society in the interests of national security, public safety or the economic well-being of the country, for the prevention of

disorder or crime, for the protection of health or morals, or for the protection of the rights and freedoms of others.

Article 9   Freedom of thought, conscience and religion

1. Everyone has the right to freedom of thought, conscience and religion; this right includes freedom to change his religion or belief and freedom, either alone or in community with others and in public or private, to manifest his religion or belief, in worship, teaching, practice and observance.

2. Freedom to manifest one's religion or beliefs shall be subject only to such limitations as are prescribed by law and are necessary in a democratic society in the interests of public safety, for the protection of public order, health or morals, or for the protection of the rights and freedoms of others.

Article 10   Freedom of expression

1. Everyone has the right to freedom of expression. This right shall include freedom to hold opinions and to receive and impart information and ideas without interference by public authority and regardless of frontiers. This Article shall not prevent States from requiring the licensing of broadcasting, television or cinema enterprises.

2. The exercise of these freedoms, since it carries with it duties and responsibilities, may be subject to such formalities, conditions, restrictions or penalties as are prescribed by law and are necessary in a democratic society, in the interests of national security, territorial integrity or public safety, for the prevention of disorder or crime, for the protection of health or morals, for the protection of the reputation or rights of others, for preventing the disclosure of information received in confidence, or for maintaining the authority and impartiality of the judiciary.

Article 12   Right to marry

Men and women of marriageable age have the right to marry and to found a family, according to the national laws governing the exercise of this right.

Article 14   Prohibition of discrimination

The enjoyment of the rights and freedom set forth In this Convention shall be secured without discrimination on any ground such as sex, race, colour, language, religion, political or other opinion, national or social origin, association with a national minority, property, birth or other status.

Health Act 1999

(1999, c. 8)

PART III MISCELLANEOUS AND SUPPLEMENTARY

Miscellaneous

60   Regulation of health care and associated professions

(1) Her Majesty may by Order in Council make provision –

    (a) modifying the regulation of any profession to which subsection (2) applies, so far as appears to Her to be necessary or expedient for the purpose of securing or improving the regulation of the profession or the services which the profession provides or to which it contributes,

(b) regulating any other profession which appears to Her to be concerned (wholly or partly) with the physical or mental health of individuals and to require regulation in pursuance of this section,

(c) modifying the functions, powers or duties of the Professional Standards Authority for Health and Social Care,

(d) modifying the list of regulatory bodies (in section 25(3) of the National Health Service Reform and Health Care Professions Act 2002) in relation to which the Authority performs its functions,

(e) modifying, as respects any such regulatory body, the range of functions of that body in relation to which the Authority performs its functions,

(2) The professions referred to in subsection (1)(a) are –

(a)   the professions regulated by the Medical Act 1983, the Dentists Act 1984, the Opticians Act 1989, the Osteopaths Act 1993 and the Chiropractors Act 1994,

(aa) the professions regulated by the Pharmacy Order 2010,

(b)   the professions regulated by the Nursing and Midwifery Order 2001,

(c)   the professions regulated by the Health and Social Work Professions Order 2001 (other than the social work profession in England),

(d)   any other profession regulated by Order in Council under this section (other than the social work profession in England).

60A   Standard of proof in fitness to practise proceedings

(1) The standard of proof applicable to any proceedings to which this subsection applies is that applicable to civil proceedings.

(2) Subsection (1) applies to any proceedings before –

(b) a committee of a regulatory body, a regulatory body itself or any officer of a regulatory body,

which relate to a person's fitness to practise a profession to which section 60(2) applies.

SCHEDULES

SCHEDULE 3   REGULATION OF HEALTH CARE AND ASSOCIATED PROFESSIONS

Matters generally within the scope of the Orders

1. An Order may make provision, in relation to any profession, for any of the following matters (among others) –

(a) the establishment and continuance of a regulatory body,

(b) keeping a register of members admitted to practice,

(c) education and training before and after admission to practice,

(d) privileges of members admitted to practice,

(e) standards of conduct and performance,

(f) discipline and fitness to practise,

(g) investigation and enforcement by or on behalf of the regulatory body,

(h) appeals,

(i) default powers exercisable by a person other than the regulatory body.

National Health Service Reform and Health Care Professions Act 2002

(2002, c. 17)

PART 2 HEALTH AND SOCIAL CARE PROFESSIONS ETC

The Professional Standards Authority for Health and Social Care

25 The Professional Standards Authority for Health and Social Care

(1) There shall be a body corporate known as the Professional Standards Authority for Health and Social Care (in this group of sections referred to as '*the Authority*').

(2) The general functions of the Authority are –

  (a) to promote the interests of users of health care, users of social care in England, users of social work services in England and other members of the public in relation to the performance of their functions by the bodies mentioned in subsection (3) (in this group of sections referred to as 'regulatory bodies'), and by their committees and officers,

  (b) to promote best practice in the performance of those functions,

  (c) to formulate principles relating to good professional self-regulation, and to encourage regulatory bodies to conform to them, and

  (d) to promote co-operation between regulatory bodies; and between them, or any of them, and other bodies performing corresponding functions.

(2A) The over-arching objective of the Authority in exercising its functions under subsection (2)(b) to (d) is the protection of the public.

(2B) The pursuit by the Authority of its over-arching objective involves the pursuit of the following objectives –

  (a) to protect, promote and maintain the health, safety and well-being of the public;

  (b) to promote and maintain public confidence in the professions regulated by the regulatory bodies;

  (c) to promote and maintain proper professional standards and conduct for members of those professions;

  (d) to promote and maintain proper standards in relation to the carrying on of retail pharmacy businesses at registered pharmacies (as defined in article 3(1) of the Pharmacy Order 2010 (S.I. 2010/231)); and

  (e) to promote and maintain proper standards and conduct for business registrants (as defined in section 36(1) of the Opticians Act 1989).

(3) The bodies referred to in subsection (2)(a) are –

  (a) the General Medical Council,

  (b) the General Dental Council,

  (c) the General Optical Council,

  (d) the General Osteopathic Council,

  (e) the General Chiropractic Council,

  (f) the General Pharmaceutical Council,

  (g) subject to section 26(6), the Pharmaceutical Society of Northern Ireland,

  (ga) the Nursing and Midwifery Council,

  (gb) the Health and Care Professions Council, and

  (j) any other regulatory body (within the meaning of Schedule 3 to the 1999 Act) established by an Order in Council under section 60 of that Act.

Adoption and Children Act 2002

(2002, c. 38)

PART 1 ADOPTION

Chapter 1 Introductory

1 Considerations applying to the exercise of powers

(1) Subsections 2-4 apply whenever a court is coming to a decision relating to the making of a parental order in relation to a child.

(2) The paramount consideration of the court must be the child's welfare, throughout his life.

(3) The court must at all times bear in mind that, in general, any delay in coming to the decision is likely to prejudice the child's welfare.

(4) The court must have regard to the following matters (among others) –

(a) the child's ascertainable wishes and feelings regarding the decision (considered in the light of the child's age and understanding),

(b) the child's particular needs,

(c) the likely effect on the child (throughout his life) of having ceased to be a member of the original family and become the subject of a parental order,

(d) the child's age, sex, background and any of the child's characteristics which the court considers relevant,

(e) any harm (within the meaning of the Children Act 1989 (c. 41)) which the child has suffered or is at risk of suffering,

(f) the relationship which the child has with relatives, and with any other person in relation to whom the court considers the relationship to be relevant.

Female Genital Mutilation Act 2003

(2003, c. 31)

1 Offence of female genital mutilation

(1) A person is guilty of an offence if he excises, infibulates or otherwise mutilates the whole or any part of a girl's labia majora, labia minora or clitoris.

(2) But no offence is committed by an approved person who performs –

(a) a surgical operation on a girl which is necessary for her physical or mental health, or

(b) a surgical operation on a girl who is in any stage of labour, or has just given birth, for purposes connected with the labour or birth.

(3) The following are approved persons –

(a) in relation to an operation falling within subsection (2)(a), a registered medical practitioner,

(b) in relation to an operation falling within subsection (2)(b), a registered medical practitioner, a registered midwife or a person undergoing a course of training with a view to becoming such a practitioner or midwife.

(4) There is also no offence committed by a person who –

(a) performs a surgical operation falling within subsection (2)(a) or (b) outside the United Kingdom, and

(b) in relation to such an operation exercises functions corresponding to those of an approved person.

(5) For the purpose of determining whether an operation is necessary for the mental health of a girl it is immaterial whether she or any other person believes that the operation is required as a matter of custom or ritual.

2   Offence of assisting a girl to mutilate her own genitalia

A person is guilty of an offence if he aids, abets, counsels or procures a girl to excise, infibulate or otherwise mutilate the whole or any part of her own labia majora, labia minora or clitoris.

3   Offence of assisting a non-UK person to mutilate overseas a girl's genitalia

(1) A person is guilty of an offence if he aids, abets, counsels or procures a person who is not a United Kingdom national or permanent United Kingdom resident to do a relevant act of female genital mutilation outside the United Kingdom.

(2) An act is a relevant act of female genital mutilation if –

(a) it is done in relation to a United Kingdom national or permanent United Kingdom resident, and

(b) it would, if done by such a person, constitute an offence under section 1.

(3) But no offence is committed if the relevant act of female genital mutilation –

(a) is a surgical operation falling within section 1(2)(a) or (b), and

(b) is performed by a person who, in relation to such an operation, is an approved person or exercises functions corresponding to those of an approved person.

Health and Social Care (Community Health and Standards) Act 2003

(2003, c. 43)

Complaints

113   Complaints about health care

(1) The Secretary of State may by regulations make provision about the handling and consideration of complaints made under the regulations about –

(a) the exercise of any of the functions of an English NHS body or a cross-border SHA;

(b) the provision of health care by or for such a body;

(c) the provision of services by such a body or any other person in pursuance of arrangements made by the body under section 75 of the National Health Service Act 2006 or section 33 of the National Health Service (Wales) Act 2006 in relation to the exercise of the health-related functions of a local authority.

(d) anything done by the National Health Service Commissioning Board or a clinical commissioning group in pursuance of arrangements made under section 7A of the National Health Service Act 2006.

(3) Regulations under this section may provide for a complaint to be considered by one or more of the following –

(a) an NHS body;

(c) an independent lay person;

(d) an independent panel established under the regulations;

(e) any other person or body.

148   Interpretation of Part 2
In this Part –
 'cross-border SHA' means a Special Health Authority not performing functions only or mainly in respect of England or only or mainly in respect of Wales;

Human Fertilisation and Embryology (Deceased Fathers) Act 2003

(2003, c. 24)

1   Certain deceased men to be registered as fathers
[See section 28 and section 29 of the Human Fertilisation and Embryology Act 1990]

3   Retrospective, transitional and transitory provision
  (1) This Act shall (in addition to any case where the sperm or embryo is used on or after the coming into force of section 1) apply to any case where the sperm of a man, or any embryo the creation of which was brought about with the sperm of a man, was used on or after 1st August 1991 and before the coming into force of that section.

  (2) Where the child concerned was born before the coming into force of section 1 of this Act, section 28(5A) or (as the case may be) (5B) of the Human Fertilisation and Embryology Act 1990 (c. 37) shall have effect as if for paragraph (e) there were substituted –
 '(e) the woman has elected in writing not later than the end of the period of six months beginning with the coming into force of this subsection for the man to be treated for the purpose mentioned in subsection (5I) below as the father of the child'.

  (3) Where the child concerned was born before the coming into force of section 1 of this Act, section 28(5C) of the Act of 1990 shall have effect as if for paragraph (f) there were substituted –
 '(f) the woman has elected in writing not later than the end of the period of six months beginning with the coming into force of this subsection for the other party to the marriage to be treated for the purpose mentioned in subsection (5I) below as the father of the child'.

  (4) Where the child concerned was born before the coming into force of section 1 of this Act, section 28(5D) of the Act of 1990 shall have effect as if for paragraph (f) there were substituted –
 '(f) the woman has elected in writing not later than the end of the period of six months beginning with the coming into force of this subsection for the man to be treated for the purpose mentioned in subsection (5I) below as the father of the child'.

  (5) Where the child concerned was born before the coming into force of section 1 of this Act, section 28 of the Act of 1990 shall have effect as if –
   (a) subsection (5E) were omitted; and
   (b) in subsection (5F) for the words from '(which requires' to 'that day)' there were substituted '(which requires an election to be made not later than the end of a period of six months)'.

  (6) Where the man who might be treated as the father of the child died before the passing of this Act –
   (a) subsections (5A) and (5B) of section 28 of the Act of 1990 shall have effect as if paragraph (d) of each subsection were omitted;
   (b) subsections (5C) and (5D) of that section of that Act shall have effect as if paragraph (e) of each subsection were omitted.

Human Tissue Act 2004

(2004, c. 30)

PART 1 REMOVAL, STORAGE AND USE OF HUMAN ORGANS AND OTHER TISSUE FOR SCHEDULED PURPOSES

1 Authorisation of activities for scheduled purposes

(1) The following activities shall be lawful if done with appropriate consent –

(a) the storage of the body of a deceased person for use for a purpose specified in Schedule 1, other than anatomical examination;

(b) the use of the body of a deceased person for a purpose so specified, other than anatomical examination;

(c) the removal from the body of a deceased person, for use for a purpose specified in Schedule 1, of any relevant material of which the body consists or which it contains;

(d) the storage for use for a purpose specified in Part 1 of Schedule 1 of any relevant material which has come from a human body;

(e) the storage for use for a purpose specified in Part 2 of Schedule 1 of any relevant material which has come from the body of a deceased person;

(f) the use for a purpose specified in Part 1 of Schedule 1 of any relevant material which has come from a human body;

(g) the use for a purpose specified in Part 2 of Schedule 1 of any relevant material which has come from the body of a deceased person.

(2) The storage of the body of a deceased person for use for the purpose of anatomical examination shall be lawful if done with the appropriate consent and after –

(a) the confirmation of the cause of death by a medical examiner in accordance with regulations under section 20(1)(f)(i) of the Coroners and Justice Act 2009 or the issue by a medical examiner of a certificate of the cause of death in accordance with regulations under section 20(1)(h)(i) of that Act ...

(3) The use of the body of a deceased person for the purpose of anatomical examination shall be lawful if done –

(a) with appropriate consent, and

(b) after the death of the person has been registered –

(i) under section 15 of the Births and Deaths Registration Act 1953.

(4) Subsections (1) to (3) do not apply to an activity of a kind mentioned there if it is done in relation to –

(a) a body to which subsection (5) applies, or

(b) relevant material to which subsection (6) applies.

(5) This subsection applies to a body if –

(a) it has been imported, or

(b) it is the body of a person who died before the day on which this section comes into force and at least one hundred years have elapsed since the date of the person's death.

(6) This subsection applies to relevant material if –

(a) it has been imported,

(b) it has come from a body which has been imported, or

(c) it is material which has come from the body of a person who died before the day on which this section comes into force and at least one hundred years have elapsed since the date of the person's death.

(7) Subsection (1)(d) does not apply to the storage of relevant material for use for the purpose of research in connection with disorders, or the functioning, of the human body if –

    (a) the material has come from the body of a living person, and

    (b) the research falls within subsection (9).

(8) Subsection (1)(f) does not apply to the use of relevant material for the purpose of research in connection with disorders, or the functioning, of the human body if –

    (a) the material has come from the body of a living person, and

    (b) the research falls within subsection (9).

(9) Research falls within this subsection if –

    (a) it is ethically approved in accordance with regulations made by the Secretary of State, and

    (b) it is to be, or is, carried out in circumstances such that the person carrying it out is not in possession, and not likely to come into possession, of information from which the person from whose body the material has come can be identified.

(9A) Subsection (1)(f) does not apply to the use of relevant material for the purpose of research where the use of the material requires consent under paragraph 6(1) or 12(1) of Schedule 3 to the Human Fertilisation and Embryology Act 1990 (use of human cells to create an embryo or a human admixed embryo) or would require such consent but for paragraphs 16 and 20 of that Schedule.

(10) The following activities shall be lawful –

    (a) the storage for use for a purpose specified in Part 2 of Schedule 1 of any relevant material which has come from the body of a living person;

    (b) the use for such a purpose of any relevant material which has come from the body of a living person;

    (c) an activity in relation to which subsection (4), (7) or (8) has effect.

(10A) In the case of an activity in relation to which subsection (8) has effect, subsection (10)(c) is to be read subject to any requirements imposed by Schedule 3 to the Human Fertilisation and Embryology Act 1990 in relation to the activity.

(11) The Secretary of State may by order –

    (a) vary or omit any of the purposes specified in Part 1 or 2 of Schedule 1, or

    (b) add to the purposes specified in Part 1 or 2 of that Schedule.

(12) Nothing in this section applies to –

    (a) the use of relevant material in connection with a device to which Directive 98/79/EC of the European Parliament and of the Council on *in vitro* diagnostic medical devices applies, where the use falls within the Directive, or

    (b) the storage of relevant material for use falling within paragraph (a).

(13) In this section, the references to a body or material which has been imported do not include a body or material which has been imported after having been exported with a view to its subsequently being re-imported.

2 'Appropriate consent': children

(1) This section makes provision for the interpretation of 'appropriate consent in section 1 in relation to an activity involving the body, or material from the body, of a person who is a child or has died a child ('the child concerned').

(2) Subject to subsection (3), where the child concerned is alive, 'appropriate consent' means his consent.

(3) Where –

    (a) the child concerned is alive,

    (b) neither a decision of his to consent to the activity, nor a decision of his not to consent to it, is in force, and

    (c) either he is not competent to deal with the issue of consent in relation to the activity or, though he is competent to deal with that issue, he fails to do so, 'appropriate consent' means the consent of a person who has parental responsibility for him.

(4) Where the child concerned has died and the activity is one to which subsection (5) applies, 'appropriate consent' means his consent in writing.

(5) This subsection applies to an activity involving storage for use, or use, for the purpose of –

(a) public display, or

(b) where the subject-matter of the activity is not excepted material, anatomical examination.

(6) Consent in writing for the purposes of subsection (4) is only valid if –

(a) it is signed by the child concerned in the presence of at least one witness who attests the signature, or

(b) it is signed at the direction of the child concerned, in his presence and in the presence of at least one witness who attests the signature.

(7) Where the child concerned has died and the activity is not one to which subsection (5) applies, 'appropriate consent' means –

(a) if a decision of his to consent to the activity, or a decision of his not to consent to it, was in force immediately before he died, his consent;

(b) if paragraph (a) does not apply –

(i) the consent of a person who had parental responsibility for him immediately before he died, or

(ii) where no person had parental responsibility for him immediately before he died, the consent of a person who stood in a qualifying relationship to him at that time.

3   'Appropriate consent': adults

(1) This section makes provision for the interpretation of 'appropriate consent' in section 1 in relation to an activity involving the body, or material from the body, of a person who is an adult or has died an adult ('the person concerned').

(2) Where the person concerned is alive, 'appropriate consent' means his consent.

(3) Where the person concerned has died and the activity is one to which subsection (4) applies, 'appropriate consent' means his consent in writing.

(4) This subsection applies to an activity involving storage for use, or use, for the purpose of –

(a) public display, or

(b) where the subject-matter of the activity is not excepted material, anatomical examination.

(5) Consent in writing for the purposes of subsection (3) is only valid if –

(a) it is signed by the person concerned in the presence of at least one witness who attests the signature,

(b) it is signed at the direction of the person concerned, in his presence and in the presence of at least one witness who attests the signature, or

(c) it is contained in a will of the person concerned made in accordance with the requirements of –

(i) section 9 of the Wills Act 1837 (c. 26).

(6) Where the person concerned has died and the activity is not one to which subsection (4) applies, 'appropriate consent' means –

(a) if a decision of his to consent to the activity, or a decision of his not to consent to it, was in force immediately before he died, his consent;

(b) if–

(i) paragraph (a) does not apply, and

(ii) he has appointed a person or persons under section 4 to deal after his death with the issue of consent in relation to the activity, consent given under the appointment;

(c) if neither paragraph (a) nor paragraph (b) applies, the consent of a person who stood in a qualifying relationship to him immediately before he died.

(7) Where the person concerned has appointed a person or persons under section 4 to deal after his death with the issue of consent in relation to the activity, the appointment shall be disregarded for the purposes of subsection (6) if no one is able to give consent under it.

(8) If it is not reasonably practicable to communicate with a person appointed under section 4 within the time available if consent in relation to the activity is to be acted on, he shall be treated for the purposes of subsection (7) as not able to give consent under the appointment in relation to it.

4 Nominated representatives

(1) An adult may appoint one or more persons to represent him after his death in relation to consent for the purposes of section 1.

(2) An appointment under this section may be general or limited to consent in relation to such one or more activities as may be specified in the appointment.

(3) An appointment under this section may be made orally or in writing.

(4) An oral appointment under this section is only valid if made in the presence of at least two witnesses present at the same time.

(5) A written appointment under this section is only valid if –
  (a) it is signed by the person making it in the presence of at least one witness who attests the signature,
  (b) it is signed at the direction of the person making it, in his presence and in the presence of at least one witness who attests the signature, or
  (c) it is contained in a will of the person making it, being a will which is made in accordance with the requirements of –
    (i) section 9 of the Wills Act 1837 (c. 26).

(6) Where a person appoints two or more persons under this section in relation to the same activity, they shall be regarded as appointed to act jointly and severally unless the appointment provides that they are appointed to act jointly.

(7) An appointment under this section may be revoked at any time.

(8) Subsections (3) to (5) apply to the revocation of an appointment under this section as they apply to the making of such an appointment.

(9) A person appointed under this section may at any time renounce his appointment.

(10) A person may not act under an appointment under this section if –
  (a) he is not an adult, or
  (b) he is of a description prescribed for the purposes of this provision by regulations made by the Secretary of State.

5 Prohibition of activities without consent etc.

(1) A person commits an offence if, without appropriate consent, he does an activity to which subsection (1), (2) or (3) of section 1 applies, unless he reasonably believes –
  (a) that he does the activity with appropriate consent, or
  (b) that what he does is not an activity to which the subsection applies.

(2) A person commits an offence if –
  (a) he falsely represents to a person whom he knows or believes is going to, or may, do an activity to which subsection (1), (2) or (3) of section 1 applies –
    (i) that there is appropriate consent to the doing of the activity, or
    (ii) that the activity is not one to which the subsection applies, and
  (b) he knows that the representation is false or does not believe it to be true.

(3) Subject to subsection (4), a person commits an offence if, when he does an activity to which section 1(2) applies, neither of the following has been signed in relation to the cause of death of the person concerned –
  (a) a certificate under section 22(1) of the Births and Deaths Registration Act 1953, and
  (b) a certificate under Article 25(2) of the Births and Deaths Registration (Northern Ireland) Order 1976 (S.I. 1976/1041 (N.I. 14)).

(4) Subsection (3) does not apply –
- (a) where the person reasonably believes –
  - (i)   that a certificate under either of those provisions has been signed in relation to the cause of death of the person concerned, or
  - (ii) that what he does is not an activity to which section 1(2) applies, or
- (b) where the person comes into lawful possession of the body immediately after death and stores it prior to its removal to a place where anatomical examination is to take place.

(5) Subject to subsection (6), a person commits an offence if, when he does an activity to which section 1(3) applies, the death of the person concerned has not been registered under either of the following provisions –
- (a) section 15 of the Births and Deaths Registration Act 1953.

(6) Subsection (5) does not apply where the person reasonably believes –
- (a) that the death of the person concerned has been registered under either of those provisions, or
- (b) that what he does is not an activity to which section 1(3) applies.

(7) A person guilty of an offence under this section shall be liable –
- (a) on summary conviction to a fine not exceeding the statutory maximum;
- (b) on conviction on indictment –
  - (i)   to imprisonment for a term not exceeding 3 years, or
  - (ii) to a fine, or
  - (iii) to both.

(8) In this section, 'appropriate consent' has the same meaning as in section 1.

6   Activities involving material from adults who lack capacity to consent
Where—
- (a) an activity of a kind mentioned in section 1(1)(d) or (f) involves material from the body of a person who –
  - (i)   is an adult, and
  - (ii) lacks capacity to consent to the activity, and
- (b) neither a decision of his to consent to the activity, nor a decision of his not to consent to it, is in force,

there shall for the purposes of this Part be deemed to be consent of his to the activity if it is done in circumstances of a kind specified by regulations made by the Secretary of State.

7   Powers to dispense with need for consent
(1) If the Authority is satisfied –
- (a) that relevant material has come from the body of a living person,
- (b) that it is not reasonably possible to trace the person from whose body the material has come ('the donor'),
- (c) that it is desirable in the interests of another person (including a future person) that the material be used for the purpose of obtaining scientific or medical information about the donor, and
- (d) that there is no reason to believe –
  - (i)   that the donor has died,
  - (ii) that a decision of the donor to refuse to consent to the use of the material for that purpose is in force, or
  - (iii) that the donor lacks capacity to consent to the use of the material for that purpose, it may direct that subsection (3) apply to the material for the benefit of the other person.

(2) If the Authority is satisfied –
- (a) that relevant material has come from the body of a living person,

(b) that it is desirable in the interests of another person (including a future person) that the material be used for the purpose of obtaining scientific or medical information about the person from whose body the material has come ('the donor'),

(c) that reasonable efforts have been made to get the donor to decide whether to consent to the use of the material for that purpose,

(d) that there is no reason to believe –

    (i) that the donor has died,

    (ii) that a decision of the donor to refuse to consent to the use of the material for that purpose is in force, or

    (iii) that the donor lacks capacity to consent to the use of the material for that purpose, and

(e) that the donor has been given notice of the application for the exercise of the power conferred by this subsection,

it may direct that subsection (3) apply to the material for the benefit of the other person.

(3) Where material is the subject of a direction under subsection (1) or (2), there shall for the purposes of this Part be deemed to be consent of the donor to the use of the material for the purpose of obtaining scientific or medical information about him which may be relevant to the person for whose benefit the direction is given.

(4) The Secretary of State may by regulations enable the High Court, in such circumstances as the regulations may provide, to make an order deeming there for the purposes of this Part to be appropriate consent to an activity consisting of –

(a) the storage of the body of a deceased person for use for the purpose of research in connection with disorders, or the functioning, of the human body,

(b) the use of the body of a deceased person for that purpose,

(c) the removal from the body of a deceased person, for use for that purpose, of any relevant material of which the body consists or which it contains,

(d) the storage for use for that purpose of any relevant material which has come from a human body, or

(e) the use for that purpose of any relevant material which has come from a human body.

8 Restriction of activities in relation to donated material

(1) Subject to subsection (2), a person commits an offence if he –

(a) uses donated material for a purpose which is not a qualifying purpose, or

(b) stores donated material for use for a purpose which is not a qualifying purpose.

(2) Subsection (1) does not apply where the person reasonably believes that what he uses, or stores, is not donated material.

(3) A person guilty of an offence under this section shall be liable –

(a) on summary conviction to a fine not exceeding the statutory maximum;

(b) on conviction on indictment –

    (i) to imprisonment for a term not exceeding 3 years, or

    (ii) to a fine, or

    (iii) to both.

(4) In subsection (1), references to a qualifying purpose are to –

(a) a purpose specified in Schedule 1,

(b) the purpose of medical diagnosis or treatment,

(c) the purpose of decent disposal, or

(d) a purpose specified in regulations made by the Secretary of State.

(5) In this section, references to donated material are to –

(a) the body of a deceased person, or

(b) relevant material which has come from a human body, which is, or has been, the subject of donation.

(6) For the purposes of subsection (5), a body, or material, is the subject of donation if authority under section 1(1) to (3) exists in relation to it.

9 Existing holdings

(1) In its application to the following activities, section 1(1) shall have effect with the omission of the words 'if done with appropriate consent' –

    (a) the storage of an existing holding for use for a purpose specified in Schedule 1;

    (b) the use of an existing holding for a purpose so specified.

(2) Subsection (1) does not apply where the existing holding is a body, or separated part of a body, in relation to which section 10(3) or (5) has effect.

(3) Section 5(1) and (2) shall have effect as if the activities mentioned in subsection (1) were not activities to which section 1(1) applies.

(4) In this section, 'existing holding' means –

    (a) the body of a deceased person, or

    (b) relevant material which has come from a human body,

held, immediately before the day on which section 1(1) comes into force, for use for a purpose specified in Schedule 1.

10 Existing anatomical specimens

(1) This section applies where a person dies during the three years immediately preceding the coming into force of section 1.

(2) Subsection (3) applies where –

    (a) before section 1 comes into force, authority is given under section 4(2) or (3) of the Anatomy Act 1984 (c. 14) for the person's body to be used for anatomical examination, and

    (b) section 1 comes into force before anatomical examination of the person's body is concluded.

(3) During so much of the relevant period as falls after section 1 comes into force, that authority shall be treated for the purposes of section 1 as appropriate consent in relation to –

    (a) the storage of the person's body, or separated parts of his body, for use for the purpose of anatomical examination, and

    (b) the use of his body, or separated parts of his body, for that purpose.

(4) Subsection (5) applies where –

    (a) before section 1 comes into force, authority is given under section 6(2) or (3) of the Anatomy Act 1984 for possession of parts (or any specified parts) of the person's body to be held after anatomical examination of his body is concluded, and

    (b) anatomical examination of the person's body is concluded –

        (i) after section 1 comes into force, but

        (i) before the end of the period of three years beginning with the date of the person's death.

(5) With effect from the conclusion of the anatomical examination of the person's body, that authority shall be treated for the purposes of section 1 as appropriate consent in relation to –

    (a) the storage for use for a qualifying purpose of a part of the person's body which –

        (i) is a part to which that authority relates, and

        (ii) is such that the person cannot be recognised simply by examination of the part, and

    (b) the use for a qualifying purpose of such a part of the person's body.

(6) Where for the purposes of section 1 there would not be appropriate consent in relation to an activity but for authority given under the Anatomy Act 1984 (c. 14) being treated for those purposes as appropriate consent in relation to the activity, section 1(1) to (3) do not authorise the doing of the activity otherwise than in accordance with that authority.

(7) In subsection (3), 'the relevant period', in relation to a person, means whichever is the shorter of –

    (a) the period of three years beginning with the date of the person's death, and

(b) the period beginning with that date and ending when anatomical examination of the per-son's body is concluded.

(8) In subsection (5), 'qualifying purpose' means a purpose specified in paragraph 6 or 9 of Schedule 1.

11 Coroners

(1) Nothing in this Part applies to anything done for purposes of functions of a coroner or under the authority of a coroner.

(2) Where a person knows, or has reason to believe, that –

(a) the body of a deceased person, or

(b) relevant material which has come from the body of a deceased person, is, or may be, required for purposes of functions of a coroner, he shall not act on authority under section 1 in relation to the body, or material, except with the consent of the coroner.

12 Interpretation of Part 1

In this Part, 'excepted material' means material which has –

(a) come from the body of a living person, or

(b) come from the body of a deceased person otherwise than in the course of use of the body for the purpose of anatomical examination.

PART 2 REGULATION OF ACTIVITIES INVOLVING HUMAN TISSUE

The Human Tissue Authority

13 The Human Tissue Authority

(1) There shall be a body corporate to be known as the Human Tissue Authority (referred to in this Act as 'the Authority').

14 Remit

(1) The following are the activities within the remit of the Authority –

(a) the removal from a human body, for use for a scheduled purpose, of any relevant material of which the body consists or which it contains;

(b) the use, for a scheduled purpose, of –

(i) the body of a deceased person, or

(ii) relevant material which has come from a human body;

(c) the storage of an anatomical specimen or former anatomical specimen;

(d) the storage (in any case not falling within paragraph (c)) of –

(i) the body of a deceased person, or

(ii) relevant material which has come from a human body, for use for a scheduled purpose;

(e) the import or export of –

(i) the body of a deceased person, or

(ii) relevant material which has come from a human body, for use for a scheduled purpose;

(f) the disposal of the body of a deceased person which has been –

(i) imported for use,

(ii) stored for use, or

(iii) used, for a scheduled purpose;

(g) the disposal of relevant material which –

(i) has been removed from a person's body for the purposes of his medical treatment,

(ii) has been removed from the body of a deceased person for the purposes of an anatomical, or post-mortem, examination,

(iii) has been removed from a human body (otherwise than as mentioned in sub-paragraph (ii)) for use for a scheduled purpose,

(iv) has come from a human body and been imported for use for a scheduled purpose, or

(v) has come from the body of a deceased person which has been imported for use for a scheduled purpose.

(h) the procurement, processing, preservation, testing, storage, distribution, import or export of tissue or cells, in so far as those activities are activities to which regulation 7(1) or (2) of the 2007 Regulations applies and are not within the remit of the Authority by virtue of paragraphs (a) to (g);

(i) the donation, testing, characterisation, procurement, preservation, transport, transplantation and disposal of human organs, in so far as those activities are activities to which regulation 5(1) of the 2012 Regulations applies and are not within the remit of the Authority by virtue of paragraphs (a) to (h).

(2) Without prejudice to the generality of subsection (1)(a) and (b), the activities within the remit of the Authority include, in particular –

(a) the carrying-out of an anatomical examination, and

(b) the making of a post-mortem examination.

(2ZA) The activities within the remit of the Authority do not include the use, for a scheduled purpose, of relevant material where the use of the material requires consent under paragraph 6(1) or 12(1) of Schedule 3 to the Human Fertilisation and Embryology Act 1990 (use of human cells to create an embryo or a human admixed embryo) or would require such consent but for paragraphs 16 and 20 of that Schedule.

(2A) Expressions used in paragraph (h) of subsection (1) and in the 2007 Regulations have the same meaning in that paragraph as in those Regulations; and the reference to activities to which regulation 7(1) or (2) of those Regulations applies is to be read subject to regulation 2(3) of those Regulations.

(3) An activity is excluded from the remit of the Authority if –

(a) it relates to the body of a person who died before the day on which this section comes into force or to material which has come from the body of such a person, and

(b) at least one hundred years have elapsed since the date of the person's death.

(4) The Secretary of State may by order amend this section for the purpose of adding to the activities within the remit of the Authority.

(5) In this section, 'relevant material', in relation to use for the scheduled purpose of transplantation, does not include blood or anything derived from blood.

15   General functions

The Authority shall have the following general functions –

(a) maintaining a statement of the general principles which it considers should be followed –

(i) in the carrying-on of activities within its remit, and

(ii) in the carrying-out of its functions in relation to such activities;

(b) providing in relation to activities within its remit such general oversight and guidance as it considers appropriate;

(c) superintending, in relation to activities within its remit, compliance with –

(i) requirements imposed by or under Part 1 or this Part, and

(ii) codes of practice under this Act;

(d) providing to the public, and to persons carrying on activities within its remit, such information and advice as it considers appropriate about the nature and purpose of such activities;

(e) monitoring developments relating to activities within its remit and advising the Secretary of State, the National Assembly for Wales and the relevant Northern Ireland department on issues relating to such developments;

(f) advising the Secretary of State, the National Assembly for Wales or the relevant Northern Ireland department on such other issues relating to activities within its remit as he, the Assembly or the department may require.

Licensing

16   Licence requirement

(1) No person shall do an activity to which this section applies otherwise than under the authority of a licence granted for the purposes of this section.

(2) This section applies to the following activities –

(a) the carrying-out of an anatomical examination;

(b) the making of a post-mortem examination;

(c) the removal from the body of a deceased person (otherwise than in the course of an activity mentioned in paragraph (a) or (b)) of relevant material of which the body consists or which it contains, for use for a scheduled purpose other than transplantation;

(d) the storage of an anatomical specimen;

(e) the storage (in any case not falling within paragraph (d)) of –

(i)   the body of a deceased person, or

(ii)   relevant material which has come from a human body, for use for a scheduled purpose;

(f) the use, for the purpose of public display, of –

(i)   the body of a deceased person, or

(ii)   relevant material which has come from the body of a deceased person.

(2A) This section does not apply to the procurement, testing, processing, preservation, storage, distribution, import or export of tissue and cells intended for human application in so far as those activities are activities to which regulation 7(1) or (2) of the 2007 Regulations applies.

(2B) Expressions used in subsection (2A) and in the 2007 Regulations have the same meaning in that subsection as in those Regulations; and the reference to activities to which regulation 7(1) or (2) of those Regulations applies is to be read subject to regulation 2(3) of those Regulations.

(3) The Secretary of State may by regulations specify circumstances in which storage of relevant material by a person who intends to use it for a scheduled purpose is excepted from sub section (2)(e)(ii).

(4) An activity is excluded from subsection (2) if –

(a) it relates to the body of a person who died before the day on which this section comes into force or to material which has come from the body of such a person, and

(b) at least one hundred years have elapsed since the date of the person's death.

(6) Schedule 3 (which makes provision about licences for the purposes of this section) has effect.

(7) In subsection (2) –

(a) references to storage do not include storage which is incidental to transportation, and

(b) 'relevant material', in relation to use for the scheduled purpose of transplantation, does not include blood or anything derived from blood.

25   Breach of licence requirement

(1) A person who contravenes section 16(1) commits an offence, unless he reasonably believes –

(a) that what he does is not an activity to which section 16 applies, or

(b) that he acts under the authority of a licence.

(2) A person guilty of an offence under subsection (1) shall be liable –

(a) on summary conviction to a fine not exceeding the statutory maximum;

(b) on conviction on indictment –

(i)   to imprisonment for a term not exceeding 3 years, or

(ii)   to a fine, or

(iii) to both.

Codes of practice

26 Preparation of codes

(1) The Authority may prepare and issue codes of practice for the purpose of –

    (a) giving practical guidance to persons carrying on activities within its remit, and

    (b) laying down the standards expected in relation to the carrying-on of such activities.

(2) The Authority shall deal under subsection (1) with the following matters –

    (a) the carrying-out of anatomical examinations;

    (b) the storage of anatomical specimens;

    (c) the storage and disposal of former anatomical specimens;

    (d) the definition of death for the purposes of this Act;

    (e) communication with the family of the deceased in relation to the making of a post-mortem examination;

    (f) the making of post-mortem examinations;

    (g) communication with the family of the deceased in relation to the removal from the body of the deceased, for use for a scheduled purpose, of any relevant material of which the body consists or which it contains;

    (h) the removal from a human body, for use for a scheduled purpose, of any relevant material of which the body consists or which it contains;

    (i) the storage for use for a scheduled purpose, and the use for such a purpose, of –

        (i) the body of a deceased person, or

        (ii) relevant material which has come from a human body;

    (j) the storage for use for a scheduled purpose, and the use for such a purpose, of an existing holding within the meaning of section 9;

    (k) the import, and the export, of –

        (i) the body of a deceased person, or

        (ii) relevant material which has come from a human body, for use for a scheduled purpose;

    (l) the disposal of relevant material which –

        (i) has been removed from a human body for use for a scheduled purpose, or

        (ii) has come from a human body and is an existing holding for the purposes of section 9.

(3) In dealing under subsection (1) with the matters mentioned in subsection (2)(h) and (i), the Authority shall, in particular, deal with consent.

(4) The Authority shall –

    (a) keep any code of practice under this section under review, and

    (b) prepare a revised code of practice when appropriate.

27 Provision with respect to consent

(1) The duty under section 26(3) shall have effect, in particular, to require the Authority to lay down the standards expected in relation to the obtaining of consent where consent falls by virtue of section 2(7)(b)(ii) or 3(6)(c) to be obtained from a person in a qualifying relationship.

(2) Subject to subsection (3), the standards required to be laid down by subsection (1) shall include provision to the effect set out in subsections (4) to (8).

(3) The standards required to be laid down by subsection (1) may include provision to different effect in relation to cases which appear to the Authority to be exceptional.

(4) The qualifying relationships for the purpose of sections 2(7)(b)(ii) and 3(6)(c) should be ranked in the following order –

    (a) spouse, civil partner or partner;

    (b) parent or child;

    (c) brother or sister;

    (d) grandparent or grandchild;

    (e) child of a person falling within paragraph (c);

    (f) stepfather or stepmother;

    (g) half-brother or half-sister;

    (h) friend of longstanding.

  (5) Relationships in the same paragraph of subsection (4) should be accorded equal ranking.

  (6) Consent should be obtained from the person whose relationship to the person concerned is accorded the highest ranking in accordance with subsections (4) and (5).

  (7) If the relationship of each of two or more persons to the person concerned is accorded equal highest ranking in accordance with subsections (4) and (5), it is sufficient to obtain the consent of any of them.

  (8) In applying the principles set out above, a person's relationship shall be left out of account if –

    (a) he does not wish to deal with the issue of consent,

    (b) he is not able to deal with that issue, or

    (c) having regard to the activity in relation to which consent is sought, it is not reasonably practicable to communicate with him within the time available if consent in relation to the activity is to be acted on.

28 Effect of codes

  (1) A failure on the part of any person to observe any provision of a code of practice under section 26 shall not of itself render the person liable to any proceedings.

  (2) The Authority may, in carrying out its functions with respect to licences, take into account any relevant observance of, or failure to observe, a code of practice under section 26, so far as dealing with a matter mentioned in any of paragraphs (a) to (c) and (e) to (j) of subsection (2) of that section.

Anatomy

30 Possession of anatomical specimens away from licensed premises

  (1) Subject to subsections (2) to (6), a person commits an offence if –

    (a) he has possession of an anatomical specimen, and

    (b) the specimen is not on premises in respect of which an anatomy licence is in force.

  (2) Subsection (1) does not apply where –

    (a) the specimen has come from premises in respect of which a storage licence is in force, and

    (b) the person –

      (i)   is authorised in writing by the designated individual to have possession of the specimen, and

      (ii) has possession of the specimen only for a purpose for which he is so authorised to have possession of it.

  (3) Subsection (1) does not apply where –

    (a) the specimen is the body of a deceased person which is to be used for the purpose of anatomical examination,

    (b) the person who has possession of the body has come into lawful possession of it immediately after the deceased's death, and

    (c) he retains possession of the body prior to its removal to premises in respect of which an anatomy licence is in force.

  (4) Subsection (1) does not apply where the person has possession of the specimen only for the purpose of transporting it to premises –

    (a) in respect of which an anatomy licence is in force, or

    (b) where the specimen is to be used for the purpose of education, training or research.

  (5) Subsection (1) does not apply where the person has possession of the specimen for purposes of functions of, or under the authority of, a coroner.

  (6) Subsection (1) does not apply where the person reasonably believes –

    (a) that what he has possession of is not an anatomical specimen,

    (b) that the specimen is on premises in respect of which an anatomy licence is in force, or

    (c) that any of subsections (2) to (5) applies.

(7) A person guilty of an offence under subsection (1) shall be liable –

    (a) on summary conviction to a fine not exceeding the statutory maximum;

    (b) on conviction on indictment –

        (i) to imprisonment for a term not exceeding 3 years, or

        (ii) to a fine, or

        (iii) to both.

(8) In this section –

'anatomy licence' means a licence authorising –

    (a) the carrying-out of an anatomical examination, or

    (b) the storage of anatomical specimens;

'storage licence' means a licence authorising the storage of anatomical specimens.

31 Possession of former anatomical specimens away from licensed premises

(1) Subject to subsections (2) to (5), a person commits an offence if –

    (a) he has possession of a former anatomical specimen, and

    (b) the specimen is not on premises in respect of which a storage licence is in force.

(2) Subsection (1) does not apply where –

    (a) the specimen has come from premises in respect of which a storage licence is in force, and

    (b) the person –

        (i) is authorised in writing by the designated individual to have possession of the specimen, and

        (ii) has possession of the specimen only for a purpose for which he is so authorised to have possession of it.

(3) Subsection (1) does not apply where the person has possession of the specimen only for the purpose of transporting it to premises –

    (a) in respect of which a storage licence is in force, or

    (b) where the specimen is to be used for the purpose of education, training or research.

(4) Subsection (1) does not apply where the person has possession of the specimen –

    (a) only for the purpose of its decent disposal, or

    (b) for purposes of functions of, or under the authority of, a coroner.

(5) Subsection (1) does not apply where the person reasonably believes –

    (a) that what he has possession of is not a former anatomical specimen,

    (b) that the specimen is on premises in respect of which a storage licence is in force, or

    (c) that any of subsections (2) to (4) applies.

(6) A person guilty of an offence under subsection (1) shall be liable –

    (a) on summary conviction to a fine not exceeding the statutory maximum;

    (b) on conviction on indictment –

        (i) to imprisonment for a term not exceeding 3 years, or

        (ii) to a fine, or

        (iii) to both.

(7) In this section, 'storage licence' means a licence authorising the storage, for use for a scheduled purpose, of relevant material which has come from a human body.

Trafficking

32 Prohibition of commercial dealings in human material for transplantation

(1) A person commits an offence if he –

    (a) gives or receives a reward for the supply of, or for an offer to supply, any controlled material;

    (b) seeks to find a person willing to supply any controlled material for reward;

(c) offers to supply any controlled material for reward;

(d) initiates or negotiates any arrangement involving the giving of a reward for the supply of, or for an offer to supply, any controlled material;

(e) takes part in the management or control of a body of persons corporate or unincorporate whose activities consist of or include the initiation or negotiation of such arrangements.

(2) Without prejudice to subsection (1)(b) and (c), a person commits an offence if he causes to be published or distributed, or knowingly publishes or distributes, an advertisement –

(a) inviting persons to supply, or offering to supply, any controlled material for reward, or

(b) indicating that the advertiser is willing to initiate or negotiate any such arrangement as is mentioned in subsection (1)(d).

(3) A person who engages in an activity to which subsection (1) or (2) applies does not commit an offence under that subsection if he is designated by the Authority as a person who may lawfully engage in the activity.

(3A) The Authority may not designate a person under subsection (3) if doing so could result in the United Kingdom being in breach of –

(a) Article 12 of Directive 2004/23/EC of the European Parliament and of the Council on setting standards of quality and safety for the donation, procurement, testing, processing, preservation, storage and distribution of human tissues and cells , or

(b) Article 13 of Directive 2010/53/EU of the European Parliament and of the Council on standards of quality and safety of human organs intended for transplantation.

(4) A person guilty of an offence under subsection (1) shall be liable –

(a) on summary conviction –

(i)   to imprisonment for a term not exceeding 12 months, or

(ii) to a fine not exceeding the statutory maximum, or

(iii) to both;

(b) on conviction on indictment –

(i)   to imprisonment for a term not exceeding 3 years, or

(ii) to a fine, or

(iii) to both.

(5) A person guilty of an offence under subsection (2) shall be liable on summary conviction –

(a) to imprisonment for a term not exceeding 51 weeks, or

(b) to a fine not exceeding level 5 on the standard scale, or

(c) to both.

(6) For the purposes of subsections (1) and (2), payment in money or money's worth to the holder of a licence shall be treated as not being a reward where –

(a) it is in consideration for transporting, removing, preparing, preserving or storing controlled material, and

(b) its receipt by the holder of the licence is not expressly prohibited by the terms of the licence.

(7) References in subsections (1) and (2) to reward, in relation to the supply of any controlled material, do not include payment in money or money's worth for defraying or reimbursing –

(a) any expenses incurred in, or in connection with, transporting, removing, preparing, preserving or storing the material,

(b) any liability incurred in respect of –

(i)   expenses incurred by a third party in, or in connection with, any of the activities mentioned in paragraph (a), or

(ii) a payment in relation to which subsection (6) has effect, or

(c) any expenses or loss of earnings incurred by the person from whose body the material comes so far as reasonably and directly attributable to his supplying the material from his body.

(8) For the purposes of this section, controlled material is any material which –

(a) consists of or includes human cells,

(b) is, or is intended to be removed, from a human body,

(c) is intended to be used for the purpose of transplantation, and

(d) is not of a kind excepted under subsection (9).

(9) The following kinds of material are excepted –

(a) gametes,

(b) embryos, and

(c) material which is the subject of property because of an application of human skill.

(10) Where the body of a deceased person is intended to be used to provide material which –

(a) consists of or includes human cells, and

(b) is not of a kind excepted under subsection (9), for use for the purpose of transplantation, the body shall be treated as controlled material for the purposes of this section.

(11) In this section –

'advertisement' includes any form of advertising whether to the public generally, to any section of the public or individually to selected persons;

'reward' means any description of financial or other material advantage.

Transplants

33   Restriction on transplants involving a live donor

(1) Subject to subsections (3) and (5), a person commits an offence if –

(a) he removes any transplantable material from the body of a living person intending that the material be used for the purpose of transplantation, and

(b) when he removes the material, he knows, or might reasonably be expected to know, that the person from whose body he removes the material is alive.

(2) Subject to subsections (3) and (5), a person commits an offence if –

(a) he uses for the purpose of transplantation any transplantable material which has come from the body of a living person, and

(b) when he does so, he knows, or might reasonably be expected to know, that the transplantable material has come from the body of a living person.

(3) The Secretary of State may by regulations provide that subsection (1) or (2) shall not apply in a case where –

(a) the Authority is satisfied –that no reward has been or is to be given in contravention of section 32, and that such other conditions as are specified in the regulations are satisfied, and

(b) such other requirements as are specified in the regulations are complied with.

(4) Regulations under subsection (3) shall include provision for decisions of the Authority in relation to matters which fall to be decided by it under the regulations to be subject, in such circumstances as the regulations may provide, to reconsideration in accordance with such procedure as the regulations may provide.

(5) Where under subsection (3) an exception from subsection (1) or (2) is in force, a person does not commit an offence under that subsection if he reasonably believes that the exception applies.

(6) A person guilty of an offence under this section is liable on summary conviction –

(a) to imprisonment for a term not exceeding 51 weeks, or

(b) to a fine not exceeding level 5 on the standard scale, or

(c) to both.

(7) In this section –

'reward' has the same meaning as in section 32;

'transplantable material' means material of a description specified by regulations made by the Secretary of State.

34   Information about transplant operations

(1) The Secretary of State may make regulations requiring such persons as may be specified in the regulations to supply to such authority as may be so specified such information as may be so specified with respect to transplants that have been or are proposed to be carried out using transplantable material removed from a human body.

(2) Any such authority shall keep a record of information supplied to it in pursuance of regulations under this section.

(3) A person commits an offence if –

(a) he fails without reasonable excuse to comply with regulations under this section, or

(b) in purported compliance with such regulations, he knowingly or recklessly supplies information which is false or misleading in a material respect.

(4) A person guilty of an offence under subsection (3)(a) is liable on summary conviction to a fine not exceeding level 3 on the standard scale.

(5) A person guilty of an offence under subsection (3)(b) is liable on summary conviction to a fine not exceeding level 5 on the standard scale.

(6) In this section, 'transplantable material' has the same meaning as in section 33.

Exceptions

39   Criminal justice purposes

(1) Subject to subsection (2), nothing in section 14(1) or 16(2) applies to anything done for purposes related to –

(a) the prevention or detection of crime, or

(b) the conduct of a prosecution.

(2) Subsection (1) does not except from section 14(1) or 16(2) the carrying-out of a post-mortem examination for purposes of functions of a coroner.

(3) The reference in subsection (2) to the carrying-out of a post-mortem examination does not include the removal of relevant material from the body of a deceased person, or from a part of the body of a deceased person, at the first place where the body or part is situated to be attended by a constable.

(4) For the purposes of subsection (1)(a), detecting crime shall be taken to include –

(a) establishing by whom, for what purpose, by what means and generally in what circumstances any crime was committed, and

(b) the apprehension of the person by whom any crime was committed; and the reference in subsection (1)(a) to the detection of crime includes any detection outside the United Kingdom of any crime or suspected crime.

(5) In subsection (1)(b), the reference to a prosecution includes a prosecution brought in respect of any crime in a country or territory outside the United Kingdom.

(6) In this section, references to crime include a reference to any conduct which –

(a) constitutes one or more criminal offences (whether under the law of a part of the United Kingdom or of a country or territory outside the United Kingdom),

(b) is, or corresponds to, any conduct which, if it all took place in any one part of the United Kingdom, would constitute one or more criminal offences.

40   Religious relics

(1) This section applies –

(a) to the use of –

(i)   the body of a deceased person, or

(ii) relevant material which has come from a human body, for the purpose of public display at a place of public religious worship or at a place associated with such a place, and

(b) to the storage of –

(i)   the body of a deceased person, or

(ii) relevant material which has come from a human body, for use for the purpose mentioned in paragraph (a).

(2) An activity to which this section applies is excluded from sections 14(1) and 16(2) if there is a connection between –

(a) the body or material to which the activity relates, and

(b) the religious worship which takes place at the place of public religious worship concerned.

(3) For the purposes of this section, a place is associated with a place of public religious worship if it is used for purposes associated with the religious worship which takes place there.

Supplementary

41 Interpretation of Part 2

(1) In this Part –

'the 2007 Regulations' means the Human Tissue (Quality and Safety for Human Application) Regulations 2007;

'the 2012 Regulations' means the Quality and Safety of Organs Intended for Transplantation Regulations 2012;

'anatomical specimen' means –

(a) the body of a deceased person to be used for the purpose of anatomical examination, or

(b) the body of a deceased person in the course of being used for the purpose of anatomical examination (including separated parts of such a body);

'designated individual', in relation to a licence, means the individual designated in the licence as the person under whose supervision the licensed activity is authorised to be carried on;

'export' means export from England, Wales or Northern Ireland to a place outside England, Wales and Northern Ireland;

'import' means import into England, Wales or Northern Ireland from a place outside England, Wales and Northern Ireland;

'scheduled purpose' means a purpose specified in Schedule 1.

(2) In this Part, references to the carrying-out of an anatomical examination are to the carrying-out of a macroscopic examination by dissection for anatomical purposes of the body of a deceased person, and, where parts of the body of a deceased person are separated in the course of such an examination, include the carrying-out of a macroscopic examination by dissection of the parts for those purposes.

(3) In this Part, references to a person to whom a licence applies are to a person to whom the authority conferred by the licence extends (as provided by section 17).

PART 3 MISCELLANEOUS AND GENERAL

Miscellaneous

43 Preservation for transplantation

(1) Where part of a body lying in a hospital, nursing home or other institution is or may be suitable for use for transplantation, it shall be lawful for the person having the control and management of the institution –

(a) to take steps for the purpose of preserving the part for use for transplantation, and

(b) to retain the body for that purpose.

(2) Authority under subsection (1)(a) shall only extend –

(a) to the taking of the minimum steps necessary for the purpose mentioned in that provision, and

(b) to the use of the least invasive procedure.

(3) Authority under subsection (1) ceases to apply once it has been established that consent making removal of the part for transplantation lawful has not been, and will not be, given.

(4) Authority under subsection (1) shall extend to any person authorised to act under the authority by –

    (a) the person on whom the authority is conferred by that subsection, or

    (b) a person authorised under this subsection to act under the authority.

(5) An activity done with authority under subsection (1) shall be treated –

    (a) for the purposes of Part 1, as not being an activity to which section 1(1) applies;

    (b) for the purposes of Part 2, as not being an activity to which section 16 applies.

(5A) Section 11(2) applies to an act on authority under subsection (1) above as it applies to an act on authority under section 1.

(6) In this section, 'body' means the body of a deceased person.

44   Surplus tissue

(1) It shall be lawful for material to which subsection (2) or (3) applies to be dealt with as waste.

(2) This subsection applies to any material which consists of or includes human cells and which has come from a person's body in the course of his –

    (a) receiving medical treatment,

    (b) undergoing diagnostic testing, or

    (c) participating in research.

(3) This subsection applies to any relevant material which –

    (a) has come from a human body, and

    (b) ceases to be used, or stored for use, for a purpose specified in Schedule 1.

(4) This section shall not be read as making unlawful anything which is lawful apart from this section.

45   Non-consensual analysis of DNA

(1) A person commits an offence if –

    (a) he has any bodily material intending –

        (i) that any human DNA in the material be analysed without qualifying consent, and

        (ii) that the results of the analysis be used otherwise than for an excepted purpose,

    (b) the material is not of a kind excepted under subsection (2), and

    (c) he does not reasonably believe the material to be of a kind so excepted.

(2) Bodily material is excepted if –

    (a) it is material which has come from the body of a person who died before the day on which this section comes into force and at least one hundred years have elapsed since the date of the person's death,

    (b) it is an existing holding and the person who has it is not in possession, and not likely to come into possession, of information from which the individual from whose body the material has come can be identified, or

    (c) it is an embryo outside the human body.

(3) A person guilty of an offence under this section –

    (a) is liable on summary conviction to a fine not exceeding the statutory maximum;

    (b) is liable on conviction on indictment –

        (i) to imprisonment for a term not exceeding 3 years, or

        (ii) to a fine, or

        (iii) to both.

(4) Schedule 4 (which makes provision for the interpretation of 'qualifying consent' and 'use for an excepted purpose' in subsection (1)(a)) has effect.

(5) In this section (and Schedule 4) – 'bodily material' means material which –

    (a) has come from a human body, and

    (b) consists of or includes human cells;

'existing holding' means bodily material held immediately before the day on which this section comes into force.

General

50   Prosecutions

No proceedings for an offence under section 5, 32 or 33 shall be instituted –

> (a) in England and Wales, except by or with the consent of the Director of Public Prosecutions.

53   'Relevant material'

(1) In this Act, 'relevant material' means material, other than gametes, which consists of or includes human cells.

(2) In this Act, references to relevant material from a human body do not include –

> (a) embryos outside the human body, or
>
> (b) hair and nail from the body of a living person.

54   General interpretation

(1) In this Act –

'adult' means a person who has attained the age of 18 years;

'anatomical examination' means macroscopic examination by dissection for anatomical purposes;

'anatomical purposes' means purposes of teaching or studying, or researching into, the gross structure of the human body;

'the Authority' has the meaning given by section 13(1);

'child', except in the context of qualifying relationships, means a person who has not attained the age of 18 years;

'licence' means a licence under paragraph 1 of Schedule 3;

'licensed activity', in relation to a licence, means the activity which the licence authorises to be carried on;

'parental responsibility' –

> (a) in relation to England and Wales, has the same meaning as in the Children Act 1989 (c. 41).

(2) In this Act –

> (a) references to material from the body of a living person are to material from the body of a person alive at the point of separation, and
>
> (b) references to material from the body of a deceased person are to material from the body of a person not alive at the point of separation.

(3) In this Act, references to transplantation are to transplantation to a human body and include transfusion.

(4) In this Act, references to decent disposal include, in relation to disposal of material which has come from a human body, disposal as waste.

(5) In this Act, references to public display, in relation to the body of a deceased person, do not include –

> (a) display for the purpose of enabling people to pay their final respects to the deceased, or
>
> (b) display which is incidental to the deceased's funeral.

(6) In this Act 'embryo' and 'gametes' have the same meaning as they have by virtue of section 1(1), (4) and (6) of the Human Fertilisation and Embryology Act 1990 in the other provisions of that Act (apart from section 4A).

(7) For the purposes of this Act, material shall not be regarded as from a human body if it is created outside the human body.

(8) For the purposes of this Act, except section 49, a person is another's partner if the two of them (whether of different sexes or the same sex) live as partners in an enduring family relationship.

(9) The following are qualifying relationships for the purposes of this Act, spouse, partner, parent, child, brother, sister, grandparent, grandchild, child of a brother or sister, stepfather, step-mother, half-brother, half-sister and friend of long standing.

SCHEDULE 1

SECTION 1   SCHEDULED PURPOSES

PART 1 PURPOSES REQUIRING CONSENT: GENERAL

(1) Anatomical examination.

(2) Determining the cause of death.

(3) Establishing after a person's death the efficacy of any drug or other treatment administered to him.

(4) Obtaining scientific or medical information about a living or deceased person which may be relevant to any other person (including a future person).

(5) Public display.

(6) Research in connection with disorders, or the functioning, of the human body.

(7) Transplantation.

PART 2 PURPOSES REQUIRING CONSENT: DECEASED PERSONS

(8) Clinical audit.

(9) Education or training relating to human health.

(10) Performance assessment.

(11) Public health monitoring.

(12) Quality assurance.

SCHEDULE 4

SECTION 45   SUPPLEMENTARY

PART 1 QUALIFYING CONSENT

Introductory

1 This Part of this Schedule makes provision for the interpretation of 'qualifying consent' in section 45(1)(a)(i).

Qualifying consent

2—(1) In relation to analysis of DNA manufactured by the body of a person who is alive, 'qualifying consent' means his consent, except where sub-paragraph (2) applies.

(2) Where –

(a) the person is a child,

(b) neither a decision of his to consent, nor a decision of his not to consent, is in force, and

(c) either he is not competent to deal with the issue of consent or, though he is competent to deal with that issue, he fails to do so,

'qualifying consent' means the consent of a person who has parental responsibility for him.

(3) In relation to analysis of DNA manufactured by the body of a person who has died an adult, 'qualifying consent' means –

(a) if a decision of his to consent, or a decision of his not to consent, was in force immediately before he died, his consent;

(b) if paragraph (a) does not apply, the consent of a person who stood in a qualifying relationship to him immediately before he died.

(4) In relation to analysis of DNA manufactured by the body of a person who has died a child, 'qualifying consent' means –

(a) if a decision of his to consent, or a decision of his not to consent, was in force immediately before he died, his consent;

(b) if paragraph (a) does not apply –

(i)   the consent of a person who had parental responsibility for him immediately before he died, or

(ii) where no person had parental responsibility for him immediately before he died, the consent of a person who stood in a qualifying relationship to him at that time.

PART 2   USE FOR AN EXCEPTED PURPOSE

Introductory

This Part of this Schedule makes provision for the interpretation of 'use for an excepted purpose in section 45(1)(a)(ii).

5—(1) Use of the results of an analysis of DNA for any of the following purposes is use for an excepted purpose –

(a) the medical diagnosis or treatment of the person whose body manufactured the DNA;

(b) purposes of functions of a coroner;

(c) purposes of functions of a procurator fiscal in connection with the investigation of deaths;

(d) the prevention or detection of crime;

(e) the conduct of a prosecution;

(f) purposes of national security;

(g) implementing an order or direction of a court or tribunal, including one outside the United Kingdom.

(2) For the purposes of sub-paragraph (1)(d), detecting crime shall be taken to include –

(a) establishing by whom, for what purpose, by what means and generally in what circumstances any crime was committed, and

(b) the apprehension of the person by whom any crime was committed; and the reference in sub-paragraph (1)(d) to the detection of crime includes any detection outside the United Kingdom of any crime or suspected crime.

(3) In sub-paragraph (1)(e), the reference to a prosecution includes a prosecution brought in respect of a crime in a country or territory outside the United Kingdom.

(4) In this paragraph, a reference to a crime includes a reference to any conduct which –

(a) constitutes one or more criminal offences (whether under the law of a part of the United Kingdom or a country or territory outside the United Kingdom),

(b) is, or corresponds to, conduct which, if it all took place in any one part of the United Kingdom, would constitute one or more criminal offences, ...

Purpose of research in connection with disorders, or functioning, of the human body

6—(1) Use of the results of an analysis of DNA for the purpose of research in connection with disorders, or the functioning, of the human body is use for an excepted purpose if the bodily material concerned is the subject of an order under sub-paragraph (2).

Purposes relating to existing holdings

7 Use of the results of an analysis of DNA for any of the following purposes is use for an excepted purpose if the bodily material concerned is an existing holding –

    (a) clinical audit;

    (b) determining the cause of death;

    (c) education or training relating to human health;

    (d) establishing after a person's death the efficacy of any drug or other treatment administered to him;

    (e) obtaining scientific or medical information about a living or deceased person which may be relevant to any other person (including a future person);

    (f) performance assessment;

    (g) public health monitoring;

    (h) quality assurance;

    (i) research in connection with disorders, or the functioning, of the human body;

    (j) transplantation.

Purposes relating to material from body of a living person

8 Use of the results of an analysis of DNA for any of the following purposes is use for an excepted purpose if the bodily material concerned is from the body of a living person –

    (a) clinical audit;

    (b) education or training relating to human health;

    (c) performance assessment;

    (d) public health monitoring;

    (e) quality assurance.

9—(1) Use of the results of an analysis of DNA for the purpose of obtaining scientific or medical information about the person whose body manufactured the DNA is use for an excepted purpose if –

    (a) the bodily material concerned is the subject of a direction under sub-paragraph (2) or (3) or an order under sub-paragraph (4) or (5), and

    (b) the information may be relevant to the person for whose benefit the direction is given or order is made.

(2) If the Authority is satisfied –

    (a) that bodily material has come from the body of a living person,

    (b) that it is not reasonably possible to trace the person from whose body the material has come ('the donor'),

    (c) that it is desirable in the interests of another person (including a future person) that DNA in the material be analysed for the purpose of obtaining scientific or medical information about the donor, and

    (d) that there is no reason to believe –

        (i) that the donor has died,

        (ii) that a decision of the donor to refuse consent to the use of the material for that purpose is in force, or

        (iii) that the donor lacks capacity to consent to the use of the material for that purpose, it may direct that this paragraph apply to the material for the benefit of the other person.

(3) If the Authority is satisfied –

    (a) that bodily material has come from the body of a living person,

    (b) that it is desirable in the interests of another person (including a future person) that DNA in the material be analysed for the purpose of obtaining scientific or medical information about the person from whose body the material has come ('the donor'),

(c) that reasonable efforts have been made to get the donor to decide whether to consent to the use of the material for that purpose,

(d) that there is no reason to believe –

    (i) that the donor has died,

    (ii) that a decision of the donor to refuse to consent to the use of the material for that purpose is in force, or

    (iii) that the donor lacks capacity to consent to the use of the material for that purpose, and

(e) that the donor has been given notice of the application for the exercise of the power conferred by this sub-paragraph,

it may direct that this paragraph apply to the material for the benefit of the other person.

(4) If the Court of Session is satisfied –

(a) that bodily material has come from the body of a living person,

(b) that it is not reasonably possible to trace the person from whose body the material has come ('the donor'),

(c) that it is desirable in the interests of another person (including a future person) that DNA in the material be analysed for the purpose of obtaining scientific or medical information about the donor, and

(d) that there is no reason to believe –

    (i) that the donor has died,

    (ii) that a decision of the donor to refuse consent to the use of the material for that purpose is in force, or

    (iii) that the donor is an incapable adult within the meaning of the Adults with Incapacity (Scotland) Act 2000 (asp 4),

it may order that this paragraph apply to the material for the benefit of the other person.

10 Use of the results of an analysis of DNA for the purpose of research in connection with disorders, or the functioning, of the human body is use for an excepted purpose if –

(a) the bodily material concerned is from the body of a living person,

(b) the research is ethically approved in accordance with regulations made by the Secretary of State, and

(c) the analysis is to be carried out in circumstances such that the person carrying it out is not in possession, and not likely to come into possession, of information from which the individual from whose body the material has come can be identified.

Purpose authorised under section 1

11 Use of the results of an analysis of DNA for a purpose specified in paragraph 7 is use for an excepted purpose if the use in England and Wales, or Northern Ireland, for that purpose of the bodily material concerned is authorised by section 1(1) or (10)(c).

Purposes relating to DNA of adults who lack capacity to consent

12—(1) Use of the results of an analysis of DNA for a purpose specified under sub-paragraph (2) is use for an excepted purpose if –

(a) the DNA has been manufactured by the body of a person who –

    (i) has attained the age of 18 years and, under the law of England and Wales or Northern Ireland, lacks capacity to consent to analysis of the DNA, or

    (ii) under the law of Scotland, is an adult with incapacity within the meaning of the Adults with Incapacity (Scotland) Act 2000, and

(b) neither a decision of his to consent to analysis of the DNA for that purpose, nor a decision of his not to consent to analysis of it for that purpose, is in force.

(2) The Secretary of State may by regulations specify for the purposes of this paragraph purposes for which DNA may be analysed.

Mental Capacity Act 2005

(2005, c. 9)

PART 1 PERSONS WHO LACK CAPACITY

The principles

1 The principles

(1) The following principles apply for the purposes of this Act.

(2) A person must be assumed to have capacity unless it is established that he lacks capacity.

(3) A person is not to be treated as unable to make a decision unless all practicable steps to help him to do so have been taken without success.

(4) A person is not to be treated as unable to make a decision merely because he makes an unwise decision.

(5) An act done, or decision made, under this Act for or on behalf of a person who lacks capacity must be done, or made, in his best interests.

(6) Before the act is done, or the decision is made, regard must be had to whether the purpose for which it is needed can be as effectively achieved in a way that is less restrictive of the person's rights and freedom of action.

Preliminary

2 People who lack capacity

(1) For the purposes of this Act, a person lacks capacity in relation to a matter if at the material time he is unable to make a decision for himself in relation to the matter because of an impairment of, or a disturbance in the functioning of, the mind or brain.

(2) It does not matter whether the impairment or disturbance is permanent or temporary.

(3) A lack of capacity cannot be established merely by reference to –

    (a) a person's age or appearance, or

    (b) a condition of his, or an aspect of his behaviour, which might lead others to make unjustified assumptions about his capacity.

(4) In proceedings under this Act or any other enactment, any question whether a person lacks capacity within the meaning of this Act must be decided on the balance of probabilities.

(5) No power which a person ('D') may exercise under this Act –

    (a) in relation to a person who lacks capacity, or

    (b) where D reasonably thinks that a person lacks capacity, is exercisable in relation to a person under 16.

3 Inability to make decisions

(1) For the purposes of section 2, a person is unable to make a decision for himself if he is unable –

    (a) to understand the information relevant to the decision,

    (b) to retain that information,

    (c) to use or weigh that information as part of the process of making the decision, or

    (d) to communicate his decision (whether by talking, using sign language or any other means).

(2) A person is not to be regarded as unable to understand the information relevant to a decision if he is able to understand an explanation of it given to him in a way that is appropriate to his circumstances (using simple language, visual aids or any other means).

(3) The fact that a person is able to retain the information relevant to a decision for a short period only does not prevent him from being regarded as able to make the decision.

(4) The information relevant to a decision includes information about the reasonably foreseeable consequences of –

    (a) deciding one way or another, or

    (b) failing to make the decision.

4 Best interests

(1) In determining for the purposes of this Act what is in a person's best interests, the person making the determination must not make it merely on the basis of –

    (a) the person's age or appearance, or

    (b) a condition of his, or an aspect of his behaviour, which might lead others to make unjustified assumptions about what might be in his best interests.

(2) The person making the determination must consider all the relevant circumstances and, in particular, take the following steps.

(3) He must consider –

    (a) whether it is likely that the person will at some time have capacity in relation to the matter in question, and

    (b) if it appears likely that he will, when that is likely to be.

(4) He must, so far as reasonably practicable, permit and encourage the person to participate, or to improve his ability to participate, as fully as possible in any act done for him and any decision affecting him.

(5) Where the determination relates to life-sustaining treatment he must not, in considering whether the treatment is in the best interests of the person concerned, be motivated by a desire to bring about his death.

(6) He must consider, so far as is reasonably ascertainable –

    (a) the person's past and present wishes and feelings (and, in particular, any relevant written statement made by him when he had capacity),

    (b) the beliefs and values that would be likely to influence his decision if he had capacity, and

    (c) the other factors that he would be likely to consider if he were able to do so.

(7) He must take into account, if it is practicable and appropriate to consult them, the views of –

    (a) anyone named by the person as someone to be consulted on the matter in question or on matters of that kind,

    (b) anyone engaged in caring for the person or interested in his welfare,

    (c) any donee of a lasting power of attorney granted by the person, and

    (d) any deputy appointed for the person by the court, as to what would be in the person's best interests and, in particular, as to the matters mentioned in subsection (6).

(8) The duties imposed by subsections (1) to (7) also apply in relation to the exercise of any powers which –

    (a) are exercisable under a lasting power of attorney, or

    (b) are exercisable by a person under this Act where he reasonably believes that another person lacks capacity.

(9) In the case of an act done, or a decision made, by a person other than the court, there is sufficient compliance with this section if (having complied with the requirements of subsections (1) to (7)) he reasonably believes that what he does or decides is in the best interests of the person concerned.

(10) 'Life-sustaining treatment' means treatment which in the view of a person providing health care for the person concerned is necessary to sustain life.

(11) 'Relevant circumstances' are those –

    (a) of which the person making the determination is aware, and

    (b) which it would be reasonable to regard as relevant.

4A   Restriction on deprivation of liberty

(1) This Act does not authorise any person ('D') to deprive any other person ('P') of his liberty.

(2) But that is subject to –

   (a) the following provisions of this section, and

   (b) section 4B.

(3) D may deprive P of his liberty if, by doing so, D is giving effect to a relevant decision of the court.

(4) A relevant decision of the court is a decision made by an order under section 16(2)(a) in relation to a matter concerning P's personal welfare.

(5) D may deprive P of his liberty if the deprivation is authorised by Schedule A1 (hospital and care home residents: deprivation of liberty).

4B   Deprivation of liberty necessary for life-sustaining treatment etc.

(1) If the following conditions are met, D is authorised to deprive P of his liberty while a decision as respects any relevant issue is sought from the court.

(2) The first condition is that there is a question about whether D is authorised to deprive P of his liberty under section 4A.

(3) The second condition is that the deprivation of liberty –

   (a) is wholly or partly for the purpose of –

      (i) giving P life-sustaining treatment, or

      (ii) doing any vital act, or

   (b) consists wholly or partly of –

      (i) giving P life-sustaining treatment, or

      (ii) doing any vital act.

(4) The third condition is that the deprivation of liberty is necessary in order to –

   (a) give the life-sustaining treatment, or

   (b) do the vital act.

(5) A vital act is any act which the person doing it reasonably believes to be necessary to prevent a serious deterioration in P's condition.

5   Acts in connection with care or treatment

(1) If a person ('D') does an act in connection with the care or treatment of another person ('P'), the act is one to which this section applies if –

   (a) before doing the act, D takes reasonable steps to establish whether P lacks capacity in relation to the matter in question, and

   (b) when doing the act, D reasonably believes –

      (i) that P lacks capacity in relation to the matter, and

      (ii) that it will be in P's best interests for the act to be done.

(2) D does not incur any liability in relation to the act that he would not have incurred if P –

   (a) had had capacity to consent in relation to the matter, and

   (b) had consented to D's doing the act.

(3) Nothing in this section excludes a person's civil liability for loss or damage, or his criminal liability, resulting from his negligence in doing the act.

(4) Nothing in this section affects the operation of sections 24 to 26 (advance decisions to refuse treatment).

6   Section 5 acts: limitations

(1) If D does an act that is intended to restrain P, it is not an act to which section 5 applies unless two further conditions are satisfied.

(2) The first condition is that D reasonably believes that it is necessary to do the act in order to prevent harm to P.

(3) The second is that the act is a proportionate response to –

   (a) the likelihood of P's suffering harm, and

   (b) the seriousness of that harm.

(4) For the purposes of this section D restrains P if he –

(a) uses, or threatens to use, force to secure the doing of an act which P resists, or

(b) restricts P's liberty of movement, whether or not P resists.

(6) Section 5 does not authorise a person to do an act which conflicts with a decision made, within the scope of his authority and in accordance with this Part, by –

(a) a donee of a lasting power of attorney granted by P, or

(b) a deputy appointed for P by the court.

(7) But nothing in subsection (6) stops a person –

(a) providing life-sustaining treatment, or

(b) doing any act which he reasonably believes to be necessary to prevent a serious deterioration in P's condition, while a decision as respects any relevant issue is sought from the court.

Lasting powers of attorney

9   Lasting powers of attorney

(1) A lasting power of attorney is a power of attorney under which the donor ('P') confers on the donee (or donees) authority to make decisions about all or any of the following –

(a) P's personal welfare or specified matters concerning P's personal welfare, and

(b) P's property and affairs or specified matters concerning P's property and affairs, and which includes authority to make such decisions in circumstances where P no longer has capacity.

(2) A lasting power of attorney is not created unless –

(a) section 10 is complied with,

(b) an instrument conferring authority of the kind mentioned in subsection (1) is made and registered in accordance with Schedule 1, and

(c) at the time when P executes the instrument, P has reached 18 and has capacity to execute it.

(4) The authority conferred by a lasting power of attorney is subject to –

(a) the provisions of this Act and, in particular, sections 1 (the principles) and 4 (best interests), and

(b) any conditions or restrictions specified in the instrument.

10   Appointment of donees

(1) A donee of a lasting power of attorney must be –

(a) an individual who has reached 18, or

(b) if the power relates only to P's property and affairs, either such an individual or a trust corporation.

11   Lasting powers of attorney: restrictions

(1) A lasting power of attorney does not authorise the donee (or, if more than one, any of them) to do an act that is intended to restrain P, unless three conditions are satisfied.

(2) The first condition is that P lacks, or the donee reasonably believes that P lacks, capacity in relation to the matter in question.

(3) The second is that the donee reasonably believes that it is necessary to do the act in order to prevent harm to P.

(4) The third is that the act is a proportionate response to –

(a) the likelihood of P's suffering harm, and

(b) the seriousness of that harm.

(7) Where a lasting power of attorney authorises the donee (or, if more than one, any of them) to make decisions about P's personal welfare, the authority –

(a) does not extend to making such decisions in circumstances other than those where P lacks, or the donee reasonably believes that P lacks, capacity,

    (b) is subject to sections 24 to 26 (advance decisions to refuse treatment), and

    (c) extends to giving or refusing consent to the carrying out or continuation of a treatment by a person providing health care for P.

  (8) But subsection (7)(c) –

    (a) does not authorise the giving or refusing of consent to the carrying out or continuation of life-sustaining treatment, unless the instrument contains express provision to that effect, and

    (b) is subject to any conditions or restrictions in the instrument.

13 Revocation of lasting powers of attorney etc.

  (1) This section applies if –

    (a) P has executed an instrument with a view to creating a lasting power of attorney, or

    (b) a lasting power of attorney is registered as having been conferred by P, and in this section references to revoking the power include revoking the instrument.

  (2) P may, at any time when he has capacity to do so, revoke the power.

General powers of the court and appointment of deputies

15 Power to make declarations

  (1) The court may make declarations as to –

    (a) whether a person has or lacks capacity to make a decision specified in the declaration;

    (b) whether a person has or lacks capacity to make decisions on such matters as are described in the declaration;

    (c) the lawfulness or otherwise of any act done, or yet to be done, in relation to that person.

    (2) 'Act' includes an omission and a course of conduct.

16 Powers to make decisions and appoint deputies: general

  (1) This section applies if a person ('P') lacks capacity in relation to a matter or matters concerning –

    (a) P's personal welfare, or

    (b) P's property and affairs.

  (2) The court may –

    (a) by making an order, make the decision or decisions on P's behalf in relation to the matter or matters, or

    (b) appoint a person (a 'deputy') to make decisions on P's behalf in relation to the matter or matters.

  (3) The powers of the court under this section are subject to the provisions of this Act and, in particular, to sections 1 (the principles) and 4 (best interests).

  (4) When deciding whether it is in P's best interests to appoint a deputy, the court must have regard (in addition to the matters mentioned in section 4) to the principles that –

    (a) a decision by the court is to be preferred to the appointment of a deputy to make a decision, and

    (b) the powers conferred on a deputy should be as limited in scope and duration as is reasonably practicable in the circumstances.

  (5) The court may make such further orders or give such directions, and confer on a deputy such powers or impose on him such duties, as it thinks necessary or expedient for giving effect to, or otherwise in connection with, an order or appointment made by it under subsection (2).

  (6) Without prejudice to section 4, the court may make the order, give the directions or make the appointment on such terms as it considers are in P's best interests, even though no application is before the court for an order, directions or an appointment on those terms.

  (7) An order of the court may be varied or discharged by a subsequent order.

  (8) The court may, in particular, revoke the appointment of a deputy or vary the powers conferred on him if it is satisfied that the deputy –

    (a) has behaved, or is behaving, in a way that contravenes the authority conferred on him by the court or is not in P's best interests, or

(b) proposes to behave in a way that would contravene that authority or would not be in P's best interests.

16A   Section 16 powers: Mental Health Act patients etc.

(1) If a person is ineligible to be deprived of liberty by this Act, the court may not include in a welfare order provision which authorises the person to be deprived of his liberty.

(2) If –

(a) a welfare order includes provision which authorises a person to be deprived of his liberty, and

(b) that person becomes ineligible to be deprived of liberty by this Act, the provision ceases to have effect for as long as the person remains ineligible.

(3) Nothing in subsection (2) affects the power of the court under section 16(7) to vary or discharge the welfare order.

(4) For the purposes of this section –

(a) Schedule 1A applies for determining whether or not P is ineligible to be deprived of liberty by this Act;

(b) 'welfare order' means an order under section 16(2)(a).

17   Section 16 powers: personal welfare

(1) The powers under section 16 as respects P's personal welfare extend in particular to –

(a) deciding where P is to live;

(b) deciding what contact, if any, P is to have with any specified persons;

(c) making an order prohibiting a named person from having contact with P;

(d) giving or refusing consent to the carrying out or continuation of a treatment by a person providing health care for P;

(e) giving a direction that a person responsible for P's health care allow a different person to take over that responsibility.

(2) Subsection (1) is subject to section 20 (restrictions on deputies).

20   Restrictions on deputies

(1) A deputy does not have power to make a decision on behalf of P in relation to a matter if he knows or has reasonable grounds for believing that P has capacity in relation to the matter.

(2) Nothing in section 16(5) or 17 permits a deputy to be given power –

(a) to prohibit a named person from having contact with P;

(b) to direct a person responsible for P's health care to allow a different person to take over that responsibility.

(4) A deputy may not be given power to make a decision on behalf of P which is inconsistent with a decision made, within the scope of his authority and in accordance with this Act, by the donee of a lasting power of attorney granted by P (or, if there is more than one donee, by any of them).

(5) A deputy may not refuse consent to the carrying out or continuation of life-sustaining treatment in relation to P.

(6) The authority conferred on a deputy is subject to the provisions of this Act and, in particular, sections 1 (the principles) and 4 (best interests).

(7) A deputy may not do an act that is intended to restrain P unless four conditions are satisfied.

(8) The first condition is that, in doing the act, the deputy is acting within the scope of an authority expressly conferred on him by the court.

(9) The second is that P lacks, or the deputy reasonably believes that P lacks, capacity in relation to the matter in question.

(10) The third is that the deputy reasonably believes that it is necessary to do the act in order to prevent harm to P.

(11) The fourth is that the act is a proportionate response to –

(a) the likelihood of P's suffering harm, and

(b) the seriousness of that harm.

(12) For the purposes of this section, a deputy restrains P if he –
    (a) uses, or threatens to use, force to secure the doing of an act which P resists, or
    (b) restricts P's liberty of movement, whether or not P resists, or if he authorises another person to do any of those things.

Advance decisions to refuse treatment

24 Advance decisions to refuse treatment: general

(1) 'Advance decision' means a decision made by a person ('P'), after he has reached 18 and when he has capacity to do so, that if –
    (a) at a later time and in such circumstances as he may specify, a specified treatment is proposed to be carried out or continued by a person providing health care for him, and
    (b) at that time he lacks capacity to consent to the carrying out or continuation of the treatment, the specified treatment is not to be carried out or continued.

(2) For the purposes of subsection (1)(a), a decision may be regarded as specifying a treatment or circumstances even though expressed in layman's terms.

(3) P may withdraw or alter an advance decision at any time when he has capacity to do so.

(4) A withdrawal (including a partial withdrawal) need not be in writing.

(5) An alteration of an advance decision need not be in writing (unless section 25(5) applies in relation to the decision resulting from the alteration).

25 Validity and applicability of advance decisions

(1) An advance decision does not affect the liability which a person may incur for carrying out or continuing a treatment in relation to P unless the decision is at the material time –
    (a) valid, and
    (b) applicable to the treatment.

(2) An advance decision is not valid if P –
    (a) has withdrawn the decision at a time when he had capacity to do so,
    (b) has, under a lasting power of attorney created after the advance decision was made, conferred authority on the donee (or, if more than one, any of them) to give or refuse consent to the treatment to which the advance decision relates, or
    (c) has done anything else clearly inconsistent with the advance decision remaining his fixed decision.

(3) An advance decision is not applicable to the treatment in question if at the material time P has capacity to give or refuse consent to it.

(4) An advance decision is not applicable to the treatment in question if –
    (a) that treatment is not the treatment specified in the advance decision,
    (b) any circumstances specified in the advance decision are absent, or
    (c) there are reasonable grounds for believing that circumstances exist which P did not anticipate at the time of the advance decision and which would have affected his decision had he anticipated them.

(5) An advance decision is not applicable to life-sustaining treatment unless –
    (a) the decision is verified by a statement by P to the effect that it is to apply to that treatment even if life is at risk, and
    (b) the decision and statement comply with subsection (6).

(6) A decision or statement complies with this subsection only if –
    (a) it is in writing,
    (b) it is signed by P or by another person in P's presence and by P's direction,
    (c) the signature is made or acknowledged by P in the presence of a witness, and
    (d) the witness signs it, or acknowledges his signature, in P's presence.

(7) The existence of any lasting power of attorney other than one of a description mentioned in subsection (2)(b) does not prevent the advance decision from being regarded as valid and applicable.

26   Effect of advance decisions

(1) If P has made an advance decision which is –

    (a) valid, and

    (b) applicable to a treatment, the decision has effect as if he had made it, and had had capacity to make it, at the time when the question arises whether the treatment should be carried out or continued.

(2) A person does not incur liability for carrying out or continuing the treatment unless, at the time, he is satisfied that an advance decision exists which is valid and applicable to the treatment.

(3) A person does not incur liability for the consequences of withholding or withdrawing a treatment from P if, at the time, he reasonably believes that an advance decision exists which is valid and applicable to the treatment.

(4) The court may make a declaration as to whether an advance decision –

    (a) exists;

    (b) is valid;

    (c) is applicable to a treatment.

(5) Nothing in an apparent advance decision stops a person –

    (a) providing life-sustaining treatment, or

    (b) doing any act he reasonably believes to be necessary to prevent a serious deterioration in P's condition, while a decision as respects any relevant issue is sought from the court.

28   Mental Health Act matters

(1) Nothing in this Act authorises anyone –

    (a) to give a patient medical treatment for mental disorder, or

    (b) to consent to a patient's being given medical treatment for mental disorder, if, at the time when it is proposed to treat the patient, his treatment is regulated by Part 4 of the Mental Health Act.

(1A) Subsection (1) does not apply in relation to any form of treatment to which section 58A of that Act (electro-convulsive therapy, etc.) applies if the patient comes within subsection (7) of that section (informal patient under 18 who cannot give consent).

(1B) Section 5 does not apply to an act to which section 64B of the Mental Health Act applies (treatment of community patients not recalled to hospital).

(2) 'Medical treatment', 'mental disorder' and 'patient' have the same meaning as in that Act.

Research

30   Research

(1) Intrusive research carried out on, or in relation to, a person who lacks capacity to consent to it is unlawful unless it is carried out –

    (a) as part of a research project which is for the time being approved by the appropriate body for the purposes of this Act in accordance with section 31, and

    (b) in accordance with sections 32 and 33.

(2) Research is intrusive if it is of a kind that would be unlawful if it was carried out –

    (a) on or in relation to a person who had capacity to consent to it, but

    (b) without his consent.

(3) A clinical trial which is subject to the provisions of clinical trials regulations is not to be treated as research for the purposes of this section.

(3A) Research is not intrusive to the extent that it consists of the use of a person's human cells to bring about the creation *in vitro* of an embryo or human admixed embryo, or the subsequent storage or use of an embryo or human admixed embryo so created.

(3B) Expressions used in subsection (3A) and in Schedule 3 to the Human Fertilisation and Embryology Act 1990 (consents to use or storage of gametes, embryos or human admixed embryos etc.) have the same meaning in that subsection as in that Schedule.

(4) 'Appropriate body', in relation to a research project, means the person, committee or other body specified in regulations made by the appropriate authority as the appropriate body in relation to a project of the kind in question.

(5) 'Clinical trials regulations' means –

    (a) the Medicines for Human Use (Clinical Trials) Regulations 2004 (S.I. 2004/1031) and any other regulations replacing those regulations or amending them, and

    (b) any other regulations relating to clinical trials and designated by the Secretary of State as clinical trials regulations for the purposes of this section.

(6) In this section, section 32 and section 34, 'appropriate authority' means –

    (a) in relation to the carrying out of research in England, the Secretary of State, and

    (b) in relation to the carrying out of research in Wales, the National Assembly for Wales.

31 Requirements for approval

(1) The appropriate body may not approve a research project for the purposes of this Act unless satisfied that the following requirements will be met in relation to research carried out as part of the project on, or in relation to, a person who lacks capacity to consent to taking part in the project ('P').

(2) The research must be connected with –

    (a) an impairing condition affecting P, or

    (b) its treatment.

(3) 'Impairing condition' means a condition which is (or may be) attributable to, or which causes or contributes to (or may cause or contribute to), the impairment of, or disturbance in the functioning of, the mind or brain.

(4) There must be reasonable grounds for believing that research of comparable effectiveness cannot be carried out if the project has to be confined to, or relate only to, persons who have capacity to consent to taking part in it.

(5) The research must –

    (a) have the potential to benefit P without imposing on P a burden that is disproportionate to the potential benefit to P, or

    (b) be intended to provide knowledge of the causes or treatment of, or of the care of persons affected by, the same or a similar condition.

(6) If the research falls within paragraph (b) of subsection (5) but not within paragraph (a), there must be reasonable grounds for believing –

    (a) that the risk to P from taking part in the project is likely to be negligible, and

    (b) that anything done to, or in relation to, P will not –

        (i)   interfere with P's freedom of action or privacy in a significant way, or

        (ii) be unduly invasive or restrictive.

(7) There must be reasonable arrangements in place for ensuring that the requirements of sections 32 and 33 will be met.

32 Consulting carers etc.

(1) This section applies if a person ('R') –

    (a) is conducting an approved research project, and

    (b) wishes to carry out research, as part of the project, on or in relation to a person ('P') who lacks capacity to consent to taking part in the project.

(2) R must take reasonable steps to identify a person who –

    (a) otherwise than in a professional capacity or for remuneration, is engaged in caring for P or is interested in P's welfare, and

    (b) is prepared to be consulted by R under this section.

(3) If R is unable to identify such a person he must, in accordance with guidance issued by the appropriate authority, nominate a person who –

    (a) is prepared to be consulted by R under this section, but

    (b) has no connection with the project.

(4) R must provide the person identified under subsection (2), or nominated under subsection (3), with information about the project and ask him –

    (a) for advice as to whether P should take part in the project, and

    (b) what, in his opinion, P's wishes and feelings about taking part in the project would be likely to be if P had capacity in relation to the matter.

(5) If, at any time, the person consulted advises R that in his opinion P's wishes and feelings would be likely to lead him to decline to take part in the project (or to wish to withdraw from it) if he had capacity in relation to the matter, R must ensure –

    (a) if P is not already taking part in the project, that he does not take part in it;

    (b) if P is taking part in the project, that he is withdrawn from it.

(6) But subsection (5)(b) does not require treatment that P has been receiving as part of the project to be discontinued if R has reasonable grounds for believing that there would be a significant risk to P's health if it were discontinued.

(7) The fact that a person is the donee of a lasting power of attorney given by P, or is P's deputy, does not prevent him from being the person consulted under this section.

(8) Subsection (9) applies if treatment is being, or is about to be, provided for P as a matter of urgency and R considers that, having regard to the nature of the research and of the particular circumstances of the case –

    (a) it is also necessary to take action for the purposes of the research as a matter of urgency, but

    (b) it is not reasonably practicable to consult under the previous provisions of this section.

(9) R may take the action if –

    (a) he has the agreement of a registered medical practitioner who is not involved in the organisation or conduct of the research project, or

    (b) where it is not reasonably practicable in the time available to obtain that agreement, he acts in accordance with a procedure approved by the appropriate body at the time when the research project was approved under section 31.

(10) But R may not continue to act in reliance on subsection (9) if he has reasonable grounds for believing that it is no longer necessary to take the action as a matter of urgency.

33 Additional safeguards

(1) This section applies in relation to a person who is taking part in an approved research project even though he lacks capacity to consent to taking part.

(2) Nothing may be done to, or in relation to, him in the course of the research –

    (a) to which he appears to object (whether by showing signs of resistance or otherwise) except where what is being done is intended to protect him from harm or to reduce or prevent pain or discomfort, or

    (b) which would be contrary to –

        (i)   an advance decision of his which has effect, or

        (ii) any other form of statement made by him and not subsequently withdrawn, of which R is aware.

(3) The interests of the person must be assumed to outweigh those of science and society.

(4) If he indicates (in any way) that he wishes to be withdrawn from the project he must be withdrawn without delay.

(5) P must be withdrawn from the project, without delay, if at any time the person conducting the research has reasonable grounds for believing that one or more of the requirements set out in section 31(2) to (7) is no longer met in relation to research being carried out on, or in relation to, P.

(6) But neither subsection (4) nor subsection (5) requires treatment that P has been receiving as part of the project to be discontinued if R has reasonable grounds for believing that there would be a significant risk to P's health if it were discontinued.

34 Loss of capacity during research project

(1) This section applies where a person ('P') –

    (a) has consented to take part in a research project begun before the commencement of section 30, but

    (b) before the conclusion of the project, loses capacity to consent to continue to take part in it.

(2) The appropriate authority may by regulations provide that, despite P's loss of capacity, research of a prescribed kind may be carried out on, or in relation to, P if –

    (a) the project satisfies prescribed requirements,

    (b) any information or material relating to P which is used in the research is of a prescribed description and was obtained before P's loss of capacity, and

    (c) the person conducting the project takes in relation to P such steps as may be prescribed for the purpose of protecting him.

(3) The regulations may, in particular, –

    (a) make provision about when, for the purposes of the regulations, a project is to be treated as having begun;

    (b) include provision similar to any made by section 31, 32 or 33.

Independent mental capacity advocate service

35 Appointment of independent mental capacity advocates

(1) The responsible authority must make such arrangements as it considers reasonable to enable persons ('independent mental capacity advocates') to be available to represent and support persons to whom acts or decisions proposed under sections 37, 38 and 39 relate or persons who fall within section 39A, 39C or 39D.

(4) In making arrangements under subsection (1), the responsible authority must have regard to the principle that a person to whom a proposed act or decision relates should, so far as practicable, be represented and supported by a person who is independent of any person who will be responsible for the act or decision.

(6) For the purpose of enabling him to carry out his functions, an independent mental capacity advocate –

    (a) may interview in private the person whom he has been instructed to represent, and

    (b) may, at all reasonable times, examine and take copies of –

        (i) any health record,

        (ii) any record of, or held by, a local authority and compiled in connection with a social services function, and

        (iii) any record held by a person registered under Part 2 of the Care Standards Act 2000 (c. 14), which the person holding the record considers may be relevant to the independent mental capacity advocate's investigation.

(6A) In subsections (1) and (4), 'the responsible authority' means –

    (a) in relation to the provision of the services of independent mental capacity advocates in the area of a local authority in England, that local authority, and

    (b) in relation to the provision of the services of independent mental capacity advocates in Wales, the Welsh Ministers.

(7) In this section, section 36 and section 37, 'the appropriate authority' means –

    (a) in relation to the provision of the services of independent mental capacity advocates in England, the Secretary of State, and

    (b) in relation to the provision of the services of independent mental capacity advocates in Wales, the National Assembly for Wales.

36 Functions of independent mental capacity advocates

(1) The appropriate authority may make regulations as to the functions of independent mental capacity advocates.

(2) The regulations may, in particular, make provision requiring an advocate to take such steps as may be prescribed for the purpose of –

    (a) providing support to the person whom he has been instructed to represent ('P') so that P may participate as fully as possible in any relevant decision;

    (b) obtaining and evaluating relevant information;

    (c) ascertaining what P's wishes and feelings would be likely to be, and the beliefs and values that would be likely to influence P, if he had capacity;

    (d) ascertaining what alternative courses of action are available in relation to P;

    (e) obtaining a further medical opinion where treatment is proposed and the advocate thinks that one should be obtained.

(3) The regulations may also make provision as to circumstances in which the advocate may challenge, or provide assistance for the purpose of challenging, any relevant decision.

37 Provision of serious medical treatment by NHS body

(1) This section applies if an NHS body –

    (a) is proposing to provide, or secure the provision of, serious medical treatment for a person ('P') who lacks capacity to consent to the treatment, and

    (b) is satisfied that there is no person, other than one engaged in providing care or treatment for P in a professional capacity or for remuneration, whom it would be appropriate to consult in determining what would be in P's best interests.

(2) But this section does not apply if P's treatment is regulated by Part 4 or 4A of the Mental Health Act.

(3) Before the treatment is provided, the NHS body must instruct an independent mental capacity advocate to represent P.

(4) If the treatment needs to be provided as a matter of urgency, it may be provided even though the NHS body has not been able to comply with subsection (3).

(5) The NHS body must, in providing or securing the provision of treatment for P, take into account any information given, or submissions made, by the independent mental capacity advocate.

(6) 'Serious medical treatment' means treatment which involves providing, withholding or withdrawing treatment of a kind prescribed by regulations made by the appropriate authority.

(7) 'NHS body' has such meaning as may be prescribed by regulations made for the purposes of this section by –

    (a) the Secretary of State, in relation to bodies in England, or

    (b) the National Assembly for Wales, in relation to bodies in Wales.

38 Provision of accommodation by NHS body

(1) This section applies if an NHS body proposes to make arrangements –

    (a) for the provision of accommodation in a hospital or care home for a person ('P') who lacks capacity to agree to the arrangements, or

    (b) for a change in P's accommodation to another hospital or care home, and is satisfied that there is no person, other than one engaged in providing care or treatment for P in a professional capacity or for remuneration, whom it would be appropriate for it to consult in determining what would be in P's best interests.

(2) But this section does not apply if P is accommodated as a result of an obligation imposed on him under the Mental Health Act.

(2A) And this section does not apply if –

    (a) an independent mental capacity advocate must be appointed under section 39A or 39C (whether or not by the NHS body) to represent P, and

    (b) the hospital or care home in which P is to be accommodated under the arrangements referred to in this section is the relevant hospital or care home under the authorisation referred to in that section.

(3) Before making the arrangements, the NHS body must instruct an independent mental capacity advocate to represent P unless it is satisfied that –
- (a) the accommodation is likely to be provided for a continuous period which is less than the applicable period, or
- (b) the arrangements need to be made as a matter of urgency.

(4) If the NHS body –
- (a) did not instruct an independent mental capacity advocate to represent P before making the arrangements because it was satisfied that subsection (3)(a) or (b) applied, but
- (b) subsequently has reason to believe that the accommodation is likely to be provided for a continuous period –
  - (i) beginning with the day on which accommodation was first provided in accordance with the arrangements, and
  - (ii) ending on or after the expiry of the applicable period,

it must instruct an independent mental capacity advocate to represent P.

(5) The NHS body must, in deciding what arrangements to make for P, take into account any information given, or submissions made, by the independent mental capacity advocate.

(6) 'Care home' has the meaning given in section 3 of the Care Standards Act 2000 (c. 14).

(7) 'Hospital' means –
- (a) in relation to England a health service hospital as defined by section 275 of the National Health Service Act 2006, and
- (b) in relation to Wales, a health service hospital as defined by section 206 of the National Health Service (Wales) Act 2006 or an independent hospital as defined by section 2 of the Care Standards Act 2000.

(8) 'NHS body' has such meaning as may be prescribed by regulations made for the purposes of this section by –
- (a) the Secretary of State, in relation to bodies in England, or
- (b) the National Assembly for Wales, in relation to bodies in Wales.

(9) 'Applicable period' means –
- (a) in relation to accommodation in a hospital, 28 days, and
- (b) in relation to accommodation in a care home, 8 weeks.

39A   Person becomes subject to Schedule A1

(1) This section applies if –
- (a) a person ('P') becomes subject to Schedule A1, and
- (b) the managing authority of the relevant hospital or care home are satisfied that there is no person, other than one engaged in providing care or treatment for P in a professional capacity or for remuneration, whom it would be appropriate to consult in determining what would be in P's best interests.

(2) The managing authority must notify the supervisory body that this section applies.

(3) The supervisory body must instruct an independent mental capacity advocate to represent P.

(4) Schedule A1 makes provision about the role of an independent mental capacity advocate appointed under this section.

(5) This section is subject to paragraph 161 of Schedule A1.

(6) For the purposes of subsection (1), a person appointed under Part 10 of Schedule A1 to be P's representative is not, by virtue of that appointment, engaged in providing care or treatment for P in a professional capacity or for remuneration.

40   Exceptions

(1) The duty imposed by sections 37(3), 38(3) or (4) or 39(4) or (5), 39A(3), 39C(3) or 39D(2) does not apply if there is –
- (a) a person nominated by P (in whatever manner) as a person to be consulted on matters to which that duty relates,

(b) a donee of a lasting power of attorney created by P who is authorised to make decisions in relation to those matters, or

(c) a deputy appointed by the court for P with power to make decisions in relation to those matters.

Miscellaneous and supplementary

42   Codes of practice

(1) The Lord Chancellor must prepare and issue one or more codes of practice –

(a) for the guidance of persons assessing whether a person has capacity in relation to any matter,

(b) for the guidance of persons acting in connection with the care or treatment of another person (see section 5),

(c) for the guidance of donees of lasting powers of attorney,

(d) for the guidance of deputies appointed by the court,

(e) for the guidance of persons carrying out research in reliance on any provision made by or under this Act (and otherwise with respect to sections 30 to 34),

(f) for the guidance of independent mental capacity advocates,

(fa) for the guidance of persons exercising functions under Schedule A1,

(fb) for the guidance of representatives appointed under Part 10 of Schedule A1,

(g) with respect to the provisions of sections 24 to 26 (advance decisions and apparent advance decisions), and

(h) with respect to such other matters concerned with this Act as he thinks fit.

(4) It is the duty of a person to have regard to any relevant code if he is acting in relation to a person who lacks capacity and is doing so in one or more of the following ways –

(a) as the donee of a lasting power of attorney,

(b) as a deputy appointed by the court,

(c) as a person carrying out research in reliance on any provision made by or under this Act (see sections 30 to 34),

(d) as an independent mental capacity advocate,

(da) in the exercise of functions under Schedule A1,

(db) as a representative appointed under Part 10 of Schedule A1,

(e) in a professional capacity,

(f) for remuneration.

(5) If it appears to a court or tribunal conducting any criminal or civil proceedings that –

(a) a provision of a code, or

(b) a failure to comply with a code, is relevant to a question arising in the proceedings, the provision or failure must be taken into account in deciding the question.

44   Ill-treatment or neglect

(1) Subsection (2) applies if a person ('D') –

(a) has the care of a person ('P') who lacks, or whom D reasonably believes to lack, capacity,

(b) is the donee of a lasting power of attorney, or an enduring power of attorney (within the meaning of Schedule 4), created by P, or

(c) is a deputy appointed by the court for P.

(2) D is guilty of an offence if he ill-treats or wilfully neglects P.

(3) A person guilty of an offence under this section is liable –

(a) on summary conviction, to imprisonment for a term not exceeding 12 months or a fine not exceeding the statutory maximum or both;

(b) on conviction on indictment, to imprisonment for a term not exceeding 5 years or a fine or both.

PART 2 THE COURT OF PROTECTION AND THE PUBLIC GUARDIAN

The Court of Protection

45 The Court of Protection

(1) There is to be a superior court of record known as the Court of Protection.

(6) The office of the Supreme Court called the Court of Protection ceases to exist.

The Public Guardian

57 The Public Guardian

(1) For the purposes of this Act, there is to be an officer, to be known as the Public Guardian.

58 Functions of the Public Guardian

(1) The Public Guardian has the following functions –

  (a) establishing and maintaining a register of lasting powers of attorney,

  (b) establishing and maintaining a register of orders appointing deputies,

  (c) supervising deputies appointed by the court,

  (d) directing a Court of Protection Visitor to visit –

  (i) a donee of a lasting power of attorney,

  (ii) a deputy appointed by the court, or

  (iii) the person granting the power of attorney or for whom the deputy is appointed ('P'), and to make a report to the Public Guardian on such matters as he may direct,

  (e) receiving security which the court requires a person to give for the discharge of his functions,

  (f) receiving reports from donees of lasting powers of attorney and deputies appointed by the court,

  (g) reporting to the court on such matters relating to proceedings under this Act as the court requires,

  (h) dealing with representations (including complaints) about the way in which a donee of a lasting power of attorney or a deputy appointed by the court is exercising his powers,

  (i) publishing, in any manner the Public Guardian thinks appropriate, any information he thinks appropriate about the discharge of his functions.

PART 3 MISCELLANEOUS AND GENERAL

Declaratory provision

62 Scope of the Act

For the avoidance of doubt, it is hereby declared that nothing in this Act is to be taken to affect the law relating to murder or manslaughter or the operation of section 2 of the Suicide Act 1961 (c. 60) (assisting suicide).

General

64 Interpretation

(1) In this Act –

'treatment' includes a diagnostic or other procedure.

SCHEDULE A1   HOSPITAL AND CARE HOME RESIDENTS: DEPRIVATION OF LIBERTY

PART 1 AUTHORISATION TO DEPRIVE RESIDENTS OF LIBERTY ETC.

1   Application of Part

(1) This Part applies if the following conditions are met.

(2) The first condition is that a person ('P') is detained in a hospital or care home – for the purpose of being given care or treatment – in circumstances which amount to deprivation of the person's liberty.

(3) The second condition is that a standard or urgent authorisation is in force.

(4) The third condition is that the standard or urgent authorisation relates –

(a) to P, and

(b) to the hospital or care home in which P is detained.

2   Authorisation to deprive P of liberty

The managing authority of the hospital or care home may deprive P of his liberty by detaining him as mentioned in paragraph 1(2).

3   No liability for acts done for purpose of depriving P of liberty

(1) This paragraph applies to any act which a person ('D') does for the purpose of detaining P as mentioned in paragraph 1(2).

(2) D does not incur any liability in relation to the act that he would not have incurred if P –

(a) had had capacity to consent in relation to D's doing the act, and

(b) had consented to D's doing the act.

4   No protection for negligent acts etc.

(1) Paragraphs 2 and 3 do not exclude a person's civil liability for loss or damage, or his criminal liability, resulting from his negligence in doing any thing.

(2) Paragraphs 2 and 3 do not authorise a person to do anything otherwise than for the purpose of the standard or urgent authorisation that is in force.

PART 3 THE QUALIFYING REQUIREMENTS

The qualifying requirements

12 (1) These are the qualifying requirements referred to in this Schedule –

(a) the age requirement;

(b) the mental health requirement;

(c) the mental capacity requirement;

(d) the best interests requirement;

(e) the eligibility requirement;

(f) the no refusals requirement.

(2) Any question of whether a person who is, or is to be, a detained resident meets the qualifying requirements is to be determined in accordance with this Part.

(3) In a case where –

(a) the question of whether a person meets a particular qualifying requirement arises in relation to the giving of a standard authorisation, and

(b) any circumstances relevant to determining that question are expected to change between the time when the determination is made and the time when the authorization is expected to come into force, those circumstances are to be taken into account as they are expected to be at the later time.

The age requirement

13   The relevant person meets the age requirement if he has reached 18.

The mental health requirement

14 (1) The relevant person meets the mental health requirement if he is suffering from mental disorder (within the meaning of the Mental Health Act, but disregarding any exclusion for persons with learning disability).

The mental capacity requirement

15 The relevant person meets the mental capacity requirement if he lacks capacity in relation to the question whether or not he should be accommodated in the relevant hospital or care home for the purpose of being given the relevant care or treatment.

The best interests requirement

16 (1) The relevant person meets the best interests requirement if all of the following conditions are met.

(2) The first condition is that the relevant person is, or is to be, a detained resident.

(3) The second condition is that it is in the best interests of the relevant person for him to be a detained resident.

(4) The third condition is that, in order to prevent harm to the relevant person, it is necessary for him to be a detained resident.

(5) The fourth condition is that it is a proportionate response to –

   (a) the likelihood of the relevant person suffering harm, and
   (b) the seriousness of that harm,

for him to be a detained resident.

The eligibility requirement

17 (1) The relevant person meets the eligibility requirement unless he is ineligible to be deprived of liberty by this Act.

(2) Schedule 1A applies for the purpose of determining whether or not P is ineligible to be deprived of liberty by this Act.

The no refusals requirement

18 The relevant person meets the no refusals requirement unless there is a refusal within the meaning of paragraph 19 or 20.

19 (1) There is a refusal if these conditions are met –

   (a) the relevant person has made an advance decision;
   (b) the advance decision is valid;
   (c) the advance decision is applicable to some or all of the relevant treatment.

(2) Expressions used in this paragraph and any of sections 24, 25 or 26 have the same meaning in this paragraph as in that section.

20 (1) There is a refusal if it would be in conflict with a valid decision of a donee or deputy for the relevant person to be accommodated in the relevant hospital or care home for the purpose of receiving some or all of the relevant care or treatment –

   (a) in circumstances which amount to deprivation of the person's liberty, or
   (b) at all.

National Health Service Act 2006

(2006, c. 41)

PART 1 PROMOTION AND PROVISION OF THE HEALTH SERVICE IN ENGLAND

The Secretary of State and the health service in England

1   Secretary of State's duty to promote comprehensive health service

(1) The Secretary of State must continue the promotion in England of a comprehensive health service designed to secure improvement –

    (a) in the physical and mental health of the people of England, and

    (b) in the prevention, diagnosis and treatment of illness.

(4) The services provided as part of the health service in England must be free of charge except in so far as the making and recovery of charges is expressly provided for by or under any enactment, whenever passed.

1A   Duty as to improvement in quality of services

(1) The Secretary of State must exercise the functions of the Secretary of State in relation to the health service with a view to securing continuous improvement in the quality of services provided to individuals for or in connection with –

    (a) the prevention, diagnosis or treatment of illness, or

    (b) the protection or improvement of public health.

(2) In discharging the duty under subsection (1) the Secretary of State must, in particular, act with a view to securing continuous improvement in the outcomes that are achieved from the provision of the services.

(3) The outcomes relevant for the purposes of subsection (2) include, in particular, outcomes which show –

    (a) the effectiveness of the services,

    (b) the safety of the services, and

    (c) the quality of the experience undergone by patients.

(4) In discharging the duty under subsection (1), the Secretary of State must have regard to the quality standards prepared by NICE under section 234 of the Health and Social Care Act 2012.

1B   Duty as to the NHS Constitution

(1) In exercising functions in relation to the health service, the Secretary of State must have regard to the NHS Constitution.

(2) In this Act, 'NHS Constitution' has the same meaning as in Chapter 1 of Part 1 of the Health Act 2009 (see section 1 of that Act).

1C   Duty as to reducing inequalities

In exercising functions in relation to the health service, the Secretary of State must have regard to the need to reduce inequalities between the people of England with respect to the benefits that they can obtain from the health service.

1D   Duty as to promoting autonomy

(1) In exercising functions in relation to the health service, the Secretary of State must have regard to the desirability of securing, so far as consistent with the interests of the health service –

    (a) that any other person exercising functions in relation to the health service or providing services for its purposes is free to exercise those functions or provide those services in the manner that it considers most appropriate, and

    (b) that unnecessary burdens are not imposed on any such person.

(2) If, in the case of any exercise of functions, the Secretary of State considers that there is a conflict between the matters mentioned in subsection (1) and the discharge by the Secretary of State of the duties under section 1, the Secretary of State must give priority to the duties under that section.

1E Duty as to research

In exercising functions in relation to the health service, the Secretary of State must promote –

(a) research on matters relevant to the health service, and

(b) the use in the health service of evidence obtained from research.

Role of the Board in the health service in England

1H The National Health Service Commissioning Board and its general functions

(1) There is to be a body corporate known as the National Health Service Commissioning Board ('the Board').

(2) The Board is subject to the duty under section 1(1) concurrently with the Secretary of State except in relation to that part of the health service that is provided in pursuance of the public health functions of the Secretary of State or local authorities.

Role of clinical commissioning groups in the health service in England

1I Clinical commissioning groups and their general functions

(1) There are to be bodies corporate known as clinical commissioning groups established in accordance with Chapter A2 of Part 2.

(2) Each clinical commissioning group has the function of arranging for the provision of services for the purposes of the health service in England in accordance with this Act.

General power

2 General power

The Secretary of State, the Board or a clinical commissioning group may do anything which is calculated to facilitate, or is conducive or incidental to, the discharge of any function conferred on that person by this Act.

2A Secretary of State's duty as to protection of public health

(1) The Secretary of State must take such steps as the Secretary of State considers appropriate for the purpose of protecting the public in England from disease or other dangers to health.

(2) The steps that may be taken under subsection (1) include –

(a) the conduct of research or such other steps as the Secretary of State considers appropriate for advancing knowledge and understanding;

(b) providing microbiological or other technical services (whether in laboratories or otherwise);

(c) providing vaccination, immunisation or screening services;

(d) providing other services or facilities for the prevention, diagnosis or treatment of illness;

(e) providing training;

(f) providing information and advice;

(g) making available the services of any person or any facilities.

2B Functions of local authorities and Secretary of State as to improvement of public health

(1) Each local authority must take such steps as it considers appropriate for improving the health of the people in its area.

(2) The Secretary of State may take such steps as the Secretary of State considers appropriate for improving the health of the people of England.

(3) The steps that may be taken under subsection (1) or (2) include –

(a) providing information and advice;

(b) providing services or facilities designed to promote healthy living (whether by helping individuals to address behaviour that is detrimental to health or in any other way);

(c)   providing services or facilities for the prevention, diagnosis or treatment of illness;

(d)   providing financial incentives to encourage individuals to adopt healthier lifestyles;

(e)   providing assistance (including financial assistance) to help individuals to minimise any risks to health arising from their accommodation or environment;

(f)   providing or participating in the provision of training for persons working or seeking to work in the field of health improvement;

(g)   making available the services of any person or any facilities.

(4) The steps that may be taken under subsection (1) also include providing grants or loans (on such terms as the local authority considers appropriate).

Arrangements for the provision of certain health services

3   Duties of clinical commissioning groups as to commissioning certain health services

(1) A clinical commissioning group must arrange for the provision of the following to such extent as it considers necessary to meet the reasonable requirements of the persons for whom it has responsibility –

(a)   hospital accommodation,

(b)   other accommodation for the purpose of any service provided under this Act,

(c)   medical, dental, ophthalmic, nursing and ambulance services,

(d)   such other services or facilities for the care of pregnant women, women who are breast-feeding and young children as the group considers are appropriate as part of the health service,

(e)   such other services or facilities for the prevention of illness, the care of persons suffering from illness and the after-care of persons who have suffered from illness as the group considers are appropriate as part of the health service,

(f)   such other services or facilities as are required for the diagnosis and treatment of illness.

(1A) For the purposes of this section, a clinical commissioning group has responsibility for –

(a)   persons who are provided with primary medical services by a member of the group, and

(b)   persons who usually reside in the group's area and are not provided with primary medical services by a member of any clinical commissioning group.

(1E) The duty in subsection (1) does not apply in relation to a service or facility if the Board has a duty to arrange for its provision.

(1F) In exercising its functions under this section and section 3A, a clinical commissioning group must act consistently with –

(a)   the discharge by the Secretary of State and the Board of their duty under section 1(1) (duty to promote a comprehensive health service), and

(b)   the objectives and requirements for the time being specified in the mandate published under section 13A.

3A   Power of clinical commissioning groups to commission certain health services

(1) Each clinical commissioning group may arrange for the provision of such services or facilities as it considers appropriate for the purposes of the health service that relate to securing improvement –

(a)   in the physical and mental health of the persons for whom it has responsibility, or

(b)   in the prevention, diagnosis and treatment of illness in those persons.

(2) A clinical commissioning group may not arrange for the provision of a service or facility under subsection (1) if the Board has a duty to arrange for its provision by virtue of section 3B or 4.

(3) Subsections (1A), (1B) and (1D) of section 3 apply for the purposes of this section as they apply for the purposes of that section.

3B Secretary of State's power to require Board to commission services

(1) Regulations may require the Board to arrange, to such extent as it considers necessary to meet all reasonable requirements, for the provision as part of the health service of –

(a) dental services of a prescribed description;

(b) services or facilities for members of the armed forces or their families;

(c) services or facilities for persons who are detained in a prison or in other accommodation of a prescribed description;

(d) such other services or facilities as may be prescribed.

(2) A service or facility may be prescribed under subsection (1)(d) only if the Secretary of State considers that it would be appropriate for the Board (rather than clinical commissioning groups) to arrange for its provision as part of the health service.

(3) In deciding whether it would be so appropriate, the Secretary of State must have regard to –

(a) the number of individuals who require the provision of the service or facility;

(b) the cost of providing the service or facility;

(c) the number of persons able to provide the service or facility;

(d) the financial implications for clinical commissioning groups if they were required to arrange for the provision of the service or facility.

(4) Before deciding whether to make regulations under this section, the Secretary of State must –

(a) obtain advice appropriate for that purpose, and

(b) consult the Board.

4 High security psychiatric services

(1) The Board must arrange for the provision of hospital accommodation and services for persons who–

(a) are liable to be detained under the Mental Health Act 1983, and

(b) in the opinion of the Secretary of State require treatment under conditions of high security on account of their dangerous, violent or criminal propensities.

(2) The hospital accommodation and services mentioned in subsection (1) are referred to in this section as 'high security psychiatric services'.

(3) High security psychiatric services may be provided –

(a) only at hospital premises at which services are provided only for the persons mentioned in subsection (1), and

(b) only by a person approved by the Secretary of State for the purposes of this subsection.

(3A) The Secretary of State may –

(a) give directions to a person who provides high security psychiatric services about the provision by that person of those services;

(b) give directions to the Board about the exercise of its functions in relation to high security psychiatric services.

(4) 'Hospital premises' means–

(a) a hospital, or

(b) any part of a hospital which is treated as a separate unit.

5 Other services

Schedule 1 makes further provision about the provision of services for the purposes of the health service in England.

Functions of Special Health Authorities

7 Functions of Special Health Authorities

(1) The Secretary of State may direct a Special Health Authority to exercise any functions of the Secretary of State or any other person which relate to the health service in England and are specified in the direction.

(1A) Subsection (1) does not apply to any function of the Secretary of State of making an order or regulations.

(1B) Before exercising the power in subsection (1) in relation to a function of a person other than the Secretary of State, the Secretary of State must consult that person.

(1C) Regulations may provide that a Special Health Authority specified in the regulations is to have such additional functions in relation to the health service in England as may be so specified.

NHS contracts

9   NHS contracts

(1) In this Act, an NHS contract is an arrangement under which one health service body ('the commissioner') arranges for the provision to it by another health service body ('the provider')of goods or services which it reasonably requires for the purposes of its functions.

(5) Whether or not an arrangement which constitutes an NHS contract would apart from this subsection be a contract in law, it must not be regarded for any purpose as giving rise to contractual rights or liabilities.

Provision of services otherwise than by the Secretary of State

12   Secretary of State's arrangements with other bodies

(1) The Secretary of State may arrange with any person or body to provide, or assist in providing anything which the Secretary of State has a duty or power to provide, or arrange for the provision of, under section 2A or 2B or Schedule 1.

(2) The bodies with whom arrangements may be made under subsection (1) include –
  (a) the Board,
  (b) clinical commissioning groups,
  (c) any other public authorities, and
  (d) voluntary organisations.

(3) The Secretary of State may make available any facilities provided by the Secretary of State under section 2A or 2B or Schedule 1 to any service provider or to any eligible voluntary organisation.

PART 2 HEALTH SERVICE BODIES

Chapter A1 The National Health Service Commissioning Board

Secretary of State's mandate to the Board

13A   Mandate to Board

(1) Before the start of each financial year, the Secretary of State must publish and lay before Parliament a document to be known as 'the mandate'.

(2) The Secretary of State must specify in the mandate –
  (a) the objectives that the Secretary of State considers the Board should seek to achieve in the exercise of its functions during that financial year and such subsequent financial years as the Secretary of State considers appropriate, and
  (b) any requirements that the Secretary of State considers it necessary to impose on the Board for the purpose of ensuring that it achieves those objectives.

(7) The Board must –
  (a) seek to achieve the objectives specified in the mandate, and
  (b) comply with any requirements so specified.

(8) Before specifying any objectives or requirements in the mandate, the Secretary of State must consult –
  (a) the Board,

(b) the Healthwatch England committee of the Care Quality Commission, and

(c) such other persons as the Secretary of State considers appropriate.

(9) Requirements included in the mandate have effect only if regulations so provide.

General duties of the Board

13C   Duty to promote NHS Constitution

(1) The Board must, in the exercise of its functions –

(a) act with a view to securing that health services are provided in a way which promotes the NHS Constitution, and

(b) promote awareness of the NHS Constitution among patients, staff and members of the public.

13D   Duty as to effectiveness, efficiency etc.

The Board must exercise its functions effectively, efficiently and economically.

13E   Duty as to improvement in quality of services

(1) The Board must exercise its functions with a view to securing continuous improvement in the quality of services provided to individuals for or in connection with –

(a) the prevention, diagnosis or treatment of illness, or

(b) the protection or improvement of public health.

(2) In discharging its duty under subsection (1), the Board must, in particular, act with a view to securing continuous improvement in the outcomes that are achieved from the provision of the services.

(3) The outcomes relevant for the purposes of subsection (2) include, in particular, outcomes which show –

(a) the effectiveness of the services,

(b) the safety of the services, and

(c) the quality of the experience undergone by patients.

(4) In discharging its duty under subsection (1), the Board must have regard to –

(a) any document published by the Secretary of State for the purposes of this section, and

(b) the quality standards prepared by NICE under section 234 of the Health and Social Care Act 2012.

13F   Duty as to promoting autonomy

(1) In exercising its functions, the Board must have regard to the desirability of securing, so far as consistent with the interests of the health service –

(a) that any other person exercising functions in relation to the health service or providing services for its purposes is free to exercise those functions or provide those services in the manner it considers most appropriate, and

(b) that unnecessary burdens are not imposed on any such person.

(2) If, in the case of any exercise of functions, the Board considers that there is a conflict between the matters mentioned in subsection (1) and the discharge by the Board of its duties under sections 1(1) and 1H(3)(b), the Board must give priority to those duties.

13G   Duty as to reducing inequalities

The Board must, in the exercise of its functions, have regard to the need to –

(a) reduce inequalities between patients with respect to their ability to access health services, and

(b) reduce inequalities between patients with respect to the outcomes achieved for them by the provision of health services.

13H   Duty to promote involvement of each patient

The Board must, in the exercise of its functions, promote the involvement of patients, and their carers and representatives (if any), in decisions which relate to –

(a) the prevention or diagnosis of illness in the patients, or

(b) their care or treatment.

13I   Duty as to patient choice

The Board must, in the exercise of its functions, act with a view to enabling patients to make choices with respect to aspects of health services provided to them.

13J   Duty to obtain appropriate advice

The Board must obtain advice appropriate for enabling it effectively to discharge its functions from persons who (taken together) have a broad range of professional expertise in –

    (a) the prevention, diagnosis or treatment of illness, and

    (b) the protection or improvement of public health.

13K   Duty to promote innovation

    (1) The Board must, in the exercise of its functions, promote innovation in the provision of health services (including innovation in the arrangements made for their provision).

    (2) The Board may make payments as prizes to promote innovation in the provision of health services.

13L   Duty in respect of research

The Board must, in the exercise of its functions, promote –

    (a) research on matters relevant to the health service, and

    (b) the use in the health service of evidence obtained from research.

13M   Duty as to promoting education and training

The Board must, in exercising its functions, have regard to the need to promote education and training for the persons mentioned in section 1F(1) so as to assist the Secretary of State in the discharge of the duty under that section.

13N   Duty as to promoting integration

    (1) The Board must exercise its functions with a view to securing that health services are provided in an integrated way where it considers that this would –

    (a) improve the quality of those services (including the outcomes that are achieved from their provision),

    (b) reduce inequalities between persons with respect to their ability to access those services, or

    (c) reduce inequalities between persons with respect to the outcomes achieved for them by the provision of those services.

    (2) The Board must exercise its functions with a view to securing that the provision of health services is integrated with the provision of health-related services or social care services where it considers that this would –

    (a) improve the quality of the health services (including the outcomes that are achieved from the provision of those services),

    (b) reduce inequalities between persons with respect to their ability to access those services, or

    (c) reduce inequalities between persons with respect to the outcomes achieved for them by the provision of those services.

    (3) The Board must encourage clinical commissioning groups to enter into arrangements with local authorities in pursuance of regulations under section 75 where it considers that this would secure –

    (a) that health services are provided in an integrated way and that this would have any of the effects mentioned in subsection (1)(a) to (c), or

    (b) that the provision of health services is integrated with the provision of health-related services or social care services and that this would have any of the effects mentioned in subsection (2)(a) to (c).

    (4) In this section –

'health-related services' means services that may have an effect on the health of individuals but are not health services or social care services;

'social care services' means services that are provided in pursuance of the social services functions of local authorities (within the meaning of the Local Authority Social Services Act 1970).

13P   Duty as respects variation in provision of health services

The Board must not exercise its functions for the purpose of causing a variation in the proportion of services provided as part of the health service that is provided by persons of a particular description if that description is by reference to –

(a) whether the persons in question are in the public or (as the case may be) private sector, or

(b) some other aspect of their status.

Public involvement

13Q   Public involvement and consultation by the Board

(1) This section applies in relation to any health services which are, or are to be, provided pursuant to arrangements made by the Board in the exercise of its functions ('commissioning arrangements').

(2) The Board must make arrangements to secure that individuals to whom the services are being or may be provided are involved (whether by being consulted or provided with information or in other ways) –

(a) in the planning of the commissioning arrangements by the Board,

(b) in the development and consideration of proposals by the Board for changes in the commissioning arrangements where the implementation of the proposals would have an impact on the manner in which the services are delivered to the individuals or the range of health services available to them, and

(c) in decisions of the Board affecting the operation of the commissioning arrangements where the implementation of the decisions would (if made) have such an impact.

(3) The reference in subsection (2)(b) to the delivery of services is a reference to their delivery at the point when they are received by users.

13R   Information on safety of services provided by the health service

(1) The Board must establish and operate systems for collecting and analysing information relating to the safety of the services provided by the health service.

(2) The Board must make information collected by virtue of subsection (1), and any other information obtained by analysing it, available to such persons as the Board considers appropriate.

(4) The Board must give advice and guidance, to such persons as it considers appropriate, for the purpose of maintaining and improving the safety of the services provided by the health service.

(5) The Board must monitor the effectiveness of the advice and guidance given by it under subsection (4).

(6) A clinical commissioning group must have regard to any advice or guidance given to it under subsection (4).

13S   Guidance in relation to processing of information

(1) The Board must publish guidance for registered persons on the practice to be followed by them in relation to the processing of –

(a) patient information, and

(b) any other information obtained or generated in the course of the provision of the health service.

(2) Registered persons who carry on an activity which involves, or is connected with, the provision of health care must have regard to any guidance published under this section.

(3) In this section, 'patient information', 'processing' and 'registered person' have the same meaning as in section 20A of the Health and Social Care Act 2008.

Business plan and report

13T   Business plan

(1) Before the start of each financial year, the Board must publish a business plan setting out how it proposes to exercise its functions in that year and each of the next two financial years.

13U   Annual report

(1) As soon as practicable after the end of each financial year, the Board must publish an annual report on how it has exercised its functions during the year.

13W   Board's power to generate income, etc.

(1) The Board has power to do anything specified in section 7(2) of the Health and Medicines Act 1988 (provision of goods, services, etc.) for the purpose of making additional income available for improving the health service.

(2) The Board may exercise a power conferred by subsection (1) only to the extent that its exercise does not to any significant extent interfere with the performance by the Board of its functions.

13X   Power to make grants etc.

(1) The Board may make payments by way of grant or loan to a voluntary organisation which provides or arranges for the provision of services which are similar to the services in respect of which the Board has functions.

Interpretation

13Z4   Interpretation

(1) In this Chapter –

'the health service' means the health service in England;

'health services' means services provided as part of the health service and, in sections 13O and 13Q, also includes services that are to be provided as part of the health service.

Chapter A2   Clinical Commissioning Groups

Establishment of clinical commissioning groups

14A   General duties of Board in relation to clinical commissioning groups

(1) The Board must exercise its functions under this Chapter so as to ensure that at any time after the day specified by order of the Secretary of State for the purposes of this section each provider of primary medical services is a member of a clinical commissioning group.

(2) The Board must exercise its functions under this Chapter so as to ensure that at any time after the day so specified the areas specified in the constitutions of clinical commissioning groups –

    (a) together cover the whole of England, and

    (b) do not coincide or overlap.

(3) For the purposes of this Chapter, 'provider of primary medical services' means a person who is a party to an arrangement mentioned in subsection (4).

(4) The arrangements mentioned in this subsection are –

    (a) a general medical services contract to provide primary medical services of a prescribed description,

    (b) arrangements under section 83(2) for the provision of primary medical services of a prescribed description,

    (c) section 92 arrangements for the provision of primary medical services of a prescribed description.

14B   Applications for the establishment of clinical commissioning groups

(1) An application for the establishment of a clinical commissioning group may be made to the Board.

(2) The application may be made by any two or more persons each of whom –

    (a) is or wishes to be a provider of primary medical services, and

    (b) wishes to be a member of the clinical commissioning group.

14L   Governing bodies of clinical commissioning groups

(1) A clinical commissioning group must have a governing body.

14P   Duty to promote NHS Constitution

(1) Each clinical commissioning group must, in the exercise of its functions –

    (a) act with a view to securing that health services are provided in a way which promotes the NHS Constitution, and

    (b) promote awareness of the NHS Constitution among patients, staff and members of the public.

14Q   Duty as to effectiveness, efficiency etc.

Each clinical commissioning group must exercise its functions effectively, efficiently and economically.

14R   Duty as to improvement in quality of services

(1) Each clinical commissioning group must exercise its functions with a view to securing continuous improvement in the quality of services provided to individuals for or in connection with the prevention, diagnosis or treatment of illness.

(2) In discharging its duty under subsection (1), a clinical commissioning group must, in particular, act with a view to securing continuous improvement in the outcomes that are achieved from the provision of the services.

(3) The outcomes relevant for the purposes of subsection (2) include, in particular, outcomes which show –

    (a) the effectiveness of the services,

    (b) the safety of the services, and

    (c) the quality of the experience undergone by patients.

(4) In discharging its duty under subsection (1), a clinical commissioning group must have regard to any guidance published under section 14Z8.

14S   Duty in relation to quality of primary medical services

Each clinical commissioning group must assist and support the Board in discharging its duty under section 13E so far as relating to securing continuous improvement in the quality of primary medical services.

14T   Duties as to reducing inequalities

Each clinical commissioning group must, in the exercise of its functions, have regard to the need to –

    (a) reduce inequalities between patients with respect to their ability to access health services, and

    (b) reduce inequalities between patients with respect to the outcomes achieved for them by the provision of health services.

14U   Duty to promote involvement of each patient

(1) Each clinical commissioning group must, in the exercise of its functions, promote the involvement of patients, and their carers and representatives (if any), in decisions which relate to–

    (a) the prevention or diagnosis of illness in the patients, or

    (b) their care or treatment.

14V   Duty as to patient choice

Each clinical commissioning group must, in the exercise of its functions, act with a view to enabling patients to make choices with respect to aspects of health services provided to them.

14W   Duty to obtain appropriate advice

(1) Each clinical commissioning group must obtain advice appropriate for enabling it effectively to discharge its functions from persons who (taken together) have a broad range of professional expertise in –

(a) the prevention, diagnosis or treatment of illness, and

(b) the protection or improvement of public health.

14X   Duty to promote innovation

Each clinical commissioning group must, in the exercise of its functions, promote innovation in the provision of health services (including innovation in the arrangements made for their provision).

14Y   Duty in respect of research

Each clinical commissioning group must, in the exercise of its functions, promote –

(a) research on matters relevant to the health service, and

(b) the use in the health service of evidence obtained from research.

14Z   Duty as to promoting education and training

Each clinical commissioning group must, in exercising its functions, have regard to the need to promote education and training for the persons mentioned in section 1F(1) so as to assist the Secretary of State in the discharge of the duty under that section.

14Z1   Duty as to promoting integration

(1) Each clinical commissioning group must exercise its functions with a view to securing that health services are provided in an integrated way where it considers that this would –

(a) improve the quality of those services (including the outcomes that are achieved from their provision),

(b) reduce inequalities between persons with respect to their ability to access those services, or

(c) reduce inequalities between persons with respect to the outcomes achieved for them by the provision of those services.

(2) Each clinical commissioning group must exercise its functions with a view to securing that the provision of health services is integrated with the provision of health-related services or social care services where it considers that this would –

(a) improve the quality of the health services (including the outcomes that are achieved from the provision of those services),

(b) reduce inequalities between persons with respect to their ability to access those services, or

(c) reduce inequalities between persons with respect to the outcomes achieved for them by the provision of those services.

Public involvement

14Z2   Public involvement and consultation by clinical commissioning groups

(1) This section applies in relation to any health services which are, or are to be, provided pursuant to arrangements made by a clinical commissioning group in the exercise of its functions ('commissioning arrangements').

(2) The clinical commissioning group must make arrangements to secure that individuals to whom the services are being or may be provided are involved (whether by being consulted or provided with information or in other ways) –

(a) in the planning of the commissioning arrangements by the group,

(b) in the development and consideration of proposals by the group for changes in the commissioning arrangements where the implementation of the proposals would have an impact on the manner in which the services are delivered to the individuals or the range of health services available to them, and

    (c) in decisions of the group affecting the operation of the commissioning arrangements where the implementation of the decisions would (if made) have such an impact.

  (3) The clinical commissioning group must include in its constitution –

    (a) a description of the arrangements made by it under subsection (2), and

    (b) a statement of the principles which it will follow in implementing those arrangements.

  (6) The reference in subsection (2)(b) to the delivery of services is a reference to their delivery at the point when they are received by users.

14Z8   Guidance on commissioning by the Board

  (1) The Board must publish guidance for clinical commissioning groups on the discharge of their commissioning functions.

  (2) Each clinical commissioning group must have regard to guidance under this section.

  (3) The Board must consult the Healthwatch England committee of the Care Quality Commission –

    (a) before it first publishes guidance under this section, and

    (b) before it publishes any revised guidance containing changes that are, in the opinion of the Board, significant.

14Z10   Power of Board to provide assistance or support

  (1) The Board may provide assistance or support to a clinical commissioning group.

  (2) The assistance that may be provided includes –

    (a) financial assistance, and

    (b) making the services of the Board's employees or any other resources of the Board available to the clinical commissioning group.

Commissioning plans and reports

14Z11   Commissioning plan

  (1) Before the start of each relevant period, a clinical commissioning group must prepare a plan setting out how it proposes to exercise its functions in that period.

  (4) The clinical commissioning group must publish the plan.

  (5) The clinical commissioning group must give a copy of the plan to the Board before the date specified by the Board in a direction.

  (6) The clinical commissioning group must give a copy of the plan to each relevant Health and Wellbeing Board.

14Z14   Opinion of Health and Wellbeing Boards on commissioning plans

  (1) A relevant Health and Wellbeing Board –

    (a) may give the Board its opinion on whether a plan published by a clinical commissioning group under section 14Z11(4) or 14Z12(2) takes proper account of each joint health and wellbeing strategy published by the Health and Wellbeing Board which relates to the period (or any part of the period) to which the plan relates, and

    (b) if it does so, must give the clinical commissioning group a copy of its opinion.

  (2) In this section, 'joint health and wellbeing strategy' has the same meaning as in section 14Z13.

14Z15   Reports by clinical commissioning groups

  (1) In each financial year other than its first financial year, a clinical commissioning group must prepare a report (an 'annual report') on how it has discharged its functions in the previous financial year.

14Z16   Performance assessment of clinical commissioning groups

  (1) The Board must conduct a performance assessment of each clinical commissioning group in respect of each financial year.

Intervention powers

14Z21   Power to give directions, dissolve clinical commissioning groups etc.

(1) This section applies if the Board is satisfied that –

    (a) a clinical commissioning group is failing or has failed to discharge any of its functions, or

    (b) there is a significant risk that a clinical commissioning group will fail to do so.

(2) The Board may direct the clinical commissioning group to discharge such of those functions, and in such manner and within such period or periods, as may be specified in the direction.

(3) The Board may direct –

    (a) the clinical commissioning group, or

    (b) the accountable officer of the group,

to cease to perform any functions for such period or periods as may be specified in the direction.

(4) The Board may –

    (a) terminate the appointment of the clinical commissioning group's accountable officer, and

    (b) appoint another person to be its accountable officer.

(6) The Board may vary the constitution of the clinical commissioning group, including doing so by –

    (a) varying its area,

    (b) adding any person who is a provider of primary medical services to the list of members, or

    (c) removing any person from that list.

(7) The Board may dissolve the clinical commissioning group.

Chapter 3 NHS trusts

25   NHS trusts

(1) The Secretary of State may by order establish bodies, called National Health Service trusts ('NHS trusts'), to provide goods and services for the purposes of the health service.

(2) An order under subsection (1) is referred to in this Act as 'an NHS trust order'.

26   General duty of NHS trusts

An NHS trust must exercise its functions effectively, efficiently and economically.

Chapter 4 Special Health Authorities

28   Special Health Authorities

(1) The Secretary of State may by order establish special bodies for the purpose of exercising any functions which may be conferred on them by or under this Act.

(3) A body established under this section is called a Special Health Authority.

Chapter 5 NHS foundation trusts

Introductory

30   NHS foundation trusts

(1) An NHS foundation trust is a public benefit corporation the function of which is to provide in accordance with this Chapter goods and services for the purposes of the health service in England.

Authorisation

33   Applications by NHS trusts

(1) An NHS trust may make an application to the regulator for authorisation to become an NHS foundation trust, if the application is supported by the Secretary of State.

39   Register of NHS foundation trusts

(1) The regulator must continue to maintain a register of NHS foundation trusts.

Functions

43   Provision of goods and services

(1) The principal purpose of an NHS foundation trust is the provision of goods and services for the purposes of the health service in England.

(2) An NHS foundation trust may provide goods and services for any purposes related to –

(a) the provision of services provided to individuals for or in connection with the prevention, diagnosis or treatment of illness, and

(b) the promotion and protection of public health.

(2A) An NHS foundation trust does not fulfil its principal purpose unless, in each financial year, its total income from the provision of goods and services for the purposes of the health service in England is greater than its total income from the provision of goods and services for any other purposes.

(3) An NHS foundation trust may also carry on activities other than those mentioned in subsection (2) for the purpose of making additional income available in order better to carry on its principal purpose.

44   Power to charge for accommodation etc.

(6) According to the nature of its functions, an NHS foundation trust may, in the case of patients being provided with goods and services for the purposes of the health service, make accommodation or further services available for patients who give undertakings (or for whom undertakings are given) to pay any charges imposed by the NHS foundation trust in respect of the accommodation or services.

(7) An NHS foundation trust may exercise the power conferred by subsection (6) only to the extent that its exercise does not to any significant extent interfere with the performance by the NHS foundation trust of its functions.

Miscellaneous

63   General duty of NHS foundation trusts

An NHS foundation trust must exercise its functions effectively, efficiently and economically.

Chapter 6   Miscellaneous

Intervention orders and default powers

66   Intervention orders

(1) This section applies to –

(a) NHS trusts, and

(b) Special Health Authorities.

(2) If the Secretary of State–

(a) considers that a body to which this section applies is not performing one or more of its functions adequately or at all, or that there are significant failings in the way the body is being run, and

(b) is satisfied that it is appropriate for him to intervene under this section,

he may make an order under this section in respect of the body (an 'intervention order').

Co-operation between NHS bodies

72   Co-operation between NHS bodies

(1) It is the duty of NHS bodies to co-operate with each other in exercising their functions.

(2) For the purposes of this section, NICE is an NHS body.

(3) For the purposes of this section, the Health and Social Care Information Centre is an NHS body.

PART 4 MEDICAL SERVICES

Duty of the Board in relation to primary medical services

83 Primary medical services

(1) The Board must, to the extent that it considers necessary to meet all reasonable requirements, exercise its powers so as to secure the provision of primary medical services throughout England.

(2) The Board may (in addition to any other power conferred on it) make such arrangements for the provision of primary medical services as it considers appropriate; and it may, in particular, make contractual arrangements with any person.

(2A) Arrangements made for the purposes of subsection (1) or (2) may include arrangements for the performance of a service outside England.

(3) The Board must publish information about such matters as may be prescribed in relation to the primary medical services provided under this Act.

(5) Regulations may provide that services of a prescribed description must, or must not, be regarded as primary medical services for the purposes of this Act.

(6) Regulations under this section may in particular describe services by reference to the manner or circumstances in which they are provided.

General medical services contracts

84 General medical services contracts: introductory

(1) The Board may enter into a contract under which primary medical services are provided in accordance with the following provisions of this Part.

(2) A contract under this section is called in this Act a 'general medical services contract'.

(3) A general medical services contract may make such provision as may be agreed between the Board and the contractor or contractors in relation to –
    (a) the services to be provided under the contract,
    (b) remuneration under the contract, and
    (c) any other matters.

(4) The services to be provided under a general medical services contract may include –
    (a) services which are not primary medical services,
    (b) services to be provided outside England.

(5) In this Part, 'contractor', in relation to a general medical services contract, means any person entering into the contract with the Primary Care Trust.

85 Requirement to provide certain primary medical services

(1) A general medical services contract must require the contractor or contractors to provide, for his or their patients, primary medical services of such descriptions as may be prescribed.

(2) Regulations under subsection (1) may in particular describe services by reference to the manner or circumstances in which they are provided.

86 Persons eligible to enter into GMS contracts

(1) The Board may, subject to such conditions as may be prescribed, enter into a general medical services contract with –
    (a) a medical practitioner,
    (b) two or more individuals practising in partnership where the conditions in subsection (2) are satisfied, or
    (c) a company limited by shares where the conditions in subsection (3) are satisfied.

(2) The conditions referred to in subsection (1)(b) are that –
    (a) at least one partner is a medical practitioner, and
    (b) any partner who is not a medical practitioner is either –
        (i) an NHS employee,

(ii) a section 92 employee, section 107 employee, section 50 employee, section 64 employee, section 17C employee or Article 15B employee,

(iii) a health care professional who is engaged in the provision of services under this Act or the National Health Service (Wales) Act 2006 (c. 42), or

(iv) an individual falling within section 93(1)(d).

(3) The conditions referred to in subsection (1)(c) are that –

(a) at least one share in the company is both legally and beneficially owned by a medical practitioner, and

(b) any share which is not so owned is both legally and beneficially owned by a person referred to in subsection (2)(b).

(4) Regulations may make provision as to the effect, in relation to a general medical services contract entered into by individuals practising in partnership, of a change in the membership of the partnership.

(5) In this section –

'health care professional', 'NHS employee', 'section 92 employee', 'section 107 employee', 'section 50 employee', 'section 64 employee', 'section 17C employee' and 'Article 15B employee' have the meaning given by section 93.

87   GMS contracts: payments

(1) The Secretary of State may give directions as to payments to be made under general medical services contracts.

(2) A general medical services contract must require payments to be made under the contract in accordance with directions under this section.

(3) Directions under subsection (1) may in particular –

(a) provide for payments to be made by reference to compliance with standards or the achievement of levels of performance,

(b) provide for payments to be made by reference to –

(i) any scheme or scale specified in the direction, or

(ii) a determination made by any person in accordance with factors specified in the direction,

(c) provide for the making of payments in respect of individual practitioners,

(d) provide that the whole or any part of a payment is subject to conditions (and may provide that payments are payable by the Board only if it is satisfied as to certain conditions),

(e) make provision having effect from a date before the date of the direction, provided that, having regard to the direction as a whole, the provision is not detrimental to the persons to whose remuneration it relates.

(4) Before giving a direction under subsection (1), the Secretary of State –

(a) must consult any body appearing to him to be representative of persons to whose remuneration the direction would relate, and

(b) may consult such other persons as he considers appropriate.

(5) 'Payments' includes fees, allowances, reimbursements, loans and repayments.

88   GMS contracts: prescription of drugs, etc.

(1) A general medical services contract must contain provision requiring the contractor or contractors to comply with any directions given by the Secretary of State for the purposes of this section as to the drugs, medicines or other substances which may or may not be ordered for patients in the provision of medical services under the contract.

89   GMS contracts: other required terms

(1) A general medical services contract must contain such provision as may be prescribed (in addition to the provision required by the preceding provisions of this Part).

90   GMS contracts: disputes and enforcement

(1) Regulations may make provision for the resolution of disputes as to the terms of a proposed general medical services contract.

Performance of primary medical services

91   Persons performing primary medical services

(1) Regulations may provide that a health care professional of a prescribed description may not perform any primary medical service for which the Board is responsible unless he is included in a list maintained under the regulations by the Board.

(2) For the purposes of this section –

(a) 'health care professional' means a person who is a member of a profession regulated by a body mentioned in section 25(3) of the National Health Service Reform and Health Care Professions Act 2002,

(b) the Board is responsible for a medical service if it provides the service, or secures its provision, by or under any enactment.

Other arrangements for the provision of primary medical services

92   Arrangements by the Board for the provision of primary medical services

(1) The Board may make agreements, other than arrangements pursuant to section 83(2) or general medical services contracts, under which primary medical services are provided.

94   Regulations about section 92 arrangements

(1) The Secretary of State may make regulations about the provision of services in accordance with section 92 arrangements.

(2) The regulations must include provision for participants other than the Board to withdraw from section 92 arrangements if they wish to do so.

Local Medical Committees

97   Local Medical Committees

(1) The Board may recognise a committee formed for an area which it is satisfied is representative of –

(a) the persons to whom subsection (2) applies, and

(b) the persons to whom subsection (3) applies.

(2) This subsection applies to –

(a) each medical practitioner who, under a general medical services contract entered into by him, is providing primary medical services in the area for which the committee is formed, and

(b) each medical practitioner who, under a general ophthalmic services contract entered into by him, is providing primary ophthalmic services in that area.

(3) This subsection applies to each other medical practitioner –

(a) who is performing primary medical services or primary ophthalmic services in the area for which the committee is formed –

(ii) in accordance with section 92 arrangements, or

(iii) under a general medical services contract or a general ophthalmic services contract, and

(b) who has notified the Board that he wishes to be represented by the committee (and has not notified it that he wishes to cease to be so represented).

(4) A committee recognised under this section is called the Local Medical Committee for the area for which it is formed.

PART 9 CHARGING

Power to charge generally

172   Charges for drugs, medicines or appliances, or pharmaceutical services

(1) Regulations may provide for the making and recovery in such manner as may be prescribed of such charges as may be prescribed in respect of –

  (a) the supply under this Act (otherwise than under Chapter 1 of Part 7) of drugs, medicines or appliances (including the replacement and repair of those appliances), and

  (b) such of the pharmaceutical services referred to in that Chapter as may be prescribed.

(2) Regulations under this section may in particular make provision in relation to the supply of contraceptive substances and appliances under paragraph 8 of Schedule 1.

173   Exemptions from general charging

(1) No charge may be made under regulations under section 172(1) in respect of –

  (a) the supply of any drug, medicine or appliance for a patient who is resident in hospital,

  (b) the supply of any drug or medicine for the treatment of sexually transmitted disease (otherwise than in the provision of primary medical services or in accordance with a pilot scheme established under section 134(1) of this Act or an LPS scheme),

  (c) the supply of any appliance (otherwise than in pursuance of paragraph 8(d) of Schedule 1) for a person who is under 16 years of age or is under 19 years of age and receiving qualifying full-time education, or

  (d) the replacement or repair of any appliance in consequence of a defect in the appliance as supplied.

PART 12   PUBLIC INVOLVEMENT AND SCRUTINY

Chapter 2   Public involvement and consultation

242   Public involvement and consultation

(1) This section applies to –

  (a) relevant English bodies, and

  (b) relevant Welsh bodies.

(1A) In this section –

'relevant English body' means –

  (c) an NHS trust that is not a relevant Welsh body, or

  (d) an NHS foundation trust;

'relevant Welsh body' means an NHS trust all or most of whose hospitals, establishments and facilities are in Wales.

(1B) Each relevant English body must make arrangements, as respects health services for which it is responsible, which secure that users of those services, whether directly or through representatives, are involved (whether by being consulted or provided with information, or in other ways) in –

  (a) the planning of the provision of those services,

  (b) the development and consideration of proposals for changes in the way those services are provided, and

  (c) decisions to be made by that body affecting the operation of those services.

(1C) Subsection (1B)(b) applies to a proposal only if implementation of the proposal would have an impact on –

  (a) the manner in which the services are delivered to users of those services, or

  (b) the range of health services available to those users.

(1D) Subsection (1B)(c) applies to a decision only if implementation of the decision (if made) would have an impact on –

    (a) the manner in which the services are delivered to users of those services, or

    (b) the range of health services available to those users.

(1E) The reference in each of subsections (1C)(a) and (1D)(a) to the delivery of services is to their delivery at the point when they are received by users.

(1F) For the purposes of subsections (1B) to (1E),

    (a) 'health services' does not include pharmaceutical services or local pharmaceutical services, and

    (b) a person is a 'user' of any health services if the person is someone to whom those services are being or may be provided.

(1G) A relevant English body must have regard to any guidance given by the Secretary of State as to the discharge of the body's duty under subsection (1B).

(1H) The guidance mentioned in subsection (1G) includes (in particular) –

    (a) guidance given by the Secretary of State as to when, or how often, involvement under arrangements under subsection (1B) is to be carried out;

    (b) guidance given by the Secretary of State as to the form to be taken by such involvement in any case specified by the guidance.

(2) Each relevant Welsh body must make arrangements with a view to securing, as respects health services for which it is responsible, that persons to whom those services are being or may be provided are, directly or through representatives, involved in and consulted on –

    (a) the planning of the provision of those services,

    (b) the development and consideration of proposals for changes in the way those services are provided, and

    (c) decisions to be made by that body affecting the operation of those services.

(3) For the purposes of this section a body is responsible for health services –

    (a) if the body provides or will provide those services to individuals, or

    (b) if another person provides, or will provide, those services to individuals –

        (i) at that body's direction,

        (ii) on its behalf, or

        (iii) in accordance with an agreement or arrangements made by that body with that other person,

and references in this section to the provision of services include references to the provision of services jointly with another person.

PART 13 MISCELLANEOUS

Duty to keep under review

247C Secretary of State's duty to keep health service functions under review

(1) The Secretary of State must keep under review the effectiveness of the exercise by the bodies mentioned in subsection (2) of functions in relation to the health service in England.

(2) The bodies mentioned in this subsection are –

    (a) the Board;

    (b) Monitor;

    (c) the Care Quality Commission and its Healthwatch England committee;

    (d) the National Institute for Health and Care Excellence;

    (e) the Health and Social Care Information Centre;

    (f) Special Health Authorities.

Annual report

247D Secretary of State's annual report

(1) The Secretary of State must publish an annual report on the performance of the health service in England.

(2) The report must include the Secretary of State's assessment of the effectiveness of the discharge of the duties under sections 1A and 1C.

(3) The Secretary of State must lay any report prepared under this section before Parliament.

Patient information

251 Control of patient information

(1) The Secretary of State may by regulations make such provision for and in connection with requiring or regulating the processing of prescribed patient information for medical purposes as he considers necessary or expedient –

(a) in the interests of improving patient care, or

(b) in the public interest.

(2) Regulations under subsection (1) may, in particular, make provision –

(a) for requiring prescribed communications of any nature which contain patient information to be disclosed by health service bodies in prescribed circumstances –

(i) to the person to whom the information relates,

(ii) (where it relates to more than one person) to the person to whom it principally relates, or

(iii) to a prescribed person on behalf of any such person as is mentioned in sub-paragraph (i) or (ii), in such manner as may be prescribed,

(b) for requiring or authorising the disclosure or other processing of prescribed patient information to or by persons of any prescribed description subject to compliance with any prescribed conditions (including conditions requiring prescribed undertakings to be obtained from such persons as to the processing of such information),

(c) for securing that, where prescribed patient information is processed by a person in accordance with the regulations, anything done by him in so processing the information must be taken to be lawfully done despite any obligation of confidence owed by him in respect of it,

(d) for creating offences punishable on summary conviction by a fine not exceeding level 5 on the standard scale or such other level as is prescribed or for creating other procedures for enforcing any provisions of the regulations.

(3) Subsections (1) and (2) are subject to subsections (4) to (7).

(6) Regulations under subsection (1) may not make provision for requiring the processing of confidential patient information solely or principally for the purpose of determining the care and treatment to be given to particular individuals.

(7) Regulations under this section may not make provision for or in connection with the processing of prescribed patient information in a manner inconsistent with any provision made by or under the Data Protection Act 1998 (c 29).

(8) Subsection (7) does not affect the operation of provisions made under subsection (2)(c).

(10) In this section 'patient information' means –

(a) information (however recorded) which relates to the physical or mental health or condition of an individual, to the diagnosis of his condition or to his care or treatment, and

(b) information (however recorded) which is to any extent derived, directly or indirectly, from such information, whether or not the identity of the individual in question is ascertainable from the information.

(11) For the purposes of this section, patient information is 'confidential patient information' where –

> (a) the identity of the individual in question is ascertainable –
>> (i)   from that information, or
>> (ii) from that information and other information which is in the possession of, or is likely to come into the possession of, the person processing that information, and
> (b) that information was obtained or generated by a person who, in the circumstances, owed an obligation of confidence to that individual.

(12) In this section 'medical purposes' means the purposes of any of –

> (a) preventative medicine, medical diagnosis, medical research, the provision of care and treatment and the management of health and social care services, and
> (b) informing individuals about their physical or mental health or condition, the diagnosis of their condition or their care and treatment.

(13) In this section –

'health service body' means any body (including a government department) or person engaged in the provision of the health service that is prescribed, or of a description prescribed, for the purposes of this definition,

'processing', in relation to information, means the use, disclosure or obtaining of the information or the doing of such other things in relation to it as may be prescribed for the purposes of this definition.

Universities

258   University clinical teaching and research

(1) The functions under this Act of the Secretary of State, the Board and each clinical commissioning group must be exercised so as to secure that there are made available such facilities as he considers are reasonably required by any university which has a medical or dental school, in connection with –

> (a) clinical teaching, and
> (b) research connected with clinical medicine or clinical dentistry.

Price of medical supplies

262   Power to control prices

(1) The Secretary of State may, after consultation with the industry body –

> (a) limit any price which may be charged by any manufacturer or supplier for the supply of any health service medicine, and
> (b) provide for any amount representing sums charged by that person for that medicine in excess of the limit to be paid to the Secretary of State within a specified period.

(2) The powers conferred by this section are not exercisable at any time in relation to a manufacturer or supplier to whom at that time a voluntary scheme applies.

263   Statutory schemes

(1) The Secretary of State may, after consultation with the industry body, make a scheme (referred to in this section and section 264 as a statutory scheme) for the purpose of –

> (a) limiting the prices which may be charged by any manufacturer or supplier for the supply of any health service medicines, or
> (b) limiting the profits which may accrue to any manufacturer or supplier in connection with the manufacture or supply of any health service medicines.

(2) A statutory scheme may, in particular, make any provision mentioned in subsections (3) to (6).

(3) The scheme may require any manufacturer or supplier to whom it applies to –

> (a) record and keep information, and
> (b) provide information to the Secretary of State.

(4) The scheme may provide for any amount representing sums charged by any manufacturer or supplier to whom the scheme applies, in excess of the limits determined under the scheme, for health service medicines covered by the scheme to be paid by that person to the Secretary of State within a specified period.

(5) The scheme may provide for any amount representing the profits, in excess of the limits determined under the scheme, accruing to any manufacturer or supplier to whom the scheme applies in connection with the manufacture or supply of health service medicines covered by the scheme to be paid by that person to the Secretary of State within a specified period.

(6) The scheme may –

  (a) prohibit any manufacturer or supplier to whom the scheme applies from increasing, without the approval of the Secretary of State, any price charged by him for the supply of any health service medicine covered by the scheme, and

  (b) provide for any amount representing any increase in contravention of that prohibition in the sums charged by that person for that medicine, so far as the increase is attributable to supplies to the health service, to be paid to the Secretary of State within a specified period.

(7) A statutory scheme may not apply to a manufacturer or supplier to whom a voluntary scheme applies.

265 Enforcement

(1) Regulations may provide for a person who contravenes any provision of regulations or directions under sections 261 to 264 to be liable to pay a penalty to the Secretary of State.

(2) The penalty may be –

  (a) a single penalty not exceeding £100,000, or

  (b) a daily penalty not exceeding £10,000 for every day on which the contravention occurs or continues.

Use of facilities in private practice

267 Permission for use of facilities in private practice

(1) A person to whom this section applies who wishes to use any relevant health service accommodation or facilities for the purpose of providing medical, dental, pharmaceutical, ophthalmic or chiropody services to non-resident private patients may apply in writing to the Secretary of State for permission under this section.

(2) Any application for permission under this section must specify –

  (a) which of the relevant health service accommodation or facilities the applicant wishes to use for the purpose of providing services to such patients, and

  (b) which of the kinds of services mentioned in subsection (1) he wishes the permission to cover.

(3) On receiving an application under this section the Secretary of State –

  (a) must consider whether anything for which permission is sought would interfere with the giving of full and proper attention to persons seeking or afforded access otherwise than as private patients to any services provided under this Act, and

  (b) must grant the permission applied for unless in his opinion anything for which permission is sought would so interfere.

(4) Any grant of permission under this section is on such terms (including terms as to the payment of charges for the use of the relevant health service accommodation or facilities pursuant to the permission) as the Secretary of State may from time to time determine.

(5) The persons to whom this section applies are –

  (a) medical practitioners, registered pharmacists or other persons who provide pharmaceutical services under Chapter 1 of Part 7,

  (b) chiropodists who provide services under this Act at premises where services are provided under that Chapter,

(c) persons providing primary medical services, primary dental services or primary ophthalmic services under a general medical services contract, a general dental services contract or a general ophthalmic services contract, or in accordance with section 92 arrangements or section 107 arrangements.

(6) 'Relevant health service accommodation or facilities', in relation to a person to whom this section applies, means –

(a) any accommodation or facilities available at premises provided by the Secretary of State by virtue of this Act, being accommodation or facilities which that person is authorised to use for purposes of this Act, or

(b) in the case of a person to whom this section applies by virtue of subsection (5)(b), accommodation or facilities which that person is authorised to use for purposes of this Act at premises where services are provided under Chapter 1 of Part 7.

PART 14 SUPPLEMENTARY

275 Interpretation

(1) In this Act (except where the context otherwise requires) –

'the Board' means the National Health Service Commissioning Board,

'clinical commissioning group' means a body established under section 14D of this Act,

'facilities' includes the provision of (or the use of) premises, goods, materials, vehicles, plant or apparatus,

'the FHSAA' means the Family Health Services Appeal Authority,

'functions' includes powers and duties,

'goods' include accommodation,

'the health service' means the health service continued under section 1(1) and under section 1 (1) of the National Health Service (Wales) Act 2006,

'health service hospital' means a hospital vested in the Secretary of State for the purposes of his functions under this Act or vested in an NHS trust or an NHS foundation trust,

'hospital' means –

(a) any institution for the reception and treatment of persons suffering from illness,

(b) any maternity home, and

(c) any institution for the reception and treatment of persons during convalescence or persons requiring medical rehabilitation, and includes clinics, dispensaries and outpatient departments maintained in connection with any such home or institution, and 'hospital accommodation' must be construed accordingly,

'illness' includes any disorder or disability of the mind and any injury or disability requiring medical or dental treatment or nursing,

'Local Health Board' means a body established under section 11 of the National Health Service (Wales) Act 2006 (c. 42),

'medical' includes surgical,

'medical practitioner' means a registered medical practitioner within the meaning of Schedule 1 to the Interpretation Act 1978 (c. 30),

'medicine' includes such chemical re-agents as are included in a list approved by the Secretary of State for the purposes of section 126,

'modifications' includes additions, omissions and amendments,

'NHS body' means –

(a) the Board,

(b) a clinical commissioning group,

(c) a Special Health Authority,

(d) an NHS trust,

(e) an NHS foundation trust.

'NICE' means the National Institute for Health and Care Excellence,

'officer' includes servant,

'patient' includes a woman who is pregnant or breast-feeding or who has recently given birth,

'prescribed' means prescribed by regulations made by the Secretary of State,

'property' includes rights,

'regulations' means regulations made by the Secretary of State,

'the regulator' means Monitor,

'university' includes a university college,

'voluntary organisation' means a body the activities of which are carried on otherwise than for profit, but does not include any public or local authority.

(2) In this Act (except where the context otherwise requires) any reference to a body established under this Act or the National Health Service (Wales) Act 2006 includes a reference to a body continued in existence by virtue of this Act or that Act.

278   Short title, extent and application

(2) Subject to this section, this Act extends to England and Wales only.

(3) Sections 261 to 266 in Part 13 (price of medical supplies) extend also to Scotland and Northern Ireland.

NHS Redress Act 2006

(2006, c. 44)

England

1   Power to establish redress scheme

(1) The Secretary of State may by regulations establish a scheme for the purpose of enabling redress to be provided without recourse to civil proceedings in circumstances in which this section applies.

(2) This section applies where under the law of England and Wales qualifying liability in tort on the part of a body or other person mentioned in subsection (3) arises in connection with the provision, as part of the health service in England, of qualifying services.

(3) The bodies and other persons referred to are –

    (a)   the Secretary of State,

    (aa) the National Health Service Commissioning Board,

    (ab) a clinical commissioning group,

    (d)   a body or other person providing, or arranging for the provision of, services whose provision is the subject of arrangements with a body or other person mentioned in paragraph (a), (aa) or (ab).

(4) The reference in subsection (2) to qualifying liability in tort is to liability in tort owed –

(a) in respect of or consequent upon personal injury or loss arising out of or in connection with breach of a duty of care owed to any person in connection with the diagnosis of illness, or the care or treatment of any patient, and

(b) in consequence of any act or omission by a health care professional.

(5) For the purposes of subsection (2), services are qualifying services if –

(a) they are provided in a hospital (in England or elsewhere), or

(b) they are of such other description (including a description involving provision outside England) as the Secretary of State may specify by regulations.

(11) In this section, 'hospital' has the same meaning as in the National Health Service Act 2006.

2 Application of scheme

(1) Subject to subsection (2), a scheme may make such provision defining its application as the Secretary of State thinks fit.

(2) A scheme must provide that it does not apply in relation to a liability that is or has been the subject of civil proceedings.

3 Redress under scheme

(1) Subject to subsections (2) and (5), a scheme may make such provision as the Secretary of State thinks fit about redress under the scheme.

(2) A scheme must provide for redress ordinarily to comprise –

(a) the making of an offer of compensation in satisfaction of any right to bring civil proceedings in respect of the liability concerned,

(b) the giving of an explanation,

(c) the giving of an apology, and

(d) the giving of a report on the action which has been, or will be, taken to prevent similar cases arising, but may specify circumstances in which one or more of those forms of redress is not required.

(3) A scheme may, in particular –

(a) make provision for the compensation that may be offered to take the form of entry into a contract to provide care or treatment or of financial compensation, or both;

(b) make provision about the circumstances in which different forms of compensation may be offered.

(4) A scheme that provides for financial compensation to be offered may, in particular –

(a) make provision about the matters in respect of which financial compensation may be offered;

(b) make provision with respect to the assessment of the amount of any financial compensation.

(5) A scheme that provides for financial compensation to be offered –

(a) may specify an upper limit on the amount of financial compensation that may be included in an offer under the scheme;

(b) if it does not specify a limit under paragraph (a), must specify an upper limit on the amount of financial compensation that may be included in such an offer in respect of pain and suffering;

(c) may not specify any other limit on what may be included in such an offer by way of financial compensation.

4 Commencement of proceedings under scheme

(1) A scheme may make such provision as the Secretary of State thinks fit about the commencement of proceedings under the scheme.

(3) A scheme may, in particular, make provision –

(a) about who may commence proceedings under the scheme;

(b) about how proceedings under the scheme may be commenced;

(c) for time limits in relation to the commencement of proceedings under the scheme;

(d) about circumstances in which proceedings under the scheme may not be commenced;

(e) requiring proceedings under the scheme to be commenced in specified circumstances;

(f) for notification of the commencement of proceedings under the scheme in specified circumstances.

5 Duty to consider potential application of scheme

(1) The Secretary of State may by regulations make provision requiring any body or other person mentioned in subsection (2) –

(a) to consider, in such circumstances as the regulations may provide, whether a case that the body or other person is investigating or reviewing involves liability to which a scheme applies, and

(b) if it appears that it does, to take such steps as the regulations may provide.

(2) The bodies and other persons referred to are –

(a) any body or other person to whose liability a scheme applies, and

(b) the Care Quality Commission.

6 Proceedings under scheme

(1) Subject to subsections (3) to (6), a scheme may make such provision as the Secretary of State thinks fit about proceedings under the scheme.

(2) A scheme may, in particular, make provision –

(a) about the investigation of cases under the scheme (including provision for the overseeing of the investigation by an individual of a specified description);

(b) about the making of decisions about the application of the scheme;

(c) for time limits in relation to acceptance of an offer of compensation under the scheme;

(d) about the form and content of settlement agreements under the scheme;

(e) for settlement agreements under the scheme to be subject in cases of a specified description to approval by a court;

(f) about the termination of proceedings under the scheme.

(3) A scheme must –

(a) make provision for the findings of an investigation of a case under the scheme to be recorded in a report, and

(b) subject to subsection (4), make provision for a copy of the report to be provided on request to the individual seeking redress.

(4) A scheme may provide that no copy of an investigation report need be provided –

(a) before an offer is made under the scheme or proceedings under the scheme are terminated, or

(b) in such other circumstances as may be specified.

(5) A scheme must provide for a settlement agreement under the scheme to include a waiver of the right to bring civil proceedings in respect of the liability to which the settlement relates.

(6) A scheme must provide for the termination of proceedings under the scheme if the liability to which the proceedings relate becomes the subject of civil proceedings.

7 Suspension of limitation period

(1) A scheme must make provision for the period during which a liability is the subject of proceedings under the scheme to be disregarded for the purposes of calculating whether any relevant limitation period has expired.

(2) In subsection (1), the reference to any relevant limitation period is to any period of time for the bringing of civil proceedings in respect of the liability which is prescribed by or under the Limitation Act 1980 or any other enactment.

(3) A scheme may define for the purposes of provision in pursuance of subsection (1) when liability is the subject of proceedings under the scheme.

8   Legal advice etc.

(1) Subject to subsections (2) and (4), a scheme may make such provision as the Secretary of State thinks fit –

    (a) for the provision of legal advice without charge to individuals seeking redress under the scheme;

    (b) for the provision in connection with proceedings under the scheme of other services, including the services of medical experts.

(2) A scheme must make such provision as the Secretary of State considers appropriate in order to secure that individuals to whom an offer under the scheme is made have access to legal advice without charge in relation to –

    (a) the offer, and

    (b) any settlement agreement.

(3) Provision under subsection (1)(a) or (2) about who may provide the legal advice may operate by reference to whether a potential provider is included in a list prepared by a specified person.

(4) A scheme that makes provision for the provision of the services of medical experts must provide for such experts to be instructed jointly by the scheme authority and the individual seeking redress under the scheme.

9   Assistance for individuals seeking redress under scheme

(1) It is the duty of the Secretary of State to arrange, to such extent as he considers necessary to meet all reasonable requirements, for the provision of assistance (by way of representation or otherwise) to individuals seeking, or intending to seek, redress under a scheme.

(2) The Secretary of State may make such other arrangements as he thinks fit for the provision of assistance to individuals in connection with cases which are the subject of proceedings under a scheme.

(3) The Secretary of State may make payments to any person in pursuance of arrangements under this section.

(4) In making arrangements under this section, the Secretary of State must have regard to the principle that the provision of services under the arrangements in connection with a particular case should, so far as practicable, be independent of any person to whose conduct the case relates or who is involved in dealing with the case.

10   Scheme members

(1) Subject to subsection (3), a scheme may make such provision as the Secretary of State thinks fit –

    (a) about membership of the scheme on the part of any body or other person to whose liability the scheme applies, and

    (b) about the functions of members in connection with the scheme.

(2) A scheme may, in particular –

    (a) require or permit a specified body or other person to be a member of the scheme;

    (b) require a member of the scheme to carry out specified functions in relation to specified proceedings under the scheme;

    (c) authorise members of the scheme to make arrangements under which functions under the scheme are carried out by one member on behalf of another;

    (d) require members of the scheme to have regard, in relation to the carrying out of functions under the scheme, to any relevant advice or other guidance issued by the scheme authority;

    (e) require, or enable the scheme authority to require, members of the scheme to keep specified records in relation to the carrying out of functions under the scheme;

    (f) require, or enable the scheme authority to require, members of the scheme to provide the authority with information or documents relevant to its functions;

(g) require members of the scheme to make payments in accordance with the scheme by way of contribution to specified costs of its operation;

(h) require a member of the scheme to charge an individual of a specified description with responsibility for overseeing the carrying out of specified functions conferred on the member under this Act;

(i) require a member of the scheme to charge an individual of a specified description with responsibility for advising the member about lessons to be learnt from cases involving the member that are dealt with under the scheme.

(3) A scheme must require a member of the scheme to prepare and publish an annual report about cases involving the member that are dealt with under the scheme and the lessons to be learnt from them.

(4) The provision that may be made under this section includes provision which has the effect that a member of a scheme who has arranged for the provision of services has functions under the scheme which relate to someone else's liability in connection with the provision of the services.

11   Scheme authority

(1) A scheme must make provision for a specified Special Health Authority (in this Act referred to as 'the scheme authority') to have such functions in connection with the scheme as the Secretary of State thinks fit.

(2) A scheme may, in particular, provide for the scheme authority to have functions in relation to –

(a) proceedings under the scheme;

(b) payments under settlement agreements under the scheme;

(c) the provision in connection with the scheme of advice or other guidance about specified matters;

(d) the provision in connection with the scheme of legal advice without charge;

(e) the assessment and payment of contributions by members of the scheme;

(f) the monitoring of the carrying out by members of the scheme of their functions under it;

(g) the provision to the Independent Regulator of Foundation Trusts of reports with respect to failure by NHS foundation trusts to carry out functions under the scheme;

(h) the publication of annual data about the scheme.

12   General duty to promote resolution under scheme

A scheme must include provision requiring the scheme authority and the members of the scheme, in carrying out their functions under the scheme, to have regard in particular to the desirability of redress being provided without recourse to civil proceedings.

13   Duties of co-operation

(1) The scheme authority under a scheme and the Care Quality Commission must co-operate with each other where it appears to them that it is appropriate to do so for the efficient and effective discharge of their respective functions.

(2) The scheme authority under a scheme and the National Patient Safety Agency must cooperate with each other where it appears to them that it is appropriate to do so for the efficient and effective discharge of their respective functions.

14   Complaints

(1) The Secretary of State may by regulations make provision about the handling and consideration of complaints made under the regulations about maladministration by any body or other person –

(a) in the exercise of functions under a scheme,

(b) in the exercise of other functions relating to proceedings under a scheme, or

(c) in connection with a settlement agreement entered into under a scheme.

(2) Regulations under subsection (1) must provide for complaints to be considered by –

    (a) the scheme authority, or

    (b) a member of the scheme.

(3) Without prejudice to the generality of subsection (1), regulations under that subsection may make the following provision.

(4) The regulations may make provision about –

    (a) the persons who may make a complaint;

    (b) the complaints which may, or may not, be made under the regulations;

    (c) the persons to whom complaints may be made;

    (d) complaints which need not be considered;

    (e) the period within which complaints must be made;

    (f) the procedures to be followed in making, handling and considering a complaint;

    (g) matters which are excluded from consideration;

    (h) the making of a report or recommendations about a complaint;

    (i) the action to be taken as a result of a complaint.

(5) The regulations may impose on the scheme authority, or a member of the scheme, obligations with respect to producing, or making available to the public, information about the procedures to be followed under the regulations.

(6) The regulations may also –

    (a) provide for different parts or aspects of a complaint to be treated differently;

    (b) require the production of information or documents in order to enable a complaint to be properly considered;

    (c) authorise the disclosure of information or documents relevant to a complaint to a person who is considering a complaint under the regulations, notwithstanding any rule of common law that would otherwise prohibit or restrict the disclosure.

(7) The regulations may make provision about complaints which raise both matters falling to be considered under the regulations and matters falling to be considered under other statutory complaints procedures, including in particular provision for enabling such a complaint to be made under the regulations.

(8) The regulations may, in relation to complaints in connection with a scheme which are made or purport to be made under the regulations, make provision for securing –

    (a) that any matters raised in such complaints which fall to be considered under other statutory complaints procedures are referred to the body or other person operating the appropriate procedures;

    (b) that any such matters are treated as if they had been raised in a complaint made under the appropriate procedures.

(9) In subsections (7) and (8), 'statutory complaints procedures' means complaints procedures established by or under any enactment.

Supplementary

18 Interpretation

(1) In this Act –

'health service' has the same meaning as in the National Health Service Act 2006;

'illness' has the same meaning as in the National Health Service Act 2006;

'patient' has the same meaning as in the National Health Service Act 2006;

'personal injury' includes any disease and any impairment of a person's physical or mental health;

'scheme', except in section 1, means a scheme established under that section;

Health and Social Care Act 2008

(2008, c. 14)

PART 1 THE CARE QUALITY COMMISSION

Chapter 1 Introductory

1 The Care Quality Commission

(1) There is to be a body corporate known as the Care Quality Commission (referred to in this Part as 'the Commission').

(2) The Commission for Healthcare Audit and Inspection, the Commission for Social Care Inspection and the Mental Health Act Commission are dissolved.

2 The Commission's functions

(2) Those functions include –

(a) registration functions under Chapter 2,

(b) review and investigation functions under Chapter 3, and

(c) functions under the Mental Health Act 1983 (c. 20).

3 The Commission's objectives

(1) The main objective of the Commission in performing its functions is to protect and promote the health, safety and welfare of people who use health and social care services.

(2) The Commission is to perform its functions for the general purpose of encouraging –

(a) the improvement of health and social care services,

(b) the provision of health and social care services in a way that focuses on the needs and experiences of people who use those services, and

(c) the efficient and effective use of resources in the provision of health and social care services.

4   Matters to which the Commission must have regard

(1) In performing its functions the Commission must have regard to –

(a) views expressed by or on behalf of members of the public about health and social care services,

(b) experiences of people who use health and social care services and their families and friends,

(c) views expressed by Local Healthwatch organisations or Local Healthwatch Contractors about the provision of health and social care services,

(d) the need to protect and promote the rights of people who use health and social care services (including, in particular, the rights of children, of persons detained under the Mental Health Act 1983, of persons who are deprived of their liberty in accordance with the Mental Capacity Act 2005, and of other vulnerable adults),

(e) the need to ensure that action by the Commission in relation to health and social care services is proportionate to the risks against which it would afford safeguards and is targeted only where it is needed,

(f) any developments in approaches to regulatory action, and

(g) best practice among persons performing functions comparable to those of the Commission (including the principles under which regulatory action should be transparent, accountable and consistent).

(3) In subsection (1)(c), 'Local Healthwatch contractor' has the meaning given by section 223 of the Local Government and Public Involvement in Health Act 2007.

5   Statement on user involvement

(1) The Commission must publish a statement describing how it proposes to –

(a) promote awareness among service users and carers of its functions,

(b) promote and engage in discussion with service users and carers about the provision of health and social care services and about the way in which the Commission exercises its functions,

(c) ensure that proper regard is had to the views expressed by service users and carers, and

(d) arrange for any of its functions to be exercised by, or with the assistance of, service users and carers.

Chapter 2   Registration in respect of provision of health or social care

Introductory

8   'Regulated activity'

(1) In this Part 'regulated activity' means an activity of a prescribed kind.

(2) An activity may be prescribed for the purposes of subsection (1) only if –

(a) the activity involves, or is connected with, the provision of health or social care in, or in relation to, England, and

(b) the activity does not involve the carrying on of any establishment or agency, within the meaning of the Care Standards Act 2000, for which Her Majesty's Chief Inspector of Education, Children's Services and Skills is the registration authority under that Act.

(3) For the purposes of subsection (2), activities connected with the provision of health or social care include, in particular –

(a) the supply of staff who are to provide such care;

(b) the provision of transport or accommodation for those who require such care;

(c) the provision of advice in respect of such care.

9 'Health or social care'

(1) This section has effect for the interpretation of this Part.

(2) 'Health care' includes all forms of health care provided for individuals, whether relating to physical or mental health, and also includes procedures that are similar to forms of medical or surgical care but are not provided in connection with a medical condition.

(3) 'Social care' includes all forms of personal care and other practical assistance provided for individuals who by reason of age, illness, disability, pregnancy, childbirth, dependence on alcohol or drugs, or any other similar circumstances, are in need of such care or other assistance.

(4) 'Health or social care' means health care or social care.

Registration of persons carrying on regulated activities

10   Requirement to register as a service provider

(1) Any person who carries on a regulated activity without being registered under this Chapter in respect of the carrying on of that activity is guilty of an offence.

(3) In the following provisions of this Part, the registration of a person under this Chapter in respect of the carrying on of a regulated activity by that person is referred to as registration 'as a service provider' in respect of that activity.

(4) A person guilty of an offence under this section is liable –

   (a) on summary conviction, to a fine not exceeding £50,000, or to imprisonment for a term not exceeding 12 months, or to both;

   (b) on conviction on indictment, to a fine, or to imprisonment for a term not exceeding 12 months, or to both.

(5) In relation to an offence committed before the commencement of section 154(1) of the Criminal Justice Act 2003 (c. 44), the reference in subsection (4)(a) to 12 months is to be read as a reference to 6 months.

11   Applications for registration as a service provider

(1) A person seeking to be registered under this Chapter as a service provider must make an application to the Commission.

Information to be available to public

38   Provision of copies of registers

(1) Subject to subsection (3), the Commission must secure that copies of any register kept for the purposes of this Chapter are available at its offices for inspection at all reasonable times by any person.

(2) Subject to subsections (3) and (4), any person who asks the Commission for a copy of, or an extract from, a register kept for the purposes of this Chapter is entitled to have one.

(3) Regulations may provide that subsections (1) and (2) do not apply –

   (a) in such circumstances as may be prescribed, or

   (b) to such parts of a register as may be prescribed.

Chapter 3 Quality of health and social care

Reviews and investigations

46   Reviews and performance assessments

(1) The Commission must, in respect of such regulated activities and such registered service providers as may be prescribed –

   (a) conduct reviews of the carrying on of the regulated activities by the service providers,

   (b) assess the performance of the service providers following each such review, and

   (c) publish a report of its assessment.

48   Special reviews and investigations

(1) The Commission may conduct any special review or investigation, and must do so if the Secretary of State so requests; but the Commission may not conduct a review or investigation under subsection (2)(ba) or (bb) without the approval of the Secretary of State.

(2) A special review or investigation is a review (other than a review under section 46) of or an investigation into –

    (a)   the provision of NHS care,

    (b)   the provision of adult social services,

    (ba)   the exercise of the functions of the National Health Service Commissioning Board or a clinical commissioning group in arranging for the provision of NHS care under the National Health Service Act 2006 or section 117 of the Mental Health Act 1983,

    (bb)   the exercise of the functions of English local authorities in arranging for the provision of adult social services, or

    (c)   the exercise of functions by English Health Authorities.

(3) Such a review or investigation may relate –

    (a)   to the overall provision of NHS care or adult social services or to the provision of NHS care or adult social services of a particular description;

    (b)   to the overall exercise of functions or to the exercise of functions of a particular description;

    (c)   to the provision of care or services or the exercise of functions by bodies or persons generally or by particular bodies or persons.

(4) Where the Commission conducts a review or investigation under this section, it must publish a report.

(5) The Commission must consider whether the report raises anything on which it ought to give advice to the Secretary of State under section 53(2).

Chapter 5 Further functions

53   Information and advice

(1) The Commission must keep the Secretary of State informed about the following matters –

    (a)   the provision of NHS care;

    (b)   the provision of adult social services;

    (c)   the carrying on of regulated activities.

(2) The Commission may at any time give the Secretary of State advice on anything connected with those matters.

54   Studies as to economy, efficiency etc.

(1) The Commission may undertake or promote comparative or other studies designed to enable it to make recommendations –

    (a)   for improving economy, efficiency and effectiveness in any activity mentioned in subsection (2),

    (b)   for improving the management, other than the financial management, of an English NHS body, or

    (c)   for improving the management of an English local authority in its provision of adult social services.

(2) Those activities are –

    (a)   the provision of health care by an English NHS provider,

    (c)   the provision of adult social services by an English local authority, and

    (d)   the making of arrangements by an English local authority for the provision of adult social services.

(3) The Commission may also undertake or promote studies designed to enable it to prepare reports as to the impact of –

    (a)   the operation of any particular statutory provisions, or

(b) any directions or guidance given by a Minister of the Crown (whether pursuant to any such provisions or otherwise), on economy, efficiency and effectiveness in an activity mentioned in subsection (2)(c) or (d).

55 Publication of results of studies under s. 54

(1) The Commission must publish –

(a) any recommendations made by it under subsection (1) of section 54, and

(b) the result of any studies undertaken or promoted under that section.

57 Reviews of data, studies and research

(1) The Commission may review –

(a) studies and research undertaken by others, or the quality of data obtained by others, in relation to the provision of NHS care or adult social services or the carrying on of regulated activities,

(b) the methods used in undertaking such studies and research or in collecting and analysing such data, and

(c) the validity of conclusions drawn from such studies and research or from such data.

58 Publication of information

(1) The Commission may make available to the public information relating to –

(a) the provision of NHS care;

(b) the provision of adult social services;

(c) the carrying on of regulated activities.

(2) Subsection (1) is subject to sections 76 and 79(2).

Chapter 6 Miscellaneous and general

Inspections

60 Inspections

(1) The Commission may for the purposes of its regulatory functions carry out inspections of –

(a) the carrying on of a regulated activity,

(b) the provision of NHS care,

(c) the provision of adult social services, or

(d) the exercise of functions by an English NHS body.

(2) For the purposes of this Part, the 'regulatory functions' of the Commission are its functions under Chapters 2, 3 and 5 except –

(a) its functions under section 53 (information and advice),

(b) its functions under section 57 (reviews of data, studies and research), and

(c) its functions under regulations under section 59 (additional functions) to the extent that the regulations provide that they are not to be treated as regulatory functions for the purposes of this Part.

Inquiries

75 Inquiries

(1) The Secretary of State may cause an inquiry to be held into any matter connected with the exercise by the Commission of any of its functions.

(2) Before an inquiry is begun, the Secretary of State may give a direction that it be held in private.

(3) Where no such direction has been given, the person holding the inquiry may decide to hold it, or any part of it, in private.

Information

80 Code of practice on confidential personal information

(1) The Commission must prepare and publish a code in respect of the practice it proposes to follow in relation to confidential personal information.

(2) The code must in particular make provision –
  (a) about the obtaining by the Commission of information which, once obtained, will be confidential personal information, and
  (b) about the handling, use and disclosure by the Commission of confidential personal information.

(3) Before publishing the code, the Commission must consult –
  (a) the National Health Service Commissioning Board, and
  (b) such other persons as it considers appropriate.

(5) In this section 'confidential personal information' means information which –
  (a) is obtained by the Commission on terms or in circumstances requiring it to be held in confidence, and
  (b) relates to and identifies an individual.

(6) For the purposes of subsection (5)(b), information obtained by the Commission is to be treated as identifying an individual if the individual can be identified from a combination of –
  (a) the information, and
  (b) other information obtained by the Commission.

Human Fertilisation and Embryology Act 2008

(2008, c. 22)

PART 2 PARENTHOOD IN CASES INVOLVING ASSISTED REPRODUCTION

Meaning of 'mother'

33   Meaning of 'mother'

(1) The woman who is carrying or has carried a child as a result of the placing in her of an embryo or of sperm and eggs, and no other woman, is to be treated as the mother of the child.

(2) Subsection (1) does not apply to any child to the extent that the child is treated by virtue of adoption as not being the woman's child.

(3) Subsection (1) applies whether the woman was in the United Kingdom or elsewhere at the time of the placing in her of the embryo or the sperm and eggs.

Application of sections 35 to 47

34   Application of sections 35 to 47

(1) Sections 35 to 47 apply, in the case of a child who is being or has been carried by a woman (referred to in those sections as 'W') as a result of the placing in her of an embryo or of sperm and eggs or her artificial insemination, to determine who is to be treated as the other parent of the child.

(2) Subsection (1) has effect subject to the provisions of sections 39, 40 and 46 limiting the purposes for which a person is treated as the child's other parent by virtue of those sections.

Meaning of 'father'

35   Woman married to a man at time of treatment

(1) If –
  (a) at the time of the placing in her of the embryo or of the sperm and eggs or of her artificial insemination, W was a party to a marriage with a man, and

(b) the creation of the embryo carried by her was not brought about with the sperm of the other party to the marriage,

then, subject to section 38(2) to (4), the other party to the marriage is to be treated as the father of the child unless it is shown that he did not consent to the placing in her of the embryo or the sperm and eggs or to her artificial insemination (as the case may be).

(2) This section applies whether W was in the United Kingdom or elsewhere at the time mentioned in subsection (1)(a).

36 Treatment provided to woman where agreed fatherhood conditions apply

If no man is treated by virtue of section 35 as the father of the child and no woman is treated by virtue of section 42 as a parent of the child but –

(a) the embryo or the sperm and eggs were placed in W, or W was artificially inseminated, in the course of treatment services provided in the United Kingdom by a person to whom a licence applies,

(b) at the time when the embryo or the sperm and eggs were placed in W, or W was artificially inseminated, the agreed fatherhood conditions (as set out in section 37) were satisfied in relation to a man, in relation to treatment provided to W under the licence,

(c) the man remained alive at that time, and

(d) the creation of the embryo carried by W was not brought about with the man's sperm,

then, subject to section 38(2) to (4), the man is to be treated as the father of the child.

37 The agreed fatherhood conditions

(1) The agreed fatherhood conditions referred to in section 36(b) are met in relation to a man ('M') in relation to treatment provided to W under a licence if, but only if, –

(a) M has given the person responsible a notice stating that he consents to being treated as the father of any child resulting from treatment provided to W under the licence,

(b) W has given the person responsible a notice stating that she consents to M being so treated,

(c) neither M nor W has, since giving notice under paragraph (a) or (b), given the person responsible notice of the withdrawal of M's or W's consent to M being so treated,

(d) W has not, since the giving of the notice under paragraph (b), given the person responsible –

(i) a further notice under that paragraph stating that she consents to another man being treated as the father of any resulting child, or

(ii) a notice under section 44(1)(b) stating that she consents to a woman being treated as a parent of any resulting child, and

(e) W and M are not within prohibited degrees of relationship in relation to each other.

(2) A notice under subsection (1)(a), (b) or (c) must be in writing and must be signed by the person giving it.

38 Further provision relating to sections 35 and 36

(1) Where a person is to be treated as the father of the child by virtue of section 35 or 36, no other person is to be treated as the father of the child.

(2) In England and Wales and Northern Ireland, sections 35 and 36 do not affect any presumption, applying by virtue of the rules of common law, that a child is the legitimate child of the parties to a marriage.

(3) In Scotland, sections 35 and 36 do not apply in relation to any child who, by virtue of any enactment or other rule of law, is treated as the child of the parties to a marriage.

(4) Sections 35 and 36 do not apply to any child to the extent that the child is treated by virtue of adoption as not being the man's child.

39   Use of sperm, or transfer of embryo, after death of man providing sperm

(1) If –

(a) the child has been carried by W as a result of the placing in her of an embryo or of sperm and eggs or her artificial insemination,

(b) the creation of the embryo carried by W was brought about by using the sperm of a man after his death, or the creation of the embryo was brought about using the sperm of a man before his death but the embryo was placed in W after his death,

(c) the man consented in writing (and did not withdraw the consent) –

(i) to the use of his sperm after his death which brought about the creation of the embryo carried by W or (as the case may be) to the placing in W after his death of the embryo which was brought about using his sperm before his death, and

(ii) to being treated for the purpose mentioned in subsection (3) as the father of any resulting child,

(d) W has elected in writing not later than the end of the period of 42 days from the day on which the child was born for the man to be treated for the purpose mentioned in subsection (3) as the father of the child, and

(e) no-one else is to be treated –

(i) as the father of the child by virtue of section 35 or 36 or by virtue of section 38(2) or (3), or

(ii) as a parent of the child by virtue of section 42 or 43 or by virtue of adoption, then the man is to be treated for the purpose mentioned in subsection (3) as the father of the child.

(2) Subsection (1) applies whether W was in the United Kingdom or elsewhere at the time of the placing in her of the embryo or of the sperm and eggs or of her artificial insemination.

(3) The purpose referred to in subsection (1) is the purpose of enabling the man's particulars to be entered as the particulars of the child's father in a relevant register of births.

(4) In the application of this section to Scotland, for any reference to a period of 42 days there is substituted a reference to a period of 21 days.

40   Embryo transferred after death of husband etc. who did not provide sperm

(1) If –

(a) the child has been carried by W as a result of the placing in her of an embryo,

(b) the embryo was created at a time when W was a party to a marriage with a man,

(c) the creation of the embryo was not brought about with the sperm of the other party to the marriage,

(d) the other party to the marriage died before the placing of the embryo in W,

(e) the other party to the marriage consented in writing (and did not withdraw the consent) –

(i) to the placing of the embryo in W after his death, and

(ii) to being treated for the purpose mentioned in subsection (4) as the father of any resulting child,

(f) W has elected in writing not later than the end of the period of 42 days from the day on which the child was born for the man to be treated for the purpose mentioned in subsection (4) as the father of the child, and

(g) no-one else is to be treated –

(i) as the father of the child by virtue of section 35 or 36 or by virtue of section 38(2) or (3), or

(ii) as a parent of the child by virtue of section 42 or 43 or by virtue of adoption,

then the man is to be treated for the purpose mentioned in subsection (4) as the father of the child.

(2) If –

(a) the child has been carried by W as a result of the placing in her of an embryo,

(b) the embryo was not created at a time when W was a party to a marriage or a civil partnership but was created in the course of treatment services provided to W in the United Kingdom by a person to whom a licence applies,

(c) a man consented in writing (and did not withdraw the consent) –

(i)   to the placing of the embryo in W after his death, and

(ii) to being treated for the purpose mentioned in subsection (4) as the father of any resulting child,

(d) the creation of the embryo was not brought about with the sperm of that man,

(e) the man died before the placing of the embryo in W,

(f) immediately before the man's death, the agreed fatherhood conditions set out in section 37 were met in relation to the man in relation to treatment proposed to be provided to W in the United Kingdom by a person to whom a licence applies,

(g) W has elected in writing not later than the end of the period of 42 days from the day on which the child was born for the man to be treated for the purpose mentioned in subsection (4) as the father of the child, and

(h) no-one else is to be treated –

(i)   as the father of the child by virtue of section 35 or 36 or by virtue of section 38(2) or (3), or

(ii) as a parent of the child by virtue of section 42 or 43 or by virtue of adoption,

then the man is to be treated for the purpose mentioned in subsection (4) as the father of the child.

(3) Subsections (1) and (2) apply whether W was in the United Kingdom or elsewhere at the time of the placing in her of the embryo.

(4) The purpose referred to in subsections (1) and (2) is the purpose of enabling the man's particulars to be entered as the particulars of the child's father in a relevant register of births.

(5) In the application of this section to Scotland, for any reference to a period of 42 days there is substituted a reference to a period of 21 days.

41   Persons not to be treated as father

(1) Where the sperm of a man who had given such consent as is required by paragraph 5 of Schedule 3 to the 1990 Act (consent to use of gametes for purposes of treatment services or non-medical fertility services) was used for a purpose for which such consent was required, he is not to be treated as the father of the child.

(2) Where the sperm of a man, or an embryo the creation of which was brought about with his sperm, was used after his death, he is not, subject to section 39, to be treated as the father of the child.

(3) Subsection (2) applies whether W was in the United Kingdom or elsewhere at the time of the placing in her of the embryo or of the sperm and eggs or of her artificial insemination.

Cases in which woman to be other parent

42   Woman in civil partnership or marriage to a woman at time of treatment

(1) If at the time of the placing in her of the embryo or the sperm and eggs or of her artificial insemination, W was a party to a civil partnership or a marriage with another woman, then subject to section 45(2) to (4), the other party to the civil partnership or marriage is to be treated as a parent of the child unless it is shown that she did not consent to the placing in W of the embryo or the sperm and eggs or to her artificial insemination (as the case may be).

(2) This section applies whether W was in the United Kingdom or elsewhere at the time mentioned in subsection (1).

43 Treatment provided to woman who agrees that second woman is to be parent

If no man is treated by virtue of section 35 as the father of the child and no woman is treated by virtue of section 42 as a parent of the child but –

    (a) the embryo or the sperm and eggs were placed in W, or W was artificially inseminated, in the course of treatment services provided in the United Kingdom by a person to whom a licence applies,

    (b) at the time when the embryo or the sperm and eggs were placed in W, or W was artificially inseminated, the agreed female parenthood conditions (as set out in section 44) were met in relation to another woman, in relation to treatment provided to W under that licence, and

    (c) the other woman remained alive at that time,

then, subject to section 45(2) to (4), the other woman is to be treated as a parent of the child.

44 The agreed female parenthood conditions

(1) The agreed female parenthood conditions referred to in section 43(b) are met in relation to another woman ('P') in relation to treatment provided to W under a licence if, but only if, –

    (a) P has given the person responsible a notice stating that P consents to P being treated as a parent of any child resulting from treatment provided to W under the licence,

    (b) W has given the person responsible a notice stating that W agrees to P being so treated,

    (c) neither W nor P has, since giving notice under paragraph (a) or (b), given the person responsible notice of the withdrawal of P's or W's consent to P being so treated,

    (d) W has not, since the giving of the notice under paragraph (b), given the person responsible –

        (i) a further notice under that paragraph stating that W consents to a woman other than P being treated as a parent of any resulting child, or

        (ii) a notice under section 37(1)(b) stating that W consents to a man being treated as the father of any resulting child, and

    (e) W and P are not within prohibited degrees of relationship in relation to each other.

(2) A notice under subsection (1)(a), (b) or (c) must be in writing and must be signed by the person giving it.

45 Further provision relating to sections 42 and 43

(1) Where a woman is treated by virtue of section 42 or 43 as a parent of the child, no man is to be treated as the father of the child.

(2) In England and Wales and Northern Ireland, sections 42 and 43 do not affect any presumption, applying by virtue of the rules of common law, that a child is the legitimate child of the parties to a marriage.

(3) In Scotland, sections 42 and 43 do not apply in relation to any child who, by virtue of any enactment or other rule of law, is treated as the child of the parties to a marriage.

(4) Sections 42 and 43 do not apply to any child to the extent that the child is treated by virtue of adoption as not being the woman's child.

46 Embryo transferred after death of civil partner or intended female parent

(1) If –

    (a) the child has been carried by W as the result of the placing in her of an embryo,

    (b) the embryo was created at a time when W was a party to a civil partnership or marriage with another woman,

    (c) the other party to the civil partnership or marriage died before the placing of the embryo in W,

    (d) the other party to the civil partnership or marriage consented in writing (and did not withdraw the consent) –

        (i)   to the placing of the embryo in W after the death of the other party, and

        (ii) to being treated for the purpose mentioned in subsection (4) as the parent of any resulting child,

    (e) W has elected in writing not later than the end of the period of 42 days from the day on which the child was born for the other party to the civil partnership or marriage to be treated for the purpose mentioned in subsection (4) as the parent of the child, and

    (f) no one else is to be treated –

        (i)   as the father of the child by virtue of section 35 or 36 or by virtue of section 45(2) or (3), or

        (ii) as a parent of the child by virtue of section 42 or 43 or by virtue of adoption,

then the other party to the civil partnership or marriage is to be treated for the purpose mentioned in subsection (4) as a parent of the child.

    (2) If –

    (a) the child has been carried by W as the result of the placing in her of an embryo,

    (b) the embryo was not created at a time when W was a party to a marriage or a civil partnership, but was created in the course of treatment services provided to W in the United Kingdom by a person to whom a licence applies,

    (c) another woman consented in writing (and did not withdraw the consent) –

        (i)   to the placing of the embryo in W after the death of the other woman, and

        (ii) to being treated for the purpose mentioned in subsection (4) as the parent of any resulting child,

    (d) the other woman died before the placing of the embryo in W,

    (e) immediately before the other woman's death, the agreed female parenthood conditions set out in section 44 were met in relation to the other woman in relation to treatment proposed to be provided to W in the United Kingdom by a person to whom a licence applies,

    (f) W has elected in writing not later than the end of the period of 42 days from the day on which the child was born for the other woman to be treated for the purpose mentioned in subsection (4) as the parent of the child, and

    (g) no one else is to be treated –

        (i)   as the father of the child by virtue of section 35 or 36 or by virtue of section 45(2) or (3), or

        (ii) as a parent of the child by virtue of section 42 or 43 or by virtue of adoption,

then the other woman is to be treated for the purpose mentioned in subsection (4) as a parent of the child.

    (3) Subsections (1) and (2) apply whether W was in the United Kingdom or elsewhere at the time of the placing in her of the embryo.

    (4) The purpose referred to in subsections (1) and (2) is the purpose of enabling the deceased woman's particulars to be entered as the particulars of the child's other parent in a relevant register of births.

    (5) In the application of subsections (1) and (2) to Scotland, for any reference to a period of 42 days there is substituted a reference to a period of 21 days.

47 Woman not to be other parent merely because of egg donation

A woman is not to be treated as the parent of a child whom she is not carrying and has not carried, except where she is so treated –

    (a) by virtue of section 42 or 43, or

    (b) by virtue of section 46 (for the purpose mentioned in subsection (4) of that section), or

    (c) by virtue of adoption.

Effect of sections 33 to 47

48   Effect of sections 33 to 47

(1) Where by virtue of section 33, 35, 36, 42 or 43 a person is to be treated as the mother, father or parent of a child, that person is to be treated in law as the mother, father or parent (as the case may be) of the child for all purposes.

(2) Where by virtue of section 33, 38, 41, 45 or 47 a person is not to be treated as a parent of the child, that person is to be treated in law as not being a parent of the child for any purpose.

(3) Where section 39(1) or 40(1) or (2) applies, the deceased man –

    (a) is to be treated in law as the father of the child for the purpose mentioned in section 39(3) or 40(4), but

    (b) is to be treated in law as not being the father of the child for any other purpose.

(4) Where section 46(1) or (2) applies, the deceased woman –

    (a) is to be treated in law as a parent of the child for the purpose mentioned in section 46(4), but

    (b) is to be treated in law as not being a parent of the child for any other purpose.

(5) Where any of subsections (1) to (4) has effect, references to any relationship between two people in any enactment, deed or other instrument or document (whenever passed or made) are to be read accordingly.

(6) In relation to England and Wales and Northern Ireland, a child who –

    (a) has a parent by virtue of section 42, or

    (b) has a parent by virtue of section 43 who is at any time during the period beginning with the time mentioned in section 43(b) and ending with the time of the child's birth a party to a civil partnership with the child's mother,

is the legitimate child of the child's parents.

References to parties to marriage or civil partnership

49   Meaning of references to parties to a marriage

(1) The references in sections 35 to 47 to the parties to a marriage at any time there referred to –

    (a) are to the parties to a marriage subsisting at that time, unless a judicial separation was then in force, but

    (b) include the parties to a void marriage if either or both of them reasonably believed at that time that the marriage was valid; and for the purposes of those sections it is to be presumed, unless the contrary is shown, that one of them reasonably believed at that time that the marriage was valid.

(2) In subsection (1)(a) 'judicial separation' includes a legal separation obtained in a country outside the British Islands and recognised in the United Kingdom.

50   Meaning of references to parties to a civil partnership

(1) The references in sections 35 to 47 to the parties to a civil partnership at any time there referred to –

    (a) are to the parties to a civil partnership subsisting at that time, unless a separation order was then in force, but

    (b) include the parties to a void civil partnership if either or both of them reasonably believed at that time that the civil partnership was valid; and for the purposes of those sections it is to be presumed, unless the contrary is shown, that one of them reasonably believed at that time that the civil partnership was valid.

(2) The reference in section 48(6)(b) to a civil partnership includes a reference to a void civil partnership if either or both of the parties reasonably believed at the time when they registered as civil partners of each other that the civil partnership was valid; and for this purpose it is to be presumed, unless the contrary is shown, that one of them reasonably believed at that time that the civil partnership was valid.

(3) In subsection (1)(a), 'separation order' means –

    (a) a separation order under section 37(1)(d) or 161(1)(d) of the Civil Partnership Act 2004 (c. 33),

    (b) a decree of separation under section 120(2) of that Act, or

    (c) a legal separation obtained in a country outside the United Kingdom and recognized in the United Kingdom.

Interpretation of references to father etc. where woman is other parent

53   Interpretation of references to father etc.

(1) Subsections (2) and (3) have effect, subject to subsections (4) and (6), for the interpretation of any enactment, deed or any other instrument or document (whenever passed or made).

(2) Any reference (however expressed) to the father of a child who has a parent by virtue of section 42 or 43 is to be read as a reference to the woman who is a parent of the child by virtue of that section.

(3) Any reference (however expressed) to evidence of paternity is, in relation to a woman who is a parent by virtue of section 42 or 43, to be read as a reference to evidence of parentage.

Parental orders

54   Parental orders

(1) On an application made by two people ('the applicants'), the court may make an order providing for a child to be treated in law as the child of the applicants if –

    (a) the child has been carried by a woman who is not one of the applicants, as a result of the placing in her of an embryo or sperm and eggs or her artificial insemination,

    (b) the gametes of at least one of the applicants were used to bring about the creation of the embryo, and

    (c) the conditions in subsections (2) to (8) are satisfied.

(2) The applicants must be –

    (a) husband and wife,

    (b) civil partners of each other, or

    (c) two persons who are living as partners in an enduring family relationship and are not within prohibited degrees of relationship in relation to each other.

(3) Except in a case falling within subsection (11), the applicants must apply for the order during the period of 6 months beginning with the day on which the child is born.

(4) At the time of the application and the making of the order –

    (a) the child's home must be with the applicants, and

    (b) either or both of the applicants must be domiciled in the United Kingdom or in the Channel Islands or the Isle of Man.

(5) At the time of the making of the order both the applicants must have attained the age of 18.

(6) The court must be satisfied that both –

    (a) the woman who carried the child, and

    (b) any other person who is a parent of the child but is not one of the applicants (including any man who is the father by virtue of section 35 or 36 or any woman who is a parent by virtue of section 42 or 43), have freely, and with full understanding of what is involved, agreed unconditionally to the making of the order.

(7) Subsection (6) does not require the agreement of a person who cannot be found or is incapable of giving agreement; and the agreement of the woman who carried the child is ineffective for the purpose of that subsection if given by her less than six weeks after the child's birth.

(8) The court must be satisfied that no money or other benefit (other than for expenses reasonably incurred) has been given or received by either of the applicants for or in consideration of –

    (a) the making of the order,

    (b) any agreement required by subsection (6),

(c) the handing over of the child to the applicants, or

(d) the making of arrangements with a view to the making of the order,

unless authorised by the court.

(10) Subsection (1)(a) applies whether the woman was in the United Kingdom or elsewhere at the time of the placing in her of the embryo or the sperm and eggs or her artificial insemination.

General

57   Repeals and transitional provision relating to Part 2

(1) Sections 33 to 48 have effect only in relation to children carried by women as a result of the placing in them of embryos or of sperm and eggs, or their artificial insemination (as the case may be), after the commencement of those sections.

(2) Sections 27 to 29 of the 1990 Act (which relate to status) do not have effect in relation to children carried by women as a result of the placing in them of embryos or of sperm and eggs, or their artificial insemination (as the case may be), after the commencement of sections 33 to 48.

(3) Section 30 of the 1990 Act (parental orders in favour of gamete donors) ceases to have effect.

58   Interpretation of Part 2

(2) For the purposes of this Part, two persons are within prohibited degrees of relationship if one is the other's parent, grandparent, sister, brother, aunt or uncle; and in this subsection references to relationships –

(a) are to relationships of the full blood or half blood or, in the case of an adopted person, such of those relationships as would subsist but for adoption, and

(b) include the relationship of a child with his adoptive, or former adoptive, parents, but do not include any other adoptive relationships.

(3) Other expressions used in this Part and in the 1990 Act have the same meaning in this Part as in that Act.

Health and Social Care Act 2012

(2012, c. 7)

PART 3 REGULATION OF HEALTH AND ADULT SOCIAL CARE SERVICES

Chapter 1 Monitor

61   Monitor

(1) The body corporate known as the Independent Regulator of NHS Foundation Trusts –

(a) is to continue to exist, and

(b) is to be known as Monitor.

62   General duties

(1) The main duty of Monitor in exercising its functions is to protect and promote the interests of people who use health care services by promoting provision of health care services which –

(a) is economic, efficient and effective, and

(b) maintains or improves the quality of the services.

(2) In carrying out its main duty, Monitor must have regard to the likely future demand for health care services.

(3) Monitor must exercise its functions with a view to preventing anti-competitive behaviour in the provision of health care services for the purposes of the NHS which is against the interests of people who use such services.

(4) Monitor must exercise its functions with a view to enabling health care services provided for the purposes of the NHS to be provided in an integrated way where it considers that this would –

  (a) improve the quality of those services (including the outcomes that are achieved from their provision) or the efficiency of their provision,

  (b) reduce inequalities between persons with respect to their ability to access those services, or

  (c) reduce inequalities between persons with respect to the outcomes achieved for them by the provision of those services.

(5) Monitor must exercise its functions with a view to enabling the provision of health care services provided for the purposes of the NHS to be integrated with the provision of health-related services or social care services where it considers that this would –

  (a) improve the quality of those health care services (including the outcomes that are achieved from their provision) or the efficiency of their provision,

  (b) reduce inequalities between persons with respect to their ability to access those health care services, or

  (c) reduce inequalities between persons with respect to the outcomes achieved for them by the provision of those health care services.

(6) Monitor must, in carrying out its duties under subsections (4) and (5), have regard to the way in which –

  (a) the National Health Service Commissioning Board carries out its duties under section 13N of the National Health Service Act 2006, and

  (b) clinical commissioning groups carry out their duties under section 14Z1 of that Act.

(7) Monitor must secure that people who use health care services, and other members of the public, are involved to an appropriate degree in decisions that Monitor makes about the exercise of its functions (other than decisions it makes about the exercise of its functions in a particular case).

(8) Monitor must obtain advice appropriate for enabling it effectively to discharge its functions from persons who (taken together) have a broad range of professional expertise in –

  (a) the prevention, diagnosis or treatment of illness (within the meaning of the National Health Service Act 2006), and

  (b) the protection or improvement of public health.

(9) Monitor must exercise its functions in a manner consistent with the performance by the Secretary of State of the duty under section 1(1) of the National Health Service Act 2006 (promotion of comprehensive health service).

(10) Monitor must not exercise its functions for the purpose of causing a variation in the proportion of health care services provided for the purposes of the NHS that is provided by persons of a particular description if that description is by reference to –

  (a) whether the persons in question are in the public or (as the case may be) private sector, or

  (b) some other aspect of their status.

64   General duties: supplementary

(1) This section applies for the purposes of this Part.

(2) 'Anti-competitive behaviour' means behaviour which would (or would be likely to) prevent, restrict or distort competition and a reference to preventing anti-competitive behaviour includes a reference to eliminating or reducing the effects (or potential effects) of the behaviour.

(3) 'Health care' means all forms of health care provided for individuals, whether relating to physical or mental health, with a reference in this Part to health care services being read accordingly; and for the purposes of this Part it does not matter if a health care service is also an adult social care service (as to which, see section 65).

(4) 'The NHS' means the comprehensive health service continued under section 1(1) of the National Health Service Act 2006, except the part of it that is provided in pursuance of the public health functions (within the meaning of that Act) of the Secretary of State or local authorities.

(5) A reference to the provision of health care services for the purposes of the NHS is a reference to their provision for those purposes in accordance with that Act.

(6) Nothing in section 62 requires Monitor to do anything in relation to the supply to persons who provide health care services of goods that are to be provided as part of those services.

66   Matters to have regard to in exercise of functions

(1) In exercising its functions, Monitor must have regard, in particular, to the need to maintain the safety of people who use health care services.

(2) Monitor must, in exercising its functions, also have regard to the following matters in so far as they are consistent with the matter referred to in subsection (1) –

    (a) the desirability of securing continuous improvement in the quality of health care services provided for the purposes of the NHS and in the efficiency of their provision,

    (b) the need for commissioners of health care services for the purposes of the NHS to ensure that the provision of access to the services for those purposes operates fairly,

    (c) the need for commissioners of health care services for the purposes of the NHS to ensure that people who require health care services for those purposes are provided with access to them,

    (d) the need for commissioners of health care services for the purposes of the NHS to make the best use of resources when doing so,

    (e) the desirability of persons who provide health care services for the purposes of the NHS co-operating with each other in order to improve the quality of health care services provided for those purposes,

    (f) the need to promote research into matters relevant to the NHS by persons who provide health care services for the purposes of the NHS,

    (g) the need for high standards in the education and training of health care professionals who provide health care services for the purposes of the NHS, and

    (h) where the Secretary of State publishes a document for the purposes of section 13E of the National Health Service Act 2006 (improvement of quality of services), any guidance published by the Secretary of State on the parts of that document which the Secretary of State considers to be particularly relevant to Monitor's exercise of its functions.

68   Duty to review regulatory burdens

(1) Monitor must keep the exercise of its functions under review and secure that in exercising its functions it does not –

    (a) impose burdens which it considers to be unnecessary, or

    (b) maintain burdens which it considers to have become unnecessary.

Chapter 3 Licensing

Licensing requirement

81   Requirement for health service providers to be licensed

(1) Any person who provides a health care service for the purposes of the NHS must hold a licence under this Chapter.

83   Exemption regulations

(1) Regulations (referred to in this section and section 84 as 'exemption regulations') may provide for the grant of exemptions from the requirement under section 81 in respect of –

    (a) a prescribed person or persons of a prescribed description;

(b) the provision of a prescribed health care service or a health care service of a prescribed description.

85 Application for licence

(1) A person seeking to hold a licence under this Chapter must make an application to Monitor.

93 Register of licence holders

(1) Monitor must maintain and publish a register of licence holders.

PART 8 THE NATIONAL INSTITUTE FOR HEALTH AND CARE EXCELLENCE

Establishment and general duties

232 The National Institute for Health and Care Excellence

(1) There is to be a body corporate known as the National Institute for Health and Care Excellence (referred to in this Part as 'NICE').

233 General duties

(1) In exercising its functions NICE must have regard to –
  (a) the broad balance between the benefits and costs of the provision of health services or of social care in England,
  (b) the degree of need of persons for health services or social care in England, and
  (c) the desirability of promoting innovation in the provision of health services or of social care in England.

(2) NICE must exercise its functions effectively, efficiently and economically.

(3) In this Part –

'health services' means services which must or may be provided as part of the health service in England;

'social care' includes all forms of personal care and other practical assistance provided for individuals who, by reason of age, illness, disability, pregnancy, childbirth, dependence on alcohol or drugs, or any other similar circumstances, are in need of such care or other assistance.

Functions: quality standards

234 Quality standards

(1) The relevant commissioner may direct NICE to prepare statements of standards in relation to the provision of –
  (a) NHS services,
  (b) public health services, or
  (c) social care in England.

(2) In this Part such a statement is referred to as a 'quality standard'.

(3) In preparing a quality standard NICE must consult the public and, for that purpose, may publish drafts of the standard.

(4) NICE must keep a quality standard under review and may revise it as it considers appropriate.

(10) In this section 'the relevant commissioner' –
  (a) in relation to a quality standard in relation to the provision of NHS services, means the Board, and
  (b) in relation to a quality standard in relation to the provision of public health services or of social care in England, means the Secretary of State,

and a reference to the relevant commissioner in relation to a joint quality standard is a reference to both the Secretary of State and the Board.

236   Advice or guidance to the Secretary of State or the Board

(1) NICE must give advice or guidance to the Secretary of State or the Board on any quality matter referred to it by the Secretary of State or (as the case may be) the Board.

PART 12 FINAL PROVISIONS

308   Extent

(1) Subject to subsections (2) to (5), this Act extends to England and Wales only.

Care Act 2014

(2014, c. 23)

Safeguarding adults at risk of abuse or neglect

42   Enquiry by local authority

(1) This section applies where a local authority has reasonable cause to suspect that an adult in its area (whether or not ordinarily resident there) –

  (a) has needs for care and support (whether or not the authority is meeting any of those needs),

  (b) is experiencing, or is at risk of, abuse or neglect, and

  (c) as a result of those needs is unable to protect himself or herself against the abuse or neglect or the risk of it.

(2) The local authority must make (or cause to be made) whatever enquiries it thinks necessary to enable it to decide whether any action should be taken in the adult's case (whether under this Part or otherwise) and, if so, what and by whom.

(3) 'Abuse' includes financial abuse; and for that purpose 'financial abuse' includes –

  (a) having money or other property stolen,

  (b) being defrauded,

  (c) being put under pressure in relation to money or other property, and

  (d) having money or other property misused.

43   Safeguarding Adults Boards

(1) Each local authority must establish a Safeguarding Adults Board (an 'SAB') for its area.

(2) The objective of an SAB is to help and protect adults in its area in cases of the kind described in section 42(1).

(3) The way in which an SAB must seek to achieve its objective is by co-ordinating and ensuring the effectiveness of what each of its members does.

(4) An SAB may do anything which appears to it to be necessary or desirable for the purpose of achieving its objective.

44   Safeguarding adults reviews

(1) An SAB must arrange for there to be a review of a case involving an adult in its area with needs for care and support (whether or not the local authority has been meeting any of those needs) if –

  (a) there is reasonable cause for concern about how the SAB, members of it or other persons with relevant functions worked together to safeguard the adult, and

  (b) condition 1 or 2 is met.

(2) Condition 1 is met if –

  (a) the adult has died, and

  (b) the SAB knows or suspects that the death resulted from abuse or neglect (whether or not it knew about or suspected the abuse or neglect before the adult died).

(3) Condition 2 is met if –
> (a) the adult is still alive, and
> (b) the SAB knows or suspects that the adult has experienced serious abuse or neglect.

(4) An SAB may arrange for there to be a review of any other case involving an adult in its area with needs for care and support (whether or not the local authority has been meeting any of those needs).

(5) Each member of the SAB must co-operate in and contribute to the carrying out of a review under this section with a view to –
> (a) identifying the lessons to be learnt from the adult's case, and
> (b) applying those lessons to future cases.

Chapter 2 Health Research Authority

Establishment

109   The Health Research Authority

(1) There is to be a body corporate called the Health Research Authority (referred to in this Act as 'the HRA').

General functions

110   The HRA's functions

(1) The main functions of the HRA are –
> (a) functions relating to the co-ordination and standardisation of practice relating to the regulation of health and social care research (see section 111);
> (b) functions relating to research ethics committees (see sections 112 to 115);
> (c) functions as a member of the United Kingdom Ethics Committee Authority (see section 116 and the Medicines for Human Use (Clinical Trials) Regulations 2004 (S.I. 2004/1031));
> (d) functions relating to approvals for processing confidential information relating to patients (see section 117 and the Health Service (Control of Patient Information) Regulations 2002 (S.I. 2002/1438)).

(2) The main objective of the HRA in exercising its functions is –
> (a) to protect participants and potential participants in health or social care research and the general public by encouraging research that is safe and ethical, and
> (b) to promote the interests of those participants and potential participants and the general public by facilitating the conduct of research that is safe and ethical (including by promoting transparency in research).

(3) Health research is research into matters relating to people's physical or mental health; but a reference to health research does not include a reference to anything authorised under the Animals (Scientific Procedures) Act 1986.

(4) Social care research is research into matters relating to personal care or other practical assistance for individuals aged 18 or over who are in need of care or assistance because of age, physical or mental illness, disability, pregnancy, childbirth, dependence on alcohol or drugs or other similar circumstances; and 'illness' has the meaning given by section 275(1) of the National Health Service Act 2006.

(6) A reference to research that is ethical is a reference to research that conforms to generally accepted ethical standards.

(7) Promoting transparency in research includes promoting –
> (a) the registration of research;
> (b) the publication and dissemination of research findings and conclusions;
> (c) the provision of access to data on which research findings or conclusions are based;
> (d) the provision of information at the end of research to participants in the research;
> (e) the provision of access to tissue used in research, for use in future research.

112   The HRA's policy on research ethics committees

(1) The HRA must ensure that research ethics committees it recognises or establishes under this Chapter provide an efficient and effective means of assessing the ethics of health and social care research.

(2) A research ethics committee is a group of persons which assesses the ethics of research involving individuals; and the ways in which health or social care research might involve individuals include, for example –

(a) by obtaining information from them;

(b) by obtaining bodily tissue or fluid from them;

(c) by using information, tissue or fluid obtained from them on a previous occasion;

(d) by requiring them to undergo a test or other process (including xenotransplantation).

(3) For the purposes of subsection (1), the HRA –

(a) must publish a document (called 'the REC policy document') which specifies the requirements which it expects research ethics committees it recognises or establishes under this Chapter to comply with, and

(b) must monitor their compliance with those requirements.

(4) The HRA may do such other things in relation to research ethics committees it recognises or establishes under this Chapter as it considers appropriate; it may, for example –

(a) co-ordinate their work;

(b) allocate work to them;

(c) develop and maintain training programmes designed to ensure that their members and staff can carry out their work effectively;

(d) provide them with advice and help (including help in the form of financial assistance).

(5) The requirements in the REC policy document may, for example, relate to –

(a) membership;

(b) proceedings;

(c) staff;

(d) accommodation and facilities;

(e) expenses;

(f) objectives and functions;

(g) accountability;

(h) procedures for challenging decisions.

(6) The HRA must ensure that the requirements imposed on research ethics committees in the REC policy document do not conflict with the requirements imposed on them by the Medicines for Human Use (Clinical Trials) Regulations 2004 (S.I. 2004/1031).

113   Approval of research

(1) The HRA must publish guidance about –

(a) the cases in which, in its opinion, good practice requires a person proposing to conduct health or social care research that involves individuals to obtain the approval of a research ethics committee recognised or established by the HRA under this Chapter, and

(b) the cases in which an enactment requires a person proposing to conduct research of that kind to obtain that approval.

115   Establishment by the HRA

(1) The HRA may establish research ethics committees which have the following functions –

(a) approving research of the kind referred to in section 113(1);

(b) giving such other approvals as enactments require.

(2) The HRA must ensure that a research ethics committee established under this section complies with the requirements set out in the REC policy document.

(3) The HRA may abolish a research ethics committee established under this section.

Social Action, Responsibility and Heroism Act 2015

(2015, c. 3)

1 When this Act applies

This Act applies when a court, in considering a claim that a person was negligent or in breach of statutory duty, is determining the steps that the person was required to take to meet a standard of care.

2 Social action

The court must have regard to whether the alleged negligence or breach of statutory duty occurred when the person was acting for the benefit of society or any of its members.

3 Responsibility

The court must have regard to whether the person, in carrying out the activity in the course of which the alleged negligence or breach of statutory duty occurred, demonstrated a predominantly responsible approach towards protecting the safety or other interests of others.

4 Heroism

The court must have regard to whether the alleged negligence or breach of statutory duty occurred when the person was acting heroically by intervening in an emergency to assist an individual in danger.

5 Extent, commencement and short title

(1) This Act extends to England and Wales only.

Consumer Rights Act 2015

(2015, c.15)

2 Key definitions

(2) 'Trader' means a person acting for purposes relating to that person's trade, business, craft or profession, whether acting personally or through another person acting in the trader's name or on the trader's behalf.

(3) 'Consumer' means an individual acting for purposes that are wholly or mainly outside that individual's trade, business, craft or profession.

(7) 'Business' includes the activities of any government department or local or public authority.

49 Service to be performed with reasonable care and skill

(1) Every contract to supply a service is to be treated as including a term that the trader must perform the service with reasonable care and skill.

50 Information about the trader or service to be binding

(1) Every contract to supply a service is to be treated as including as a term of the contract anything that is said or written to the consumer, by or on behalf of the trader, about the trader or the service, if –

    (a) it is taken into account by the consumer when deciding to enter into the contract, or

    (b) it is taken into account by the consumer when making any decision about the service after entering into the contract.

(2) Anything taken into account by the consumer as mentioned in subsection (1)(a) or (b) is subject to –

    (a) anything that qualified it and was said or written to the consumer by the trader on the same occasion, and

(b) any change to it that has been expressly agreed between the consumer and the trader (before entering into the contract or later).

(4) A change to any of the information mentioned in subsection (3), made before entering into the contract or later, is not effective unless expressly agreed between the consumer and the trader.

57   Liability that cannot be excluded or restricted

(1) A term of a contract to supply services is not binding on the consumer to the extent that it would exclude the trader's liability arising under section 49 (service to be performed with reasonable care and skill).

(2) Subject to section 50(2), a term of a contract to supply services is not binding on the consumer to the extent that it would exclude the trader's liability arising under section 50 (information about trader or service to be binding).

(3) A term of a contract to supply services is not binding on the consumer to the extent that it would restrict the trader's liability arising under any of sections 49 and 50 and, where they apply, sections 51 and 52 (reasonable price and reasonable time), if it would prevent the consumer in an appropriate case from recovering the price paid or the value of any other consideration. (If it would not prevent the consumer from doing so, Part 2 (unfair terms) may apply.)

(4) That also means that a term of a contract to supply services is not binding on the consumer to the extent that it would –

(a) exclude or restrict a right or remedy in respect of a liability under any of sections 49 to 52,

(b) make such a right or remedy or its enforcement subject to a restrictive or onerous condition,

(c) allow a trader to put a person at a disadvantage as a result of pursuing such a right or remedy, or

(d) exclude or restrict rules of evidence or procedure.

(5) The references in subsections (1) to (3) to excluding or restricting a liability also include preventing an obligation or duty arising or limiting its extent.

PART 2 UNFAIR TERMS

61   Contracts and notices covered by this Part

(1) This Part applies to a contract between a trader and a consumer.

(3) A contract to which this Part applies is referred to in this Part as a 'consumer contract'.

(4) This Part applies to a notice to the extent that it –

(a) relates to rights or obligations as between a trader and a consumer, or

(b) purports to exclude or restrict a trader's liability to a consumer.

(7) A notice to which this Part applies is referred to in this Part as a 'consumer notice'.

(8) In this section 'notice' includes an announcement, whether or not in writing, and any other communication or purported communication.

62   Requirement for contract terms and notices to be fair

(1) An unfair term of a consumer contract is not binding on the consumer.

(2) An unfair consumer notice is not binding on the consumer.

(3) This does not prevent the consumer from relying on the term or notice if the consumer chooses to do so.

(4) A term is unfair if, contrary to the requirement of good faith, it causes a significant imbalance in the parties' rights and obligations under the contract to the detriment of the consumer.

(5) Whether a term is fair is to be determined –
  (a) taking into account the nature of the subject matter of the contract, and
  (b) by reference to all the circumstances existing when the term was agreed and to all of the other terms of the contract or of any other contract on which it depends.

(6) A notice is unfair if, contrary to the requirement of good faith, it causes a significant imbalance in the parties' rights and obligations to the detriment of the consumer.

(7) Whether a notice is fair is to be determined –
  (a) taking into account the nature of the subject matter of the notice, and
  (b) by reference to all the circumstances existing when the rights or obligations to which it relates arose and to the terms of any contract on which it depends.

(8) This section does not affect the operation of –
  (c) section 57 (exclusion of liability: services contracts), or
  (d) section 65 (exclusion of negligence liability).

63 Contract terms which may or must be regarded as unfair

(1) Part 1 of Schedule 2 contains an indicative and non-exhaustive list of terms of consumer contracts that may be regarded as unfair for the purposes of this Part.

64 Exclusion from assessment of fairness

(1) A term of a consumer contract may not be assessed for fairness under section 62 to the extent that –
  (a) it specifies the main subject matter of the contract, or
  (b) the assessment is of the appropriateness of the price payable under the contract by comparison with the goods, digital content or services supplied under it.

(2) Subsection (1) excludes a term from an assessment under section 62 only if it is transparent and prominent.

(3) A term is transparent for the purposes of this Part if it is expressed in plain and intelligible language and (in the case of a written term) is legible.

(4) A term is prominent for the purposes of this section if it is brought to the consumer's attention in such a way that an average consumer would be aware of the term.

(5) In subsection (4) 'average consumer' means a consumer who is reasonably well-informed, observant and circumspect.

(6) This section does not apply to a term of a contract listed in Part 1 of Schedule 2.

65 Bar on exclusion or restriction of negligence liability

(1) A trader cannot by a term of a consumer contract or by a consumer notice exclude or restrict liability for death or personal injury resulting from negligence.

(2) Where a term of a consumer contract, or a consumer notice, purports to exclude or restrict a trader's liability for negligence, a person is not to be taken to have voluntarily accepted any risk merely because the person agreed to or knew about the term or notice.

(3) In this section 'personal injury' includes any disease and any impairment of physical or mental condition.

(4) In this section 'negligence' means the breach of –
  (a) any obligation to take reasonable care or exercise reasonable skill in the performance of a contract where the obligation arises from an express or implied term of the contract,
  (b) a common law duty to take reasonable care or exercise reasonable skill …

(5) It is immaterial for the purposes of subsection (4) –
  (a) whether a breach of duty or obligation was inadvertent or intentional, or
  (b) whether liability for it arises directly or vicariously.

67   Effect of an unfair term on the rest of a contract

Where a term of a consumer contract is not binding on the consumer as a result of this Part, the contract continues, so far as practicable, to have effect in every other respect.

68   Requirement for transparency

(1) A trader must ensure that a written term of a consumer contract, or a consumer notice in writing, is transparent.

(2) A consumer notice is transparent for the purposes of subsection (1) if it is expressed in plain and intelligible language and it is legible.

Statutory Instruments

Abortion Regulations 1991

(SI 1991, No. 499)

Interpretation

2 In these Regulations 'the Act' means the Abortion Act 1967;
'practitioner' means a registered medical practitioner.

Certificate of opinion

3 (1) Any opinion to which section 1 of the Act refers shall be certified –

(a) in the case of a pregnancy terminated in accordance with section 1(1) of the Act, either –

   (i)   in the form set out in Part I of Schedule 1 to these Regulations; or

   (ii) in a certificate signed and dated by both practitioners jointly or in separate certificates signed and dated by each practitioner stating: –

(a) the full name and address of each practitioner;

(b) the full name and address of the pregnant woman;

(c) whether or not each practitioner has seen or examined, or seen and examined, the pregnant woman; and

(d) that each practitioner is of the opinion formed in good faith that at least one and the same ground mentioned in paragraph (a) to (d) of section 1(1) of the Act is fulfilled,

(b) in the case of a pregnancy terminated in accordance with section 1(4) of the Act, either –

   (i)   in the form set out in Part II of Schedule 1 to these Regulations; or

   (ii) in a certificate giving the full name and address of the practitioner and containing the full name and address of the pregnant woman and stating that the practitioner is of the opinion formed in good faith that one of the grounds mentioned in section 1(4) of the Act is fulfilled.

(2) Any certificate of an opinion referred to in section 1(1) of the Act shall be given before the commencement of the treatment for the termination of the pregnancy to which it relates.

(3) Any certificate of an opinion referred to in section 1(4) of the Act shall be given before the commencement of the treatment for the termination of the pregnancy to which it relates or, if that is not reasonably practicable, not later than 24 hours after such termination.

(4) Any such certificate as is referred to in paragraphs (2) and (3) of this regulation shall be preserved by the practitioner who terminated the pregnancy to which it relates for a period of not less than three years beginning with the date of the termination.

(5) A certificate which is no longer to be preserved shall be destroyed by the person in whose custody it then is.

Notice of termination of pregnancy and information relating to the termination

4—(1) Any practitioner who terminates a pregnancy in England or Wales shall give to the appropriate Chief Medical Officer –

(a) notice of the termination, and

(b) such other information relating to the termination as is specified in Schedule 2 to these Regulations,

and shall do so by sending them to him or her within 14 days of the termination either in a sealed envelope or by an electronic communication transmitted by an electronic communications system used solely for the transfer of confidential information to him or her.

(2) The appropriate Chief Medical Officer is –

(a) where the pregnancy was terminated in England, the Chief Medical Officer of the Department of Health, Richmond House, 79 Whitehall, London, SW1A 2NS; or

(b) where the pregnancy was terminated in Wales, the Chief Medical Officer for Wales, Welsh Assembly Government, Cathays Park, Cardiff CF1 3NQ.

Restriction on disclosure of information

5 A notice given or any information furnished to a Chief Medical Officer in pursuance of these Regulations shall not be disclosed except that disclosure may be made –

(a) for the purposes of carrying out their duties –

(i) to an officer of the Department of Health authorised by the Chief Medical Officer of that Department, or to an officer of the Welsh Assembly Government authorised by the Chief Medical Officer of that Office, as the case may be, or

(ii) to the National Statistician duly appointed under section 5 of the Statistics and Registration Service Act 2007 or an employee of the Statistics Board (established under section 1 of that Act) authorised by the National Statistician; or

(iii) to an individual authorised by the Chief Medical Officer who is engaged in setting up, maintaining and supporting a computer system used for the purpose of recording, processing and holding such notice or information;

(b) for the purposes of carrying out his duties in relation to offences under the Act or the law relating to abortion, to the Director of Public Prosecutions or a member of his staff authorised by him; or

(c) for the purposes of investigating whether an offence has been committed under the Act or the law relating to abortion, to a police officer not below the rank of superintendent or a person authorised by him; or

(d) pursuant to a court order, for the purposes of proceedings which have begun; or

(e) for the purposes of bona fide scientific research; or

(f) to the practitioner who terminated the pregnancy; or

(g) to a practitioner, with the consent in writing of the woman whose pregnancy was terminated; or

(h) when requested by the President of the General Medical Council for the purpose of investigating whether the fitness to practise of the practitioner is impaired, to the President of the General Medical Council or a member of its staff authorised by him –

(i) to the woman whose pregnancy was terminated, on her supplying to the Chief Medical Officer written details of her date of birth, the date and place of the termination and a copy of the certificate of registration of her birth certified as a true copy of the original by a solicitor or a practitioner.

Regulation 3(1)

SCHEDULE 1

PART I

<u>**IN CONFIDENCE**</u> **<u>CERTIFICATE A</u>**

<u>ABORTION ACT 1967</u>

Not to be destroyed within three years of the date of operation

**Certificate to be completed before an abortion is
performed under Section 1(1) of the Act**

I, ...

(Name and qualifications of practitioner in block capitals)

of ....

....

(Full address of practitioner)

Have/have not* seen/and examined* the pregnant woman to whom this certificate relates at

....

....

(full address of place at which patient was seen or examined)

on ....

and I ....

(Name and qualifications of practitioner in block capitals)

of ....

....

(Full address of practitioner)

Have/have not* seen/and examined* the pregnant woman to whom this certificate relates at

....

....

(Full address of place at which patient was seen or examined)

on ....

We hereby certify that we are of the opinion, formed in good faith, that in the case

of ....

(Full name of pregnant woman in block capitals)

of ....

....

(Usual place of residence of pregnant woman in block capitals)

(Ring appropriate letter(s))

A — the continuance of the pregnancy would involve risk to the life of the pregnant woman greater than if the pregnancy were terminated;

B — the termination is necessary to prevent grave permanent injury to the physical or mental health of the pregnant woman;

C — the pregnancy has NOT exceeded its 24th week and that the continuance of the pregnancy would involve risk, greater than if the pregnancy were terminated, of injury to the physical or mental health of the pregnant woman;

D — the pregnancy has NOT exceeded its 24th week and that the continuance of the pregnancy would involve risk, greater than if the pregnancy were terminated, of injury to the physical or mental health of any existing child(ren) of the family of the pregnant woman;

E — there is a substantial risk that if the child were born it would suffer from such physical or mental abnormalities as to be seriously handicapped.

This certificate of opinion is given before the commencement of the treatment for the termination of pregnancy to which it refers and relates to the circumstances of the pregnant woman's individual case.

Signed ....   **Date** ....

Signed ....   **Date** ....

* Delete as appropriate   DxDH005329 4/94 C8000 CC38806   Form HSA1 (revised 1991)

PART II

IN CONFIDENCE   **Certificate B**

Not to be destroyed within three years of the date of operation

ABORTION ACT 1967

**Certificate to be completed in relation to abortion performed
in emergency under Section I (4) of the Act**

I, ...

(Name and qualifications of practitioner in block capitals)

of ....

....

(Full address of practitioner)

hereby certify that I *am/was of the opinion formed in good faith that it *is/was necessary

immediately to terminate the pregnancy of

....

(Full name of pregnant woman in block capitals)

of ....

....

(Usual place of residence of pregnant woman in block capitals)

(Ring appropriate number)

In order I.   to save the life of the pregnant woman : or

2.   to prevent grave permanent injury to the physical or mental health of the
pregnant woman.

This certificate of opinion is given :—

(Ring appropriate letter)

A.   before the commencement of the treatment for the termination of the pregnancy to

which it relates ; or, if that is not reasonably practicable, then

B.   not later than 24 hours after such termination.

Signed ....

Date..

*Delete as appropriate

FORM H.S.A. 2   15985 8003903 30m (2) 11/79 WPLtd Gp709

16468 PC1 10k 2P AUG 99 (0)

Regulation 4   **SCHEDULE 2**

Information to be supplied in an Abortion Notification

1. Full name and address (including postcode) of the practitioner who terminated the pregnancy and the General Medical Council registration number of the practitioner.

2. In non-emergency cases particulars of the practitioners who gave a certificate of opinion pursuant to section 1(1) of the Act and whether they saw or examined, or saw and examined the patient before giving the certificate.

3. Patient's details –
   (a) patient's hospital or clinic number or National Health Service number or (if unavailable) patient's full name;
   (b) date of birth;
   (c) in the case of a patient resident in the United Kingdom, her full postcode or, if the postcode is unavailable, her address;
   (d) in the case of a patient resident outside the United Kingdom, her country of residence;
   (e) ethnicity (if disclosed by the patient);
   (f) marital status; and
   (g) parity.

4. Name and address of place of termination.

5. Whether the termination was paid for privately or not.

6. Date and method of foeticide if appropriate.

7. In a case where the termination is by surgery –
   (a) date of termination;
   (b) the method of termination used; and
   (c) in cases where the dates are different, the date of admission to the place of termination and the date of discharge from the place of termination.

8. In a case where the termination is by non-surgical means –
   (a) the date of treatment with antiprogestrone;
   (b) the date of treatment with prostaglandin;
   (c) the date on which the termination is confirmed;
   (d) in cases where the place of treatment with prostaglandin is different from the place of treatment with antiprogestrone, the name and address at which the prostaglandin was administered;
   (e) details of other agents used and the date of administration; and
   (f) the date of discharge if an overnight stay is required.

9. Number of complete weeks of gestation.

10. The ground(s) certified for terminating the pregnancy contained in the certificate of opinion given pursuant to section 1(1) of the Act together with the following additional information in the case of –
    (a) the ground specified in paragraph (a), whether or not there was a risk to the patient's mental health and if not, her main medical conditions;
    (b) the grounds specified in paragraphs (b) and (c), the main medical condition(s) of the patient;
    (c) the ground specified in paragraph (d), any foetal abnormalities diagnosed, together with method of diagnosis used, and any other reasons for termination.

11. The ground(s) certified for terminating the pregnancy contained in the certificate of opinion given pursuant to section 1(4) of the Act and the patient's main medical conditions.

12. In cases of selective termination the original number of foetuses and the number of foetuses remaining.

13. Whether or not the patient was offered chlamydia screening.

14. Particulars of any complications experienced by the patient up to the date of discharge.

15. In the case of the death of the patient the date and cause of death.

Access to Health Records (Control of Access) Regulations 1993

(SI 1993, No. 746)

1   Citation, commencement and interpretation

(2) In these Regulations, 'the Act' means the Access to Health Records Act 1990.

2   Restriction of right of access to health records

Access shall not be given under section 3(2) of the Act to any part of a health record which would disclose information showing that an identifiable individual was, or may have been, born in consequence of treatment services within the meaning of the Human Fertilisation and Embryology Act 1990.

Data Protection (Subject Access Modification) (Health) Order 2000

(SI 2000, No. 413)

2   Interpretation

In this Order –

'the Act' means the Data Protection Act 1998;

'the appropriate health professional' means –

(a) the health professional who is currently or was most recently responsible for the clinical care of the data subject in connection with the matters to which the information which is the subject of the request relates; or

(b) where there is more than one such health professional, the health professional who is the most suitable to advise on the matters to which the information which is the subject of the request relates; or

(c) where –

(i) there is no health professional available falling within paragraph (a) or (b), or

(ii) the data controller is the Secretary of State and data to which this Order applies are processed in connection with the exercise of the functions conferred on him by or under the Child Support Act 1991 and the Child Support Act 1995 or his functions in relation to social security or war pensions, a health professional who has the necessary experience and qualifications to advise on the matters to which the information which is the subject of the request relates;

'care' includes examination, investigation, diagnosis and treatment;

'request' means a request made under section 7;

'section 7' means section 7 of the Act.

3   Personal data to which Order applies

(1) Subject to paragraph (2), this Order applies to personal data consisting of information as to the physical or mental health or condition of the data subject.

(2) This Order does not apply to any data which are exempted from section 7 by an order made under section 38(1) of the Act.

4   Exemption from the subject information provisions

(1) Personal data falling within paragraph (2) and to which this Order applies are exempt from the subject information provisions.

(2) This paragraph applies to personal data processed by a court and consisting of information supplied in a report or other evidence given to the court by a local authority, Health and Social Services Board, Health and Social Services Trust, probation officer or other person in the course of any proceedings to which the Family Proceedings Courts (Children Act 1989) Rules 1991, the Magistrates' Courts (Children and Young Persons) Rules 1992, the Magistrates' Courts (Criminal Justice (Children)) Rules (Northern Ireland) 1999, the Act of Sederunt (Child Care and Maintenance Rules) 1997 or the Children's Hearings (Scotland) Rules 1996, the Children's Hearings (Scotland) Act 2011 (Rules of Procedure in Children's Hearings) Rules 2013 or the Family Procedure Rules 2010 apply where, in accordance with a provision of any of those Rules, the information may be withheld by the court in whole or in part from the data subject.

5   Exemptions from section 7

(1) Personal data to which this Order applies are exempt from section 7 in any case to the extent to which the application of that section would be likely to cause serious harm to the physical or mental health or condition of the data subject or any other person.

(2) Subject to article 7(1), a data controller who is not a health professional shall not withhold information constituting data to which this Order applies on the ground that the exemption in paragraph (1) applies with respect to the information unless the data controller has first consulted the person who appears to the data controller to be the appropriate health professional on the question whether or not the exemption in paragraph (1) applies with respect to the information.

(3) Where any person falling within paragraph (4) is enabled by or under any enactment or rule of law to make a request on behalf of a data subject and has made such a request, personal data to which this Order applies are exempt from section 7 in any case to the extent to which the application of that section would disclose information.

  (a) provided by the data subject in the expectation that it would not be disclosed to the person making the request;

  (b) obtained as a result of any examination or investigation to which the data subject consented in the expectation that the information would not be so disclosed; or

  (c) which the data subject has expressly indicated should not be so disclosed, provided that sub-paragraphs (a) and (b) shall not prevent disclosure where the data subject has expressly indicated that he no longer has the expectation referred to therein.

(4) A person falls within this paragraph if –

  (a) except in relation to Scotland, the data subject is a child, and that person has parental responsibility for that data subject;

  (b) in relation to Scotland, the data subject is a person under the age of sixteen, and that person has parental responsibilities for that data subject; or

  (c) the data subject is incapable of managing his own affairs and that person has been appointed by a court to manage those affairs.

6   Modification of section 7 relating to data controllers who are not health professionals

(1) Subject to paragraph (2) and article 7(3), section 7 of the Act is modified so that a data controller who is not a health professional shall not communicate information constituting data to which this Order applies in response to a request unless the data controller has first consulted the person who appears to the data controller to be the appropriate health professional on the question whether or not the exemption in article 5(1) applies with respect to the information.

(2) Paragraph (1) shall not apply to the extent that the request relates to information which the data controller is satisfied has previously been seen by the data subject or is already within the knowledge of the data subject.

7   Additional provision relating to data controllers who are not health professionals

(1) Subject to paragraph (2), article 5(2) shall not apply in relation to any request where the data controller has consulted the appropriate health professional prior to receiving the request and obtained in writing from that appropriate health professional an opinion that the exemption in article 5(1) applies with respect to all of the information which is the subject of the request.

(2) Paragraph (1) does not apply where the opinion either –

    (a) was obtained before the period beginning six months before the relevant day (as defined by section 7(10) of the Act) and ending on that relevant day, or

    (b) was obtained within that period and it is reasonable in all the circumstances to re-consult the appropriate health professional.

(3) Article 6(1) shall not apply in relation to any request where the data controller has consulted the appropriate health professional prior to receiving the request and obtained in writing from that appropriate health professional an opinion that the exemption in article 5(1) does not apply with respect to all of the information which is the subject of the request.

8   Further modifications of section 7

In relation to data to which this Order applies –

    (a) section 7(4) of the Act shall have effect as if there were inserted after paragraph (b) of that subsection 'or, (c) the information is contained in a health record and the other individual is a health professional who has compiled or contributed to the health record or has been involved in the care of the data subject in his capacity as a health professional';

    (b) section 7(9) shall have effect as if –

        (i) there was substituted –

'(9) If a court is satisfied on the application of –

    (a) any person who has made a request under the foregoing provisions of this section, or

    (b) any other person to whom serious harm to his physical or mental health or condition would be likely to be caused by compliance with any such request in contravention of those provisions, that the data controller in question is about to comply with or has failed to comply with the request in contravention of those provisions, the court may order him not to comply or, as the case may be, to comply with the request.'; and

        (ii) the reference therein to a contravention of the foregoing provisions of that section included a reference to a contravention of the provisions contained in this Order.

Health Service (Control of Patient Information) Regulations 2002

(SI 2002, No. 1438)

1   Citation, commencement, interpretation and extent

(2) In these Regulations –

'the Act' means the Health and Social Care Act 2001;

'public authority' has the same meaning as in section 3(1) of the Freedom of Information Act 2000;

'research ethics committee' means –

    (a) a research ethics committee recognised or established by or on behalf of the Health Research Authority under the Care Act 2014 …

(3) Any notice given under these Regulations shall be –

    (a) in writing; or

    (b) transmitted by electronic means in a legible form which is capable of being used for subsequent reference.

2   Medical purposes related to the diagnosis or treatment of neoplasia

(1) Subject to paragraphs (2) to (4) and regulation 7, confidential patient information relating to patients referred for the diagnosis or treatment of neoplasia may be processed for medical purposes which comprise or include –

(a) the surveillance and analysis of health and disease;

(b) the monitoring and audit of health and health related care provision and outcomes where such provision has been made;

(c) the planning and administration of the provision made for health and health related care;

(d) medical research approved by research ethics committees;

(e) the provision of information about individuals who have suffered from a particular disease or condition where –

(i)   that information supports an analysis of the risk of developing that disease or condition; and

(ii)   it is required for the counselling and support of a person who is concerned about the risk of developing that disease or condition.

(2) For the purposes of this regulation, 'processing' includes (in addition to the use, disclosure or obtaining of information) any operations, or set of operations, which are undertaken in order to establish or maintain databases for the purposes set out in paragraph (1), including –

(a) the recording and holding of information;

(b) the retrieval, alignment and combination of information;

(c) the organisation, adaption or alteration of information;

(d) the blocking, erasure and destruction of information.

(3) The processing of confidential patient information for the purposes specified in paragraph (1) may be undertaken by persons who (either individually or as members of a class) are –

(a) approved by the Secretary of State, and

(b) authorised by the person who lawfully holds the information.

(4) Where the Secretary of State considers that it is necessary in the public interest that confidential patient information is processed for a purpose specified in paragraph (1), he may give notice to any person who is approved and authorised under paragraph (3) to require that person to process that information for that purpose and any such notice may require that the information is processed forthwith or within such period as is specified in the notice.

(5) A person who processes confidential patient information under this regulation shall inform the Patient Information Advisory Group of that processing and shall make available to the Secretary of State such information as he may require to assist him in the investigation and audit of that processing and in his annual consideration of the provisions of these Regulations which is required by section 60(4) of the Act.

3   Communicable disease and other risks to public health

(1) Subject to paragraphs (2) and (3) and regulation 7, confidential patient information may be processed with a view to –

(a) diagnosing communicable diseases and other risks to public health;

(b) recognising trends in such diseases and risks;

(c) controlling and preventing the spread of such diseases and risks;

(d) monitoring and managing –

(i)   outbreaks of communicable disease;

(ii)   incidents of exposure to communicable disease;

(iii) the delivery, efficacy and safety of immunisation programmes;

(iv) adverse reactions to vaccines and medicines;

(v)   risks of infection acquired from food or the environment (including water supplies);

(vi) the giving of information to persons about the diagnosis of communicable disease and risks of acquiring such disease.

(2) For the purposes of this regulation, 'processing' includes any operations, or set of operations set out in regulation 2(2) which are undertaken for the purposes set out in paragraph (1)

(3) The processing of confidential patient information for the purposes specified in paragraph (1) may be undertaken by –

    (b) persons employed or engaged for the purposes of the health service;

    (c) other persons employed or engaged by a Government Department or other public authority in communicable disease surveillance.

(4) Where the Secretary of State considers that it is necessary to process patient information for a purpose specified in paragraph (1), he may give notice to any body or person specified in paragraph (2) to require that person or body to process that information for that purpose and any such notice may require that the information is processed forthwith or within such period as is specified in the notice.

(5) Where confidential information is processed under this regulation, the bodies and persons specified in paragraph (2) shall make available to the Secretary of State such information as he may require to assist him in the investigation and audit of that processing and in his annual consideration of the provisions of these Regulations which is required by section 60(4) of the Act.

4   Modifying the obligation of confidence

Anything done by a person that is necessary for the purpose of processing confidential patient information in accordance with these Regulations shall be taken to be lawfully done despite any obligation of confidence owed by that person in respect of it.

5   Approval for processing information

(1) Subject to regulation 7, confidential patient information may be processed for medical purposes in the circumstances set out in the Schedule to these Regulations provided that the processing has been approved –

    (a) in the case of medical research, by the Health Research Authority, and

    (b) in any other case, by the Secretary of State.

(2) The Health Research Authority may not give an approval under paragraph (1)(a) unless a research ethics committee has approved the medical research concerned.

(3) The Health Research Authority shall put in place and operate a system for reviewing decisions it makes under paragraph (1)(a).

6   Registration

(1) Where an approval granted by the Health Research Authority or the Secretary of State under regulation 5 permits the transfer of confidential patient information between persons who may determine the purposes for which, and the manner in which, the information may be processed, it or he shall record in a register the name and address of each of those persons together with the particulars specified in paragraph (2).

(2) The following particulars are specified for inclusion in each entry in the register –

    (a) a description of the confidential patient information to which the approval relates;

    (b) the medical purposes for which the information may be processed;

    (c) the provisions in the Schedule to these Regulations under which the information may be processed; and

    (d) such other particulars as the Health Research Authority or (as the case may be) the Secretary of State may consider appropriate to enter in the register.

(3) The Health Research Authority shall retain the particulars of each entry it records in the register, and the Secretary of State shall retain the particulars of each entry he records in the register, for so long as confidential patient information may be processed under an approval and for not less than 12 months after the termination of an approval.

(4) The Health Research Authority shall, in such manner and to such extent as it considers appropriate, publish entries it records in the register; and the Secretary of State shall, in such manner and to such extent as he considers appropriate, publish entries he records in the register.

7   Restrictions and exclusions

(1) Where a person is in possession of confidential patient information under these Regulations, he shall not process that information more than is necessary to achieve the purposes for which he is permitted to process that information under these Regulations and, in particular, he shall –

    (a) so far as it is practical to do so, remove from the information any particulars which identify the person to whom it relates which are not required for the purposes for which it is, or is to be, processed;

    (b) not allow any person access to that information other than a person who, by virtue of his contract of employment or otherwise, is involved in processing the information for one or more of those purposes and is aware of the purpose or purposes for which the information may be processed;

    (c) ensure that appropriate technical and organisational measures are taken to prevent unauthorised processing of that information;

    (d) review at intervals not exceeding 12 months the need to process confidential patient information and the extent to which it is practicable to reduce the confidential patient information which is being processed;

    (e) on request by any person or body, make available information on the steps taken to comply with these Regulations.

(2) No person shall process confidential patient information under these Regulations unless he is a health professional or a person who in the circumstances owes a duty of confidentiality which is equivalent to that which would arise if that person were a health professional.

For the purposes of paragraph (2) 'health professional' has the same meaning as in section 69(1) of the Data Protection Act 1998.

8   Enforcement procedure

(1) Any person who does not comply with a requirement imposed on him under regulation 2(4) or (5), 3(4) or (5) or 7 may be subject to a civil penalty of not exceeding £5000.

(2) The Secretary of State may determine whether any person has not complied with such a requirement and he may assess whether it is appropriate to impose the maximum civil penalty, a lesser penalty or no penalty having regard to the seriousness of any non-compliance, the circumstances of any person who has not complied and the need to ensure the compliance in respect of any such future requirements.

(3) Any penalty payable under this regulation shall be recoverable by the Secretary of State as a civil debt.

Regulations 5 and 6(2)(c)   THE SCHEDULE

General provisions

Circumstances in which confidential patient information may be processed for medical purposes under regulation 5 of these Regulations.

1. The processing of confidential patient information for medical purposes with a view to making the patient in question less readily identifiable from that information.

2. The processing of confidential patient information that relates to the present or past geographical locations of patients (including where necessary information from which patients may be identified) which is required for medical research into the locations at which disease or other medical conditions may occur.

3. The processing of confidential patient information to enable the lawful holder of that information to identify and contact patients for the purpose of obtaining consent –

    (a) to participate in medical research;

    (b) to use the information for the purposes of medical research, or

    (c) to allow the use of tissue or other samples for medical purposes.

   4. The processing of confidential patient information for medical purposes from more than one source with a view to –
   (a) linking information from more than one of those sources;
   (b) validating the quality or completeness of –
      (i)   confidential patient information, or
      (ii) data derived from such information;
   (c) avoiding the impairment of the quality of data derived from confidential patient information by incorrect linkage or the unintentional inclusion of the same information more than once.
   5. The audit, monitoring and analysing of the provision made by the health service for patient care and treatment.
   6. The granting of access to confidential patient information for one or more of the above purposes.

National Health Service (General Medical Services Contracts) Regulations 2004

(SI 2004, No. 291)

PART I GENERAL

2   Interpretation

SCHEDULE 6 OTHER CONTRACTUAL TERMS

PART I GENERAL

Interpretation
   2.—(1) In these Regulations –
   'the Act' means the National Health Service Act 1977; [sic]
   'the 1990 Act' means the National Health Service and Community Care Act 1990;
   'the Board' means the National Health Service Commissioning Board;
   'Care Quality Commission' means the body established by section 1 of the Health and Social Care Act 2008;
   'CCG' means a clinical commissioning group;
   'contract' means, except where the context otherwise requires, a general medical services contract under section 28Q of the Act;
   'contractor's list of patients' means the list prepared and maintained by the Board under paragraph 14 of Schedule 6;
   'general medical practitioner' means, unless the context otherwise requires a medical practitioner whose name is included in the General Practitioner Register kept by the General Medical Council;
   'medical performers list' means the list of medical practitioners maintained and published by the Board in accordance with section 91 (persons performing primary medical services) of the 2006 Act;

Regulation 26   **SCHEDULE 6**

OTHER CONTRACTUAL TERMS

PART I PROVISION OF SERVICES

Premises
   1. Subject to any plan which is included in the contract pursuant to regulation 18(3), the contractor shall ensure that the premises used for the provision of services under the contract are –
   (a) suitable for the delivery of those services; and
   (b) sufficient to meet the reasonable needs of the contractor's patients.

Attendance at practice premises

2.—(1) The contractor shall take steps to ensure that any patient who –

(a) has not previously made an appointment; and

(b) attends at the practice premises during the normal hours for essential services, is provided with such services by an appropriate health care professional during that surgery period except in the circumstances specified in sub-paragraph (2).

(2) The circumstances referred to in sub-paragraph (1) are that –

(a) it is more appropriate for the patient to be referred elsewhere for services under the Act; or

(b) he is then offered an appointment to attend again within a time which is appropriate and reasonable having regard to all the circumstances and his health would not thereby be jeopardised.

Attendance outside practice premises

3.—(1) In the case of a patient whose medical condition is such that in the reasonable opinion of the contractor –

(a) attendance on the patient is required; and

(b) it would be inappropriate for him to attend at the practice premises, the contractor shall provide services to that patient at whichever in its judgement is the most appropriate of the places set out in sub-paragraph (2).

(2) The places referred to in sub-paragraph (1) are –

(a) the place recorded in the patient's medical records as being his last home address;

(b) such other place as the contractor has informed the patient and the Board is the place where it has agreed to visit and treat the patient; or

(c) some other place in the contractor's practice area.

(3) Nothing in this paragraph prevents the contractor from –

(a) arranging for the referral of a patient without first seeing the patient, in a case where the medical condition of that patient makes that course of action appropriate; or

(b) visiting the patient in circumstances where this paragraph does not place it under an obligation to do so.

PART II PATIENTS

List of patients

14. The Board shall prepare and keep up to date a list of the patients –

(a) who have been accepted by the contractor for inclusion in its list of patients under paragraph 15 and who have not subsequently been removed from that list under paragraphs 19 to 27; and

(b) who have been assigned to the contractor under paragraph 32 or 33 and whose assignment has not subsequently been rescinded.

Patient preference of practitioner

18. (1) Where the contractor has accepted an application for inclusion in its list of patients, it shall –

(a) notify the patient (or, in the case of a child or an adult who lacks capacity, the person who made the application on their behalf) of the patient's right to express a preference to receive services from a particular performer or class of performer either generally or in relation to any particular condition; and

(b) record in writing any such preference expressed by or on behalf of the patient.

(2) The contractor shall endeavour to comply with any reasonable preference expressed under sub-paragraph (1) but need not do so if the preferred performer –

(a) has reasonable grounds for refusing to provide services to the patient; or

(b) does not routinely perform the service in question within the practice.

PART III PRESCRIBING AND DISPENSING

Excessive prescribing

46.—(1) The contractor shall not prescribe drugs, medicines or appliances whose cost or quantity, in relation to any patient, is, by reason of the character of the drug, medicine or appliance in question in excess of that which was reasonably necessary for the proper treatment of that patient.

(2) In considering whether a contractor has breached its obligations under sub-paragraph (1) the Board must seek the views of the Local Medical Committee (if any) for the area in which the contractor provides services under the contract.

PART IV PERSONS WHO PERFORM SERVICES

Conditions for employment and engagement

60.—(1) Before employing or engaging any person to assist it in the provision of services under the contract, the contractor shall take reasonable care to satisfy itself that the person in question is both suitably qualified and competent to discharge the duties for which he is to be employed or engaged.

(2) The duty imposed by sub-paragraph (1) is in addition to the duties imposed by paragraphs 57 to 59.

(3) When considering the competence and suitability of any person for the purpose of sub-paragraph (1), the contractor shall have regard, in particular, to –
    (a) that person's academic and vocational qualifications;
    (b) his education and training; and
    (c) his previous employment or work experience.

Level of skill

67. The contractor shall carry out its obligations under the contract with reasonable care and skill.

PART V RECORDS, INFORMATION, NOTIFICATIONS AND RIGHTS OF ENTRY

Patient records

73.—(1) In this paragraph, 'computerised records' means records created by way of entries on a computer.

(2) The contractor shall keep adequate records of its attendance on and treatment of its patients and shall do so –
    (a) on forms supplied to it for the purpose by the Board; or
    (b) with the written consent of the Board, by way of computerised records, or in a combination of those two ways.

(3) The contractor shall include in the records referred to in sub-paragraph (2) clinical reports sent in accordance with paragraph 7 of this Schedule or from any other health care professional who has provided clinical services to a person on its list of patients.

(6) The contractor shall send the complete records relating to a patient to the Board –
    (a) where a person on its list dies, before the end of the period of 14 days beginning with the date on which it was informed by the Board of the death, or (in any other case) before the end of the period of one month beginning with the date on which it learned of the death; or
    (b) in any other case where the person is no longer registered with the contractor, as soon as possible at the request of the Board.

Confidentiality of personal data

75. The contractor shall nominate a person with responsibility for practices and procedures relating to the confidentiality of personal data held by it.

Practice leaflet

76. The contractor shall –

    (a) compile a document (in this paragraph called a practice leaflet) which shall include the information specified in Schedule 10;

    (b) review its practice leaflet at least once in every period of 12 months and make any amendments necessary to maintain its accuracy; and

    (c) make available a copy of the leaflet, and any subsequent updates, to its patients and prospective patients.

Friends and family test

76ZA.—(1) A contractor must give all patients who use the contractor's practice the opportunity to provide feedback about the service received from the practice through the Friends and Family Test.

    (2) The contractor must –

    (a) report the results of completed Friends and Family Tests to the Board; and

    (b) publish the results of such completed Tests,

in the manner approved by the Board.

    (3) In this paragraph, 'Friends and Family Test' means the arrangements that a contractor is required by the Board to implement to enable its patients to provide anonymous feedback about the patient experience at the contractor's practice.

Notifications to the Board

82. In addition to any requirements of notification elsewhere in the regulations, the contractor shall notify the Board in writing, as soon as reasonably practicable, of –

    (a) any serious incident that, in the reasonable opinion of the contractor, affects or is likely to affect the contractor's performance of its obligations under the contract;

    (b) any circumstances which give rise to the Board's right to terminate the contract under paragraph 111, 112 or 113(1);

    (c) any appointments system which it proposes to operate and the proposed discontinuance of any such system;

    (d) any change of which it is aware in the address of a registered patient; and

    (e) the death of any patient of which it is aware.

Notification of deaths

87.—(1) The contractor shall report in writing to the Board the death on its practice premises of any patient no later than the end of the first working day after the date on which the death occurred.

    (2) The report shall include –

    (a) the patient's full name;

    (b) the patient's National Health Service number where known;

    (c) the date and place of death;

    (d) a brief description of the circumstances, as known, surrounding the death;

    (e) the name of any medical practitioner or other person treating the patient whilst on the practice premises; and

    (f) the name, where known, of any other person who was present at the time of the death.

    (3) The contractor shall send a copy of the report referred to in sub-paragraph (1) to any other Primary Care Trust in whose area the deceased was resident at the time of his death.

PART VI COMPLAINTS

Complaints procedure

Complaints procedure

92.—(1) The contractor shall establish and operate a complaints procedure to deal with any complaints in relation to any matter reasonably connected with the provision of services under the contract.

(2) In respect of complaints made on or after 1 April 2009, the complaints procedure required by sub-paragraph (1) shall comply with the requirements of the Local Authority Social Services and National Health Service Complaints (England) Regulations 2009.

PART IX MISCELLANEOUS

Clinical governance

121.—(1) The contractor shall have an effective system of clinical governance which shall include appropriate standard operating procedures in relation to the management and use of controlled drugs.

(2) The contractor shall nominate a person who will have responsibility for ensuring the effective operation of the system of clinical governance.

(3) The person nominated under sub-paragraph (2) shall be a person who performs or manages services under the contract.

(4) In this paragraph 'system of clinical governance' means a framework through which the contractor endeavours continuously to improve the quality of its services and safeguard high standards of care by creating an environment in which clinical excellence can flourish.

Medicines for Human Use (Clinical Trials) Regulations 2004

(SI 2004, No. 1031)

PART I INTRODUCTORY PROVISIONS

Interpretation

2.—(1) In these Regulations –

'the 2012 Regulations' means the Human Medicines Regulations 2012;

'the Act' means the Medicines Act 1968;

'adult' means a person who has attained the age of 16 years;

'adverse event' means any untoward medical occurrence in a subject to whom a medicinal product has been administered, including occurrences which are not necessarily caused by or related to that product;

'adverse reaction' means any untoward and unintended response in a subject to an investigational medicinal product which is related to any dose administered to that subject;

'chief investigator' means –

(a) in relation to a clinical trial conducted at a single trial site, the investigator for that site, or

(b) in relation to a clinical trial conducted at more than one trial site, the authorised health professional, whether or not he is an investigator at any particular site, who takes primary responsibility for the conduct of the trial;

'clinical trial' means any investigation in human subjects, other than a non-interventional trial, intended –

(a) to discover or verify the clinical, pharmacological or other pharmacodynamic effects of one or more medicinal products,

(b) to identify any adverse reactions to one or more such products, or

(c) to study absorption, distribution, metabolism and excretion of one or more such products, with the object of ascertaining the safety or efficacy of those products;

'Commission Directive 2003/94/EC' means Commission Directive 2003/94/EC laying down the principles and guidelines of good manufacturing practice for medicinal products for human use and for investigational medicinal products for human use;

'the Commission on Human Medicines' means the Commission on Human Medicines within the meaning of regulation 9 of the 2012 Regulations;

'conditions and principles of good clinical practice' means the conditions and principles specified in Schedule 1;

'conducting a clinical trial' includes –

(a) administering, or giving directions for the administration of, an investigational medicinal product to a subject for the purposes of that trial,

(b) giving a prescription for an investigational medicinal product for the purposes of that trial,

(c) carrying out any other medical or nursing procedure in relation to that trial, and

(d) carrying out any test or analysis –

(i)   to discover or verify the clinical, pharmacological or other pharmacodynamic effects of the investigational medicinal products administered in the course of the trial,

(ii) to identify any adverse reactions to those products, or

(iii) to study absorption, distribution, metabolism and excretion of those products, but does not include any activity undertaken prior to the commencement of the trial which consists of making such preparations for the trial as are necessary or expedient;

'the Directive' means Directive 2001/20/EC of the European Parliament and of the Council on the approximation of the laws, regulations and administrative provisions of the Member States relating to the implementation of good clinical practice in the conduct of clinical trials on medicinal products for human use;

'Directive 2001/83/EC' means Directive 2001/83/EC of the European Parliament and of the Council on the Community code relating to medicinal products for human use, as amended;

'the European Medicines Agency' means the European Agency for the Evaluation of Medicinal Products established by Council Regulation (EEC) No. 2309/93 laying down Community procedures for the authorisation and supervision of medicinal products for human and veterinary use and establishing a European Agency for the Evaluation of Medicinal Products;

'ethics committee' means –

(a) a committee established or recognised in accordance with Part 2,

(b) the Ethics Committee constituted by regulations made by the Scottish Ministers under section 51(6) of the Adults with Incapacity (Scotland) Act 2000, or

(c) the Gene Therapy Advisory Committee;

'the GCP Directive' means Commission Directive 2005/28/EC laying down principles and detailed guidelines for good clinical practice as regards investigational medicinal products for human use, as well as the requirements for authorisation of the manufacturing or importation of such products;

'the Gene Therapy Advisory Committee' means the Gene Therapy Advisory Committee appointed by the Secretary of State to –

(a) consider and advise on the acceptability of proposals for gene therapy research on human subjects, on ethical grounds, and

(b) provide advice on developments in gene therapy research and their implications;

'health care' means services for or in connection with the prevention, diagnosis or treatment of illness;

'informed consent' shall be construed in accordance with paragraph 3 of Part 1 of Schedule 1;

'investigational medicinal product' means a pharmaceutical form of an active substance or placebo being tested, or to be tested, or used, or to be used, as a reference in a clinical trial, and includes a medicinal product which has a marketing authorisation but is, for the purposes of the trial –

(a) used or assembled (formulated or packaged) in a way different from the form of the product authorised under the authorisation,

(b) used for an indication not included in the summary of product characteristics under the authorisation for that product, or

(c) used to gain further information about the form of that product as authorised under the authorisation;

'investigator' means, in relation to a clinical trial, the authorised health professional responsible for the conduct of that trial at a trial site, and if the trial is conducted by a team of authorised health professionals at a trial site, the investigator is the leader responsible for that team;

'licensing authority' shall be construed in accordance with regulation 6 of the 2012 Regulations;

'medicinal product' means a medicinal product within the meaning of regulation 2(1) of the 2012 Regulations;

'minor' means a person under the age of 16 years;

'non-interventional trial' means a study of one or more medicinal products which have a marketing authorisation, where the following conditions are met –

(a) the products are prescribed in the usual manner in accordance with the terms of that authorisation,

(b) the assignment of any patient involved in the study to a particular therapeutic strategy is not decided in advance by a protocol but falls within current practice,

(c) the decision to prescribe a particular medicinal product is clearly separated from the decision to include the patient in the study,

(d) no diagnostic or monitoring procedures are applied to the patients included in the study, other than those which are ordinarily applied in the course of the particular therapeutic strategy in question, and

(e) epidemiological methods are to be used for the analysis of the data arising from the study; 'Phase I trial' means a clinical trial to study the pharmacology of an investigational medicinal product when administered to humans, where the sponsor and investigator have no knowledge of any evidence that the product has effects likely to be beneficial to the subjects of the trial;

'the principles and guidelines of good manufacturing practice' means the principles and guidelines of good manufacturing practice set out in Commission Directive 2003/94/EC;

'protocol' means a document that describes the objectives, design, methodology, statistical considerations and organisation of a clinical trial;

'serious adverse event', 'serious adverse reaction' or 'unexpected serious adverse reaction' means any adverse event, adverse reaction or unexpected adverse reaction, respectively, that –

    (a) results in death,

    (b) is life-threatening,

    (c) requires hospitalisation or prolongation of existing hospitalisation,

    (d) results in persistent or significant disability or incapacity, or

    (a) consists of a congenital anomaly or birth defect;

'sponsor' shall be construed in accordance with regulation 3;

'subject' means, in relation to a clinical trial, an individual, whether a patient or not, who participates in a clinical trial –

    (a) as a recipient of an investigational medicinal product or of some other treatment or product, or

    (b) without receiving any treatment or product, as a control;

'third country' means a country or territory outside the European Economic Area;

'trial site' means a hospital, health centre, surgery or other establishment or facility at or from which a clinical trial, or any part of such a trial, is conducted;

'unexpected adverse reaction' means an adverse reaction the nature and severity of which is not consistent with the information about the medicinal product in question set out –

    (a) in the case of a product with a marketing authorization, in the summary of product characteristics for that product,

    (b) in the case of any other investigational medicinal product, in the investigator's brochure relating to the trial in question.

Sponsor of a clinical trial

3.—(1) In these Regulations, subject to the following paragraphs, 'sponsor' means, in relation to a clinical trial, the person who takes responsibility for the initiation, management and financing (or arranging the financing) of that trial.

    (11) A person who is a sponsor of a clinical trial in accordance with this regulation must –

    (a) be established in an EEA State, or

    (b) have a legal representative who is so established.

PART II ETHICS COMMITTEES

United Kingdom Ethics Committees Authority

5.—(1) The body responsible for establishing, recognising and monitoring ethics committees in the United Kingdom in accordance with these Regulations is the United Kingdom Ethics Committees Authority, which is a body consisting of –

    (a) the Health Research Authority;

    (b) the National Assembly for Wales;

    (c) the Scottish Ministers; and

    (d) the Department for Health, Social Services and Public Safety for Northern Ireland.

Establishment of ethics committees

6.—(1) The Authority may establish ethics committees to act –

    (a) for the entire United Kingdom or for such areas of the United Kingdom; and

(b) in relation to such descriptions or classes of clinical trials, as the Authority consider appropriate.

PART III AUTHORISATION FOR CLINICAL TRIALS AND ETHICS COMMITTEE OPINION

Requirement for authorisation and ethics committee opinion

12.—(1) No person shall –
(a) start a clinical trial or cause a clinical trial to be started; or
(b) conduct a clinical trial,
unless the conditions specified in paragraph (3) are satisfied.

(2) No person shall –
(a) recruit an individual to be a subject in a trial;
(b) issue an advertisement for the purpose of recruiting individuals to be subjects in a trial, unless the condition specified in paragraph (3)(a) has been satisfied.

(3) The conditions referred to in paragraphs (1) and (2) are –
(a) an ethics committee to which an application in relation to the trial may be made in accordance with regulation 14 or an appeal panel appointed under Schedule 4 has given a favourable opinion in relation to the clinical trial; and
(b) the clinical trial has been authorised by the licensing authority.

Application for ethics committee opinion

14.—(1) An application for an ethics committee opinion in relation to a clinical trial shall be made by the chief investigator for that trial.

(2) A chief investigator for a trial shall make an application for an ethics committee opinion in relation to that trial to one ethics committee only, regardless of the number of trial sites at which the trial is to be conducted.

(5) An application for an ethics committee opinion in relation to a clinical trial involving medicinal products for gene therapy, other than a trial falling within paragraph (4), shall be made to the Gene Therapy Advisory Committee.

Ethics committee opinion

15.—(1) Except as provided for in paragraph (4A) (which removes the requirement on the Gene Therapy Advisory Committee to give an opinion) and subject to paragraphs (3) and (4) (which suspend and disapply time limits respectively), an ethics committee shall give an opinion in relation to the clinical trial to which a valid application relates within the specified period beginning with the date of receipt of the valid application.

(2) Where following receipt of a valid application it appears to the committee that further information is required in order to give an opinion on a trial, the committee may, within the specified period and before giving its opinion, send a notice in writing to the applicant requesting that he furnishes the committee with that information.

(5) In preparing its opinion, the committee shall consider, in particular, the following matters –
(a) the relevance of the clinical trial and its design;
(b) whether the evaluation of the anticipated benefits and risks as required under paragraph 10 of Part 2 of Schedule 1 is satisfactory and whether the conclusions are justified;
(c) the protocol;
(d) the suitability of the investigator and supporting staff;
(e) the investigator's brochure or, where the investigational medicinal product has a marketing authorization and the product is to be used in accordance with the terms of that authorization, the summary of product characteristics relating to that product;
(f) the quality of the facilities for the trial;

(g)   the adequacy and completeness of the written information to be given, and the procedure to be followed, for the purpose of obtaining informed consent to the subjects' participation in the trial;

(h)   if the subjects are to include minors or persons incapable of giving informed consent, whether the research is justified having regard to the conditions and principles specified in Part 4 or Part 5 respectively of Schedule 1;

(i)   provision for indemnity or compensation in the event of injury or death attributable to the clinical trial;

(j)   any insurance or indemnity to cover the liability of the investigator or sponsor;

(k)   the amounts, and, where appropriate, the arrangements, for rewarding or compensating investigators and subjects;

(l)   the terms of any agreement between the sponsor and the owner or occupier of the trial site which are relevant to the arrangements referred to in sub-paragraph (k); and

(m)   the arrangements for the recruitment of subjects.

(6) If –

(a) any subject of the clinical trial is to be a minor; and

(b) the committee does not have a member with professional expertise in paediatric care, it shall, before giving its opinion, obtain advice on the clinical, ethical and psychosocial problems in the field of paediatric care which may arise in relation to that trial.

(7) If –

(a) any subject to the clinical trial is to be an adult incapable by reason of physical and mental incapacity to give informed consent to participation in the trial; and

(b) the committee does not have a member with professional expertise in the treatment of –

    (i)   the disease to which the trial relates, and

    (ii)   the patient population suffering that disease,

it shall, before giving its opinion, obtain advice on the clinical, ethical and pyschosocial problems in the field of that disease and patient population which may arise in relation to that trial.

(10)   In this regulation –

'the specified period' means –

(a) in the case of a clinical trial involving a medicinal product for gene therapy or somatic cell therapy or a medicinal product containing a genetically modified organism or a tissue engineered product –

    (i)   where a specialist group or committee is consulted, 180 days, or

    (ii)   where there is no such consultation, 90 days; or

(b) in any other case, 60 days.

'specialist group or committee' means a group or committee whose functions include the pro-vision of advice on ethical or scientific issues in relation to –

(a) tissue engineered products;

(b) in the case of medicinal products for gene therapy or somatic cell therapy, the use of such therapies in the treatment of humans; or

(c) in the case of medicinal products containing genetically modified organisms, the administration of such products to humans.

Review and appeal relating to ethics committee opinion

16.—(1) This regulation applies where a chief investigator for a trial has been notified by the ethics committee to which he made an application in accordance with regulation 14 that the committee's opinion in relation to that trial is not favourable.

(3) Where the opinion was given by an ethics committee other than the Gene Therapy Advisory Committee, the chief investigator may within 90 days of being notified that the committee's opinion is not favourable, give a notice to the United Kingdom Ethics Committees Authority –

(a) stating his wish to appeal against the opinion; and

(b) setting out his representations with respect to that opinion.

(4) Where the opinion was given by the Gene Therapy Advisory Committee, the chief investigator may, within 14 days of being notified of that opinion –

(a) give a notice in writing to the Committee requiring the Committee to review its opinion; or

(b) give a notice in writing to the United Kingdom Ethics Committee Authority –

(i)   stating his wish to appeal against the opinion; and

(ii)   setting out his representations with respect to that opinion.

(5) Where the Gene Therapy Advisory Committee is required by a notice under paragraph (4) to review its opinion, it must do so within 60 days of receipt of the notice.

(6) On a review pursuant to paragraph (5), the Gene Therapy Advisory Committee may vary or confirm their opinion and shall give notice in writing to the chief investigator of the variation or confirmation.

(7) If the Gene Therapy Advisory Committee confirm their opinion pursuant to paragraph (6), a chief investigator may within the 14 days of being notified of the confirmation give notice in writing to the United Kingdom Ethics Committees Authority –

(a) stating his wish to appeal against the Committee's opinion; and

(b) setting out his representations with respect to that opinion.

Request for authorisation to conduct a clinical trial

17.—(1)   A request for authorisation to conduct a clinical trial shall be made to the licensing authority by the sponsor of the trial.

PART IV GOOD CLINICAL PRACTICE AND THE CONDUCT OF CLINICAL TRIALS

Good clinical practice and protection of clinical trial subjects

28.—(1) No person shall –

(a) conduct a clinical trial; or

(b) perform the functions of the sponsor of a clinical trial (whether that person is the sponsor or is acting under arrangements made with that sponsor),

otherwise than in accordance with the conditions and principles of good clinical practice.

(2) Subject to paragraph (5), the sponsor of a clinical trial shall put and keep in place arrangements for the purpose of ensuring that with regard to that trial the conditions and principles of good clinical practice are satisfied or adhered to.

(3) Subject to paragraphs (4) and (5), the sponsor of a clinical trial shall ensure that –

(a) the investigational medicinal products used in the trial, and

(b) any devices used for the administration of such products, are made available to the subjects of the trial free of charge.

Conduct of trial in accordance with clinical trial authorisation etc.

29. Subject to regulation 30, no person shall conduct a clinical trial otherwise than in accordance with –

(a) the protocol relating to that trial, as may be amended from time to time in accordance with regulations 22 to 25;

(b) the terms of –

(i)   the request for authorisation to conduct that trial,

(ii)   the application for an ethics committee opinion in relation to that trial, and

(iii) any particulars or documents, other than the protocol, accompanying that request or that application, as may be amended from time to time in accordance with regulations 22 to 25; and

(c) any conditions imposed by the licensing authority under regulation 18(2) or (6), 19(8), 20(5), 24 (5) or Schedule 5.

Notification of serious breaches

29A.—(1) The sponsor of a clinical trial shall notify the licensing authority in writing of any serious breach of –

    (a) the conditions and principles of good clinical practice in connection with that trial; or

    (b) the protocol relating to that trial, as amended from time to time in accordance with regulations 22 to 25, within 7 days of becoming aware of that breach.

(2) For the purposes of this regulation, a 'serious breach' is a breach which is likely to effect to a significant degree –

    (a) the safety or physical or mental integrity of the subjects of the trial; or

    (b) the scientific value of the trial.

Urgent safety measures

30.—(1) The sponsor and investigator may take appropriate urgent safety measures in order to protect the subjects of a clinical trial against any immediate hazard to their health or safety.

(2) If measures are taken pursuant to paragraph (1), the sponsor shall –

    (a) where paragraph (3) applies, as soon as possible; and

    (b) in any other case, immediately, and in any event no later than 3 days from the date the measures are taken,

give written notice to the licensing authority and the relevant ethics committee of the measures taken and the circumstances giving rise to those measures.

Suspension or termination of clinical trial

31.—(1) If, in relation to a clinical trial –

    (a) the licensing authority have objective grounds for considering that –

        (i) any condition, restriction or limitation which applies to the conduct of the trial and is set out in the request for authorisation or the particulars or documents accompanying that request, or

        (ii) any condition imposed by the licensing authority under regulation 18(2) or (6), 19 (8), 20(5), 24 (5) or Schedule 5, is no longer satisfied (either generally or at a particular trial site); or

    (b) the licensing authority have information raising doubts about the safety or scientific validity of the trial, or the conduct of the trial at a particular trial site, the licensing authority may, by a notice served in accordance with paragraph (2), require that the trial, or the conduct of the trial at a particular trial site, be suspended or terminated.

PART V PHARMACOVIGILANCE

Notification of adverse events

32.—(1) An investigator shall report any serious adverse event which occurs in a subject at a trial site at which he is responsible for the conduct of a clinical trial immediately to the sponsor.

(2) An immediate report under paragraph (1) may be made orally or in writing.

(3) Following the immediate report of a serious adverse event, the investigator shall make a detailed written report on the event.

Notification of suspected unexpected serious adverse reactions

33.—(1) A sponsor shall ensure that all relevant information about a suspected unexpected serious adverse reaction which occurs during the course of a clinical trial in the United Kingdom and is fatal or life-threatening is –

    (a) recorded; and

    (b) reported as soon as possible to –

        (i)   the licensing authority,

(ii) the competent authorities of any EEA State, other than the United Kingdom, in which the trial is being conducted, and

(iii) the relevant ethics committee,

and in any event not later that 7 days after the sponsor was first aware of the reaction.

(5) A sponsor shall ensure that, in relation to each clinical trial in the United Kingdom for which he is the sponsor, the investigators responsible for the conduct of a trial are informed of any suspected unexpected serious adverse reaction which occurs in relation to an investigational medicinal product used in that trial, whether that reaction occurs during the course of that trial or another trial for which the sponsor is responsible.

Clinical trials conducted in third countries

34. If a clinical trial is being conducted at a trial site in a third country in addition to sites in the United Kingdom, the sponsor of that trial shall ensure that all suspected unexpected serious adverse reactions occurring at that site are entered into the European database established in accordance with Article 11 of the Directive.

Annual list of suspected serious adverse reactions and safety report

35.—(1) As soon as practicable after the end of the reporting year, a sponsor shall, in relation to each investigational medicinal product tested in clinical trials in the United Kingdom for which he is the sponsor furnish the licensing authority and the relevant ethics committees with –

(a) a list of all the suspected serious adverse reactions which have occurred during that year in relation to –

(i) those trials, whether at trial sites in the United Kingdom or elsewhere, or

(ii) any other trials relating to that product which are conducted outside the United Kingdom and for which he is the sponsor, including those reactions relating to any investigational medicinal product used as a placebo or as a reference in those trials; and

(b) a report on the safety of the subjects of those trials.

PART VIII ENFORCEMENT AND RELATED PROVISIONS

Offences

49.—(1) Any person who contravenes any of the following provisions –

(a)   regulation 3A;

(aa) regulation 12(1) and (2);

(b)   regulation 13(1);

(c)   regulation 27;

(d)   regulation 28(1) to (3);

(e)   regulation 29;

(ee) regulation 29A;

(f)   regulation 30(2);

(ff) regulation 31A(1) to (3) and (5) to (10);

(g)   regulation 32(1), (3), and (5) to (9);

(h)   regulation 33(1) to (5);

(i)   regulation 34;

(j)   regulation 35(1);

(k)   regulation 36(1);

(l)   regulation 42; and

(m)   regulation 43(1) and (6), shall be guilty of an offence.

False or misleading information

50.—(1) Any person who in the course of –

    (a) making an application for an ethics committee opinion;

    (b) making a request for authorisation to conduct a clinical trial; or

    (c) making an application for the grant or variation of a manufacturing authorisation,

provides to the licensing authority or an ethics committee any relevant information which is false or misleading in a material particular shall be guilty of an offence.

    (2) Any person who –

    (a) is conducting a clinical trial authorised in accordance with these Regulations;

    (b) is a sponsor of such a clinical trial;

    (c) while acting under arrangements made with a sponsor of such a clinical trial, performs the functions of that sponsor; or

    (d) holds a manufacturing authorisation,

and who, for the purposes of these Regulations, provides to the licensing authority or an ethics committee any relevant information which is false or misleading in a material particular shall be guilty of an offence.

    (4) In this regulation, 'relevant information' means any information which is relevant to an evaluation of –

    (a) the safety, quality or efficacy of an investigational medicinal product;

    (b) the safety or scientific validity of a clinical trial; or

    (c) whether, with regard to a clinical trial, the conditions and principles of good clinical practice are being satisfied or adhered to.

Defence of due diligence

51.—(1) A person does not commit an offence under these Regulations if he took all reasonable precautions and exercised all due diligence to avoid the commission of that offence.

    (2) Where evidence is adduced which is sufficient to raise an issue with respect to that defence, the court or jury shall assume that the defence is satisfied unless the prosecution proves beyond reasonable doubt that it is not.

Penalties

52. A person guilty of an offence under these Regulations shall be liable –

    (a) on summary conviction to a fine not exceeding the statutory maximum or to imprisonment for a term not exceeding three months or to both;

    (b) on conviction on indictment to a fine or to imprisonment for a term not exceeding two years or to both.

Regulation 2(1)   ## SCHEDULE 1

CONDITIONS AND PRINCIPLES OF GOOD CLINICAL PRACTICE AND THE PROTECTION OF CLINICAL TRIAL SUBJECTS

PART I APPLICATION AND INTERPRETATION

1.—(1) The conditions and principles specified in Part 2 apply to all clinical trials.

    (2) If any subject of a clinical trial is –

    (a) an adult able to give informed consent, or

    (b) an adult who has given informed consent to taking part in the clinical trial prior to the onset of incapacity, the conditions and principles specified in Part 3 apply in relation to that subject.

(3) Subject to sub-paragraphs (6) and (7), if any subject of a clinical trial is a minor, the conditions and principles specified in Part 4 apply in relation to that subject.

(4) Subject to sub-paragraphs (6) and (7), if any subject –

(a) is an adult unable by virtue of physical or mental incapacity to give informed consent, and

(b) did not, prior to the onset of incapacity, give or refuse to give informed consent to taking part in the clinical trial, the conditions and principles specified in Part 5 apply in relation to that subject.

(5) If any person –

(a) is an adult unable by virtue of physical or mental incapacity to give informed consent, and

(b) has, prior to the onset of incapacity, refused to give informed consent to taking part in the clinical trial, that person cannot be included as a subject in the clinical trial.

(6) Sub-paragraph (7) applies if treatment is being, or is about to be, provided for a subject who is a minor or an incapacitated adult as a matter of urgency and, having regard to the nature of the clinical trial and of the particular circumstances of the case –

(a) it is also necessary to take action for the purposes of the clinical trial as a matter of urgency; but

(b) it is not reasonably practicable to meet the conditions set out in paragraphs 1 to 5 of Part 4 in the case of a minor or paragraphs 1 to 5 of Part 5 in the case of an incapacitated adult.

(7) Where this sub-paragraph applies, paragraphs 1 to 5 of Part 4 in the case of a minor or paragraphs 1 to 5 of Part 5 in the case of an incapacitated adult shall not apply in relation to the subject if the action specified in sub-paragraph (6) is carried out in accordance with a procedure approved by an ethics committee or by an appeal panel appointed under Schedule 4 at the time it gave its favourable opinion.

3.—(1) For the purposes of this Schedule, a person gives informed consent to take part, or that a subject is to take part, in a clinical trial only if his decision –

(c) is given freely after that person is informed of the nature, significance, implications and risks of the trial; and

(d) either –

(i)   is evidenced in writing, dated and signed, or otherwise marked, by that person so as to indicate his consent, or

(ii) if the person is unable to sign or to mark a document so as to indicate his consent, is given orally in the presence of at least one witness and recorded in writing.

(2) For the purposes of this Schedule, references to informed consent –

(a) shall be construed in accordance with paragraph (1); and

(b) include references to informed consent given or refused by an adult unable by virtue of physical or mental incapacity to give informed consent, prior to the onset of that incapacity.

PART 2 CONDITIONS AND PRINCIPLES WHICH APPLY TO ALL CLINICAL TRIALS

Principles based on Articles 2 to 5 of the GCP Directive

1. The rights, safety and well-being of the trial subjects shall prevail over the interests of science and society.

2. Each individual involved in conducting a trial shall be qualified by education, training and experience to perform his tasks.

3. Clinical trials shall be scientifically sound and guided by ethical principles in all their aspects.

4. The necessary procedures to secure the quality of every aspect of the trial shall be complied with.

5. The available non-clinical and clinical information on an investigational medicinal product shall be adequate to support the proposed clinical trial.

6. Clinical trials shall be conducted in accordance with the principles of the Declaration of Helsinki.

7. The protocol shall provide for the definition of inclusion and exclusion of subjects participating in a clinical trial, monitoring and publication policy.

8. The investigator and sponsor shall consider all relevant guidance with respect to commencing and conducting a clinical trial.

9. All clinical information shall be recorded, handled and stored in such a way that it can be accurately reported, interpreted and verified, while the confidentiality of records of the trial subjects remains protected.

Conditions based on Article 3 of the Directive

10. Before the trial is initiated, foreseeable risks and inconveniences have been weighed against the anticipated benefit for the individual trial subject and other present and future patients. A trial should be initiated and continued only if the anticipated benefits justify the risks.

11. The medical care given to, and medical decisions made on behalf of, subjects shall always be the responsibility of an appropriately qualified doctor or, when appropriate, of a qualified dentist.

12. A trial shall be initiated only if an ethics committee and the licensing authority comes to the conclusion that the anticipated therapeutic and public health benefits justify the risks and may be continued only if compliance with this requirement is permanently monitored.

13. The rights of each subject to physical and mental integrity, to privacy and to the protection of the data concerning him in accordance with the Data Protection Act 1998 are safeguarded.

14. Provision has been made for insurance or indemnity to cover the liability of the investigator and sponsor which may arise in relation to the clinical trial.

PART 3 CONDITIONS WHICH APPLY IN RELATION TO AN ADULT ABLE TO CONSENT OR WHO HAS GIVEN CONSENT PRIOR TO THE ONSET OF INCAPACITY

1. The subject has had an interview with the investigator, or another member of the investigating team, in which he has been given the opportunity to understand the objectives, risks and inconveniences of the trial and the conditions under which it is to be conducted.

2. The subject has been informed of his right to withdraw from the trial at any time.

3. The subject has given his informed consent to taking part in the trial.

4. The subject may, without being subject to any resulting detriment, withdraw from the clinical trial at any time by revoking his informed consent.

5. The subject has been provided with a contact point where he may obtain further information about the trial.

PART 4 CONDITIONS AND PRINCIPLES WHICH APPLY IN RELATION TO A MINOR

Conditions

1. A person with parental responsibility for the minor or, if by reason of the emergency nature of the treatment provided as part of the trial no such person can be contacted prior to the proposed inclusion of the subject in the trial, a legal representative for the minor has had an interview with the investigator, or another member of the investigating team, in which he has been given the opportunity to understand the objectives, risks and inconveniences of the trial and the conditions under which it is to be conducted.

2. That person or legal representative has been provided with a contact point where he may obtain further information about the trial.

3. That person or legal representative has been informed of the right to withdraw the minor from the trial at any time.

4. That person or legal representative has given his informed consent to the minor taking part in the trial.

5. That person with parental responsibility or the legal representative may, without the minor being subject to any resulting detriment, withdraw the minor from the trial at any time by revoking his informed consent.

6. The minor has received information according to his capacity of understanding, from staff with experience with minors, regarding the trial, its risks and its benefits.

7. The explicit wish of a minor who is capable of forming an opinion and assessing the information referred to in the previous paragraph to refuse participation in, or to be withdrawn from, the clinical trial at any time is considered by the investigator.

8. No incentives or financial inducements are given –
  (a) to the minor; or
  (b) to a person with parental responsibility for that minor or, as the case may be, the minor's legal representative, except provision for compensation in the event of injury or loss.

9. The clinical trial relates directly to a clinical condition from which the minor suffers or is of such a nature that it can only be carried out on minors.

10. Some direct benefit for the group of patients involved in the clinical trial is to be obtained from that trial.

11. The clinical trial is necessary to validate data obtained –
  (a) in other clinical trials involving persons able to give informed consent, or
  (b) by other research methods.

12. The corresponding scientific guidelines of the European Medicines Agency are followed.

Principles

13. Informed consent given by a person with parental responsibility or a legal representative to a minor taking part in a clinical trial shall represent the minor's presumed will.

14. The clinical trial has been designed to minimise pain, discomfort, fear and any other foreseeable risk in relation to the disease and the minor's stage of development.

15. The risk threshold and the degree of distress have to be specially defined and constantly monitored.

16. The interests of the patient always prevail over those of science and society.

PART 5 CONDITIONS AND PRINCIPLES WHICH APPLY IN RELATION TO AN INCAPACITATED ADULT

Conditions

1. The subject's legal representative has had an interview with the investigator, or another member of the investigating team, in which he has been given the opportunity to understand the objectives, risks and inconveniences of the trial and the conditions under which it is to be conducted.

2. The legal representative has been provided with a contact point where he may obtain further information about the trial.

3. The legal representative has been informed of the right to withdraw the subject from the trial at any time.

4. The legal representative has given his informed consent to the subject taking part in the trial.

5. The legal representative may, without the subject being subject to any resulting detriment, withdraw the subject from the trial at any time by revoking his informed consent.

6. The subject has received information according to his capacity of understanding regarding the trial, its risks and its benefits.

7. The explicit wish of a subject who is capable of forming an opinion and assessing the information referred to in the previous paragraph to refuse participation in, or to be withdrawn from, the clinical trial at any time is considered by the investigator.

8. No incentives or financial inducements are given to the subject or their legal representative, except provision for compensation in the event of injury or loss.

9. There are grounds for expecting that administering the medicinal product to be tested in the trial will produce a benefit to the subject outweighing the risks or produce no risk at all.

10. The clinical trial is essential to validate data obtained –
   (a) in other clinical trials involving persons able to give informed consent, or
   (b) by other research methods.

11. The clinical trial relates directly to a life-threatening or debilitating clinical condition from which the subject suffers.

Principles

12. Informed consent given by a legal representative to an incapacitated adult in a clinical trial shall represent that adult's presumed will.

13. The clinical trial has been designed to minimise pain, discomfort, fear and any other foreseeable risk in relation to the disease and the cognitive abilities of the patient.

14. The risk threshold and the degree of distress have to be specially defined and constantly monitored.

15. The interests of the patient always prevail over those of science and society.

Regulations 7(1)(b), 8(a) and 9   **SCHEDULE 2**

ADDITIONAL PROVISIONS RELATING TO ETHICS COMMITTEES

Interpretation

In this Schedule –

1. 'expert member' means a member of an ethics committee who –
   (a) is a health care professional,
   (b) has professional qualifications or experience relating to the conduct of, or use of statistics in clinical research, unless those professional qualifications or experience relate only to the ethics of clinical research or medical treatment, or
   (c) is not a health care professional, but has been a registered medical practitioner or a person registered in the dentists register under the Dentists Act 1984;

'lay member' means a member of an ethics committee, other than an expert member.

Membership

3.—(1) An ethics committee shall consist of –
   (a) expert members; and
   (b) lay members.

   (2) An ethics committee shall have no more than 18 members.

   (3) The members of an ethics committee shall be appointed by the appointing authority.

   (4) A person shall not be eligible for appointment as a lay member of an ethics committee if, in the course of his employment or business, he –
   (a) provides medical, dental or nursing care, or
   (b) conducts clinical research.

(5) An appointing authority shall, in relation to an ethics committee, exercise their power under sub-paragraph (3) so as to ensure that –

    (a) at least one third of the total membership shall be lay members; and

    (b) at least half of the lay members must be persons who are not, or who never have been –

        (i)   health care professionals,

        (ii) persons involved in the conduct of clinical research, other than as a subject of such research, or

        (iii) a chairman, member or director of –

            (aa) a health service body, or

            (bb) a body, other than a health service body, which provides health care.

Human Fertilisation and Embryology Authority (Disclosure of Donor Information) Regulations 2004

(SI 2004, No. 1511)

Citation, commencement and interpretation

1.—(2) In these Regulations –

'the Act' means the Human Fertilisation and Embryology Act 1990;

'applicant' means a person who has requested information under section 31ZA of the Act;

'donor' means the person who has provided the sperm, eggs or embryos that have been used for treatment services in consequence of which the applicant was, or may have been, born.

Information that the Authority is required to give

2.—(1) Subject to paragraphs 3(A) and (4), the information contained in the register which the Authority is required to give an applicant by virtue of section 31ZA(2)(a) of the Act is any information to which paragraph (2) or (3) applies.

(2) This paragraph applies to information as to –

    (a) the sex, height, weight, ethnic group, eye colour, hair colour, skin colour, year of birth, country of birth and marital status of the donor;

    (b) whether the donor was adopted;

    (c) the ethnic group or groups of the donor's parents;

    (d) the screening tests carried out on the donor and information on his personal and family medical history;

    (e) where the donor has a child, the sex of that child and where the donor has children, the number of those children and the sex of each of them;

    (f) the donor's religion, occupation, interests and skills and why the donor provided sperm, eggs or embryos;

    (g) matters contained in any description of himself as a person which the donor has provided;

    (h) any additional matter which the donor has provided with the intention that it be made available to an applicant;

but does not include information which may identify the donor by itself or in combination with any other information which is in, or is likely to come into, the possession of the applicant.

(3) This paragraph applies to information from which the donor may be identified which he provides after 31st March 2005 to a person to whom a licence applies, being information as to –

    (a) any matter specified in sub-paragraphs (a) to (h) of paragraph (2);

    (b) the surname and each forename of the donor and, if different, the surname and each forename of the donor used for the registration of his birth;

    (c) the date of birth of the donor and the town or district in which he was born;

     (d) the appearance of the donor;

     (e) the last known postal address of the donor.

  (3A) Where a request is made under section 31ZA(2)(a) of the Act and the applicant has not attained the age of 18 when the applicant gives notice to the Authority under section 31ZA(1) of the Act, the information that the Authority is required to give the applicant is the information to which paragraph (2) applies (and accordingly not information from which the donor may be identified).

  (4) The information which the Authority is required to give to the applicant does not include any information which at the time of his request the applicant indicates that he does not wish to receive.

Human Tissue Act 2004 (Persons who Lack Capacity to Consent and Transplants) Regulations 2006

(SI 2006, No. 1659)

PART 1 PRELIMINARY

Interpretation

    2. In these Regulations –

'the Act' means the Human Tissue Act 2004;

'the Authority' means the Human Tissue Authority;

'the clinical trials regulations' means –

     (a) the Medicines for Human Use (Clinical Trials) Regulations 2004 and any other regulations replacing those regulations or amending them, and

     (b) any other regulations relating to clinical trials and designated by the Secretary of State as clinical trials regulations for the purposes of section 30(5) of the Mental Capacity Act 2005 (research);

'donor' and 'recipient' have the meaning given by regulation 11;

'intrusive research' means research of a kind that would be unlawful if it was carried out

     (a) on or in relation to a person who had capacity to consent to it, but

     (b) without his consent;

'organ' means a differentiated part of the human body, formed by different tissues, that maintains its structure, vascularisation and capacity to develop physiological functions with a significant level of autonomy, and part of an organ is also considered to be an organ if its function is to be used for the same purpose as the entire organ in the human body, maintaining the requirement of structure and vascularisation;

'transplantable material' has the meaning given by –

     (a) regulation 9 for the purposes of section 34 of the Act (information about transplant operations), and

     (b) regulation 10 for the purposes of section 33 of the Act (restrictions on transplants involving a live donor).

PART 2 PERSONS WHO LACK CAPACITY TO CONSENT

Storage and use of relevant material

Deemed consent to storage and use of relevant material: England and Wales

    3.—(1) This regulation applies in any case falling within paragraphs (a) and (b) of section 6 of the Act (storage and use involving material from adults who lack capacity to consent).

(2) An adult ('P') who lacks capacity to consent to an activity of a kind mentioned in section 1(1) (d) or (f) of the Act (storage or use of material for purposes specified in Schedule 1) which involves material from P's body, is deemed to have consented to the activity where –

    (a) the activity is done for a purpose specified in paragraph 4 or 7 of Part 1 of Schedule 1 to the Act (the purposes of obtaining information relevant to another person and of transplantation) by a person who is acting in what he reasonably believes to be P's best interests;

    (b) the activity is done for the purpose of a clinical trial which is authorised and conducted in accordance with the clinical trials regulations;

    (c) the activity is done on or after the relevant commencement date for the purpose of intrusive research which is carried out in accordance with the requirements of section 30(1) (a) and (b) of the Mental Capacity Act 2005 (approval by appropriate body and compliance with sections 32 and 33 of that Act);

    (d) the activity is done on or after the relevant commencement date for the purpose of intrusive research –

        (i) section 34 of the Mental Capacity Act 2005 (loss of capacity during research project) applies in relation to that research, and

        (ii) the activity is carried out in accordance with regulations made under section 34(2) of that Act; or

    (e) the activity is done before the relevant commencement date for the purpose of research which, before that date, is ethically approved within the meaning of regulation 8.

Analysis of DNA

Purposes for which DNA may be analysed without consent: England and Wales

5.—(1) This regulation applies for the purposes of paragraph 12 of Schedule 4 to the Act (excepted purposes relating to DNA of adults who lack capacity to consent).

(2) In any case falling within sub-paragraph (1)(a)(i) and (b) of that paragraph (DNA manufactured by the body of a person who under the law of England and Wales lacks capacity to consent), the purposes for which DNA manufactured by the body of a person ('P') who lacks capacity to consent to analysis of the DNA may be analysed are –

    (a) any purpose which the person carrying out the analysis reasonably believes to be in P's best interests;

    (b) the purposes of a clinical trial which is authorised and conducted in accordance with the clinical trials regulations;

    (c) the purposes of intrusive research which is carried out on or after the relevant commencement date in accordance with the requirements of section 30(1)(a) and (b) of the Mental Capacity Act 2005 (approval by appropriate body and compliance with sections 32 and 33 of that Act);

    (d) the purposes of intrusive research –

        (i) which is carried out on or after the relevant commencement date,

        (ii) in relation to which section 34 of the Mental Capacity Act 2005 (loss of capacity during research project) applies, and

        (iii) which is carried out in accordance with regulations made under section 34(2) of that Act; or

    (e) research which is carried out before the relevant commencement date and which, before that date, is ethically approved within the meaning of regulation 8.

Ethical approval

Ethical approval for the purposes of regulations 3 to 6

8.—(1) Research is ethically approved within the meaning of this regulation if approval is given by a research ethics authority in the circumstances specified in paragraph (2).

(2) The circumstances are that –

    (a) the research is in connection with disorders, or the functioning, of the human body,

    (b) there are reasonable grounds for believing that research of comparable effectiveness cannot be carried out if the research has to be confined to, or relate only to, persons who have capacity to consent to taking part in it, and

    (c) there are reasonable grounds for believing that research of comparable effectiveness cannot be carried out in circumstances such that the person carrying out the research is not in possession, and not likely to come into possession, of information from which the person from whose body the defined material has come can be identified.

(3) 'Defined material'–

    (a) in relation to ethical approval for the purposes of regulations 3(2)(e) and 4(2)(c), means the relevant material involved in an activity of a kind mentioned in section 1(1) (d) or (f) of the Act, and

    (b) in relation to ethical approval for the purposes of regulations 5(2)(e) and 6(2)(c), means the bodily material in relation to which an analysis of DNA is to be carried out.

(4) 'Research ethics authority' has the meaning given by regulation 2 of the Human Tissue Act 2004 (Ethical Approval, Exceptions from Licensing and Supply of Information about Transplants) Regulations 2006.

PART 3 TRANSPLANTS

Meaning of transplantable material for the purposes of section 34 of the Act

9. For the purposes of section 34 of the Act (information about transplant operations) 'transplantable material' means –

    (a) the whole or part of any of the following organs if it is to be used for the same purpose as the entire organ in the human body –

        (i) kidney,

        (ii) heart,

        (iii) lung or a lung lobe,

        (iv) pancreas,

        (v) liver,

        (vi) bowel,

        (vii) larynx,

    (b) face, or

    (c) limb.

Meaning of transplantable material for the purposes of section 33 of the Act

10.—(1) Subject to paragraphs (2) and (3), for the purposes of section 33 of the Act (restriction on transplants involving a live donor), 'transplantable material' means –

    (a) an organ, or part of an organ if it is to be used for the same purpose as the entire organ in the human body,

    (b) bone marrow, and

    (c) peripheral blood stem cells, where that material is removed from the body of a living person with the intention that it be transplanted into another person.

(2) The material referred to in paragraph (1)(a) is not transplantable material for the purposes of section 33 of the Act in a case where the primary purpose of removal of the material is the medical treatment of the person from whose body the material is removed.

(3) The material referred to in paragraph (1)(b) and (c) is transplantable material for the purposes of section 33 of the Act only in a case where the person from whose body the material is removed is –

(a) an adult who lacks the capacity, or

(b) a child who is not competent, to consent to removal of the transplantable material.

Cases in which restriction on transplants involving a live donor is disapplied

11.—(1) Section 33(1) and (2) of the Act (offences relating to transplants involving a live donor) shall not apply in any case involving transplantable material from the body of a living person ('the donor') if the requirements of paragraphs (2) to (6) are met.

(2) A registered medical practitioner who has clinical responsibility for the donor must have caused the matter to be referred to the Authority and where that referral concerns an organ, the referral must state that the registered medical practitioner, or a person acting under the supervision of that registered medical practitioner –

(a) is satisfied that the donor's health and medical history are suitable for the purposes of donation; and

(b) has –

(i) provided the donor with the information the donor requires to understand the consequences of donation, and

(ii) endeavoured to obtain information from the donor that is relevant to transplantation.

(2A) In paragraph (2)(b), in cases where the person giving consent is different from the donor, the references to donor shall be read as if they were a references to the person giving consent.

(3) The Authority must be satisfied that –

(a) no reward has been or is to be given in contravention of section 32 of the Act (prohibition of commercial dealings in human material for transplantation), and

(b) when the transplantable material is removed –

(i) consent for its removal for the purpose of transplantation has been given, or

(ii) its removal for that purpose is otherwise lawful.

(4) The Authority must take the report referred to in paragraph (6) into account in making its decision under paragraph (3).

(5) The Authority shall give notice of its decision under paragraph (3) to –

(a) the donor of the transplantable material or any person acting on his behalf,

(b) the person to whom it is proposed to transplant the transplantable material ('the recipient') or any person acting on his behalf, and

(c) the registered medical practitioner who caused the matter to be referred to the Authority under paragraph (2).

(6) Subject to paragraph (7), one or more qualified persons must have conducted separate interviews with each of the following –

(a) the donor,

(b) if different from the donor, the person giving consent, and

(c) the recipient, and reported to the Authority on the matters specified in paragraphs (8) and (9).

(7) Paragraph (6) does not apply in any case where the removal of the transplantable material for the purpose of transplantation is authorised by an order made in any legal proceedings before a court.

(8) The matters that must be covered in the report of each interview under paragraph (6) are –

(a) any evidence of duress or coercion affecting the decision to give consent,

(b) any evidence of an offer of a reward, and

(c) any difficulties of communication with the person interviewed and an explanation of how those difficulties were overcome.

(9) The following matters must be covered in the report of the interview with the donor and, where relevant, the other person giving consent –

(a) the information given to the person interviewed as to the nature of the medical procedure for, and the risk involved in, the removal of the transplantable material,

    (b) the full name of the person who gave that information and his qualification to give it, and

    (c) the capacity of the person interviewed to understand –

        (i)   the nature of the medical procedure and the risk involved, and

        (ii)   that the consent may be withdrawn at any time before the removal of the transplantable material.

(10) A person shall be taken to be qualified to conduct an interview under paragraph (6) if –

    (a) he appears to the Authority to be suitably qualified to conduct the interview,

    (b) he does not have any connection with any of the persons to be interviewed, or with a person who stands in a qualifying relationship to any of those persons, which the Authority considers to be of a kind that might raise doubts about his ability to act impartially, and

    (c) in the case of an interview with the donor or other person giving consent, he is not the person who gave the information referred to in paragraph (9)(a).

Decisions of the Authority: procedure for certain cases

12.—(1) In any case to which paragraph (2), (3) or (4) applies, the Authority's decision as to the matters specified in regulation 11(3) shall be made by a panel of no fewer than 3 members of the Authority.

(2) A case falls within this paragraph if –

    (a) the donor of the transplantable material is a child, and

    (b) the material is an organ or part of an organ if it is to be used for the same purpose as an entire organ in the human body.

(3) A case falls within this paragraph if –

    (a) the donor of the transplantable material is an adult who lacks capacity to consent to removal of the material, and

    (b) the material is an organ or part of an organ if it is to be used for the same purpose as an entire organ in the human body.

(4) A case falls within this paragraph if –

    (a) the donor of the transplantable material is an adult who has capacity to consent to removal of the material, and

    (b) the case involves –

        (i)   paired donations,

        (ii)   pooled donations, or

        (iii) a non-directed altruistic donation.

(5) In this regulation –

'non-directed altruistic donation' means the removal (in circumstances not amounting to a paired or pooled donation) of transplantable material from a donor for transplant to a person who is not genetically related to the donor or known to him;

'paired donations' means an arrangement under which –

    (a) transplantable material is removed from a donor ('D') for transplant to a person who is not genetically related or known to D, and

    (b) transplantable material is removed from another person for transplant to a person who is genetically related or known to D; and

'pooled donations' means a series of paired donations of transplantable material, each of which is linked to another in the same series (for example, transplantable material from D is transplanted to the wife of another person ('E'), transplantable material from E is transplanted to the partner of a third person ('F') and transplantable material from F is transplanted to D's son).

Right to reconsideration of Authority's decision

13.—(1) The Authority may reconsider any decision made by it under regulation 11(3) if it is satisfied that –

    (a) any information given for the purpose of the decision was in any material respect false or misleading, or

    (b) there has been any material change of circumstances since the decision was made.

(2) A specified person may in any case require the Authority to reconsider any decision made by it under regulation 11(3).

(3) 'Specified persons', in relation to such a decision, are –

  (a) the donor of the transplantable material or any person acting on his behalf,
  (b) the recipient of the material or any person acting on his behalf, and
  (c) the registered medical practitioner who caused the matter to be referred to the Authority under regulation 11(2).

Mental Capacity Act 2005 (Independent Mental Capacity Advocates) (General) Regulations 2006

(SI 2006, No. 1832)

Interpretation

2.—(1) In these Regulations –

'the Act' means the Mental Capacity Act 2005; and

'IMCA' means an independent mental capacity advocate.

(2) In these Regulations, references to instructions given to a person to act as an IMCA are to instructions given under sections 37 to 39 of the Act or under regulations made by virtue of section 41 of the Act.

Meaning of serious medical treatment

4.—(1) This regulation defines serious medical treatment for the purposes of section 37 of the Act. (2) Serious medical treatment is treatment which involves providing, withdrawing or withholding treatment in circumstances where –

  (a) in a case where a single treatment is being proposed, there is a fine balance between its benefits to the patient and the burdens and risks it is likely to entail for him,
  (b) in a case where there is a choice of treatments, a decision as to which one to use is finely balanced, or
  (c) what is proposed would be likely to involve serious consequences for the patient.

Functions of an independent mental capacity advocate

6.—(1) This regulation applies where an IMCA has been instructed by an authorised person to represent a person ('P').

(2) 'Authorised person' means a person who is required or enabled to instruct an IMCA under sections 37 to 39 of the Act or under regulations made by virtue of section 41 of the Act.

(3) The IMCA must determine in all the circumstances how best to represent and support P.

(4) In particular, the IMCA must –

  (a) verify that the instructions were issued by an authorised person;
  (b) to the extent that it is practicable and appropriate to do so –
    (i) interview P, and
    (ii) examine the records relevant to P to which the IMCA has access under section 35 (6) of the Act;
  (c) to the extent that it is practicable and appropriate to do so, consult –
    (i) persons engaged in providing care or treatment for P in a professional capacity or for remuneration, and
    (ii) other persons who may be in a position to comment on P's wishes, feelings, beliefs or values; and
  (d) take all practicable steps to obtain such other information about P, or the act or decision that is proposed in relation to P, as the IMCA considers necessary.

(5) The IMCA must evaluate all the information he has obtained for the purpose of –

    (a) ascertaining the extent of the support provided to P to enable him to participate in making any decision about the matter in relation to which the IMCA has been instructed;

    (b) ascertaining what P's wishes and feelings would be likely to be, and the beliefs and values that would be likely to influence P, if he had capacity in relation to the proposed act or decision;

    (c) ascertaining what alternative courses of action are available in relation to P;

    (d) where medical treatment is proposed for P, ascertaining whether he would be likely to benefit from a further medical opinion.

(6) The IMCA must prepare a report for the authorised person who instructed him.

(7) The IMCA may include in the report such submissions as he considers appropriate in relation to P and the act or decision which is proposed in relation to him.

Challenges to decisions affecting persons who lack capacity

7.—(1) This regulation applies where –

    (a) an IMCA has been instructed to represent a person ('P') in relation to any matter, and

    (b) a decision affecting P (including a decision as to his capacity) is made in that matter.

(8) The IMCA has the same rights to challenge the decision as he would have if he were a person (other than an IMCA) engaged in caring for P or interested in his welfare.

Mental Health (Hospital, Guardianship and Treatment) (England) Regulations 2008

(SI 2008, No. 1184)

PART 1 INTERPRETATION

2.—(1) In these Regulations –

'the Act' means the Mental Health Act 1983;

'the Commission' means the Care Quality Commission;

'guardianship patient' means a person who is subject to guardianship under the Act;

'private guardian', in relation to a patient, means a person, other than a local social services authority, who acts as guardian under the Act;

'responsible registered establishment' is a registered establishment which is a responsible hospital;

PART 3 FUNCTIONS OF GUARDIANS AND NEAREST RELATIVES

Duties of private guardians

22.—(1) It shall be the duty of a private guardian –

    (a) to appoint a registered medical practitioner to act as the nominated medical attendant of the patient;

    (b) to notify the responsible local social services authority of the name and address of the nominated medical attendant;

    (c) in exercising the powers and duties of a private guardian conferred or imposed by the Act and these Regulations, to comply with such directions as that authority may give;

    (d) to furnish that authority with all such reports or other information with regard to the patient as the authority may from time to time require;

    (e) to notify that authority –

        (i) on the reception of the patient into guardianship, of the private guardian's address and the address of the patient,

        (ii) except in a case to which paragraph (f) applies, of any permanent change of either address, before or not later than 7 days after the change takes place;

    (f) on any permanent change of the private guardian's address, where the new address is in the area of a different local social services authority, to notify that authority –

        (i) of that address and that of the patient,

        (ii) of the particulars mentioned in paragraph (b),

and to notify the authority which was formerly responsible of the permanent change in the private guardian's address;

    (g) in the event of the death of the patient, or the termination of the guardianship by discharge, transfer or otherwise, to notify the responsible local social services authority as soon as reasonably practicable.

Visits to patients subject to guardianship

23. The responsible local social services authority shall arrange for every patient received into guardianship under the Act to be visited at such intervals as the authority may decide, but –

    (a) in any case at intervals of not more than 3 months, and

    (b) at least one such visit in any year shall be made by an approved clinician or a practitioner approved by the Secretary of State for the purposes of section 12 (general provisions as to medical recommendations).

Performance of functions of nearest relative

24.—(1) Subject to the conditions of paragraph (7), any person other than –

    (a) the patient;

    (b) a person mentioned in section 26(5) (persons deemed not to be the nearest relative), or

    (c) a person in respect of whom the court has made an order on the grounds set out in section 29(3)(b) to (e) (which sets out the grounds on which an application to the court for the appointment of a person to exercise the functions of a nearest relative may be made) for so long as an order under that section is in effect,

may be authorised in accordance with paragraph (2) to act on behalf of the nearest relative in respect of the matters mentioned in paragraph (3).

(2) Subject to paragraph (8), the authorisation mentioned in paragraph (1) must be given in writing by the nearest relative.

(3) The matters referred to in paragraph (1) are the performance in respect of the patient of the functions conferred upon the nearest relative under –

    (a) Part 2 of the Act (as modified by Schedule 1 to the Act as the case may be), and

    (b) section 66 (applications to tribunals).

(4) An authorisation given under paragraph (1) shall take effect upon its receipt by the person authorised.

(5) Subject to the conditions of paragraph (7), the nearest relative of a patient may give notice in writing revoking that authorisation.

(6) Any revocation of such authorisation shall take effect upon the receipt of the notice by the person authorised.

(7) The conditions mentioned in paragraphs (1) and (5) are that the nearest relative shall immediately notify –

    (a) the patient;

    (b) in the case of a patient liable to be detained in a hospital, the managers of that hospital;

    (c) in the case of a patient subject to guardianship, the responsible local social services authority and the private guardian, if any;

(d) in the case of a community patient, the managers of the responsible hospital, of the authorisation or, as the case may be, its revocation.

(8) An authorisation or notification referred to in this regulation may be transmitted by means of electronic communication if the recipient agrees.

PART 5 CONSENT TO TREATMENT

Consent to treatment

27.—(1) For the purposes of section 57 (treatment requiring consent and a second opinion) –

(a) the form of treatment to which that section shall apply, in addition to the treatment mentioned in subsection (1)(a)of that section (any surgical operation for destroying brain tissue or for destroying the functioning of brain tissue), shall be the surgical implantation of hormones for the purpose of reducing male sexual drive, …

(3) For the purposes of section 58A (electro-convulsive therapy, etc.) –

(a) the form of treatment to which that section shall apply, in addition to the administration of electro-convulsive therapy mentioned in subsection (1)(a) of that section, shall be the administration of medicine as part of that therapy; …

(4) Section 58A does not apply to treatment by way of the administration of medicine as part of electro-convulsive therapy where that treatment falls within section 62(1)(a) or (b) (treatment immediately necessary to save the patient's life or to prevent a serious deterioration in the patient's condition).

PART 6 TREATMENT OF COMMUNITY PATIENTS NOT RECALLED TO HOSPITAL

28.—(2) Treatment of a patient to whom section 64B(3)(b) or section 64E(3)(b) applies (adult and child patients for whom treatment is immediately necessary), may include treatment by way of administration of medicine as part of electro-convulsive therapy but only where that treatment falls within section 64C(5)(a) or (b) (treatment immediately necessary to save the patient's life or to prevent a serious deterioration in the patient's condition).

(3) Treatment of a patient to whom section 64G (emergency treatment for patients lacking capacity or competence) applies may include treatment by way of the administration of medicine as part of electro-convulsive therapy but only where that treatment falls within section 64G(5)(a) or (b) (treatment immediately necessary to save the patient's life or to prevent a serious deterioration in the patient's condition).

Tribunal Procedure (First-tier Tribunal) (Health, Education and Social Care Chamber) Rules 2008

(SI 2008, No. 2699)

PART 1 INTRODUCTION

Citation, commencement, application and interpretation

1.—(3) In these Rules –

'the 2007 Act' means the Tribunals, Courts and Enforcement Act 2007;

'mental health case' means proceedings brought under the Mental Health Act 1983 …

'nearest relative' has the meaning set out in section 26 of the Mental Health Act 1983;

'party' means –

(a) in a mental health case, the patient, the responsible authority, the Secretary of State (if the patient is a restricted patient or in a reference under rule 32(8) (seeking approval under section 86 of the Mental Health Act 1983)), and any other person who starts a mental health case by making an application;

'patient' means the person who is the subject of a mental health case;

'responsible authority' means –

(a) in relation to a patient detained under the Mental Health Act 1983 in a hospital within the meaning of Part 2 of that Act, the managers (as defined in section 145 of that Act);

(b) in relation to a patient subject to guardianship, the responsible local social services authority (as defined in section 34(3) of the Mental Health Act 1983);

(c) in relation to a community patient, the managers of the responsible hospital (as defined in section 145 of the Mental Health Act 1983);

'restricted patient' has the meaning set out in section 79(1) of the Mental Health Act 1983;

'Tribunal' means the First-tier Tribunal ...

PART 2 GENERAL POWERS AND PROVISIONS

Representatives

11.—(7) In a mental health case, if the patient has not appointed a representative, the Tribunal may appoint a legal representative for the patient where –

(a) the patient has stated that they do not wish to conduct their own case or that they wish to be represented; or

(b) the patient lacks the capacity to appoint a representative but the Tribunal believes that it is in the patient's best interests for the patient to be represented.

(8) In a mental health case a party may not appoint as a representative, or be represented or assisted at a hearing by –

(a) a person liable to be detained or subject to guardianship, or who is a community patient, under the Mental Health Act 1983; or

(b) a person receiving treatment for mental disorder at the same hospital as the patient.

PART 4 PROCEEDINGS BEFORE THE TRIBUNAL IN MENTAL HEALTH CASES

Before the hearing

Procedure in mental health cases

32.—(1) An application or reference must be –

(a) made in writing;

(b) signed (in the case of an application, by the applicant or any person authorised by the applicant to do so); and

(c) sent or delivered to the Tribunal so that it is received within the time specified in the Mental Health Act 1983 ...

(2) An application must, if possible, include –

(a) the name, address and date of birth of the patient;

(b) if the application is made by the patient's nearest relative, the name, address and relationship to the patient of the patient's nearest relative;

(c) the provision under which the patient is detained, liable to be detained, subject to guardianship, or a community patient;

    (d) whether the person making the application has appointed a representative or intends to do so, and the name and address of any representative appointed;

    (e) the name and address of the responsible authority in relation to the patient.

(3) Subject to rule 14(2) (withholding evidence likely to cause harm), when the Tribunal receives a document from any party it must send a copy of that document to each other party.

(4) If the patient is a conditionally discharged patient –

    (a) upon being notified by the Tribunal of an application, the Secretary of State must immediately provide to the Tribunal the names and addresses of the responsible clinician and any social supervisor in relation to the patient; and

    (b) upon being notified by the Tribunal of an application or reference, the responsible clinician and any social supervisor named by the Secretary of State under this rule must send or deliver the documents specified in the relevant practice direction to the Tribunal so that they are received by the Tribunal as soon as practicable and in any event within 3 weeks.

(5) In proceedings under section 66(1)(a) of the Mental Health Act 1983 (application for admission for assessment), on the earlier of receipt of the copy of the application or a request from the Tribunal, the responsible authority must send or deliver to the Tribunal –

    (a) the application for admission;

    (b) the medical recommendations on which the application is founded;

    (c) such of the information specified in the relevant practice direction as is within the knowledge of the responsible authority and can reasonably be provided in the time available; and

    (d) such of the documents specified in the relevant practice direction as can reasonably be provided in the time available.

(6) If paragraph (4) or (5) does not apply, the responsible authority must send or deliver a statement containing the information and documents required by the relevant practice direction to the Tribunal so that it is received by the Tribunal as soon as practicable and in any event within 3 weeks after the responsible authority received a copy of the application or reference.

(7) If the patient is a restricted patient the responsible authority must also send the statement under paragraph (6) to the Secretary of State, and the Secretary of State must send a statement of any further relevant information to the Tribunal as soon as practicable and in any event –

    (a) in proceedings under section 75(1) of the Mental Health Act 1983, within 2 weeks after the Secretary of State received the relevant authority's statement; or

    (b) otherwise, within 3 weeks after the Secretary of State received the relevant authority's statement.

(8) If the Secretary of State wishes to seek the approval of the Tribunal under section 86(3) of the Mental Health Act 1983 (removal of alien patients), the Secretary of State must refer the patient's case to the Tribunal and the provisions of these Rules applicable to references under that Act apply to the proceedings.

Notice of proceedings to interested persons

33. When the Tribunal receives the information required by rule 32(4), (5) or (6) (procedure in mental health cases) the Tribunal must give notice of the proceedings –

    (a) where the patient is subject to the guardianship of a private guardian, to the guardian;

    (b) where there is an extant order of the Court of Protection, to that court;

    (c) subject to a patient with capacity to do so requesting otherwise, where any person other than the applicant is named by the authority as exercising the functions of the nearest relative, to that person; and

    (e) to any other person who, in the opinion of the Tribunal, should have an opportunity of being heard.

Medical examination of the patient

34.—(1) Where paragraph (2) applies, an appropriate member of the Tribunal must, so far as practicable, examine the patient in order to form an opinion of the patient's mental condition, and may do so in private.

(2) This paragraph applies –

(a) in proceedings under section 66(1)(a) of the Mental Health Act 1983 (application in respect of an admission for assessment), unless the Tribunal is satisfied that the patient does not want such an examination;

(b) in any other case, if the patient or the patient's representative has informed the Tribunal in writing, not less than 14 days before the hearing, that –

(i) the patient; or

(ii) if the patient lacks the capacity to make such a decision, the patient's representative, wishes there to be such an examination; or

(c) if the Tribunal has directed that there be such an examination.

Hearings

Restrictions on disposal of proceedings without a hearing

35.—(1) Subject to the following paragraphs, the Tribunal must hold a hearing before making a decision which disposes of proceedings.

(2) This rule does not apply to a decision under Part 5.

(3) The Tribunal may make a decision on a reference under section 68 of the Mental Health Act 1983 (duty of managers of hospitals to refer cases to tribunal) without a hearing if the patient is a community patient aged 18 or over and either –

(a) the patient has stated in writing that the patient does not wish to attend or be represented at a hearing of the reference and the Tribunal is satisfied that the patient has the capacity to decide whether or not to make that decision; or

(b) the patient's representative has stated in writing that the patient does not wish to attend or be represented at a hearing of the reference.

(4) The Tribunal may dispose of proceedings without a hearing under rule 8(3) (striking out a party's case).

Entitlement to attend a hearing

36.—(1) Subject to rule 38(4) (exclusion of a person from a hearing), each party to proceedings is entitled to attend a hearing.

(2) Any person notified of the proceedings under rule 33 (notice of proceedings to interested persons) may –

(a) attend and take part in a hearing to such extent as the Tribunal considers proper; or

(b) provide written submissions to the Tribunal.

Time and place of hearings

37.—(1) In proceedings under section 66(1)(a) of the Mental Health Act 1983 the hearing of the case must start within 7 days after the date on which the Tribunal received the application notice.

(2) In proceedings under section 75(1) of that Act, the hearing of the case must start at least 5 weeks but no more than 8 weeks after the date on which the Tribunal received the reference.

(3) The Tribunal must give reasonable notice of the time and place of the hearing (including any adjourned or postponed hearing), and any changes to the time and place of the hearing, to –

(a) each party entitled to attend a hearing; and

(b) any person who has been notified of the proceedings under rule 33 (notice of proceedings to interested persons).

(4) The period of notice under paragraph (3) must be at least 21 days, except that –

(a) in proceedings under section 66(1)(a) of the Mental Health Act 1983 the period must be at least 3 working days; and

(b) the Tribunal may give shorter notice –
  (i)   with the parties' consent; or
  (ii) in urgent or exceptional circumstances.

Public and private hearings

38.—(1) All hearings must be held in private unless the Tribunal considers that it is in the interests of justice for the hearing to be held in public.

(2) If a hearing is held in public, the Tribunal may give a direction that part of the hearing is to be held in private.

(3) Where a hearing, or part of it, is to be held in private, the Tribunal may determine who is permitted to attend the hearing or part of it.

(4) The Tribunal may give a direction excluding from any hearing, or part of it –
  (a) any person whose conduct the Tribunal considers is disrupting or is likely to disrupt the hearing;
  (b) any person whose presence the Tribunal considers is likely to prevent another person from giving evidence or making submissions freely;
  (c) any person who the Tribunal considers should be excluded in order to give effect to a direction under rule 14(2) (withholding information likely to cause harm); or
  (d) any person where the purpose of the hearing would be defeated by the attendance of that person.

(5) The Tribunal may give a direction excluding a witness from a hearing until that witness gives evidence.

Hearings in a party's absence

39.—(1) Subject to paragraph (2), if a party fails to attend a hearing the Tribunal may proceed with the hearing if the Tribunal –
  (a) is satisfied that the party has been notified of the hearing or that reasonable steps have been taken to notify the party of the hearing; and
  (b) considers that it is in the interests of justice to proceed with the hearing.

(2) The Tribunal may not proceed with a hearing that the patient has failed to attend unless the Tribunal is satisfied that –
  (a) the patient –
    (i)   has decided not to attend the hearing; or
    (ii) is unable to attend the hearing for reasons of ill health; and
  (b) an examination under rule 34 (medical examination of the patient) –
    (i)   has been carried out; or
    (ii) is impractical or unnecessary.

Local Authority Social Services and National Health Service Complaints (England) Regulations 2009

(SI 2009, No. 309)

Interpretation

2.—(1) In these Regulations –
'the 1993 Act' means the Health Service Commissioners Act 1993;
'the 2004 Regulations' means the National Health Service (Complaints) Regulations 2004;
'the 2006 Act' means the National Health Service Act 2006;
'complaints manager' means the person designated in accordance with regulation 4(1)(b);
'general medical services contractor' means a person or body who has entered into a general medical services contract with the National Health Service Commissioning Board in accordance with section 84 of the 2006 Act;

'relevant complaints procedure' means –

    (b) any complaints procedure that may at any time be or have been required respectively by any of the following provisions –

        (i) paragraph 92 of Schedule 6 to the National Health Service (General Medical Services Contracts) Regulations 2004;

        (ii) paragraph 86 of Schedule 5 to the National Health Service (Personal Medical Services Agreements) Regulations 2004;

'responsible body' means a local authority, NHS body, primary care provider or independent provider.

Arrangements for the handling and consideration of complaints

3.—(1) Each responsible body must make arrangements ('arrangements for dealing with complaints') in accordance with these Regulations for the handling and consideration of complaints.

(2) The arrangements for dealing with complaints must be such as to ensure that –

    (a) complaints are dealt with efficiently;

    (b) complaints are properly investigated;

    (c) complainants are treated with respect and courtesy;

    (d) complainants receive, so far as is reasonably practical –

        (i) assistance to enable them to understand the procedure in relation to complaints; or

        (ii) advice on where they may obtain such assistance;

    (e) complainants receive a timely and appropriate response;

    (f) complainants are told the outcome of the investigation of their complaint; and

    (g) action is taken if necessary in the light of the outcome of a complaint.

Responsibility for complaints arrangements

4.—(1) Each responsible body must designate –

    (a) a person, in these Regulations referred to as a responsible person, to be responsible for ensuring compliance with the arrangements made under these Regulations, and in particular ensuring that action is taken if necessary in the light of the outcome of a complaint; and

    (b) a person, in these Regulations referred to as a complaints manager, to be responsible for managing the procedures for handling and considering complaints in accordance with the arrangements made under these Regulations.

(4) The responsible person is to be –

    (a) in the case of a local authority or NHS body, the person who acts as the chief executive officer of the authority or body;

    (b) in the case of any other responsible body, the person who acts as the chief executive officer of the body or, if none –

        (i) the person who is the sole proprietor of the responsible body;

        (ii) where the responsible body is a partnership, a partner; or

        (iii) in any other case, a director of the responsible body, or a person who is responsible for managing the responsible body.

(5) The complaints manager may be –

    (a) a person who is not an employee of the responsible body;

    (b) the same person as the responsible person;

    (c) a complaints manager designated by another responsible body under paragraph (1)(b).

Persons who may make complaints

5.—(1) A complaint may be made by –

    (a) a person who receives or has received services from a responsible body; or

    (b) a person who is affected, or likely to be affected, by the action, omission or decision of the responsible body which is the subject of the complaint.

(2) A complaint may be made by a person (in this regulation referred to as a representative) acting on behalf of a person mentioned in paragraph (1) who –

(a) has died;

(b) is a child;

(c) is unable to make the complaint themselves because of –

(i) physical incapacity; or

(ii) lack of capacity within the meaning of the Mental Capacity Act 2005; or

(d) has requested the representative to act on their behalf.

(3) Where a representative makes a complaint on behalf of a child, the responsible body to which the complaint is made –

(a) must not consider the complaint unless it is satisfied that there are reasonable grounds for the complaint being made by a representative instead of the child; and

(b) if it is not so satisfied, must notify the representative in writing, and state the reason for its decision.

(4) This paragraph applies where –

(a) a representative makes a complaint on behalf of –

(i) a child; or

(ii) a person who lacks capacity within the meaning of the Mental Capacity Act 2005; and

(b) the responsible body to which the complaint is made is satisfied that the representative is not conducting the complaint in the best interests of the person on whose behalf the complaint is made.

(5) Where paragraph (4) applies –

(a) the complaint must not be considered or further considered under these Regulations; and

(b) the responsible body must notify the representative in writing, and state the reason for its decision.

(6) In these Regulations any reference to a complainant includes a reference to a representative.

Complaints about the provision of health services

7.—(1) This regulation applies to a complaint which is –

(a) made to a clinical commissioning group or the National Health Service Commissioning Board in accordance with these Regulations on or after 1 April 2013;

(b) about the services provided by the group or Board; and

(c) not specified in regulation 8(1).

(2) In this regulation, 'provider' means an NHS body, primary care provider or independent provider.

(3) Where a clinical commissioning group or the National Health Service Commissioning Board receives a complaint to which this regulation applies –

(a) the group or Board must ask the complainant whether the complainant consents to details of the complaint being sent to the provider; and

(b) if the complainant so consents, the group or Board must as soon as reasonably practicable send details of the complaint to the provider.

(4) If the clinical commissioning group or the National Health Service Commissioning Board considers that it is appropriate for the group or Board to deal with the complaint –

(a) it must so notify the complainant and the provider; and

(b) it must continue to handle the complaint in accordance with these Regulations.

(5) If the clinical commissioning group or the National Health Service Commissioning Board considers that it is more appropriate for the complaint to be dealt with by the provider, and the complainant consents –

(a) the group or Board must so notify the complainant and the provider;

(b) when the provider receives the notification given to it under sub-paragraph (a) –

(i) the provider must handle the complaint in accordance with these Regulations; and

(ii) the complainant is deemed to have made the complaint to the provider under these Regulations.

Time limit for making a complaint

12.—(1) Except as mentioned in paragraph (2), a complaint must be made not later than 12 months after –

(a) the date on which the matter which is the subject of the complaint occurred; or

(b) if later, the date on which the matter which is the subject of the complaint came to the notice of the complainant.

(2) The time limit in paragraph (1) shall not apply if the responsible body is satisfied that –

(a) the complainant had good reasons for not making the complaint within that time limit; and

(b) notwithstanding the delay, it is still possible to investigate the complaint effectively and fairly.

Procedure before investigation

13.—(1) A complaint may be made orally, in writing or electronically.

(2) Where a complaint is made orally, the responsible body to which the complaint is made must –

(a) make a written record of the complaint; and

(b) provide a copy of the written record to the complainant.

(3) Except where regulation 6(5) or 7(1) applies in relation to a complaint, the responsible body must acknowledge the complaint not later than 3 working days after the day on which it receives the complaint.

(5) Where regulation 7(1) applies to a complaint –

(a) the clinical commissioning group or the National Health Service Commissioning Board which receives the complaint must acknowledge the complaint not later than 3 working days after the day on which it receives it; and

(b) where a responsible body receives notification given to it under regulation 7(5)(a), it must acknowledge the complaint not later than 3 working days after the day on which it receives the notification.

(6) The acknowledgement may be made orally or in writing.

(7) At the time it acknowledges the complaint, the responsible body must offer to discuss with the complainant, at a time to be agreed with the complainant –

(a) the manner in which the complaint is to be handled; and

(b) the period ('the response period') within which –

(i) the investigation of the complaint is likely to be completed; and

(ii) the response required by regulation 14(2) is likely to be sent to the complainant.

(8) If the complainant does not accept the offer of a discussion under paragraph (7), the responsible body must –

(a) determine the response period specified in paragraph (7)(b); and

(b) notify the complainant in writing of that period.

Investigation and response

14.—(1) A responsible body to which a complaint is made must –

(a) investigate the complaint in a manner appropriate to resolve it speedily and efficiently; and

(b) during the investigation, keep the complainant informed, as far as reasonably practicable, as to the progress of the investigation.

(2) As soon as reasonably practicable after completing the investigation, the responsible body must send the complainant in writing a response, signed by the responsible person, which includes –

(a) a report which includes the following matters –

(i) an explanation of how the complaint has been considered; and

          (ii) the conclusions reached in relation to the complaint, including any matters for which the complaint specifies, or the responsible body considers, that remedial action is needed; and

    (b) confirmation as to whether the responsible body is satisfied that any action needed in consequence of the complaint has been taken or is proposed to be taken;

    (c) where the complaint relates wholly or in part to the functions of a local authority, details of the complainant's right to take their complaint to a Local Commissioner under the Local Government Act 1974; and

    (d) except where the complaint relates only to the functions of a local authority, details of the complainant's right to take their complaint to the Health Service Commissioner under the 1993 Act.

(3) In paragraph (4), 'relevant period' means the period of 6 months commencing on the day on which the complaint was received, or such longer period as may be agreed before the expiry of that period by the complainant and the responsible body.

(4) If the responsible body does not send the complainant a response in accordance with paragraph (2) within the relevant period, the responsible body must –

    (a) notify the complainant in writing accordingly and explain the reason why; and

    (b) send the complainant in writing a response in accordance with paragraph (2) as soon as reasonably practicable after the relevant period.

Publicity

16. Each responsible body must make information available to the public as to –

    (a) its arrangements for dealing with complaints; and

    (b) how further information about those arrangements may be obtained.

Monitoring

17. For the purpose of monitoring the arrangements under these Regulations each responsible body must maintain a record of the following matters –

    (a) each complaint received;

    (b) the subject matter and outcome of each complaint; and

    (c) where the responsible body informed the complainant of –

          (i) the response period specified in regulation 13(7)(b); or

          (ii) any amendment to that period,

whether a report of the outcome of the investigation was sent to the complainant within that period or any amended period.

Annual reports

18.—(1) Each responsible body must prepare an annual report for each year which must –

    (a) specify the number of complaints which the responsible body received;

    (b) specify the number of complaints which the responsible body decided were well-founded;

    (c) specify the number of complaints which the responsible body has been informed have been referred to –

          (i) the Health Service Commissioner to consider under the 1993 Act; or

          (ii) the Local Commissioner to consider under the Local Government Act 1974; and

    (d) summarise –

          (i) the subject matter of complaints that the responsible body received;

          (ii) any matters of general importance arising out of those complaints, or the way in which the complaints were handled;

          (iii) any matters where action has been or is to be taken to improve services as a consequence of those complaints.

(3) Each responsible body must ensure that its annual report is available to any person on request.

(4) This paragraph applies to a responsible body which is –

(a) an NHS body other than a clinical commissioning group or the National Health Service Commissioning Board; or

(b) a primary care provider or an independent provider,

and which in any year provides, or agrees to provide, services under arrangements with a clinical commissioning group or the National Health Service Commissioning Board.

(5) Where paragraph (4) applies to a responsible body, the responsible body must send a copy of its annual report to the Primary Care Trust which arranged for the provision of the services by the responsible body.

(7) The copy of the annual report required to be sent in accordance with paragraph (5) or (6) must be sent as soon as reasonably practicable after the end of the year to which the report relates.

National Health Service (Performers Lists) (England) Regulations 2013

(SI 2013, No. 335)

PART 1 GENERAL PROVISIONS AS TO PERFORMERS LISTS

2 Interpretation

In these Regulations –

'the 2006 Act' means the National Health Service Act 2006;

'the Board' means the National Health Service Commissioning Board established by section 1H of the 2006 Act (the National Health Service Commissioning Board and its general functions);

'GP Register' means the register kept by virtue of section 34C of the Medical Act 1983 (the general practitioner register);

'health service list' means –

(a) a list referred to in section 159(1) of the 2006 Act (national disqualification), including that section as enacted immediately before the transfer date;

(b) a dental list, an ophthalmic list, or a medical list;

(c) a medical supplementary list, a dental supplementary list or an ophthalmic supplementary list; or

(d) a services list;

'list' means, unless the context otherwise requires, a health service list or an equivalent list;

'medical list' means a list prepared by a Primary Care Trust under regulation 4 of the National Health Service (General Medical Services) Regulations 1992 (medical list);

'medical performers list' means, unless the context otherwise requires, the list prepared, maintained and published by the Board pursuant to regulation 3(1)(a);

'Practitioner' means a medical practitioner, dental practitioner or ophthalmic practitioner;

'performers list' means, unless the context otherwise requires, a list referred to in regulation 3(1);

'register of medical practitioners' has the meaning given to it by section 2(2) of the Medical Act 1983 (registration of medical practitioners);

'regulatory body' means a body anywhere in the world which regulates or licenses any profession of which the Practitioner is or has been a member and includes a body which regulates or licenses the education, training or qualifications of that profession;

'relevant body' means, in relation to a Practitioner, the body for the time being mentioned in section 25(3) of the National Health Service Reform and Health Care Professions Act 2002 (regulatory bodies), which regulates the profession of the Practitioner;

'relevant performers list' means –

(a) in the case of a medical practitioner, the medical performers list;

3   Performers lists

(1) The Board is to prepare, maintain and publish, in accordance with this Part as modified or supplemented by the relevant Part –

(a) a medical performers list;

(2) The performers lists must be made available by the Board for public inspection.

14   Removal from a performers list

(1) The Board must remove a Practitioner from a performers list where the grounds in regulations 28(1), 35(1) or 41(1) apply or where it becomes aware that the Practitioner –

(a) has been convicted in the United Kingdom of murder;

(b) is subject to a national disqualification which disqualifies the Practitioner from inclusion in the performers list in question;

(c) has died; or

(d) is no longer registered with the Practitioner's relevant body.

(2) Where the Board is notified by the First-tier Tribunal that it has considered an appeal by a Practitioner against conditions imposed under regulation 10 and has decided to remove the Practitioner instead, the Board is to remove the Practitioner from the performers list and must immediately notify the Practitioner that it has done so.

(3) The Board may remove a Practitioner from a performers list where any one of the following is satisfied –

(a) the Practitioner has been convicted in the United Kingdom of a criminal offence (other than murder), committed on or after the day prescribed in the relevant Part, and has been sentenced to a term of imprisonment (whether suspended or not) of over six months;

(b) the Practitioner's continued inclusion in that performers list would be prejudicial to the efficiency of the services which those included in that performers list perform ('an efficiency case');

(c) the Practitioner –

(i) has (whether on the Practitioner's own or together with another person) by an act or omission caused, or risked causing, detriment to any health scheme by securing or trying to secure for the Practitioner or another person any financial or other benefit, and

(ii) knew that the Practitioner or the other person was not entitled to the benefit ('a fraud case'); or

(d) the Practitioner is unsuitable to be included in that performers list ('an unsuitability case').

PART 2   MEDICAL PERFORMERS LIST

23   Interpretation

In this Part –

'both registers' means the register of medical practitioners and the GP Register;

'Fitness to Practise Panel' means a Fitness to Practise Panel of the General Medical Council;

'foundation training scheme' means postgraduate medical education and training necessary for the award of a CCT in general practice;

'general medical practitioner' means a registered medical practitioner –

(a) who is a GP Registrar; or

(b) whose name is included in the GP Register;

'GP Registrar' means a registered medical practitioner who is being trained in general practice by a GP Trainer, whether as part of training leading to a CCT or otherwise;

'GP Trainer' means a general medical practitioner, other than a GP Registrar, who is approved by the General Medical Council under section 34I(1)(c) of the Medical Act 1983 (postgraduate medical education and training: approvals) for the purposes of providing training to a GP Registrar;

'health case' has the meaning given in section 35E(4) of the Medical Act 1983 (provisions supplementary to function of a fitness to practise panel);

'Interim Orders Panel' means an interim orders panel of the General Medical Council;

'licensed medical practitioner' means a medical practitioner who holds a license to practise;

24   Medical performers list

(1) A medical practitioner may not perform any primary medical services unless that medical practitioner is a general medical practitioner and is included in the medical performers list.

This is subject to paragraphs (2) to (5).

(2) A licensed medical practitioner, who is provisionally registered under section 15 (provisional registration), 15A (provisional registration for EEA nationals etc) or 21 (provisional registration of EEA national etc with certain overseas qualifications) of the Medical Act 1983, may perform primary medical services, when the medical practitioner is not included in the medical performers list, while acting in the course of the medical practitioner's employment as part of an acceptable programme for provisionally registered doctors within the meaning of section 10A of the Medical Act 1983 (programmes for provisionally registered doctors) in a medical practice which is a recognised practice setting for the purposes of section 44D of that Act (approved practice settings).

(3) A registered medical practitioner who falls within paragraph (4) may perform primary medical services when not included in the medical performers list in so far as the performance of those services constitutes a part of a programme of post-registration supervised clinical practice approved by the General Medical Council ('a post-registration programme').

(4) A registered medical practitioner falls within this paragraph if that medical practitioner –

(a) is not a GP Registrar;

(b) is undertaking a post-registration programme;

(c) has notified the Board at least 24 hours before commencing any part of such a programme in England; and

(d) has, with that notification, provided the Board with sufficient evidence to satisfy it that the medical practitioner is undergoing a post-registration programme.

(5) A GP Registrar, who has applied in accordance with these Regulations to the Board for inclusion in the medical performers list, may perform primary medical services, despite not being included in that list, until the first of the following arises –

(a) the date on which the Board notifies that GP Registrar of its decision on the application for inclusion; or

(b) the end of a period of 3 months, starting with the date on which that GP Registrar begins a foundation training scheme.

28   Grounds for removal from the medical performers list

(1) In addition to the grounds in regulation 14(1), the Board must remove a medical practitioner from the medical performers list where it becomes aware that –

(a) the medical practitioner's name is no longer included in the GP Register;

(b) the medical practitioner's registration in the register of medical practitioners has been suspended under section 35D(2)(b), (10)(b) or (12), or section 38(1) of the Medical Act 1983 or by virtue of rules made under paragraph 5A(3) of Schedule 4 to that Act;

(c) the medical practitioner's licence to practice has been withdrawn except where this has been withdrawn as a result of an interim suspension order made under section 41A(1)(a) of the Medical Act 1983; or

(d) if the medical practitioner is a GP Registrar, the medical practitioner is in breach of an undertaking provided in accordance with regulation 26(3) and has failed to withdraw

from the list after the Board has given the medical practitioner 28 days notice requesting the medical practitioner to do so.
This is subject to paragraph (2).

(2) Paragraph (1)(b) does not apply where a direction that a medical practitioner's registration be suspended is made in a health case.

(3) For the purposes of regulation 14(3)(a), the day prescribed in this Part is 3rd November 2003 or, if the medical practitioner had been included in a medical list or a medical supplementary list, 14th December 2001.

Health and Social Care Act 2008 (Regulated Activities) Regulations 2014

(SI 2014, No. 2936)

2   Interpretation

(1) In these Regulations –

'the Act' means the Health and Social Care Act 2008;

'the 1983 Act' means the Mental Health Act 1983;

'the 2005 Act' means the Mental Capacity Act 2005;

'the 2006 Act' means the National Health Service Act 2006;

'the 2010 Regulations' means the Health and Social Care Act 2008 (Regulated Activities) Regulations 2010;

'local anaesthesia' means any anaesthesia other than general, spinal or epidural anaesthesia, and also excludes the administration of a regional nerve block;

'medical practitioner' means a registered medical practitioner;

'nominated individual' must be construed in accordance with regulation 6(2);

'nurse' means a registered nurse;

'nursing care' means any services provided by a nurse and involving –

(a) the provision of care, or

(b) the planning, supervision or delegation of the provision of care,

other than any services which, having regard to their nature and the circumstances in which they are provided, do not need to be provided by a nurse;

'personal care' means –

(a) physical assistance given to a person in connection with –

(i)   eating or drinking (including the maintenance of established parenteral nutrition),

(ii) toileting (including in relation to the process of menstruation),

(iii) washing or bathing,

(iv) dressing,

(v)   oral care, or

(vi) the care of skin, hair and nails (with the exception of nail care provided by a person registered with the Health and Care Professions Council as a chiropodist or podiatrist pursuant to article 5 of the 2001 Order), or

(b) the prompting, together with supervision, of a person, in relation to the performance of any of the activities listed in paragraph (a), where that person is unable to make a decision for themselves in relation to performing such an activity without such prompting and supervision;

'registered manager' means, in respect of a regulated activity, a person registered with the Commission under Chapter 2 of Part 1 of the Act as a manager in respect of that activity;

'registered person' means, in respect of a regulated activity, a person who is the service provider or registered manager in respect of that activity;

'relevant person', except in regulation 20, means the service user or, where the service user is under 16 and not competent to make a decision in relation to their care or treatment, a person lawfully acting on their behalf;

'treatment', except in paragraph 5 of Schedule 1, includes –

    (a) a diagnostic or screening procedure carried out for medical purposes,

    (b) the ongoing assessment of a service user's mental or physical state,

    (c) nursing, personal and palliative care, and

    (d) the giving of vaccinations and immunisations;

'vulnerable adult' has the same meaning as in section 60(1) (interpretation) of the Safeguarding Vulnerable Groups Act 2006.

3   Prescribed activities

(1) Subject to paragraphs (3) and (4), the activities specified in Schedule 1 are prescribed as regulated activities for the purposes of section 8(1) of the Act.

(2) An activity which is ancillary to, or is carried on wholly or mainly in relation to, a regulated activity shall be treated as part of that activity.

8   General

(1) A registered person must comply with regulations 9 to 20A in carrying on a regulated activity.

9   Person-centred care

(1) The care and treatment of service users must –

    (a) be appropriate,

    (b) meet their needs, and

    (c) reflect their preferences.

(2) But paragraph (1) does not apply to the extent that the provision of care or treatment would result in a breach of regulation 11.

(5) If the service user is 16 or over and lacks capacity in relation to a matter to which this regulation applies, paragraphs (1) to (3) are subject to any duty on the registered person under the 2005 Act in relation to that matter.

(6) But if Part 4 or 4A of the 1983 Act applies to a service user, care and treatment must be provided in accordance with the provisions of that Act.

10   Dignity and respect

(1) Service users must be treated with dignity and respect.

(2) Without limiting paragraph (1), the things which a registered person is required to do to comply with paragraph (1) include in particular –

    (a) ensuring the privacy of the service user;

    (b) supporting the autonomy, independence and involvement in the community of the service user;

    (c) having due regard to any relevant protected characteristics (as defined in section 149(7) of the Equality Act 2010) of the service user.

11   Need for consent

(1) Care and treatment of service users must only be provided with the consent of the relevant person.

(2) Paragraph (1) is subject to paragraphs (3) and (4).

(3) If the service user is 16 or over and is unable to give such consent because they lack capacity to do so, the registered person must act in accordance with the 2005 Act.

(4) But if Part 4 or 4A of the 1983 Act applies to a service user, the registered person must act in accordance with the provisions of that Act.

(5) Nothing in this regulation affects the operation of section 5 of the 2005 Act, as read with section 6 of that Act (acts in connection with care or treatment).

12   Safe care and treatment

(1) Care and treatment must be provided in a safe way for service users.

(2) Without limiting paragraph (1), the things which a registered person must do to comply with that paragraph include –

(a) assessing the risks to the health and safety of service users of receiving the care or treatment;

(b) doing all that is reasonably practicable to mitigate any such risks;

(c) ensuring that persons providing care or treatment to service users have the qualifications, competence, skills and experience to do so safely;

(d) ensuring that the premises used by the service provider are safe to use for their intended purpose and are used in a safe way;

(e) ensuring that the equipment used by the service provider for providing care or treatment to a service user is safe for such use and is used in a safe way;

(f) where equipment or medicines are supplied by the service provider, ensuring that there are sufficient quantities of these to ensure the safety of service users and to meet their needs;

(g) the proper and safe management of medicines;

(h) assessing the risk of, and preventing, detecting and controlling the spread of, infections, including those that are health care associated;

(i) where responsibility for the care and treatment of service users is shared with, or transferred to, other persons, working with such other persons, service users and other appropriate persons to ensure that timely care planning takes place to ensure the health, safety and welfare of the service users.

13   Safeguarding service users from abuse and improper treatment

(1) Service users must be protected from abuse and improper treatment in accordance with this regulation.

(2) Systems and processes must be established and operated effectively to prevent abuse of service users.

(3) Systems and processes must be established and operated effectively to investigate, immediately upon becoming aware of, any allegation or evidence of such abuse.

(4) Care or treatment for service users must not be provided in a way that –

(a) includes discrimination against a service user on grounds of any protected characteristic (as defined in section 4 of the Equality Act 2010) of the service user,

(b) includes acts intended to control or restrain a service user that are not necessary to prevent, or not a proportionate response to, a risk of harm posed to the service user or another individual if the service user was not subject to control or restraint,

(c) is degrading for the service user, or

(d) significantly disregards the needs of the service user for care or treatment.

(5) A service user must not be deprived of their liberty for the purpose of receiving care or treatment without lawful authority.

(6) For the purposes of this regulation –

'abuse' means –

(a) any behaviour towards a service user that is an offence under the Sexual Offences Act 2003,

(b) ill-treatment (whether of a physical or psychological nature) of a service user,

(c) theft, misuse or misappropriation of money or property belonging to a service user, or

(d) neglect of a service user.

(7) For the purposes of this regulation, a person controls or restrains a service user if that person –

(a) uses, or threatens to use, force to secure the doing of an act which the service user resists, or

(b) restricts the service user's liberty of movement, whether or not the service user resists,

including by use of physical, mechanical or chemical means.

14   Meeting nutritional and hydration needs

(1) The nutritional and hydration needs of service users must be met.

(2) Paragraph (1) applies where –

    (a) care or treatment involves –

        (i)   the provision of accommodation by the service provider, or

        (ii) an overnight stay for the service user on premises used by the service for the purposes of carrying on a regulated activity, or

    (b) the meeting of the nutritional or hydration needs of service users is part of the arrangements made for the provision of care or treatment by the service provider.

(3) But paragraph (1) does not apply to the extent that the meeting of such nutritional or hydration needs would –

    (a) result in a breach of regulation 11, or

    (b) not be in the service user's best interests.

(4) For the purposes of paragraph (1), 'nutritional and hydration needs' means –

    (a) receipt by a service user of suitable and nutritious food and hydration which is adequate to sustain life and good health,

    (b) receipt by a service user of parenteral nutrition and dietary supplements when prescribed by a health care professional,

    (c) the meeting of any reasonable requirements of a service user for food and hydration arising from the service user's preferences or their religious or cultural background, and

    (d) if necessary, support for a service user to eat or drink.

(5) Section 4 of the 2005 Act (best interests) applies for the purposes of determining the best interests of a service user who is 16 or over under this regulation as it applies for the purposes of that Act.

16   Receiving and acting on complaints

(1) Any complaint received must be investigated and necessary and proportionate action must be taken in response to any failure identified by the complaint or investigation.

(2) The registered person must establish and operate effectively an accessible system for identifying, receiving, recording, handling and responding to complaints by service users and other persons in relation to the carrying on of the regulated activity.

(3) The registered person must provide to the Commission, when requested to do so and by no later than 28 days beginning on the day after receipt of the request, a summary of –

    (a) complaints made under such complaints system,

    (b) responses made by the registered person to such complaints and any further correspondence with the complainants in relation to such complaints, and

    (c) any other relevant information in relation to such complaints as the Commission may request.

18   Staffing

(1) Sufficient numbers of suitably qualified, competent, skilled and experienced persons must be deployed in order to meet the requirements of this Part.

20   Duty of candour

(1) Registered persons must act in an open and transparent way with relevant persons in relation to care and treatment provided to service users in carrying on a regulated activity.

(2) As soon as reasonably practicable after becoming aware that a notifiable safety incident has occurred a registered person must –

    (a) notify the relevant person that the incident has occurred in accordance with paragraph (3), and

    (b) provide reasonable support to the relevant person in relation to the incident, including when giving such notification.

(3) The notification to be given under paragraph (2)(a) must –

(a) be given in person by one or more representatives of the registered person,

(b) provide an account, which to the best of the registered person's knowledge is true, of all the facts the registered person knows about the incident as at the date of the notification,

(c) advise the relevant person what further enquiries into the incident the registered person believes are appropriate,

(d) include an apology, and

(e) be recorded in a written record which is kept securely by the registered person.

(4) The notification given under paragraph (2)(a) must be followed by a written notification given or sent to the relevant person containing –

(a) the information provided under paragraph (3)(b),

(b) details of any enquiries to be undertaken in accordance with paragraph (3)(c),

(c) the results of any further enquiries into the incident, and

(d) an apology.

(5) But if the relevant person cannot be contacted in person or declines to speak to the representative of the registered person –

(a) paragraphs (2) to (4) are not to apply, and

(b) a written record is to be kept of attempts to contact or to speak to the relevant person.

(6) The registered person must keep a copy of all correspondence with the relevant person under paragraph (4).

(7) In this regulation –

'apology' means an expression of sorrow or regret in respect of a notifiable safety incident;

'moderate harm' means –

(a) harm that requires a moderate increase in treatment, and

(b) significant, but not permanent, harm;

'moderate increase in treatment' means an unplanned return to surgery, an unplanned re-admission, a prolonged episode of care, extra time in hospital or as an outpatient, cancelling of treatment, or transfer to another treatment area (such as intensive care);

'notifiable safety incident' has the meaning given in paragraphs (8) and (9);

'prolonged pain' means pain which a service user has experienced, or is likely to experience, for a continuous period of at least 28 days;

'prolonged psychological harm' means psychological harm which a service user has experienced, or is likely to experience, for a continuous period of at least 28 days;

'relevant person' means the service user or, in the following circumstances, a person lawfully acting on their behalf –

(a) on the death of the service user,

(b) where the service user is under 16 and not competent to make a decision in relation to their care or treatment, or

(c) where the service user is 16 or over and lacks capacity in relation to the matter;

'severe harm' means a permanent lessening of bodily, sensory, motor, physiologic or intellectual functions, including removal of the wrong limb or organ or brain damage, that is related directly to the incident and not related to the natural course of the service user's illness or underlying condition.

(8) In relation to a health service body, 'notifiable safety incident' means any unintended or unexpected incident that occurred in respect of a service user during the provision of a regulated activity that, in the reasonable opinion of a health care professional, could result in, or appears to have resulted in –

(a) the death of the service user, where the death relates directly to the incident rather than to the natural course of the service user's illness or underlying condition, or

(b) severe harm, moderate harm or prolonged psychological harm to the service user.

(9) In relation to any other registered person, 'notifiable safety incident' means any unintended or unexpected incident that occurred in respect of a service user during the provision of a regulated activity that, in the reasonable opinion of a health care professional –

(a) appears to have resulted in –

  (i) the death of the service user, where the death relates directly to the incident rather than to the natural course of the service user's illness or underlying condition,

  (ii) an impairment of the sensory, motor or intellectual functions of the service user which has lasted, or is likely to last, for a continuous period of at least 28 days,

  (iii) changes to the structure of the service user's body,

  (iv) the service user experiencing prolonged pain or prolonged psychological harm, or

  (v) the shortening of the life expectancy of the service user; or

(b) requires treatment by a health care professional in order to prevent –

  (i) the death of the service user, or

  (ii) any injury to the service user which, if left untreated, would lead to one or more of the outcomes mentioned in sub-paragraph (a).

22   Offences

(1) It is an offence for a registered person to fail to comply with any of the requirements in the following regulations, as read with regulation 8 –

(a) regulation 11,

(b) regulation 16(3)

(c) regulation 17(3)

(d) regulation 20(2)(a) and (3), or

(e) regulation 20A.

(2) A registered person commits an offence if the registered person fails to comply with a requirement of regulation 12, 13(1) to (4) or 14, as read with regulation 8, and such failure results in –

(a) avoidable harm (whether of a physical or psychological nature) to a service user,

(b) a service user being exposed to a significant risk of such harm occurring, or

(c) in a case of theft, misuse or misappropriation of money or property, any loss by a service user of the money or property concerned.

(4) But it is a defence for a registered person to prove that they took all reasonable steps and exercised all due diligence to prevent the breach of any of those regulations that has occurred.

23   Offences: penalties

(4) A person guilty of an offence under regulation 22(1) for breach of regulation 11 or an offence under regulation 22(2) is liable on summary conviction to a fine.

(5) A person guilty of an offence under regulation 22(1) for breach of regulation 16(3), 17(3) or 20(2)(a) and (3) is liable, on summary conviction, to a fine not exceeding level 4 on the standard scale.

National Health Service (Clinical Negligence Scheme) Regulations 2015

(SI 2015, No. 559)

1   Citation, commencement and application

(3) These Regulations apply to England only.

2   Interpretation

(1) In these Regulations –

'the 1996 Regulations' means the National Health Service (Clinical Negligence Scheme) Regulations 1996;

'the 2006 Act' means the National Health Service Act 2006;

'the 2012 Act' means the Health and Social Care Act 2012;

'the appointed day' means the date on which these Regulations come into force;

'a CCG' means a clinical commissioning group;

'eligible body' means a body specified in sub-paragraphs (a) to (l) of regulation 4(1);

'insolvency' has the meaning given in section 247(1) of the Insolvency Act 1986 (meaning of 'insolvency' and 'go into liquidation');

'membership year', in respect of any eligible body, means any 12 month period starting on 1st April during which the body is a member of the Scheme;

'relevant function' means –

(a) arranging for the provision of services for the purposes of the health service;

(b) providing services for the purposes of the health service;

(c) exercising functions in relation to the health service;

(d) exercising powers under, or by virtue of, section 7 of the Health and Medicines Act 1988

(e) exercising powers under section 13W, 14Z5, 43(3) or 44 of, or paragraphs 19 and 20 of Schedule 4 to, the 2006 Act;

(f) exercising powers under section 243 or 270 of the 2012 Act; or

(g) exercising powers by virtue of section 240(1)(a) or (b) of the 2012 Act;

'relevant health services' –

(a) means health services provided in England for the purposes of the health service, but

(b) does not include primary care services;

'the Scheme' means the scheme known as the Clinical Negligence Scheme for Trusts

The Scheme

3   Clinical Negligence Scheme for Trusts

(1) The Scheme is to continue to have effect as if it had been established under these Regulations

(2) The purpose of the Scheme is to enable eligible bodies to make provision to meet liabilities to which the Scheme applies.

(3) An eligible body may participate in the Scheme only if it is a member of the Scheme.

(4) The Secretary of State will continue to administer the Scheme.

4   Eligible bodies

(1) The bodies which are eligible to be members of the Scheme are –

(a) the Board;

(b) a CCG;

(c) a Special Health Authority;

(d) the Care Quality Commission;

(e) Health Education England;

(f) the Health Research Authority;

(g) the Health and Social Care Information Centre;

(h) NICE;

(i) an NHS trust;

(j) an NHS foundation trust;

(k) a local authority which provides, or arranges the provision of, relevant health services under an arrangement made between the local authority and either –

(i)   the Secretary of State; or

(ii) a body specified in sub-paragraph (a) to (c), (i) or (j);

(l) any body ('B') not specified in sub-paragraphs (a) to (k) which provides relevant health services in the circumstances specified in paragraph (2), (3) or (4).

(2) The circumstances specified in this paragraph are where the relevant health services are provided under an arrangement made between B and the Board, a CCG or a Special Health Authority.

(3) The circumstances specified in this paragraph are where the relevant health services –

(a) are provided under an arrangement made between B and another body which is not a member of the Scheme; and

(b) are also the subject of an arrangement made between that other body and the Board, a CCG or a Special Health Authority.

(4) The circumstances specified in this paragraph are where the relevant health services –

    (a) are provided under an arrangement made between B and another body which is not a member of the Scheme; and

    (b) are also the subject of –

        (i) an arrangement made between that other body and a further body which is not a member of the Scheme;

        (ii) any further arrangement or arrangements which may have been entered into between bodies which are not members of the Scheme; and

        (iii) an arrangement made between the Board, a CCG or a Special Health Authority and a body falling within paragraph (i) or (ii).

Liabilities to which the Scheme applies

8   Liabilities of members

(1) Subject to paragraph (4), the Scheme applies to any liability in tort under the law of England and Wales which a member of the Scheme owes to a third party in respect of or consequent upon personal injury or loss as specified in paragraph (2).

(2) The personal injury or loss referred to in paragraph (1) is personal injury or loss arising out of or in connection with any breach of a duty of care which –

    (a) the member owes to any person in connection with the diagnosis of any illness or the care or treatment of any patient; and

    (b) is in consequence of any act or omission specified in paragraph (3).

(3) The act or omission referred to in paragraph (2) is an act or omission to act on the part of –

    (a) a person employed or engaged by the member in connection with any relevant function of the member; or

    (b) an employee or agent of a person engaged by the member in connection with any such function.

Payments into the Scheme

11   Determination of amounts payable by members

(1) The Secretary of State must determine the amount which each member of the Scheme must pay to the Secretary of State in respect of each membership year.

12   Duty of members to make contributions to the Scheme

(1) Each member of the Scheme must, in respect of each membership year, pay to the Secretary of State the amount determined in respect of the member under regulation 11(1) (determination of amounts payable by members).

Payments out of the Scheme

14   Payments out of the Scheme: liabilities of members

(1) Where a payment falls to be made by a member of the Scheme in connection with a claim in respect of a liability to which the Scheme applies, the Secretary of State may pay to the member or on the member's behalf an amount determined by the Secretary of State under regulation 18.

(2) No payment may be made under paragraph (1) –

    (a) in respect of any liability of the member which is excluded from the Scheme by any of paragraphs (3) to (5); or

    (b) in respect of any liability of, or payment by, the member which is excluded from the Scheme by regulation 16 (exclusions from the Scheme).

(3) Any liability which was incurred by an eligible body before it became a member of the Scheme is excluded from the Scheme unless –

    (a) the claim by a third party against the eligible body in respect of the liability was made after the start of its membership of the Scheme;

(b) the Secretary of State is satisfied that the eligible body informed the Secretary of State before the end of the qualifying period that the claim had been made;

(c) the Secretary of State agreed before the start of the eligible body's membership that any liability of the body that results from a claim to which sub-paragraphs (a) and (b) apply should not be excluded from the Scheme; and

(d) that agreement remains in force at the date on which the claim against the eligible body falls to be met.

(4) Any liability of a member which falls to be met after the member gives notice of cancellation under regulation 6(2) (cancellation of membership by a member) but before membership has ceased is excluded from the Scheme unless the Secretary of State is satisfied that the liability would have fallen to be met at that time irrespective of the member's decision to give such a notice.

(5) Any liability of a body ('B') which falls to be met after its membership of the Scheme has ceased is excluded from the Scheme unless –

(a) the claim by a third party against B in respect of the liability was made before B's membership ceased;

(b) the Secretary of State is satisfied that B informed the Secretary of State before the end of the qualifying period that the claim had been made;

(c) the Secretary of State agreed before B's membership ceased that any liability of B that results from a claim to which sub-paragraphs (a) and (b) apply should not be excluded from the Scheme; and

(d) that agreement remained in force on the date on which B's membership ceased.

(6) In paragraph (3)(b) and (5)(b), the 'qualifying period' is the period of 14 days starting with the date on which the member became aware that a claim had been made or, if earlier, the date on which the Secretary of State considers that the member ought to have become aware that a claim had been made.

18   Determining the amount of any payment to be made out of the Scheme

(1) In respect of each liability to which the Scheme applies, the Secretary of State must determine the amount of any payment which is to be made under regulation 14(1) or 15(1) (payments out of the Scheme in respect of liabilities of members and former members).

(2) In determining the amount of the payment to be made in circumstances specified in each of paragraphs (3) to (8), the Secretary of State must have regard to the relevant matters specified in that paragraph.

(3) Where an award of damages has been made by a Court against the member, the relevant matters are the amount of –

(a) the award;

(b) the legal and associated costs awarded to the claimant; and

(c) any legal and associated costs incurred by or on behalf of the member.

(4) Where legal proceedings are the subject of a settlement agreed to by the member, the relevant matters are the amount of –

(a) any sum paid or payable by the member in relation to the claimant's claim for damages;

(b) the member's contribution towards any legal and associated costs incurred by the claimant; and

(c) any legal and associated costs incurred by or on behalf of the member.

(5) Where, in any legal proceedings, a Court has declined to award damages against the member, the relevant matters are –

(a) the amount of any legal and associated costs incurred by or on behalf of the member; and

(b) the extent to which those costs are not recoverable either from the claimant or from the Legal Aid Agency under regulations made by virtue of section 26(5) of the Legal Aid, Sentencing and Punishment of Offenders Act 2012(**a**) (costs in civil proceedings).

(6) Where a member has, otherwise than in the course of legal proceedings, agreed to make a payment in settlement of a claim, the relevant matters are the amount of –

(a) the payment agreed; and

(b) any legal or associated costs incurred by or on behalf of the member in connection with the claim.

(7) Where, otherwise than in the course of legal proceedings, a member has agreed to make any contribution towards legal or associated costs incurred by a person in connection with that person's claim against the member in respect of a liability to which the Scheme applies, the relevant matters are the amount of –

(a) that contribution; and

(b) any legal or associated costs incurred by or on behalf of the member in connection with the claim.

(8) Where a member has agreed to be bound by the determination of any person or body as to the making of a payment by that member in respect of a liability to which the Scheme applies, the relevant matters are the amount of –

(a) the payment;

(b) any legal or associated costs incurred by the claimant in connection with the claim; and

(c) any legal or associated costs incurred by or on behalf of the member in connection with the claim.

Part III

Department of Health Guidelines

NHS Indemnity: Arrangements for Clinical Negligence Claims in the NHS

[*The following guidance was issued with Health Service Guideline (96)48.*]

Executive summary

Introduction

This is a summary of the main points contained within *NHS Indemnity Arrangements for clinical negligence claims in the NHS,* issued under cover of HSG 96/48. The booklet includes a Q&A section covering the applicability of NHS indemnity to common situations and an annex on sponsored trials. It covers NHS indemnity for clinical negligence but not for any other liability such as product liability, employers liability or liability for NHS trust board members.

Clinical negligence

Clinical negligence is defined as 'a breach of duty of care by members of the health care professions employed by NHS bodies or by others consequent on decisions or judgements made by members of those professions acting in their professional capacity in the course of their employment, and which are admitted as negligent by the employer or are determined as such through the legal process'. The term health care professional includes hospital doctors, dentists, nurses, midwives, health visitors, pharmacy practitioners, registered ophthalmic or dispensing opticians (working in a hospital setting), members of professions allied to medicine and dentistry, ambulance personnel, laboratory staff and relevant technicians.

Main principles

NHS bodies are vicariously liable for the negligent acts and Omissions of their employees and should have arrangements for meeting this liability. NHS Indemnity applies where

    (a) the negligent health care professional was:
        (i)   working under a contract of employment and the negligence occurred in the course of that employment;
        (ii) not working under a contract of employment but was contracted to an NHS body to provide services to persons to whom that NHS body owed a duty of care;
        (iii) neither of the above but otherwise owed a duty of care to the persons injured;
    (b) persons, not employed under a contract of employment and who may or may not be a health care professional, who owe a duty of care to the persons injured. These include locums; medical academic staff with honorary contracts; students; those conducting clinical trials; charitable volunteers; persons undergoing further professional education, training and examinations; students and staff working on income generation projects.

Where these principles apply, NHS bodies should accept full financial liability where negligent harm has occurred, and not seek to recover their costs from the health care professional involved.

Who is not covered

NHS Indemnity does not apply to family health service practitioners working under contracts for services, eg GPs (including fundholders), general dental practitioners, family dentists, pharmacists or optometrists; other self employed health care professionals eg independent midwives; employees of FHS practices; employees of private hospitals; local education authorities; voluntary agencies. Exceptions to the normal cover arrangements are set out in the main document.

Circumstances covered

NHS Indemnity covers negligent harm caused to patients or healthy volunteers in the following circumstances: whenever they are receiving an established treatment, whether or not in accordance with an agreed guideline or protocol; whenever they are receiving a novel or unusual treatment which, in the judgement of the health care professional, is appropriate for that particular patient; whenever they are subjects as patients or healthy volunteers of clinical research aimed at benefitting patients now or in the future.

Expenses met

Where negligence is alleged, NHS bodies are responsible for meeting: the legal and administrative costs of defending the claim or, if appropriate, of reaching a settlement; the plaintiffs costs, as agreed by the two parties or as awarded by the court; the damages awarded either as a one-off payment or as a structured settlement.

Clinical negligence—definition

1. Clinical negligence is defined as:

    'A breach of duty of care by members of the health care professions employed by NHS bodies or by others consequent on decisions or judgments made by members of those professions acting in their professional capacity in the course of employment, and which are admitted as negligent by the employer or are determined as such through the legal process.'[1]

2. In this definition 'breach of duty of care' has its legal meaning. NHS bodies will need to take legal advice in individual cases, but the general position will be that the following must all apply before liability for negligence exists:

    2.1 There must have been a duty of care owed to the person treated by the relevant professional(s);

    2.2 The standard of care appropriate to such duty must not have been attained and therefore the duty breached, whether by action or inaction, advice given or failure to advise;

    2.3 Such a breach must be demonstrated to have caused the injury and therefore the resulting loss complained about by the patient;

    2.4 Any loss sustained as a result of the injury and complained about by the person treated must be of a kind that the courts recognise and for which they allow compensation; and

    2.5 The injury and resulting loss complained about by the person treated must have been reasonably foreseeable as a possible consequence of the breach.

3. This booklet is concerned with NHS Indemnity for clinical negligence and does not cover indemnity for any other liability such as product liability, employers liability or liability for NHS trust board members.

Other terms

4. Throughout this guidance:

    4.1 The terms 'an NHS body' and 'NHS bodies' include Health Authorities, Special Health Authorities and NHS Trusts but excludes all GP practices whether fundholding or not, general dental practices, pharmacies and opticians' practices.

---

[1] The NHS (Clinical Negligence Scheme) Regulations 1996, which established the Clinical Negligence Scheme for Trusts, defines clinical negligence in terms of '... a liability in tort owed by a member to a third party in respect of or consequent upon personal injury or loss arising out of or in connection with any breach of a duty of care owed by that body to any person in connection with the diagnosis of any illness, or the care or treatment of any patient, in consequence of any act or omission to act on the part of a person employed or engaged by a member in connection with any relevant function of the member.'

4.2 The term 'health care professional' includes:

Doctors, dentists, nurses, midwives, health visitors, hospital pharmacy practitioners, registered ophthalmic or registered dispensing opticians working in a hospital setting, members of professions supplementary to medicine and dentistry, ambulance personnel, laboratory staff and relevant technicians.

Principles

5. NHS bodies are legally liable for the negligent acts and omissions of their employees (the principle of vicarious liability), and should have arrangements for meeting this liability. NHS Indemnity applies where:

5.1 the negligent health care professional was working under a contract of employment (as opposed to a contract for services) and the negligence occurred in the course of that employment; or

5.2 the negligent health care professional, although not working under a contract of employment, was contracted to an NHS body to provide services to persons to whom that NHS body owed a duty of care.

6. Where the principles outlined in paragraph 5 apply, NHS bodies should accept full financial liability where negligent harm has occurred. They should not seek to recover their costs either in part or in full from the health care professional concerned or from any indemnities they may have. NHS bodies may carry this risk entirely or spread it through membership of the Clinical Negligence Scheme for Trusts (CNST—see EL(95)40).

Who is covered

7. NHS Indemnity covers the actions of staff in the course of their NHS employment. It also covers people in certain other categories whenever the NHS body owes a duty of care to the person harmed, including, for example, locums, medical academic staff with honorary contracts, students, those conducting clinical trials, charitable volunteers and people undergoing further professional education, training and examinations. This includes staff working on income generation projects. GPs or dentists who are directly employed by Health Authorities, e.g. as Public Health doctors (including port medical officers and medical inspectors of immigrants at UK air/sea ports), are covered.

8. Examples of the applicability of NHS Indemnity to common situations are set out in question and answer format in Annex A.

Who is not covered

9. NHS Indemnity does not apply to general medical and dental practitioners working under contracts for services. General practitioners, including GP fundholders, are responsible for making their own indemnity arrangements, as are other self-employed health care professionals such as independent midwives. Neither does NHS Indemnity apply to employees of general practices, whether fundholding or not, or to employees of private hospitals (even when treating NHS patients) local education authorities or voluntary agencies.

10. Examples of circumstances in which independent practitioners or staff who normally work for private employers are covered by NHS Indemnity are given in Annex A. The NHS Executive advises independent practitioners to check their own indemnity position.

11. Examples of circumstances in which NHS employees are not covered by NHS Indemnity are also given in Annex A.

Circumstances covered

12. NHS bodies owe a duty of care to healthy volunteers or patients treated or undergoing tests which they administer. NHS Indemnity covers negligent harm caused to these people in the following circumstances:

12.1 whenever they are receiving an established treatment, whether of not in accordance with an agreed guideline or protocol;

12.2 whenever they are receiving a novel or unusual treatment which in the clinical judgment of the health care professional is appropriate for the particular patient;

12.3 whenever they are subjects of clinical research aimed at benefitting patients now or in the future, whether as patients or as healthy volunteers. (Special arrangements, including the availability of no-fault indemnity apply where research is sponsored by pharmaceutical companies. See Annex B.)

Expenses met

13 Where negligence is alleged NHS bodies are responsible for meeting:

13.1 the legal and administrative costs of defending the claim and, if appropriate, of reaching a settlement, including the cost of any mediation;

13.2 where appropriate, plaintiff's costs, either as agreed between the parties or as awarded by a court of law;

13.3 the damages agreed or awarded, whether as a one-off payment or a structured settlement.

Claims management principles

14. NHS bodies should take the essential decisions on the handling of claims of clinical negligence against their staff, using professional defence organisations or others as their agents and advisers as appropriate.*

Financial support arrangements

15. Details of the Clinical Negligence Scheme for Trusts (CNST) were announced in EL(95)40 on 29 March 1995.

16. All financial arrangements in respect of clinical negligence costs for NHS bodies have been reviewed and guidance on transitional arrangements (for funding clinical accidents which happened before 1 April 1995), was issued on 27 November 1995 under cover of FDL(95)56. FDL(96)36 provided further guidance on a number of detailed questions.

ANNEX A QUESTIONS AND ANSWERS ON NHS INDEMNITY

Below are replies to some of the questions most commonly asked about NHS Indemnity

1   Who is covered by NHS Indemnity?

NHS bodies are liable at law for the negligent acts and omissions of their staff in the course of their NHS employment. Under NHS Indemnity, NHS bodies take direct responsibility for costs and damages arising from clinical negligence where they (as employers) are vicariously liable for the acts and omissions of their health care professional staff.

2   Would health care professionals opting to work under contracts for services rather than as employees of the NHS be covered?

Where an NHS body is responsible for *providing* care to patients NHS Indemnity will apply whether the health care professional involved is an employee or not. For example a doctor working under a contract for services with an NHS Trust would be covered because the Trust has responsibility for the care of its patients. A consultant undertaking contracted NHS work in a private hospital would also be covered.

3   Does this include clinical academics and research workers?

NHS bodies are vicariously liable for the work done by university medical staff and other research workers (e.g. employees of the MRC) under their honorary contracts, but not for pre-clinical or other work in the university.

---

* **Editors' note:** The handling of claims for clinical negligence has subsequently been taken over by the NHS Litigation Authority, although 'NHS bodies' remain legally responsible for meeting claims.

4   Are GP practices covered?

GP's whether fundholders or not [and who are not employed by Health Authorities as public health doctors], are independent practitioners and therefore they and their employed staff are not covered by NHS Indemnity.

5   Is a hospital doctor doing a GP locum covered?

This would not be the responsibility of the NHS body since it would be outside the contract of employment. The hospital doctor and the general practitioners concerned should ensure that there is appropriate professional liability cover.

6   Is a GP seeing a patient in hospital covered?

AGP providing medical care to patients in hospital under a contractual arrangement, e.g. where the GP was employed as a clinical assistant, will be covered by NHS Indemnity, as will a GP who provides services in NHS hospitals under staff fund contracts (known as 'bed funds'). Where there is no such contractual arrangement, and the NHS body provides facilities for patient(s) who continue to be the clinical responsibility of the GP, the GP would be responsible and professional liability cover would be appropriate. However, junior medical staff, nurses or members of the professions supplementary to medicine involved in the care of a GP's patients in NHS hospitals under their contract of employment would be covered.

7   Are GP trainees working in general practice covered?

In general practice the responsibility for training and for paying the salary of a GP trainee rests with the trainer. While the trainee is receiving a salary in general practice it is advisable that both the trainee and the trainer, and indeed other members of the practice, should have appropriate professional liability cover as NHS indemnity will not apply.

8   Are NHS employees working under contracts with
GP fundholders covered?

If their employing NHS body has agreed a contract to provide services to a GP fundholding practice's patients, NHS employees will be working under the terms of their contracts of employment and NHS Indemnity will cover them. If NHS employees themselves contract with GP fundholders (or any other independent body) to do work outside their NHS contract of employment they should ensure that they have separate indemnity cover.

9   Is academic general practice covered?

The Department his no plans to extend NHS Indemnity to academic departments of general practice. In respect of general medical services, Health Authorities' payments of fees and allowances include an element for expenses, of which medical defence subscriptions are a part.

10   Is private work in NHS hospitals covered by NHS Indemnity?

NHS bodies will not be responsible for a health care professional's private practice, even in an NHS hospital. However, where junior medical staff, nurses or members of professions supplementary to medicine are involved in the care of private patients in NHS hospitals, they would normally be doing so is part of their NHS contract, and would therefore be covered. It remains advisable that health professionals who might be involved in work outside the scope of his or her NHS employment should have professional liability cover.

11   Is Category 2 work covered?

Category 2 work (e.g. reports for insurance companies) is by definition not undertaken for the employing NHS body and is therefore not covered by NHS Indemnity. Unless the work is carried out on behalf of the employing NHS body, professional liability cover would be needed.

12   Are disciplinary proceedings of statutory bodies covered?

NHS bodies are not financially responsible for the defence of staff involved in disciplinary proceedings conducted by statutory bodies such as the GMC (doctors), UKCC (nurses and midwives), GDC (dentists)

CPSM (professions supplementary to medicine) and RPSGB (pharmacists). It is the responsibility of the practitioner concerned to take out professional liability cover against such an eventuality.

13   Are clinical trials covered?

In the case of negligent harm, health care professionals undertaking clinical trials or studies on volunteers, whether healthy or patients, in the course of their NHS employment are covered by NHS Indemnity. Similarly, for a trial not involving medicines, the NHS body would take financial responsibility unless the trial were covered by such other indemnity as may have been agreed between the NHS body and those responsible for the trial. In any case, NHS bodies should ensure that they are informed of clinical trials in which their staff are taking part in their NHS employment and that these trials have the required Research Ethics Committee approval. For non-negligent harm, see question 16 below.

14   Is harm resulting from a fault in the drug/equipment covered?

Where harm is caused due to a fault in the manufacture of a drug or piece of equipment then, under the terms of the Consumer Protection Act 1987, it is no defence for the producer to show that he exercised reasonable care. Under normal circumstances, therefore, NHS indemnity would not apply unless there was a question whether the health care professional either knew or should reasonably have known that the drug/equipment was faulty but continued to use it. Strict liability could apply if the drug/equipment had been manufactured by an NHS body itself, for example a prototype as part of a research programme.

15   Are Local Research Ethics Committees (LRECs) covered?

Under the Department's guidelines an LREC is appointed by the Health Authority to provide independent advice to NHS bodies within its area on the ethics of research proposals. The Health Authority should take financial responsibility for members' acts and omissions in the course of performance of their duties as LREC members.

16   Is there liability for non-negligent harm?

Apart from liability for defective products, legal liability does not arise where a person is harmed but no one has acted negligently. An example of this would be unexpected side-effects of drugs during clinical trials. In exceptional circumstances (and within the delegated limit of £50,000) NHS bodies may consider whether an ex-gratia payment could be offered. NHS bodies may not offer advance indemnities or take out commercial insurance for non-negligent harm.

17   What arrangements can non-NHS bodies make for non-negligent harm?

Arrangements will depend on the status of the non-NHS body. Arrangements for clinical trials sponsored by the pharmaceutical industry are set out in Annex B. Other independent sector sponsors of clinical research involving NHS patients (e.g. universities and medical research charities) may also make arrangements to indemnity research subjects for non-negligent harm. Public sector research funding bodies such as the Medical Research Council (MRC) may not offer advance indemnities nor take out commercial insurance for non-negligent harm. The MRC offers the assurance that it will give sympathetic consideration to claims in respect of non-negligent harm arising from an MRC funded trial. NHS bodies should not make ex-gratia payments for non-negligent harm where research is sponsored by a non-NHS body.

18   Would health care professionals be covered if they were working other than in accordance with the duties of their post?

Health care professionals would be covered by NHS Indemnity for actions in the course of NHS employment, and this should be interpreted liberally. For work not covered in this way health care professionals may have a civil, or even, in extreme circumstances, criminal liability for their actions.

19   Are health care professionals attending accident victims ('Good Samaritan' acts) covered?

'Good Samaritan' acts are not part of the health care professional's work for the employing body. Medical defence organisations are willing to provide low-cost cover against the (unusual) event of anyone performing such an act being sued for negligence. Ambulance services can, with the agreement of staff, include an additional term in the individual employee contracts to the effect that the member of staff is expected to provide assistance in any emergency outside of duty hours where it is appropriate to do so.

20   Are NHS staff in public health medicine or in community health services doing work for local authorities covered? Are occupational physicians covered?

Staff working in public health medicine, clinical medical officers or therapists carrying out local authority functions under their NHS contract would be acting in the course of their NHS employment. They will therefore be covered by NHS Indemnity. The same principle applies to occupational physicians employed by NHS bodies.

21   Are NHS staff working for other agencies, e.g. the Prison Service, covered?

In general, NHS bodies are not financially responsible for the acts of NHS staff when they are working on an individual contractual basis for other agencies. (Conversely, they are responsible where, for example, a Ministry of Defence doctor works in an NHS hospital.) Either the non-NHS body commissioning the work would be responsible, or the health care professional should have separate indemnity cover. However, NHS Indemnity should cover work for which the NHS body pays the health care professional a fee, such as domiciliary visits, and family planning services.

22   Are former NHS staff covered?

NHS Indemnity will cover staff who have subsequently left the Service (e.g. on retirement) provided the liability arose in respect of acts or omissions in the course of their NHS employment, regardless of when the claim was notified. NHS bodies may seek the co-operation of former staff in providing statements in the defence of a case.

23   Are NHS staff offering services to voluntary bodies such as the Red Cross or hospices covered?

The NHS body would be responsible for the actions of its staff only if it were contractually responsible for the clinical staffing of the voluntary body. If not, the staff concerned may wish to ensure that they have separate indemnity cover.

24   Do NHS bodies provide cover for locums?

NHS bodies take financial responsibility for the acts and omissions of a locum health care professional, whether 'internal' or provided by an external agency, doing the work of a colleague who would be covered.

25   What are the arrangements for staff employed by one trust working in another?

This depends on the contractual arrangements. If the work is being done as part of a formal agreement between the trusts, then the staff involved will be acting within their normal NHS duties and, unless the agreement states otherwise, the employing trust will be liable. The NHS Executive does not recommend the use of ad hoc arrangements, e.g. a doctor in one trust asking a doctor in another to provide an informal second opinion, unless there is an agreement between the trusts as to which of them will accept liability for the 'visiting' doctor in such circumstances.

26   Are private sector rotations for hospital staff covered?

The medical staff of independent hospitals are responsible for their own professional liability cover, subject to the requirements of the hospital managers. If NHS staff in the training grades work in independent hospitals as part of their NHS training, they would be covered by NHS Indemnity, provided that such work was covered by an NHS contract of employment.

27   Are voluntary workers covered?

Where volunteers work in NHS bodies, they are covered by NHS Indemnity. NHS managers should be aware of all voluntary activity going on in their organisations and should wherever possible confirm volunteers' indemnity position in writing.

28   Are students covered?

NHS Indemnity applies where students are working under the supervision of NHS employees. This should be made clear in the agreement between the NHS body and the students' educational body. This will apply to students of all the health care professions and to school students on, for example, work experience placements. Students working in NHS premises, under supervision of medical academic staff employed by universities holding honorary contracts, are also covered. Students who spend time in a primary care setting will only be covered if this is part of an NHS contract. Potential students making preliminary visits and school placements should be adequately supervised and should not become involved in any clinical work. Therefore, no clinical negligence should arise on their part.

In the unlikely event of a school making a negligent choice of work placement for a pupil to work in the NHS, then the school, and not NHS indemnity, should pick up the legal responsibility for the actions of that pupil. The contractual arrangement between the NHS and the school should make this clear.

29   Are health care professional undergoing on-the-job training covered?

Where an NHS body's staff are providing on-the-job training (e.g. refresher or skills updating courses) for health care professionals, the trainees are covered by NHS Indemnity whether they are normally employed by the NHS or not.

30   Are independent midwives covered?

Independent midwives are self-employed practitioners. In common with all other health care professionals working outside the NHS, they are responsible for making their own indemnity arrangements.

31   Are overseas doctors who have come to the UK temporarily, perhaps to demonstrate a new technique, covered?

The NHS body which has invited the overseas doctor will owe a duty of care to the patients on whom the technique is demonstrated and so NHS Indemnity will apply. NHS bodies, therefore, need to make sure that they are kept informed of any such demonstration visits which are proposed and of the nature of the technique to be demonstrated. Where visiting clinicians are not formally registered as students, or are not employees, an honorary contract should be arranged.

32   Are staff who are qualified in another member state of the European Union covered?

Staff qualified in another member state of the European Union, and who are undertaking an adaptation period in accordance with EEC directive 89/48EEC and the European Communities (Recognition of Professional Qualifications) Regulations 1991 which implements EEC Directive 89/48/EEC) and EEC Directive 92/51/EEC, must be treated in a manner consistent with their qualified status in another member state, and should be covered.

Part IV

General Medical Council

The following section contains extracts from guidance published by the General Medical Council which sets out the principles of good practice that the GMC expects doctors to adhere to. The GMC revises its guidance periodically so please check the GMC's website for updated editions: www.gmc-uk.org where you can also read and download the guidance in full.

Good medical practice*

[*Some references omitted.*]

Professionalism in action

1 Patients need good doctors. Good doctors make the care of their patients their first concern: they are competent, keep their knowledge and skills up to date, establish and maintain good relationships with patients and colleagues,[1] are honest and trustworthy, and act with integrity and within the law.

2 Good doctors work in partnership with patients and respect their rights to privacy and dignity. They treat each patient as an individual. They do their best to make sure all patients receive good care and treatment that will support them to live as well as possible, whatever their illness or disability.

3 *Good medical practice* describes what is expected of all doctors registered with the General Medical Council (GMC). It is your responsibility to be familiar with *Good medical practice* and the explanatory guidance which supports it, and to follow the guidance they contain.

4 You must use your judgement in applying the principles to the various situations you will face as a doctor, whether or not you hold a licence to practise, whatever field of medicine you work in, and whether or not you routinely see patients. You must be prepared to explain and justify your decisions and actions.

5 In *Good medical practice*, we use the terms 'you must' and 'you should' in the following ways.
- 'You must' is used for an overriding duty or principle.
- 'You should' is used when we are providing an explanation of how you will meet the overriding duty.
- 'You should' is also used where the duty or principle will not apply in all situations or circumstances, or where there are factors outside your control that affect whether or how you can follow the guidance.

6 To maintain your licence to practise, you must demonstrate, through the revalidation process, that you work in line with the principles and values set out in this guidance. Serious or persistent failure to follow this guidance will put your registration at risk.

Domain 1: Knowledge, skills and performance

Develop and maintain your professional performance

7 You must be competent in all aspects of your work, including management, research and teaching.

8 You must keep your professional knowledge and skills up to date.

9 You must regularly take part in activities that maintain and develop your competence and performance.

10 You should be willing to find and take part in structured support opportunities offered by your employer or contracting body (for example, mentoring). You should do this when you join an organisation and whenever your role changes significantly throughout your career.

11 You must be familiar with guidelines and developments that affect your work.

12 You must keep up to date with, and follow, the law, our guidance and other regulations relevant to your work.

13 You must take steps to monitor and improve the quality of your work.

Apply knowledge and experience to practice

14 You must recognise and work within the limits of your competence.

14.1 You must have the necessary knowledge of the English language to provide a good standard of practice and care in the UK.

15 You must provide a good standard of practice and care. If you assess, diagnose or treat patients, you must:

  a adequately assess the patient's conditions, taking account of their history (including the symptoms and psychological, spiritual, social and cultural factors), their views and values; where necessary, examine the patient

  b promptly provide or arrange suitable advice, investigations or treatment where necessary

  c refer a patient to another practitioner when this serves the patient's needs.

16 In providing clinical care you must:

  a prescribe drugs or treatment, including repeat prescriptions, only when you have adequate knowledge of the patient's health and are satisfied that the drugs or treatment serve the patient's needs

  b provide effective treatments based on the best available evidence

  c take all possible steps to alleviate pain and distress whether or not a cure may be possible

  d consult colleagues where appropriate

  e respect the patient's right to seek a second opinion

  f check that the care or treatment you provide for each patient is compatible with any other treatments the patient is receiving, including (where possible) self-prescribed over-the-counter medications

  g wherever possible, avoid providing medical care to yourself or anyone with whom you have a close personal relationship.

17 You must be satisfied that you have consent or other valid authority before you carry out any examination or investigation, provide treatment or involve patients or volunteers in teaching or research.

18 You must make good use of the resources available to you.

Record your work clearly, accurately and legibly

19 Documents you make (including clinical records) to formally record your work must be clear, accurate and legible. You should make records at the same time as the events you are recording or as soon as possible afterwards.

20 You must keep records that contain personal information about patients, colleagues or others securely, and in line with any data protection requirements.

21 Clinical records should include:
   a relevant clinical findings
   b the decisions made and actions agreed, and who is making the decisions and agreeing the actions
   c the information given to patients
   d any drugs prescribed or other investigation or treatment
   e who is making the record and when.

Domain 2: Safety and quality

Contribute to and comply with systems to protect patients

22 You must take part in systems of quality assurance and quality improvement to promote patient safety. This includes:
   a taking part in regular reviews and audits of your work and that of your team, responding constructively to the outcomes, taking steps to address any problems and carrying out further training where necessary
   b regularly reflecting on your standards of practice and the care you provide
   c reviewing patient feedback where it is available.

23 To help keep patients safe you must:
   a contribute to confidential inquiries
   b contribute to adverse event recognition
   c report adverse incidents involving medical devices that put or have the potential to put the safety of a patient, or another person, at risk
   d report suspected adverse drug reactions
   e respond to requests from organisations monitoring public health.
When providing information for these purposes you should still respect patients' confidentiality.

Respond to risks to safety

24 You must promote and encourage a culture that allows all staff to raise concerns openly and safely.

25 You must take prompt action if you think that patient safety, dignity or comfort is or may be seriously compromised.
   a If a patient is not receiving basic care to meet their needs, you must immediately tell some-one who is in a position to act straight away.
   b If patients are at risk because of inadequate premises, equipment[2] or other resources, poli-cies or systems, you should put the matter right if that is possible. You must raise your con-cern in line with our guidance and your workplace policy. You should also make a record of the steps you have taken.
   c If you have concerns that a colleague may not be fit to practise and may be putting patients at risk, you must ask for advice from a colleague, your defence body or us. If you are still concerned you must report this, in line with our guidance and your workplace policy, and make a record of the steps you have taken.

26 You must offer help if emergencies arise in clinical settings or in the community, taking account of your own safety, your competence and the availability of other options for care.

27 Whether or not you have vulnerable[3] adults or children and young people as patients, you should consider their needs and welfare and offer them help if you think their rights have been abused or denied.

---

[2] Follow the guidance in paragraph 23c if the risk arises from an adverse incident involving a medical device.
[3] Some patients are likely to be more vulnerable than others because of their illness, disability or frailty or because of their current cir-cumstances, such as bereavement or redundancy. You should treat children and young people under 18 years as vulnerable. Vulnerability can be temporary or permanent.

Protect patients and colleagues from any risk posed by your health

28 If you know or suspect that you have a serious condition that you could pass on to patients, or if your judgement or performance could be affected by a condition or its treatment, you must consult a suitably qualified colleague. You must follow their advice about any changes to your practice they consider necessary. You must not rely on your own assessment of the risk to patients.

29 You should be immunised against common serious communicable diseases (unless otherwise contraindicated).

30 You should be registered with a general practitioner outside your family.

Domain 3: Communication, partnership and teamwork

Communicate effectively

31 You must listen to patients, take account of their views, and respond honestly to their questions.

32 You must give patients[4] the information they want or need to know in a way they can understand. You should make sure that arrangements are made, wherever possible, to meet patients' language and communication needs.

33 You must be considerate to those close to the patient and be sensitive and responsive in giving them information and support.

34 When you are on duty you must be readily accessible to patients and colleagues seeking information, advice or support.

Work collaboratively with colleagues to maintain or improve patient care

35 You must work collaboratively with colleagues, respecting their skills and contributions.

36 You must treat colleagues fairly and with respect.

37 You must be aware of how your behaviour may influence others within and outside the team.

38 Patient safety may be affected if there is not enough medical cover. So you must take up any post you have formally accepted, and work your contractual notice period before leaving a job, unless the employer has reasonable time to make other arrangements.

Teaching, training, supporting and assessing

39 You should be prepared to contribute to teaching and training doctors and students.

40 You must make sure that all staff you manage have appropriate supervision.

41 You must be honest and objective when writing references, and when appraising or assessing the performance of colleagues, including locums and students. References must include all information relevant to your colleagues' competence, performance and conduct.

42 You should be willing to take on a mentoring role for more junior doctors and other healthcare professionals.

43 You must support colleagues who have problems with their performance or health. But you must put patient safety first at all times.

Continuity and coordination of care

44 You must contribute to the safe transfer of patients between healthcare providers and between health and social care providers. This means you must:

   a share all relevant information with colleagues involved in your patients' care within and outside the team, including when you hand over care as you go off duty, and when you delegate care or refer patients to other health or social care providers,

---

[4] Patients here includes those people with the legal authority to make healthcare decisions on a patient's behalf.

   b check, where practical, that a named clinician or team has taken over responsibility when your role in providing a patient's care has ended. This may be particularly important for patients with impaired capacity or who are vulnerable for other reasons.

45 When you do not provide your patients' care yourself, for example when you are off duty, or you delegate the care of a patient to a colleague, you must be satisfied that the person providing care has the appropriate qualifications, skills and experience to provide safe care for the patient.

Establish and maintain partnerships with patients

46 You must be polite and considerate.

47 You must treat patients as individuals and respect their dignity and privacy.

48 You must treat patients fairly and with respect whatever their life choices and beliefs.

49 You must work in partnership with patients, sharing with them the information they will need to make decisions about their care, including:

   a their condition, its likely progression and the options for treatment, including associated risks and uncertainties

   b the progress of their care, and your role and responsibilities in the team

   c who is responsible for each aspect of patient care, and how information is shared within teams and among those who will be providing their care

   d any other information patients need if they are asked to agree to be involved in teaching or research.

50 You must treat information about patients as confidential. This includes after a patient has died.

51 You must support patients in caring for themselves to empower them to improve and maintain their health. This may, for example, include:

   a advising patients on the effects of their life choices and lifestyle on their health and well-being

   b supporting patients to make lifestyle changes where appropriate.

52 You must explain to patients if you have a conscientious objection to a particular procedure. You must tell them about their right to see another doctor and make sure they have enough information to exercise that right. In providing this information you must not imply or express disapproval of the patient's lifestyle, choices or beliefs. If it is not practical for a patient to arrange to see another doctor, you must make sure that arrangements are made for another suitably qualified colleague to take over your role.

Show respect for patients

53 You must not use your professional position to pursue a sexual or improper emotional relationship with a patient or someone close to them.

54 You must not express your personal beliefs (including political, religious and moral beliefs) to patients in ways that exploit their vulnerability or are likely to cause them distress.

55 You must be open and honest with patients if things go wrong. If a patient under your care has suffered harm or distress, you should:

   a put matters right (if that is possible)

   b offer an apology

   c explain fully and promptly what has happened and the likely short-term and long-term effects.

Domain 4: Maintaining trust

Treat patients and colleagues fairly and without discrimination

56 You must give priority to patients on the basis of their clinical need if these decisions are within your power. If inadequate resources, policies or systems prevent you from doing this, and patient safety, dignity or comfort may be seriously compromised, you must follow the guidance in paragraph 25b.

57 The investigations or treatment you provide or arrange must be based on the assessment you and your patient make of their needs and priorities, and on your clinical judgement about the likely effectiveness of the treatment options. You must not refuse or delay treatment because you believe that a patient's actions or lifestyle have contributed to their condition.

58 You must not deny treatment to patients because their medical condition may put you at risk. If a patient poses a risk to your health or safety, you should take all available steps to minimise the risk before providing treatment or making other suitable alternative arrangements for providing treatment.

59 You must not unfairly discriminate against patients or colleagues by allowing your personal views[5] to affect your professional relationships or the treatment you provide or arrange. You should challenge colleagues if their behaviour does not comply with this guidance, and follow the guidance in paragraph 25c if the behaviour amounts to abuse or denial of a patient's or colleague's rights.

60 You must consider and respond to the needs of disabled patients and should make reasonable adjustments[6] to your practice so they can receive care to meet their needs.

61 You must respond promptly, fully and honestly to complaints and apologise when appropriate. You must not allow a patient's complaint to adversely affect the care or treatment you provide or arrange.

62 You should end a professional relationship with a patient only when the breakdown of trust between you and the patient means you cannot provide good clinical care to the patient.

63 You must make sure you have adequate insurance or indemnity cover so that your patients will not be disadvantaged if they make a claim about the clinical care you have provided in the UK.

64 If someone you have contact with in your professional role asks for your registered name and/or GMC reference number, you must give this information to them.

Act with honesty and integrity

Honesty

65 You must make sure that your conduct justifies your patients' trust in you and the public's trust in the profession.

66 You must always be honest about your experience, qualifications and current role.

67 You must act with honesty and integrity when designing, organising or carrying out research, and follow national research governance guidelines and our guidance.

Communicating information

68 You must be honest and trustworthy in all your communication with patients and colleagues. This means you must make clear the limits of your knowledge and make reasonable checks to make sure any information you give is accurate.

69 When communicating publicly, including speaking to or writing in the media, you must maintain patient confidentiality. You should remember when using social media that communications intended for friends or family may become more widely available.

70 When advertising your services, you must make sure the information you publish is factual and can be checked, and does not exploit patients' vulnerability or lack of medical knowledge.

---

[5] This includes your views about a patient's or colleague's lifestyle, culture or their social or economic status, as well as the characteristics protected by legislation: age, disability, gender reassignment, race, marriage and civil partnership, pregnancy and maternity, religion or belief, sex and sexual orientation.

[6] 'Reasonable adjustments' does not only mean changes to the physical environment. It can include, for example, being flexible about appointment time or length, and making arrangements for those with communication difficulties such as impaired hearing. For more information see the EHRC website (www.equalityhumanrights.com/advice-and-guidance).

71 You must be honest and trustworthy when writing reports, and when completing or signing forms, reports and other documents. You must make sure that any documents you write or sign are not false or misleading.

    a You must take reasonable steps to check the information is correct.

    b You must not deliberately leave out relevant information.

Openness and legal or disciplinary proceedings

72 You must be honest and trustworthy when giving evidence to courts or tribunals. You must make sure that any evidence you give or documents you write or sign are not false or misleading.

    a You must take reasonable steps to check the information.

    b You must not deliberately leave out relevant information.

73 You must cooperate with formal inquiries and complaints procedures and must offer all relevant information while following the guidance in *Confidentiality*.

74 You must make clear the limits of your competence and knowledge when giving evidence or acting as a witness.

75 You must tell us without delay if, anywhere in the world:

    a you have accepted a caution from the police or been criticised by an official inquiry

    b you have been charged with or found guilty of a criminal offence

    c another professional body has made a finding against your registration as a result of fitness to practise procedures.

76 If you are suspended by an organisation from a medical post, or have restrictions placed on your practice, you must, without delay, inform any other organisations you carry out medical work for and any patients you see independently.

Honesty in financial dealings

77 You must be honest in financial and commercial dealings with patients, employers, insurers and other organisations or individuals.

78 You must not allow any interests you have to affect the way you prescribe for, treat, refer or commission services for patients.

79 If you are faced with a conflict of interest, you must be open about the conflict, declaring your interest formally, and you should be prepared to exclude yourself from decision making.

80 You must not ask for or accept—from patients, colleagues or others—any inducement, gift or hospitality that may affect or be seen to affect the way you prescribe for, treat or refer patients or commission services for patients. You must not offer these inducements.

Further guidance on Good medical practice

0–18 years: guidance for all doctors*

[Excerpt and some footnotes and Appendices omitted.]

In *0–18 years: guidance for all doctors*, the terms 'you must' and 'you should' are used in the following ways:

'You must' is used for an overriding duty or principle

'You should' is used when we are providing an explanation of how you will meet the overriding duty

'You should' is also used where the duty or principle will not apply in all situations or circumstances, or where there are factors outside your control that affect whether or how you can comply with the guidance.

Serious or persistent failure to follow this guidance will put your registration at risk.

Introduction

1 This guidance is for all doctors, but it may also be useful for children, young people[1], those with an interest in their care, and anyone else who wants to know what guidance doctors are given.

2 The guidance is for all doctors, whether or not they routinely see children and young people as patients. Doctors should also be aware of the needs and welfare of children and young people when they see patients:

    (a) who are parents or carers[2]

    (b) who are cared for by children or young people, or

    (c) who may represent a danger to children or young people.

3 *Good Medical Practice* states that doctors must safeguard and protect the health and well-being of children and young people. Well-being includes treating children and young people as individuals and respecting their views, as well as considering their physical and emotional welfare.

4 When treating children and young people, doctors must also consider parents and others close to them; but their patient must be the doctor's first concern.

5 When treating adults who care for, or pose risks to, children and young people, the adult patient must be the doctor's first concern; but doctors must also consider and act in the best interests of children and young people.

6 Children and young people may be particularly vulnerable and need to be protected from harm; they can often find it difficult accessing services or defending their rights; and they often rely on others for their well-being. They may have particular communication needs and may need help to make decisions.

7 Children and young people are individuals with rights that should be respected. This means listening to them and taking into account what they have to say about things that affect them. It also means respecting their decisions and confidentiality.

8 Doctors should always act in the best interests of children and young people. This should be the guiding principle in all decisions which may affect them. But identifying their best interests is not always easy. This is particularly the case in relation to treatment that does not have proven health benefits or when competent young people refuse treatment that is clearly in their medical interests. There can also be a conflict between child protection and confidentiality, both of which are vitally important to the welfare of children and young people.

9 Reaching satisfactory answers to these challenging questions may mean considering a number of difficult ethical and legal issues. The purpose of this guidance is to help doctors balance competing interests and make decisions that are ethical, lawful and for the good of children and young people.

10 The law relating to children and young people is complex and differs across the UK. Doctors who have children and young people as patients will need some understanding of the law as it applies where they practise. Summaries of the law contained in this guidance cannot be a substitute for up-to-date legal advice in individual cases.

11 When in doubt as to their responsibilities, doctors should seek the advice of experienced colleagues, named or designated doctors for child protection, or professional or regulatory bodies.

Assessing best interests

12 An assessment of best interests will include what is clinically indicated in a particular case. You should also consider:

    (a) the views of the child or young person, so far as they can express them, including any previously expressed preferences;

    (b) the views of parents;

---

[1] See Appendix 1 for who we mean by children and young people [*omitted*].

[2] See Appendix 2 for who guidance on who has parental responsibility and roles of parents and carers [*omitted*].

(c) the views of others close to the child or young person;

(d) the cultural, religious or other beliefs and values of the child or parents;

(e) the views of other healthcare professionals involved in providing care to the child or young person, and of any other professionals who have an interest in their welfare; and

(f) which choice, if there is more than one, will least restrict the child or young person's future options.

13 This list is not exhaustive. The weight you attach to each point will depend on the circumstances, and you should consider any other relevant information. You should not make unjustified assumptions about a child or young person's best interests based on irrelevant or discriminatory factors, such as their behaviour, appearance or disability.

Communication

14 Effective communication between doctors and children and young people is essential to the provision of good care. You should find out what children, young people and their parents want and need to know, what issues are important to them, and what opinions or fears they have about their health or treatment. In particular you should:

(a) involve children and young people in discussions about their care;

(b) be honest and open with them and their parents, while respecting confidentiality;

(c) listen to and respect their views about their health, and respond to their concerns and preferences;

(d) explain things using language or other forms of communication they can understand;

(e) consider how you and they use non-verbal communication, and the surroundings in which you meet them;

(f) give them opportunities to ask questions, and answer these honestly and to the best of your ability;

(g) do all you can to make open and truthful discussion possible, taking into account that this can be helped or hindered by the involvement of parents or other people; and

(h) give them the same time and respect that you would give to adult patients.

15 You should make it clear that you are available to see children and young people on their own if that is what they want. You should avoid giving the impression (whether directly, through reception staff or in any other way) that they cannot access services without a parent. You should think carefully about the effect the presence of a chaperone can have. Their presence can deter young people from being frank and from asking for help.

16 You should take children and young people's views seriously and not dismiss or appear to dismiss their concerns or contributions. Disabled children and young people can feel particularly disadvantaged in this respect.

17 Children and young people usually want or need to know about their illnesses and what is likely to happen to them in the future. You should provide information that is easy to understand and appropriate to their age and maturity about:

(a) their conditions;

(b) the purpose of investigations and treatments you propose and what that involves, including pain, anaesthetics and stays in hospital;

(c) the chances of success and the risks of different treatment options, including not having treatment;

(d) who will be mainly responsible for and involved in their care; and

(e) their right to change their minds or to ask for a second opinion.

18 You should not overburden children and young people or their parents, but give them information at an appropriate time and pace, and check their understanding of key points.

19 You should talk directly and listen to children and young people who are able to take part in discussions about their care. Young people who are able to understand what is being said and who can speak for themselves resent being spoken about when they are present. But younger children might not be able to understand what their illness or proposed treatment is likely to involve, even when explained in straightforward terms.

20 You should only keep the type of information described in paragraph 17 from children or young people if:

    (a) it would cause them serious harm (and not just upset them or make them more likely to want to refuse treatment); or

    (b) they ask you to, because they would prefer someone else to make decisions for them.

21 You have the same duty of confidentiality to children and young people as you have to adults. But parents often want and need information about their children's care so that they can make decisions or provide care and support. Children and young people are usually happy for information to be shared with their parents. This sharing of information is often in the best interests of children and young people, particularly if their health would benefit from special care or ongoing treatment, such as a special diet or regular medication. Parents are usually the best judges of their children's best interests and should make important decisions up until children are able to make their own decisions. You should share relevant information with parents in accordance with the law and the guidance in paragraphs 27, 28 and 42 to 55.

Making decisions

22 You can provide medical treatment to a child or young person with their consent if they are competent to give it, or with the consent of a parent or the court. You can provide emergency treatment without consent to save the life of, or prevent serious deterioration in the health of, a child or young person.

23 You should involve children and young people as much as possible in decisions about their care, even when they are not able to make decisions on their own.

Assessing the capacity to consent

24 You must decide whether a young person is able to understand the nature, purpose and possible consequences of investigations or treatments you propose, as well as the consequences of not having treatment. Only if they are able to understand, retain, use and weigh this information, and communicate their decision to others can they consent to that investigation or treatment. That means you must make sure that all relevant information has been provided and thoroughly discussed before deciding whether or not a child or young person has the capacity to consent.

25 The capacity to consent depends more on young people's ability to understand and weigh up options than on age. When assessing a young person's capacity to consent, you should bear in mind that:

    (a) at 16 a young person can be presumed to have the capacity to consent (see paragraphs 30 to 33);

    (b) a young person under 16 may have the capacity to consent, depending on their maturity and ability to understand what is involved.

26 It is important that you assess maturity and understanding on an individual basis and with regard to the complexity and importance of the decision to be made. You should remember that a young person who has the capacity to consent to straightforward, relatively risk-free treatment may not necessarily have the capacity to consent to complex treatment involving high risks or serious con-sequences.[3] The capacity to consent can also be affected by their physical and emotional development and by changes in their health and treatment.

---

[3] See paragraphs 70–71 for guidance on advice and treatment for contraception, abortion and sexually transmitted infections.

Children and young people who lack the capacity to consent

27 If a child lacks the capacity to consent, you should ask for their parent's consent. It is usually sufficient to have consent from one parent. If parents cannot agree and disputes cannot be resolved informally, you should seek legal advice about whether you should apply to the court.

28 The legal framework for the treatment of 16- and 17-year-olds who lack the capacity to consent differs across the UK:

(a) In England, Wales and Northern Ireland, parents can consent to investigations and treatment that are in the young person's best interests.

(b) In England and Wales, treatment can also be provided in the young person's best interests without parental consent, although the views of parents may be important in assessing the young person's best interests (see paragraphs 12 and 13).

(c) In Northern Ireland, treatment can be provided in the young person's best interests if a parent cannot be contacted, although you should seek legal advice about applying for court approval for significant (other than emergency) interventions.

(d) In Scotland, 16- and 17-year-olds who do not have the capacity to consent are treated as adults who lack capacity and treatment may be given to safeguard or promote their health.

Young people who have the capacity to consent

29 You should encourage young people to involve their parents in making important decisions, but you should usually abide by any decision they have the capacity to make themselves (see paragraphs 30 to 33 and paragraphs 46 to 52). You should also consider involving other members of the multi-disciplinary team, an independent advocate or a named or designated doctor for child protection if their involvement would help young people in making decisions.

If a young person refuses treatment

30 Respect for young people's views is important in making decisions about their care. If they refuse treatment, particularly treatment that could save their life or prevent serious deterioration in their health, this presents a challenge that you need to consider carefully.

31 Parents cannot override the competent consent of a young person to treatment that you consider is in their best interests. But you can rely on parental consent when a child lacks the capacity to consent. In Scotland parents cannot authorise treatment a competent young person has refused. In England, Wales and Northern Ireland, the law on parents overriding young people's competent refusal is complex. You should seek legal advice if you think treatment is in the best interests of a competent young person who refuses.

32 You must carefully weigh up the harm to the rights of children and young people of overriding their refusal against the benefits of treatment, so that decisions can be taken in their best interests. In these circumstances, you should consider involving other members of the multi-disciplinary team, an independent advocate, or a named or designated doctor for child protection. Legal advice may be helpful in deciding whether you should apply to the court to resolve disputes about best interests that cannot be resolved informally.

33 You should also consider involving these same colleagues before seeking legal advice if parents refuse treatment that is clearly in the best interests of a child or young person who lacks capacity, or if both a young person with capacity and their parents refuse such treatment. For further guidance on these issues see GMC guidance on consent and withholding and withdrawing life-prolonging treatments.

Procedures undertaken mainly for religious, cultural, social or emotional reasons

34 Both the GMC and the law permit doctors to undertake procedures that do not offer immediate or obvious therapeutic benefits for children or young people, so long as they are in their best interests (see paragraphs 12 and 13) and performed with consent (see paragraph 27).

35 To assess their best interests you should consider the religious and cultural beliefs and values of the child or young person and their parents as well as any social, psychological and emotional benefits. This may be relevant in circumcision of male children for religious or cultural reasons, or surgical correction of physical characteristics that do not endanger the child's life or health.

Research

36 Research involving children and young people can benefit all children; but they may be vulnerable because they cannot always recognise their best interests, express their needs or defend their rights.

37 Children or young people should be involved in research only when research on adults cannot provide the same benefits. They can be involved in research that has either:

    (a) potential benefits for children or young people generally, as long as the research does not go against their best interests or involves only minimal or low risk of harm (this would be research that involves, for example, asking questions or taking blood samples, the assessment of the risk depending on the view of the child or young person); or

    (b) potential therapeutic benefits for them that outweigh any foreseeable risks, which should be kept as low as possible.

38 Children and young people should not usually be involved in research if they object or appear to object in either words or actions, even if their parents consent. If they are able to consent for themselves, you should still consider involving their parents, depending on the nature of the research.

39 You must not put pressure on children, young people or their parents to consent to research in the expectation of therapeutic, financial or any other benefit.

40 Before involving children or young people in research, you should seek advice and get the necessary approval from a relevant research ethics committee, the Medical Research Council or a medical royal college. For further information see GMC guidance on research.

Donation, transplantation, organ and tissue storage and use

41 The Human Tissue Act 2004 and Human Tissue (Scotland) Act 2006 were passed following inquiries into the storage of children's organs and tissue without the proper consent. The Acts make consent central to the lawful storage and use of children and young people's organs and tissue, and to the removal of such material after death. The Human Tissue Authority regulates and issues codes of practice on activities covered by the Act in England, Wales and Northern Ireland. Scottish ministers have those powers in Scotland.

Principles of confidentiality

42 Respecting patient confidentiality is an essential part of good care; this applies when the patient is a child or young person as well as when the patient is an adult. Without the trust that confidentiality brings, children and young people might not seek medical care and advice, or they might not tell you all the facts needed to provide good care.

43 The same duties of confidentiality apply when using, sharing or disclosing information about children and young people as about adults. You should:

    (a) disclose information that identifies the patient only if this is necessary to achieve the purpose of the disclosure—in all other cases you should anonymise the information before disclosing it;

    (b) inform the patient[4] about the possible uses of their information, including how it could be used to provide their care and for clinical audit

---

[4] or, where appropriate, those with parental responsibility for the patient.

    (c) ask for the patient's[5] consent before disclosing information that could identify them, if the information is needed for any other purpose, other than in the exceptional circumstances described in this guidance;

    (d) keep disclosures to the minimum necessary.

For further information see GMC guidance on confidentiality.

Sharing information with the consent of the child or young person

44 Sharing information with the right people can help to protect children and young people from harm and ensure that they get the help they need. It can also reduce the number of times they are asked the same questions by different professionals. By asking for their consent to share relevant information, you are showing them respect and involving them in decisions about their care.

45 If children and young people are able to take part in decision-making, you should explain why it is that you need to share information, and ask for their consent. They will usually be happy for you to talk to their parents and others involved in their care or treatment.

Sharing information without consent

46 If a child or young person does not agree to disclosure there are still circumstances in which you should disclose information:

    (a) when there is an overriding public interest in the disclosure;

    (b) when you judge that the disclosure is in the best interests of a child or young person who does not have the maturity or understanding to make a decision about disclosure; and

    (c) when disclosure is required by law.

Public interest

47 You can disclose, without consent, information that identifies the child or young person, in the public interest. A disclosure is in the public interest if the benefits that are likely to arise from the release of information outweigh both the child or young person's interest in keeping the information confidential and society's interest in maintaining trust between doctors and patients. You must make this judgement case by case, by weighing up the various interests involved.

48 When considering whether disclosure would be justified you should:

    (a) tell the child or young person what you propose to disclose and why, unless that would undermine the purpose or place the child or young person at increased risk of harm;

    (b) ask for consent to the disclosure, if you judge the young person to be competent to make the decision, unless it is not practical to do so.

49 If a child or young person refuses consent, or if it is not practical to ask for consent, you should consider the benefits and possible harms that may arise from disclosure. You should consider any views given by the child or young person on why you should not disclose the information. But you should disclose information if this is necessary to protect the child or young person, or someone else, from risk of death or serious harm. Such cases may arise, for example, if:

    (a) a child or young person is at risk of neglect or sexual, physical or emotional abuse (see paragraphs 56 to 63);

    (b) the information would help in the prevention, detection or prosecution of serious crime, usually crime against the person;

    (c) a child or young person is involved in behaviour that might put them or others at risk of serious harm, such as serious addiction, self-harm or joy-riding.

50 If you judge that disclosure is justified, you should disclose the information promptly to an appropriate person or authority and record your discussions and reasons. If you judge that disclosure is not justified, you should record your reasons for not disclosing.

---

[5] or, where appropriate, those with parental responsibility for the patient.

Disclosures when a child lacks the capacity to consent

51 Children will usually be accompanied by parents or other adults involved in their care, and you can usually tell if a child agrees to information being shared by their behaviour. Occasionally, children who lack the capacity to consent will share information with you on the understanding that their parents are not informed. You should usually try to persuade the child to involve a parent in such circumstances. If they refuse and you consider it is necessary in the child's best interests for the information to be shared (for example, to enable a parent to make an important decision, or to provide proper care for the child), you can disclose information to parents or appropriate authorities. You should record your discussions and reasons for sharing the information.

Disclosures required by law

52 You must disclose information as required by law. You must also disclose information when directed to do so by a court.

Access to medical records by children, young people and their parents

53 Young people with capacity have the legal right to access their own health records and can allow or prevent access by others, including their parents.[6] In Scotland, anyone aged 12 or over is legally presumed to have such capacity. A child might of course achieve capacity earlier or later. In any event you should usually let children access their own health records. But they should not be given access to information that would cause them serious harm or any information about another person without the other person's consent.

54 You should let parents access their child's medical records if the child or young person consents, or lacks capacity, and it does not go against the child's best interests. If the records contain information given by the child or young person in confidence you should not normally disclose the information without their consent.

55 Divorce or separation does not affect parental responsibility and you should allow both parents reasonable access to their children's health records.

Child protection

56 Doctors play a crucial role in protecting children from abuse and neglect. You may be told or notice things that teachers and social workers, for example, may not. You may have access to confidential information that causes you to have concern for the safety or well-being of children.

57 Early identification of risks can help children and young people get the care and support they need to be healthy, safe and happy, and to achieve their potential.

58 If you work with children or young people, you should have the knowledge and skills to identify abuse and neglect. You should be aware of the use of frameworks for assessing children and young people's needs, the work of Local Safeguarding Children's Boards and Child Protection Committees, and policies, procedures and organisations that work to protect children and promote their welfare.

59 Children, young people and parents may not want you to disclose information about them if they think they will be denied help, blamed or made to feel ashamed. They might have had bad experiences or fear contact with the police or social services. You should help them understand the importance and benefits of sharing information. But you must not delay sharing relevant information with an appropriate person or authority if delay would increase the risk to the child or young person or to other children or young people.

60 Confidentiality is important and information sharing should be proportionate to the risk of harm. You may share some limited information, with consent if possible, to decide if there is a risk

---

[6] There are circumstances in which disclosures may be made to parents and others without consent (see paragraphs 46–52).

that would justify further disclosures. A risk might only become apparent when a number of people with niggling concerns share them. If in any doubt about whether to share information, you should seek advice from an experienced colleague, a named or designated doctor for child protection, or a Caldicott Guardian. You can also seek advice from a professional body, defence organisation or the GMC. You will be able to justify raising a concern, even if it turns out to be groundless, if you have done so honestly, promptly, on the basis of reasonable belief, and through the appropriate channels.

61 Your first concern must be the safety of children and young people. You must inform an appropriate person or authority promptly of any reasonable concern that children or young people are at risk of abuse or neglect, when that is in a child's best interests or necessary to protect other children or young people. You must be able to justify a decision not to share such a concern, having taken advice from a named or designated doctor for child protection or an experienced colleague, or a defence or professional body.

You should record your concerns, discussions and reasons for not sharing information in these circumstances.

62 You should participate fully in child protection procedures, attend meetings whenever practical and co-operate with requests for information about child abuse and neglect. This includes Serious Case Reviews set up to identify why a child has been seriously harmed, to learn lessons from mistakes and to improve systems and services for children and their families. When the overall purpose of a review is to protect other children or young people from a risk of serious harm, you should share relevant information, even when a child or young person or their parents do not consent, or if it is not possible to ask for consent. You must be prepared to justify your decision not to share information in such cases.

63 You should make sure that there are clear and well-understood policies and procedures for sharing information with agencies you work with closely or often. You should have an understanding of the roles, policies and practices of other agencies and professionals. This includes understanding the circumstances in which they consider disclosure to be justified. Teachers, social workers, police, youth offending teams and others all have different relationships with children and young people. They also have different cultures, policies and guidance on sharing information. You should understand and respect these differences but remember the particular responsibilities you have as a doctor and the importance of trust in your relationship with your patients.

Sexual activity

64 A confidential sexual health service is essential for the welfare of children and young people. Concern about confidentiality is the biggest deterrent to young people asking for sexual health advice. That in turn presents dangers to young people's own health and to that of the community, particularly other young people.

65 You can disclose relevant information when this is in the public interest (see paragraphs 47 to 50). If a child or young person is involved in abusive or seriously harmful sexual activity, you must protect them by sharing relevant information with appropriate people or agencies, such as the police or social services, quickly and professionally.

66 You should consider each case on its merits and take into account young people's behaviour, living circumstances, maturity, serious learning disabilities, and any other factors that might make them particularly vulnerable.

67 You should usually share information about sexual activity involving children under 13, who are considered in law to be unable to consent. You should discuss a decision not to disclose with a named or designated doctor for child protection and record your decision and the reasons for it.

68 You should usually share information about abusive or seriously harmful sexual activity involving any child or young person, including that which involves:

    (a)   a young person too immature to understand or consent;

    (b)   big differences in age, maturity or power between sexual partners;

    (c)   a young person's sexual partner having a position of trust;

(d) force or the threat of force, emotional or psychological pressure, bribery or payment, either to engage in sexual activity or to keep it secret;

(e) drugs or alcohol used to influence a young person to engage in sexual activity when they otherwise would not;

(f) a person known to the police or child protection agencies as having had abusive relationships with children or young people.

69 You may not be able to judge if a relationship is abusive without knowing the identity of a young person's sexual partner, which the young person might not want to reveal. If you are concerned that a relationship is abusive, you should carefully balance the benefits of knowing a sexual partner's identity against the potential loss of trust in asking for or sharing such information.

Contraception, abortion and sexually transmitted infections (STIs)

70 You can provide contraceptive, abortion and STI advice and treatment, without parental knowledge or consent, to young people under 16 provided that:

(a) they understand all aspects of the advice and its implications;

(b) you cannot persuade the young person to tell their parents or to allow you to tell them;

(c) in relation to contraception and STIs, the young person is very likely to have sex with or without such treatment;

(d) their physical or mental health is likely to suffer unless they receive such advice or treatment; and

(e) it is in the best interests of the young person to receive the advice and treatment without parental knowledge or consent.

71 You should keep consultations confidential even if you decide not to provide advice or treatment (for example, if your patient does not understand your advice or the implications of treatment), other than in the exceptional circumstances outlined in paragraphs 46 to 52 and paragraphs 64 to 69.

Conscientious objections

72 If carrying out a particular procedure or giving advice about it conflicts with your religious or moral beliefs, and this conflict might affect the treatment or advice you provide, you must explain this to the patient and tell them they have the right to see another doctor. You should make sure that information about alternative services is readily available to all patients. Children and young people in particular may have difficulty in making alternative arrangements themselves, so you must make sure that arrangements are made for another suitably qualified colleague to take over your role as quickly as possible.

Suitability to work with children and young people

73 Children are not miniature adults. Good clinical care for children relies on specially trained clinical staff together with equipment, facilities and an environment appropriate to children's needs. If you have children and young people as patients, you should make sure you have the appropriate training and experience in the clinical care of children in your specialty. You should take steps to make sure that, wherever possible, you and members of your team have access to the appropriate premises, equipment and other resources necessary to provide good care. If you also have adults as patients, you should audit separately the care you provide to children and young people.

74 If you are responsible for recruiting or employing people, or if you otherwise control who can work with children or young people in your care, you should make sure that their suitability is checked. NHS Employers (part of the NHS Confederation) issues advice on good employment practice, including pre- and post-employment, Criminal Records Bureau, alert notice, vetting and barring scheme and other checks.

75 You should follow the GMC's guidance on raising concerns about patient safety if you have concerns that children or young people are, or may be, at risk of harm because of a colleague's conduct, performance or health.

Complaints

76 You should always take children and young people's complaints seriously. You should help them to complain if their rights or interests have been denied or abused, or if they are unhappy with the care they have received or because they have been denied care.

Prescribing medicines

77 If you prescribe medicines for children, you should be familiar with the current guidance published in the British National Formulary for Children.

For further information see GMC guidance on good practice in prescribing medicines.

Consent: patients and doctors making decisions together*

[*Annexes omitted.*]

How the guidance applies to you

This guidance is addressed to doctors, but may also help patients and the public to understand what to expect of their doctors. In this guidance the terms 'you must' and 'you should' are used in the following ways:

'you must' is used for an overriding duty or principle 'you should' is used when we are providing an explanation of how you will meet the overriding duty,

'you should' is also used where the duty or principle will not apply in all situations or circumstances, or where there are factors outside your control that affect whether or how you can comply with the guidance.

The guidance is not, and cannot be, exhaustive. So you should use your judgement to apply the principles it sets out to the situations you face in your own practice. You must work in partnership with your patients. You should discuss with them their condition and treatment options in a way they can understand, and respect their right to make decisions about their care.

You should see getting their consent as an important part of the process of discussion and decision-making, rather than as something that happens in isolation.

In deciding how much information to share with your patients you should take account of their wishes. The information you share should be in proportion to the nature of their condition, the complexity of the proposed investigation or treatment, and the seriousness of any potential side effects, complications or other risks.

Serious or persistent failure to follow this guidance will put your registration at risk. You must, therefore, be prepared to explain and justify your actions.

PART 1: PRINCIPLES

1 All healthcare involves decisions made by patients and those providing their care. This guidance sets out principles for good practice in making decisions. The principles apply to all decisions about care: from the treatment of minor and self-limiting conditions, to major interventions with significant risks or side effects. The principles also apply to decisions about screening.[1]

2 Whatever the context in which medical decisions are made, you must work in partnership with your patients to ensure good care. In so doing, you must:

    (a) listen to patients and respect their views about their health;

    (b) discuss with patients what their diagnosis, prognosis, treatment and care involve;

    (c) share with patients the information they want or need in order to make decisions;

    (d) maximise patients' opportunities, and their ability, to make decisions for themselves; and

    (e) respect patients' decisions.

Partnership

3 For a relationship between doctor and patient to be effective, it should be a partnership based on openness, trust and good communication. Each person has a role to play in making decisions about treatment or care.

4 No single approach to discussions about treatment or care will suit every patient, or apply in all circumstances. Individual patients may want more or less information or involvement in making decisions depending on their circumstances or wishes. And some patients may need additional support to understand information and express their views and preferences.

5 If patients have capacity to make decisions for themselves, a basic model applies:

    (a) The doctor and patient make an assessment of the patient's condition, taking into account the patient's medical history, views, experience and knowledge.

    (b) The doctor uses specialist knowledge and experience and clinical judgement, and the patient's views and understanding of their condition, to identify which investigations or treatments are likely to result in overall benefit for the patient. The doctor explains the options to the patient, setting out the potential benefits, risks, burdens and side effects of each option, including the option to have no treatment. The doctor may recommend a particular option, which they believe to be best for the patient, but they must not put pressure on the patient to accept their advice.

    (c) The patient weighs up the potential benefits, risks and burdens of the various options as well as any non-clinical issues that are relevant to them. The patient decides whether to accept any of the options and, if so, which one. They also have the right to accept or refuse an option for a reason that may seem irrational to the doctor, or for no reason at all.[2]

    (d) If the patient asks for a treatment that the doctor considers would not be of overall benefit to them, the doctor should discuss the issues with the patient and explore the reasons for their request. If, after discussion, the doctor still considers that the treatment would not be of overall benefit to the patient, they do not have to provide the treatment. But they should explain their reasons to the patient, and explain any other options that are available, including the option to seek a second opinion.

6 If patients are not able to make decisions for themselves, the doctor must work with those close to the patient and with other members of the healthcare team. The doctor must take into account any views or preferences expressed by the patient and must follow the law on decision-making when a patient lacks capacity.[3]

---

[1] Testing of healthy or asymptomatic people to detect genetic predispositions or early signs of debilitating or life-threatening conditions.

[2] Mental health laws across the UK set out the circumstances in which an individual may be compulsorily assessed and treated for a mental disorder, without their consent. See the legal annex for more information about the legislation across the UK.

[3] See paragraphs 62–63 and the legal annex for an overview of the relevant legislation.

PART 2: MAKING DECISIONS ABOUT INVESTIGATIONS AND TREATMENT

Sharing information and discussing treatment options

7 The exchange of information between doctor and patient is central to good decision-making. How much information you share with patients will vary, depending on their individual circumstances. You should tailor your approach to discussions with patients according to:

(a) their needs, wishes and priorities;

(b) their level of knowledge about, and understanding of, their condition, prognosis and the treatment options;

(c) the nature of their condition;

(d) the complexity of the treatment; and

(e) the nature and level of risk associated with the investigation or treatment.

8 You should not make assumptions about:

(a) the information a patient might want or need;

(b) the clinical or other factors a patient might consider significant; or

(c) a patient's level of knowledge or understanding of what is proposed.

9 You must give patients the information they want or need about:

(a) the diagnosis and prognosis;

(b) any uncertainties about the diagnosis or prognosis, including options for further investigations;

(c) options for treating or managing the condition, including the option not to treat;

(d) the purpose of any proposed investigation or treatment and what it will involve;

(e) the potential benefits, risks and burdens, and the likelihood of success, for each option; this should include information, if available, about whether the benefits or risks are affected by which organisation or doctor is chosen to provide care;

(f) whether a proposed investigation or treatment is part of a research programme or is an innovative treatment designed specifically for their benefit;[4]

(g) the people who will be mainly responsible for and involved in their care, what their roles are, and to what extent students may be involved;

(h) their right to refuse to take part in teaching or research;

(i) their right to seek a second opinion;

(j) any bills they will have to pay;

(k) any conflicts of interest that you, or your organisation, may have;

(l) any treatments that you believe have greater potential benefit for the patient than those you or your organisation can offer.

10 You should explore these matters with patients, listen to their concerns, ask for and respect their views, and encourage them to ask questions.

11 You should check whether patients have understood the information they have been given, and whether or not they would like more information before making a decision. You must make it clear that they can change their mind about a decision at any time.

Answering questions

12 You must answer patients' questions honestly and, as far as practical, answer as fully as they wish.

---

[4] The patient should be told how the proposed treatment differs from the usual methods, why it is being offered, and if there are any additional risks or uncertainties. If you are considering prescribing unlicensed medicines or medicines for use off-label, you must follow the guidance in paragraphs 19–24 of Good practice in prescribing medicines.

Reasons for not sharing information with patients

13 No one else can make a decision on behalf of an adult who has capacity.[5] If a patient asks you to make decisions on their behalf or wants to leave decisions to a relative, partner, friend, carer or another person close to them, you should explain that it is still important that they understand the options open to them, and what the treatment will involve. If they do not want this information, you should try to find out why.

14 If, after discussion, a patient still does not want to know in detail about their condition or the treatment, you should respect their wishes, as far as possible. But you must still give them the information they need in order to give their consent to a proposed investigation or treatment. This is likely to include what the investigation or treatment aims to achieve and what it will involve, for example: whether the procedure is invasive; what level of pain or discomfort they might experience, and what can be done to minimise it; anything they should do to prepare for the investigation or treatment; and if it involves any serious risks.

15 If a patient insists that they do not want even this basic information, you must explain the potential consequences of them not having it, particularly if it might mean that their consent is not valid. You must record the fact that the patient has declined this information. You must also make it clear that they can change their mind and have more information at any time.

16 You should not withhold information necessary for making decisions for any other reason, including when a relative, partner, friend or carer asks you to, unless you believe that giving it would cause the patient serious harm. In this context 'serious harm' means more than that the patient might become upset or decide to refuse treatment.

17 If you withhold information from the patient you must record your reason for doing so in the patient's medical records, and you must be prepared to explain and justify your decision. You should regularly review your decision, and consider whether you could give information to the patient later, without causing them serious harm.

Sharing information

18 How you discuss a patient's diagnosis, prognosis and treatment options is often as important as the information itself. You should:

   (a) share information in a way that the patient can understand and, whenever possible, in a place and at a time when they are best able to understand and retain it;
   (b) give information that the patient may find distressing in a considerate way;
   (c) involve other members of the healthcare team in discussions with the patient, if appropriate;
   (d) give the patient time to reflect, before and after they make a decision, especially if the information is complex or what you are proposing involves significant risks;
   (e) make sure the patient knows if there is a time limit on making their decision, and who they can contact in the healthcare team if they have any questions or concerns.

19 You should give information to patients in a balanced way. If you recommend a particular treatment or course of action, you should explain your reasons for doing so. But you must not put pressure on a patient to accept your advice.

20 You may need to support your discussions with patients by using written material, or visual or other aids. If you do, you must make sure the material is accurate and up to date.

21 You should check whether the patient needs any additional support to understand information, to communicate their wishes, or to make a decision. You should bear in mind that some barriers to understanding and communication may not be obvious; for example, a patient may have

---

[5] A patient has capacity if they can understand, retain, use and weigh up the information needed to make a decision, and can communicate their wishes—see paragraphs 71–74 on assessing capacity. If your patient is under 18 you must follow the guidance in paragraphs 54–56 and the GMC's guidance, 0–18 years: guidance for all doctors. In certain circumstances, a patient with capacity can be treated without their consent for a mental disorder, subject to the provisions of relevant mental health legislation—see the legal annex for more information about legislation across the UK.

unspoken anxieties, or may be affected by pain or other underlying problems. You must make sure, wherever practical, that arrangements are made to give the patient any necessary support. This might include, for example: using an advocate or interpreter; asking those close to the patient about the patient's communication needs; or giving the patient a written or audio record of the discussion and any decisions that were made.

Involving families, carers and advocates

22 You should accommodate a patient's wishes if they want another person, such as a relative, partner, friend, carer or advocate, to be involved in discussions or to help them make decisions. In these circumstances, you should follow the guidance in paragraphs 7–21.

Obstacles to sharing information

23 It is sometimes difficult, because of pressures on your time or the limited resources available, to give patients as much information or support in making decisions as you, or they, would like. To help in this, you should consider the role that other members of the healthcare team might play, and what other sources of information and support are available. These may be, for example, patient information leaflets, advocacy services, expert patient programmes, or support groups for people with specific conditions.

24 You should do your best to make sure that patients with additional needs, such as those with disabilities, have the time and support they need to make a decision. In all cases, you must treat patients fairly and not discriminate against them.

25 If you think that limits on your ability to give patients the time or information they need is seriously compromising their ability to make an informed decision, you should raise your concerns with your employing or contracting authority. See paragraph 6 of Good Medical Practice and the supplementary guidance, Raising concerns about patient safety.[6]

Responsibility for seeking a patient's consent

26 If you are the doctor undertaking an investigation or providing treatment, it is your responsibility to discuss it with the patient. If this is not practical, you can delegate the responsibility to someone else, provided you make sure that the person you delegate to:

    (a)   is suitably trained and qualified;

    (b)   has sufficient knowledge of the proposed investigation or treatment, and understands the risks involved;

    (c)   understands, and agrees to act in accordance with, the guidance in this booklet.

27 If you delegate, you are still responsible for making sure that the patient has been given enough time and information to make an informed decision, and has given their consent, before you start any investigation or treatment.

Discussing side effects, complications and other risks

28 Clear, accurate information about the risks of any proposed investigation or treatment, presented in a way patients can understand, can help them make informed decisions. The amount of information about risk that you should share with patients will depend on the individual patient and what they want or need to know. Your discussions with patients should focus on their individual situation and the risk to them.

29 In order to have effective discussions with patients about risk, you must identify the adverse outcomes that may result from the proposed options. This includes the potential outcome of taking no action. Risks can take a number of forms, but will usually be:

    (a)   side effects,

    (b)   complications, and

---

[6] See also paragraph 19 of Management for doctors and the supplementary guidance, Accountability in Multi-disciplinary and Multi-Agency Mental Health Teams for more guidance on steps doctors can take to clarify responsibility and lines of accountability.

(c) failure of an intervention to achieve the desired aim.

Risks can vary from common but minor side effects, to rare but serious adverse outcomes possibly resulting in permanent disability or death.

30 In assessing the risk to an individual patient, you must consider the nature of the patient's condition, their general health and other circumstances. These are variable factors that may affect the likelihood of adverse outcomes occurring.

31 You should do your best to understand the patient's views and preferences about any proposed investigation or treatment, and the adverse outcomes they are most concerned about. You must not make assumptions about a patient's understanding of risk or the importance they attach to different outcomes. You should discuss these issues with your patient.[7]

32 You must tell patients if an investigation or treatment might result in a serious adverse outcome,[8] even if the likelihood is very small. You should also tell patients about less serious side effects or complications if they occur frequently, and explain what the patient should do if they experience any of them.

33 You must give information about risk in a balanced way. You should avoid bias, and you should explain the expected benefits as well as the potential burdens and risks of any proposed investigation or treatment.

34 You must use clear, simple and consistent language when discussing risks with patients. You should be aware that patients may understand information about risk differently from you. You should check that the patient understands the terms that you use, particularly when describing the seriousness, frequency and likelihood of an adverse outcome. You should use simple and accurate written information or visual or other aids to explain risk, if they will help the patient to understand.

35 If a patient does not want to know about the possible risks of a proposed investigation or treatment, you must follow the guidance in paragraphs 13–17.

36 You must keep up to date with developments in your area of practice, which may affect your knowledge and understanding of the risks associated with the investigations or treatments that you provide.

Making decisions

The scope of decisions

37 You must explain clearly to patients the scope of any decisions to be made. This will apply particularly if:

(a) treatment will be provided in stages, with the possibility that changes or adjustments might be needed;

(b) different doctors or healthcare professionals will provide particular parts of an investigation or treatment, such as anaesthesia and surgery;

(c) a number of different investigations or treatments are involved;

(d) uncertainty about the diagnosis or the options might only be resolved when the investigation or treatment has started, when the patient may be unable to make decisions.[9]

38 In such cases, you should discuss and agree with the patient how decisions will be made about whether to make changes to the investigation or treatment plan. You should establish whether the patient agrees to all or only parts of the proposed plan. If they agree only to parts of it, you should make sure that there is a clear process through which they can be involved in making decisions at a later stage.

---

[7] See Explaining the risks and benefits of treatment options, Royal College of Physicians Patient and Carer Involvement Steering Group, www.rcplondon.ac.uk/college/PIU/piu_risk.asp.

[8] An adverse outcome resulting in death, permanent or long-term physical disability or disfigurement, medium or long-term pain, or admission to hospital; or other outcomes with a long-term or permanent effect on a patient's employment, social or personal life.

[9] Note for pathologists and radiologists: there may be times when uncertainty about a diagnosis can only be resolved by investigations which were not specifically ordered as part of the original request for testing. If these investigations appear to fall outside the scope of the original consent given by the patient, or there are particular sensitivities around the condition for which the pathologist or radiologist wishes to test, they must contact the treating doctor and establish whether further discussion with, and consent from, the patient is necessary before proceeding.

39 You must not exceed the scope of the authority given by a patient, except in an emergency. If an emergency arises, you must follow the guidance in paragraph 79.

Making decisions about potential future events

40 You should discuss with patients the possibility of additional problems coming to light during an investigation or treatment when they might not be in a position to make a decision about how to proceed. If there is a significant risk of a particular problem arising, you should ask in advance what the patient would like you to do if it does arise. You should also ask if there are any procedures they object to, or which they would like more time to think about.

Ensuring that decisions are voluntary

41 Patients may be put under pressure by employers, insurers, relatives or others, to accept a particular investigation or treatment. You should be aware of this and of other situations in which patients may be vulnerable. Such situations may be, for example, if they are resident in a care home, subject to mental health legislation, detained by the police or immigration services, or in prison.

42 You should do your best to make sure that such patients have considered the available options and reached their own decision. If they have a right to refuse treatment, you should make sure that they know this and are able to refuse if they want to.

Respecting a patient's decisions

43 You must respect a patient's decision to refuse an investigation or treatment, even if you think their decision is wrong or irrational.[10] You should explain your concerns clearly to the patient and outline the possible consequences of their decision. You must not, however, put pressure on a patient to accept your advice. If you are unsure about the patient's capacity to make a decision, you must follow the guidance in Part 3.

Expressions of consent

44 Before accepting a patient's consent, you must consider whether they have been given the information they want or need, and how well they understand the details and implications of what is proposed. This is more important than how their consent is expressed or recorded.

45 Patients can give consent orally or in writing, or they may imply consent by complying with the proposed examination or treatment, for example, by rolling up their sleeve to have their blood pressure taken.

46 In the case of minor or routine investigations or treatments, if you are satisfied that the patient understands what you propose to do and why, it is usually enough to have oral or implied consent.

47 In cases that involve higher risk, it is important that you get the patient's written consent. This is so that everyone involved understands what was explained and agreed.

48 By law you must get written consent for certain treatments, such as fertility treatment and organ donation. You must follow the laws and codes of practice that govern these situations.

49 You should also get written consent from a patient if:
    (a) the investigation or treatment is complex or involves significant risks;
    (b) there may be significant consequences for the patient's employment, or social or personal life;
    (c) providing clinical care is not the primary purpose of the investigation or treatment; or
    (d) the treatment is part of a research programme or is an innovative treatment designed specifically for their benefit.

---

[10] If the patient has a mental disorder, you should note the exceptions in the Mental Health Act 1983 (as amended by the Mental Health Act 2007), the Mental Health (NI) Order 1986, and the Mental Health (Care and Treatment) (Scotland) Act 2003. They allow compulsory treatment for mental disorder in certain circumstances, without consent, even if the patient has capacity. See the legal annex for more information.

50 If it is not possible to get written consent, for example, in an emergency or if the patient needs the treatment to relieve serious pain or distress, you can rely on oral consent. But you must still give the patient the information they want or need to make a decision. You must record the fact that they have given consent, in their medical records.

Recording decisions

51 You must use the patient's medical records or a consent form to record the key elements of your discussion with the patient. This should include the information you discussed, any specific requests by the patient, any written, visual or audio information given to the patient, and details of any decisions that were made.

Reviewing decisions

52 Before beginning treatment, you or a member of the healthcare team should check that the patient still wants to go ahead; and you must respond to any new or repeated concerns or questions they raise. This is particularly important if:

(a) significant time has passed since the initial decision was made;

(b) there have been material changes in the patient's condition, or in any aspect of the proposed investigation or treatment; or

(c) new information has become available, for example about the risks of treatment or about other treatment options.

53 You must make sure that patients are kept informed about the progress of their treatment, and are able to make decisions at all stages, not just in the initial stage. If the treatment is ongoing, you should make sure that there are clear arrangements in place to review decisions and, if necessary, to make new ones.

Involving children and young people in making decisions

54 You should involve children and young people as much as possible in discussions about their care, even if they are not able to make decisions on their own.

55 A young person's ability to make decisions depends more on their ability to understand and weigh up options, than on their age. When assessing a young person's capacity to make decisions, you should bear in mind that:

(a) a young person under 16 may have capacity to make decisions, depending on their maturity and ability to understand what is involved;

(b) at 16 a young person can be presumed to have capacity to make most decisions about their treatment and care.

56 You must follow the guidance in 0–18 years: guidance for all doctors, and in particular the section Making decisions (paragraphs 22–41). It gives advice on involving children and young people in decisions, assessing capacity and best interests, and what to do if they refuse treatment. It also explains the different legal requirements across the UK for decision-making involving children and young people.

Advance care planning

57 If a patient:

(a) has a condition that will affect the length or quality of their life, or

(b) has a condition that will impair their capacity as it progresses, such as dementia, or

(c) is otherwise facing a situation in which loss or impairment of capacity is a foreseeable possibility you should encourage them to think about what they might want for themselves in the event that they cannot make their own decisions, and to discuss their wishes and concerns with you and the healthcare team.

58 Such discussions might cover:

(a) the patient's wishes, preferences or fears in relation to their future care, including any treatments they would want to refuse, and under what circumstances;

(b) the feelings, beliefs or values that may be influencing the patient's preferences and decisions;

(c) the relatives, friends, carers or representatives that the patient would like to be involved in decisions about their care; and

(d) interventions that are likely to become necessary in an emergency, such as cardio-pulmo-nary resuscitation (CPR).

59 You should approach such discussions sensitively. If the patient agrees, you should consider involving other members of the healthcare team, people who are close to the patient or an advocate.

60 If a patient wants to nominate someone to make decisions on their behalf if they lose capacity, or if they want to refuse a particular treatment, you should explain that there may be ways to formalise these wishes and recommend that they get independent advice on how to do this.

61 You must record the discussion and any decisions the patient makes. You should make sure that a record of the plan is made available to the patient and others involved in their care, so that everyone is clear about what has been agreed. This is particularly important if the patient has made an advance decision to refuse treatment.[11] You should bear in mind that care plans need to be reviewed and updated as the situation or the patient's views change.

PART 3: CAPACITY ISSUES

The legal framework

62 Making decisions about treatment and care for patients who lack capacity is governed in England and Wales by the Mental Capacity Act 2005, and in Scotland by the Adults with Incapacity (Scotland) Act 2000. The legislation sets out the criteria and procedures to be followed in making decisions when patients lack capacity to make these decisions for themselves. It also grants legal authority to certain people to make decisions on behalf of patients who lack capacity.[12] In Northern Ireland, there is currently no relevant primary legislation; and decision-making for patients without capacity is governed by the common law, which requires that decisions must be made in a patient's best interests.[13] There is more information about legislation and case law in the legal annex to this guidance.[14]

63 The guidance that follows is consistent with the law across the UK. It is important that you keep up to date with, and comply with, the laws and codes of practice that apply where you work. If you are unsure about how the law applies in a particular situation, you should consult your defence body or professional association, or seek independent legal advice.

Presumption of capacity

64 You must work on the presumption that every adult patient has the capacity to make decisions about their care, and to decide whether to agree to, or refuse, an examination, investigation or treatment. You must only regard a patient as lacking capacity once it is clear that, having been given all appropriate help and support, they cannot understand, retain, use or weigh up the information needed to make that decision, or communicate their wishes.

---

[11] The Mental Capacity Act 2005 requires advance decisions to refuse life-sustaining treatment to be in writing. Advance decisions to refuse other types of treatment may be written or verbal but, if verbal, they should be recorded in a person's healthcare record (see Mental Capacity Act 2005 Code of Practice, chapter 9). It may be helpful under the provisions of the Adults with Incapacity (Scotland) Act 2000, for a written record to be made of a person's advance decision to refuse medical treatment (see Code of Practice for those authorised to carry out medical treatment or research under Part 5 of the Act, paragraphs 2.27–2.30).

[12] Individuals with powers of attorney that cover health and welfare decisions (England, Wales and Scotland), court-appointed deputies (England and Wales) or guardians with welfare powers (Scotland) can, in certain circumstances, make decisions on behalf of a person who does not have capacity. See the legal annex for more information.

[13] In Northern Ireland, there is currently no legal provision for someone else to consent to treatment on behalf of patients without capacity.

[14] If you are treating a patient who lacks capacity and who also has a mental disorder, you should be aware of how the mental health legislation across the UK interacts with the law on mental capacity. See Other sources of information and guidance. [*Omitted.*]

65 You must not assume that a patient lacks capacity to make a decision solely because of their age, disability, appearance, behaviour, medical condition (including mental illness), their beliefs, their apparent inability to communicate, or the fact that they make a decision that you disagree with.

Maximising a patient's ability to make decisions

66 A patient's ability to make decisions may depend on the nature and severity of their condition, or the difficulty or complexity of the decision. Some patients will always be able to make simple decisions, but may have difficulty if the decision is complex or involves a number of options. Other patients may be able to make decisions at certain times but not others, because fluctuations in their condition impair their ability to understand, retain or weigh up information, or communicate their wishes.

67 If a patient's capacity is affected in this way, you must follow the guidance in paragraphs 18–21, taking particular care to give the patient the time and support they need to maximise their ability to make decisions for themselves. For example, you will need to think carefully about the extra support needed by patients with dementia or learning disabilities.

68 You must take all reasonable steps to plan for foreseeable changes in a patient's capacity to make decisions. This means that you should:

    (a) discuss treatment options in a place and at a time when the patient is best able to understand and retain the information;

    (b) ask the patient if there is anything that would help them remember information, or make it easier to make a decision, such as bringing a relative, partner, friend, carer or advocate to consultations, or having written or audio information about their condition or the proposed investigation or treatment;

    (c) speak to those close to the patient and to other healthcare staff about the best ways of communicating with the patient, taking account of confidentiality issues.

69 If a patient is likely to have difficulty retaining information, you should offer them a written record of your discussions, detailing what decisions were made and why.

70 You should record any decisions that are made, wherever possible while the patient has capacity to understand and review them. You must bear in mind that advance refusals of treatment may need to be recorded, signed and witnessed.

Assessing capacity

71 You must assess a patient's capacity to make a particular decision at the time it needs to be made. You must not assume that because a patient lacks capacity to make a decision on a particular occasion, they lack capacity to make any decisions at all, or will not be able to make similar decisions in the future.

72 You must take account of the advice on assessing capacity in the Codes of Practice that accompany the Mental Capacity Act 2005 and the Adults with Incapacity (Scotland) Act 2000 and other relevant guidance. If your assessment is that the patient's capacity is borderline, you must be able to show that it is more likely than not that they lack capacity.

73 If your assessment leaves you in doubt about the patient's capacity to make a decision, you should seek advice from:

    (a) nursing staff or others involved in the patient's care, or those close to the patient, who may be aware of the patient's usual ability to make decisions and their particular communication needs;

    (b) colleagues with relevant specialist experience, such as psychiatrists, neurologists, or speech and language therapists.

74 If you are still unsure about the patient's capacity to make a decision, you must seek legal advice with a view to asking a court to determine capacity.

Making decisions when a patient lacks capacity

75 In making decisions about the treatment and care of patients who lack capacity, you must:
   (a) make the care of your patient your first concern;
   (b) treat patients as individuals and respect their dignity;
   (c) support and encourage patients to be involved, as far as they want to and are able, in decisions about their treatment and care; and
   (d) treat patients with respect and not discriminate against them.

76 You must also consider:
   (a) whether the patient's lack of capacity is temporary or permanent;
   (b) which options for treatment would provide overall clinical benefit for the patient;
   (c) which option, including the option not to treat, would be least restrictive of the patient's future choices;
   (d) any evidence of the patient's previously expressed preferences, such as an advance statement or decision;[15]
   (e) the views of anyone the patient asks you to consult, or who has legal authority to make a decision on their behalf,[16] or has been appointed to represent them;[17]
   (f) the views of people close to the patient on the patient's preferences, feelings, beliefs and values, and whether they consider the proposed treatment to be in the patient's best interests;[18]
   (g) what you and the rest of the healthcare team know about the patient's wishes, feelings, beliefs and values.

Resolving disagreements

77 You should aim to reach a consensus about a patient's treatment and care, allowing enough time for discussions with those who have an interest in the patient's welfare. Sometimes disagreements arise between members of the healthcare team, or between the healthcare team and those close to the patient. It is usually possible to resolve them, for example by involving an independent advocate, consulting a more experienced colleague, holding a case conference, or using local mediation services. You should take into account the different decision-making roles and authority of those you consult, and the legal framework for resolving disagreements.[19]

78 If, having taken these steps, there is still significant disagreement, you should seek legal advice on applying to the appropriate court or statutory body for review or for an independent ruling. Patients, those authorised to act for them, and those close to them, should be informed as early as possible of any decision to start such proceedings so that they have the opportunity to participate or be represented.

The scope of treatment in emergencies

79 When an emergency arises in a clinical setting[20] and it is not possible to find out a patient's wishes, you can treat them without their consent, provided the treatment is immediately necessary to save their life or to prevent a serious deterioration of their condition. The treatment you provide must be the least restrictive of the patient's future choices. For as long as the patient lacks capacity, you should provide ongoing care on the basis of the guidance in paragraphs 75–76. If the patient

---

[15] See paragraphs 2.28–2.29 of the Code of Practice for persons authorised to carry out medical treatment or research under Part 5 of the Adults with Incapacity (Scotland) Act 2000, or Chapter 9 of the Mental Capacity Act 2005 Code of Practice.

[16] Welfare attorneys and court appointed guardians (Scotland), holders of lasting powers of attorney and court-appointed deputies (England and Wales).

[17] Independent Mental Capacity Advocates in England and Wales.

[18] In England and in Wales, if you are proposing serious medical treatment (see paragraphs 10.42–10.50 of the Mental Capacity Act 2005 Code of Practice) and there is nobody other than paid staff who can represent the views of a patient who lacks the capacity to consent to that serious medical treatment, and that treatment is provided or funded by the NHS, an Independent Mental Capacity Advocate must be instructed to represent and support the patient.

[19] See Chapter 3 of the Code of Practice for persons authorised to carry out medical treatment or research under Part 5 of the Adults with Incapacity (Scotland) Act 2000, or Chapter 15 of the Mental Capacity Act 2005 Code of Practice.

[20] Paragraph 11 of *Good medical practice* says that doctors must offer assistance in an emergency, wherever it arises, taking account of their own safety, their competence and the availability of other options for care.

regains capacity while in your care, you should tell them what has been done, and why, as soon as they are sufficiently recovered to understand.

[*Legal annex omitted.*]

Confidentiality*

[*Excerpts, endnotes omitted.*]

Principles

6. Confidentiality is central to trust between doctors and patients. Without assurances about confidentiality, patients may be reluctant to seek medical attention or to give doctors the information they need in order to provide good care. But appropriate information sharing is essential to the efficient provision of safe, effective care, both for the individual patient and for the wider community of patients.

7. You should make sure that information is readily available to patients explaining that, unless they object, their personal information may be disclosed for the sake of their own care and for local clinical audit. Patients usually understand that information about them has to be shared within the healthcare team to provide their care. But it is not always clear to patients that others who support the provision of care might also need to have access to their personal information. And patients may not be aware of disclosures to others for purposes other than their care, such as service planning or medical research. You must inform patients about disclosures for purposes they would not reasonably expect, or check that they have already received information about such disclosures.

8. Confidentiality is an important duty, but it is not absolute. You can disclose personal information if:

 (a) it is required by law (see paragraphs 17 to 23)
 (b) the patient consents - either implicitly for the sake of their own care (see paragraphs 25 to 31) or expressly for other purposes (see paragraphs 32 to 35)
 (c) it is justified in the public interest (see paragraphs 36 to 56).

9. When disclosing information about a patient, you must:

 (a) use anonymised or coded information if practicable and if it will serve the purpose
 (b) be satisfied that the patient:
   (i) has ready access to information that explains that their personal information might be disclosed for the sake of their own care, or for local clinical audit, and that they can object, and
   (ii) has not objected
 (c) get the patient's express consent if identifiable information is to be disclosed for purposes other than their care or local clinical audit, unless the disclosure is required by law or can be justified in the public interest
 (d) keep disclosures to the minimum necessary, and
 (e) keep up to date with, and observe, all relevant legal requirements, including the common law and data protection legislation.

10. When you are satisfied that information should be disclosed, you should act promptly to disclose all relevant information.

11. You should respect, and help patients to exercise, their legal rights to:

 (a) be informed about how their information will be used, and
 (b) have access to, or copies of, their health records.

Protecting information

12. You must make sure that any personal information about patients that you hold or control is effectively protected at all times against improper disclosure. The UK health departments publish guidance on how long health records should be kept and how they should be disposed of. You should follow the guidance whether or not you work in the NHS.

13. Many improper disclosures are unintentional. You should not share identifiable information about patients where you can be overheard, for example in a public place or in an internet chat forum. You should not share passwords or leave patients' records, either on paper or on screen, unattended or where they can be seen by other patients, unauthorised healthcare staff, or the public.

14. Unless they have a relevant management role, doctors are not expected to assess the security standards of large-scale computer systems provided for their use in the NHS or in other managed healthcare environments. You should familiarise yourself with and follow policies and procedures designed to protect patients' privacy where you work and when using computer systems provided for your use. This includes policies on the use of laptops and portable media storage devices. You must not abuse your access privileges and must limit your access to information you have a legitimate reason to view.

15. If you are responsible for the management of patient records or other patient information, you should make sure that they are held securely and that any staff you manage are trained and understand their responsibilities. You should make use of professional expertise when selecting and developing systems to record, access and send electronic data. You should make sure that administrative information, such as names and addresses, can be accessed separately from clinical information so that sensitive information is not displayed automatically.

16. If you are concerned about the security of personal information in premises or systems provided for your use, you should follow the advice in *Good Medical Practice on Raising concerns about patient safety* (GMP, 2006) including concerns about confidentiality and information governance.

Disclosures required by law

Disclosures required by statute

17. You must disclose information to satisfy a specific statutory requirement, such as notification of a known or suspected case of certain infectious diseases.

18. Various regulatory bodies have statutory powers to access patients' records as part of their duties to investigate complaints, accidents or health professionals' fitness to practise. You should satisfy yourself that any disclosure sought is required by law or can be justified in the public interest. Many regulatory bodies have codes of practice governing how they will access and use personal information.

19. Whenever practicable, you should inform patients about such disclosures, unless that would undermine the purpose, even if their consent is not required.

20. Patient records or other personal information may be required by the GMC or other statutory regulators for an investigation into a healthcare professional's fitness to practise. If information is requested, but not required by law, or if you are referring concerns about a health professional to a regulatory body, you must, if practicable, seek the patient's express consent before disclosing personal information. If a patient refuses to consent, or if it is not practicable to seek their consent, you should contact the appropriate regulatory body, to help you decide whether the disclosure can be justified in the public interest.

Disclosures to courts or in connection with litigation

21. You must disclose information if ordered to do so by a judge or presiding officer of a court. You should object to the judge or the presiding officer if attempts are made to compel you to disclose what appears to you to be irrelevant information, such as information about a patient's relative who is not involved in the proceedings.

22. You must not disclose personal information to a third party such as a solicitor, police officer or officer of a court without the patient's express consent, unless it is required by law or can be justified in the public interest.

Disclosing information with consent

24. Seeking a patient's consent to disclosure of information shows respect, and is part of good communication between doctors and patients.

Circumstances in which patients may give implied consent to disclosure

Sharing information within the healthcare team or with others providing care

25. Most patients understand and accept that information must be shared within the healthcare team in order to provide their care. You should make sure information is readily available to patients explaining that, unless they object, personal information about them will be shared within the healthcare team, including administrative and other staff who support the provision of their care.

26. This information can be provided in leaflets, posters, on websites, and face to face and should be tailored to patients' identified needs as far as practicable. Posters might be of little assistance to patients with sight impairment or who do not read English, for example. In reviewing the information provided to patients, you should consider whether patients would be surprised to learn about how their information is being used and disclosed.

27. You must respect the wishes of any patient who objects to particular information being shared within the healthcare team or with others providing care, unless disclosure would be justified in the public interest. If a patient objects to a disclosure that you consider essential to the provision of safe care, you should explain that you cannot refer them or otherwise arrange for their treatment without also disclosing that information.

28. You must make sure that anyone you disclose personal information to understands that you are giving it to them in confidence, which they must respect. All staff members receiving personal information in order to provide or support care are bound by a legal duty of confidence, whether or not they have contractual or professional obligations to protect confidentiality.

29. Circumstances may arise in which a patient cannot be informed about the disclosure of information, for example in a medical emergency. In such a case you should pass relevant information promptly to those providing the patient's care. If and when the patient is capable of understanding, you should inform them how their personal information was disclosed if it was in a way they would not reasonably expect.

Local clinical audit

30. All doctors in clinical practice have a duty to participate in clinical audit and to contribute to National Confidential Inquiries. If an audit is to be undertaken by the team that provided care, or those working to support them, such as clinical audit staff, you may disclose identifiable information, provided you are satisfied that the patient:

    (a) has ready access to information that explains that their personal information may be disclosed for local clinical audit, and that they have the right to object, and

    (b) has not objected.

31. If a patient does object you should explain why the information is needed and how this may benefit their own, and others' care. If it is not possible to provide safe care without disclosing information for audit, you should explain this to the patient and the options open to them.

32. If clinical audit is to be undertaken, but not by the team that provided care or those who support them, the information should be anonymised or coded. If this is not practicable, or if identifiable information is essential to the audit, you should disclose the information only if you have the patient's express consent. (See the guidance on Research and other secondary uses in paragraphs 40 to 50.)

Disclosures for which express consent should be sought

33. As a general rule, you should seek a patient's express consent before disclosing identifiable information for purposes other than the provision of their care or local clinical audit, such as financial audit and insurance or benefits claims.

34. If you are asked to provide information to third parties, such as a patient's insurer or employer or a government department or an agency assessing a claimant's entitlement to benefits, either following an examination or from existing records, you should:

    (a) be satisfied that the patient has sufficient information about the scope, purpose and likely consequences of the examination and disclosure, and the fact that relevant information cannot be concealed or withheld

    (b) obtain or have seen written consent to the disclosure from the patient or a person properly authorised to act on the patient's behalf; you may accept an assurance from an officer of a government department or agency or a registered health professional acting on their behalf that the patient or a person properly authorised to act on their behalf has consented

    (c) only disclose factual information you can substantiate, presented in an unbiased manner, relevant to the request; so you should not usually disclose the whole record, although it may be relevant to some benefits paid by government departments and to other assessments of patients' entitlement to pensions or other health-related benefits, and

    (d) offer to show your patient, or give them a copy of, any report you write about them for employment or insurance purposes before it is sent, unless:

      (i) they have already indicated they do not wish to see it

      (ii) disclosure would be likely to cause serious harm to the patient or anyone else

      (iii) disclosure would be likely to reveal information about another person who does not consent.

35. If a patient refuses consent, or if it is not practicable to get their consent, information can still be disclosed if it is required by law or can be justified in the public interest (see paragraphs 36 to 56). If the purpose is covered by a regulation made under section 251 of the *NHS Act 2006*, disclosures can also be made without a patient's consent, but not if the patient has objected.

Disclosures in the public interest

36. There is a clear public good in having a confidential medical service. The fact that people are encouraged to seek advice and treatment, including for communicable diseases, benefits society as a whole as well as the individual. Confidential medical care is recognised in law as being in the public interest. However, there can also be a public interest in disclosing information: to protect individuals or society from risks of serious harm, such as serious communicable diseases or serious crime; or to enable medical research, education or other secondary uses of information that will benefit society over time.

37. Personal information may, therefore, be disclosed in the public interest, without patients' consent, and in exceptional cases where patients have withheld consent, if the benefits to an individual or to society of the disclosure outweigh both the public and the patient's interest in keeping the information confidential. You must weigh the harms that are likely to arise from non-disclosure of information against the possible harm both to the patient, and to the overall trust between doctors and patients, arising from the release of that information.

38. Before considering whether a disclosure of personal information would be justified in the public interest, you must be satisfied that identifiable information is necessary for the purpose, or that it is not reasonably practicable to anonymise or code it. In such cases, you should still seek the patient's consent unless it is not practicable to do so, for example because:

    (a) the patient is not competent to give consent, in which case you should consult the patient's welfare attorney, court-appointed deputy, guardian or the patient's relatives, friends or carers (see paragraphs 57 to 63)

(b) you have reason to believe that seeking consent would put you or others at risk of serious harm

(c) seeking consent would be likely to undermine the purpose of the disclosure, for example, by prejudicing the prevention or detection of serious crime, or

(d) action must be taken quickly, for example, in the detection or control of outbreaks of some communicable diseases, and there is insufficient time to contact the patient.

39. You should inform the patient that a disclosure will be made in the public interest, even if you have not sought consent, unless to do so is impracticable, would put you or others at risk of serious harm, or would prejudice the purpose of the disclosure. You must document in the patient's record your reasons for disclosing information without consent and any steps you have taken to seek the patient's consent, to inform them about the disclosure, or your reasons for not doing so.

Research and other secondary uses

40. Research, epidemiology, public health surveillance, health service planning and education and training are among the important secondary uses made of patient information. Each of these uses can serve important public interests.

41. For many secondary uses, it will be sufficient and practicable to disclose only anonymised or coded information. When identifiable information is needed, or it is not practicable to remove identifiable information, it will often be perfectly practicable to get patients' express consent.

42. You may disclose identifiable information without consent if it is required by law, if it is approved under section 251 of the *NHS Act 2006*, or if it can be justified in the public interest and it is either:

(a) necessary to use identifiable information, or

(b) not practicable to anonymise or code the information and, in either case, not practicable to seek consent (or efforts to seek consent have been unsuccessful).

43. In considering whether it is practicable to seek consent you should take account of:

(a) the age of records and the likely traceability of patients

(b) the number of records, and

(c) the possibility of introducing bias because of a low response rate or because particular groups of patients refuse, or do not respond to, requests to use their information.

44. When considering whether the public interest in disclosures for secondary uses outweighs patients' and the public interest in keeping the information confidential, you must consider:

(a) the nature of the information to be disclosed

(b) what use will be made of the information

(c) how many people will have access to the information

(d) the confidentiality and security arrangements in place to protect the information from further disclosure

(e) the advice of a Caldicott Guardian or similar expert adviser, who is not directly connected with the use for which disclosure is being considered, and

(f) the potential for distress or harm to patients.

45. When considering applications for support under section 251 of the *NHS Act 2006* in England and Wales, the National Information Governance Board considers:

(a) the feasibility of doing the research or other activity with patients' consent or by using anonymised or coded information, and

(b) whether the use of identifiable information would benefit patients or the public sufficiently to outweigh patients' right to privacy.

48. It might not be practicable for the healthcare team, or those who usually support them, to anonymise or code information or to seek patients' express consent:

(a) for the disclosure of identifiable information for important secondary uses, or

(b) so that suitable patients can be recruited to clinical trials or other approved research projects.

49. If that is the case:
   (a) identifiable information may be sent to a 'safe haven', where they exist and have the capabilities and are otherwise suitable to process the information (including anonymising or coding it) and to manage the disclosure of information for secondary uses or, if that is not practicable
   (b) the task of anonymising or coding the information or seeking patients' consent to disclosure can be delegated to someone incorporated into the healthcare team on a temporary basis and bound by legal and contractual obligations of confidentiality.

50. You should only disclose identifiable information for research if that research is approved by a Research Ethics Committee. You should alert Research Ethics Committees to disclosures of identifiable information without consent when applying for approval for research projects.

Disclosures to protect the patient

51. It may be appropriate to encourage patients to consent to disclosures you consider necessary for their protection, and to warn them of the risks of refusing to consent; but you should usually abide by a competent adult patient's refusal to consent to disclosure, even if their decision leaves them, but nobody else, at risk of serious harm. You should do your best to provide patients with the information and support they need to make decisions in their own interests, for example, by arranging contact with agencies to support victims of domestic violence.

52. Disclosure without consent may be justified if it is not practicable to seek a patient's consent. See paragraph 38 for examples, and paragraph 63 for guidance on disclosures to protect a patient who lacks capacity to consent.

Disclosures to protect others

53. Disclosure of personal information about a patient without consent may be justified in the public interest if failure to disclose may expose others to a risk of death or serious harm. You should still seek the patient's consent to disclosure if practicable and consider any reasons given for refusal.

54. Such a situation might arise, for example, when a disclosure would be likely to assist in the prevention, detection or prosecution of serious crime, especially crimes against the person. When victims of violence refuse police assistance, disclosure may still be justified if others remain at risk, for example, from someone who is prepared to use weapons, or from domestic violence when children or others may be at risk.

55. If a patient's refusal to consent to disclosure leaves others exposed to a risk so serious that it outweighs the patient's and the public interest in maintaining confidentiality, or if it is not practicable or safe to seek the patient's consent, you should disclose information promptly to an appropriate person or authority. You should inform the patient before disclosing the information, if practicable and safe, even if you intend to disclose without their consent.

56. You should participate in procedures set up to protect the public from violent and sex offenders. You should co-operate with requests for relevant information about patients who may pose a risk of serious harm to others.

Disclosures about patients who lack capacity to consent

57. There is advice on assessing a patient's mental capacity in our guidance *Consent: patients and doctors making decisions together* and in the *Adults with Incapacity (Scotland) Act 2000* and *Mental Capacity Act 2005* codes of practice. There is no specific mental capacity legislation for Northern Ireland.

58. For advice in relation to children and young people, see our guidance *0-18 years: guidance for all doctors*.

59. When making decisions about whether to disclose information about a patient who lacks capacity, you must:
   (a) make the care of the patient your first concern

   (b) respect the patient's dignity and privacy, and

   (c) support and encourage the patient to be involved, as far as they want and are able, in decisions about disclosure of their personal information.

60. You must also consider:

   (a) whether the patient's lack of capacity is permanent or temporary and, if temporary, whether the decision to disclose could reasonably wait until they regain capacity

   (b) any evidence of the patient's previously expressed preferences

   (c) the views of anyone the patient asks you to consult, or who has legal authority to make a decision on their behalf, or has been appointed to represent them

   (d) the views of people close to the patient on the patient's preferences, feelings, beliefs and values, and whether they consider the proposed disclosure to be in the patient's best interests, and

   (e) what you and the rest of the healthcare team know about the patient's wishes, feelings, beliefs and values.

61. If a patient who lacks capacity asks you not to disclose personal information about their condition or treatment, you should try to persuade them to allow an appropriate person to be involved in the consultation. If they refuse, and you are convinced that it is essential in their best interests, you may disclose relevant information to an appropriate person or authority. In such a case you should tell the patient before disclosing the information and, if appropriate, seek and carefully consider the views of an advocate or carer. You should document in the patient's record your discussions and the reasons for deciding to disclose the information.

62. You may need to share personal information with a patient's relatives, friends or carers to enable you to assess the patient's best interests. But that does not mean they have a general right of access to the patient's records or to have irrelevant information about, for example, the patient's past healthcare. You should also share relevant personal information with anyone who is authorised to make decisions on behalf of, or who is appointed to support and represent, a mentally incapacitated patient.

Disclosures when a patient may be a victim of neglect or abuse

63. If you believe that a patient may be a victim of neglect or physical, sexual or emotional abuse, and that they lack capacity to consent to disclosure, you must give information promptly to an appropriate responsible person or authority, if you believe that the disclosure is in the patient's best interests or necessary to protect others from a risk of serious harm. If, for any reason, you believe that disclosure of information is not in the best interests of a neglected or abused patient, you should discuss the issues with an experienced colleague. If you decide not to disclose information, you should document in the patient's record your discussions and the reasons for deciding not to disclose. You should be prepared to justify your decision.

Sharing information with a patient's partner, carers, relatives or friends

64. You should establish with the patient what information they want you to share, who with, and in what circumstances. This will be particularly important if the patient has fluctuating or diminished capacity or is likely to lose capacity, even temporarily. Early discussions of this nature can help to avoid disclosures that patients would object to. They can also help to avoid misunderstandings with, or causing offence to, anyone the patient would want information to be shared with.

65. If a patient lacks capacity, you should share relevant information in accordance with the advice in paragraphs 57 to 63. Unless they indicate otherwise, it is reasonable to assume that patients would want those closest to them to be kept informed of their general condition and prognosis.

66. If anyone close to the patient wants to discuss their concerns about the patient's health, you should make it clear to them that, while it is not a breach of confidentiality to listen to their concerns,

you cannot guarantee that you will not tell the patient about the conversation. You might need to share with a patient information you have received from others, for example, if it has influenced your assessment and treatment of the patient. You should not refuse to listen to a patient's partner, carers or others on the basis of confidentiality. Their views or the information they provide might be helpful in your care of the patient. You will, though, need to consider whether your patient would consider you listening to the concerns of others about your patient's health or care to be a breach of trust, particularly if they have asked you not to listen to particular people.

Genetic and other shared information

67. Genetic and some other information about your patient might at the same time also be information about others the patient shares genetic or other links with. The diagnosis of an illness in the patient might, for example, point to the certainty or likelihood of the same illness in a blood relative.

68. Most patients will readily share information about their own health with their children and other relatives, particularly if they are advised that it might help those relatives to:
    (a)   get prophylaxis or other preventative treatments or interventions
    (b)   make use of increased surveillance or other investigations, or
    (c)   prepare for potential health problems.

69. However, a patient might refuse to consent to the disclosure of information that would benefit others, for example where family relationships have broken down, or if their natural children have been adopted. In these circumstances, disclosure might still be justified in the public interest (see paragraphs 36 to 56). If a patient refuses consent to disclosure, you will need to balance your duty to make the care of your patient your first concern against your duty to help protect the other person from serious harm. If practicable, you should not disclose the patient's identity in contacting and advising others of the risks they face.

Disclosure after a patient's death

70. Your duty of confidentiality continues after a patient has died. Whether and what personal information may be disclosed after a patient's death will depend on the circumstances. If the patient had asked for information to remain confidential, you should usually respect their wishes. If you are unaware of any instructions from the patient, when you are considering requests for information you should take into account:
    (a)   whether the disclosure of information is likely to cause distress to, or be of benefit to, the patient's partner or family
    (b)   whether the disclosure will also disclose information about the patient's family or anyone else
    (c)   whether the information is already public knowledge or can be anonymised or coded, and
    (d)   the purpose of the disclosure.

71. There are circumstances in which you should disclose relevant information about a patient who has died, for example:
    (a)   to help a coroner, procurator fiscal or other similar officer with an inquest or fatal accident inquiry
    (b)   when disclosure is required by law, is authorised under section 251 of the *NHS Act 2006*, or is justified in the public interest, such as for education or research
    (c)   for National Confidential Inquiries or for local clinical audit
    (d)   on death certificates, which you must complete honestly and fully
    (e)   for public health surveillance, in which case the information should be anonymised or coded, unless that would defeat the purpose
    (f)   when a parent asks for information about the circumstances and causes of a child's death

(g) when a partner, close relative or friend asks for information about the circumstances of an adult's death, and you have no reason to believe that the patient would have objected to such a disclosure, and

(h) when a person has a right of access to records under the *Access to Health Records Act 1990* ...

72. Archived records relating to deceased patients remain subject to a duty of confidentiality, although the potential for disclosing information about, or causing distress to, surviving relatives or damaging the public's trust will diminish over time.

Good practice in research and consent to research*

[*Excerpts (and some notes omitted).*]

Good practice in research

Scope of the guidance

1 Research in this guidance refers to an attempt to derive generalisable new knowledge. Research aims to find out what is best practice by addressing clearly defined questions with systematic and rigorous methods. It includes studies that aim to generate hypotheses as well as those that aim to test them.

2 This guidance covers research with people, as well as research involving human tissue and records-based research that does not involve people directly.

3 It also applies to clinical trials, which cover a broad range of different types of research involving people.[1] For example, they can test medicines or vaccines, treatments, surgical procedures, devices, or health prevention or care. A clinical trial of investigational medicinal products is a particular type of trial that is governed by legislation. The key elements of the law for conducting a clinical trial of investigational medicinal products in the UK are set out in annex B.

4 This guidance does not apply to clinical audit or service evaluation projects, which aim to measure standards of care. Nor does it cover innovative treatments designed to benefit individual patients. These activities are covered by the standards and principles set out in *Consent: patients and doctors making decisions together* and *Confidentiality*.

Principles of good research practice

5 To protect participants and maintain public confidence in research, it is important that all research is conducted lawfully, with honesty and integrity, and in accordance with good practice.

This guidance sets out principles of good research practice, which you must follow if you are involved in research.

Law and governance

6 The law and governance arrangements that apply to research are complex and vary depending on the type of research, the participants involved, how it is funded and where in the UK it is undertaken. You must comply with the law, governance arrangements and codes of practice that apply to the research you are undertaking. The legal annexes to this guidance give more detail and

---

* © General Medical Council 2010.

[1] The World Health Organization defines a clinical trial as any research study that prospectively assigns human participants or groups of humans to one or more health-related interventions to evaluate the effects on health outcomes. Clinical trials may also be referred to as interventional trials. Interventions include but are not restricted to drugs, cells and other biological products, surgical procedures, radiologic procedures, devices, behavioural treatments, process-of-care changes, preventive care, etc. This definition includes phase I to phase IV trials.

links to further information about the relevant legal and governance framework for research (see annex A) and the key elements of the legislation that governs clinical trials of investigational medicinal products in the UK (see annex B).

Good research design and practice

7 You must make sure that research is based on a properly developed protocol that has been approved by a research ethics committee.[2] It must be prepared according to good practice guidance given by government and other research and professional bodies.

8 You must make sure that the safety, dignity and wellbeing of participants take precedence over the development of treatments and the furthering of knowledge.

9 You must make sure that foreseeable risks to participants are kept as low as possible. In addition, you must be satisfied that:

- the anticipated benefits to participants outweigh the foreseeable risks, or
- the foreseeable risks to participants are minimal if the research only has the potential to benefit others more generally.

10 You must make sure that decisions at all stages of research, especially for recruitment, are free from discrimination[3] and respect participants' equality and diversity. You should take all reasonable steps to make sure that people eligible to participate in a project are given equal access to take part and the opportunity to benefit from the research. Where appropriate, you should use patient and public involvement groups at all stages of the project to help make sure that the research is well designed and conducted.

11 You should make sure that details of a research project are registered on an eligible, publicly available database that is kept updated, where such a database exists.

12 You should be satisfied that appropriate monitoring systems are in place to make sure research is being carried out in accordance with the law and good practice.

13 You must keep your knowledge and skills up to date. If you lead a research team, you must make sure that all members of the team have the necessary skills, experience, training and support to carry out their research responsibilities as effectively as possible.

14 You should make sure that commercial and other interests do not stop or adversely affect the completion of research. If you are concerned about this you should follow the guidance on raising your concerns in paragraph 19.

Protecting participants from harm

15 You must stop research where the results indicate that participants are at risk of significant harm or, in research involving treatment required by a patient, where no benefit can be expected.

16 You must report adverse findings as soon as possible to the affected participants, to those responsible for their medical care, to the research ethics committee, and to the research sponsor or primary funder where relevant. You must make sure that bodies responsible for protecting the public, for example, the Medicines and Healthcare products Regulatory Agency, are informed.

17 You should make sure that participants are not encouraged to volunteer more frequently than is advisable or against their best interests. You should make sure that nobody takes part repeatedly in research projects if it might lead to a risk of significant harm to them. You should make sure that any necessary safeguards are in place to protect anybody who may be vulnerable to pressure to take part in research. You must follow our guidance in paragraphs 21–22 of *Consent to research* on involving vulnerable adults in research.

---

[2] Research ethics committees (RECs) have a responsibility to safeguard the rights, safety, dignity and wellbeing of people participating in research. They review applications for research and give opinions about the proposed participant involvement and whether the research is ethical. Guidance on whether research requires ethical review under either the law or the policy of the UK health departments can be found on the National Research Ethics Service website. See www.nres.npsa.nhs.uk/applications/guidance/.

[3] Restricting research participants to subgroups of the population that may be defined, for example, by age, gender, ethnicity or sexual orientation, for legitimate methodological reasons does not constitute discrimination.

18 If a participant is involved in investigations that may contribute to a cumulative long-term risk of harm, for example, radiation from X-rays or radioactive substances, you must consider any previous exposure to the risk and make sure that a record is kept about their participation.[12]

19 If you have good reason to believe that participants are at risk of significant harm by taking part in research or by the behaviour of anyone conducting research, you must report your concerns to an appropriate person in your employing or contracting body. If you remain concerned you should inform the research ethics committee and the research sponsor or primary funder. You should follow the guidance in *Raising concerns about patient* safety[4] if you are not sure when or how to raise concerns.

20 If you are responsible for acting on concerns raised by colleagues, you must make sure that reporting procedures are in place and that staff are aware of them. If a concern is brought to your attention you must take appropriate action promptly and professionally.

Honesty and integrity

21 You must conduct research honestly. If you are concerned about the quality or integrity of the research, including allegations of fraud or misconduct, you must follow the guidance in paragraph 19 on raising concerns. You must report evidence of financial or scientific fraud, or other breaches of this guidance, to an appropriate person in your employing or contracting body, and where appropriate to the GMC or other statutory regulatory bodies.

22 You must be open and honest with participants and members of the research team, including nonmedical staff, when sharing information about a research project. You must answer questions honestly and as fully as possible.

23 You must make clear, accurate and legible records of research results, as soon as possible after the data are collected. You must keep records for the appropriate period to allow adequate time for review, further research and audit, or to help resolve any concerns about the data or research project.

24 You must report research results accurately, objectively, promptly and in a way that can be clearly understood. You must make sure that research reports are properly attributed and do not contain false or misleading data. Whenever possible, you should publish research results, including adverse findings, through peer-reviewed journals.

25 You should make research findings available to those who might benefit. You should make reasonable efforts to inform participants of the outcome of the research, or make the information publicly available if it is not practical to inform participants directly.

Avoiding conflicts of interest

26 You must be open and honest in all financial and commercial matters relating to your research and its funding.

27 You must not allow your judgement about a research project to be influenced, or be seen to be influenced, at any stage, by financial, personal, political or other external interests. You must identify any actual or potential conflicts of interest that arise, and declare them as soon as possible to the research ethics committee, other appropriate bodies, and the participants, in line with the policy of your employing or contracting body.

Consent to research

28 You must get consent from participants before involving them in any research project. You must have other valid authority before involving in research adults who lack capacity, or children or young people who cannot consent for themselves.

29 You must make sure that people are informed of, and that you respect, their right to decline to take part in research and to withdraw from the research project at any time, with an assurance

---

[4] See www.gmc-uk.org/guidance/ethical_guidance/raising_concerns.asp.

that this will not adversely affect their relationship with those providing care, or the care they receive.

30 When seeking consent for research, you must follow the guidance in *Consent to research* and, where relevant, *Consent: patients and doctors making decisions together*.

Respecting confidentiality

31 You must respect participants' right to confidentiality, and make sure that any data collected as part of a research project are stored securely and in accordance with data protection and other requirements.

32 You must follow the guidance in *Confidentiality*, in particular the guidance in paragraphs 40–50 on research and other secondary uses, if you undertake records-based research that does not involve people directly.

Consent to research

Seeking consent

Valid consent

1 Seeking consent is fundamental in research involving people. Participants' consent is legally valid and professionally acceptable only if they have the capacity to decide whether to take part in the research, have been properly informed, and have agreed to participate without pressure or coercion.

2 When conducting research involving people who cannot consent for themselves, you must follow the guidance that applies, such as the advice on research involving children or young people in paragraphs 14–20 and on adults who lack capacity in paragraphs 23–35.

Right to withdraw from research

3 You must make sure that people are informed of, and that you respect, their right to decline to take part in research and to withdraw from the research project at any time, with an assurance that this will not adversely affect their relationship with those providing care or the care they receive. You should tell people if the treatment options available to them might be affected by a decision to withdraw from a research project.

Sharing information

4 You must give people the information they want or need in order to decide whether to take part in research. How much information you share with them will depend on their individual circumstances. You must not make assumptions about the information a person might want or need, or their knowledge and understanding of the proposed research project.

5 In most cases, the information people will need to decide whether to take part in research will be included in the participant information sheet. The National Research Ethics Service gives advice on the design of information sheets and consent forms, and the key points they should cover. You should follow that advice if you are developing information sheets or consent forms.[5]

6 You should give people any further information they ask for. This might include a copy of the protocol approved by a research ethics committee (subject to considerations of confidentiality, commercial privilege or the possible undermining of the purpose of the study). You should make sure people have the details of an individual or organisation they can contact to discuss the research project and get further information.

---

[5] Information & consent forms. Guidance for researchers and reviewers (National Research Ethics Service, 2009). See www.nres.npsa. nhs.uk/applications/guidance/. *Explaining research* (National Research Ethics Service, 2008). See www.nres.npsa.nhs.uk/EasySiteWeb/ GatewayLink.aspx?alId=356.

Giving information in a way that people can understand

7 You must make sure that people are given information in a way that they can understand. You should check that people understand the terms that you use and any explanation given about the proposed research method. If necessary, you should support your discussions with simple and accurate written material or visual or other aids.

8 You must make sure, whenever practical, that arrangements are made to meet people's language, communication and other support needs. It is important to make sure that people who require additional assistance are not excluded from research and from the benefits that research can offer them and the wider groups to which they belong.

Responsibility for seeking consent

9 If you are responsible for seeking consent, you must understand the research project, including what the project will involve and any anticipated benefits and foreseeable risks.

10 If you delegate the responsibility to someone else, you must make sure they have sufficient understanding of the research project, and the appropriate skills and competence to seek consent.

Recording consent

11 You should record the key elements of your discussion with people about their decision to take part in research. If practical, you should ask them, or someone with valid authority, to give written consent. It is a legal requirement to get written consent from participants in clinical trials of investigational medicinal products.[6]

Sharing information with others involved in care

12 With the participant's consent, you should usually inform their GP and other clinicians responsible for their care about their involvement in a research project, and you should provide the doctors with any other information necessary for the participant's continuing care. You should follow this advice regardless of whether the participant is a patient or a healthy volunteer.

13 If a participant objects to information being shared in this way, you should explain to them the potential consequences of not sharing information. If the participant continues to object, you must respect their wishes, unless sharing the information is justified in the public interest.

Areas requiring special consideration

Research involving children or young people

14 When considering involving children or young people in research, you must follow the advice in *0–18 years: guidance for all doctors*. It gives advice on the circumstances in which children or young people can be involved in research, effective communication with children and young people, and assessing capacity to consent. It also explains the different legal requirements across the UK for 16 and 17-year olds who lack capacity to consent.

15 There are particular considerations in relation to seeking and acting on consent for children or young people to participate in research. As part of seeking approval for the project from a research ethics committee, you must clearly explain the arrangements for getting consent and seek advice if necessary.

16 Before involving a child or young person in research you must get consent from a parent, but you should get consent from both parents, if possible, particularly if the research involves more than low or minimal risk of harm. If a parent is under 16 years of age, you must get consent from them if they have the capacity to make a decision about whether their child should take part in the research

---

[6] In clinical trials of investigational medicinal products, consent is only valid if it is recorded in writing. If the person is unable to give written consent, for example, if they have a disability which means that they cannot write, they can give consent orally in the presence of at least one witness and this must be recorded in writing.

project. If a child or young person is able to consent for themselves, you should still consider involving their parents, depending on the nature of the research.

17 You should aim to reach a consensus with parents about a child or young person's participation in research. If disagreements arise it is usually possible to resolve them informally, and you should follow the advice in paragraphs 77–78 in *Consent: patients and doctors making decisions together*. If disagreements cannot be resolved informally, you should not involve the child or young person in research, unless the treatment can be accessed only as part of a research project and you assess that it is in their best interests. In these circumstances, if the decision about entering the child or young person in research has significant consequences for the child or young person, you should seek legal advice about whether you should apply to the appropriate court for an independent ruling.

18 You should be familiar with the guidance on you must not include them in the research. Under the *Adults with Incapacity (Scotland) Act 2000*, you must get consent from any guardian or welfare attorney who has power to consent to the adult's participation in research or, if there is no such guardian or welfare attorney, from the person's nearest relative.

Emergency research

19 Circumstances may arise where involvement in research has the potential to benefit a child or young person who lacks capacity, but an urgent decision about the child's involvement needs to be made before it is possible to get consent from a parent. This may arise because a parent cannot reasonably be contacted, or they do not have capacity to consent because of their own condition or distress. In such cases you can involve a child or young person in research if you have the approval of a research ethics committee for such recruitment. You must seek the consent of a parent as soon as possible to continue involving them in the project.

20 There are specific legal requirements that relate to involving children or young people under 16 in emergency clinical trials of investigational medicinal products. Annex B contains further guidance on the legal requirements in these circumstances.

Research involving vulnerable adults

21 Some adults with capacity may be vulnerable to pressure to take part in research. You should be aware that their health or social circumstances might make them vulnerable to pressure from others. Vulnerable adults may be, for example, living in care homes or other institutions, or have learning difficulties or mental illness. In these circumstances, it is particularly important that you check whether they need any additional support to understand information or to make a decision. You must make sure that they know they have the right to decline to participate in research, and that they are able to decline if they want to. The Royal College of Physicians of London provides further guidance on involving vulnerable groups in research.[7][11]

22 You should raise concerns with a senior colleague, or your employing or contracting organisation, if systems are not in place to provide the additional support that vulnerable adults may need to make a decision about taking part in research. If you are not sure when or how to raise concerns, you should follow the guidance in *Raising concerns about patient safety*.

Research involving adults without capacity

23 This section gives guidance about specific issues in research involving adults who lack capacity. It sets out the key elements of the law that governs the involvement of people over 16 who lack capacity to consent. Annex A contains a summary of the law in this area, and annex B explains the key elements of the legislation that governs clinical trials of investigational medicinal products in the UK.

24 You must assess an adult's capacity to make a particular decision at the time it needs to be made. You must follow the guidance in part 3 of *Consent: patients and doctors making decisions*

---

[7] Guidelines on the practice of ethics committees in medical research with human participants (Royal College of Physicians, 2007).

together, which gives advice on maximising a person's ability to make decisions, and on assessing capacity.

When adults without capacity might be involved in research

25 You must only undertake research involving an adult who lacks capacity if it is related to their incapacity or its treatment. You must not involve in research adults who lack capacity if the same or similar research could be undertaken by involving only people with capacity.

26 You should only involve in research adults who lack capacity, including clinical trials of investigational medicinal products, if the research is expected to provide a benefit to them that outweighs the risks. Research, not including clinical trials of investigational medicinal products, may also involve adults who lack capacity if the research is not expected to provide a direct benefit to them but is expected to contribute to the understanding of their incapacity, leading to an indirect benefit to them or others with the same incapacity, and if the risks are minimal. This means that the person should not suffer harm or distress by taking part. In all research involving adults who lack capacity, you must make sure that the foreseeable risks are kept as low as possible.

Seeking to involve adults without capacity in research

27 You should consider the views of people close to the adult who lacks capacity to consent before involving that person in a research project. They are often best placed to know the person's wishes about taking part in research. In clinical trials of investigational medicinal products, you must get consent from a legal representative.

28 Under the *Mental Capacity Act 2005* (in England and Wales) you must consult a consultee about whether the adult who lacks capacity should take part in the research, and what they think that person's wishes would be if they had capacity to decide for themselves. If the consultee considers that they probably would not wish to take part, and use of a deceased person's organs, tissue or cells for the purposes of research. The Act does not cover the storage and use of tissue from living people for the purposes of research.

29 If you are seeking to involve an adult who has lost capacity to consent, for example, through onset or progress of a condition that has impaired their capacity, such as dementia, you should take all reasonable steps to find out whether they have previously indicated their wishes about participating in future research, including any refusal to participate. You must consider any evidence of the person's previously expressed preferences, such as an advance statement or decision.

Right to withdraw from research

30 You must make sure that a participant's right to withdraw from research is respected. You should consider any sign of objection, distress or indication of refusal, whether or not it is spoken, as implied refusal. Under the *Mental Capacity Act 2005* (in England and Wales) you should usually withdraw the participant from the research if the consultee considers that they would wish to be withdrawn. In clinical trials of investigational medicinal products, the legal representative can withdraw the participant from the trial at any time.

Loss of capacity during a research project

31 Some people with capacity will consent to take part in research, but then may lose capacity before the end of the project. If you become aware that a participant has lost capacity, you should consider carefully the benefits and harm that could occur from their continued participation in the research, and you must follow the law that applies where you work.

32 If you are seeking to involve a person in research who you believe may lose capacity during the course of the project, you should consider seeking their views about the circumstances in which they would wish to continue to participate. You should explain to them the steps that would be taken to decide whether they should continue to take part and how their wishes, if known, would be taken into account.

Research into treatment in emergencies

33 You may want to undertake urgent research into procedures or treatments used in emergencies when a person is unconscious or otherwise unable to make a decision. In an emergency situation it is not always possible to get consent to involve a person in research using the standard consent procedures.

34 The *Mental Capacity Act 2005* permits urgent research in emergencies to start when it is not practical to consult someone about involving a person who lacks capacity in research. In this situation you must either get agreement from a doctor not involved in the research, or follow a procedure approved by a research ethics committee. Similarly, you can start a clinical trial of investigational medicinal products when it needs to be undertaken urgently if you cannot get the consent of a legal representative, as long as a research ethics committee has given approval for such action. The *Adults with Incapacity (Scotland) Act 2000* provides for emergency clinical trials of investigational medicinal products but not for other types of emergency research. If this situation arises you should seek legal advice on how to proceed.

35 You must follow the law on continuing to involve in emergency research an adult who lacks capacity. You must get consent from the adult as soon as possible if they recover capacity.

Research involving human tissue

36 You must keep up to date with, and comply with, the laws and codes of practice that apply to the use in research of human organs, tissue and cells. The Human Tissue Authority (HTA) publishes a number of codes of practice,[8] including those on consent and research, which advise on the issues you should consider when seeking consent for the purpose of research.

37 In England, Wales and Northern Ireland, the Human Tissue Act 2004 requires consent to be obtained before the storage and use of a living person's organs, tissue or cells for the purpose of research in connection with disorders in, or the functioning of, the human body. In a number of specific circumstances, there are exceptions to the consent requirements; for example, a living person's organs, tissue or cells may be stored and used without consent if the researcher is unable to identify the person it has come from, and if it is used for a specific research project that has been approved by a research ethics committee. The Human Tissue Act 2004 also requires consent to be obtained for the removal, storage and use of a deceased person's organs, tissue and cells for the purpose of research in connection with disorders in, or the functioning of, the human body. Regulations made under the Human Tissue Act 2004 permit the use and storage of organs, tissue or cells from adults who lack capacity for research under certain circumstances.

38 The *Human Tissue (Scotland) Act 2006* requires authorisation to be obtained before the storage and use of a deceased person's organs, tissue or cells for the purposes of research. The Act does not cover the storage and use of tissue from living people for the purposes of research

39 The *Medicines for Human Use (Clinical Trials) Regulations 2004* apply to the use of tissue in clinical trials of investigational medicinal products.

Treatment and care towards the end of life: good practice in decision making*

[*Excerpts*.]

Guidance

1 Patients who are approaching the end of their life need high-quality treatment and care that support them to live as well as possible until they die, and to die with dignity. This guidance

---

[8] Human Tissue Authority—Codes of Practice. See www.hta.gov.uk/policiesandcodesofpractice/codesofpractice.cfm.

identifies a number of challenges in ensuring that patients receive such care, and provides a framework to support you in addressing the issues in a way that meets the needs of individual patients. Providing treatment and care towards the end of life will often involve decisions that are clinically complex and emotionally distressing; and some decisions may involve ethical dilemmas and uncertainties about the law that further complicate the decision-making process. This guidance is intended to help you, in whatever context you are working, to address these issues effectively with patients, the healthcare team and those who have an interest in the patient's welfare. It seeks to ensure that people who are close to the patient (partners, family, carers and others) are involved and supported, while the patient is receiving care and after the patient has died.

2 For the purposes of this guidance, patients are 'approaching the end of life' when they are likely to die within the next 12 months. This includes patients whose death is imminent (expected within a few hours or days) and those with:

(a) advanced, progressive, incurable conditions

(b) general frailty and co-existing conditions that mean they are expected to die within 12 months

(c) existing conditions if they are at risk of dying from a sudden acute crisis in their condition

(d) life-threatening acute conditions caused by sudden catastrophic events.

This guidance also applies to those extremely premature neonates whose prospects for survival are known to be very poor, and to patients who are diagnosed as being in a persistent vegetative state (PVS), for whom a decision to withdraw treatment may lead to their death.

3 The most challenging decisions in this area are generally about withdrawing or not starting a treatment when it has the potential to prolong the patient's life. This may involve treatments such as antibiotics for life-threatening infection, cardiopulmonary resuscitation (CPR), renal dialysis, 'artificial' nutrition and hydration (for the purpose of this guidance 'artificial' is replaced by 'clinically assisted'[1]) and mechanical ventilation. The evidence of the benefits, burdens and risks of these treatments is not always clear cut, and there may be uncertainty about the clinical effect of a treatment on an individual patient, or about the particular benefits, burdens and risks for that patient. In some circumstances these treatments may only prolong the dying process or cause the patient unnecessary distress. Given the uncertainties, you and others involved in the decision-making process may

4 In addition it is now widely agreed that high-quality treatment and care towards the end of life includes palliative care that focuses on managing pain and other distressing symptoms; providing psychological, social and spiritual support to patients; and supporting those close to the patient. However, it is not always recognised that palliative care can be provided at any stage in the progression of a patient's illness, not only in the last few days of their life.

6 It is important to note that we use the term 'overall benefit' to describe the ethical basis on which decisions are made about treatment and care for adult patients who lack capacity to decide. GMC guidance on overall benefit, applied with the decision-making principles in paragraphs 7–13, is consistent with the legal requirement to consider whether treatment 'benefits' a patient (Scotland), or is in the patient's 'best interests' (England, Wales and Northern Ireland), and to apply the other principles set out in the *Mental Capacity Act 2005* and *Adults with Incapacity (Scotland) Act 2000*.

---

[1] 'Artificial nutrition and hydration' is the phrase sometimes used in healthcare settings. However, we believe that 'clinically assisted nutrition and hydration' is a more accurate description of the use of a drip, a nasogastric tube or a tube surgically implanted into the stomach, to provide nutrition and fluids. need reassurance about what is ethically and legally permissible, especially when deciding whether to withdraw a potentially life-prolonging treatment.

Principles

Equalities and human rights

7 You must give patients who are approaching the end of their life the same quality of care as all other patients. You must treat patients and those close to them with dignity, respect and compassion, especially when they are facing difficult situations and decisions about care. You must respect their privacy and right to confidentiality.

8 Some groups of patients can experience inequalities in getting access to healthcare services and in the standard of care provided. It is known that some older people, people with disabilities and people from ethnic minorities have received poor standards of care towards the end of life. This can be because of physical, communication and other barriers, and mistaken beliefs or lack of knowledge among those providing services, about the patient's needs and interests. Equalities, capacity and human rights laws reinforce your ethical duty to treat patients fairly.

9 If you are involved in decisions about treatment and care towards the end of life, you must be aware of the *Human Rights Act 1998* and its main provisions, as your decisions are likely to engage the basic rights and principles set out in the Act.

Presumption in favour of prolonging life

10 Following established ethical and legal (including human rights) principles, decisions concerning potentially life-prolonging treatment must not be motivated by a desire to bring about the patient's death, and must start from a presumption in favour of prolonging life. This presumption will normally require you to take all reasonable steps to prolong a patient's life. However, there is no absolute obligation to prolong life irrespective of the consequences for the patient, and irrespective of the patient's views, if they are known or can be found out.

Working with the principles and decision-making models

Role of relatives, partners and others close to the patient

17 The people close to a patient can play a significant role in ensuring that the patient receives high-quality care as they near the end of life, in both community and hospital settings. Many parents, other close relatives and partners, as well as paid and unpaid carers, will be involved in discussing issues with a patient, enabling them to make choices, supporting them to communicate their wishes, or participating directly in their treatment and care. In some cases, they may have been granted legal power by the patient, or the court, to make healthcare decisions when the patient lacks capacity to make their own choices.

18 It is important that you and other members of the healthcare team acknowledge the role and responsibilities of people close to the patient. You should make sure, as far as possible, that their needs for support are met and their feelings respected, although the focus of care must remain on the patient.

19 Those close to a patient may want or need information about the patient's diagnosis and about the likely progression of the condition or disease, in order to help them provide care and recognise and respond to changes in the patient's condition. If a patient has capacity to make decisions, you should check that they agree to you sharing this information. If a patient lacks capacity to make a decision about sharing information, it is reasonable to assume that, unless they indicate otherwise, they would want those closest to them to be kept informed of relevant information about their general condition and prognosis. (There is more guidance in our booklet on *Confidentiality*.) You should check whether a patient has nominated someone close to them to be kept informed and consulted about their treatment.

20 When providing information, you must do your best to explain clinical issues in a way the person can understand, and approach difficult or potentially distressing issues about the patient's prognosis and care with tact and sensitivity. (See paragraphs 33–36 on addressing emotional difficulties and possible sources of support.)

21 When discussing the issues with people who do not have legal authority to make decisions on behalf of a patient who lacks capacity, you should make it clear that their role is to advise the healthcare team about the patient's known or likely wishes, views and beliefs. You must not give them the impression they are being asked to make the decision.

Addressing uncertainty

31 If there is a reasonable degree of uncertainty about whether a particular treatment will provide overall benefit for a patient who lacks capacity to make the decision, the treatment should be started in order to allow a clearer assessment to be made.

32 You must explain clearly to those close to the patient and the healthcare team that the treatment will be monitored and reviewed, and may be withdrawn at a later stage if it proves ineffective or too burdensome for the patient in relation to the benefits. You should explain the basis on which the decision will be made about whether the treatment will continue or be withdrawn.

Emotional difficulties in end of life decision making

33 Some members of the healthcare team, or people who are close to the patient, may find it more difficult to contemplate withdrawing a life-prolonging treatment than to decide not to start the treatment in the first place. This may be because of the emotional distress that can accompany a decision to withdraw life-prolonging treatment, or because they would feel responsible for the patient's death. However, you should not allow these anxieties to override your clinical judgement and lead you either not to start treatment that may be of some benefit to the patient, or to continue treatment that is of no overall benefit.

34 You should explain to those close to the patient that, whatever decisions are made about providing particular treatments, the patient's condition will be monitored and managed to ensure that they are comfortable and, as far as possible, free of pain and other distressing symptoms. You should also make clear that a decision to withdraw, or not to start a treatment will be reviewed in the light of changes in the clinical situation.

35 You should offer advice about any support that may be available for the patient, for those close to them and for members of the healthcare team, if they are finding the situation emotionally challenging. Sources of support include patient and carer support and advocacy services, counselling and chaplaincy services, and ethics support networks.

36 You should do your best to make sure that patients who may feel pressured by family or carers to accept or refuse particular investigations or treatments are given the time, information and help they need to reach their own decisions.

Resource constraints

37 Decisions about what treatment options can be offered may be complicated by resource constraints—such as funding restrictions on certain treatments in the NHS, or lack of availability of intensive care beds. In such circumstances, you must provide as good a standard of care as you can for the patient, while balancing sometimes competing duties towards the wider population, funding bodies and employers. There will often be no simple solution. Ideally, decisions about access to treatments should be made on the basis of an agreed local or national policy that takes account of the human rights implications. Decisions made on a case-by-case basis, without reference to agreed policy, risk introducing elements of unfair discrimination or failure to consider properly the patient's legal rights (see paragraphs 7–9).

38 If resource constraints are a factor, you must:
   (a) provide the best service possible within the resources available
   (b) be familiar with any local and national policies that set out agreed criteria for access to the particular treatment (such as national service frameworks and NICE and SIGN guidelines)

    (c) make sure that decisions about prioritising patients are fair and based on clinical need and the patient's capacity to benefit, and not simply on grounds of age, race, social status or other factors that may introduce discriminatory access to care

    (d) be open and honest with the patient (if they have capacity), or those close to them, and the rest of the healthcare team about the decision-making process and the criteria for prioritising patients in individual cases.

39 You should not withdraw or decide not to start treatment if doing so would involve significant risk for the patient and the only justification is resource constraints. If you have good reason to think that patient safety is being compromised by inadequate resources, and it is not within your power to put the matter right, you should draw the situation to the attention of the appropriate individual or organisation, following our guidance on Raising concerns about patient safety (2006).

Assessing the overall benefit of treatment options

Weighing the benefits, burdens and risks

40 The benefits of a treatment that may prolong life, improve a patient's condition or manage their symptoms must be weighed against the burdens and risks for that patient, before you can reach a view about its overall benefit. For example, it may be of no overall benefit to provide potentially life-prolonging but burdensome treatment in the last days of a patient's life when the focus of care is changing from active treatment to managing the patient's symptoms and keeping them comfortable.

41 The benefits, burdens and risks associated with a treatment are not always limited to clinical considerations, and you should be careful to take account of the other factors relevant to the circumstances of each patient.

42 Patients who have capacity will reach their own view about what personal factors they wish to consider and the weight they wish to attach to these alongside the clinical considerations.

43 In the case of patients who lack capacity, their legal proxy will make these judgements with advice from you and others involved in the patient's care. If you are responsible for making the decision about overall benefit, those close to the patient and members of the healthcare team are likely to have knowledge about the patient's wishes, values and preferences and any other personal factors that should be taken into account. (See the model for decision making in paragraph 16.) You may also find information about the patient's wishes in their notes, advance care plan or other record, such as an advance request for or refusal of treatment.

Avoiding bias

46 You must be careful not to rely on your personal views about a patient's quality of life and to avoid making judgements based on poorly informed or unfounded assumptions about the healthcare needs of particular groups, such as older people and those with disabilities.

Resolving disagreements

47 You should aim to reach a consensus about what treatment and care would be of overall benefit to a patient who lacks capacity. Disagreements may arise between you and those close to the patient, or between you and members of the healthcare team, or between the healthcare team and those close to the patient. Depending on the seriousness of any disagreement, it is usually possible to resolve it; for example, by involving an independent advocate, seeking advice from a more experienced colleague, obtaining a second opinion, holding a case conference, or using local mediation services. In working towards a consensus, you should take into account the different decision-making roles and authority of those you consult, and the legal framework for resolving disagreements.

48 If, having taken these steps, there is still significant disagreement, you should seek legal advice on applying to the appropriate statutory body for review (Scotland) or appropriate court for an independent ruling. The patient, those authorised to act for them and those close to them should be informed, as early as possible, of any decision to start such proceedings, so that they have the opportunity to participate or be represented.

49 In situations in which a patient with capacity to decide requests a treatment and does not accept your view that the treatment would not be clinically appropriate, the steps suggested above for resolving disagreement may also be helpful.

Advance care planning

The benefits

50 As treatment and care towards the end of life are delivered by multidisciplinary teams often working across local health, social care and voluntary sector services, you must plan ahead as much as possible to ensure timely access to safe, effective care and continuity in its delivery to meet the patient's needs.

51 The emotional distress and other pressures inherent in situations in which patients are approaching the end of their life sometimes lead to misunderstandings and conflict between doctors and patients and those close to them, or between members of the healthcare team. However, this can usually be avoided through early, sensitive discussion and planning about how best to manage the patient's care.

What to discuss

52 Patients whose death from their current condition is a foreseeable possibility are likely to want the opportunity (whether they are in a community or hospital setting) to decide what arrangements should be made to manage the final stages of their illness. This could include having access to palliative care, and attending to any personal and other matters that they consider important towards the end of their life.

53 If a patient in your care has a condition that will impair their capacity as it progresses, or is otherwise facing a situation in which loss or impairment of capacity is a foreseeable possibility, you should encourage them to think about what they might want for themselves should this happen, and to discuss their wishes and concerns with you and the healthcare team. Your discussions should cover:

(a) the patient's wishes, preferences or fears in relation to their future treatment and care

(b) the feelings, beliefs or values that may be influencing the patient's preferences and decisions

(c) the family members, others close to the patient or any legal proxies that the patient would like to be involved in decisions about their care

(d) interventions which may be considered or undertaken in an emergency, such as cardio-pulmonary resuscitation (CPR), when it may be helpful to make decisions in advance

(e) the patient's preferred place of care (and how this may affect the treatment options available)

(f) the patient's needs for religious, spiritual or other personal support.

54 Depending on the patient's circumstances, it may also be appropriate to create opportunities for them to talk about what they want to happen after they die. Some patients will want to discuss their wishes in relation to the handling of their body, and their beliefs or values about organ or tissue donation.

55 You must approach all such discussions sensitively. If you are unsure how best to do this or how to respond to any non-clinical issues raised by the patient, you should refer to relevant guidelines on good practice in advance care planning. If the patient agrees, you should involve in the discussions other members of the healthcare team, people who are close to the patient, or an independent advocate.

When patients do not want to know

56 Some patients may not be ready to think about their future care, or may find the prospect of doing so too distressing. However, no-one else can make a decision on behalf of an adult who has capacity. If a patient asks you to make decisions on their behalf or wants to leave decisions to a relative, partner or friend, you should explain that it is important that they understand the options open to them, and what the treatment will involve. If they do not want this information, you should try to find out why.

57 If the patient still does not want to know in detail about their condition or the treatment, you should respect their wishes as far as possible. But you must explain the importance of providing at least the basic information they need in order to give valid consent to a proposed investigation or treatment. This is likely to include what the investigation or treatment aims to achieve and what it will involve. For example, whether a procedure is invasive; what level of pain or discomfort they might experience and what can be done to minimise it; what they should do to prepare for the investigation or treatment; and whether it involves any serious risks.

58 If the patient insists that they do not want even this basic information, you must explain the potential consequences of carrying out an investigation or treatment if their consent may be open to subsequent legal challenge. You must record the fact that the patient has declined relevant information and who they asked to make the decision about treatment. You must also make it clear that they can change their mind and have more information at any time.

When others want information to be withheld from the patient

59 Apart from circumstances in which a patient refuses information, you should not withhold information necessary for making decisions (including when asked by someone close to the patient), unless you believe that giving it would cause the patient serious harm. In this context 'serious harm' means more than that the patient might become upset or decide to refuse treatment. If you withhold information from the patient, you must record your reasons for doing so in the medical records, and be prepared to explain and justify your decision. You should regularly review your decision and consider whether you could give information to the patient later, without causing them serious harm.

Formalising a patient's wishes

60 If a patient wants to nominate someone to make decisions on their behalf if they lose capacity, or if they want to make an advance refusal of a particular treatment, you should explain that there may be ways to formalise these wishes, such as appointing an attorney or making a written advance decision or directive. You should support a patient who has decided to take these steps. You should provide advice on the clinical issues and recommend that they get independent advice on how to formalise their wishes.

Recording and sharing the advance care plan

61 You must make a record of the discussion and of the decisions made. You should make sure that a record of the advance care plan is made available to the patient, and is shared with others involved in their care (provided that the patient agrees), so that everyone is clear about what has been agreed. (See also paragraphs 22–23 about working in teams and across service boundaries.) If a patient makes an advance refusal of treatment, you should encourage them to share this information with those close to them, with other doctors, and with key health and social care staff involved in their care.

62 You must bear in mind that advance care plans need to be reviewed and updated as the patient's situation or views change.

Acting on advance requests for treatment

63 When planning ahead, some patients worry that they will be unreasonably denied certain treatments towards the end of their life, and so they may wish to make an advance request for those treatments. Some patients approaching the end of life want to retain as much control as possible over the treatments they receive and may want a treatment that has some prospects of prolonging their life, even if it has significant burdens and risks.

64 When responding to a request for future treatment, you should explore the reasons for the request and the degree of importance the patient attaches to the treatment. You should explain how decisions about the overall benefit of the treatment would be influenced by the patient's current wishes if they lose capacity. You should make clear that, although future decisions cannot be bound by their request for a particular treatment, their request will be given weight by those making the decision.

65 If a patient has lost capacity to decide, you must provide any treatment you assess to be of overall benefit to the patient. When assessing overall benefit, you should take into account the patient's previous request, what you know about their other wishes and preferences, and the goals of care at that stage (for example, whether the focus has changed to palliative care), and you should consult the patient's legal proxy or those close to the patient, as set out in the decision-making model in paragraph 16. The patient's previous request must be given weight and, when the benefits, burdens and risks are finely balanced, will usually be the deciding factor.

66 If significant disagreement arises between you and the patient's legal proxy, those close to the patient, or members of the healthcare team, about what would be of overall benefit, you must take steps to resolve the disagreement (see paragraphs 47–48).

Acting on advance refusals of treatment

67 Some patients worry that towards the end of their life they may be given medical treatments that they do not want. So they may want to make their wishes clear about particular treatments in circumstances that might arise in the course of their future care. When discussing any proposed advance refusal, you should explain to the patient how such refusals would be taken into account if they go on to lose capacity to make decisions about their care.

Assessing the applicability of advance refusals

71 In relation to judgements about applicability, the following considerations apply across the UK:

- (a) whether the decision is clearly applicable to the patient's current circumstances, clinical situation and the particular treatment or treatments about which a decision is needed
- (b) whether the decision specifies particular circumstances in which the refusal of treatment should not apply
- (c) how long ago the decision was made and whether it has been reviewed or updated (this may also be a factor in assessing validity)
- (d) whether there are reasonable grounds for believing that circumstances exist which the patient did not anticipate and which would have affected their decision if anticipated, for example any relevant clinical developments or changes in the patient's personal circumstances since the decision was made.

Doubt or disagreement about the status of advance refusals

72 Advance refusals of treatment often do not come to light until a patient has lost capacity. In such cases, you should start from a presumption that the patient had capacity when the decision was made, unless there are grounds to believe otherwise.

73 If there is doubt or disagreement about the validity or applicability of an advance refusal of treatment, you should make further enquiries (if time permits) and seek a ruling from the court if necessary. In an emergency, if there is no time to investigate further, the presumption should be in favour of providing treatment, if it has a realistic chance of prolonging life, improving the patient's condition, or managing their symptoms.

74 If it is agreed, by you and those caring for the patient, that an advance refusal of treatment is invalid or not applicable, the reasons for reaching this view should be documented.

Reviewing decisions

78 A patient's condition may improve unexpectedly, or may not progress as anticipated, or their views about the benefits, burdens and risks of treatment may change over time. You should make sure that there are clear arrangements in place to review decisions. New decisions about starting or continuing with a treatment may be needed in the light of changes in the patient's condition and circumstances, and it may be necessary to seek a second opinion or, if this is not possible, advice from an experienced colleague.

Conscientious objections

79 You can withdraw from providing care if your religious, moral or other personal beliefs about providing life-prolonging treatment lead you to object to complying with:

(a) a patient's decision to refuse such treatment, or

(b) a decision that providing such treatment is not of overall benefit to a patient who lacks capacity to decide.

However, you must not do so without first ensuring that arrangements have been made for another doctor to take over your role. It is not acceptable to withdraw from a patient's care if this would leave the patient or colleagues with nowhere to turn. Refer to our guidance on *Personal Beliefs and Medical Practice* (2008) for more information.

80 If you disagree with a decision to withdraw or not to start a life-prolonging treatment on the basis of your clinical judgement about whether the treatment should be provided, you should follow the guidance in paragraphs 47–48 about resolving disagreements.

Organ donation

81 If a patient is close to death and their views cannot be determined, you should be prepared to explore with those close to them whether they had expressed any views about organ or tissue donation, if donation is likely to be a possibility.

82 You should follow any national procedures for identifying potential organ donors and, in appropriate cases, for notifying the local transplant coordinator.xiv You must take account of the requirements in relevant legislation and in any supporting codes of practice, in any discussions that you have with the patient or those close to them. You should make clear that any decision about whether the patient would be a suitable candidate for donation would be made by the transplant coordinator or team, and not by you and the team providing treatment.

Neonates, children and young people

Considering the benefits, burdens and risks of treatment

93 Identifying the best interests of children or young people who may be approaching the end of life can be challenging. This is particularly the case when there are uncertainties about the long-term outcomes of treatment, when emergencies arise, and in the case of extremely premature neonates whose prospects for survival are known to be very poor. Complex and emotionally demanding decisions may have to be made; for example, about whether to resuscitate and admit a neonate to intensive care, and whether to continue invasive intensive care or replace it with palliative care. It can be very difficult to judge when the burdens and risks, including the degree of suffering caused by treatment, outweigh the benefits of the treatment to the patient.

94 You must take account of up-to-date, authoritative clinical guidance when considering what treatment might be in a child or young person's best interests. If there are uncertainties about the range of options for managing their condition, or the likely outcomes, you should seek advice or a second opinion as early as possible from a colleague with relevant expertise (who may be from another specialty, such as palliative care, or another discipline, such as nursing).

95 Parents play an important role in assessing their child's best interests, and you should work in partnership with them when considering decisions about their child's treatment. You should support parents, and must share with them the information they want or need, in a way that they can understand, about their child's condition and options for care (subject to considerations of confidentiality). You must take account of their views when identifying options that are clinically appropriate and likely to be in the child's best interests.

96 You must be able to explain and justify the factors that you judge should be taken into account when considering decisions about what treatment might be in the best interests of a child or young person. You must not rely on your personal values when making best interests decisions. You must be careful not to make judgements based on poorly informed or unfounded assumptions about the impact of a disability on a child or young person's quality of life.

Neonates and infants

106 It may be particularly difficult to make a decision on the basis of what is in the best interests of a neonate or infant. If, when considering the benefits, burdens and risks of treatment (including resuscitation and clinically assisted nutrition and hydration) you conclude that, although providing treatment would be likely to prolong life, it would cause pain, suffering and other burdens that would outweigh any benefits and you reach a consensus with the child's parents and healthcare team that it would be in the child's best interests to withdraw, or not start the treatment, you may do so. However, in the case of decisions about clinically assisted nutrition and hydration, before you reach a definite decision to withdraw or not to start treatment, you must seek a second opinion (or, if this is not possible, advice) following the guidance at paragraph 121. Whatever decision is made, you must make sure that any distressing symptoms that the child may be experiencing are managed effectively and that the child's condition is reviewed regularly.

Meeting patients' nutrition and hydration needs

109 All patients are entitled to food and drink of adequate quantity and quality and to the help they need to eat and drink. Malnutrition and dehydration can be both a cause and consequence of ill health, so maintaining a healthy level of nutrition and hydration can help to prevent or treat illness and symptoms and improve treatment outcomes for patients. You must keep the nutrition and hydration status of your patients under review. You should be satisfied that nutrition and hydration are being provided in a way that meets your patients' needs, and that if necessary patients are being given adequate help to enable them to eat and drink.

110 If a patient refuses food or drink,[2] or has problems eating or drinking, you should first assess and address any underlying physical or psychological causes that could be improved with treatment or care. For example, some patients stop eating because of depression, or pain caused by mouth ulcers or dentures, or for other reasons that can be addressed. If a patient needs assistance in eating or drinking that is not being provided, or if underlying problems are not being effectively managed, you should take steps to rectify the situation, if you can. If you cannot, you should inform an appropriate person within the organisation that is responsible for the patient's care.

111 If you are concerned that a patient is not receiving adequate nutrition or hydration by mouth, even with support, you must carry out an assessment of their condition and their individual requirements. You must assess their needs for nutrition and hydration separately and consider what forms of clinically assisted nutrition or hydration may be required to meet their needs.

Clinically assisted nutrition and hydration

112 Clinically assisted nutrition includes intravenous feeding, and feeding by nasogastric tube and by percutaneous endoscopic gastrostomy (PEG) and radiologically inserted gastrostomy (RIG) feeding tubes through the abdominal wall. All these means of providing nutrition also provide fluids necessary to keep patients hydrated. Clinically assisted hydration can also be provided by intravenous or subcutaneous infusion of fluids through a 'drip'. The terms 'clinically assisted nutrition' and 'clinically assisted hydration' do not refer to help given to patients to eat or drink, for example by spoon feeding.

---

[2] The offer of food and drink by mouth is part of basic care (as is the offer of washing and pain relief) and must always be offered to patients who are able to swallow without serious risk of choking or aspirating food or drink. Food and drink can be refused by patients at the time it is offered, but an advance refusal of food and drink has no force.

113 Providing nutrition and hydration by tube or drip may provide symptom relief, or prolong or improve the quality of the patient's life; but they may also present problems. The current evidence about the benefits, burdens and risks of these techniques as patients approach the end of life is not clear-cut. This can lead to concerns that patients who are unconscious or semi-conscious may be experiencing distressing symptoms and complications, or otherwise be suffering either because their needs for nutrition or hydration are not being met or because attempts to meet their perceived needs for nutrition or hydration may be causing them avoidable suffering.

114 Nutrition and hydration provided by tube or drip are regarded in law as medical treat-ment32, and should be treated in the same way as other medical interventions. Nonetheless, some people see nutrition and hydration, whether taken orally or by tube or drip, as part of basic nurture for the patient that should almost always be provided. For this reason it is especially important that you listen to and consider the views of the patient and of those close to them (including their cultural and religious views) and explain the issues to be considered, including the benefits, burdens and risks of providing clinically assisted nutrition and hydration. You should make sure that patients, those close to them and the healthcare team understand that, when clinically assisted nutrition or hydration would be of overall benefit, it will always be offered; and that if a decision is taken not to provide clinically assisted nutrition or hydration, the patient will continue to receive high-quality care, with any symptoms addressed.

115 If disagreement arises between you and the patient (or those close to a patient who lacks capacity), or you and other members of the healthcare team, or between the team and those close to the patient, about whether clinically assisted nutrition or hydration should be provided, you should seek resolution following the guidance in paragraphs 47–49. You should make sure that the patient, or someone acting on their behalf, is informed and given advice on the patient's rights and how to access their own legal advice or representation.

Patients who have capacity

116 If you consider that a patient is not receiving adequate nutrition or hydration by mouth, you should follow the decision model in paragraph 14. You must assess the patient's nutrition and hydration needs separately and offer the patient those treatments you consider to be clinically appropriate because, for example, they would provide symptom relief or would be likely to prolong the patient's life. You must explain to the patient the benefits, burdens and risks associated with the treatments, so that the patient can make a decision about whether to accept them.

117 If you assess that clinically assisted nutrition or hydration would not be clinically appropriate, you must monitor the patient's condition and reassess the benefits, burdens and risks of providing clinically assisted nutrition or hydration as the patient's condition changes. If a patient asks you to provide nutrition or hydration by tube or drip, you should discuss the issues with the patient and explore the reasons for their request. You must reassess the benefits and burdens of providing the treatment requested, giving weight to the patient's wishes and values. When the benefits, burdens and risks are finely balanced, the patient's request will usually be the deciding factor. However, if after discussion you still consider that the treatment would not be clinically appropriate, you do not have to provide it. But you should explain your reasons to the patient and explain any other options that are available, including the option to seek a second opinion.

Adult patients who lack capacity

118 If a patient lacks capacity and cannot eat or drink enough to meet their nutrition or hydration needs, you must assess whether providing clinically assisted nutrition or hydration would be of overall benefit to them, following the decision model in paragraph 16 and guidance in paragraphs 40–48. Clinically assisted nutrition or hydration will usually be of overall benefit, if for example they prolong life or provide symptom relief. You must assess the patient's nutrition and hydration needs separately. You must monitor the patient's condition, and reassess the benefits, burdens and risks of providing clinically assisted nutrition or hydration as the patient's condition changes.

Adult patients who lack capacity and are not expected to die within hours or days

119 If a patient is in the end stage of a disease or condition, but you judge that their death is not expected within hours or days, you must provide clinically assisted nutrition or hydration if it would be of overall benefit to them, taking into account the patient's beliefs and values, any previous request for nutrition or hydration by tube or drip and any other views they previously expressed about their care. The patient's request must be given weight and, when the benefits, burdens and risks are finely balanced, will usually be the deciding factor.

120 You must assess the patient's nutrition and hydration needs separately. If you judge that the provision of clinically assisted nutrition or hydration would not be of overall benefit to the patient, you may conclude that the treatment should not be started at that time or should be withdrawn. You should explain your view to the patient, if appropriate, and those close to them, and respond to any questions or concerns they express.

121 In these circumstances you must make sure that the patient's interests have been thoroughly considered. This means you must take all reasonable steps to get a second opinion from a senior clinician (who might be from another discipline) who has experience of the patient's condition but who is not already directly involved in the patient's care. This opinion should be based on an examination of the patient by the clinician. In exceptional circumstances, if this is not possible for practical reasons, you must still get advice from a colleague, for example by telephone, having given them up-to-date information about the patient's condition. You should also consider seeking legal advice.

122 If you reach a consensus that clinically assisted nutrition or hydration would not be of overall benefit to the patient and the treatment is withdrawn or not started, you must make sure that the patient is kept comfortable and that any distressing symptoms are addressed. You must monitor the patient's condition and be prepared to reassess the benefits, burdens and risks of providing clinically assisted nutrition or hydration in light of changes in their condition. If clinically assisted nutrition or hydration is started or reinstated after a later assessment, and you subsequently conclude that it would not be of overall benefit to continue with the treatment, you must seek a second opinion (or, if this is not possible, seek advice), following the advice in paragraph 121.

Adult patients who lack capacity and are expected to die within hours or days

123 If a patient is expected to die within hours or days, and you consider that the burdens of providing clinically assisted nutrition or hydration outweigh the benefits they are likely to bring, it will not usually be appropriate to start or continue treatment. You must consider the patient's needs for nutrition and hydration separately.

124 If a patient has previously requested that nutrition or hydration be provided until their death, or those close to the patient are sure that this is what the patient wanted, the patient's wishes must be given weight and, when the benefits, burdens and risks are finely balanced, will usually be the deciding factor.

125 You must keep the patient's condition under review, especially if they live longer than you expected. If this is the case, you must reassess the benefits, burdens and risks of providing clinically assisted nutrition or hydration, as the patient's condition changes.

Patients in a persistent vegetative state (PVS) or similar condition

126 If you are considering withdrawing nutrition or hydration from a patient in PVS or a condition closely resembling PVS, the courts in England, Wales and Northern Ireland currently require that you approach them for a ruling. The courts in Scotland have not specified such a requirement, but you should seek legal advice on whether a court ruling may be necessary in an individual case.

Conscientious objection

127 If you have a conscientious objection to withdrawing, or not providing, clinically assisted nutrition or hydration, you should follow the guidance in paragraphs 79–80.

Cardiopulmonary resuscitation (CPR)

128 When someone suffers sudden cardiac or respiratory arrest, CPR attempts to restart their heart or breathing and restore their circulation. CPR interventions are invasive and include chest compressions, electric shock by an external or implanted defibrillator, injection of drugs and ventilation. If attempted promptly, CPR has a reasonable success rate in some circumstances. Generally, however, CPR has a very low success rate and the burdens and risks of CPR include harmful side effects such as rib fracture and damage to internal organs; adverse clinical outcomes such as hypoxic brain damage; and other consequences for the patient such as increased physical disability. If the use of CPR is not successful in restarting the heart or breathing, and in restoring circulation, it may mean that the patient dies in an undignified and traumatic manner.

When to consider making a Do Not Attempt CPR (DNACPR) decision

129 If cardiac or respiratory arrest is an expected part of the dying process and CPR will not be successful, making and recording an advance decision not to attempt CPR will help to ensure that the patient dies in a dignified and peaceful manner. It may also help to ensure that the patient's last hours or days are spent in their preferred place of care by, for example, avoiding emergency admission from a community setting to hospital. These management plans are called Do Not Attempt CPR (DNACPR) orders, or Do Not Attempt Resuscitation or Allow Natural Death decisions.

130 In cases in which CPR might be successful, it might still not be seen as clinically appropriate because of the likely clinical outcomes. When considering whether to attempt CPR, you should consider the benefits, burdens and risks of treatment that the patient may need if CPR is successful. In cases where you assess that such treatment is unlikely to be clinically appropriate, you may conclude that CPR should not be attempted. Some patients with capacity to make their own decisions may wish to refuse CPR; or in the case of patients who lack capacity it may be judged that attempting CPR would not be of overall benefit to them. However, it can be difficult to establish the patient's wishes or to get relevant information about their underlying condition to make a considered judgement at the time they suffer a cardiac or respiratory arrest and an urgent decision has to be made. So, if a patient has an existing condition that makes cardiac or respiratory arrest likely, establishing a management plan in advance will help to ensure that the patient's wishes and preferences about treatment can be taken into account and that, if appropriate, a DNACPR decision is made and recorded.

131 If a patient is admitted to hospital acutely unwell, or becomes clinically unstable in their home or other place of care, and they are at foreseeable risk of cardiac or respiratory arrest, a judgement about the likely benefits, burdens and risks of CPR should be made as early as possible.

Discussions about whether to attempt CPR

132 As with other treatments, decisions about whether CPR should be attempted must be based on the circumstances and wishes of the individual patient. This may involve discussions with the patient or with those close to them, or both, as well as members of the healthcare team. You must approach discussions sensitively and bear in mind that some patients, or those close to them, may have concerns that decisions not to attempt CPR might be influenced by poorly informed or unfounded assumptions about the impact of disability or advanced age on the patient's quality of life.

133 If a patient lacks capacity to make a decision about future CPR, the views of members of the healthcare team involved in their care may be valuable in assessing the likely clinical effectiveness of attempting CPR and whether successful CPR is likely to be of overall benefit. You should make every effort to discuss a patient's CPR status with these healthcare professionals.

When CPR will not be successful

134 If a patient is at foreseeable risk of cardiac or respiratory arrest and you judge that CPR should not be attempted, because it will not be successful in restarting the patient's heart and breathing and restoring circulation, you must carefully consider whether it is necessary or appropriate to tell the patient that a DNACPR decision has been made. You should not make assumptions

about a patient's wishes, but should explore in a sensitive way how willing they might be to know about a DNACPR decision. While some patients may want to be told, others may find discussion about interventions that would not be clinically appropriate burdensome and of little or no value. You should not withhold information simply because conveying it is difficult or uncomfortable for you or the healthcare team.

135 If you conclude that the patient does not wish to know about or discuss a DNACPR decision, you should seek their agreement to share with those close to them, with carers and with others, the information they may need to know in order to support the patient's treatment and care.

136 If a patient lacks capacity, you should inform any legal proxy and others close to the patient about the DNACPR decision and the reasons for it.

When CPR may be successful

Patients who have capacity

137 If CPR may be successful in restarting a patient's heart and breathing and restoring circulation, the benefits of prolonging life must be weighed against the potential burdens and risks. But this is not solely a clinical decision. You should offer the patient opportunities to discuss (with support if they need it) whether CPR should be attempted in the circumstances that may surround a future cardiac or respiratory arrest. You must approach this sensitively and should not force a discussion or information onto the patient if they do not want it. However, if they are prepared to talk about it, you must provide them with accurate information about the burdens and risks of CPR interventions, including the likely clinical and other outcomes if CPR is successful. This should include sensitive explanation of the extent to which other intensive treatments and procedures may not be seen as clinically appropriate after successful CPR. For example, in some cases, prolonged support for multi-organ failure in an intensive care unit may not be clinically appropriate even though the patient's heart has been restarted.

138 You should explain, in a sensitive manner, any doubts that you and the healthcare team may have about whether the burdens and risks of CPR would outweigh the benefits, including whether the level of recovery expected after successful CPR would be acceptable to the patient.

139 Some patients may wish to receive CPR when there is only a small chance of success, in spite of the risk of distressing clinical and other outcomes. If it is your considered judgement that CPR would not be clinically appropriate for the patient, you should make sure that they have accurate information about the nature of possible CPR interventions and, for example, the length of survival and level of recovery that they might realistically expect if they were successfully resuscitated. You should explore the reasons for their request and try to reach agreement; for example, limited CPR interventions could be agreed in some cases. When the benefits, burdens and risks are finely balanced, the patient's request will usually be the deciding factor. If, after discussion, you still consider that CPR would not be clinically appropriate, you are not obliged to agree to attempt it in the circumstances envisaged. You should explain your reasons and any other options that may be available to the patient, including seeking a second opinion.

Patients who lack capacity

140 If a patient lacks capacity to make a decision about future CPR, you should consult any legal proxy who has authority to make the decision for the patient. If there is no legal proxy with relevant authority, you must discuss the issue with those close to the patient and with the healthcare team. In your consultations or discussions, you must follow the decision-making model in paragraph 16. In particular, you should be clear about the role that others are being asked to take in the decision-making process. If they do not have legal authority to make the decision, you should be clear that their role is to advise you and the healthcare team about the patient. You must not give them the impression that it is their responsibility to decide whether CPR will benefit, or be in the best interests of, the patient. You should provide any legal proxy and those close to the patient, with the same information about the nature of CPR and the burdens and risks for the patient as explained in paragraphs 137–138.

141 If the legal proxy requests that CPR with a small chance of success is attempted in future, in spite of the burdens and risks, or they are sure that this is what the patient wanted, and it is your considered judgement that CPR would not be clinically appropriate and not of overall benefit for the patient, you should explore the reasons for the proxy's request. If after further discussion you still consider that attempting CPR would not be of overall benefit for the patient, you are not obliged to offer to attempt CPR in the circumstances envisaged. You should explain your reasons and any other options that may be available to the legal proxy, including their right to seek a second opinion.

Resolving disagreements

142 If there is disagreement about whether CPR should be provided, you should try to resolve it by following the guidance in paragraphs 47–49.

Recording and communicating CPR decisions

143 Any discussions with a patient, or with those close to them, about whether to attempt CPR, and any decisions made, should be documented in the patient's record or advance care plan. If a DNACPR decision is made and there has been no discussion with the patient because they indicated a wish to avoid it, or because it was your considered view that discussion with the patient was not appropriate, you should note this in the patient's records.

Treatment and care after a DNACPR decision

144 You must make it clear to the patient, to those close to them and to members of the healthcare team that a DNACPR decision applies only to CPR. It does not imply that other treatments will be stopped or withheld. Other treatment and care will be provided if it is clinically appropriate and agreed to by a patient with capacity, or if it is of overall benefit to a patient who lacks capacity.

145 A DNACPR decision should not override your clinical judgement about CPR if the patient experiences cardiac or respiratory arrest from a reversible cause, such as the induction of anaesthesia during a planned procedure, or if the circumstances of the arrest are not those envisaged when the DNACPR decision was made.

Emergencies and CPR

146 Emergencies can arise when there is no time to make a proper assessment of the patient's condition and the likely outcome of CPR; when no previous DNACPR decision is in place; and when it is not possible to find out the patient's views. In these circumstances, CPR should be attempted, unless you are certain you have sufficient information about the patient to judge that it will not be successful.

Financial and commercial arrangements and conflicts of interest*

[*Excerpts, some notes omitted.*]

Financial and commercial arrangements

Fees and charges

3. You must be honest and open in any financial arrangements with patients.
4. If you charge fees you must:
    a. tell patients about your fees, if possible before seeking their consent to treatment
    b. tell patients if any part of the fee goes to another healthcare professional.

---

5. You must not exploit patients' vulnerability or lack of medical knowledge when charging fees for treatments and services.

Gifts, bequests and donations

6. You must not encourage patients to give, lend or bequeath money or gifts that will directly or indirectly benefit you.

7. You may accept unsolicited gifts from patients or their relatives provided:

a. this does not affect, or appear to affect, the way you prescribe for, advise, treat, refer, or commission services for patients

b. you have not used your influence to pressurise or persuade patients or their relatives to offer you gifts.[1]

8. However, if you receive a gift or bequest from a patient or their relative, you should consider the potential damage this could cause to your patients' trust in you and the public's trust in the profession. You should refuse gifts or bequests where they could be perceived as an abuse of trust.

9. You must not put pressure on patients or their families to make donations to other people or organisations.

Conflicts of interest

10. Trust between you and your patients is essential to maintaining effective professional relationships, and your conduct must justify your patients' trust in you and the public's trust in the profession. Trust may be damaged if your interests affect, or are seen to affect, your professional judgement. Conflicts of interest may arise in a range of situations. They are not confined to financial interests, and may also include other personal interests.

11. Conflicts of interest are not always avoidable, and whether a particular conflict creates a serious concern will depend on the circumstances and what steps have been taken to mitigate the risks, for example, by following established procedures for declaring and managing a conflict.

12. You should:

a. use your professional judgement to identify when conflicts of interest arise

b. avoid conflicts of interest wherever possible

c. declare any conflict to anyone affected, formally and as early as possible, in line with the policies of your employer or the organisation contracting your services

d. get advice about the implications of any potential conflict of interest

e. make sure that the conflict does not affect your decisions about patient care.

13. If you are in doubt about whether there is a conflict of interest, act as though there is.

Decisions about patient care

14. If you, or someone close to you, or your employer, has a financial or commercial interest in an organisation providing healthcare such as:

- a pharmaceutical or medical devices company
- a nursing or care home
- a pharmacy or dispensary

you must not allow that interest to affect the way you prescribe for, advise, treat, refer or commission services for patients. You must be open and honest with your patients about any such interests that could be seen to affect the way you prescribe for, advise, treat, refer or commission services for them.

---

[1] The acceptance of gifts by general practitioners in all four UK countries is subject to statutory regulation. General Medical Services contract regulations state that a register should be kept of gifts from patients or their relatives which have a value of £100 or more unless the gift is unconnected with the provision of services. The register of gifts should include the donor's name and nature of the gift. NHS trusts set their own policies on gifts.

15. You must not try to influence patients' choice of healthcare services to benefit you, someone close to you, or your employer. If your organisation dispenses medicines, you must not allow your financial or commercial interests to affect the way you prescribe.

16. You must not ask for or accept any inducement, gift or hospitality that may affect or be seen to affect the way you prescribe for, advise, treat, refer or commission services for patients. You must not offer such inducements to colleagues.[2]

17. If you plan to refer a patient for investigation, treatment or care at an organisation in which you have a financial or commercial interest, you must tell the patient about that interest and make a note of this in the patient's medical record.

18. Where there is an unavoidable conflict of interest about the care of a particular patient, you should record this in the patient's medical record.

Commissioning services

19. The commissioning of services in the NHS can lead to conflicts of interest for the individual doctors involved. If you have responsibility for, or are involved in, commissioning services, you must:
   a. satisfy yourself that all decisions made are fair, transparent and comply with the law
   b. keep up to date with and follow the guidance and codes of practice[3] that govern the commissioning of services where you work
   c. formally declare any financial interest that you, or someone close to you, or your employer has in a provider company, in accordance with the governance arrangements in the jurisdiction where you work
   d. take steps to manage any conflict between your duties as a doctor and your commissioning responsibilities, for example by excluding yourself from the decision making process and any subsequent monitoring arrangements.

Incentives and inducements

Target payments and health service financial incentives

20. Preventative health measures, such as immunisation of children and screening for cervical cancer, have clear benefits for both individual patients and society, as do health monitoring schemes such as those encouraged through the Quality and Outcomes Framework. Target payments are used to encourage general practitioners to increase the number of patients involved. Although you may wish to recommend treatments and invite patients to participate in assessments, you must not put pressure on patients to participate because of the financial benefits for you.

21. Health service financial incentives and similar schemes to improve the cost-effective use of medicines have a legitimate role to play in helping to make good use of available resources. Such schemes can also benefit the wider community of patients. But you must consider the safety and needs of the individual patient for whom you prescribe. In particular, you should do the following.
   a. Consider the benefits and risks to the patient whenever you consider changing the patient's medicine for reasons of cost. One risk, for example, is that patients' adherence to medicines can be harmed by frequent switching.
   b. Inform patients before changing a medicine and tell them how the medicine should be taken.

---

[2] The promotion of medicines is controlled by a combination of statutory measures (with both criminal and civil sanctions) enforced by the Medicines and Healthcare products Regulatory Agency and self-regulation: the Prescription Medicines Code of Practice Authority is responsible for administering The Association of the British Pharmaceutical Industry's *Code of Practice*. See also the Association of British Healthcare Industries' *Code of Business Practice* for its members in the medical technology sector.

[3] See *Towards establishment: Creating responsible and accountable CCGs* (www.commissioningboard.nhs.uk/resources/resources-for-ccgs). See also www.comissioningboard.nhs.uk.

c. Consider what information, explanation and support a patient may need if a new suspected side effect of their medicine is found.

22. You should follow clinical guidelines and raise concerns[4] if you have good reason to think that patient safety is or may be seriously compromised by financial incentives and similar schemes.

Relationships with the pharmaceutical industry

23. Doctors' relationships with the pharmaceutical industry take many forms, some of which might be seen to influence the way doctors prescribe medicines. You should:

a. follow the guidance in the Medicines and Healthcare products Regulatory Agency's *Blue Guide*

b. consider the advice of the Prescription Medicines Code of Practice Authority (PMCPA).

24. The PMCPA is responsible for administering the Association of the British Pharmaceutical Industry's (ABPI's) *Code of Practice for the Pharmaceutical Industry*, which covers inducements, hospitality and other issues.

Recommending services outside healthcare

25. Some organisations providing services outside healthcare (such as insurance companies or solicitors) run schemes where payment is offered according to the number of customers referred. Generally, doctors will not have the professional expertise to make recommendations or refer to a particular organisation; their chief interest in such schemes is financial. You should not accept fees for referring patients to, or recommending the services of, particular organisations or individuals.

Maintaining a professional boundary between you and your patient*

[*Excerpts, notes omitted.*]

Doctor-patient partnership

3 Trust is the foundation of the doctor-patient partnership. Patients should be able to trust that their doctor will behave professionally towards them during consultations and not see them as a potential sexual partner.

Current patients

4 You must not pursue a sexual or improper emotional relationship with a current patient.

5 If a patient pursues a sexual or improper emotional relationship with you, you should treat them politely and considerately and try to re-establish a professional boundary. If trust has broken down and you find it necessary to end the professional relationship, you must follow the guidance in *Ending your professional relationship with a patient*.

6 You must not use your professional relationship with a patient to pursue a relationship with someone close to them. For example, you must not use home visits to pursue a relationship with a member of a patient's family.

7 You must not end a professional relationship with a patient solely to pursue a personal relationship with them.

[4] General Medical Council (2013) *Raising and acting on concerns about patient safety* London, GMC.
* © General Medical Council 2013.

Former patients

8 Personal relationships with former patients may also be inappropriate depending on factors such as:

    a the length of time since the professional relationship ended (see paragraphs 9–10)

    b the nature of the previous professional relationship

    c whether the patient was particularly vulnerable at the time of the professional relationship, and whether they are still vulnerable (see paragraphs 11–13)

    d whether you will be caring for other members of the patient's family.

You must consider these issues carefully before pursuing a personal relationship with a former patient.

Timing

9 It is not possible to specify a length of time after which it would be acceptable to begin a relationship with a former patient. However, the more recently a professional relationship with a patient ended, the less likely it is that beginning a personal relationship with that patient would be appropriate.

10 The duration of the professional relationship may also be relevant. For example, a relationship with a former patient you treated over a number of years is more likely to be inappropriate than a relationship with a patient with whom you had a single consultation.

Vulnerability of the patient

11 Some patients may be more vulnerable than others[1] and the more vulnerable someone is, the more likely it is that having a relationship with them would be an abuse of power and your position as a doctor.

12 Pursuing a relationship with a former patient is more likely to be (or be seen to be) an abuse of your position if you are a psychiatrist or a paediatrician.

13 Whatever your specialty, you must not pursue a personal relationship with a former patient who is still vulnerable. If the former patient was vulnerable at the time that you treated them, but is no longer vulnerable, you should be satisfied that:

- the patient's decisions and actions are not influenced by the previous relationship between you
- you are not (and could not be seen to be) abusing your professional position.

Social media

14 You must consider the potential risks involved in using social media and the impact that inappropriate use could have on your patients' trust in you and society's trust in the medical profession. Social media can blur the boundaries between a doctor's personal and professional lives and may change the nature of the relationship between a doctor and a patient. You must follow our guidance on the use of social media.

Help and advice

15 If you are not sure whether you are (or could be seen to be) abusing your professional position, you should seek advice about your situation from an impartial colleague, your defence body or your medical association.

---

[1] Some patients are likely to be more vulnerable than others because of their illness, disability or frailty, or because of their current circumstances (such as bereavement or redundancy). Children and young people younger than 18 years should be considered vulnerable. Vulnerability can be temporary or permanent. For more guidance on this, see the Royal College of Psychiatrists's guidance *Vulnerable Patients, Safe Doctors* (2007).

Good practice in prescribing and managing medicines and devices*

[Excerpts, some notes omitted.]

About this guidance

3　You are responsible for the prescriptions you sign and for your decisions and actions when you supply and administer medicines and devices or authorise or instruct others to do so. You must be prepared to explain and justify your decisions and actions when prescribing, administering and managing medicines.

4　'Prescribing' is used to describe many related activities, including supply of prescription only medicines, prescribing medicines, devices and dressings on the NHS and advising patients on the purchase of over the counter medicines and other remedies. It may also be used to describe written information provided for patients (information prescriptions) or advice given. While some of this guidance is particularly relevant to prescription only medicines, you should follow it in relation to the other activities you undertake, so far as it is relevant and applicable. This guidance applies to medical devices as well as to medicines.

5　Serious or persistent failure to follow this guidance will put your registration at risk.

Keeping up to date and prescribing safely

6　*Good medical practice* says that you must recognise and work within the limits of your competence and that you must keep your knowledge and skills up to date. You must maintain and develop the knowledge and skills in pharmacology and therapeutics, as well as prescribing and medicines management, relevant to your role and prescribing practice.

7　You should make use of electronic and other systems that can improve the safety of your prescribing, for example by highlighting interactions and allergies and by ensuring consistency and compatibility of medicines prescribed, supplied and administered. The Medicines and Healthcare Products Regulatory Agency's (MHRA) Drug Safety Update and the NHS Central Alert System provide information and advice to support the safer use of medicines relevant to your practice and alert you to safety information about medicines you prescribe. The National electronic Library for Medicines has extensive information on the safe, effective and efficient use of medicines. The National Prescribing Centre (now part of the National Institute for Health and Clinical Excellence (NICE)) publishes a range of materials to help you improve the safety and clinical and cost effectiveness of your prescribing. The electronic Medicines Compendium lists Summaries of Product Characteristics and Patient Information Leaflets.

8　If you are unsure about interactions or other aspects of prescribing and medicines management you should seek advice from experienced colleagues, including pharmacists, prescribing advisers and clinical pharmacologists.

9　You must be familiar with the guidance in the British National Formulary (BNF) and British National Formulary for Children (BNFC), which contain essential information to help you prescribe, monitor, supply, and administer medicines.

10　You should follow the advice in the BNF on prescription writing and make sure your prescriptions and orders are clear, in accordance with the relevant statutory requirements and include your name legibly. You should also consider including clinical indications on your prescriptions.**practice in prescribing and managing**

11　You should take account of the clinical guidelines published by the:

　　a　NICE (England)

   b Scottish Medicines Consortium and Health Improvement Scotland (including the Scottish Intercollegiate Guidelines Network) (Scotland)

   c Department for Health, Social Services and Public Safety (Northern Ireland)

   d All-Wales Medicines Strategy Group (Wales)

   e medical royal colleges and other authoritative sources of specialty specific clinical guidelines.

12 You should make sure that anyone to whom you delegate responsibility for dispensing medicines in your own practice is competent to do what you ask of them. Advice on training for dispensing support staff can be obtained from the General Pharmaceutical Council.

13 You should make sure that anyone to whom you delegate responsibility for administering medicines is competent to do what you ask of them.

Need and objectivity

14 You should prescribe medicines only if you have adequate knowledge of the patient's health and you are satisfied that they serve the patient's needs.

15 In *Consent: patients and doctors making decisions together*, we say:

- 5d. If a patient asks for a treatment that the doctor considers would not be of overall benefit to them, the doctor should discuss the issues with the patient and explore the reasons for their request. If, after discussion, the doctor still considers that the treatment would not be of overall benefit to the patient, they do not have to provide the treatment. But they should explain their reasons to the patient, and explain any other options that are available, including the option to seek a second opinion.

16 You must not prescribe medicines for your own convenience or the convenience of other health or social care professionals (for example, those caring for patients with dementia in care homes).

Prescribing for yourself or those close to you

17 Wherever possible you must avoid prescribing for yourself or anyone with whom you have a close personal relationship.

18 Controlled medicines present particular dangers, occasionally associated with drug misuse, addiction and misconduct. You must not prescribe a controlled medicine for yourself or someone close to you unless:

   a no other person with the legal right to prescribe is available to assess and prescribe without a delay which would put your, or the patient's, life or health at risk or cause unacceptable pain or distress, and

   b the treatment is immediately necessary to:

      i save a life

      ii avoid serious deterioration in health, or

      iii alleviate otherwise uncontrollable pain or distress.

19 If you prescribe for yourself or someone close to you, you must:

   a make a clear record at the same time or as soon as possible afterwards. The record should include your relationship to the patient (where relevant) and the reason it was necessary for you to prescribe.

   b tell your own or the patient's general practitioner (and others treating you or the patient, where relevant) what medicines you have prescribed and any other information necessary for continuing care, unless (in the case of prescribing for somebody close to you) they object.

Consent

20 In *Consent: patients and doctors making decisions together*, we say:

- 3. For a relationship between doctor and patient to be effective, it should be a partnership based on openness, trust and good communication. Each person has a role to play in making decisions about treatment or care.

21 Together with the patient, you should make an assessment of their condition before deciding to prescribe a medicine. You must have or take an adequate history, including:

    a any previous adverse reactions to medicines

    b recent use of other medicines, including non-prescription and herbal medicines, illegal drugs and medicines purchased online, and

    c other medical conditions.

22 You should encourage your patients to be open with you about their use of alternative remedies, illegal substances and medicines obtained online, as well as whether in the past they have taken prescribed medicines as directed.

23 You should identify the likely cause of the patient's condition and which treatments are likely to be of overall benefit to them.

24 You should reach agreement with the patient on the treatment proposed,[1] explaining:

    a the likely benefits, risks and burdens, including serious and common side effects

    b what to do in the event of a side effect or recurrence of the condition

    c how and when to take the medicine and how to adjust the dose if necessary, or how to use a medical device

    d the likely duration of treatment

    e arrangements for monitoring, follow-up and review, including further consultation, blood tests or other investigations, processes for adjusting the type or dose of medicine, and for issuing repeat prescriptions.

25 The amount of information you give to each patient will vary according to the nature of their condition, the potential risks and side effects and the patient's needs and wishes. You should check that the patient has understood the information, and encourage them to ask questions to clarify any concerns or uncertainty. You should consider the benefits of written information, information in other languages and other aids for patients with disabilities to help them understand and consider information at their own speed and to retain the information you give them.

26 You should also provide patients' carers with information about the medicines you prescribe, either with the patient's consent or, if the patient lacks capacity to consent, if it is in their best interests.

27 It is sometimes difficult, because of time pressures, to give patients as much information as you or they would like. To help with this, you should consider the role that other members of the healthcare team, including pharmacists, might play. Pharmacists can undertake medicines reviews, explain how to take medicines and offer advice on interactions and side effects. You should work with pharmacists in your organisation and/or locality to avoid the risks of overburdening or confusing patients with excessive or inconsistent information.

28 You should also refer patients to the information in patient information leaflets (PILs) and other reliable sources of relevant information. PILs are useful supplements to the information you give patients about their medicines, but they are not a substitute for that information.

29 Some patients do not take medicines prescribed for them, or do not follow the instructions on the dose to take or the time medicines should be taken. You should try to understand the reasons for this and address them by providing reassurance and information, and by negotiating with the patient to reach agreement on an appropriate course of treatment that they are able and willing to adhere to.

Sharing information with colleagues

30 You must contribute to the safe transfer of patients between healthcare providers and between health and social care providers. This means you must share all relevant information with colleagues involved in your patient's care within and outside the team, including when you hand over care as you go off duty, when you delegate care or refer patients to other health or social care

---

[1] A number of patient decision aids are available on the National Prescribing Centre website (www.npc.nhs.uk).

providers. This should include all relevant information about their current and recent use of other medicines, other conditions, allergies and previous adverse reactions to medicines.

31 It is essential for safe care that information about medicines accompanies patients (or quickly follows them, for example on emergency admission to hospital) when they transfer between care settings.

32 If you prescribe for a patient, but are not their general practitioner, you should check the completeness and accuracy of the information accompanying a referral. When an episode of care is completed, you must tell the patient's general practitioner about:

    a changes to the patient's medicines (existing medicines changed or stopped and new medicines started, with reasons)

    b length of intended treatment

    c monitoring requirements

    d any new allergies or adverse reactions identified, unless the patient objects or if privacy concerns override the duty, for example in sexual health clinics.

33 If a patient has not been referred to you by their general practitioner, you should also:

    a consider whether the information you have is sufficient and reliable enough to enable you to prescribe safely; for example, whether:

        i you have access to their medical records or other reliable information about the patient's health and other treatments they are receiving

        ii you can verify other important information by examination or testing

    b ask for the patient's consent to contact their general practitioner if you need more information or confirmation of the information you have before prescribing. If the patient objects, you should explain that you cannot prescribe for them and what their options are.

34 If you are the patient's general practitioner, you should make sure that changes to the patient's medicines (following hospital treatment, for example) are reviewed and quickly incorporated into the patient's record. This will help to avoid patients receiving inappropriate repeat prescriptions and reduce the risk of adverse interaction.

Shared care

35 Decisions about who should take responsibility for continuing care or treatment after initial diagnosis or assessment should be based on the patient's best interests, rather than on your convenience or the cost of the medicine and associated monitoring or follow-up.

36 Shared care requires the agreement of all parties, including the patient. Effective communication and continuing liaison between all parties to a shared care agreement are essential.

Prescribing at the recommendation of a professional colleague

37 If you prescribe at the recommendation of another doctor, nurse or other healthcare professional, you must satisfy yourself that the prescription is needed, appropriate for the patient and within the limits of your competence.

38 If you delegate assessment of a patients' suitability for a medicine, you must be satisfied that the person to whom you delegate has the qualifications, experience, knowledge and skills to make the assessment. You must give them enough information about the patient to carry out the assessment required. You must also make sure that they follow the guidance in paragraphs 21–29 on consent.

39 In both cases, you will be responsible for any prescription you sign.

Recommending medicines for prescription by colleagues

40 If you recommend that a colleague, for example a junior doctor or general practitioner, prescribes a particular medicine for a patient, you must consider their competence to do so. You must satisfy yourself that they have sufficient knowledge of the patient and the medicine, experience (especially in the case of junior doctors) and information to prescribe. You should be willing to answer their questions and otherwise assist them in caring for the patient, as required.

Shared care prescribing

41 If you share responsibility for a patient's care with a colleague, you must be competent to exercise your share of clinical responsibility. You should:

a keep yourself informed about the medicines that are prescribed for the patient

b be able to recognise serious and frequently occurring adverse side effects

c make sure appropriate clinical monitoring arrangements are in place and that the patient and healthcare professionals involved understand them

d keep up to date with relevant guidance on the use of the medicines and on the management of the patient's condition.

42 In proposing a shared care arrangement, specialists may advise the patient's general practitioner which medicine to prescribe. If you are recommending a new, or rarely prescribed, medicine, you should specify the dosage and means of administration, and agree a protocol for treatment. You should explain the use of unlicensed medicines, and departures from authoritative guidance or recommended treatments and provide both the general practitioner and the patient with sufficient information to permit the safe management of the patient's condition.

43 If you are uncertain about your competence to take responsibility for the patient's continuing care, you should seek further information or advice from the clinician with whom the patient's care is shared or from another experienced colleague. If you are still not satisfied, you should explain this to the other clinician and to the patient, and make appropriate arrangements for their continuing care.

Raising concerns

44 Prescribing and administration errors by doctors are common,[2] but harm is usually avoided by professional colleagues intervening before the errors can affect patients.

45 You must protect patients from risks of harm posed by colleagues' prescribing, administration and other medicines-related errors. You should question any decision or action that you consider might be unsafe.[3] You should also respond constructively to concerns raised by colleagues, patients and carers about your own practice.

Reporting adverse drug reactions, medical device adverse incidents and other patient safety incidents

46 Early, routine reporting of adverse reactions, incidents and near misses involving medicines and devices can allow performance and systems issues to be investigated, problems rectified and lessons learned.[4] You must make reports in accordance with your employer or contracting body's local clinical governance procedures.

47 You must inform the MHRA about:

a serious suspected adverse reactions to all medicines and all reactions to products marked with a Black Triangle in the BNF and elsewhere using the Yellow Card Scheme.

b adverse incidents involving medical devices, including those caused by human error that put, or have the potential to put, the safety of patients, healthcare professionals or others at risk. These incidents should also be reported to the medical device liaison officer within your organisation.

48 You should provide patients with information about how they can report suspected side effects directly to the MHRA.

---

[2] See the *EQUIP (Errors—Questioning Undergraduate Impact on Prescribing)* study and Investigating the prevalence and causes of prescribing errors in general practice: The PRACTICe study.

[3] See *Raising and acting on concerns about patient safety (2012)*.

[4] You should anonymise or code the information or seek consent, if practicable, or see our confidentiality guidance for more advice.

49 You should also:

    a check that all serious patient safety incidents are reported to the National Reporting and Learning System (in England and Wales), especially if such incidents are not automatically reported through clinical governance arrangements where you work

    b where appropriate, inform the patient's general practitioner, the pharmacy that supplied the medicine, the local controlled drugs accountable officer and the medicines manufacturers of relevant adverse drug reactions and patient safety incidents.

50 You should respond to requests from the Drug Safety Research Unit for prescription-event monitoring data and information for studies on specific safety or pharmacovigilance issues.

Reviewing medicines

51 Whether you prescribe with repeats or on a one-off basis, you must make sure that suitable arrangements are in place for monitoring, follow-up and review, taking account of the patients' needs and any risks arising from the medicines.

52 When you review a patient's medicines, you should re-assess the patient's need for unlicensed medicines (see paragraphs 67–70), for example antipsychotics used for the treatment of behavioural and psychological symptoms in dementia.

53 Reviewing medicines will be particularly important where:

    a patients may be at risk, for example, patients who are frail or have multiple illnesses.

    b medicines have potentially serious or common side effects

    c the patient is prescribed a controlled or other medicine that is commonly abused or misused

    d the BNF or other authoritative clinical guidance[5]5 recommends blood tests or other monitoring at regular intervals.

54 Pharmacists can help improve safety, efficacy and adherence in medicines use, for example by advising patients about their medicines and carrying out medicines reviews. This does not relieve you of your duty to ensure that your prescribing and medicines management is appropriate. You should consider and take appropriate action on information and advice from pharmacists and other healthcare professionals who have reviewed patients' use of medicines, especially following changes to their medicines or if they report problems with tolerance, side effects or with taking medicines as directed.

Repeat prescribing and prescribing with repeats

55 You are responsible for any prescription you sign, including repeat prescriptions for medicines initiated by colleagues, so you must make sure that any repeat prescription you sign is safe and appropriate. You should consider the benefits of prescribing with repeats to reduce the need for repeat prescribing.

56 As with any prescription, you should agree with the patient what medicines are appropriate and how their condition will be managed, including a date for review. You should make clear why regular reviews are important and explain to the patient what they should do if they:

    a suffer side effects or adverse reactions, or

    b stop taking the medicines before the agreed review date (or a set number of repeats have been issued), You must make clear records of these discussions and your reasons for repeat prescribing.

57 You must be satisfied that procedures for prescribing with repeats and for generating repeat prescriptions are secure and that:

    a the right patient is issued with the correct prescription

    b the correct dose is prescribed, particularly for patients whose dose varies during the course of treatment

---

[5] See 10 Top Tips for GPs—Strategies for safer prescribing (National Prescribing Centre, 2011).

    c the patient's condition is monitored, taking account of medicine usage and effects

    d only staff who are competent to do so prepare repeat prescriptions for authorisation

    e patients who need further examination or assessment are reviewed by an appropriate healthcare professional

    f any changes to the patient's medicines are critically reviewed and quickly incorporated into their record.

58 At each review, you should confirm that the patient is taking their medicines as directed, and check that the medicines are still needed, effective and tolerated. This may be particularly important following a hospital stay, or changes to medicines following a hospital or home visit. You should also consider whether requests for repeat prescriptions received earlier or later than expected may indicate poor adherence, leading to inadequate therapy or adverse effects.

59 When you issue repeat prescriptions or prescribe with repeats, you should make sure that procedures are in place to monitor whether the medicine is still safe and necessary for the patient. You should keep a record of dispensers who hold original repeat dispensing prescriptions so that you can contact them if necessary.

Remote prescribing via telephone, video-link or online

60 Before you prescribe for a patient via telephone, video-link or online, you must satisfy yourself that you can make an adequate assessment, establish a dialogue and obtain the patient's consent in accordance with the guidance at paragraphs 20–29.

61 You may prescribe only when you have adequate knowledge of the patient's health, and are satisfied that the medicines serve the patient's needs. You must consider:

    a the limitations of the medium through which you are communicating with the patient

    b the need for physical examination or other assessments

    c whether you have access to the patient's medical records.

62 You must undertake a physical examination of patients before prescribing non-surgical cosmetic medicinal products such as Botox, Dysport or Vistabel or other injectable cosmetic medicines. You must not therefore prescribe these medicines by telephone, video-link, or online.

63 If you are prescribing for a patient in a care or nursing home or hospice, you should communicate with the patient (or, if that is not practicable, the person caring for them) to make your assessment and to provide the necessary information and advice. You should make sure that any instructions, for example for administration or monitoring the patient's condition, are understood and send written confirmation as soon as possible.

64 If the patient has not been referred to you by their general practitioner, you do not have access to their medical records, and you have not previously provided them with face-to-face care, you must also:

    a give your name and, if you are prescribing online, your GMC number

    b explain how the remote consultation will work and what to do if they have any concerns or questions

    c follow the advice in paragraphs 30–34 on Sharing information with colleagues.

65 You should not collude in the unlawful advertising of prescription only or unlicensed medicines to the public by prescribing via websites that breach advertising regulations.

66 If you prescribe for patients who are overseas, you should consider how you or local healthcare professionals will monitor their condition. You should also have regard to differences in a product's licensed name, indications and recommended dosage regimen. You may also need to consider:

    a MHRA guidance on import/export requirements and safety of delivery,

    b whether you will need additional indemnity cover

    c whether you will need to be registered with a regulatory body in the country in which the prescribed medicines are to be dispensed.

Prescribing unlicensed medicines

67 The term 'unlicensed medicine' is used to describe medicines that are used outside the terms of their UK licence or which have no licence for use in the UK.[6] Unlicensed medicines are commonly used in some areas of medicine such as in paediatrics, psychiatry and palliative care. They are also used, less frequently, in other areas of medicine.

68 You should usually prescribe licensed medicines in accordance with the terms of their licence. However, you may prescribe unlicensed medicines where, on the basis of an assessment of the individual patient, you conclude, for medical reasons, that it is necessary to do so to meet the specific needs of the patient.

69 Prescribing unlicensed medicines may be necessary where:

    a There is no suitably licensed medicine that will meet the patient's need. Examples include (but are not limited to):

        i there is no licensed medicine applicable to the particular patient. For example, if the patient is a child and a medicine licensed only for adult patients would meet the needs of the child; or

        ii a medicine licensed to treat a condition or symptom in children would nonetheless not meet the specific assessed needs of the particular child patient, but a medicine licensed for the same condition or symptom in adults would do so; or

        iii the dosage specified for a licensed medicine would not meet the patient's need; or

        iv the patient needs a medicine in a formulation that is not specified in an applicable licence.

    b Or where a suitably licensed medicine that would meet the patient's need is not available. This may arise where, for example, there is a temporary shortage in supply; or

    c The prescribing forms part of a properly approved research project.

70 When prescribing an unlicensed medicine you must:

    a be satisfied that there is sufficient evidence or experience of using the medicine to demonstrate its safety and efficacy

    b take responsibility for prescribing the medicine and for overseeing the patient's care, monitoring, and any follow up treatment, or ensure that arrangements are made for another suitable doctor to do so

    c make a clear, accurate and legible record of all medicines prescribed and, where you are not following common practice, your reasons for prescribing an unlicensed medicine.

Information for patients about the licence for their medicines

71 You must give patients (or their parents or carers) sufficient information about the medicines you propose to prescribe to allow them to make an informed decision.

72 Some medicines are routinely used outside the terms of their licence, for example in treating children. In emergencies or where there is no realistic alternative treatment and such information is likely to cause distress, it may not be practical or necessary to draw attention to the licence. In other cases, where prescribing unlicensed medicines is supported by authoritative clinical guidance, it may be sufficient to describe in general terms why the medicine is not licensed for the proposed use or patient population. You must always answer questions from patients (or their parents or carers) about medicines fully and honestly.

73 If you intend to prescribe unlicensed medicines where that is not routine or if there are suitably licensed alternatives available, you should explain this to the patient, and your reasons for doing so.

74 You should be careful about using medical devices for purposes for which they were not intended.

---

[6] Further information about licensing of medicines can be found at http://www.mhra.gov.uk/Howweregulate/Medicines/index.htm.

Sports medicine

75 You must not prescribe or collude in the provision of medicines or treatment with the intention of improperly enhancing an individual's performance in sport. This does not preclude the provision of any care or treatment where your intention is to protect or improve the patient's health.

Personal beliefs and medical practice*

[Excerpts, some notes omitted.]

Personal beliefs and values in medical practice

3 We recognise that personal beliefs and cultural practices are central to the lives of doctors and patients, and that all doctors have personal values that affect their day-to-day practice. We don't wish to prevent doctors from practising in line with their beliefs and values, as long as they also follow the guidance in *Good medical practice*. Neither do we wish to prevent patients from receiving care that is consistent with, or meets the requirements of, their beliefs and values.

Doctors' personal beliefs

4 Doctors may practise medicine in accordance with their beliefs, provided that they act in accordance with relevant legislation and:
- do not treat patients unfairly
- do not deny patients access to appropriate medical treatment or services
- do not cause patients distress.

If any of these circumstances is likely to arise, we expect doctors to provide effective patient care, advice or support in line with *Good medical practice,* whatever their personal beliefs.[1]

Legal issues

5 As *Good medical practice* makes clear, doctors must keep up to date with and follow the law relevant to their work. For example, the *Equality Act 2010* and parallel legislation in Northern Ireland prohibit doctors from discriminating, directly or indirectly, against others, or from harassing them, on grounds of a protected characteristic, when they provide medical services. In addition, some legislation:
- a specifically entitles doctors to exercise a conscientious objection to providing certain treatments or procedures
- b allows or prohibits particular treatments or procedures.

6 The law does not require doctors to provide treatments or procedures that they have assessed as not being clinically appropriate or not of overall benefit to the patient.

7 The legal annex** provides information about some relevant legislation. You should seek legal advice if you are unsure whether, by exercising a conscientious objection, you are contravening the law in the country where you work.

Conscientious objection

8 You may choose to opt out of providing a particular procedure because of your personal beliefs and values, as long as this does not result in direct or indirect discrimination against, or harassment of, individual patients or groups of patients. This means you must not refuse to treat a

---

* © General Medical Council 2013.
[1] For example, if you are the only doctor legally able to sign a cremation certificate, you should not refuse to do so on the basis of your own personal or religious objection to cremation.
** **Editors' note:** omitted.

particular patient or group of patients because of your personal beliefs or views about them.[2] And you must not refuse to treat the health consequences of lifestyle choices to which you object because of your beliefs.[3]

9 Employing and contracting bodies are entitled to require doctors to fulfil contractual requirements[4] that may restrict doctors' freedom to work in accordance with their conscience. This is a matter between doctors and their employing or contracting bodies.

10 If, having taken account of your legal and ethical obligations, you wish to exercise a conscientious objection to particular services or procedures, you must do your best to make sure that patients who may consult you about it are aware of your objection in advance. You can do this by making sure that any printed material about your practice and the services you provide explains if there are any services you will not normally provide because of a conscientious objection.

11 You should also be open with employers, partners or colleagues about your conscientious objection. You should explore with them how you can practise in accordance with your beliefs without compromising patient care and without overburdening colleagues.

12 Patients have a right to information about their condition and the options open to them. If you have a conscientious objection to a treatment or procedure that may be clinically appropriate for the patient, you must do the following.

   a Tell the patient that you do not provide the particular treatment or procedure, being careful not to cause distress. You may wish to mention the reason for your objection, but you must be careful not to imply any judgement of the patient.

   b Tell the patient that they have a right to discuss their condition and the options for treatment (including the option that you object to) with another practitioner who does not hold the same objection as you and can advise them about the treatment or procedure you object to.

   c Make sure that the patient has enough information to arrange to see another doctor who does not hold the same objection as you.

13 If it's not practical for a patient to arrange to see another doctor, you must make sure that arrangements are made—without delay—for another suitably qualified colleague to advise, treat or refer the patient. You must bear in mind the patient's vulnerability and act promptly to make sure they are not denied appropriate treatment or services. If the patient has a disability, you should make reasonable adjustments to your practice to allow them to receive care to meet their needs. In emergencies, you must not refuse to provide treatment necessary to save the life of, or prevent serious deterioration in the health of, a person because the treatment conflicts with your personal beliefs.

14 You will not necessarily need to end a consultation with your patient because you have an objection to a treatment or procedure that may be appropriate for them. However, if you feel (or the patient feels) that your conscientious objection prevents you from making an objective assessment, you should suggest again that the patient seeks advice and treatment elsewhere.

15 You must not obstruct patients from accessing services or leave them with nowhere to turn.

16 Whatever your personal beliefs about the procedure in question, you must be respectful of the patient's dignity and views.

How could a patient's personal beliefs affect their healthcare?

17 Patients' personal beliefs may lead them to:
   • ask for a procedure for mainly religious, cultural or social reasons
   • refuse treatment that you judge to be of overall benefit to them.

---

[2] For example, this means that you must not refuse to provide a patient with medical services because the patient is proposing to undergo, is undergoing, or has undergone gender reassignment. However, you may decide not to provide or refer any patients (including patients proposing to undergo gender reassignment) for particular services to which you hold a conscientious objection, for example, treatments that cause infertility.

[3] For example, this means that while you may decide not to provide contraception (including emergency contraception) services to any patient, you cannot be willing to prescribe it only for women who live in accordance with your beliefs (eg by prescribing for married women but not for unmarried women).

[4] Except where those requirements are inconsistent with legislation or where the law provides protection on grounds of conscience.

Procedures provided for mainly religious or cultural reasons

18 If patients (or those with parental responsibility for them) ask for a procedure, such as circumcision of male children, for mainly religious or cultural reasons, you should discuss with them the benefits, risks and side effects of the procedure. You should usually provide procedures[5] that patients request and that you assess to be of overall benefit to the patient. If the patient is a child, you should usually provide a procedure or treatment that you assess to be in their best interests. In all circumstances, you will also need the patient's or parental consent.

19 In assessing what is of overall benefit to adult patients, you must take into account their cultural, religious or other beliefs and values. For further advice on assessing overall benefit, see our guidance *Consent: patients and doctors making decisions together* and *Treatment and care towards the end of life: good practice in decision making.*

20 If the patient is a child, you must proceed on the basis of the best interests of the child and with consent. Assessing best interests will include the child's and/or the parents' cultural, religious or other beliefs and values. You should get the child's consent if they have the maturity and understanding to give it. If not, you should get consent from all those with parental responsibility. If you cannot get consent for a procedure, for example, because the parents cannot agree and disputes cannot be resolved informally, you should:

- inform the child's parents that you cannot provide the service unless you have authorisation from the court
- advise the child's parents to seek legal advice on applying to the court.

21 If you judge that a procedure is not in the best interests of a child, you must explain this to the child (if he or she can understand) and to their parents. If you do not believe that the procedure is of overall benefit to an adult patient, you must explain this to them. You are not obliged to provide treatments in such cases. If you hold objections to the procedure as a result of your religious or moral beliefs, you should follow our advice on conscientious objection (paragraphs 8–16).

22 If you agree to perform any procedure for religious or cultural reasons, you must meet the same standards of practice required for performing therapeutic procedures including:

- having the necessary skills and experience to perform the procedure and use appropriate measures, including anaesthesia, to minimise pain and discomfort both during and after the procedure
- keeping your knowledge and skills up to date
- ensuring conditions are hygienic
- providing appropriate aftercare.

23 If you are carrying out circumcision, or another procedure, for religious reasons, you should explain to the patient (or, in the case of children, their parents) that they may invite their religious adviser to be present during the procedure to give advice on how it should be performed to meet the requirements of their faith.

Patients who refuse treatment

24 You must respect a competent patient's decision to refuse an investigation or treatment, even if you think their decision is wrong or irrational. You may advise the patient of your clinical opinion, but you must not put pressure on them to accept your advice.[6] You must be careful that your words and actions do not imply judgement of the patient or their beliefs and values.

25 If you have a conscientious objection—for example, to the withdrawal of life-prolonging treatment—you should follow the guidance in paragraphs 79–80 and 47–48 of our guidance *Treatment and care towards the end of life: good practice in decision making.*

---

[5] Where you have the knowledge, skills and experience to do so safely.

[6] For example, many Jehovah's Witnesses have strong objections to the use of blood and blood products, and may refuse them even if they may die as a result. Hospital liaison committees established by the Watch Tower Society (the governing body of Jehovah's Witnesses) can advise on current Society policy. They also keep details of hospitals and doctors who are experienced in 'bloodless' medical procedures.

26 If the patient is a child who lacks capacity to make a decision, and both parents refuse treatment on the grounds of their religious or moral beliefs, you must discuss their concerns and look for treatment options that will accommodate their beliefs. You should involve the child in a way appropriate to their age and maturity. If following a discussion of all the options you cannot reach an agreement, and treatment is essential to preserve life or prevent serious deterioration in health, you should seek advice on approaching the court.

27 In an emergency, you can provide treatment that is immediately necessary to save life or prevent deterioration in health without consent or, in exceptional circumstances, against the wishes of a person with parental responsibility.

28 For further advice on consent to treatment involving children and adults, including adults who lack capacity, see our guidance *Consent: patients and doctors making decisions together* and *0–18 years: guidance for all doctors*.

Talking to patients about personal beliefs

29 In assessing a patient's conditions and taking a history, you should take account of spiritual, religious, social and cultural factors, as well as their clinical history and symptoms (see *Good medical practice* paragraph 15a). It may therefore be appropriate to ask a patient about their personal beliefs. However, you must not put pressure on a patient to discuss or justify their beliefs, or the absence of them.

30 During a consultation, you should keep the discussion relevant to the patient's care and treatment. If you disclose any personal information to a patient, including talking to a patient about personal beliefs, you must be very careful not to breach the professional boundary that exists between you. These boundaries are essential to maintaining a relationship of trust between a doctor and a patient.

31 You may talk about your own personal beliefs only if a patient asks you directly about them, or indicates they would welcome such a discussion. You must not impose your beliefs and values on patients, or cause distress by the inappropriate or insensitive expression of them.

Part V

Codes of Practice and Policy Guidance

A Code of Practice for the Diagnosis and Confirmation of Death*

(Academy of Medical Royal Colleges, 2008)

[Excerpts, footnotes omitted]

This Code of Practice has been approved by the Academy of Medical Royal Colleges as a statement of current practice in the diagnosis and confirmation of death. It does not (and could not) seek to provide guidance for every single clinical situation where a doctor is required to diagnose death or to be a comprehensive statement of clinical and/or legal obligations for medical staff towards their patients in this complex area of practice. Doctors and other healthcare workers should bear in mind the need to consider the Guidance carefully and, using their own clinical judgment, to consider whether it is appropriate to any individual case. Any medical professional who has concerns about interpretation of the Guidance or whether it should be followed in any clinical situation should discuss the matter with professional colleagues, seek advice from their employer's ethics committee or legal advisors, or contact their Medical Defence Organisation.

2. Diagnosis and confirmation of death

Death entails the irreversible loss of those essential characteristics which are necessary to the existence of a living human person and, thus, the definition of death should be regarded as the irreversible loss of the capacity for consciousness, combined with irreversible loss of the capacity to breathe. This may be secondary to a wide range of underlying problems in the body, for example, cardiac arrest.

2.1 Death following the irreversible cessation of brain-stem function

The irreversible cessation of brain-stem function whether induced by intra-cranial events or the result of extra-cranial phenomena, such as hypoxia, will produce this clinical state and therefore irreversible cessation of the integrative function of the brain-stem equates with the death of the individual and allows the medical practitioner to diagnose death.

Three things should be noted in this regard:

First, the irreversible loss of the capacity for consciousness does not by itself entail individual death. Patients in the vegetative state (VS) have also lost this capacity (see section 6.9). The difference between them and patients who are declared dead by virtue of irreversible cessation of brain-stem function is that the latter cannot continue to breathe unaided without respiratory support, along with other life-sustaining biological interventions. This also means that even if the body of the deceased remains on respiratory support, the loss of integrated biological function will inevitably lead to deterioration and organ necrosis within a short time.

Second, the diagnosis of death because of cessation of brain-stem function does not entail the cessation of all neurological activity in the brain. What does follow from such a diagnosis is that none of these potential activities indicates any form of consciousness associated with human life,

---

* Reproduced by kind permission of the Academy of Medical Royal Colleges.

particularly the ability to feel, to be aware of, or to do, anything. Where such residual activity exists, it will not do so for long due to the rapid breakdown of other bodily functions.

Third, there may also be some residual reflex movement of the limbs after such a diagnosis. However, as this movement is independent of the brain and is controlled through the spinal cord, it is neither indicative of the ability to feel, be aware of, or to respond to, any stimulus, nor to sustain respiration or allow other bodily functions to continue.

In short, while there are some ways in which parts of the body may continue to show signs of biological activity after a diagnosis of irreversible cessation of brain-stem function, these have no moral relevance to the declaration of death for the purpose of the immediate withdrawal of all forms of supportive therapy. It is for this reason that patients with such activity can no longer benefit from supportive treatment and legal certification of their death is appropriate.

The current position in law is that there is no statutory definition of death in the United Kingdom. Subsequent to the proposal of the 'brain death criteria' by the Conference of Medical Royal Colleges in 1976, the courts in England and Northern Ireland have adopted these criteria as part of the law for the diagnosis of death. There is no reason to believe that courts in other parts of the United Kingdom would not follow this approach.

Section 26(2)(d) of the Human Tissue Act 2004 empowers the Human Tissue Authority to develop a series of Codes of Practice, including the definition of death for the purposes of that Act only. The Codes published thus far are available at www.hta.gov.uk/guidance/codes_of_practice.cfm

4.   Diagnosis and confirmation of death in a patient in coma

When managing a patient in coma, treatment decisions must be made in the patient's best interests. The first objective for the healthcare team is to determine the cause and depth of coma, to maintain life while this is being done (respecting any valid advance decision to refuse treatment), and attempt to restore function. Such measures are often successful, but when the brain-stem has been damaged in such a way, and to such a degree, that its integrative functions (which include the neural control of cardiac and pulmonary function and consciousness) are irreversibly destroyed, death of the individual has occurred and the heart will inevitably stop beating subsequently, although the time over which this occurs may vary considerably (see 6.4).

When death has been diagnosed by the methods to be described, the patient is dead even though respiration and circulation can be artificially maintained successfully for a limited period of time. The appropriate course of action is then to consider withdrawal of mechanical respiratory support, the ethical justification for which has passed, and to allow the heart to stop. This imposes an unnecessary and distressing vigil on the relatives, partners and carers, who should be kept fully informed by the local care team of the diagnosis, the inevitable outcome and the likely sequence of events.

6.   The diagnosis of death following irreversible cessation of brain-stem function

6.9   The vegetative state

Problems relating to the diagnosis and management of the vegetative state (VS) must not be confused with those relating to death, and the Guidelines endorsed by the Conference of Medical Royal Colleges emphasise the important differences. Brain-stem death is not part of the VS, which has been defined as a clinical condition of unawareness of self and environment in which the patient breathes spontaneously, has a stable circulation, and shows cycles of eye closure and opening which may simulate sleep and waking.

7.   Management of the patient

It is important that decisions made on behalf of living patients, who lack the capacity to make decisions for themselves, are made in line with the Mental Capacity Act and take account of the patient's best interests. The implications of this requirement are laid out in the MCA Code of Practice [http://www.publicguardian.gov.uk/mca/code-of-practice.htm]. This Code of Practice refers both to an individual before death who lacks capacity and after death has been diagnosed and confirmed, when the question of best interests no longer arises.

7.1   Maintenance of therapy

The maintenance of normal homoeostasis by attempting to ensure adequate fluid intake, electrolyte balance, normal blood pressure, the monitoring of urine output by catheter collection and the use of other therapeutic agents, is part of the standard medical care of the patient where death has not been conclusively established.

7.2   Cessation of respiration

Some patients, who are thought to have sustained irreversible brain damage and are receiving partial ventilatory assistance, may continue to make respiratory efforts, precluding the confirmation of death. In such patients it is important to decide at an early stage whether it is appropriate to initiate full mechanical ventilation at the onset of apnoea, to allow the exclusion of other causes for the deterioration and to allow the confirmation of death by confirming the irreversible cessation of brain-stem function. If this course of action is not considered appropriate in the evaluation of the benefit of further treatment aimed at sustaining life, then neither is the partial ventilatory support being provided. In such a case, withdrawing ventilatory assistance following discussion with the patient's relatives or relevant others may be the most appropriate course as being in the best interests of the patient.

7.3   Elective ventilation

Where a patient has been intubated and ventilated as part of a resuscitation (e.g. a cardiac arrest or multiple injury) or in order to facilitate an investigation (such as a CT head scan), additional information may subsequently become available that was not known at the time of the decision to intubate and ventilate. This new information may be related to the patient's pre-existing medical conditions or may be related to the present condition (e.g. a CT scan showing gross cerebral trauma or cerebral haemorrhage). With the new information, it may become clear that, whether or not death of the brain has actually occurred, the patient's condition is inevitably going to be fatal. In such a case, withdrawal of ventilatory support, ideally following discussion with the patient's relatives, may be the most appropriate course. If further intensive care is not considered appropriate because it can be of no benefit, nor in the patient's best interests, then neither is a continuation of the respiratory support being provided. In deciding which relative to involve in decisions of this nature, we recommend following the recommendations made in the Mental Capacity Act, outlined in 7.2.

The patient will usually (but not invariably) start to make some respiratory effort for a period of time following withdrawal of ventilatory support. In this situation, although further active treatment is inappropriate, transfer to a Critical Care Unit may allow the family to spend time with their dying relative, during which palliative care can be provided in an environment that is dignified for the patient and supportive for the relatives. A similar situation exists in the case of a spontaneously breathing baby with a lethal congenital anomaly such as anencephaly. In both these situations endotracheal intubation and artificial ventilation of the patient should only be initiated and maintained to further the patient's benefit and not as a means of preserving organ function.

Policy for Prosecutors in Respect of Cases of Encouraging or Assisting Suicide

(Issued by the Director of Public Prosecutions, February 2010)

[Excerpts.]

Introduction

1.   A person commits an offence under section 2 of the Suicide Act 1961 if he or she does an act capable of encouraging or assisting the suicide or attempted suicide of another person, and that act was intended to encourage or assist suicide or an attempt at suicide. This offence is referred to in this policy as 'encouraging or assisting suicide'. The consent of the Director of Public Prosecutions (DPP) is required before an individual may be prosecuted.

2. The offence of encouraging or assisting suicide carries a maximum penalty of 14 years' imprisonment. This reflects the seriousness of the offence.

3. Committing or attempting to commit suicide is not, however, of itself, a criminal offence.

4. This policy is issued as a result of the decision of the Appellate Committee of the House of Lords in R *(on the application of Purdy) v Director of Public Prosecutions* reported at [2009] UKHL 45, which required the DPP 'to clarify what his position is as to the factors that he regards as relevant for and against prosecution' (paragraph 55) in cases of encouraging and assisting suicide.

5. The case of *Purdy* did not change the law: only Parliament can change the law on encouraging or assisting suicide.

6. This policy does not in any way 'decriminalise' the offence of encouraging or assisting suicide. Nothing in this policy can be taken to amount to an assurance that a person will be immune from prosecution if he or she does an act that encourages or assists the suicide or the attempted suicide of another person.

7. For the purposes of this policy, the term 'victim' is used to describe the person who commits or attempts to commit suicide. Not everyone may agree that this is an appropriate description but, in the context of the criminal law, it is the most suitable term to use.

8. This policy applies when the act that constitutes the encouragement or assistance is committed in England and Wales; any suicide or attempted suicide as a result of that encouragement or assistance may take place anywhere in the world, including in England and Wales.

The decision-making process

13. Prosecutors must apply the Full Code Test as set out in the Code for Crown Prosecutors in cases of encouraging or assisting suicide. The Full Code Test has two stages: (i) the evidential stage; and (ii) the public interest stage. The evidential stage must be considered before the public interest stage. A case which does not pass the evidential stage must not proceed, no matter how serious or sensitive it may be. Where there is sufficient evidence to justify a prosecution, prosecutors must go on to consider whether a prosecution is required in the public interest.

14. The DPP will only consent to a prosecution for an offence of encouraging or assisting suicide in a case where the Full Code Test is met.

Encouraging or assisting suicide and murder or manslaughter distinguished

32. The act of suicide requires the victim to take his or her own life.

33. It is murder or manslaughter for a person to do an act that ends the life of another, even if he or she does so on the basis that he or she is simply complying with the wishes of the other person concerned.

34. So, for example, if a victim attempts to commit suicide but succeeds only in making him or herself unconscious, a person commits murder or manslaughter if he or she then does an act that causes the death of the victim, even if he or she believes that he or she is simply carrying out the victim's express wish.

Explaining the law

35. For the avoidance of doubt, a person who does not do anything other than provide information to another which sets out or explains the legal position in respect of the offence of encouraging or assisting suicide under section 2 of the Suicide Act 1961 does not commit an offence under that section.

The public interest stage

36. It has never been the rule that a prosecution will automatically follow where the evidential stage of the Full Code Test is satisfied. This was recognised by the House of Lords in the *Purdy* case where Lord Hope stated that: '[i]t has long been recognised that a prosecution does not follow automatically whenever an offence is believed to have been committed' (paragraph 44). He went on to endorse the approach adopted by Sir Hartley Shawcross, the Attorney General in 1951, when

he stated in the House of Commons that: '[i]t has never been the rule ... that criminal offences must automatically be the subject of prosecution'.

37. Accordingly, where there is sufficient evidence to justify a prosecution, prosecutors must go on to consider whether a prosecution is required in the public interest.

38. In cases of encouraging or assisting suicide, prosecutors must apply the public interest factors set out in the Code for Crown Prosecutors and the factors set out in this policy in making their decisions. A prosecution will usually take place unless the prosecutor is sure that there are public interest factors tending against prosecution which outweigh those tending in favour.

39. Assessing the public interest is not simply a matter of adding up the number of factors on each side and seeing which side has the greater number. Each case must be considered on its own facts and on its own merits. Prosecutors must decide the importance of each public interest factor in the circumstances of each case and go on to make an overall assessment. It is quite possible that one factor alone may outweigh a number of other factors which tend in the opposite direction. Although there may be public interest factors tending against prosecution in a particular case, prosecutors should consider whether nonetheless a prosecution should go ahead and for those factors to be put to the court for consideration when sentence is passed.

40. The absence of a factor does not necessarily mean that it should be taken as a factor tending in the opposite direction. For example, just because the victim was not 'under 18 years of age' does not transform the 'factor tending in favour of prosecution' into a 'factor tending against prosecution'.

41. It may sometimes be the case that the only source of information about the circumstances of the suicide and the state of mind of the victim is the suspect. Prosecutors and investigators should make sure that they pursue all reasonable lines of further enquiry in order to obtain, wherever possible, independent verification of the suspect's account.

42. Once all reasonable enquiries are completed, if the reviewing prosecutor is doubtful about the suspect's account of the circumstances of the suicide or the state of mind of the victim which may be relevant to any factor set out below, he or she should conclude that there is insufficient information to support that factor.

Public interest factors tending in favour of prosecution

43. A prosecution is more likely to be required if:
   1. the victim was under 18 years of age;
   2. the victim did not have the capacity (as defined by the Mental Capacity Act 2005) to reach an informed decision to commit suicide;
   3. the victim had not reached a voluntary, clear, settled and informed decision to commit suicide;
   4. the victim had not clearly and unequivocally communicated his or her decision to commit suicide to the suspect;
   5. the victim did not seek the encouragement or assistance of the suspect personally or on his or her own initiative;
   6. the suspect was not wholly motivated by compassion; for example, the suspect was motivated by the prospect that he or she or a person closely connected to him or her stood to gain in some way from the death of the victim;
   7. the suspect pressured the victim to commit suicide;
   8. the suspect did not take reasonable steps to ensure that any other person had not pressured the victim to commit suicide;
   9. the suspect had a history of violence or abuse against the victim;
   10. the victim was physically able to undertake the act that constituted the assistance him or herself;
   11. the suspect was unknown to the victim and encouraged or assisted the victim to commit or attempt to commit suicide by providing specific information via, for example, a website or publication;
   12. the suspect gave encouragement or assistance to more than one victim who were not known to each other;

13. the suspect was paid by the victim or those close to the victim for his or her encouragement or assistance;

14. the suspect was acting in his or her capacity as a medical doctor, nurse, other healthcare professional, a professional carer [whether for payment or not], or as a person in authority, such as a prison officer, and the victim was in his or her care;

15. the suspect was aware that the victim intended to commit suicide in a public place where it was reasonable to think that members of the public may be present;

16. the suspect was acting in his or her capacity as a person involved in the management or as an employee (whether for payment or not) of an organisation or group, a purpose of which is to provide a physical environment (whether for payment or not) in which to allow another to commit suicide.

44. On the question of whether a person stood to gain, (paragraph 43(6) see above), the police and the reviewing prosecutor should adopt a common sense approach. It is possible that the suspect may gain some benefit - financial or otherwise - from the resultant suicide of the victim after his or her act of encouragement or assistance. The critical element is the motive behind the suspect's act. If it is shown that compassion was the only driving force behind his or her actions, the fact that the suspect may have gained some benefit will not usually be treated as a factor tending in favour of prosecution. However, each case must be considered on its own merits and on its own facts.

Public interest factors tending against prosecution

45. A prosecution is less likely to be required if:

1. the victim had reached a voluntary, clear, settled and informed decision to commit suicide;

2. the suspect was wholly motivated by compassion;

3. the actions of the suspect, although sufficient to come within the definition of the offence, were of only minor encouragement or assistance;

4. the suspect had sought to dissuade the victim from taking the course of action which resulted in his or her suicide;

5. the actions of the suspect may be characterised as reluctant encouragement or assistance in the face of a determined wish on the part of the victim to commit suicide;

6. the suspect reported the victim's suicide to the police and fully assisted them in their enquiries into the circumstances of the suicide or the attempt and his or her part in providing encouragement or assistance.

46. The evidence to support these factors must be sufficiently close in time to the encouragement or assistance to allow the prosecutor reasonably to infer that the factors remained operative at that time. This is particularly important at the start of the specific chain of events that immediately led to the suicide or the attempt.

47. These lists of public interest factors are not exhaustive and each case must be considered on its own facts and on its own merits.

48. If the course of conduct goes beyond encouraging or assisting suicide, for example, because the suspect goes on to take or attempt to take the life of the victim, the public interest factors tending in favour of or against prosecution may have to be evaluated differently in the light of the overall criminal conduct.

Mental Health Act 1983 Code of Practice (2015)

[*Excerpts, footnotes omitted.*]

Chapter 1   Guiding principles

1.1 It is essential that all those undertaking functions under the Act understand the five sets of overarching principles which should always be considered when making decisions in relation to care, support or treatment provided under the Act. This chapter provides an explanation of the overarching principles and stresses that they should be considered when making decisions under the Act. Although all are of equal importance the weight given to each principle in reaching a particular decision will depend on context and the nature of the decision being made.

The five overarching principles are:

Least restrictive option and maximising independence

Where it is possible to treat a patient safely and lawfully without detaining them under the Act, the patient should not be detained. Wherever possible a patient's independence should be encouraged and supported with a focus on promoting recovery wherever possible.

Empowerment and involvement

Patients should be fully involved in decisions about care, support and treatment. The views of families, carers and others, if appropriate, should be fully considered when taking decisions. Where decisions are taken which are contradictory to views expressed, professionals should explain the reasons for this.

Respect and dignity

Patients, their families and carers should be treated with respect and dignity and listened to by professionals.

Purpose and effectiveness

Decisions about care and treatment should be appropriate to the patient, with clear therapeutic aims, promote recovery and should be performed to current national guidelines and/or current, available best practice guidelines.

Efficiency and equity

Providers, commissioners and other relevant organisations should work together to ensure that the quality of commissioning and provision of mental healthcare services are of high quality and are given equal priority to physical health and social care services. All relevant services should work together to facilitate timely, safe safe and supportive discharge from detention.

Least restrictive option and maximising independence

1.2 Where it is possible to treat a patient safely and lawfully without detaining them under the Act, the patient should not be detained.

1.3 Commissioners, providers and other relevant agencies should work together to prevent mental health crises and, where possible, reduce the use of detention through prevention and early intervention by commissioning a range of services that are accessible, responsive and as high quality as other health emergency services.

1.4 If the Act is used, detention should be used for the shortest time necessary in the least restrictive hospital setting available, and be delivered as close as reasonably possible to a location that the patient identifies they would like to be close to (eg their home or close to a family member or carer). In cases where the patient lacks capacity to make a decision about the location they would like to be close to, a best interests decision on the location should be taken. This will promote recovery and enable the patient to maintain contact with family, friends, and their community.

1.5 Any restrictions should be the minimum necessary to safely provide the care or treatment required having regard to whether the purpose for the restriction can be achieved in a way that is less restrictive of the person's rights and freedom of action.

1.6 Restrictions that apply to all patients in a particular setting (blanket or global restrictions) should be avoided. There may be settings where there will be restrictions on all patients that are necessary for their safety or for that of others. Any such restrictions should have a clear justification for the particular hospital, group or ward to which they apply. Blanket restrictions should never be for the convenience of the provider. Any such restrictions, should be agreed by hospital managers, be documented with the reasons for such restrictions clearly described and subject to governance procedures that exist in the relevant organisation.

Empowerment and involvement

1.7 Patients should be given the opportunity to be involved in planning, developing and reviewing their own care and treatment to help ensure that it is delivered in a way that is as appropriate and effective for them as possible. Wherever possible, care plans should be produced in consultation with the patient.

1.8 A patient's views, past and present wishes and feelings (whether expressed at the time or in advance), should be considered so far as they are reasonably ascertainable. Patients should be encouraged and supported to develop advance statements of wishes and feeling and express their views about future care and treatment when they are well.

1.9 The patient's choices and views should be fully recorded. Where a decision in the care plan is contrary to the wishes of the patient or others the reasons for this should be transparent, explained to them and fully documented.

1.10 Patients should be enabled to participate in decision-making as far as they are capable of doing so. Consideration should be given to what assistance or support a patient may need to participate in decision-making and any such assistance or support should be provided, to ensure maximum involvement possible. This includes being given sufficient information about their care and treatment in a format that is easily understandable to them.

1.11 Patients should be encouraged and supported in involving carers (unless there are particular reasons to the contrary). Professionals should fully consider their views when making decisions.

1.12 Patients should be informed of the support that an advocate can provide, including carers or, if they are eligible, an independent mental health advocate (IMHA) (or an independent mental capacity advocate (IMCA) where relevant). Local authorities should ensure that timely access to IMHAs is available and that IMHAs have appropriate training and skills to support the patient effectively including where a patient has particular needs.

Respect and dignity

1.13 Patients and carers should be treated with respect and dignity. Practitioners performing functions under the Act should respect the rights and dignity of patients and their carers, while also ensuring their safety and that of others.

1.14 People taking decisions under the Act must recognise and respect the diverse needs, values and circumstances of each patient, including their age, disability, gender reassignment, marriage and civil partnership, pregnancy and maternity, race, religion or belief, sex and sexual orientation, and culture. There must be no unlawful discrimination.

Purpose and effectiveness

1.15 Care, support and treatment given under the Act should be given in accordance with up-to-date national guidance and/or current best practice from professional bodies, where this is available. Treatment should address an individual patient's needs, taking account of their circumstances and preferences where appropriate.

1.16 Patients should be offered treatment and care in environments that are safe for them, staff and any visitors and are supportive and, therapeutic. Practitioners should deliver a range of treatments which focus on positive clinical and personal outcomes, where appropriate. Care plans for detained patients should focus on maximisingprofessionals should consider the broad range of interventions and services needed to promote recovery not only in hospital but after a patient leaves hospital, including maintaining relationships, housing, opportunities for meaningful daytime activity and employment opportunities,

1.17 Physical healthcare needs should be assessed and addressed including promotion of healthy living and steps taken to reduce any potential side effects associated with treatments.

Efficiency and equity

1.18 Commissioners and providers, including their staff, should give equal priority to mental health as they do to physical health conditions.

1.19 Where patients are subject to compulsory detention, health and social care agencies should work together to deliver a programme of care that, as far as practicable, minimises the duration of detention, facilitates safe discharge from hospital and takes into account the patient's wishes.

1.20 Commissioners, providers and other relevant organisations should establish effective relationships to ensure efficient working with accountability defined through joint governance arrangements. Joint working should be used to minimise delay in care planning needed to facilitate discharge.

1.21 Commissioners, providers and other relevant organisations should ensure that their staff have sufficient skills, information and knowledge about the Act and provision of services to support all their patients. There should be clear mechanisms for accessing specialist support for those with additional needs.

Using the principles

1.22 All decisions must be lawful and informed by good professional practice. Lawfulness necessarily includes compliance with the Human Rights Act 1998 (HRA) and Equality Act 2010.

1.23 All five sets of principles are of equal importance, and should inform any decision made under the Act. The weight given to each principle in reaching a particular decision will need to be balanced in different ways according to the circumstances and nature of each particular decision. The guidance in the Code is based on these principles and reference is made to them throughout the Code.

1.24 Commissioners, providers, professionals and others providing care under the Act should document, and justify, any decision to depart from the Code or a particular guiding principle. The Care Quality Commission will look for evidence of this during their inspections and commissioners can use it as part of their contract monitoring.

Chapter 2   Mental disorder definition

Figure 1: Clinically recognised conditions which could fall within the Act's definition of mental disorder

- Affective disorders, such as depression and bipolar disorder
- Schizophrenia and delusional disorders
- Neurotic, stress-related and somatoform disorders, such as anxiety, phobic disorders, obsessive compulsive disorders, post-traumatic stress disorder and hypochondriacal disorders
- Organic mental disorders such as dementia and delirium (however caused)
- Personality and behavioural changes caused by brain injury or damage (however acquired)
- Personality disorders (see paragraphs 2.19–2.20 and chapter 21)
- Mental and behavioural disorders caused by psychoactive substance use (see paragraphs 2.9–2.13)
- Eating disorders, non-organic sleep disorders and non-organic sexual disorders
- Learning disabilities (see paragraphs 2.14–2.18 and chapter 20)
- Autistic spectrum disorders (including Asperger's syndrome) (see paragraphs 2.14–2.18 and chapter 20)
- Behavioural and emotional disorders of children and young people

(Note: this list is not exhaustive)

2.7 Care must always be taken to avoid diagnosing, or failing to diagnose, mental disorder on the basis of preconceptions about people or failure to appreciate cultural and social differences. What may be indicative of mental disorder in one person, given their background and individual circumstances, may be nothing of the sort in another person.

2.8 Difference should not be confused with disorder. No-one may be considered to be mentally disordered solely because of their political, religious or cultural beliefs, values or opinions, unless there are proper clinical grounds to believe that they are the symptoms or manifestations of a disability or disorder of the mind. The same is true of a person's involvement, or likely involvement, in illegal, anti-social or 'immoral' behaviour. Beliefs, behaviours or actions which do not result from a disorder or disability of the mind are not a basis for compulsory measures under the Act, even if they appear unusual or cause other people alarm, distress or danger.

Chapter 14   Applications for detention in hospital

14.7 Before it is decided that admission to hospital is necessary, consideration must be given to whether there are alternative means of providing the care and treatment which the patient requires. This includes consideration of whether there might be other effective forms of care or treatment which the patient would be willing to accept and of whether guardianship would be appropriate instead.

14.8 In all cases, consideration should be given to:
- the patient's wishes and view of their own needs
- the patient's age and physical health
- any past wishes or feelings expressed by the patient
- the patient's cultural background
- the patient's social and family circumstances
- the impact that any future deterioration or lack of improvement in the patient's condition would have on their children, other relatives or carers, especially those living with the patient, including an assessment of their ability and willingness to cope, and
- the effect on the patient, and those close to the patient, of a decision to admit or not to admit under the Act.

Alternatives to detention under the Act

14.11 In deciding whether it is necessary to detain patients, doctors and AMHPs must always consider the alternative ways of providing the treatment or care they need. Decision-makers should always consider whether there are less restrictive alternatives to detention under the Act, which may include:
- informal admission to hospital of a patient based on that person's consent (see chapter 19 for guidance on consent to informal admission for children and young people)
- treatment under the Mental Capacity Act (MCA) if the person lacks capacity to consent to admission and treatment. If a deprivation of liberty occurs, or is likely to occur, either the Act, a DoLS authorisation or a deprivation of liberty order by the Court of Protection must be in place (see chapter 13)
- management in the community—eg by a crisis and support team, in a crisis house or with a host family (see chapter 29 on community patients), or
- guardianship (see chapter 30 and 31).

14.12 In considering whether it is necessary for the person to be detained under the Act, decision-makers must consider whether the person has capacity to consent to or refuse admission and treatment. This should be assessed in accordance with the MCA, which makes clear that a person must be assumed to have capacity unless it is established that they do not.

14.13 Professionals must consider available alternatives, having regard to all the relevant circumstances, to identify the least restrictive way of best achieving the proposed assessment or treatment. This will include considering what is the person's best interests (if the person lacks capacity, this will be determined in accordance with the MCA).

Patients with capacity to give or to refuse consent to admission

14.14 When a patient needs to be in hospital, informal admission is usually appropriate when a patient who has the capacity to give or to refuse consent is consenting to admission. (See chapter 19 for guidance on when parents might consent to admission on behalf of children and young people.)

14.15 This should not be regarded as an absolute rule, especially if the reason for considering admission is that the patient presents a clear risk to themselves or others because of their mental disorder.

14.16 Compulsory admission should, in particular, be considered where a patient's current mental state, together with reliable evidence of past experience, indicates a strong likelihood that they will have a change of mind about informal admission, either before or after they are admitted, with a resulting risk to their health or safety or to the safety of other people.

14.17 The threat of detention must not be used to coerce a patient to consent to admission to hospital or to treatment (and is likely to invalidate any apparent consent).

14.18 If consideration is being given to the informal admission of a patient who is subject to Secretary of State for Justice restrictions, the Mental Health Casework Section (MHCS) of the Ministry of Justice should be contacted. Further advice is provided in chapter 22 and on the Ministry of Justice website.

Patients who lack capacity to give or to refuse consent to admission or treatment

14.19 Where the criteria for detention under the Act are met, the situations where an application for detention should be made under the Act instead of relying on the DoLS include where:

- the patient has made a valid and applicable advance decision to refuse treatment which includes a necessary element of the treatment for which they are to be admitted to hospital (see chapter 9)
- the use of the DoLS would conflict with a decision of the person's attorney, deputy, guardian or the Court of Protection, or
- the patient is objecting to being admitted to (or remaining in) hospital for mental health treatment.

14.20 In that last case, whether a patient is objecting has to be considered in the round, taking into account all the circumstances, so far as they are reasonably ascertainable. The decision to be made is whether the patient objects to treatment—the reasonableness of that objection is not the issue. In many cases the patient will be perfectly able to state their objection. In other cases doctors and AMHPs will need to consider the patient's behaviour, wishes, feelings, views, beliefs and values, both present and past, so far as they can be ascertained. If there is reason to think that a patient would object, if able to do so, then the patient should be taken to be objecting.

14.21 Even if providing appropriate care or treatment will not unavoidably involve a deprivation of liberty, in some cases it may be necessary to detain a patient under the Act rather than rely on the MCA. For example, where the patient:

- has, by means of a valid and applicable advance decision, refused a necessary element of the treatment required, or
- lacks capacity to make decisions on some elements of the care and treatment they need, but has capacity to decide about a vital element—eg admission to hospital—and has either already refused it or is likely to do so.

14.22 Whether or not the DoLS could be used, other reasons why it may be necessary to detain a patient under the Act and not rely on the MCA alone include the following:

- the patient's lack of capacity to consent or refuse is fluctuating or temporary and the patient is not expected to consent to admission or treatment when they regain capacity. This may be particularly relevant to patients having acute psychotic, manic or depressive episodes

- •. degree of restraint may need to be used which is justified by the risk to other people but which is not permissible under the MCA$_3$ because, exceptionally, it cannot be said to be proportionate to the risk to the patient personally, and
- there is some other specific identifiable risk that the person might not receive the treatment they need if the MCA is relied on and either the person or others might potentially suffer harm as a result.

14.23 Otherwise, if the MCA can be used safely and effectively to assess or treat a patient, it is likely to be difficult to demonstrate that the criteria for detaining the patient under the Act are met.

14.24 For further information on the DoLS, see chapter 13, the MCA Code of Practice and its supplementary DoLS Code.

Chapter 19   Children and young people under the age of 18

General considerations

19.4 In addition to the Act, those responsible for the care of children and young people in hospital should be familiar with other relevant legislation, including the Children Acts 1989 and 2004, the MCA and the HRA. They should also be aware of the United Nations Convention on the Rights of the Child (UNCRC), and keep up-to-date with relevant case law and guidance.

19.5 When making decisions in relation to the care and treatment of children and young people, practitioners should keep the following points in mind:

- the best interests of the child or young person must always be a significant consideration
- everyone who works with children has a responsibility for keeping them safe and to take prompt action if welfare needs or safeguarding concerns are identified
- all practitioners and agencies are expected to contribute to whatever actions are needed to safeguard and promote a child or young person's welfare
- the developmental process from childhood to adulthood, particularly during adolescence, involves significant changes in a wide range of areas, such as physical, emotional and cognitive development—these factors need to be taken into account, in addition to the child and young person's personal circumstances, when assessing whether a child or young person has a mental disorder
- children and young people should always be kept as fully informed as possible and should receive clear and detailed information concerning their care and treatment, explained in a way they can understand and in a format that is appropriate to their age
- the child or young person's views, wishes and feelings should always be sought, their views taken seriously and professionals should work with them collaboratively in deciding on how to support that child or young person's needs
- any intervention in the life of a child or young person that is considered necessary by reason of their mental disorder should be the least restrictive option and the least likely to expose them to the risk of any stigmatisation, consistent with effective care and treatment, and it should also result in the least possible separation from family, carers, friends and community or interruption of their education
- where hospital admission is necessary, the child or young person should be placed as near to their home as reasonably practicable, recognising that placement further away from home increases the separation between the child or young person and their family, carers, friends, community and school
- all children and young people should receive the same access to educational provision as their peers
- children and young people have as much right to expect their dignity to be respected as anyone else, and
- children and young people have as much right to privacy and confidentiality as anyone else.

Safeguarding children and young people where admission to hospital is not appropriate

19.17 There is no minimum age limit for detention in hospital under the Act. It may be used to detain children or young people who need to be admitted to hospital for assessment and/or treatment of their mental disorder, when they cannot be admitted and/or treated on an informal basis (…), and where the criteria for detention under the Act are met.

19.18 Where practitioners conclude that admission to hospital is not the appropriate course of action, consideration must be given to alternative means of care and support that will meet the needs of the child or young person. The appropriate action will usually be to refer the child or young person's case to the relevant local authority's children's services, in accordance with local protocols for interagency working to safeguard and promote the welfare of children and young people.

19.19 In cases where admission to hospital under the Act is not appropriate, but the child or young person has significant needs which mean that the level and type of intervention is likely to amount to a deprivation of liberty, their placement in secure accommodation under section 25 of the Children Act 1989 may be required. This will be a matter for the local authority children's services to consider in the light of the provisions of section 25 of the Children Act 1989, and relevant Children Act 1989 guidance. Children who are not Gillick competent (…) or young people who lack capacity (…) whose needs are severe and long-term, and where deprivation of liberty is one necessary element of their education or care, may also be accommodated in other placements.

Human Fertilisation and Embryology Authority Code of Practice (8th edition)*

(2015)

[*Excerpts.*]

REGULATORY PRINCIPLES FOR LICENSED CENTRES

Regulatory principles

The HFEA expects the person responsible to ensure that their licensed centre demonstrates adherence to the following principles when carrying out activities licensed under the Human Fertilisation and Embryology Act.

Licensed centres must:

1. treat prospective and current patients and donors fairly, and ensure that all licensed activities are conducted in a non-discriminatory way

2. have respect for the privacy, confidentiality, dignity, comfort and well being of prospective and current patients and donors

3. have respect for the special status of the embryo when conducting licensed activities

4. take account of the welfare of any child who may be born as a result of the licensed treatment provided by the centre, and of any other child who may be affected by that birth

5. give prospective and current patients and donors sufficient, accessible and up-to-date information to enable them to make informed decisions

6. ensure that patients and donors have provided all relevant consents before carrying out any licensed activity

---

* Reproduced with permission from the Human Fertilisation and Embryology Authority. The Authority regularly amends and updates the Code and the latest version may be found on their website: http://www.hfea.gov.uk/.

7. conduct all licensed activities with skill and care and in an appropriate environment, in line with good clinical practice, to ensure optimum outcomes and minimum risk for patients, donors and offspring

8. ensure that all premises, equipment, processes and procedures used in the conduct of licensed activities are safe, secure and suitable for the purpose

9. ensure that all staff engaged in licensed activity are competent and recruited in sufficient numbers to guarantee safe clinical and laboratory practice

10. maintain accurate records and information about all licensed activities

11. report all adverse incidents (including serious adverse events and serious adverse reactions) and near misses to the HFEA, investigate all complaints properly, and share lessons learned appropriately

12. ensure that all licensed research by the centre meets ethical standards, and is done only where there is both a clear scientific justification and no viable alternative to the use of embryos, and

13. conduct all licensed activities with regard for the regulatory framework governing treatment and research involving gametes or embryos within the UK, including:
- maintaining up-to-date awareness and understanding of legal obligations
- responding promptly to requests for information and documents from the HFEA, and
- co-operating fully with inspections and investigations by the HFEA or other agencies responsible for law enforcement or regulation of healthcare.

5   Consent to treatment, storage, donation and disclosure of information
Consent to use and storage of gametes and embryos

5.1 The centre should obtain written informed consent from a person before it carries out the following procedures:
- (a) using their gametes for their own treatment or their partner's treatment, or
- (b) using their gametes for research and training.

5.8 The centre should give anyone seeking treatment or considering donation or storage enough time to reflect on their decisions before obtaining their consent. The centre should give them an opportunity to ask questions and receive further information, advice and guidance.

5.9 If the possibility of donating gametes or embryos for the treatment of others, or donating embryos for research or training purposes, arises during the course of treatment, the centre should allow potential donors enough time to consider the implications and to receive counselling before giving consent.

5.10 The centre should ensure that consent is:
- (a) given voluntarily (without pressure to accept treatment or agree to donation)
- (b) given by a person who has capacity to do so, as defined by the Mental Capacity Act 2005 (England and Wales), or the Age of Legal Capacity (Scotland) Act 1991 and the Adults with Incapacity (Scotland) Act 2000, and
- (c) taken by a person authorised by the centre to do so.

5.11 The centre should ensure that anyone giving consent declares that:
- (a) they were given enough information to enable them to understand the nature, purpose and implications of the treatment or donation
- (b) they were given a suitable opportunity to receive proper counselling about the implications of the proposed procedures
- (c) they were given information about the procedure for varying or withdrawing consent, and
- (d) the information they have given in writing is correct and complete.

5.12 Treatment centres should take all reasonable steps to verify the identity of anyone accepted for treatment, including partners who may not visit the centre during treatment. If a patient's identity is in doubt, the centre should verify their identity, including examining photographic evidence such as a passport or a photocard driving licence. The centre should record this evidence in the patient's medical records.

5.13 To avoid the possibility of misrepresentation or mistake, the centre should check the identities of patients (and their partners, if applicable) against identifying information in the medical records. This should be done at each consultation, examination, treatment or donation.

Additional consent requirements for using gametes and embryos

5.21 Consent to the use of gametes or embryos for the treatment of others should state the number of families that may have children using the donated gametes or embryos.

5.22 When an individual gives consent to the use of gametes for the treatment of others, the centre need not get consent from the donor's partner or spouse. However, if the donor is married, in a civil partnership or in a long-term relationship, the centre should encourage them to seek their partner's support for the donation of their gametes.

5.23 Men who wish to donate embryos originally created for the treatment of their partner and themselves, and those people considering treatment with such embryos, should be:

(a) informed of the uncertain legal status of men donating embryos created originally for the treatment of their partner and themselves, when the embryos are used in the treatment of a single woman

(b) referred to information on the HFEA's website on this issue, and

(c) advised to seek independent legal advice before consenting to donate their embryos or being treated with the embryos.

Variation and withdrawal of consent

5.37 The centre should check the identity of anyone withdrawing or varying consent against identifying information held in the medical records. The centre should also ensure that the person withdrawing or varying consent has been given sufficient information to enable them to make an informed decision about doing so.

5.38 The centre should have procedures for dealing with disputes that may arise when one gamete provider withdraws their consent to the use or storage of gametes or embryos in treatment. In this situation the centre should stop treatment and notify all relevant parties. Centres should provide information about counselling or mediation services as appropriate.

7   Multiple births

Limits on egg and embryo transfer

7.4 The centre should not transfer more than three eggs or two embryos in any treatment cycle if:

(a) the woman is to receive treatment using her own eggs, or embryos created using her own eggs (fresh or cryopreserved), and

(b) the woman is aged under 40 at the time of transfer.

7.5 The centre should not transfer more than four eggs or three embryos in any treatment cycle if:

(a) the woman is to receive treatment using her own eggs, or embryos created using her own eggs (fresh or cryopreserved), and

(b) the woman is aged 40 or over at the time of transfer.

7.6 If a woman is to receive treatment using donated eggs or embryos, or embryos created with donated eggs, the centre should not transfer more than three eggs or two embryos in a treatment cycle. This is regardless of the procedure used and the woman's age at the time of transfer.

8   Welfare of the child

Scope of the welfare of the child provision

8.1 This guidance note applies to all fertility treatments regulated by the HFEA, including IUI. Centres providing treatments that are not regulated by the HFEA but that fall within the definition of 'treatment services' (see above) may also find this guidance note helpful.

The welfare of the child assessment process

8.2 The centre should have documented procedures to ensure that proper account is taken of the welfare of any child who may be born as a result of treatment services, and any other child who may be affected by the birth.

8.3 The centre should assess each patient and their partner (if they have one) before providing any treatment, and should use this assessment to decide whether there is a risk of significant harm or neglect to any child referred to in 8.2.

8.4 If the child is not to be raised by the carrying mother (ie, in a surrogacy arrangement), the centre should assess both those commissioning the surrogacy arrangement and the surrogate (and the surrogate's partner, if she has one) in case there is a breakdown in the surrogacy arrangement.

8.5 Assessments do not need to be done on gamete or embryo donors, or in cases where gametes are being stored for later use.

8.7 Those seeking treatment are entitled to a fair assessment. The centre is expected to consider the wishes of all those involved, and the assessment must be done in a non-discriminatory way. In particular, patients should not be discriminated against on grounds of gender, race, disability, sexual orientation, religious belief or age.

Factors to take into account during the assessment process

8.10 The centre should consider factors that are likely to cause a risk of significant harm or neglect to any child who may be born or to any existing child of the family. These factors include any aspects of the patient's or (if they have one) their partner's:

  (a) past or current circumstances that may lead to any child mentioned above experiencing serious physical or psychological harm or neglect, for example:
    (i) previous convictions relating to harming children
    (ii) child protection measures taken regarding existing children, or
    (iii) violence or serious discord in the family environment

  (b) past or current circumstances that are likely to lead to an inability to care throughout childhood for any child who may be born, or that are already seriously impairing the care of any existing child of the family, for example:
    (i) mental or physical conditions
    (ii) drug or alcohol abuse
    (iii) medical history, where the medical history indicates that any child who may be born is likely to suffer from a serious medical condition, or
    (iv) circumstances that the centre considers likely to cause serious harm to any child mentioned above.

8.11 When considering a child's need for supportive parenting, centres should consider the following definition:

'Supportive parenting is a commitment to the health, well being and development of the child. It is presumed that all prospective parents will be supportive parents, in the absence of any reasonable cause for concern that any child who may be born, or any other child, may be at risk of significant harm or neglect. Where centres have concern as to whether this commitment exists, they may wish to take account of wider family and social networks within which the child will be raised.'

8.12 If the child will not be raised by the carrying mother, the centre should take into account the possibility of a breakdown in the surrogacy arrangement and whether this is likely to cause a risk of significant harm or neglect to any child who may be born or any existing children in the surrogate's family.

Refusing treatment

8.15 The centre should refuse treatment if it:

  (a) concludes that any child who may be born or any existing child of the family is likely to be at risk of significant harm or neglect, or
  (b) cannot obtain enough information to conclude that there is no significant risk.

8.16 In deciding whether to refuse treatment, the centre should:

    (a) take into account the views of all staff who have been involved with caring for the patient (and their partner if they have one), and

    (b) give the patient (and their partner if they have one) the opportunity to respond to the reason or reasons for refusal before the centre makes a final decision.

8.17 If treatment is refused, the centre should explain, in writing, to the patient (and their partner if they have one):

    (a) why treatment has been refused

    (b) any circumstances that may enable the centre to reconsider its decision

    (c) any remaining options, and

    (d) opportunities for obtaining appropriate counselling.

10   Embryo testing and sex selection

Preimplantation genetic diagnosis for heritable conditions

10.5 When deciding if it is appropriate to provide PGD in particular cases, the centre should consider the circumstances of those seeking treatment rather than the particular heritable condition.

10.6 The use of PGD should be considered only where there is a significant risk of a serious genetic condition being present in the embryo. When deciding if it is appropriate to provide PGD in particular cases, the seriousness of the condition in that case should be discussed between the people seeking treatment and the clinical team. The perception of the level of risk for those seeking treatment will also be an important factor for the centre to consider.

10.7 The centre should consider the following factors when deciding if PGD is appropriate in particular cases:

    (a) the views of the people seeking treatment in relation to the condition to be avoided, including their previous reproductive experience

    (b) the likely degree of suffering associated with the condition

    (c) the availability of effective therapy, now and in the future

    (d) the speed of degeneration in progressive disorders

    (e) the extent of any intellectual impairment

    (f) the social support available, and

    (g) the family circumstances of the people seeking treatment.

Preimplantation genetic diagnosis for histocompatibility (tissue typing)

10.22 When deciding whether to use preimplantation tissue typing, the centre should consider the circumstances of each case individually, rather than the fact that the procedure is sought to provide tissue to treat a particular condition.

10.23 When deciding on the appropriateness of preimplantation tissue typing in a particular situation, the centre should consider the condition of the affected child, including:

    (a) the degree of suffering associated with their condition

    (b) the speed of degeneration in progressive disorders

    (c) the extent of any intellectual impairment

    (d) their prognosis, considering all treatment options available

    (e) the availability of alternative sources of tissue for treating them, now and in the future, and

    (f) the availability of effective therapy for them, now and in the future.

10.24 The centre should also consider the possible consequences for any child who may be born as a result, including:

    (a) any possible risks associated with embryo biopsy

    (b) the likely long-term emotional and psychological implications

    (c) whether they are likely to require intrusive surgery as a result of the treatment of the affected child (and whether this is likely to be repeated), and

    (d) any complications or predispositions associated with the tissue type to be selected.

10.25 The centre should also consider the family circumstances of the people seeking treatment, including:

    (a) their previous reproductive experience

    (b) their views and the affected child's views of the condition

    (c) the likelihood of a successful outcome, taking into account:

        (i) their reproductive circumstances (ie, the number of embryos likely to be available for testing in each treatment cycle, the number likely to be suitable for transfer, whether carrier embryos may be transferred, and the likely number of cycles)

        (ii) the likely outcome of treatment for the affected child

    (d) the consequences of an unsuccessful outcome

    (e) the demands of IVF/preimplantation testing treatment on them while caring for an affected child, and

    (f) the extent of social support available.

11 Donor recruitment, assessment and screening

Advertising

11.1 Advertising and publicity materials should be designed and written with regard to the sensitive issues involved in recruiting donors.

Age of prospective donors

11.2 Centres should refer to the relevant professional guidelines on age limits before accepting gametes for the treatment of others.

Note: Current professional guidelines state that eggs should not be taken from donors aged 36 or over, and sperm should not be taken from donors aged 41 or over.

11.3 For donated eggs, the relevant age limit should be observed unless there are exceptional reasons not to do so. The centre should record any such reasons in the patient's medical records.

11.4 For donated sperm, the relevant age limit should normally be observed. However, due to less substantial evidence on age limits for sperm donors, centres should assess the possible effect of the donor's age on a case-by-case basis. The centre should record in the patient's medical records the reasons for using a donor above the recommended age limit.

11.5 For donated embryos, the guidance above applies to both gamete providers.

11.6 Gametes for the treatment of others should not be taken from anyone under the age of 18.

Information for prospective donors

11.32 Before any consents or samples are obtained from a prospective donor, the recruiting centre should provide information about:

    (a) the screening that will be done, and why it is necessary

    (b) the possibility that the screening may reveal unsuspected conditions (eg, low sperm count, genetic anomalies or HIV infection) and the practical implications ...

    (m) the possibility that a donor-conceived person who is disabled as a result of an inherited condition that the donor knew about, or ought reasonably to have known about, but failed to disclose, may be able to sue the donor for damages.

Giving donors information about children born as a result of their donation

11. 37 The centre should inform donors that anyone born as a result of their donation will have access to the following non-identifying information provided by them, from the age of 16:

    (a) physical description (height, weight, and eye, hair and skin colours)

    (b) year and country of birth

    (c) ethnic group

    (d) whether the donor had any genetic children when they registered, and the number and sex of those children

    (e) other details the donor may have chosen to supply (eg, occupation, religion and interests)

    (f) the ethnic group(s) of the donor's parents

(g) whether the donor was adopted or donor conceived (if they are aware of this)
(h) marital status (at the time of donation)
(i)   details of any screening tests and medical history
(j)   skills
(k) reason for donating
(l)   goodwill message, and
(m) description of themselves as a person (pen portrait).

11.38 The centre should also inform donors who register or re-register after 31 March 2005 that anyone born as a result of their donation will have access to the following identifying information, from the age of 18:

(a) full names (and any previous names)
(b) date of birth, and town or district where born, and
(c) last known postal address (or address at time of registration).

11.39 The centre should inform identifiable donors that it will make a reasonable attempt to contact and forewarn them before disclosing identifiable details to anyone born as a result of their donation. The centre should encourage donors to provide up-to-date contact details to facilitate this.

Consent

11.45 The centre is not required to obtain the consent of the donor's partner or spouse. However, if the donor is married, in a civil partnership or in a long-term relationship, the centre should encourage them to seek their partner's support for the donation of their gametes.

13 Payments for donors
Payments for donors

13.1 Advertising or publicity aimed at recruiting gamete or embryo donors, or at encouraging donation, should not refer to the possibility of financial gain or similar advantage, although it may refer to compensation permitted under relevant HFEA Directions.

13.2 The person responsible has a duty to assure themselves that no payments or benefits (except those in line with relevant HFEA Directions) have been given or promised to the donor by another agency or intermediary, including introductory agencies.

13.3 Donors may be compensated with a fixed amount of money, as specified in HFEA Directions, which reasonably covers any financial losses incurred in connection with donating gametes provided to that centre.

13.4 If donors have incurred expenses (not including loss of earnings) that exceed the amounts specified in HFEA Directions, the centre may compensate donors with excess expenses in line with HFEA Directions.

13.5 The centre should ensure that donors understand that donating gametes and embryos is voluntary and unpaid and that they may be compensated only in line with relevant HFEA Directions.

13.6 If an egg donor becomes ill as a direct result of donating, the centre may also reimburse their reasonable expenses arising from the illness.

15 Procuring, processing and transporting gametes and embryos
Processing and disposal of gametes and embryos

15.13 The centre should take account of the special status of the human embryo when the development of an embryo is to be brought to an end. Terminating the development of embryos and disposing of the remaining material should be approached with appropriate sensitivity, having regard to the interests of the gamete providers and anyone for whose treatment the embryos were being kept.

20 Donor-assisted conception
Information for people seeking treatment with donated gametes and embryos

20.6 Women should not be treated with gametes, or with embryos derived from gametes, of more than one man or more than one woman during any treatment cycle.

The importance of informing children of their donor origins

20.7 The centre should tell people who seek treatment with donated gametes or embryos that it is best for any resulting child to be told about their origin early in childhood. There is evidence that finding out suddenly, later in life, about donor origins can be emotionally damaging to children and to family relations.

20.8 The centre should encourage and prepare patients to be open with their children from an early age about how they were conceived. The centre should give patients information about how counselling may allow them to explore the implications of treatment, in particular how information may be shared with any resultant children.

Access to information for donors, donor-conceived people and parents

20.10 The centre should inform people seeking treatment with donated gametes or embryos that the donor will be able to request the following information about any children born as a result of their donated gametes or embryos:

(a) the number of children born

(b) their sex, and

(c) their year of birth.

20.11 The centre should inform people seeking treatment with donated gametes or embryos that any resulting children will have access to the following non-identifying information about the donor (if the donor has provided it) from the age of 16:

(a) physical description (height, weight, and eye, hair and skin colours)

(b) year and country of birth

(c) ethnic group

(d) whether the donor had any genetic children when they registered, and the number and sex of those children

(e) other details the donor may have chosen to supply (eg, occupation, religion and interests)

(f) the ethnic group(s) of the donor's parents

(g) whether the donor was adopted or donor conceived (if they are aware of this)

(h) marital status (at the time of donation)

(i) details of any screening tests and medical history

(j) skills

(k) reason for donating

(l) goodwill message, and

(m) description of themselves as a person (pen portrait)

20.12 The centre should inform people seeking treatment with gametes or embryos donated after 31 March 2005, or with those donated before this date by a donor who subsequently re-registered as identifiable, that any children born as a result of the donation will have access to the following identifying information about the donor, from the age of 18:

(a) full names (and any previous names)

(b) date of birth, and town or district where born, and

(c) last known postal address (or address at time of registration).

Age of Legal Capacity (Scotland) Act 1991

(1991, c. 50)

Age of legal capacity

1.—(1) As from the commencement of this Act –

    (a) a person under the age of 16 years shall, subject to section 2 below, have no legal capacity to enter into any transaction;

    (b) a person of or over the age of 16 years shall have legal capacity to enter into any transaction.

Exceptions to general rule

2.—(4) A person under the age of 16 years shall have legal capacity to consent on his own behalf to any surgical, medical or dental procedure or treatment where, in the opinion of a qualified medical practitioner attending him, he is capable of understanding the nature and possible consequences of the procedure or treatment.

Adults with Incapacity (Scotland) Act 2000

(2000, asp 4)

PART 1

General

1 General principles and fundamental definitions

    (1) The principles set out in subsections (2) to (4) shall be given effect to in relation to any intervention in the affairs of an adult under or in pursuance of this Act, including any order made in or for the purpose of any proceedings under this Act for or in connection with an adult.

    (2) There shall be no intervention in the affairs of an adult unless the person responsible for authorising or effecting the intervention is satisfied that the intervention will benefit the adult and that such benefit cannot reasonably be achieved without the intervention.

    (3) Where it is determined that an intervention as mentioned in subsection (1) is to be made, such intervention shall be the least restrictive option in relation to the freedom of the adult, consistent with the purpose of the intervention.

    (4) In determining if an intervention is to be made and, if so, what intervention is to be made, account shall be taken of –

(a) the present and past wishes and feelings of the adult so far as they can be ascertained by any means of communication, whether human or by mechanical aid (whether of an interpretative nature or otherwise) appropriate to the adult;

(b) the views of the nearest relative and the primary carer of the adult, in so far as it is reasonable and practicable to do so;

(c) the views of –

    (i) any guardian, continuing attorney or welfare attorney of the adult who has powers relating to the proposed intervention; and

    (ii) any person whom the sheriff has directed to be consulted, in so far as it is reasonable and practicable to do so; and

(d) the views of any other person appearing to the person responsible for authorising or effecting the intervention to have an interest in the welfare of the adult or in the proposed intervention, where these views have been made known to the person responsible, in so far as it is reasonable and practicable to do so.

(5) Any guardian, continuing attorney, welfare attorney or manager of an establishment exercising functions under this Act or under any order of the sheriff in relation to an adult shall, in so far as it is reasonable and practicable to do so, encourage the adult to exercise whatever skills he has concerning his property, financial affairs or personal welfare, as the case may be, and to develop new such skills.

(6) For the purposes of this Act, and unless the context otherwise requires – 'adult' means a person who has attained the age of 16 years;

'incapable' means incapable of –

(a) acting; or

(b) making decisions; or

(c) communicating decisions; or

(d) understanding decisions; or

(e) retaining the memory of decisions, as mentioned in any provision of this Act, by reason of mental disorder or of inability to communicate because of physical disability; but a person shall not fall within this definition by reason only of a lack or deficiency in a faculty of communication if that lack or deficiency can be made good by human or mechanical aid (whether of an interpretative nature or otherwise); and

'incapacity' shall be construed accordingly.

Part VII

International

Declaration of Geneva, 1948*

At the time of being admitted as a member of the medical profession I solemnly pledge myself to consecrate my life to the service of humanity: I will give to my teachers the respect and gratitude which is their due; I will practice my profession with conscience and dignity; The health and life of my patient will be my first consideration; I will respect the secrets which are confided in me; I will maintain by all means in my power, the honor and the noble traditions of the medical profession; My colleagues will be my brothers: I will not permit considerations of religion, nationality, race, party politics or social standing to intervene between my duty and my patient; I will maintain the utmost respect for human life, from the time of its conception, even under threat, I will not use my medical knowledge contrary to the laws of humanity; I make these promises solemnly, freely and upon my honor ...

(The Second General Assembly of the World Medical Association 1948)

The Nuremberg Code

Trials of War Criminals before the Nuremberg Military Tribunals under Control Council Law No. 10: Nuremberg October 1946–April 1949. Washington: U.S. Government Printing Office (n.d.), vol. 2, pp. 181–182.

Permissible Medical Experiments

1. The voluntary consent of the human subject is absolutely essential. This means that the person involved should have legal capacity to give consent; should be so situated as to be able to exercise free power of choice, without the intervention of any element of force, fraud, deceit, duress, over-reaching, or other ulterior form of constraint or coercion; and should have sufficient knowledge and comprehension of the elements of the subject matter involved as to enable him to make an understanding and enlightened decision. This latter element requires that before the acceptance of an affirmative decision by the experimental subject there should be made known to him the nature, duration, and purpose of the experiment; the method and means by which it is to be conducted; all inconveniences and hazards reasonably to be expected; and the effects upon his health or person which may possibly come from his participation in the experiment.

The duty and responsibility for ascertaining the quality of the consent rests upon each individual who initiates, directs or engages in the experiment. It is a personal duty and responsibility which may not be delegated to another with impunity.

2. The experiment should be such as to yield fruitful results for the good of society, unprocurable by other methods or means of study, and not random and unnecessary in nature.

3. The experiment should be so designed and based on the results of animal experimentation and a knowledge of the natural history of the disease or other problem under study that the anticipated results will justify the performance of the experiment.

4. The experiment should be so conducted as to avoid all unnecessary physical and mental suffering and injury.

5. No experiment should be conducted where there is an a priori reason to believe that death or disabling injury will occur; except, perhaps, in those experiments where the experimental physicians also serve as subjects.

6. The degree of risk to be taken should never exceed that determined by the humanitarian importance of the problem to be solved by the experiment.

7. Proper preparations should be made and adequate facilities provided to protect the experimental subject against even remote possibilities of injury, disability, or death.

8. The experiment should be conducted only by scientifically qualified persons. The highest degree of skill and care should be required through all stages of the experiment of those who conduct or engage in the experiment.

9. During the course of the experiment the human subject should be at liberty to bring the experiment to an end if he has reached the physical or mental state where continuation of the experiment seems to him to be impossible.

10. During the course of the experiment the scientist in charge must be prepared to terminate the experiment at any stage, if he has probably cause to believe, in the exercise of the good faith, superior skill and careful judgment required of him that a continuation of the experiment is likely to result in injury, disability, or death to the experimental subject.

International Covenant on Economic, Social and Cultural Rights*

Adopted by General Assembly resolution 2200A (XXI) of 16 December 1966

Article 12

1. The States Parties to the present Covenant recognize the right of everyone to the enjoyment of the highest attainable standard of physical and mental health.

2. The steps to be taken by the States Parties to the present Covenant to achieve the full realization of this right shall include those necessary for:
   (a) The provision for the reduction of the stillbirth-rate and of infant mortality and for the healthy development of the child;
   (b) The improvement of all aspects of environmental and industrial hygiene;
   (c) The prevention, treatment and control of epidemic, endemic, occupational and other diseases;
   (d) The creation of conditions which would assure to all medical service and medical attention in the event of sickness.

Convention on the Rights of the Child 1989*

Adopted and opened for signature, ratification and accession by General Assembly resolution 44/25 of 20 November 1989

PART I

Article 1

For the purposes of the present Convention, a child means every human being below the age of eighteen years unless under the law applicable to the child, majority is attained earlier.

Article 3

1. In all actions concerning children, whether undertaken by public or private social welfare institutions, courts of law, administrative authorities or legislative bodies, the best interests of the child shall be a primary consideration.

2. States Parties undertake to ensure the child such protection and care as is necessary for his or her well-being, taking into account the rights and duties of his or her parents, legal guardians, or other individuals legally responsible for him or her, and, to this end, shall take all appropriate legislative and administrative measures.

3. States Parties shall ensure that the institutions, services and facilities responsible for the care or protection of children shall conform with the standards established by competent authorities, particularly in the areas of safety, health, in the number and suitability of their staff, as well as competent supervision.

Article 5

States Parties shall respect the responsibilities, rights and duties of parents or, where applicable, the members of the extended family or community as provided for by local custom, legal guardians or other persons legally responsible for the child, to provide, in a manner consistent with the evolving capacities of the child, appropriate direction and guidance in the exercise by the child of the rights recognized in the present Convention.

Article 6

1. States Parties recognize that every child has the inherent right to life.

2. States Parties shall ensure to the maximum extent possible the survival and development of the child.

Article 12

1. States Parties shall assure to the child who is capable of forming his or her own views the right to express those views freely in all matters affecting the child, the views of the child being given due weight in accordance with the age and maturity of the child.

2. For this purpose, the child shall in particular be provided the opportunity to be heard in any judicial and administrative proceedings affecting the child, either directly, or through a representative or an appropriate body, in a manner consistent with the procedural rules of national law.

Article 13

1. The child shall have the right to freedom of expression; this right shall include freedom to seek, receive and impart information and ideas of all kinds, regardless of frontiers, either orally, in writing or in print, in the form of art, or through any other media of the child's choice.

2. The exercise of this right may be subject to certain restrictions, but these shall only be such as are provided by law and are necessary:

    (a) For respect of the rights or reputations of others; or

    (b) For the protection of national security or of public order, or of public health or morals.

Article 14

1. States Parties shall respect the right of the child to freedom of thought, conscience and religion.

2. States Parties shall respect the rights and duties of the parents and, when applicable, legal guardians, to provide direction to the child in the exercise of his or her right in a manner consistent with the evolving capacities of the child.

3. Freedom to manifest one's religion or beliefs may be subject only to such limitations as are prescribed by law and are necessary to protect public safety, order, health or morals, or the fundamental rights and freedoms of others.

Article 16

1. No child shall be subjected to arbitrary or unlawful interference with his or her privacy, family, or correspondence, nor to unlawful attacks on his or her honour and reputation.

2. The child has the right to the protection of the law against such interference or attacks.

Article 18

1. States Parties shall use their best efforts to ensure recognition of the principle that both parents have common responsibilities for the upbringing and development of the child. Parents or, as the case may be, legal guardians, have the primary responsibility for the upbringing and development of the child. The best interests of the child will be their basic concern.

2. For the purpose of guaranteeing and promoting the rights set forth in the present Convention, States Parties shall render appropriate assistance to parents and legal guardians in the performance of their child-rearing responsibilities and shall ensure the development of institutions, facilities and services for the care of children.

3. States Parties shall take all appropriate measures to ensure that children of working parents have the right to benefit from child-care services and facilities for which they are eligible.

Article 19

1. States Parties shall take all appropriate legislative, administrative, social and educational measures to protect the child from all forms of physical or mental violence, injury or abuse, neglect or negligent treatment, maltreatment or exploitation, including sexual abuse, while in the care of parent(s), legal guardian(s) or any other person who has the care of the child.

Article 23

1. States Parties recognize that a mentally or physically disabled child should enjoy a full and decent life, in conditions which ensure dignity, promote self-reliance and facilitate the child's active participation in the community.

2. States Parties recognize the right of the disabled child to special care and shall encourage and ensure the extension, subject to available resources, to the eligible child and those responsible for his or her care, of assistance for which application is made and which is appropriate to the child's condition and to the circumstances of the parents or others caring for the child.

3. Recognizing the special needs of a disabled child, assistance extended in accordance with paragraph 2 of the present article shall be provided free of charge, whenever possible, taking into account the financial resources of the parents or others caring for the child, and shall be designed to ensure that the disabled child has effective access to and receives education, training, health care services, rehabilitation services, preparation for employment and recreation opportunities in a manner conducive to the child's achieving the fullest possible social integration and individual development, including his or her cultural and spiritual development

4. States Parties shall promote, in the spirit of international cooperation, the exchange of appropriate information in the field of preventive health care and of medical, psychological and functional treatment of disabled children, including dissemination of and access to information concerning methods of rehabilitation, education and vocational services, with the aim of enabling States Parties to improve their capabilities and skills and to widen their experience in these areas. In this regard, particular account shall be taken of the needs of developing countries.

Article 24

1. States Parties recognize the right of the child to the enjoyment of the highest attainable standard of health and to facilities for the treatment of illness and rehabilitation of health. States Parties shall strive to ensure that no child is deprived of his or her right of access to such health care services.

2. States Parties shall pursue full implementation of this right and, in particular, shall take appropriate measures:

   (a) To diminish infant and child mortality;
   (b) To ensure the provision of necessary medical assistance and health care to all children with emphasis on the development of primary health care;
   (c) To combat disease and malnutrition, including within the framework of primary health care, through, inter alia, the application of readily available technology and through the provision of adequate nutritious foods and clean drinking-water, taking into consideration the dangers and risks of environmental pollution;
   (d) To ensure appropriate pre-natal and post-natal health care for mothers;
   (e) To ensure that all segments of society, in particular parents and children, are informed, have access to education and are supported in the use of basic knowledge of child health and nutrition, the advantages of breastfeeding, hygiene and environmental sanitation and the prevention of accidents;
   (f) To develop preventive health care, guidance for parents and family planning education and services.

3. States Parties shall take all effective and appropriate measures with a view to abolishing traditional practices prejudicial to the health of children.

4. States Parties undertake to promote and encourage international co-operation with a view to achieving progressively the full realization of the right recognized in the present article. In this regard, particular account shall be taken of the needs of developing countries.

Article 25

States Parties recognize the right of a child who has been placed by the competent authorities for the purposes of care, protection or treatment of his or her physical or mental health, to a periodic review of the treatment provided to the child and all other circumstances relevant to his or her placement.

Universal Declaration on the Human Genome and Human Rights*

UNESCO, 29th Session, 11 November 1997

A. Human dignity and the human genome

Article 1

The human genome underlies the fundamental unity of all members of the human family, as well as the recognition of their inherent dignity and diversity. In a symbolic sense, it is the heritage of humanity.

Article 2

   (a) Everyone has a right to respect for their dignity and for their rights regardless of their genetic characteristics.
   (b) That dignity makes it imperative not to reduce individuals to their genetic characteristics and to respect their uniqueness and diversity.

Article 3

The human genome, which by its nature evolves, is subject to mutations. It contains potentialities that are expressed differently according to each individual's natural and social environment, including the individual's state of health, living conditions, nutrition and education.

Article 4

The human genome in its natural state shall not give rise to financial gains.

B. Rights of the persons concerned

Article 5

(a) Research, treatment or diagnosis affecting an individual's genome shall be undertaken only after rigorous and prior assessment of the potential risks and benefits pertaining thereto and in accordance with any other requirement of national law.

(b) In all cases, the prior, free and informed consent of the person concerned shall be obtained. If the latter is not in a position to consent, consent or authorization shall be obtained in the manner prescribed by law, guided by the person's best interest.

(c) The right of each individual to decide whether or not to be informed of the results of genetic examination and the resulting consequences should be respected.

(d) In the case of research, protocols shall, in addition, be submitted for prior review in accordance with relevant national and international research standards or guidelines.

(e) If according to the law a person does not have the capacity to consent, research affecting his or her genome may only be carried out for his or her direct health benefit, subject to the authorization and the protective conditions prescribed by law. Research which does not have an expected direct health benefit may only be undertaken by way of exception, with the utmost restraint, exposing the person only to a minimal risk and minimal burden and if the research is intended to contribute to the health benefit of other persons in the same age category or with the same genetic condition, subject to the conditions prescribed by law, and provided such research is compatible with the protection of the individual's human rights.

Article 6

No one shall be subjected to discrimination based on genetic characteristics that is intended to infringe or has the effect of infringing human rights, fundamental freedoms and human dignity.

Article 7

Genetic data associated with an identifiable person and stored or processed for the purposes of research or any other purpose must be held confidential in the conditions set by law.

Article 8

Every individual shall have the right, according to international and national law, to just reparation for any damage sustained as a direct and determining result of an intervention affecting his or her genome.

Article 9

In order to protect human rights and fundamental freedoms, limitations to the principles of consent and confidentiality may only be prescribed by law, for compelling reasons within the bounds of public international law and the international law of human rights.

C. Research on the human genome

Article 10

No research or research applications concerning the human genome, in particular in the fields of biology, genetics and medicine, should prevail over respect for the human rights, fundamental freedoms and human dignity of individuals or, where applicable, of groups of people.

Article 11

Practices which are contrary to human dignity, such as reproductive cloning of human beings, shall not be permitted. States and competent international organizations are invited to co-operate in identifying such practices and in taking, at national or international level, the measures necessary to ensure that the principles set out in this Declaration are respected.

Article 12

(a) Benefits from advances in biology, genetics and medicine, concerning the human genome, shall be made available to all, with due regard for the dignity and human rights of each individual.

(b) Freedom of research, which is necessary for the progress of knowledge, is part of freedom of thought. The applications of research, including applications in biology, genetics and medicine, concerning the human genome, shall seek to offer relief from suffering and improve the health of individuals and humankind as a whole.

D. Conditions for the exercise of scientific activity

Article 13

The responsibilities inherent in the activities of researchers, including meticulousness, caution, intellectual honesty and integrity in carrying out their research as well as in the presentation and utilization of their findings, should be the subject of particular attention in the framework of research on the human genome, because of its ethical and social implications. Public and private science policy-makers also have particular responsibilities in this respect.

Article 14

States should take appropriate measures to foster the intellectual and material conditions favourable to freedom in the conduct of research on the human genome and to consider the ethical, legal, social and economic implications of such research, on the basis of the principles set out in this Declaration.

Article 15

States should take appropriate steps to provide the framework for the free exercise of Research on the human genome with due regard for the principles set out in this Declaration, in order to safeguard respect for human rights, fundamental freedoms and human dignity and to protect public health. They should seek to ensure that research results are not used for non-peaceful purposes.

Article 16

States should recognize the value of promoting, at various levels, as appropriate, the establishment of independent, multidisciplinary and pluralist ethics committees to assess the ethical, legal and social issues raised by research on the human genome and its applications.

E. Solidarity and international co-operation

Article 17

States should respect and promote the practice of solidarity towards individuals, families and population groups who are particularly vulnerable to or affected by disease or disability of a genetic character. They should foster, inter alia, research on the identification, prevention and treatment of genetically based and genetically influenced diseases, in particular rare as well as endemic diseases which affect large numbers of the world's population.

Article 18

States should make every effort, with due and appropriate regard for the principles set out in this Declaration, to continue fostering the international dissemination of scientific knowledge concerning the human genome, human diversity and genetic research and, in that regard, to foster scientific and cultural co-operation, particularly between industrialized and developing countries.

Article 19

 (a) In the framework of international co-operation with developing countries, states should seek to encourage measures enabling:

  (i) assessment of the risks and benefits pertaining to research on the human genome to be carried out and abuse to be prevented;

  (ii) the capacity of developing countries to carry out research on human biology and genetics, taking into consideration their specific problems, to be developed and strengthened;

  (iii) developing countries to benefit from the achievements of scientific and technological research so that their use in favour of economic and social progress can be to the benefit of all;

  (iv) the free exchange of scientific knowledge and information in the areas of biology, genetics and medicine to be promoted.

 (b) Relevant international organizations should support and promote the initiatives taken by states for the above-mentioned purposes.

F. Promotion of the principles set out in the Declaration

Article 20

States should take appropriate measures to promote the principles set out in the Declaration, through education and relevant means, inter alia through the conduct of research and training in interdisciplinary fields and through the promotion of education in bioethics, at all levels, in particular for those responsible for science policies.

Article 21

States should take appropriate measures to encourage other forms of research, training and information dissemination conducive to raising the awareness of society and all of its members of their responsibilities regarding the fundamental issues relating to the defence of human dignity which may be raised by research in biology, in genetics and in medicine, and its applications. They should also undertake to facilitate on this subject an open international discussion, ensuring the free expression of various sociocultural, religious and philosophical opinions.

G. Implementation of the Declaration

Article 22

States should make every effort to promote the principles set out in this Declaration and should, by means of all appropriate measures, promote their implementation.

Article 23

States should take appropriate measures to promote, through education, training and information dissemination, respect for the above-mentioned principles and to foster their recognition and effective application. States should also encourage exchanges and networks among independent ethics committees, as they are established, to foster full collaboration.

Article 24

The International Bioethics Committee of UNESCO should contribute to the dissemination of the principles set out in this Declaration and to the further examination of issues raised by their applications and by the evolution of the technologies in question. It should organize appropriate consultations with parties concerned, such as vulnerable groups. It should make recommendations, in accordance with UNESCO's statutory procedures, addressed to the General Conference and give advice concerning the follow-up of this Declaration, in particular regarding the identification of practices that could be contrary to human dignity, such as germ-line interventions.

Article 25

Nothing in this Declaration may be interpreted as implying for any state, group or person any claim to engage in any activity or to perform any act contrary to human rights and fundamental freedoms, including the principles set out in this Declaration.

Convention for the Protection of Human Rights and Dignity of the Human Being with regard to the Application of Biology and Medicine: Convention on Human Rights and Biomedicine 1997*

Chapter I General provisions

Article 1   Purpose and object

Parties to this Convention shall protect the dignity and identity of all human beings and guarantee everyone, without discrimination, respect for their integrity and other rights and fundamental freedoms with regard to the application of biology and medicine.

Each Party shall take in its internal law the necessary measures to give effect to the provisions of this Convention.

Article 2   Primacy of the human being

The interests and welfare of the human being shall prevail over the sole interest of society or science.

Article 3   Equitable access to health care

Parties, taking into account health needs and available resources, shall take appropriate measures with a view to providing, within their jurisdiction, equitable access to health care of appropriate quality.

Article 4   Professional standards

Any intervention in the health field, including research, must be carried out in accordance with relevant professional obligations and standards.

Chapter II Consent

Article 5   General rule

An intervention in the health field may only be carried out after the person concerned has given free and informed consent to it.

This person shall beforehand be given appropriate information as to the purpose and nature of the intervention as well as on its consequences and risks.

The person concerned may freely withdraw consent at any time.

Article 6   Protection of persons not able to consent

1. Subject to Articles 17 and 20 below, an intervention may only be carried out on a person who does not have the capacity to consent, for his or her direct benefit.

2. Where, according to law, a minor does not have the capacity to consent to an intervention, the intervention may only be carried out with the authorisation of his or her representative or an authority or a person or body provided for by law.

---

* Reproduced with permission from the Council of Europe. An explanatory report to accompany this legal text can be found on their website: http://www.coe.int/.
European Treaty Series—No. 164

The opinion of the minor shall be taken into consideration as an increasingly determining factor in proportion to his or her age and degree of maturity.

3. Where, according to law, an adult does not have the capacity to consent to an intervention because of a mental disability, a disease or for similar reasons, the intervention may only be carried out with the authorisation of his or her representative or an authority or a person or body provided for by law.

The individual concerned shall as far as possible take part in the authorisation procedure.

4. The representative, the authority, the person or the body mentioned in paragraphs 2 and 3 above shall be given, under the same conditions, the information referred to in Article 5.

5. The authorisation referred to in paragraphs 2 and 3 above may be withdrawn at any time in the best interests of the person concerned.

Article 7   Protection of persons who have a mental disorder

Subject to protective conditions prescribed by law, including supervisory, control and appeal procedures, a person who has a mental disorder of a serious nature may be subjected, without his or her consent, to an intervention aimed at treating his or her mental disorder only where, without such treatment, serious harm is likely to result to his or her health.

Article 8   Emergency situation

When because of an emergency situation the appropriate consent cannot be obtained, any medically necessary intervention may be carried out immediately for the benefit of the health of the individual concerned.

Article 9   Previously expressed wishes

The previously expressed wishes relating to a medical intervention by a patient who is not, at the time of the intervention, in a state to express his or her wishes shall be taken into account.

Chapter III Private life and right to information

Article 10   Private life and right to information

1. Everyone has the right to respect for private life in relation to information about his or her health.

2. Everyone is entitled to know any information collected about his or her health. However, the wishes of individuals not to be so informed shall be observed.

3. In exceptional cases, restrictions may be placed by law on the exercise of the rights contained in paragraph 2 in the interests of the patient.

Chapter IV Human genome

Article 11   Non-discrimination

Any form of discrimination against a person on grounds of his or her genetic heritage is prohibited.

Article 12   Predictive genetic tests

Tests which are predictive of genetic diseases or which serve either to identify the subject as a carrier of a gene responsible for a disease or to detect a genetic predisposition or susceptibility to a disease may be performed only for health purposes or for scientific research linked to health purposes, and subject to appropriate genetic counselling.

Article 13   Interventions on the human genome

An intervention seeking to modify the human genome may only be undertaken for preventive, diagnostic or therapeutic purposes and only if its aim is not to introduce any modification in the genome of any descendants.

Article 14   Non-selection of sex

The use of techniques of medically assisted procreation shall not be allowed for the purpose of choosing a future child's sex, except where serious hereditary sex-related disease is to be avoided.

Chapter V   Scientific research

Article 15   General rule

Scientific research in the field of biology and medicine shall be carried out freely, subject to the provisions of this Convention and the other legal provisions ensuring the protection of the human being.

Article 16   Protection of persons undergoing research

Research on a person may only be undertaken if all the following conditions are met:

    i   there is no alternative of comparable effectiveness to research on humans;

    ii the risks which may be incurred by that person are not disproportionate to the potential benefits of the research;

    iii the research project has been approved by the competent body after independent examination of its scientific merit, including assessment of the importance of the aim of the research, and multidisciplinary review of its ethical acceptability;

    iv the persons undergoing research have been informed of their rights and the safeguards prescribed by law for their protection;

    v   the necessary consent as provided for under Article 5 has been given expressly, specifically and is documented. Such consent may be freely withdrawn at any time.

Article 17   Protection of persons not able to consent to research

1. Research on a person without the capacity to consent as stipulated in Article 5 may be undertaken only if all the following conditions are met:

    i   the conditions laid down in Article 16, sub-paragraphs i to iv, are fulfilled;

    ii the results of the research have the potential to produce real and direct benefit to his or her health;

    iii research of comparable effectiveness cannot be carried out on individuals capable of giving consent;

    iv the necessary authorisation provided for under Article 6 has been given specifically and in writing; and

    v the person concerned does not object.

2. Exceptionally and under the protective conditions prescribed by law, where the research has not the potential to produce results of direct benefit to the health of the person concerned, such research may be authorised subject to the conditions laid down in paragraph 1, sub-paragraphs i, iii, iv and v above, and to the following additional conditions:

    i   the research has the aim of contributing, through significant improvement in the scientific understanding of the individual's condition, disease or disorder, to the ultimate attainment of results capable of conferring benefit to the person concerned or to other persons in the same age category or afflicted with the same disease or disorder or having the same condition;

    ii the research entails only minimal risk and minimal burden for the individual concerned.

Article 18   Research on embryos in vitro

1. Where the law allows research on embryos *in vitro*, it shall ensure adequate protection of the embryo.

2. The creation of human embryos for research purposes is prohibited.

Chapter VI Organ and tissue removal from living donors for transplantation purposes

Article 19 General rule

1. Removal of organs or tissue from a living person for transplantation purposes may be carried out solely for the therapeutic benefit of the recipient and where there is no suitable organ or tissue available from a deceased person and no other alternative therapeutic method of comparable effectiveness.

2. The necessary consent as provided for under Article 5 must have been given expressly and specifically either in written form or before an official body.

Article 20 Protection of persons not able to consent to organ removal

1. No organ or tissue removal may be carried out on a person who does not have the capacity to consent under Article 5.

2. Exceptionally and under the protective conditions prescribed by law, the removal of regenerative tissue from a person who does not have the capacity to consent may be authorised provided the following conditions are met:

    i   there is no compatible donor available who has the capacity to consent;

    ii   the recipient is a brother or sister of the donor;

    iii   the donation must have the potential to be life-saving for the recipient;

    iv   the authorisation provided for under paragraphs 2 and 3 of Article 6 has been given specifically and in writing, in accordance with the law and with the approval of the competent body;

    v   the potential donor concerned does not object.

Chapter VII Prohibition of financial gain and disposal of a part of the human body

Article 21 Prohibition of financial gain

The human body and its parts shall not, as such, give rise to financial gain.

Article 22 Disposal of a removed part of the human body

When in the course of an intervention any part of a human body is removed, it may be stored and used for a purpose other than that for which it was removed, only if this is done in conformity with appropriate information and consent procedures.

Chapter VIII Infringements of the provisions of the Convention

Article 23 Infringement of the rights or principles

The Parties shall provide appropriate judicial protection to prevent or to put a stop to an unlawful infringement of the rights and principles set forth in this Convention at short notice.

Article 24 Compensation for undue damage

The person who has suffered undue damage resulting from an intervention is entitled to fair compensation according to the conditions and procedures prescribed by law.

Article 25 Sanctions

Parties shall provide for appropriate sanctions to be applied in the event of infringement of the provisions contained in this Convention.

Chapter IX Relation between this convention and other provisions

Article 26 Restrictions on the exercise of the rights

1. No restrictions shall be placed on the exercise of the rights and protective provisions contained in this Convention other than such as are prescribed by law and are necessary in a democratic society in the interest of public safety, for the prevention of crime, for the protection of public health or for the protection of the rights and freedoms of others.

2. The restrictions contemplated in the preceding paragraph may not be placed on Articles 11, 13, 14, 16, 17, 19, 20 and 21.

Article 27 Wider protection

None of the provisions of this Convention shall be interpreted as limiting or otherwise affecting the possibility for a Party to grant a wider measure of protection with regard to the application of biology and medicine than is stipulated in this Convention.

Chapter X Public debate

Article 28 Public debate

Parties to this Convention shall see to it that the fundamental questions raised by the developments of biology and medicine are the subject of appropriate public discussion in the light, in particular, of relevant medical, social, economic, ethical and legal implications, and that their possible application is made the subject of appropriate consultation.

Chapter XI Interpretation and follow-up of the Convention

Article 29 Interpretation of the Convention

The European Court of Human Rights may give, without direct reference to any specific proceedings pending in a court, advisory opinions on legal questions concerning the interpretation of the present Convention at the request of:

- the Government of a Party, after having informed the other Parties;
- the Committee set up by Article 32, with membership restricted to the Representatives of the Parties to this Convention, by a decision adopted by a two-thirds majority of votes cast.

Article 30 Reports on the application of the Convention

On receipt of a request from the Secretary General of the Council of Europe any Party shall furnish an explanation of the manner in which its internal law ensures the effective implementation of any of the provisions of the Convention.

Additional Protocol to the Convention for the Protection of Human Rights and Dignity of the Human Being with regard to the Application of Biology and Medicine, on the Prohibition of Cloning Human Beings*

(Paris, 12.I.1998)

European Treaty Series—No. 168

---

* Reproduced with permission from the Council of Europe. An explanatory report to accompany this legal text can be found on their website: http://www.coe.int/.

Article 1

1. Any intervention seeking to create a human being genetically identical to another human being, whether living or dead, is prohibited.

2. For the purpose of this article, the term human being 'genetically identical' to another human being means a human being sharing with another the same nuclear gene set.

Article 2

No derogation from the provisions of this Protocol shall be made under Article 26, paragraph 1, of the Convention.

Additional Protocol to the Convention on Human Rights and Biomedicine concerning Transplantation of Organs and Tissues of Human Origin*

(Strasbourg, 24.I.2002)

European Treaty Series—No. 186

Chapter I Object and scope

Article 1   Object

Parties to this Protocol shall protect the dignity and identity of everyone and guarantee, without discrimination, respect for his or her integrity and other rights and fundamental freedoms with regard to transplantation of organs and tissues of human origin.

Article 2   Scope and definitions

1. This Protocol applies to the transplantation of organs and tissues of human origin carried out for therapeutic purposes.

2. The provisions of this Protocol applicable to tissues shall apply also to cells, including haem-atopoietic stem cells.

3. The Protocol does not apply:
   a. to reproductive organs and tissue;
   b. to embryonic or foetal organs and tissues;
   c. to blood and blood derivatives.

4. For the purposes of this Protocol:
   – the term 'transplantation' covers the complete process of removal of an organ or tissue from one person and implantation of that organ or tissue into another person, including all procedures for preparation, preservation and storage;
   – subject to the provisions of Article 20, the term 'removal' refers to removal for the purposes of implantation.

Chapter II General provisions

Article 3   Transplantation system

Parties shall guarantee that a system exists to provide equitable access to transplantation services for patients.

Subject to the provisions of Chapter III, organs and, where appropriate, tissues shall be allocated only among patients on an official waiting list, in conformity with transparent, objective and duly

---

* Reproduced with permission from the Council of Europe. An explanatory report to accompany this legal text can be found on their website: http://www.coe.int/.

justified rules according to medical criteria. The persons or bodies responsible for the allocation decision shall be designated within this framework.

In case of international organ exchange arrangements, the procedures must also ensure justified, effective distribution across the participating countries in a manner that takes into account the solidarity principle within each country.

The transplantation system shall ensure the collection and recording of the information required to ensure traceability of organs and tissues.

Article 4   Professional standards

Any intervention in the field of organ or tissue transplantation must be carried out in accordance with relevant professional obligations and standards.

Article 5   Information for the recipient

The recipient and, where appropriate, the person or body providing authorisation for the implantation shall beforehand be given appropriate information as to the purpose and nature of the implantation, its consequences and risks, as well as on the alternatives to the intervention.

Article 6   Health and safety

All professionals involved in organ or tissue transplantation shall take all reasonable measures to minimise the risks of transmission of any disease to the recipient and to avoid any action which might affect the suitability of an organ or tissue for implantation.

Article 7   Medical follow-up

Appropriate medical follow-up shall be offered to living donors and recipients after transplantation.

Article 8   Information for health professionals and the public

Parties shall provide information for health professionals and for the public in general on the need for organs and tissues. They shall also provide information on the conditions relating to removal and implantation of organs and tissues, including matters relating to consent or authorisation, in particular with regard to removal from deceased persons.

Chapter III   Organ and tissue removal from living persons

Article 9   General rule

Removal of organs or tissue from a living person may be carried out solely for the therapeutic benefit of the recipient and where there is no suitable organ or tissue available from a deceased person and no other alternative therapeutic method of comparable effectiveness.

Article 10   Potential organ donors

Organ removal from a living donor may be carried out for the benefit of a recipient with whom the donor has a close personal relationship as defined by law, or, in the absence of such relationship, only under the conditions defined by law and with the approval of an appropriate independent body.

Article 11   Evaluation of risks for the donor

Before organ or tissue removal, appropriate medical investigations and interventions shall be carried out to evaluate and reduce physical and psychological risks to the health of the donor. The removal may not be carried out if there is a serious risk to the life or health of the donor.

Article 12   Information for the donor

The donor and, where appropriate, the person or body providing authorisation according to Article 14, paragraph 2, of this Protocol, shall beforehand be given appropriate information as to the purpose and nature of the removal as well as on its consequences and risks. They shall also be informed of the rights and the safeguards prescribed by law for the protection of the donor. In particular, they shall be informed of the right to have access to independent advice about such risks by a health professional having appropriate experience and who is not involved in the organ or tissue removal or subsequent transplantation procedures.

Article 13   Consent of the living donor

Subject to Articles 14 and 15 of this Protocol, an organ or tissue may be removed from a living donor only after the person concerned has given free, informed and specific consent to it either in written form or before an official body.

　　The person concerned may freely withdraw consent at any time.

Article 14   Protection of persons not able to consent to organ or tissue removal

　　1. No organ or tissue removal may be carried out on a person who does not have the capacity to consent under Article 13 of this Protocol.

　　2. Exceptionally, and under the protective conditions prescribed by law, the removal of regenerative tissue from a person who does not have the capacity to consent may be authorised provided the following conditions are met:

　　　i　there is no compatible donor available who has the capacity to consent;
　　　ii　the recipient is a brother or sister of the donor;
　　　iii　the donation has the potential to be life-saving for the recipient;
　　　iv　the authorisation of his or her representative or an authority or a person or body provided for by law has been given specifically and in writing and with the approval of the competent body;
　　　v　the potential donor concerned does not object.

Article 15   Cell removal from a living donor

The law may provide that the provisions of Article 14, paragraph 2, indents ii and iii, shall not apply to cells insofar as it is established that their removal only implies minimal risk and minimal burden for the donor.

Chapter IV Organ and tissue removal from deceased persons

Article 16   Certification of death

Organs or tissues shall not be removed from the body of a deceased person unless that person has been certified dead in accordance with the law.

　　The doctors certifying the death of a person shall not be the same doctors who participate directly in removal of organs or tissues from the deceased person, or subsequent transplantation procedures, or having responsibilities for the care of potential organ or tissue recipients.

Article 17   Consent and authorisation

　　Organs or tissues shall not be removed from the body of a deceased person unless consent or authorisation required by law has been obtained.

　　The removal shall not be carried out if the deceased person had objected to it.

Article 18   Respect for the human body

During removal the human body must be treated with respect and all reasonable measures shall be taken to restore the appearance of the corpse.

Article 19   Promotion of donation

Parties shall take all appropriate measures to promote the donation of organs and tissues.

Chapter V Implantation of an organ or tissue removed for a purpose other than donation for implantation

Article 20   Implantation of an organ or tissue removed for a purpose other than donation for implantation

　　1. When an organ or tissue is removed from a person for a purpose other than donation for implantation, it may only be implanted if the consequences and possible risks have been explained to

that person and his or her informed consent, or appropriate authorisation in the case of a person not able to consent, has been obtained.

2. All the provisions of this Protocol apply to the situations referred to in paragraph 1, except for those in Chapter III and IV.

Chapter VI Prohibition of financial gain

Article 21   Prohibition of financial gain

1. The human body and its parts shall not, as such, give rise to financial gain or comparable advantage.

The aforementioned provision shall not prevent payments which do not constitute a financial gain or a comparable advantage, in particular:
- compensation of living donors for loss of earnings and any other justifiable expenses caused by the removal or by the related medical examinations;
- payment of a justifiable fee for legitimate medical or related technical services rendered in connection with transplantation;
- compensation in case of undue damage resulting from the removal of organs or tissues from living persons.

2. Advertising the need for, or availability of, organs or tissues, with a view to offering or seeking financial gain or comparable advantage, shall be prohibited.

Article 22   Prohibition of organ and tissue trafficking

Organ and tissue trafficking shall be prohibited.

Chapter VII Confidentiality

Article 23   Confidentiality

1. All personal data relating to the person from whom organs or tissues have been removed and those relating to the recipient shall be considered to be confidential. Such data may only be collected, processed and communicated according to the rules relating to professional confidentiality and personal data protection.

2. The provisions of paragraph 1 shall be interpreted without prejudice to the provisions making possible, subject to appropriate safeguards, the collection, processing and communication of the necessary information about the person from whom organs or tissues have been removed or the recipient(s) of organs and tissues in so far as this is required for medical purposes, including traceability, as provided for in Article 3 of this Protocol.

Chapter VIII Infringements of the provisions of the Protocol

Article 24   Infringements of rights or principles

Parties shall provide appropriate judicial protection to prevent or to put a stop to an unlawful infringement of the rights and principles set forth in this Protocol at short notice.

Article 25   Compensation for undue damage

The person who has suffered undue damage resulting from transplantation procedures is entitled to fair compensation according to the conditions and procedures prescribed by law.

Article 26   Sanctions

Parties shall provide for appropriate sanctions to be applied in the event of infringement of the provisions contained in this Protocol.

Chapter IX Co-operation between Parties

Article 27   Co-operation between Parties

Parties shall take appropriate measures to ensure that there is efficient co-operation between them on organ and tissue transplantation, *inter alia* through information exchange.

In particular, they shall undertake appropriate measures to facilitate the rapid and safe transportation of organs and tissues to and from their territory.

Optional Protocol to the Convention against Torture and other Cruel, Inhuman or Degrading Treatment or Punishment*

Adopted 18 December 2002 by General Assembly resolution A/RES/57/199.

PART I GENERAL PRINCIPLES

Article 1

The objective of the present Protocol is to establish a system of regular visits undertaken by independent international and national bodies to places where people are deprived of their liberty, in order to prevent torture and other cruel, inhuman or degrading treatment or punishment.

Article 2

1. A Subcommittee on Prevention of Torture and Other Cruel, Inhuman or Degrading Treatment or Punishment of the Committee against Torture (hereinafter referred to as the Subcommittee on Prevention) shall be established and shall carry out the functions laid down in the present Protocol.

2. The Subcommittee on Prevention shall carry out its work within the framework of the Charter of the United Nations and shall be guided by the purposes and principles thereof, as well as the norms of the United Nations concerning the treatment of people deprived of their liberty.

3. Equally, the Subcommittee on Prevention shall be guided by the principles of confidentiality, impartiality, non-selectivity, universality and objectivity.

Article 3

Each State Party shall set up, designate or maintain at the domestic level one or several visiting bodies for the prevention of torture and other cruel, inhuman or degrading treatment or punishment (hereinafter referred to as the national preventive mechanism).

Article 4

1. Each State Party shall allow visits, in accordance with the present Protocol, by the mechanisms referred to in articles 2 and 3 to any place under its jurisdiction and control where persons are or may be deprived of their liberty, either by virtue of an order given by a public authority or at its instigation or with its consent or acquiescence (hereinafter referred to as places of detention). These visits shall be undertaken with a view to strengthening, if necessary, the protection of these persons against torture and other cruel, inhuman or degrading treatment or punishment.

2. For the purposes of the present Protocol, deprivation of liberty means any form of detention or imprisonment or the placement of a person in a public or private custodial setting which that person is not permitted to leave at will by order of any judicial, administrative or other authority.

PART III MANDATE OF THE SUBCOMMITTEE ON PREVENTION

Article 11

1. The Subcommittee on Prevention shall:
   (a) Visit the places referred to in article 4 and make recommendations to States Parties concerning the protection of persons deprived of their liberty against torture and other cruel, inhuman or degrading treatment or punishment;
   (b) In regard to the national preventive mechanisms:
      (i)   Advise and assist States Parties, when necessary, in their establishment;
      (ii) Maintain direct, and if necessary confidential, contact with the national preventive mechanisms and offer them training and technical assistance with a view to strengthening their capacities;
      (iii) Advise and assist them in the evaluation of the needs and the means necessary to strengthen the protection of persons deprived of their liberty against torture and other cruel, inhuman or degrading treatment or punishment;
      (iv) Make recommendations and observations to the States Parties with a view to strengthening the capacity and the mandate of the national preventive mechanisms for the prevention of torture and other cruel, inhuman or degrading treatment or punishment;
   (c) Cooperate, for the prevention of torture in general, with the relevant United Nations organs and mechanisms as well as with the international, regional and national institutions or organizations working towards the strengthening of the protection of all persons against torture and other cruel, inhuman or degrading treatment or punishment.

Article 12

In order to enable the Subcommittee on Prevention to comply with its mandate as laid down in article 11, the States Parties undertake:
   (a) To receive the Subcommittee on Prevention in their territory and grant it access to the places of detention as defined in article 4 of the present Protocol;
   (b) To provide all relevant information the Subcommittee on Prevention may request to evaluate the needs and measures that should be adopted to strengthen the protection of persons deprived of their liberty against torture and other cruel, inhuman or degrading treatment or punishment;
   (c) To encourage and facilitate contacts between the Subcommittee on Prevention and the national preventive mechanisms;
   (d) To examine the recommendations of the Subcommittee on Prevention and enter into dialogue with it on possible implementation measures.

Article 14

1. In order to enable the Subcommittee on Prevention to fulfil its mandate, the States Parties to the present Protocol undertake to grant it:
   (a) Unrestricted access to all information concerning the number of persons deprived of their liberty in places of detention as defined in article 4, as well as the number of places and their location;
   (b) Unrestricted access to all information referring to the treatment of those persons as well as their conditions of detention;
   (c) Subject to paragraph 2 below, unrestricted access to all places of detention and their installations and facilities;
   (d) The opportunity to have private interviews with the persons deprived of their liberty without witnesses, either personally or with a translator if deemed necessary, as well as

with any other person who the Subcommittee on Prevention believes may supply relevant information;

(e) The liberty to choose the places it wants to visit and the persons it wants to interview.

2. Objection to a visit to a particular place of detention may be made only on urgent and compelling grounds of national defence, public safety, natural disaster or serious disorder in the place to be visited that temporarily prevent the carrying out of such a visit. The existence of a declared state of emergency as such shall not be invoked by a State Party as a reason to object to a visit.

Article 15

No authority or official shall order, apply, permit or tolerate any sanction against any person or organization for having communicated to the Subcommittee on Prevention or to its delegates any information, whether true or false, and no such person or organization shall be otherwise prejudiced in any way.

Article 16

1. The Subcommittee on Prevention shall communicate its recommendations and observations confidentially to the State Party and, if relevant, to the national preventive mechanism.

2. The Subcommittee on Prevention shall publish its report, together with any comments of the State Party concerned, whenever requested to do so by that State Party. If the State Party makes part of the report public, the Subcommittee on Prevention may publish the report in whole or in part. However, no personal data shall be published without the express consent of the person concerned.

3. The Subcommittee on Prevention shall present a public annual report on its activities to the Committee against Torture.

4. If the State Party refuses to cooperate with the Subcommittee on Prevention according to articles 12 and 14, or to take steps to improve the situation in the light of the recommendations of the Subcommittee on Prevention, the Committee against Torture may, at the request of the Subcommittee on Prevention, decide, by a majority of its members, after the State Party has had an opportunity to make its views known, to make a public statement on the matter or to publish the report of the Subcommittee on Prevention.

PART IV NATIONAL PREVENTIVE MECHANISMS

Article 17

Each State Party shall maintain, designate or establish, at the latest one year after the entry into force of the present Protocol or of its ratification or accession, one or several independent national preventive mechanisms for the prevention of torture at the domestic level. Mechanisms established by decentralized units may be designated as national preventive mechanisms for the purposes of the present Protocol if they are in conformity with its provisions.

Article 18

1. The States Parties shall guarantee the functional independence of the national preventive mechanisms as well as the independence of their personnel.

2. The States Parties shall take the necessary measures to ens ure that the experts of the national preventive mechanism have the required capabilities and professional knowledge. They shall strive for a gender balance and the adequate representation of ethnic and minority groups in the country.

3. The States Parties undertake to make available the necessary resources for the functioning of the national preventive mechanisms.

4. When establishing national preventive mechanisms, States Parties shall give due consideration to the Principles relating to the status of national institutions for the promotion and protection of human rights.

Article 19

The national preventive mechanisms shall be granted at a minimum the power:

    (a) To regularly examine the treatment of the persons deprived of their liberty in places of detention as defined in article 4, with a view to strengthening, if necessary, their protection against torture and other cruel, inhuman or degrading treatment or punishment;

    (b) To make recommendations to the relevant authorities with the aim of improving the treatment and the conditions of the persons deprived of their liberty and to prevent torture and other cruel, inhuman or degrading treatment or punishment, taking into consideration the relevant norms of the United Nations;

    (c) To submit proposals and observations concerning existing or draft legislation.

Article 20

In order to enable the national preventive mechanisms to fulfil their mandate, the States Parties to the present Protocol undertake to grant them:

    (a) Access to all information concerning the number of persons deprived of their liberty in places of detention as defined in article 4, as well as the number of places and their location;

    (b) Access to all information referring to the treatment of those persons as well as their conditions of detention;

    (c) Access to all places of detention and their installations and facilities;

    (d) The opportunity to have private interviews with the persons deprived of their liberty without witnesses, either personally or with a translator if deemed necessary, as well as with any other person who the national preventive mechanism believes may supply relevant information;

    (e) The liberty to choose the places they want to visit and the persons they want to interview;

    (f) The right to have contacts with the Subcommittee on Prevention, to send it information and to meet with it.

Article 21

1. No authority or official shall order, apply, permit or tolerate any sanction against any person or organization for having communicated to the national preventive mechanism any information, whether true or false, and no such person or organization shall be otherwise prejudiced in any way.

2. Confidential information collected by the national preventive mechanism shall be privileged. No personal data shall be published without the express consent of the person concerned.

Article 22

The competent authorities of the State Party concerned shall examine the recommendations of the national preventive mechanism and enter into a dialogue with it on possible implementation measures.

Article 23

The States Parties to the present Protocol undertake to publish and disseminate the annual reports of the national preventive mechanisms.

PART VII FINAL PROVISIONS

Article 30

No reservations shall be made to the present Protocol.

Article 32

The provisions of the present Protocol shall not affect the obligations of States Parties to the four Geneva Conventions of 12 August 1949 and the Additional Protocols thereto of 8 June 1977, nor the opportunity available to any State Party to authorize the International Committee of the Red Cross to visit places of detention in situations not covered by international humanitarian law.

Directive 2004/23/EC of the European Parliament and of the Council of 31 March 2004 on setting standards of quality and safety for the donation, procurement, testing, processing, preservation, storage and distribution of human tissues and cells*

Chapter I General provisions

Article 1 Objective
This Directive lays down standards of quality and safety for human tissues and cells intended for human applications, in order to ensure a high level of protection of human health.

Article 2 Scope
1. This Directive shall apply to the donation, procurement, testing, processing, preservation, storage and distribution of human tissues and cells intended for human applications and of manufactured products derived from human tissues and cells intended for human applications. Where such manufactured products are covered by other directives, this Directive shall apply only to donation, procurement and testing.

2. This Directive shall not apply to:
   (a) tissues and cells used as an autologous graft within the same surgical procedure;
   (b) blood and blood components as defined by Directive 2002/98/EC;
   (c) organs or parts of organs if it is their function to be used for the same purpose as the entire organ in the human body.

Article 3 Definitions
For the purposes of this Directive:
   (a) 'cells' means individual human cells or a collection of human cells when not bound by any form of connective tissue;
   (b) 'tissue' means all constituent parts of the human body formed by cells;
   (c) 'donor' means every human source, whether living or deceased, of human cells or tissues;
   (d) 'donation' means donating human tissues or cells intended for human applications;
   (e) 'organ' means a differentiated and vital part of the human body, formed by different tissues, that maintains its structure, vascularisation and capacity to develop physiological functions with an important level of autonomy;
   (f) 'procurement' means a process by which tissue or cells are made available;
   (g) 'processing' means all operations involved in the preparation, manipulation, preservation and packaging of tissues or cells intended for human applications;
   (h) 'preservation' means the use of chemical agents, alterations in environmental conditions or other means during processing to prevent or retard biological or physical deterioration of cells or tissues;
   (i) 'quarantine' means the status of retrieved tissue or cells, or tissue isolated physically or by other effective means, whilst awaiting a decision on their acceptance or rejection;
   (j) 'storage' means maintaining the product under appropriate controlled conditions until distribution;
   (k) 'distribution' means transportation and delivery of tissues or cells intended for human applications;

(l) 'human application' means the use of tissues or cells on or in a human recipient and extra-corporal applications;

(m) 'serious adverse event' means any untoward occurrence associated with the procurement, testing, processing, storage and distribution of tissues and cells that might lead to the transmission of a communicable disease, to death or life-threatening, disabling or incapacitating conditions for patients or which might result in, or prolong, hospitalization or morbidity;

(n) 'serious adverse reaction' means an unintended response, including a communicable disease, in the donor or in the recipient associated with the procurement or human application of tissues and cells that is fatal, life-threatening, disabling, incapacitating or which results in, or prolongs, hospitalisation or morbidity;

(o) 'tissue establishment' means a tissue bank or a unit of a hospital or another body where activities of processing, preservation, storage or distribution of human tissues and cells are undertaken. It may also be responsible for procurement or testing of tissues and cells;

(p) 'allogeneic use' means cells or tissues removed from one person and applied to another;

(q) 'autologous use' means cells or tissues removed from and applied in the same person.

Chapter II Obligations on Member States' authorities

Article 5 Supervision of human tissue and cell procurement

1. Member States shall ensure that tissue and cell procurement and testing are carried out by persons with appropriate training and experience and that they take place in conditions accredited, designated, authorised or licensed for that purpose by the competent authority or authorities.

2. The competent authority or authorities shall take all necessary measures to ensure that tissue and cell procurement complies with the requirements referred to in Article 28(b), (e) and (f). The tests required for donors shall be carried out by a qualified laboratory accredited, designated, authorised or licensed by the competent authority or authorities.

Chapter III Donor selection and evaluation

Article 12 Principles governing tissue and cell donation

1. Member States shall endeavour to ensure voluntary and unpaid donations of tissues and cells. Donors may receive compensation, which is strictly limited to making good the expenses and inconveniences related to the donation. In that case, Member States define the conditions under which compensation may be granted.

Member States shall report to the Commission on these measures before 7 April 2006 and thereafter every three years. On the basis of these reports the Commission shall inform the European Parliament and the Council of any necessary further measures it intends to take at Community level.

2. Member States shall take all necessary measures to ensure that any promotion and publicity activities in support of the donation of human tissues and cells comply with guidelines or legislative provisions laid down by the Member States. Such guidelines or legislative provisions shall include appropriate restrictions or prohibitions on advertising the need for, or availability of, human tissues and cells with a view to offering or seeking financial gain or comparable advantage. Member States shall endeavour to ensure that the procurement of tissues and cells as such is carried out on a nonprofit basis.

Article 13 Consent

1. The procurement of human tissues or cells shall be authorised only after all mandatory consent or authorization requirements in force in the Member State concerned have been met.

2. Member States shall, in keeping with their national legislation, take all necessary measures to ensure that donors, their relatives or any persons granting authorisation on behalf of the donors are provided with all appropriate information as referred to in the Annex.

Article 14   Data protection and confidentiality

1. Member States shall take all necessary measures to ensure that all data, including genetic information, collated within the scope of this Directive and to which third parties have access, have been rendered anonymous so that neither donors nor recipients remain identifiable.

2. For that purpose, they shall ensure that:

(a) data security measures are in place, as well as safeguards against any unauthorised data additions, deletions or modifications to donor files or deferral records, and transfer of information;

(b) procedures are in place to resolve data discrepancies; and

(c) no unauthorised disclosure of information occurs, whilst guaranteeing the traceability of donations.

3. Member States shall take all necessary measures to ensure that the identity of the recipient (s) is not disclosed to the donor or his family and vice versa, without prejudice to legislation in force in Member States on the conditions for disclosure, notably in the case of gametes donation.

Annex   Information to be provided on the donation of cells and/or tissues

A. Living donors

1. The person in charge of the donation process shall ensure that the donor has been properly informed of at least those aspects relating to the donation and procurement process outlined in paragraph 3. Information must be given prior to the procurement.

2. The information must be given by a trained person able to transmit it in an appropriate and clear manner, using terms that are easily understood by the donor.

3 information must cover: the purpose and nature of the procurement, its consequences and risks; analytical tests, if they are performed; recording and protection of donor data, medical confidentiality; therapeutic purpose and potential benefits and information on the applicable safeguards intended to protect the donor.

4. The donor must be informed that he/she has the right to receive the confirmed results of the analytical tests, clearly explained.

5. Information must be given on the necessity for requiring the applicable mandatory consent, certification and authorisation in order that the tissue and/or cell procurement can be carried out.

B. Deceased donors

1. All information must be given and all necessary consents and authorisations must be obtained in accordance with the legislation in force in Member States.

2. The confirmed results of the donor's evaluation must be communicated and clearly explained to the relevant persons in accordance with the legislation in Member States.

United Nations Declaration on Human Cloning*

A/RES/59/280 March 2005

The General Assembly … Solemnly declares the following:

(a) Member States are called upon to adopt all measures necessary to protect adequately human life in the application of life sciences;

(b) Member States are called upon to prohibit all forms of human cloning inasmuch as they are incompatible with human dignity and the protection of human life;

(c) Member States are further called upon to adopt the measures necessary to prohibit the application of genetic engineering techniques that may be contrary to human dignity;

(d) Member States are called upon to take measures to prevent the exploitation of women in the application of life sciences;

(e) Member States are also called upon to adopt and implement without delay national legislation to bring into effect paragraphs (a) to (d);

(f) Member States are further called upon, in their financing of medical research, including of life sciences, to take into account the pressing global issues such as HIV/AIDS, tuberculosis and malaria, which affect in particular the developing countries.

Additional Protocol to the Convention on Human Rights and Biomedicine concerning Biomedical Research*

European Treaty Series—No. 195

Opened for signature 25 January 2005

Article 1   Object and purpose

Parties to this Protocol shall protect the dignity and identity of all human beings and guarantee everyone, without discrimination, respect for their integrity and other rights and fundamental freedoms with regard to any research involving interventions on human beings in the field of biomedicine.

Article 2   Scope

1. This Protocol covers the full range of research activities in the health field involving interventions on human beings.

2. This Protocol does not apply to research on embryos in vitro. It does apply to research on foetuses and embryos in vivo.

3. For the purposes of this Protocol, the term 'intervention' includes:
   i.   a physical intervention, and
   ii. any other intervention in so far as it involves a risk to the psychological health of the person concerned.

Article 3   Primacy of the human being

The interests and welfare of the human being participating in research shall prevail over the sole interest of society or science.

Article 4   General rule

Research shall be carried out freely, subject to the provisions of this Protocol and the other legal provisions ensuring the protection of the human being.

Article 5   Absence of alternatives

Research on human beings may only be undertaken if there is no alternative of comparable effectiveness.

Article 6   Risks and benefits

1. Research shall not involve risks and burdens to the human being disproportionate to its potential benefits.

2. In addition, where the research does not have the potential to produce results of direct benefit to the health of the research participant, such research may only be undertaken if the research entails no more than acceptable risk and acceptable burden for the research participant. This shall be without prejudice to the provision contained in Article 15 paragraph 2, sub-paragraph ii for the protection of persons not able to consent to research.

---

* Reproduced with permission from the Council of Europe. An explanatory report to accompany this legal text can be found on their website: http://www.coe.int/.

Article 7   Approval

Research may only be undertaken if the research project has been approved by the competent body after independent examination of its scientific merit, including assessment of the importance of the aim of research, and multidisciplinary review of its ethical acceptability.

Article 8   Scientific quality

Any research must be scientifically justified, meet generally accepted criteria of scientific quality and be carried out in accordance with relevant professional obligations and standards under the supervision of an appropriately qualified researcher.

Article 9   Independent examination by an ethics committee

1. Every research project shall be submitted for independent examination of its ethical acceptability to an ethics committee. Such projects shall be submitted to independent examination in each State in which any research activity is to take place.

2. The purpose of the multidisciplinary examination of the ethical acceptability of the research project shall be to protect the dignity, rights, safety and well-being of research participants. The assessment of the ethical acceptability shall draw on an appropriate range of expertise and experience adequately reflecting professional and lay views.

3. The ethics committee shall produce an opinion containing reasons for its conclusion.

Article 10   Independence of the ethics committee

1. Parties to this Protocol shall take measures to assure the independence of the ethics committee. That body shall not be subject to undue external influences.

2. Members of the ethics committee shall declare all circumstances that might lead to a conflict of interest. Should such conflicts arise, those involved shall not participate in that review.

Article 11   Information for the ethics committee

1. All information which is necessary for the ethical assessment of the research project shall be given in written form to the ethics committee.

2. In particular, information on items contained in the appendix to this Protocol shall be provided, in so far as it is relevant for the research project.

Article 12   Undue influence

The ethics committee must be satisfied that no undue influence, including that of a financial nature, will be exerted on persons to participate in research. In this respect, particular attention must be given to vulnerable or dependent persons.

Article 13   Information for research participants

1. The persons being asked to participate in a research project shall be given adequate information in a comprehensible form. This information shall be documented.

2. The information shall cover the purpose, the overall plan and the possible risks and benefits of the research project, and include the opinion of the ethics committee. Before being asked to consent to participate in a research project, the persons concerned shall be specifically informed, according to the nature and purpose of the research:

    i.   of the nature, extent and duration of the procedures involved, in particular, details of any burden imposed by the research project;

    ii. of available preventive, diagnostic and therapeutic procedures;

    iii. of the arrangements for responding to adverse events or the concerns of research participants;

    iv. of arrangements to ensure respect for private life and ensure the confidentiality of personal data;

    v. of arrangements for access to information relevant to the participant arising from the research and to its overall results;

    vi. of the arrangements for fair compensation in the case of damage;

vii. of any foreseen potential further uses, including commercial uses, of the research results, data or biological materials;

viii. of the source of funding of the research project.

3. In addition, the persons being asked to participate in a research project shall be informed of the rights and safeguards prescribed by law for their protection, and specifically of their right to refuse consent or to withdraw consent at any time without being subject to any form of discrimination, in particular regarding the right to medical care.

Article 14   Consent

1. No research on a person may be carried out, subject to the provisions of both Chapter V and Article 19, without the informed, free, express, specific and documented consent of the person. Such consent may be freely withdrawn by the person at any phase of the research.

2. Refusal to give consent or the withdrawal of consent to participation in research shall not lead to any form of discrimination against the person concerned, in particular regarding the right to medical care.

3. Where the capacity of the person to give informed consent is in doubt, Arrangements shall be in place to verify whether or not the person has such capacity.

Article 15   Protection of persons not able to consent to research

1. Research on a person without the capacity to consent to research may be undertaken only if all the following specific conditions are met:

  i.   the results of the research have the potential to produce real and direct benefit to his or her health;

  ii. research of comparable effectiveness cannot be carried out on individuals capable of giving consent;

  iii. the person undergoing research has been informed of his or her rights and the safeguards prescribed by law for his or her protection, unless this person is not in a state to receive the information;

  iv. the necessary authorisation has been given specifically and in writing by the legal representative or an authority, person or body provided for by law, and after having received the information required by Article 16, taking into account the person's previously expressed wishes or objections. An adult not able to consent shall as far as possible take part in the authorisation procedure. The opinion of a minor shall be taken into consideration as an increasingly determining factor in proportion to age and degree of maturity;

  v.   the person concerned does not object.

2. Exceptionally and under the protective conditions prescribed by law, where the research has not the potential to produce results of direct benefit to the health of the person concerned, such research may be authorised subject to the conditions laid down in paragraph 1, sub-paragraphs ii, iii, iv, and v above, and to the following additional conditions:

  i.   the research has the aim of contributing, through significant improvement in the scientific understanding of the individual's condition, disease or disorder, to the ultimate attainment of results capable of conferring benefit to the person concerned or to other persons in the same age category or afflicted with the same disease or disorder or having the same condition;

  ii. the research entails only minimal risk and minimal burden for the individual concerned; and any consideration of additional potential benefits of the research shall not be used to justify an increased level of risk or burden.

3. Objection to participation, refusal to give authorisation or the withdrawal of authorisation to participate in research shall not lead to any form of discrimination against the person concerned, in particular regarding the right to medical care.

Article 16   Information prior to authorisation

1. Those being asked to authorise participation of a person in a research project shall be given adequate information in a comprehensible form. This information shall be documented.

2. The information shall cover the purpose, the overall plan and the possible risks and benefits of the research project, and include the opinion of the ethics committee. They shall further be informed of the rights and safeguards prescribed by law for the protection of those not able to consent to research and specifically of the right to refuse or to withdraw authorisation at any time, without the person concerned being subject to any form of discrimination, in particular regarding the right to medical care. They shall be specifically informed according to the nature and purpose of the research of the items of information listed in Article 13.

3. The information shall also be provided to the individual concerned, unless this person is not in a state to receive the information.

Article 17   Research with minimal risk and minimal burden

1. For the purposes of this Protocol it is deemed that the research bears a minimal risk if, having regard to the nature and scale of the intervention, it is to be expected that it will result, at the most, in a very slight and temporary negative impact on the health of the person concerned.

2. It is deemed that it bears a minimal burden if it is to be expected that the discomfort will be, at the most, temporary and very slight for the person concerned. In assessing the burden for an individual, a person enjoying the special confidence of the person concerned shall assess the burden where appropriate.

Article 18   Research during pregnancy or breastfeeding

1. Research on a pregnant woman which does not have the potential to produce results of direct benefit to her health, or to that of her embryo, foetus or child after birth, may only be undertaken if the following additional conditions are met:

    i.   the research has the aim of contributing to the ultimate attainment of results capable of conferring benefit to other women in relation to reproduction or to other embryos, foetuses or children;

    ii.   research of comparable effectiveness cannot be carried out on women who are not pregnant;

    iii. the research entails only minimal risk and minimal burden.

2. Where research is undertaken on a breastfeeding woman, particular care shall be taken to avoid any adverse impact on the health of the child.

Article 19   Research on persons in emergency clinical situations

1. The law shall determine whether, and under which protective additional conditions, research in emergency situations may take place when:

    i.   a person is not in a state to give consent, and

    ii.   because of the urgency of the situation, it is impossible to obtain in a sufficiently timely manner, authorisation from his or her representative or an authority or a person or body which would in the absence of an emergency situation be called upon to give authorisation.

2. The law shall include the following specific conditions:

    i.   research of comparable effectiveness cannot be carried out on persons in non-emergency situations;

    ii.   the research project may only be undertaken if it has been approved specifically for emergency situations by the competent body;

    iii. any relevant previously expressed objections of the person known to the researcher shall be respected;

    iv. where the research has not the potential to produce results of direct benefit to the health of the person concerned, it has the aim of contributing, through significant improvement in the scientific understanding of the individual's condition, disease or disorder, to the ultimate attainment of results capable of conferring benefit to the person concerned or to other persons in the same category or afflicted with the same disease or disorder or having the same condition, and entails only minimal risk and minimal burden.

3. Persons participating in the emergency research project or, if applicable, their representatives shall be provided with all the relevant information concerning their participation in the research project as soon as possible. Consent or authorisation for continued participation shall be requested as soon as reasonably possible.

Article 20   Research on persons deprived of liberty

Where the law allows research on persons deprived of liberty, such persons may participate in a research project in which the results do not have the potential to produce direct benefit to their health only if the following additional conditions are met:

    i.   research of comparable effectiveness cannot be carried out without the participation of persons deprived of liberty;

    ii.   the research has the aim of contributing to the ultimate attainment of results capable of conferring benefit to persons deprived of liberty;

    iii. the research entails only minimal risk and minimal burden.

Article 21   Minimisation of risk and burden

1. All reasonable measures shall be taken to ensure safety and to minimise risk and burden for the research participants.

2. Research may only be carried out under the supervision of a clinical professional who possesses the necessary qualifications and experience.

Article 22   Assessment of health status

1. The researcher shall take all necessary steps to assess the state of health of human beings prior to their inclusion in research, to ensure that those at increased risk in relation to participation in a specific project be excluded.

2. Where research is undertaken on persons in the reproductive stage of their lives, particular consideration shall be given to the possible adverse impact on a current or future pregnancy and the health of an embryo, foetus or child.

Article 23   Non-interference with necessary clinical interventions

1. Research shall not delay nor deprive participants of medically necessary preventive, diagnostic or therapeutic procedures.

2. In research associated with prevention, diagnosis or treatment, participants assigned to control groups shall be assured of proven methods of prevention, diagnosis or treatment.

3. The use of placebo is permissible where there are no methods of proven effectiveness, or where withdrawal or withholding of such methods does not present an unacceptable risk or burden.

Article 23   Non-interference with necessary clinical interventions

1. Research shall not prevent or delay nor deprive participants of medically necessary preventive, diagnostic or therapeutic procedures.

2. In research associated with prevention, diagnosis or treatment, participants assigned to control groups shall be assured of proven methods of prevention diagnosis or treatment.

3. The use of placebo is permissible where there are no methods of proven effectiveness, or where withdrawal or withholding of such methods does not present an unacceptable risk or burden.

Article 24   New developments

1. Parties to this Protocol shall take measures to ensure that the research project is re-examined if this is justified in the light of scientific developments or events arising in the course of the research.

2. The purpose of the re-examination is to establish whether:
  i.   the research needs to be discontinued or if changes to the research project are necessary for the research to continue;
  ii.   research participants, or if applicable their representatives, need to be informed of the developments or events;
  iii. additional consent or authorisation for participation is required.

  2. Any new information relevant to their participation shall be conveyed to the research participants, or, if applicable, to their representatives, in a timely manner.

  3. The competent body shall be informed of the reasons for any premature termination of a research project.

Article 25   Confidentiality

  1. Any information of a personal nature collected during biomedical research shall be considered as confidential and treated according to the rules relating to the protection of private life.

  2. The law shall protect against inappropriate disclosure of any other information related to a research project that has been submitted to an ethics committee in compliance with this Protocol.

Article 26   Right to information

  1. Research participants shall be entitled to know any information collected on their health in conformity with the provisions of Article 10 of the Convention.

  2. Other personal information collected for a research project will be accessible to them in conformity with the law on the protection of individuals with regard to processing of personal data.

Article 27   Duty of care

If research gives rise to information of relevance to the current or future health or quality of life of research participants, this information must be offered to them. That shall be done within a framework of health care or counselling. In communication of such information, due care must be taken in order to protect confidentiality and to respect any wish of a participant not to receive such information.

Article 28   Availability of results

  1. On completion of the research, a report or summary shall be submitted to the ethics committee or the competent body.

  2. The conclusions of the research shall be made available to participants in reasonable time, on request.

  3. The researcher shall take appropriate measures to make public the results of research in reasonable time.

Article 29   Research in States not parties to this Protocol

Sponsors or researchers within the jurisdiction of a Party to this Protocol that plan to undertake or direct a research project in a State not party to this Protocol shall ensure that, without prejudice to the provisions applicable in that State, the research project complies with the principles on which the provisions of this Protocol are based. Where necessary, the Party shall take appropriate measures to that end.

APPENDIX TO THE ADDITIONAL PROTOCOL ON BIOMEDICAL RESEARCH

Information to be given to the ethics committee

Information on the following items shall be provided to the ethics committee, in so far as it is relevant for the research project:

Description of the project

i. the name of the principal researcher, qualifications and experience of researchers and, where appropriate, the clinically responsible person, and funding arrangements;

ii. the aim and justification for the research based on the latest state of scientific knowledge;

iii. methods and procedures envisaged, including statistical and other analytical techniques;

iv. a comprehensive summary of the research project in lay language;

v. a statement of previous and concurrent submissions of the research project for assessment or approval and the outcome of those submissions;

Participants, consent and information

vi. justification for involving human beings in the research project;

vii. the criteria for inclusion or exclusion of the categories of persons for participation in the research project and how those persons are to be selected and recruited;

viii. reasons for the use or the absence of control groups;

ix. a description of the nature and degree of foreseeable risks that may be incurred through participating in research;

x. the nature, extent and duration of the interventions to be carried out on the research participants, and details of any burden imposed by the research project;

xi. arrangements to monitor, evaluate and react to contingencies that may have con- sequences for the present or future health of research participants;

xii. the timing and details of information for those persons who would participate in the research project and the means proposed for provision of this information;

xiii. documentation intended to be used to seek consent or, in the case of persons not able to consent, authorisation for participation in the research project;

xiv. arrangements to ensure respect for the private life of those persons who would participate in research and ensure the confidentiality of personal data;

xv. arrangements foreseen for information which may be generated and be relevant to the present or future health of those persons who would participate in research and their family members;

Other information

xvi. details of all payments and rewards to be made in the context of the research project;

xvii. details of all circumstances that might lead to conflicts of interest that may affect the independent judgement of the researchers;

xviii. details of any foreseen potential further uses, including commercial uses, of the research results, data or biological materials;

xix. details of all other ethical issues, as perceived by the researcher;

xx. details of any insurance or indemnity to cover damage arising in the context of the research project.

The ethics committee may request additional information necessary for evaluation of the research project.

Convention on the Rights of Persons with Disabilities*

Adopted December 2006 by General Assembly Resolution A/RES/61/106

Article 1   Purpose

The purpose of the present Convention is to promote, protect and ensure the full and equal enjoyment of all human rights and fundamental freedoms by all persons with disabilities, and to promote respect for their inherent dignity.

Persons with disabilities include those who have long-term physical, mental, intellectual or sensory impairments which in interaction with various barriers may hinder their full and effective participation in society on an equal basis with others.

Article 2   Definitions

For the purposes of the present Convention:

'Communication' includes languages, display of text, Braille, tactile communication, large print, accessible multimedia as well as written, audio, plain-language, human-reader and augmentative and alternative modes, means and formats of communication, including accessible information and communication technology;

'Language' includes spoken and signed languages and other forms of non spoken languages;

'Discrimination on the basis of disability' means any distinction, exclusion or restriction on the basis of disability which has the purpose or effect of impairing or nullifying the recognition, enjoyment or exercise, on an equal basis with others, of all human rights and fundamental freedoms in the political, economic, social, cultural, civil or any other field. It includes all forms of discrimination, including denial of reasonable accommodation;

'Reasonable accommodation' means necessary and appropriate modification and adjustments not imposing a disproportionate or undue burden, where needed in a particular case, to ensure to persons with disabilities the enjoyment or exercise on an equal basis with others of all human rights and fundamental freedoms;

'Universal design' means the design of products, environments, programmes and services to be usable by all people, to the greatest extent possible, without the need for adaptation or specialized design. 'Universal design' shall not exclude assistive devices for particular groups of persons with disabilities where this is needed.

Article 3   General principles

The principles of the present Convention shall be:

- a. Respect for inherent dignity, individual autonomy including the freedom to make one's own choices, and independence of persons;
- b. Non-discrimination;
- c. Full and effective participation and inclusion in society;
- d. Respect for difference and acceptance of persons with disabilities as part of human diversity and humanity;
- e. Equality of opportunity;
- f. Accessibility;
- g. Equality between men and women;
- h. Respect for the evolving capacities of children with disabilities and respect for the right of children with disabilities to preserve their identities.

Article 4   General obligations

1. States Parties undertake to ensure and promote the full realization of all human rights and fundamental freedoms for all persons with disabilities without discrimination of any kind on the basis of disability. To this end, States Parties undertake:

- a. To adopt all appropriate legislative, administrative and other measures for the implementation of the rights recognized in the present Convention;
- b. To take all appropriate measures, including legislation, to modify or abolish existing laws, regulations, customs and practices that constitute discrimination against persons with disabilities;
- c. To take into account the protection and promotion of the human rights of persons with disabilities in all policies and programmes;
- d. To refrain from engaging in any act or practice that is inconsistent with the present Convention and to ensure that public authorities and institutions act in conformity with the present Convention;

e. To take all appropriate measures to eliminate discrimination on the basis of disability by any person, organization or private enterprise;

f. To undertake or promote research and development of universally designed goods, services, equipment and facilities, as defined in article 2 of the present Convention, which should require the minimum possible adaptation and the least cost to meet the specific needs of a person with disabilities, to promote their availability and use, and to promote universal design in the development of standards and guidelines;

g. To undertake or promote research and development of, and to promote the availability and use of new technologies, including information and communications technologies, mobility aids, devices and assistive technologies, suitable for persons with disabilities, giving priority to technologies at an affordable cost;

h. To provide accessible information to persons with disabilities about mobility aids, devices and assistive technologies, including new technologies, as well as other forms of assistance, support services and facilities;

i. To promote the training of professionals and staff working with persons with disabilities in the rights recognized in this Convention so as to better provide the assistance and services guaranteed by those rights.

2. With regard to economic, social and cultural rights, each State Party undertakes to take measures to the maximum of its available resources and, where needed, within the framework of international cooperation, with a view to achieving progressively the full realization of these rights, without prejudice to those obligations contained in the present Convention that are immediately applicable according to international law.

3. In the development and implementation of legislation and policies to implement the present Convention, and in other decision-making processes concerning issues relating to persons with disabilities, States Parties shall closely consult with and actively involve persons with disabilities, including children with disabilities, through their representative organizations.

4. Nothing in the present Convention shall affect any provisions which are more conducive to the realization of the rights of persons with disabilities and which may be contained in the law of a State Party or international law in force for that State. There shall be no restriction upon or derogation from any of the human rights and fundamental freedoms recognized or existing in any State Party to the present Convention pursuant to law, conventions, regulation or custom on the pretext that the present Convention does not recognize such rights or freedoms or that it recognizes them to a lesser extent.

5. The provisions of the present Convention shall extend to all parts of federal states without any limitations or exceptions.

Article 5   Equality and non-discrimination

1. States Parties recognize that all persons are equal before and under the law and are entitled without any discrimination to the equal protection and equal benefit of the law.

2. States Parties shall prohibit all discrimination on the basis of disability and guarantee to persons with disabilities equal and effective legal protection against discrimination on all grounds.

3. In order to promote equality and eliminate discrimination, States Parties shall take all appropriate steps to ensure that reasonable accommodation is provided.

4. Specific measures which are necessary to accelerate or achieve de facto equality of persons with disabilities shall not be considered discrimination under the terms of the present Convention.

Article 6   Women with disabilities

1. States Parties recognize that women and girls with disabilities are subject to multiple discrimination, and in this regard shall take measures to ensure the full and equal enjoyment by them of all human rights and fundamental freedoms.

2. States Parties shall take all appropriate measures to ensure the full development, advancement and empowerment of women, for the purpose of guaranteeing them the exercise and enjoyment of the human rights and fundamental freedoms set out in the present Convention.

Article 7   Children with disabilities

1. States Parties shall take all necessary measures to ensure the full enjoyment by children with disabilities of all human rights and fundamental freedoms on an equal basis with other children.

2. In all actions concerning children with disabilities, the best interests of the child shall be a primary consideration.

3. States Parties shall ensure that children with disabilities have the right to express their views freely on all matters affecting them, their views being given due weight in accordance with their age and maturity, on an equal basis with other children, and to be provided with disability and age-appropriate assistance to realize that right.

Article 8   Awareness-raising

1. States Parties undertake to adopt immediate, effective and appropriate measures:
   a. To raise awareness throughout society, including at the family level, regarding persons with disabilities, and to foster respect for the rights and dignity of persons with disabilities;
   b. To combat stereotypes, prejudices and harmful practices relating to persons with disabilities, including those based on sex and age, in all areas of life;
   c. To promote awareness of the capabilities and contributions of persons with disabilities.

Measures to this end include:
   a. Initiating and maintaining effective public awareness campaigns designed:
      i.   To nurture receptiveness to the rights of persons with disabilities;
      ii.   To promote positive perceptions and greater social awareness towards persons with disabilities;
      iii. To promote recognition of the skills, merits and abilities of persons with disabilities, and of their contributions to the workplace and the labour market;
   b. Fostering at all levels of the education system, including in all children from an early age, an attitude of respect for the rights of persons with disabilities;
   c. Encouraging all organs of the media to portray persons with disabilities in a manner consistent with the purpose of the present Convention;
   d. Promoting awareness-training programmes regarding persons with disabilities and the rights of persons with disabilities.

Article 10   Right to life

States Parties reaffirm that every human being has the inherent right to life and shall take all necessary measures to ensure its effective enjoyment by persons with disabilities on an equal basis with others.

Article 12   Equal recognition before the law

1. States Parties reaffirm that persons with disabilities have the right to recognition everywhere as persons before the law.

2. States Parties shall recognize that persons with disabilities enjoy legal capacity on an equal basis with others in all aspects of life.

3. States Parties shall take appropriate measures to provide access by persons with disabilities to the support they may require in exercising their legal capacity.

4. States Parties shall ensure that all measures that relate to the exercise of legal capacity provide for appropriate and effective safeguards to prevent abuse in accordance with international human rights law. Such safeguards shall ensure that measures relating to the exercise of legal capacity respect the rights, will and preferences of the person, are free of conflict of interest and undue influence, are proportional and tailored to the person's circumstances, apply for the shortest time

possible and are subject to regular review by a competent, independent and impartial authority or judicial body. The safeguards shall be proportional to the degree to which such measures affect the person's rights and interests.

5. Subject to the provisions of this article, States Parties shall take all appropriate and effective measures to ensure the equal right of persons with disabilities to own or inherit property, to control their own financial affairs and to have equal access to bank loans, mortgages and other forms of financial credit, and shall ensure that persons with disabilities are not arbitrarily deprived of their property.

Article 13   Access to justice

1. States Parties shall ensure effective access to justice for persons with disabilities on an equal basis with others, including through the provision of procedural and age-appropriate accommodations, in order to facilitate their effective role as direct and indirect participants, including as witnesses, in all legal proceedings, including at investigative and other preliminary stages.

2. In order to help to ensure effective access to justice for persons with disabilities, States Parties shall promote appropriate training for those working in the field of administration of justice, including police and prison staff.

Article 14   Liberty and security of the person

1. States Parties shall ensure that persons with disabilities, on an equal basis with others:
    a.   Enjoy the right to liberty and security of person;
    b.   Are not deprived of their liberty unlawfully or arbitrarily, and that any deprivation of liberty is in conformity with the law, and that the existence of a disability shall in no case justify a deprivation of liberty.

2. States Parties shall ensure that if persons with disabilities are deprived of their liberty through any process, they are, on an equal basis with others, entitled to guarantees in accordance with international human rights law and shall be treated in compliance with the objectives and principles of this Convention, including by provision of reasonable accommodation.

Article 15   Freedom from torture or cruel, inhuman or degrading treatment or punishment

1. No one shall be subjected to torture or to cruel, inhuman or degrading treatment or punishment. In particular, no one shall be subjected without his or her free consent to medical or scientific experimentation.

2. States Parties shall take all effective legislative, administrative, judicial or other measures to prevent persons with disabilities, on an equal basis with others, from being subjected to torture or cruel, inhuman or degrading treatment or punishment.

Article 16   Freedom from exploitation, violence and abuse

1. States Parties shall take all appropriate legislative, administrative, social, educational and other measures to protect persons with disabilities, both within and outside the home, from all forms of exploitation, violence and abuse, including their gender-based aspects.

2. States Parties shall also take all appropriate measures to prevent all forms of exploitation, violence and abuse by ensuring, inter alia, appropriate forms of gender- and age-sensitive assistance and support for persons with disabilities and their families and caregivers, including through the provision of information and education on how to avoid, recognize and report instances of exploitation, violence and abuse. States Parties shall ensure that protection services are age-, gender- and disability-sensitive.

3. In order to prevent the occurrence of all forms of exploitation, violence and abuse, States Parties shall ensure that all facilities and programmes designed to serve persons with disabilities are effectively monitored by independent authorities.

4. States Parties shall take all appropriate measures to promote the physical, cognitive and psychological recovery, rehabilitation and social reintegration of persons with disabilities who become

victims of any form of exploitation, violence or abuse, including through the provision of protection services. Such recovery and reintegration shall take place in an environment that fosters the health, welfare, self-respect, dignity and autonomy of the person and takes into account gender- and age-specific needs.

5. States Parties shall put in place effective legislation and policies, including women- and child-focused legislation and policies, to ensure that instances of exploitation, violence and abuse against persons with disabilities are identified, investigated and, where appropriate, prosecuted.

Article 17   Protecting the integrity of the person
Every person with disabilities has a right to respect for his or her physical and mental integrity on an equal basis with others.

Article 18   Liberty of movement and nationality
2. Children with disabilities shall be registered immediately after birth and shall have the right from birth to a name, the right to acquire a nationality and, as far as possible, the right to know and be cared for by their parents.

Article 19   Living independently and being included in the community
States Parties to this Convention recognize the equal right of all persons with disabilities to live in the community, with choices equal to others, and shall take effective and appropriate measures to facilitate full enjoyment by persons with disabilities of this right and their full inclusion and participation in the community, including by ensuring that:
   a. Persons with disabilities have the opportunity to choose their place of residence and where and with whom they live on an equal basis with others and are not obliged to live in a particular living arrangement;
   b. Persons with disabilities have access to a range of in-home, residential and other community support services, including personal assistance necessary to support living and inclusion in the community, and to prevent isolation or segregation from the community;
   c. Community services and facilities for the general population are available on an equal basis to persons with disabilities and are responsive to their needs.

Article 21   Freedom of expression and opinion, and access to information
States Parties shall take all appropriate measures to ensure that persons with disabilities can exercise the right to freedom of expression and opinion, including the freedom to seek, receive and impart information and ideas on an equal basis with others and through all forms of communication of their choice, as defined in article 2 of the present Convention, including by:
   a. Providing information intended for the general public to persons with disabilities in accessible formats and technologies appropriate to different kinds of disabilities in a timely manner and without additional cost;
   b. Accepting and facilitating the use of sign languages, Braille, augmentative and alternative communication, and all other accessible means, modes and formats of communication of their choice by persons with disabilities in official interactions;
   c. Urging private entities that provide services to the general public, including through the Internet, to provide information and services in accessible and usable formats for persons with disabilities;
   d. Encouraging the mass media, including providers of information through the Internet, to make their services accessible to persons with disabilities;
   e. Recognizing and promoting the use of sign languages.

Article 22   Respect for privacy
1. No person with disabilities, regardless of place of residence or living arrangements, shall be subjected to arbitrary or unlawful interference with his or her privacy, family, home or correspondence or other types of communication or to unlawful attacks on his or her honour and reputation.

Persons with disabilities have the right to the protection of the law against such interference or attacks.

2. States Parties shall protect the privacy of personal, health and rehabilitation information of persons with disabilities on an equal basis with others.

Article 23   Respect for home and the family

1. States Parties shall take effective and appropriate measures to eliminate discrimination against persons with disabilities in all matters relating to marriage, family, parenthood and relationships, on an equal basis with others, so as to ensure that:

  a. The right of all persons with disabilities who are of marriageable age to marry and to found a family on the basis of free and full consent of the intending spouses is recognized;
  b. The rights of persons with disabilities to decide freely and responsibly on the number and spacing of their children and to have access to age-appropriate information, reproductive and family planning education are recognized, and the means necessary to enable them to exercise these rights are provided;
  c. Persons with disabilities, including children, retain their fertility on an equal basis with others.

2. States Parties shall ensure the rights and responsibilities of persons with disabilities, with regard to guardianship, wardship, trusteeship, adoption of children or similar institutions, where these concepts exist in national legislation; in all cases the best interests of the child shall be paramount. States Parties shall render appropriate assistance to persons with disabilities in the performance of their child-rearing responsibilities.

3. States Parties shall ensure that children with disabilities have equal rights with respect to family life. With a view to realizing these rights, and to prevent concealment, abandonment, neglect and segregation of children with disabilities, States Parties shall undertake to provide early and comprehensive information, services and support to children with disabilities and their families.

4. States Parties shall ensure that a child shall not be separated from his or her parents against their will, except when competent authorities subject to judicial review determine, in accordance with applicable law and procedures, that such separation is necessary for the best interests of the child. In no case shall a child be separated from parents on the basis of a disability of either the child or one or both of the parents.

5. States Parties shall, where the immediate family is unable to care for a child with disabilities, undertake every effort to provide alternative care within the wider family, and failing that, within the community in a family setting.

Article 25   Health

States Parties recognize that persons with disabilities have the right to the enjoyment of the highest attainable standard of health without discrimination on the basis of disability. States Parties shall take all appropriate measures to ensure access for persons with disabilities to health services that are gender-sensitive, including health-related rehabilitation. In particular, States Parties shall:

  a. Provide persons with disabilities with the same range, quality and standard of free or affordable health care and programmes as provided to other persons, including in the area of sexual and reproductive health and population-based public health programmes;
  b. Provide those health services needed by persons with disabilities specifically because of their disabilities, including early identification and intervention as appropriate, and services designed to minimize and prevent further disabilities, including among children and older persons;
  c. Provide these health services as close as possible to people's own communities, including in rural areas;

d. Require health professionals to provide care of the same quality to persons with disabilities as to others, including on the basis of free and informed consent by, inter alia, raising awareness of the human rights, dignity, autonomy and needs of persons with disabilities through training and the promulgation of ethical standards for public and private health care;

e. Prohibit discrimination against persons with disabilities in the provision of health insurance, and life insurance where such insurance is permitted by national law, which shall be provided in a fair and reasonable manner;

f. Prevent discriminatory denial of health care or health services or food and fluids on the basis of disability.

Article 26   Habilitation and rehabilitation

1. States Parties shall take effective and appropriate measures, including through peer support, to enable persons with disabilities to attain and maintain maximum independence, full physical, mental, social and vocational ability, and full inclusion and participation in all aspects of life. To that end, States Parties shall organize, strengthen and extend comprehensive habilitation and rehabilitation services and programmes, particularly in the areas of health, employment, education and social services, in such a way that these services and programmes:

a. Begin at the earliest possible stage, and are based on the multidisciplinary assessment of individual needs and strengths;

b. Support participation and inclusion in the community and all aspects of society, are voluntary, and are available to persons with disabilities as close as possible to their own communities, including in rural areas.

2. States Parties shall promote the development of initial and continuing training for professionals and staff working in habilitation and rehabilitation services.

3. States Parties shall promote the availability, knowledge and use of assistive devices and technologies, designed for persons with disabilities, as they relate to habilitation and rehabilitation.

Additional Protocol to the Convention on Human Rights and Biomedicine concerning Genetic Testing for Health Purposes*

(27.XI.2008)

Council of Europe Treaty Series—No. 203

Chapter I   Object and scope

Article 1   Object and purpose

Parties to this Protocol shall protect the dignity and identity of all human beings and guarantee everyone, without discrimination, respect for their integrity and other rights and fundamental freedoms with regard to the tests to which this Protocol applies in accordance with Article 2.

Article 2   Scope

1. This Protocol applies to tests, which are carried out for health purposes, involving analysis of biological samples of human origin and aiming specifically to identify the genetic characteristics of

---

* Reproduced with permission from the Council of Europe. An explanatory report to accompany this legal text can be found on their website: http://www.coe.int/.

a person which are inherited or acquired during early prenatal development (hereinafter referred to as 'genetic tests').

    2. This Protocol does not apply:

        (a) to genetic tests carried out on the human embryo or foetus;

        (b) to genetic tests carried out for research purposes.

    3. For the purposes of paragraph 1:

        (a) 'analysis' refers to:

            (i)   chromosomal analysis,

            (ii) DNA or RNA analysis,

            (iii) analysis of any other element enabling information to be obtained which is equivalent to that obtained with the methods referred to in sub-paragraphs a.i. and a.ii.;

        (b) 'biological samples' refers to:

            (i)   biological materials removed for the purpose of the test concerned,

            (ii) biological materials previously removed for another purpose.

Chapter II General provisions

Article 3 Primacy of the human being

The interests and welfare of the human being concerned by genetic tests covered by this Protocol shall prevail over the sole interest of society or science.

Article 4 Non-discrimination and non-stigmatisation

    1. Any form of discrimination against a person, either as an individual or as a member of a group on grounds of his or her genetic heritage is prohibited.

    2. Appropriate measures shall be taken in order to prevent stigmatisation of persons or groups in relation to genetic characteristics.

Chapter III Genetic services

Article 5 Quality of genetic services

Parties shall take the necessary measures to ensure that genetic services are of appropriate quality. In particular, they shall see to it that:

    (a) genetic tests meet generally accepted criteria of scientific validity and clinical validity;

    (b) a quality assurance programme is implemented in each laboratory and that laboratories are subject to regular monitoring;

    (c) persons providing genetic services have appropriate qualifications to enable them to perform their role in accordance with professional obligations and standards.

Article 6 Clinical utility

Clinical utility of a genetic test shall be an essential criterion for deciding to offer this test to a person or a group of persons.

Article 7 Individualised supervision

    1. A genetic test for health purposes may only be performed under individualised medical supervision.

    2. Exceptions to the general rule referred to in paragraph 1 may be allowed by a Party, subject to appropriate measures being provided, taking into account the way the test will be carried out, to give effect to the other provisions of this Protocol.

   However, such an exception may not be made with regard to genetic tests with important implications for the health of the persons concerned or members of their family or with important implications concerning procreation choices.

Chapter IV Information, genetic counselling and consent

Article 8   Information and genetic counseling

1. When a genetic test is envisaged, the person concerned shall be provided with prior appropriate information in particular on the purpose and the nature of the test, as well as the implications of its results.

2. For predictive genetic tests as referred to in Article 12 of the Convention on Human Rights and Biomedicine, appropriate genetic counselling shall also be available for the person concerned.

The tests concerned are:
- tests predictive of a monogenic disease,
- tests serving to detect a genetic predisposition or genetic susceptibility to a disease,
- tests serving to identify the subject as a healthy carrier of a gene responsible for a disease.

The form and extent of this genetic counselling shall be defined according to the implications of the results of the test and their significance for the person or the members of his or her family, including possible implications concerning procreation choices.

Genetic counselling shall be given in a non-directive manner.

Article 9   Consent

1. A genetic test may only be carried out after the person concerned has given free and informed consent to it.

Consent to tests referred to in Article 8, paragraph 2, shall be documented.

2. The person concerned may freely withdraw consent at any time.

Chapter V Persons not able to consent

Article 10   Protection of persons not able to consent

Subject to Article 13 of this Protocol, a genetic test on a person who does not have the capacity to consent may only be carried out for his or her direct benefit.

Where, according to law, a minor does not have the capacity to consent, a genetic test on this person shall be deferred until attainment of such capacity unless that delay would be detrimental to his or her health or well-being.

Article 11   Information prior to authorisation, genetic counselling and support

1. When a genetic test is envisaged in respect of a person not able to consent, the person, authority or body whose authorisation is required shall be provided with prior appropriate information in particular with regard to the purpose and the nature of the test, as well as the implications of its results.

Appropriate prior information shall also be provided to the person not able to consent in respect of whom the test is envisaged, to the extent of his or her capacity to understand.

A qualified person shall be available to answer possible questions by the person, authority or body whose authorisation is required, and, if appropriate, the person in respect of whom the test is envisaged.

2. The provisions of Article 8, paragraph 2, shall apply in the case of persons not able to consent to the extent of their capacity to understand.

Where relevant, appropriate support shall be available for the person whose authorisation is required.

Article 12   Authorisation

1. Where, according to law, a minor does not have the capacity to consent to a genetic test, that test may only be carried out with the authorisation of his or her representative or an authority or a person or body provided for by law.

The opinion of the minor shall be taken into consideration as an increasingly determining factor in proportion to his or her age and degree of maturity.

2. Where, according to law, an adult does not have the capacity to consent to a genetic test because of a mental disability, a disease or for similar reasons, that test may only be carried out with the authorisation of his or her representative or an authority or a person or body provided for by law.

Wishes relating to a genetic test expressed previously by an adult at a time where he or she had capacity to consent shall be taken into account.

The individual concerned shall, to the extent of his or her capacity to understand, take part in the authorisation procedure.

3. Authorisation to tests referred to in Article 8, paragraph 2, shall be documented.

4. The authorisation referred to in paragraphs 1 and 2 above may be withdrawn at any time in the best interests of the person concerned.

Chapter VI Tests for the benefit of family members

Article 13   Tests on persons not able to consent

Exceptionally, and by derogation from the provisions of Article 6, paragraph 1, of the Convention on Human Rights and Biomedicine and of Article 10 of this Protocol, the law may allow a genetic test to be carried out, for the benefit of family members, on a person who does not have the capacity to consent, if the following conditions are met:

- (a) the purpose of the test is to allow the family member(s) concerned to obtain a preventive, diagnostic or therapeutic benefit that has been independently evaluated as important for their health, or to allow them to make an informed choice with respect to procreation;
- (b) the benefit envisaged cannot be obtained without carrying out this test;
- (c) the risk and burden of the intervention are minimal for the person who is undergoing the test;
- (d) the expected benefit has been independently evaluated as substantially outweighing the risk for private life that may arise from the collection, processing or communication of the results of the test;
- (e) the authorisation of the representative of the person not able to consent, or an authority or a person or body provided for by law has been given;
- (f) the person not able to consent shall, in proportion to his or her capacity to understand and degree of maturity, take part in the authorisation procedure. The test shall not be carried out if this person objects to it.

Article 14   Tests on biological materials when it is not possible to contact the person concerned

When it is not possible, with reasonable efforts, to contact a person for a genetic test for the benefit of his or her family member(s) on his or her biological material previously removed for another purpose, the law may allow the test to be carried out in accordance with the principle of proportionality, where the expected benefit cannot be otherwise obtained and where the test cannot be deferred.

Provisions shall be made, in accordance with Article 22 of the Convention on Human Rights and Biomedicine, for the case where the person concerned has expressly opposed such test.

Article 15   Tests on deceased persons

A genetic test for the benefit of other family members may be carried out on biological samples:

- – removed from the body of a deceased person, or
- – removed, when he or she was alive, from a person now deceased, only if the consent or authorisation required by law has been obtained.

Chapter VII Private life and right to information

Article 16   Respect for private life and right to information

1. Everyone has the right to respect for his or her private life, in particular to protection of his or her personal data derived from a genetic test.

2. Everyone undergoing a genetic test is entitled to know any information collected about his or her health derived from this test.

The conclusions drawn from the test shall be accessible to the person concerned in a comprehensible form.

3. The wish of a person not to be informed shall be respected.

4. In exceptional cases, restrictions may be placed by law on the exercise of the rights contained in paragraphs 2 and 3 above in the interests of the person concerned.

Article 17   Biological samples

Biological samples referred to in Article 2 shall only be used and stored in such conditions as to ensure their security and the confidentiality of the information which can be obtained therefrom.

Article 18   Information relevant to family members

Where the results of a genetic test undertaken on a person can be relevant to the health of other family members, the person tested shall be informed.

Chapter VIII Genetic screening programmes for health purposes

Article 19   Genetic screening programmes for health purposes

A health screening programme involving the use of genetic tests may only be implemented if it has been approved by the competent body. This approval may only be given after independent evaluation of its ethical acceptability and fulfillment of the following specific conditions:

(a) the programme is recognised for its health relevance for the whole population or section of population concerned;

(b) the scientific validity and effectiveness of the programme have been established;

(c) appropriate preventive or treatment measures in respect of the disease or disorder which is the subject of the screening, are available to the persons concerned;

(d) appropriate measures are provided to ensure equitable access to the programme;

(e) the programme provides measures to adequately inform the population or section of population concerned of the existence, purposes and means of accessing the screening programme as well as the voluntary nature of participation in it.

Chapter IX Public information

Article 20   Public information

Parties shall take appropriate measures to facilitate access for the public to objective general information on genetic tests, including their nature and the potential implications of their results.

Chapter X Relation between this Protocol and other provisions and re-examination of the Protocol

Article 21   Relation between this Protocol and the Convention

As between the Parties, the provisions of Articles 1 to 20 of this Protocol shall be regarded as additional articles to the Convention on Human Rights and Biomedicine, and all the provisions of the Convention shall apply accordingly.

Article 22   Wider protection
None of the provisions of this Protocol shall be interpreted as limiting or otherwise affecting the possibility for a Party to grant persons concerned by genetic testing for health purposes a wider measure of protection than is stipulated in this Protocol.

World Medical Association Declaration of Helsinki: Ethical Principles for Medical Research involving Human Subjects*

(2008)

A. Introduction

1. The World Medical Association (WMA) has developed the Declaration of Helsinki as a statement of ethical principles for medical research involving human subjects, including research on identifiable human material and data.

The Declaration is intended to be read as a whole and each of its constituent paragraphs should not be applied without consideration of all other relevant paragraphs.

2. Although the Declaration is addressed primarily to physicians, the WMA encourages other participants in medical research involving human subjects to adopt these principles.

3. It is the duty of the physician to promote and safeguard the health of patients, including those who are involved in medical research. The physician's knowledge and conscience are dedicated to the fulfillment of this duty.

4. The Declaration of Geneva of the WMA binds the physician with the words, 'The health of my patient will be my first consideration', and the International Code of Medical Ethics declares that, 'A physician shall act in the patient's best interest when providing medical care.'

5. Medical progress is based on research that ultimately must include studies involving human subjects. Populations that are underrepresented in medical research should be provided appropriate access to participation in research.

6. In medical research involving human subjects, the well-being of the individual research subject must take precedence over all other interests.

7. The primary purpose of medical research involving human subjects is to understand the causes, development and effects of diseases and improve preventive, diagnostic and therapeutic interventions (methods, procedures and treatments). Even the best current interventions must be evaluated continually through research for their safety, effectiveness, efficiency, accessibility and quality.

8. In medical practice and in medical research, most interventions involve risks and burdens.

9. Medical research is subject to ethical standards that promote respect for all human subjects and protect their health and rights. Some research populations are particularly vulnerable and need special protection. These include those who cannot give or refuse consent for themselves and those who may be vulnerable to coercion or undue influence.

10. Physicians should consider the ethical, legal and regulatory norms and standards for research involving human subjects in their own countries as well as applicable international norms and standards. No national or international ethical, legal or regulatory requirement should reduce or eliminate any of the protections for research subjects set forth in this Declaration.

B. Principles for all medical research

11. It is the duty of physicians who participate in medical research to protect the life, health, dignity, integrity, right to self-determination, privacy, and confidentiality of personal information of research subjects.

12. Medical research involving human subjects must conform to generally accepted scientific principles, be based on a thorough knowledge of the scientific literature, other relevant sources of information, and adequate laboratory and, as appropriate, animal experimentation. The welfare of animals used for research must be respected.

13. Appropriate caution must be exercised in the conduct of medical research that may harm the environment.

14. The design and performance of each research study involving human subjects must be clearly described in a research protocol. The protocol should contain a statement of the ethical considerations involved and should indicate how the principles in this Declaration have been addressed. The protocol should include information regarding funding, sponsors, institutional affiliations, other potential conflicts of interest, incentives for subjects and provisions for treating and/or compensating subjects who are harmed as a consequence of participation in the research study. The protocol should describe arrangements for post-study access by study subjects to interventions identified as beneficial in the study or access to other appropriate care or benefits.

15. The research protocol must be submitted for consideration, comment, guidance and approval to a research ethics committee before the study begins. This committee must be independent of the researcher, the sponsor and any other undue influence. It must take into consideration the laws and regulations of the country or countries in which the research is to be performed as well as applicable international norms and standards but these must not be allowed to reduce or eliminate any of the protections for research subjects set forth in this Declaration. The committee must have the right to monitor ongoing studies. The researcher must provide monitoring information to the committee, especially information about any serious adverse events. No change to the protocol may be made without consideration and approval by the committee.

16. Medical research involving human subjects must be conducted only by individuals with the appropriate scientific training and qualifications. Research on patients or healthy volunteers requires the supervision of a competent and appropriately qualified physician or other health care professional. The responsibility for the protection of research subjects must always rest with the physician or other health care professional and never the research subjects, even though they have given consent.

17. Medical research involving a disadvantaged or vulnerable population or community is only justified if the research is responsive to the health needs and priorities of this population or community and if there is a reasonable likelihood that this population or community stands to benefit from the results of the research.

18. Every medical research study involving human subjects must be preceded by careful assessment of predictable risks and burdens to the individuals and communities involved in the research in comparison with foreseeable benefits to them and to other individuals or communities affected by the condition under investigation.

19. Every clinical trial must be registered in a publicly accessible database before recruitment of the first subject.

20. Physicians may not participate in a research study involving human subjects unless they are confident that the risks involved have been adequately assessed and can be satisfactorily managed. Physicians must immediately stop a study when the risks are found to outweigh the potential benefits or when there is conclusive proof of positive and beneficial results.

21. Medical research involving human subjects may only be conducted if the importance of the objective outweighs the inherent risks and burdens to the research subjects.

22. Participation by competent individuals as subjects in medical research must be voluntary. Although it may be appropriate to consult family members or community leaders, no competent individual may be enrolled in a research study unless he or she freely agrees.

23. Every precaution must be taken to protect the privacy of research subjects and the confidentiality of their personal information and to minimize the impact of the study on their physical, mental and social integrity.

24. In medical research involving competent human subjects, each potential subject must be adequately informed of the aims, methods, sources of funding, any possible conflicts of interest, institutional affiliations of the researcher, the anticipated benefits and potential risks of the study and the discomfort it may entail, and any other relevant aspects of the study. The potential subject must be informed of the right to refuse to participate in the study or to withdraw consent to participate at any time without reprisal. Special attention should be given to the specific information needs of individual potential subjects as well as to the methods used to deliver the information. After ensuring that the potential subject has understood the information, the physician or another appropriately qualified individual must then seek the potential subject's freely-given informed consent, preferably in writing. If the consent cannot be expressed in writing, the non-written consent must be formally documented and witnessed.

25. For medical research using identifiable human material or data, physicians must normally seek consent for the collection, analysis, storage and/or reuse. There may be situations where consent would be impossible or impractical to obtain for such research or would pose a threat to the validity of the research. In such situations the research may be done only after consideration and approval of a research ethics committee.

26. When seeking informed consent for participation in a research study the physician should be particularly cautious if the potential subject is in a dependent relationship with the physician or may consent under duress. In such situations the informed consent should be sought by an appropriately qualified individual who is completely independent of this relationship.

27. For a potential research subject who is incompetent, the physician must seek informed consent from the legally authorized representative. These individuals must not be included in a research study that has no likelihood of benefit for them unless it is intended to promote the health of the population represented by the potential subject, the research cannot instead be performed with competent persons, and the research entails only minimal risk and minimal burden.

28. When a potential research subject who is deemed incompetent is able to give assent to decisions about participation in research, the physician must seek that assent in addition to the consent of the legally authorized representative. The potential subject's dissent should be respected.

29. Research involving subjects who are physically or mentally incapable of giving consent, for example, unconscious patients, may be done only if the physical or mental condition that prevents giving informed consent is a necessary characteristic of the research population. In such circumstances the physician should seek informed consent from the legally authorized representative. If no such representative is available and if the research cannot be delayed, the study may proceed without informed consent provided that the specific reasons for involving subjects with a condition that renders them unable to give informed consent have been stated in the research protocol and the study has been approved by a research ethics committee. Consent to remain in the research should be obtained as soon as possible from the subject or a legally authorized representative.

30. Authors, editors and publishers all have ethical obligations with regard to the publication of the results of research. Authors have a duty to make publicly available the results of their research on human subjects and are accountable for the completeness and accuracy of their reports. They should adhere to accepted guidelines for ethical reporting. Negative and inconclusive as well as positive results should be published or otherwise made publicly available. Sources of funding, institutional affiliations and conflicts of interest should be declared in the publication. Reports of research not in accordance with the principles of this Declaration should not be accepted for publication.

C. Additional principles for medical research combined with medical care

31. The physician may combine medical research with medical care only to the extent that the research is justified by its potential preventive, diagnostic or therapeutic value and if the physician has good reason to believe that participation in the research study will not adversely affect the health of the patients who serve as research subjects.

32. The benefits, risks, burdens and effectiveness of a new intervention must be tested against those of the best current proven intervention, except in the following circumstances:

- The use of placebo, or no treatment, is acceptable in studies where no current proven intervention exists; or
- Where for compelling and scientifically sound methodological reasons the use of placebo is necessary to determine the efficacy or safety of an intervention and the patients who receive placebo or no treatment will not be subject to any risk of serious or irreversible harm. Extreme care must be taken to avoid abuse of this option.

33. At the conclusion of the study, patients entered into the study are entitled to be informed about the outcome of the study and to share any benefits that result from it, for example, access to interventions identified as beneficial in the study or to other appropriate care or benefits.

34. The physician must fully inform the patient which aspects of the care are related to the research. The refusal of a patient to participate in a study or the patient's decision to withdraw from the study must never interfere with the patient-physician relationship.

35. In the treatment of a patient, where proven interventions do not exist or have been ineffective, the physician, after seeking expert advice, with informed consent from the patient or a legally authorized representative, may use an unproven intervention if in the physician's judgement it offers hope of saving life, re-establishing health or alleviating suffering. Where possible, this intervention should be made the object of research, designed to evaluate its safety and efficacy. In all cases, new information should be recorded and, where appropriate, made publicly available.

Directive 2010/45/EU of the European Parliament and of the Council of 7 July 2010 on standards of quality and safety of human organs intended for transplantation*

(Official Journal L 207, 06/08/2010 P. 0014–0029)

Chapter I Subject Matter, Scope and Definitions

Article 1   Subject Matter
This Directive lays down rules to ensure standards of quality and safety for human organs (hereinafter 'organs') intended for transplantation to the human body, in order to ensure a high level of human health protection.

Article 2   Scope
1. This Directive applies to the donation, testing, characterisation, procurement, preservation, transport and transplantation of organs intended for transplantation.

2. Where such organs are used for research purposes, this Directive only applies where they are intended for transplantation into the human body.

Article 3   Definitions
For the purposes of this Directive, the following definitions apply:
- (a) 'authorisation' means authorisation, accreditation, designation, licensing or registration, depending on the concepts used and the practices in place in each Member State;
- (b) 'competent authority' means an authority, body, organisation and/or institution responsible for implementing the requirements of this Directive;
- (c) 'disposal' means the final placement of an organ where it is not used for transplantation;
- (d) 'donor' means a person who donates one or several organs, whether donation occurs during lifetime or after death;

(e) 'donation' means donating organs for transplantation;

(f) 'donor characterisation' means the collection of the relevant information on the characteristics of the donor needed to evaluate his/her suitability for organ donation, in order to undertake a proper risk assessment and minimise the risks for the recipient, and optimise organ allocation;

(g) 'European organ exchange organisation' means a non-profit organisation, whether public or private, dedicated to national and cross-border organ exchange, in which the majority of its member countries are Member States;

(h) 'organ' means a differentiated part of the human body, formed by different tissues, that maintains its structure, vascularisation, and capacity to develop physiological functions with a significant level of autonomy. A part of an organ is also considered to be an organ if its function is to be used for the same purpose as the entire organ in the human body, maintaining the requirements of structure and vascularisation;

(i) 'organ characterisation' means the collection of the relevant information on the characteristics of the organ needed to evaluate its suitability, in order to undertake a proper risk assessment and minimise the risks for the recipient, and optimise organ allocation;

(j) 'procurement' means a process by which the donated organs become available;

(k) 'procurement organisation' means a healthcare establishment, a team or a unit of a hospital, a person, or any other body which undertakes or coordinates the procurement of organs, and is authorised to do so by the competent authority under the regulatory framework in the Member State concerned;

(l) 'preservation' means the use of chemical agents, alterations in environmental conditions or other means to prevent or retard biological or physical deterioration of organs from procurement to transplantation;

(m) 'recipient' means a person who receives a transplant of an organ;

(n) 'serious adverse event' means any undesired and unexpected occurrence associated with any stage of the chain from donation to transplantation that might lead to the transmission of a communicable disease, to death or life-threatening, disabling or incapacitating conditions for patients or which results in, or prolongs, hospitalisation or morbidity;

(o) 'serious adverse reaction' means an unintended response, including a communicable disease, in the living donor or in the recipient that might be associated with any stage of the chain from donation to transplantation that is fatal, life-threatening, disabling, incapacitating, or which results in, or prolongs, hospitalisation or morbidity;

(p) 'operating procedures' means written instructions describing the steps in a specific process, including the materials and methods to be used and the expected end outcome;

(q) 'transplantation' means a process intended to restore certain functions of the human body by transferring an organ from a donor to a recipient;

(r) 'transplantation centre' means a healthcare establishment, a team or a unit of a hospital or any other body which undertakes the transplantation of organs and is authorised to do so by the competent authority under the regulatory framework in the Member State concerned;

(s) 'traceability' means the ability to locate and identify the organ at each stage in the chain from donation to transplantation or disposal, including the ability to:

- identify the donor and the procurement organisation,

- identify the recipient(s) at the transplantation centre(s), and

- locate and identify all relevant non-personal information relating to products and materials coming into contact with that organ.

Chapter II The Quality and Safety of Organs

Article 4 Framework for quality and safety

1. Member States shall ensure that a framework for quality and safety is established to cover all stages of the chain from donation to transplantation or disposal, in compliance with the rules laid down in this Directive.

2. The framework for quality and safety shall provide for the adoption and implementation of operating procedures for:

(a) the verification of donor identity;

(b) the verification of the details of the donor's or the donor's family's consent, authorisation or absence of any objection, in accordance with the national rules that apply where donation and procurement take place;

(c) the verification of the completion of the organ and donor characterisation in accordance with Article 7 and the Annex;

(d) the procurement, preservation, packaging and labelling of organs in accordance with Articles 5, 6 and 8;

(e) the transportation of organs in accordance with Article 8;

(f) ensuring traceability, in accordance with Article 10, guaranteeing compliance with the Union and national provisions on the protection of personal data and confidentiality;

(g) the accurate, rapid and verifiable reporting of serious adverse events and reactions in accordance with Article 11(1);

(h) the management of serious adverse events and reactions in accordance with Article 11(2).

The operating procedures referred to in points (f), (g) and (h) shall specify, inter alia, the responsibilities of procurement organisations, European organ exchange organisations and transplantation centres.

3. In addition, the framework for quality and safety shall ensure that the healthcare personnel involved at all stages of the chain from donation to transplantation or disposal are suitably qualified or trained and competent, and shall develop specific training programmes for such personnel.

Article 5 Procurement organisations

1. Member States shall ensure that the procurement takes place in, or is carried out by, procurement organisations that comply with the rules laid down in this Directive.

2. Member States shall, upon the request of the Commission or another Member State, provide information on the national requirements for the authorisation of procurement organisations.

Article 6 Organ procurement

1. Member States shall ensure that medical activities in procurement organisations, such as donor selection and evaluation, are performed under the advice and the guidance of a doctor of medicine as referred to in Directive 2005/36/EC of the European Parliament and of the Council of 7 September 2005 on the recognition of professional qualifications.

2. Member States shall ensure that procurement takes place in operating theatres, which are designed, constructed, maintained and operated in accordance with adequate standards and best medical practices so as to ensure the quality and safety of the organs procured.

3. Member States shall ensure that procurement material and equipment are managed in accordance with relevant Union, international and national legislation, standards and guidelines on the sterilisation of medical devices.

Article 7 Organ and donor characterisation

1. Member States shall ensure that all procured organs and donors thereof are characterised before transplantation through the collection of the information set out in the Annex....

2. Notwithstanding paragraph 1, if according to a risk-benefit analysis in a particular case, including in life-threatening emergencies, the expected benefits for the recipient outweigh the risks

posed by incomplete data, an organ may be considered for transplantation even where not all of the minimum data specified in Part A of the Annex are available.

3. In order to meet the quality and safety requirements laid down in this Directive, the medical team shall endeavour to obtain all necessary information from living donors and for that purpose shall provide them with the information they need to understand the consequences of donation. In the case of deceased donation, where possible and appropriate, the medical team shall endeavour to obtain such information from relatives of the deceased donor or other persons. The medical team shall also endeavour to make all parties from whom information is requested aware of the importance of the swift transmission of that information.

4. The tests required for organ and donor characterisation shall be carried out by laboratories with suitably qualified or trained and competent personnel and adequate facilities and equipment.

6. Where organs are exchanged between Member States, those Member States shall ensure that the information on organ and donor characterisation, as specified in the Annex, is transmitted to the other Member State with which the organ is exchanged, in conformity with the procedures established by the Commission pursuant to Article 29.

Article 9   Transplantation centres

1. Member States shall ensure that transplantation takes place in, or is carried out by, transplantation centres that comply with the rules laid down in this Directive.

2. The competent authority shall indicate in the authorisation which activities the transplantation centre concerned may undertake.

3. The transplantation centre shall verify before proceeding to transplantation that:
(a) the organ and donor characterisation are completed and recorded in accordance with Article 7 and the Annex;
(b) the conditions of preservation and transport of shipped organs have been maintained.

4. Member States shall, upon the request of the Commission or another Member State, provide information on the national requirements for the authorisation of transplantation centres.

Article 10   Traceability

1. Member States shall ensure that all organs procured, allocated and transplanted on their territory can be traced from the donor to the recipient and vice versa in order to safeguard the health of donors and recipients.

2. Member States shall ensure the implementation of a donor and recipient identification system that can identify each donation and each of the organs and recipients associated with it. With regard to such a system, Member States shall ensure that confidentiality and data security measures are in place in compliance with Union and national provisions, as referred to in Article 16.

3. Member States shall ensure that:
(a) the competent authority or other bodies involved in the chain from donation to transplantation or disposal keep the data needed to ensure traceability at all stages of the chain from donation to transplantation or disposal and the information on organ and donor characterisation as specified in the Annex, in accordance with the framework for quality and safety;
(b) data required for full traceability is kept for a minimum of 30 years after donation. Such data may be stored in electronic form.

4. Where organs are exchanged between Member States, those Member States shall transmit the necessary information to ensure the traceability of organs, in conformity with the procedures established by the Commission pursuant to Article 29.

Article 11   Reporting system and management concerning serious adverse events and reactions

1. Member States shall ensure that there is a reporting system in place to report, investigate, register and transmit relevant and necessary information concerning serious adverse events that may influence the quality and safety of organs and that may be attributed to the testing,

characterisation, procurement, preservation and transport of organs, as well as any serious adverse reaction observed during or after transplantation which may be connected to those activities.

Article 12   Healthcare personnel

Member States shall ensure that healthcare personnel directly involved in the chain from donation to the transplantation or disposal of organs are suitably qualified or trained and competent to perform their tasks and are provided with the relevant training, as referred to in Article 4(3).

Chapter III Donor and Recipient Protection and Donor Selection and Evaluation

Article 13   Principles governing organ donation

1. Member States shall ensure that donations of organs from deceased and living donors are voluntary and unpaid.

2. The principle of non-payment shall not prevent living donors from receiving compensation, provided it is strictly limited to making good the expenses and loss of income related to the donation. Member States shall define the conditions under which such compensation may be granted, while avoiding there being any financial incentives or benefit for a potential donor.

3. Member States shall prohibit advertising the need for, or availability of, organs where such advertising is with a view to offering or seeking financial gain or comparable advantage.

4. Member States shall ensure that the procurement of organs is carried out on a non-profit basis.

Article 14   Consent requirements

The procurement of organs shall be carried out only after all requirements relating to consent, authorisation or absence of any objection in force in the Member State concerned have been met.

Article 15   Quality and safety aspects of living donation

1. Member States shall take all necessary measures to ensure the highest possible protection of living donors in order to fully guarantee the quality and safety of organs for transplantation.

2. Member States shall ensure that living donors are selected on the basis of their health and medical history, by suitably qualified or trained and competent professionals. Such assessments may provide for the exclusion of persons whose donation could present unacceptable health risks.

3. Member States shall ensure that a register or record of the living donors is kept, in accordance with Union and national provisions on the protection of the personal data and statistical confidentiality.

4. Member States shall endeavour to carry out the follow-up of living donors and shall have a system in place in accordance with national provisions, in order to identify, report and manage any event potentially relating to the quality and safety of the donated organ, and hence of the safety of the recipient, as well as any serious adverse reaction in the living donor that may result from the donation.

Article 16   Protection of personal data, confidentiality and security of processing

Member States shall ensure that the fundamental right to protection of personal data is fully and effectively protected in all organ donation and transplantation activities, in conformity with Union provisions on the protection of personal data, such as Directive 95/46/EC, and in particular Article 8(3), Articles 16 and 17 and Article 28(2) thereof. Pursuant to Directive 95/46/EC, Member States shall take all necessary measures to ensure that:

    (a) the data processed are kept confidential and secure in accordance with Articles 16 and 17 of Directive 95/46/EC. Any unauthorised accessing of data or systems that makes identification of donor or recipients possible shall be penalised in accordance with Article 23 of this Directive;

(b) donors and recipients whose data are processed within the scope of this Directive are not identifiable, except as permitted by Article 8(2) and (3) of Directive 95/46/EC, and national provisions implementing that Directive. Any use of systems or data that makes the identification of donors or recipients possible with a view to tracing donors or recipients other than for the purposes permitted by Article 8(2) and (3) of Directive 95/46/EC, including medical purposes, and by national provisions implementing that Directive shall be penalised in accordance with Article 23 of this Directive;

(c) the principles relating to data quality, as set out in Article 6 of Directive 95/46/EC, are met.

Chapter IV Obligations of Competent Authorities and Exchange of Information

Article 18   Records and reports concerning procurement organisations and transplantation centres

1. Member States shall ensure that the competent authority:

(a) keeps a record of the activities of procurement organisations and transplantation centres, including aggregated numbers of living and deceased donors, and the types and quantities of organs procured and transplanted, or otherwise disposed of in accordance with Union and national provisions on the protection of personal data and statistical confidentiality;

(b) draws up and makes publicly accessible an annual report on activities referred to in point (a);

(c) establishes and maintains an updated record of procurement organisations and transplantation centres.

2. Member States shall, upon the request of the Commission or another Member State, provide information on the record of procurement organisations and transplantation centres.

Chapter V Organ Exchange with Third Countries and European Organ Exchange Organisations

Article 20   Organ exchange with third countries

1. Member States shall ensure that organ exchange with third countries is supervised by the competent authority. For this purpose, the competent authority and European organ exchange organisations may conclude agreements with counterparts in third countries.

2. The supervision of organ exchange with third countries may be delegated by the Member States to European organ exchange organisations.

3. Organ exchange, as referred to in paragraph 1, shall be allowed only where the organs:

(a) can be traced from the donor to the recipient and vice versa;

(b) meet quality and safety requirements equivalent to those laid down in this Directive.

Chapter VI General Provisions

Article 23   Penalties

Member States shall lay down the rules on penalties applicable to infringements of the national provisions adopted pursuant to this Directive and shall take all measures necessary to ensure that the penalties are implemented. The penalties provided for must be effective, proportionate and dissuasive. Member States shall notify those provisions to the Commission by 27 August 2012 and shall notify it without delay of any subsequent amendments affecting them.

Article 24 Adaptation of the Annex

The Commission may adopt delegated acts in accordance with Article 25 and subject to the conditions of Articles 26, 27 and 28 in order to:

(a) supplement or amend the minimum data set specified in Part A of the Annex only in exceptional situations where it is justified by a serious risk to human health considered as such on the basis of the scientific progress;

(b) supplement or amend the complementary data set specified in Part B of the Annex in order to adapt it to scientific progress and international work carried out in the field of quality and safety of organs intended for transplantation.

Article 31 Transposition

1. Member States shall bring into force the laws, regulations and administrative provisions necessary to comply with this Directive by 27 August 2012. They shall forthwith inform the Commission thereof.

ANNEX

ORGAN AND DONOR CHARACTERISATION

PART A MINIMUM DATA SET

Minimum data—information for the characterisation of organs and donors, which has to be collected for each donation in accordance with second subparagraph of Article 7(1) and without prejudice to Article 7(2).

Minimum data set:

The establishment where the procurement takes place and other general data; Type of donor; Blood group; Gender; Cause of death; Date of death; Date of birth or estimated age; Weight; Height; Past or present history of IV drug abuse; Past or present history of malignant neoplasia; Present history of other transmissible disease; HIV; HCV; HBV tests; Basic information to evaluate the function of the donated organ

PART B COMPLEMENTARY DATA SET

Complementary data—information for the characterisation of organs and donors to be collected in addition to minimum data specified in Part A, based on the decision of the medical team, taking into account the availability of such information and the particular circumstances of the case, in accordance with the second subparagraph of Article 7(1).

Complementary data set:

General data: Contact details of the procurement organisation/the establishment where the procurement takes place necessary for coordination, allocation and traceability of the organs from donors to recipients and vice versa.

Donor data: Demographic and anthropometrical data required in order to guarantee an appropriate matching between the donor/organ and the recipient.

Donor medical history: Medical history of the donor, in particular the conditions which might affect the suitability of the organs for transplantation and imply the risk of disease transmission.

Physical and clinical data: Data from clinical examination which are necessary for the evaluation of the physiological maintenance of the potential donor as well as any finding revealing conditions which remained undetected during the examination of the donor's medical history and which might affect the suitability of organs for transplantation or might imply the risk of disease transmission.

Laboratory parameters: Data needed for the assessment of the functional characterisation of the organs and for the detection of potentially transmissible diseases and of possible contraindications with respect to organ donation.

Image tests: Image explorations necessary for the assessment of the anatomical status of the organs for transplantation.

Therapy: Treatments administered to the donor and relevant for the assessment of the functional status of the organs and the suitability for organ donation, in particular the use of antibiotics, ino-tropic support or transfusion therapy.

Index